Case Studies in Finance

Managing for Corporate Value Creation

Case Studies in Finance

Managing for Corporate Value Creation

Seventh Edition

Robert F. Bruner
Kenneth M. Eades
Michael J. Schill

UNIVERSITY *of* VIRGINIA

DARDEN SCHOOL OF BUSINESS

McGraw-Hill
Irwin

The *McGraw-Hill* Companies

CASE STUDIES IN FINANCE: MANAGING FOR CORPORATE VALUE CREATION,
SEVENTH EDITION
International Edition 2014

Exclusive rights by McGraw-Hill Education (Asia), for manufacture and export. This book cannot be
re-exported from the country to which it is sold by McGraw-Hill. This International Edition is not to
be sold or purchased in North America and contains content that is different from its North American
version.

Published by McGraw-Hill, a business unit of The McGraw-Hill Companies, Inc., 1221 Avenue of the
Americas, New York, NY 10020. Copyright © 2014 by The McGraw-Hill Companies, Inc. Previous
editions © 2002, 1989, and 1975. All rights reserved. No part publication may be reproduced or
distributed in any form or by any means, or stored in a database or retrieval system, without the prior
written consent of The McGraw-Hill Companies, Inc., including, but not limited to, in any network or
other electronic storage or transmission, or broadcast for distance learning.
Some ancillaries, including electronic and print components, may not be available to customers outside
the United States.

10 09 08 07 06 05 04 03 02 01
20 15 14 13
CTP   SLP

When ordering this title, use ISBN 978-1-259-07094-5 or MHID 1-259-07094-8

The Internet addresses listed in the text were accurate at the time of publication. The inclusion of a
website does not indicate an endorsement by the authors or McGraw-Hill, and McGraw-Hill does not
guarantee the accuracy of the information presented at these sites.

Printed in Singapore

www.mhhe.com

The McGraw-Hill/Irwin Series in Finance, Insurance and Real Estate

Stephen A. Ross
Franco Modigliani Professor of Finance and Economics
Sloan School of Management
Massachusetts Institute of Technology
Consulting Editor

FINANCIAL MANAGEMENT

In dedication to
our wives

Barbara M. Bruner
Kathy N. Eades
Mary Ann H. Schill

and to our children

About the Authors

Robert F. Bruner is Dean of the Darden Graduate School of Business Administration, Distinguished Professor of Business Administration and Charles C. Abbott Professor of Business Administration at the University of Virginia. He has taught and written in various areas, including corporate finance, mergers and acquisitions, investing in emerging markets, innovation, and technology transfer. In addition to *Case Studies in Finance,* his books include *Finance Interactive,* multimedia tutorial software in Finance (Irwin/McGraw-Hill 1997), *The Portable MBA* (Wiley 2003), *Applied Mergers and Acquisitions,* (Wiley, 2004), *Deals from Hell: M&A Lessons that Rise Above the Ashes* (Wiley, 2005) and *The Panic of 1907* (Wiley, 2007). He has been recognized in the United States and Europe for his teaching and case writing. *BusinessWeek* magazine cited him as one of the "masters of the MBA classroom." He is the author or co-author of over 400 case studies and notes. His research has been published in journals such as *Financial Management, Journal of Accounting and Economics, Journal of Applied Corporate Finance, Journal of Financial Economics, Journal of Financial and Quantitative Analysis,* and *Journal of Money, Credit, and Banking.* Industrial corporations, financial institutions, and government agencies have retained him for counsel and training. He has been on the faculty of the Darden School since 1982, and has been a visiting professor at various schools including Columbia, INSEAD, and IESE. Formerly he was a loan officer and investment analyst for First Chicago Corporation. He holds the B.A. degree from Yale University and the M.B.A. and D.B.A. degrees from Harvard University. Copies of his papers and essays may be obtained from his website, http://www.darden.virginia.edu/web/Faculty-Research/Directory/Full-time/Robert-F-Bruner/. He may be reached via email at brunerr@virginia.edu.

Kenneth M. Eades is Professor of Business Administration and Area Coordinator of the Finance Department of the Darden Graduate School of Business Administration at the University of Virginia. He has taught a variety of corporate finance topics including: capital structure, dividend policy, risk management, capital investments and firm valuation. His research interests are in the area of corporate finance where he has published articles in *The Journal of Finance, Journal of Financial Economics, Journal of Financial and Quantitative Analysis,* and *Financial Management.* In addition to *Case Studies in Finance,* his books include *The Portable MBA* (Wiley 2010) *Finance Interactive,* a multimedia tutorial software in Finance (Irwin/McGraw-Hill 1997) and *Case Studies in Financial Decision Making* (Dryden Press, 1994). He has written numerous case studies as well as a web-based, interactive tutorial on the pricing of financial derivatives. He has received the Wachovia Award for Excellence in Teaching Materials and the Wachovia Award for Excellence in Research. Mr. Eades is active in executive education programs at the Darden School and has served as a consultant to a number of corporations and institutions; including many commercial banks and investment banks; Fortune 500 companies and the Internal Revenue Service. Prior to joining Darden in 1988, Professor Eades was a member of the faculties at The University of Michigan and the Kellogg School of Management at Northwestern University. He has a B.S. from the University of Kentucky and Ph.D. from Purdue University. His website is http://www.darden.virginia.edu/web/Faculty-Research/Directory/Full-time/Kenneth-M-Eades/ and he may be reached via email at eades@virginia.edu.

Michael J. Schill is Associate Professor of Business Administration of the Darden Graduate School of Business Administration at the University of Virginia where he teaches corporate finance and investments. His research spans empirical questions in corporate finance, investments, and international finance. He is the author of numerous articles that have been published in leading finance journals such as *Journal of Business, Journal of Finance, Journal of Financial Economics,* and *Review of Financial Studies,* and cited by major media outlets such as *The Wall Street Journal.* Some of his recent research projects investigate the market pricing of firm growth and the corporate gains to foreign stock exchange listing or foreign currency borrowing. He has been on the faculty of the Darden School since 2001 and was previously with the University of California, Riverside, as well as a visiting professor at Cambridge and Melbourne. Prior to his doctoral work, he was a management consultant with Marakon Associates in Stamford and London. He continues to be active in consulting and executive education for major corporations. He received a B.S. degree from Brigham Young University, an M.B.A. from INSEAD, and a Ph.D. from University of Washington. More details are available from his website, http://www.darden.virginia.edu/web/Faculty-Research/Directory/Full-time/ Michael-J-Schill/. He may be reached via email at schill@virginia.edu.

Contents

Setting Some Themes

Financial Analysis and Forecasting

Estimating the Cost of Capital

Capital Budgeting and Resource Allocation

Management of the Firm's Equity: Dividends and Repurchases

Management of the Corporate Capital Structure

Analysis of Financing Tactics: Leases, Options, and Foreign Currency

Valuing the Enterprise: Acquisitions and Buyouts

The half-decade from 2008 to 2013 forced a series of "teachable moments" into the consciousness of leaders in both business and government. More such moments may be in the offing, given the unresolved issues stemming from the global financial crisis. What lessons shall we draw from these moments? And how shall we teach the lessons so that the next generation of leaders can implement wiser policies?

One theme implicit in most critiques and policy recommendations of this period entails *the consequences of financial illiteracy*. At few other times in financial history have we seen so strong an affirmation of Derek Bok's famous argument, "If you think education is expensive, try ignorance." The actions and behavior of consumers, investors, financial intermediaries, and regulators suggest ignorance (naïve or otherwise) of such basic financial concepts as time value of money, risk-adjusted returns, cost of capital, capital adequacy, solvency, optionality, capital market efficiency, and so on. If ignorance is bliss, teachers of finance face a delirious world.

Now more than ever, the case method of teaching corporate finance is critical to meeting the diverse educational challenges of our day. The cases presented in this volume address the richness of the problems that practitioners face and help to develop the student in three critical areas:

- *Knowledge.* The conceptual and computational building blocks of finance are the necessary foundation for professional competence. The cases in this volume afford solid practice with the breadth and depth of this foundational knowledge. And they link the practical application of tools and concepts to a *contextual setting* for analysis. Such real-world linkage is an important advantage of case studies over textbook problem sets.

- *Skills.* Case studies demand decisions and recommendations. Too many analysts are content to calculate or estimate without helping a decision-maker fully understand the implications of the analysis. By placing the student in the position of the decision-maker, the case study promotes confidence and competence in making decisions. Furthermore, class discussions of cases promote skills in communication, selling and defending ideas, giving feedback, negotiating, and getting results through teamwork—these are social skills that are best learned in face-to-face engagement.

- *Attributes of character.* Popular outrage over the crisis focused on *shady ethics*. The duty of agents, diligence in the execution of professional responsibilities, breaches of trust, the temptations of self-dealing, and outright fraud intrude into retrospective assessments of what might otherwise be dry and technical analyses of the last decade. It is no longer possible or desirable to teach finance as a purely technical subject devoid of ethical considerations. Ultimately, teaching is a moral act: by choosing worthy problems, modeling behavior, and challenging the thinking of students, the teacher strengthens students in ways that are vitally important for the future of society. The case method builds attributes of character such as work ethic and persistence; empathy for classmates and decision-makers; social awareness of the consequences of decisions and the challenging context for decision-makers; and accountability for one's work. When students are challenged orally to explain their work, the ensuing discussion reveals the moral dilemmas that confront the decision maker. At the core of transformational teaching with cases is growth in integrity. As Aristotle said, "Character is destiny," a truism readily apparent in the ruinous aftermath of the global financial crisis.

As with the sixth edition of this book, I must commend my colleagues, Kenneth Eades and Michael Schill, who brought this seventh edition to the public. They are accomplished scholars in Finance and masterful teachers—above all, they are devoted to the quality of the learning experience for students. Their efforts in preparing this volume will enrich the learning for countless students and help teachers world-wide to rise to the various challenges of the post-crisis world.

Robert F. Bruner
Dean and Charles C. Abbott Professor of Business Administration
Distinguished Professor of Business Administration
Darden Graduate School of Business Administration
University of Virginia
Charlottesville, Virginia
October 8, 2012

Preface

The inexplicable is all around us. So is the incomprehensible. So is the unintelligible. Interviewing Babe Ruth* in 1928, I put it to him "People come and ask what's your system for hitting home runs—that so?" "Yes," said the Babe, "and all I can tell 'em is I pick a good one and sock it. I get back to the dugout and they ask me what it was I hit and I tell 'em I don't know except it looked good."
  —Carl Sandburg†

Managers are not confronted with problems that are independent of each other, but with dynamic situations that consist of complex systems of changing problems that interact with each other. I call such situations messes . . . Managers do not solve problems: they manage messes.
  —Russell Ackoff‡

Orientation of the Book

Practitioners tell us that much in finance is inexplicable, incomprehensible, and unintelligible. Like Babe Ruth, their explanations for their actions often amount to "I pick a good one and sock it." Fortunately for a rising generation of practitioners, tools and concepts of Modern Finance provide a language and approach for excellent performance. The aim of this book is to illustrate and exercise the application of these tools and concepts in a messy world.

Focus on Value

The subtitle of this book is *Managing for Corporate Value Creation.* Economics teaches us that value creation should be an enduring focus of concern because value is the foundation of survival and prosperity of the enterprise. The focus on value also helps managers understand the impact of the firm on the world around it. These cases harness and exercise this economic view of the firm. It is the special province of finance to highlight value as a legitimate concern for managers. The cases in this book exercise valuation analysis over a wide range of assets, debt, equities, and options, and a wide range of perspectives, such as investor, creditor, and manager.

Linkage to Capital Markets

An important premise of these cases is that managers should take cues from the capital markets. The cases in this volume help the student learn to look at the capital markets in four ways. First, they illustrate important players in the capital markets such as individual exemplars like Warren Buffett and Bill Miller and institutions like

---

*George Herman "Babe" Ruth (1895–1948) was one of the most famous players in the history of American baseball, leading the league in home runs for 10 straight seasons, setting a record of 60 home runs in one season, and hitting 714 home runs in his career. Ruth was also known as the "Sultan of Swat."

†Carl Sandburg, "Notes for Preface," in *Harvest Poems* (New York: Harcourt Brace Jovanovich, 1960), p.11.

‡Russell Ackoff, "The Future of Operational Research is Past," *Journal of Operational Research Society,* 30, 1 (Pergamon Press, Ltd., 1979): 93–104.

investment banks, commercial banks, rating agencies, hedge funds, merger arbitrageurs, private equity firms, lessors of industrial equipment, and so on. Second, they exercise the students' abilities to interpret capital market conditions across the economic cycle. Third, they explore the design of financial securities, and illuminate the use of exotic instruments in support of corporate policy. Finally, they help students understand the implications of transparency of the firm to investors, and the impact of news about the firm in an efficient market.

Respect for the Administrative Point of View

The real world is messy. Information is incomplete, arrives late, or is reported with error. The motivations of counterparties are ambiguous. Resources often fall short. These cases illustrate the immense practicality of finance theory in sorting out the issues facing managers, assessing alternatives, and illuminating the effects of any particular choice. A number of the cases in this book present practical ethical dilemmas or moral hazards facing managers—indeed, this edition features a chapter, "Ethics in Finance" right at the beginning, where ethics belongs. Most of the cases (and teaching plans in the associated instructor's manual) call for *action plans* rather than mere analyses or descriptions of a problem.

Contemporaneity

All of the cases in this book are set in the year 2000 or after and 40 percent are set in 2006 or later. A substantial proportion (25 percent) of these cases and technical notes are new, or significantly updated. The mix of cases reflects the global business environment: 45 percent of the cases in this book are set outside the United States, or have strong cross-border elements. Finally the blend of cases continues to reflect the growing role of women in managerial ranks: 28 percent of the cases present women as key protagonists and decision-makers. Generally, these cases reflect the increasingly diverse world of business participants.

Plan of the Book

The cases may be taught in many different combinations. The sequence indicated by the table of contents corresponds to course designs used at Darden. Each cluster of cases in the Table of Contents suggests a concept module, with a particular orientation.

1. **Setting Some Themes.** These cases introduce basic concepts of value creation, assessment of performance against a capital market benchmark, and capital market efficiency that reappear throughout a case course. The numerical analysis required of the student is relatively light. The synthesis of case facts into an important framework or perspective is the main challenge. The case, "Warren E. Buffett, 2005," sets the nearly universal theme of this volume: the need to think like an investor. "Bill Miller and Value Trust," explores a basic question about performance measurement: what is the right benchmark against which to evaluate success? "Ben & Jerry's Homemade, Inc." invites a consideration of "value" and the ways to measure it. The case entitled, "The Battle for Value, 2004: FedEx Corp. vs. United Parcel Service, Inc." uses

"economic profit" (or EVA®) to explore the origins of value creation and destruction, and its competitive implications for the future. A new case, "Genzyme and Relational Investors: Science and Business Collide?", poses the dilemma of managing a public company when the objectives of the shareholders are not always easily aligned with the long-term objectives of the company.

2. **Financial Analysis and Forecasting.** In this section, students are introduced to the crucial skills of financial-statement analysis, break-even analysis, ratio analysis, and financial statement forecasting. The section starts with a note, "The Thoughtful Forecaster", that provides a helpful introduction to financial state-ment analysis and student guidance on generating rational financial forecasts. The case, "Value Line Publishing: October 2002", provides students an exposure to financial modeling with electronic spreadsheets. "Horniman Horticulture" uses a financial model to build intuition for the relevancy of corporate cash flow and the financial effects of firm growth. The case, "Krispy Kreme Doughnuts, Inc.," confronts issues regarding the quality of reported financial results. "Guna Fibres" asks the students to consider a variety of working capital decisions, including the impact of seasonal demand upon financing needs. Other cases address issues in the analysis of working-capital management, and credit analysis.

3. **Estimating the Cost of Capital.** This module begins with a discussion of "best practices" among leading firms. The cases exercise skills in estimating the cost of capital for firms and their business segments. The cases aim to exercise and solidify students' mastery of the capital asset pricing model, the dividend-growth model, and the weighted average cost of capital formula. "Roche Holdings AG: Funding the Genentech Acquisition" is a new case that invites students to estimate the appropriate cost of debt in the largest debt issuance in history. The case provides an introduction to the concept of estimating required returns. "Nike, Inc.: Cost of Capital" presents an introductory exercise in the estimation of the weighted average cost of capital. "Teletech Corporation, 2005," explores the implications of mean-variance analysis to business segments within a firm, and gives a useful foundation for discussing value-additivity. "The Boeing 7E7," presents a dramatic exercise in the estimation of a discount rate for a major corporate project.

4. **Capital Budgeting and Resource Allocation.** The focus of these cases is the evaluation of investment opportunities and entire capital budgets. The analytical challenges range from simple time value of money problems ("The Investment Detective") to setting the entire capital budget for a resource-constrained firm ("Target Corporation"). Key issues in this module include the estimation of Free Cash Flows, the comparison of various investment criteria (NPV, IRR, payback, and equivalent annuities), the treatment of issues in mutually exclusive invest-ments, and capital budgeting under rationing. This module features several new cases. The first is "The Procter and Gamble Company: Crest Whitestrips Ad-vanced Seal", which asks the student to value a new product launch but then con-sider the financial implications of a variety of alternative launch scenarios. The second new case, "Jacobs Division", presents students an opportunity to consider the implications of strategic planning processes. And finally, "UVa Hospital System: The Long-term Acute Care Hospital Project", is an analysis of investment

decision within a not-for-profit environment. In addition to forecasting and valuing the project's cash flows, students must assess whether NPV and IRR are appropriate metrics for an organization that does not have stockholders.

5. **Management of the Firm's Equity: Dividends and Repurchases.** This module seeks to develop practical principles about dividend policy and share issues by drawing on concepts about dividend irrelevance, signaling, investor clienteles, bonding, and agency costs. The first case, "Gainesboro Machine Tools Corporation", concerns a company that is changing its business strategy and considering a change in its dividend policy. The case serves as a comprehensive introduction to corporate financial policy and themes in managing the right side of the balance sheet. The second case is new to this edition. "AutoZone, Inc." is a leading auto parts retailer that has been repurchasing shares over many years. The case serves as an excellent example of how share repurchases impact the balance sheet and presents the student with the challenge of assessing the impact upon the company's stock price.

6. **Management of the Corporate Capital Structure.** The problem of setting capital structure targets is introduced in this module. Prominent issues are the use and creation of debt tax shields, the role of industry economics and technology, the influence of corporate competitive strategy, the tradeoffs between debt policy, dividend policy, and investment goals, and the avoidance of costs of distress. The case, "California Pizza Kitchen," addresses the classic dilemma entailed in optimizing the use of debt tax shields and providing financial flexibility—this theme is extended in another case, "Deluxe Corporation" that asks how much flexibility a firm needs. "Horizon Lines, Inc." is a new case about a company facing default on a debt covenant that will prompt the need for either Chapter 11 protection or a voluntary financial restructuring.

7. **Analysis of Financing Tactics: Leases, Options, and Foreign Currency.** While the preceding module is concerned with setting debt targets, this module addresses a range of tactics a firm might use to pursue those targets, hedge risk, and exploit market opportunities. Included are domestic and international debt offerings, leases, currency hedges, warrants, and convertibles. With these cases, students will exercise techniques in securities valuation, including the use of option-pricing theory. For example, "Baker Adhesives" explores the concept of exchange-rate risk and the management of that risk with a forward-contract hedge and a money-market hedge. "MoGen, Inc" presents the pricing challenges associated with a convertible bond as well as a complex hedging strategy to change the conversion price of the convertible through the purchase of options and issuance of warrants. A new case, "J&L Railroad", presents a commodity risk problem for which students are asked to propose a specific hedging strategy using financial contracts offered on the open market or from a commercial bank.

8. **Valuing the Enterprise: Acquisitions and Buyouts.** This module begins with an extensive introduction to firm valuation in the note "Methods of Valuation: Mergers and Acquisitions." The focus of the note includes valuation using DCF and multiples. This edition features four new cases in this module. The first new case, "American Greetings", is provides a straightforward firm valuation in the context of a repurchase decision and is designed to be an introduction to firm

valuation. The second new case is "Rosetta Stone: Pricing the 2009 IPO", provides an alternative IPO valuation case to the JetBlue case with additional focus on valuation with market multiples. "Sun Microsystems" is the third new addition to the module and presents traditional takeover valuation case with opportunities to evaluate merger synergies and cost of capital implications. Several of the cases demand an analysis that spans several stakeholders. For example, "Hershey Foods Corporation," presents the high profile story of when the Hershey Trust Company put Hershey Foods up for sale. The case raises a number of challenging valuation and governance issues. "The Timken Company" deals with an acquisition that requires the student to conduct a challenging valuation analysis of Torrington as well as develop a financing strategy for the deal. The module also features a merger negotiation exercise ("Flinder Valves and Controls Inc.") that provides an engaging venue for investigating the distribution of joint value in a merger negotiation. Thus, the comprehensive nature of cases in this module makes them excellent vehicles for end-of-course classes, student term papers, and/or presentations by teams of students.

This edition offers a number of cases that give insights about investing or financing decisions in emerging markets. These include "Guna Fibres Ltd.," "Star River Electronics Ltd.," and "Baker Adhesives."

Summary of Changes for this Edition

The seventh edition represents a substantial change from the sixth edition.

This edition offers 13 new or significantly updated cases in this edition, or 25 percent of the total. In the interest of presenting a fresh and contemporary collection, older cases have been updated and/or replaced with new case situations such that all the cases are set in 2000 or later and 40 percent are set in 2006 or later. Several of the favorite "classic" cases from the first six editions are available online from Irwin/McGraw-Hill, from where instructors who adopt this edition may copy them for classroom use. All cases and teaching notes have been edited to sharpen the opportunities for student analysis.

The book continues with a strong international aspect (24 of the cases, 45 percent, are set outside the United States or feature significant cross-border issues). Also, the collection continues to feature female decision-makers and protagonists prominently (15, or 28 percent, of the cases).

Supplements

The case studies in this volume are supported by various resources that help make student engagement a success:

- Spreadsheet files support student and instructor preparation of the cases. They are located on the book's website at www.mhhe.com/bruner7e

- A guide to the novice on case preparation, "Note to the Student: How to Study and Discuss Cases" in this volume.

- The instructor's resource manual provides counterparty roles for two negotiation exercises and also presents detailed discussions of case outcomes, one of which is designed to be used as second class period for the case. These supplemental materials can significantly extend student learning and expand the opportunities for classroom discussion.

- An instructor's resource manual of about 800 pages in length containing teaching notes for each case. Each teaching note includes suggested assignment questions, a hypothetical teaching plan, and a prototypical finished case analysis.

- Website addresses in many of the teaching notes. These provide a convenient avenue for updates on the performance of undisguised companies appearing in the book.

- Notes in the instructor's manual on how to design a case method course, on using computers with cases, and on preparing to teach a case.

- A companion book by Robert Bruner titled, *Socrates' Muse: Reflections on Excellence in Case Discussion Leadership* (Irwin/McGraw-Hill, 2002), is available to instructors who adopt the book for classroom use. This book offers useful tips on case method teaching.

- Several "classic" cases and their associated teaching notes were among the most popular and durable cases in previous editions of *Case Studies in Finance*. Instructors adopting this volume for classroom use may request permission to reproduce them for their courses.

Acknowledgments

This book would not be possible without the contributions of many other people. Colleagues at Darden who have taught, co-authored, contributed to, or commented on these cases are Brandt Allen, Yiorgos Allayannis, Sam Bodily, Karl-Adam Bonnier, Susan Chaplinsky, John Colley, Bob Conroy, Mark Eaker, Richard Evans, Bob Fair, Paul Farris, Jim Freeland, Sherwood Frey, Bob Harris, Jared Harris, Mark Haskins, Michael Ho, Marc Lipson, Elena Loutskina, Pedro Matos, Matt McBrady, Charles Meiburg, Jud Reis, William Sihler and Robert Spekman. We are grateful for their collegiality and for the support for our casewriting efforts from the Darden School Foundation, the L. White Matthews Fund for Finance Casewriting, the Batten Institute, the Citicorp Global Scholars Program, Columbia Business School, INSEAD, and the University of Melbourne.

Colleagues at other schools provided worthy insights and encouragement toward the development of the seven editions of *Case Studies in Finance*. We are grateful to the following persons (listed with the schools with which they were associated at the time of our correspondence or work with them):

Michael Adler, *Columbia*

Raj Aggarwal, *John Carroll*

Turki Alshimmiri, *Kuwait Univ.*

Ed Altman, *NYU*

James Ang, *Florida State*

Paul Asquith, *M.I.T.*

Bob Barnett, *North Carolina State*

Geert Bekaert, *Stanford*

Michael Berry, *James Madison*

Randy Billingsley, *VPI&SU*

Gary Blemaster, *Georgetown*

Rick Boebel, Univ. Otago, *New Zealand*

Oyvind Bohren, *BI, Norway*

John Boquist, *Indiana*

Michael Brennan, *UCLA*

Duke Bristow, *UCLA*

Ed Burmeister, *Duke*

Kirt Butler, *Michigan State*

Don Chance, *VPI&SU*

Andrew Chen, *Southern Methodist*

Barbara J. Childs, *Univ. of Texas at Austin*

C. Roland Christensen, *Harvard*

Thomas E. Copeland, *McKinsey*

Jean Dermine, *INSEAD*

Michael Dooley, *UVA Law*

Barry Doyle, *University of San Francisco*

Bernard Dumas, *INSEAD*

Craig Dunbar, *Western Ontario*

Peter Eisemann, *Georgia State*

Javier Estrada, *IESE*

Ben Esty, *Harvard*

Thomas H. Eyssell, *Missouri*

Pablo Fernandez, *IESE*

Kenneth Ferris, *Thunderbird*

John Finnerty, *Fordham*

Joseph Finnerty, *Illinois*

Steve Foerster, *Western Ontario*

Günther Franke, *Konstanz*

Bill Fulmer, *George Mason*

Louis Gagnon, *Queens*

Dan Galai, *Jerusalem*

Jim Gentry, *Illinois*

Stuart Gilson, *Harvard*

Robert Glauber, *Harvard*

Mustafa Gultekin, *North Carolina*

Benton Gup, *Alabama*

Jim Haltiner, *William & Mary*

Rob Hansen, *VPI&SU*

Philippe Haspeslagh, *INSEAD*

Gabriel Hawawini, *INSEAD*

Pekka Hietala, *INSEAD*

Rocky Higgins, *Washington*

Pierre Hillion, *INSEAD*

Laurie Simon Hodrick, *Columbia*

John Hund, *Texas*

Daniel Indro, *Kent State*

Thomas Jackson, *UVA Law*

Pradeep Jalan, *Regina*

Michael Jensen, *Harvard*

Sreeni Kamma, *Indiana*

Steven Kaplan, *Chicago*

Andrew Karolyi, *Western Ontario*

James Kehr, *Miami Univ. Ohio*

Kathryn Kelm, *Emporia State*

Carl Kester, *Harvard*

Naveen Khanna, *Michigan State*

Herwig Langohr, *INSEAD*

Dan Laughhunn, *Duke*

Ken Lehn, *Pittsburgh*

Saul Levmore, *UVA Law*

Wilbur Lewellen, *Purdue*

Scott Linn, *Oklahoma*

Dennis Logue, *Dartmouth*

Paul Mahoney, *UVA Law*

Paul Malatesta, *Washington*

Wesley Marple, *Northeastern*

Felicia Marston, *UVA (McIntire)*

John Martin, *Texas*

Ronald Masulis, *Vanderbilt*

John McConnell, *Purdue*

Richard McEnally, *North Carolina*

Catherine McDonough, *Babson*

Wayne Mikkelson, *Oregon*

Michael Moffett, *Thunderbird*

Nancy Mohan, *Dayton*

Ed Moses, *Rollins*

Charles Moyer, *Wake Forest*

David W. Mullins, Jr., *Harvard*

James T. Murphy, *Tulane*

Chris Muscarella, *Penn State*

Robert Nachtmann, *Pittsburgh*

Tom C. Nelson, *University of Colorado*

Ben Nunnally, *UNC-Charlotte*

Robert Parrino, *Texas (Austin)*

Luis Pereiro, *Universidad Torcuato di Tella*

Pamela Peterson, *Florida State*

Larry Pettit, *Virginia (McIntire)*

Tom Piper, *Harvard*

Gordon Philips, *Maryland*

John Pringle, *North Carolina*

Ahmad Rahnema, *IESE*

Al Rappaport, *Northwestern*

Allen Rappaport, *Northern Iowa*

Raghu Rau, *Purdue*

David Ravenscraft, *North Carolina*

Henry B. Reiling, *Harvard*

Lee Remmers, *INSEAD*

Jay Ritter, *Michigan*

Richard Ruback, *Harvard*

Jim Schallheim, *Utah*

Art Selander, *Southern Methodist*

Israel Shaked, *Boston*

Dennis Sheehan, *Penn State*

J.B. Silvers, *Case Western*

Betty Simkins, *Oklahoma State*

Luke Sparvero, *Texas*

Richard Stapleton, *Lancaster*

Laura Starks, *Texas*

Jerry Stevens, *Richmond*

John Strong, *William & Mary*

Marti Subrahmanyam, *NYU*

Anant Sundaram, *Thunderbird*

Rick Swasey, *Northeastern*

Bob Taggart, *Boston College*

Udin Tanuddin, *Univ. Surabaya, Indonesia*

Anjan Thakor, *Indiana*

Thomas Thibodeau, *Southern Methodist*

Clifford Thies, *Shenandoah Univ.*

James G. Tompkins, *Kenesaw State*

Walter Torous, *UCLA*

Max Torres, *IESE*

Nick Travlos, *Boston College*

Lenos Trigeorgis, *Cyprus*

George Tsetsekos, *Drexel*

Peter Tufano, *Harvard*

James Van Horne, *Stanford*

Nick Varaiya, *San Diego State*

Theo Vermaelen, *INSEAD*

Michael Vetsuypens, *Southern Methodist*

Claude Viallet, *INSEAD*

Ingo Walter, *NYU*

Sam Weaver, *Lehigh*

J.F. Weston, *UCLA*

Peter Williamson, *Dartmouth*

Brent Wilson, *Brigham Young*

Kent Womack, *Dartmouth*

Karen Wruck, *Ohio State*

Fred Yeager, *St. Louis*

Betty Yobaccio, *Framingham State*

Marc Zenner, *North Carolina*

We are also grateful to the following practitioners (listed here with affiliated companies at the time of our work with them):

Tom Adams, *Rosetta Stone*

Norm Bartczak, *Center for Financial Strategy*

Bo Brookby, *First Wachovia*

Alison Brown, *Compass Records*

W.L. Lyons Brown, *Brown-Forman*

Bliss Williams Browne, *First Chicago*

George Bruns, *BankBoston*

Ian Buckley, *Henderson Investors*

Ned Case, *General Motors*

Phil Clough, *ABS Capital*

Daniel Cohrs, *Marriott*

David Crosby, *Johnson & Johnson*

Jinx Dennett, *BankBoston*

Barbara Dering, *Bank of New York*

Ty Eggemeyer, *McKinsey*

Geoffrey Elliott, *Morgan Stanley*

Glenn Eisenberg, *The Timken Company*

Louis Elson, *Palamon Capital Partners*

Christine Eosco, *BankBoston*

Larry Fitzgerald, *UVA Health System*

Catherine Friedman, *Morgan Stanley*

Carl Frischkorn, *Threshold Sports*

Carrie Galeotafiore, *Value Line Publishing*

Charles Griffith, *AlliedSignal*

Ian Harvey, *BankBoston*

David Herter, *Fleet Boston*

Christopher Howe, *Kleinwort Benson*

Paul Hunn, *Manufacturers Hanover*

Kristen Huntley, *Morgan Stanley*

James Gelly, *General Motors*

Ed Giera, *General Motors*

Betsy Hatfield, *Bank Boston*

Denis Hamboyan, *Bank Boston*

John Hulbert, *Target Corp.*

Thomas Jasper, *Salomon Brothers*

Andrew Kalotay, *Salomon Brothers*

Lisa Levine, *Equipment Leasing*

Mary Lou Kelley, *McKinsey*

Francesco Kestenholz, *UBS*

Daniel Lentz, *Procter and Gamble*

Eric Linnes, *Kleinwort Benson*

Peter Lynch, *Fidelity Investments*

Dar Maanavi, *Merrill Lynch*

Mary McDaniel, *SNL Securities*

Jean McTighe, *BankBoston*

Frank McTigue, *McTigue Associates*

David Meyer, *J.P. Morgan*

Michael Melloy, *Planet*

Jeanne Mockard, *Putnam Investments*

Pascal Montiero de Barros, *Planet*

Lin Morison, *BankBoston*

John Muleta, *PSINet*

Dennis Neumann, *Bank of New York*

John Newcomb, *BankBoston*

Ralph Norwood, *Polaroid*

Marni Gislason Obernauer, *J.P. Morgan*

John Owen, *JetBlue Airways*

Michael Pearson, *McKinsey*

Nancy Preis, *Kleinwort Benson*

Joe Prendergast, *First Wachovia*

Luis Quartin-Bastos, *Planet*

Jack Rader, *FMA*

Christopher Reilly, *S.G. Warburg*

Emilio Rottoli, *Glaxo*

Gerry Rooney, *NationsBank*

Craig Ruff, *AIMR*

Barry Sabloff, *First Chicago*

Linda Scheuplein, *J.P. Morgan*

Doug Scovanner, *Target Corp.*

Keith Shaughnessy, *Bank Boston*

Jack Sheehan, *Johnstown*

Katrina Sherrerd, *AIMR*

John Smetanka, *Security Pacific*

John Smith, *General Motors*

Raj Srinath, *AMTRAK*

Rick Spangler, *First Wachovia*

Kirsten Spector, *BankBoston*

Martin Steinmeyer, *MediMedia*

Bill Stilley, Adenosine *Therapeutics*

Stephanie Summers, *Lehman Brothers*

Sven-Ivan Sundqvist, *Dagens Nyheter*

Patrick Sweeney, *Servervault*

Henri Termeer, *Genzyme*

Ward J. Timken, Jr., *The Timken Company*

Peter Thorpe, *Citicorp.*

Katherine Updike, *Excelsior*

Tom Verdoorn, *Land O'Lakes*

Frank Ward, *Corp. Performance Systems*

David Wake Walker, *Kleinwort Benson*

Garry West, *Compass Records*

Ulrich Wiechmann, *UWINC*

Ralph Whitworth, *Relational Investors*

Scott Williams, *McKinsey*

Harry You, *Salomon Brothers*

Richard Zimmermann, *Hershey Foods*

Research assistants working under our direction have helped gather data and prepare drafts. Research assistants who contributed to various cases in this and previous editions include Darren Berry, Justin Brenner, Anna Buchanan, Anne Campbell, Drew Chambers, Jessica Chan, Vladimir Kolcin, Lucas Doe, Brett Durick, David Eichler, Ali Erarac, Rick Green, Daniel Hake, Dennis Hall, Jerry Halpin, Peter Hennessy, Nili Mehta, Casey Opitz, Katarina Paddack, Suprajj Papireddy, Chad Rynbrandt, John Sherwood, Elizabeth Shumadine, Jane Sommers-Kelly, Thien Pham, Carla Stiassni, Sanjay Vakharia, Larry Weatherford, and Steve Wilus. We give special acknowledgement to Sean Carr who played a multifaceted role in the production of the previous edition. It was his efforts that not only made the fifth edition a reality, but also positioned us so well to complete this edition. We have supervised numerous others in the development of individual cases—those worthy contributors are recognized in the first footnote of each case.

A busy professor soon learns the wisdom in the adage, "Many hands make work light." we are very grateful to the staff of the Darden School for its support in this project. Excellent editorial assistance at Darden was provided by Stephen Smith and Catherine Wiese (Darden's nonpareil editors) and their associates in Darden Business Publishing and the Darden Case Collection, Sherry Alston, Amy Lemley, Heidi White, and Beth Woods. Ginny Fisher gave stalwart secretarial support. Valuable library research support was given by Karen Marsh King and Susan Norrisey. The patience, care, and dedication of these people are richly appreciated.

At McGraw-Hill/Irwin, Chuck Synovec has served as Executive Editor for this book. Mike Junior, now Vice President, recruited Bob Bruner into this project years ago; the legacy of that early vision-setting continues in this edition. Lisa Bruflodt was the project manager, and Casey Rasch served as Editorial Coordinator on this edition.

Of all the contributors, our wives, Barbara M. Bruner, Kathy N. Eades, and Mary Ann H. Schill as well as our children have endured great sacrifices as the result of our work on this book. As Milton said, "They also serve who only stand and wait." Development of this seventh edition would not have been possible without their fond patience.

All these acknowledgments notwithstanding, responsibility for these materials is ours. We welcome suggestions for their enhancement. Please let us know of your experience with these cases, either through McGraw-Hill/Irwin, or at the coordinates given below.

Robert F. Bruner
Dean,
Charles C. Abbott Professor of Business Administration and
Distinguished Professor of Business Administration
Darden Graduate School of Business
University of Virginia
brunerr@virginia.edu[§]

Kenneth M. Eades
Paul Tudor Jones Research Professor of Business Administration
Darden Graduate School of Business
University of Virginia
eades@virginia.edu*

Michael J. Schill
Associate Professor of Business Administration
Darden Graduate School of Business
University of Virginia
schill@virginia.edu*

Individual copies of all the Darden cases in this and previous editions may be obtained promptly from McGraw-Hill/Irwin's Create (http://create.mcgraw-hill.com) or from Darden Business Publishing (telephone: 800-246-3367; https://store.darden. virginia.edu/). Proceeds from these case sales support case writing efforts. Please respect the copyrights on these materials.

[§]Students should know that we are unable to offer any comments that would assist their preparation of these cases without the prior express request of their instructors.

Note to the Student: How to Study and Discuss Cases

Get a good idea and stay with it. Dog it and work at it until it's done, and done right.
—Walt Disney

You enroll in a "case-method" course, pick up the book of case studies or the stack of loose-leaf cases, and get ready for the first class meeting. If this is your first experience with case discussions, the odds are that you are clueless and a little anxious about how to prepare for this course. That is fairly normal, but something you should try to break through quickly in order to gain the maximum benefit from your studies. Quick breakthroughs come from a combination of good attitude, good "infrastructure," and good execution—this note offers some tips.

Good Attitude

Students learn best that which they teach themselves. Passive and mindless learning is ephemeral. Active, mindful learning simply sticks. The case method makes learning sticky by placing you in situations that require the invention of tools and concepts *in your own terms*. The most successful case-method students share a set of characteristics that drive self-teaching:

1. **Personal initiative, self-reliance:** Case studies rarely suggest how to proceed. Professors are more like guides on a long hike: They can't carry you, but they can show you the way. You must arrive at the destination under your own power. You must figure out the case on your own. To teach yourself means that you must sort ideas out in ways that make sense to you personally. To teach yourself is to give yourself two gifts: the idea you are trying to learn and greater self-confidence in your own ability to master the world.

2. **Curiosity, a zest for exploration as an end in itself:** Richard P. Feynman, who won the Nobel Prize in Physics in 1965, was once asked whether his key discovery was worth it. He replied, "[The Nobel Prize is] a pain in the [neck]. . . . I don't like honors. . . . The prize is the pleasure of finding the thing out, the kick in the discovery, the observation that other people use it [my work]—those are the real things; the honors are unreal to me."[1]

3. **A willingness to take risks:** Risk-taking is at the heart of all learning. Usually, one learns more from failures than from successes. Banker Walter Wriston once said, "Good judgment comes from experience. Experience comes from bad judgment."

4. **Patience and persistence:** Case studies are messy, a realistic reflection of the fact that managers don't manage problems, they manage messes. Initially, reaching a solution will seem to be the major challenge. But once you reach *a* solution, you may discover other possible solutions and then face the choice among the best alternatives.

5. **An orientation to community and discussion:** Much of the power of the case method derives from a willingness to *talk* with others about your ideas and your points of confusion. This is one of the paradoxes of the case method: You must teach yourself, but not in a vacuum. The poet T. S. Eliot said, "There is no life not lived in community." Talking seems like such an inefficient method of sorting through the case, but if exploration is an end in itself, then talking is the only way. Furthermore, talking is an excellent means of testing your own mastery of ideas, of rooting out points of confusion, and, generally, of preparing yourself for professional life.

6. **Trust in the process:** The learnings from a case-method course are impressive. They arrive cumulatively over time. In many cases, the learnings continue well after the course has finished. Occasionally, those learnings hit you with the force of a tsunami. But generally, the learnings creep in quietly but powerfully like the tide. After the case course, you will look back and see that your thinking, mastery, and appreciation have changed dramatically. The key point is that you should not measure the success of your progress on the basis of any single case discussion. Trust that, in the cumulative work over many cases, you will gain the mastery you seek.

Good Infrastructure

"Infrastructure" consists of all the resources that the case-method student can call upon. Some of this is simply given to you by the professor: case studies, assignment questions, supporting references to textbooks or articles, and computer data or models. But you can go much further to help yourself. Consider these steps:

1. **Find a quiet place to study. Spend at least 90 minutes there for each case study.** Each case has subtleties to it that you will miss unless you can concentrate. After two or three visits, your quiet place will take on the attributes of a habit:

---

[1]Richard P. Feynman, *The Pleasure of Finding Things Out* (Cambridge, Mass.: Perseus Publishing, 1999), 12.

You will slip into a working attitude more easily. Be sure to spend enough time in the quiet place to give yourself a chance to really engage the case.

2. **Get a business dictionary.** If you are new to business and finance, some of the terms will seem foreign; if English is not your first language, *many* of the terms will seem foreign, if not bizarre. Get into the habit of looking up terms that you don't know. The benefit of this becomes cumulative.

3. **Skim a business newspaper each day, read a business magazine, follow the markets.** Reading a newspaper or magazine helps build a *context* for the case study you are trying to solve at the moment, and helps you make connections between the case study and current events. The terminology of business and finance that you see in the publications helps to reinforce your use of the dictionary, and hastens your mastery of the terms that you will see in the cases. Your learning by reading business periodicals is cumulative. Some students choose to follow a good business-news Web site on the Internet. Those Web sites have the virtue of being inexpensive and efficient, but they tend to screen too much. Having the printed publication in your hands and leafing through it help the process of *discovery*, which is the whole point of the exercise.

4. **Learn the basics of spreadsheet modeling on a computer.** Many case studies now have supporting data available for analysis in *Microsoft Excel* spreadsheet files. Analyzing the data on a computer rather than by hand both speeds up your work and extends your reach.

5. **Form a study group.** The ideas in many cases are deep; the analysis can get complex. *You will learn more and perform better in class participation by discussing the cases together in a learning team.* Your team should devote an average of an hour to each case. High-performance teams show a number of common attributes:

   a. The members commit to the success of the team.

   b. The team plans ahead, leaving time for contingencies.

   c. The team meets regularly.

   d. Team members show up for meetings and are *prepared* to contribute.

   e. There may or may not be a formal leader, but the assignments are clear. Team members meet their assigned obligations.

6. **Get to know your professor.** In the case method, students inevitably learn more from one another than from the instructor. But the teacher is part of the learning infrastructure, too: a resource to be used wisely. Never troll for answers in advance of a case discussion. Do your homework; use classmates and learning teams to clear up most of your questions so that you can focus on the meatiest issues with the teacher. Be very organized and focused about what you would like to discuss. Remember that teachers like to learn, too: If you reveal a new insight about a case or bring a clipping about a related issue in current events, both the professor and the student can gain from their time together. Ultimately, the best payoff to the professor is the "aha" in the student's eyes when he or she masters an idea.

Good Execution

Good attitude and infrastructure must be employed properly—one needs good execution. The extent to which a student learns depends on how the case study is approached. What can one do to gain the maximum from the study of those cases?

1. **Reading the case.** The very first time you read any case, look for the forest, not the trees. This requires that your first reading be quick. Do not begin taking notes on the first round; instead, read the case like a magazine article. The first few paragraphs of a well-constructed case usually say something about the problem—read those carefully. Then quickly read the rest of the case, mainly seeking a sense of the scope of the problems and what information the case contains to help resolve them. Leaf through the exhibits, looking for what information they hold rather than for any analytical insights. At the conclusion of the first pass, read any supporting articles or notes that your instructor may have recommended.

2. **Getting into the case situation. Develop your "awareness."** With the broader perspective in mind, the second and more detailed reading will be more productive. The reason is that as you now encounter details, your mind will be able to organize them in some useful fashion rather than inventorying them randomly. Making links among case details is necessary for solving the case. At this point, you can take notes that will set up your analysis.

   The most successful students project themselves into the position of the decision-maker because this perspective helps them link case details as well as develop a stand on the case problem. Assignment questions may help you do this, but it is a good idea to get into the habit of doing it yourself. Here are the kinds of questions you might try to answer in preparing every case:

   - Who are the protagonists in the case? Who must take action on the problem? What do they have at stake? What pressures are they under?

   - What business is the company in? What is the nature of its product? What is the nature of demand for that product? What is the firm's distinctive competence? With whom does it compete?[2] What is the structure of the industry? Is the firm comparatively strong or weak? In what ways?

   - What are the goals of the firm? What is the firm's strategy in pursuit of those goals? (The goals and strategy may be explicitly stated, or they may be implicit in the way the firm does business.) What are the firm's apparent functional policies in marketing (e.g., push versus pull strategy), production (e.g., labor relations, use of new technology, distributed production versus centralized), and finance (e.g., the use of debt financing, payment of dividends)? Financial

---

[2]Think broadly about competitors. In *A Connecticut Yankee in King Arthur's Court,* Mark Twain wrote, "The best swordsman in the world doesn't need to fear the second best swordsman in the world; no, the person for him to be afraid of is some ignorant antagonist who has never had a sword in his hand before; he doesn't do the thing he ought to do, and so the expert isn't prepared for him; he does the thing he ought not to do; and it often catches the expert out and ends him on the spot."

and business strategies can be inferred from an analysis of the financial ratios and a sources-and-uses-of-funds statement.

- How well has the firm performed in pursuit of its goals? (The answer to this question calls for simple analysis using financial ratios, such as the DuPont system, compound growth rates, and measures of value creation.)

The larger point of this phase of your case preparation is to broaden your awareness of the issues. Warren Buffett, perhaps the most successful investor in history, said, "Any player unaware of the fool in the market probably *is* the fool in the market." Awareness is an important attribute of successful managers.

3. **Defining the problem.** A common trap for many executives is to assume that the issue at hand is the real problem most worthy of their time, rather than a symptom of some larger problem that *really* deserves their time. For instance, a lender is often asked to advance funds to help tide a firm over a cash shortfall. Careful study may reveal that the key problem is not a cash shortfall, but rather product obsolescence, unexpected competition, or careless cost management. Even in cases where the decision is fairly narrowly defined (e.g., a capital-expenditure choice), the "problem" generally turns out to be the believability of certain key assumptions. Students who are new to the case method tend to focus narrowly in defining problems and often overlook the influence that the larger setting has on the problem. In doing that, the student develops narrow specialist habits, never achieving the general-manager perspective. It is useful and important for you to define the problem yourself and, in the process, validate the problem as suggested by the protagonist in the case.

4. **Analysis: run the numbers and go to the heart of the matter.** Virtually all finance cases require numerical analysis. This is good because figure-work lends rigor and structure to your thinking. But some cases, reflecting reality, invite you to explore blind alleys. If you are new to finance, even those explorations will help you learn.[3] The best case students develop an instinct for where to devote their analysis. Economy of effort is desirable. If you have invested wisely in problem definition, economical analysis tends to follow. For instance, a student might assume that a particular case is meant to exercise financial forecasting skills and will spend two or more hours preparing a detailed forecast, instead of preparing a simpler forecast in one hour and conducting a sensitivity analysis based on key assumptions in the next hour. An executive rarely thinks of a situation as having to do with a forecasting method or discounting or any other technique, but rather thinks of it as a problem of judgment, deciding on which people or concepts or environmental conditions to bet. The best case analyses get down to the *key bets* on which the executive is wagering the prosperity of the firm and his or her career. Get to the business issues quickly, and avoid lengthy churning through relatively unimportant calculations.

---

[3]Case analysis is often iterative: An understanding of the big issues invites an analysis of details—then the details may restructure the big issues and invite the analysis of other details. In some cases, getting to the heart of the matter will mean just such iteration.

5. **Prepare to participate: take a stand.** To develop analytical insights without making recommendations is useless to executives and drains the case-study experience of some of its learning power. A stand means having a point of view about the problem, a recommendation, and an analysis to back up both of them. The lessons most worth learning all come from taking a stand. From that truth flows the educative force of the case method. In the typical case, the student is projected into the position of an executive who must do something in response to a problem. It is this choice of what to do that constitutes the executive's stand. Over the course of a career, an executive who takes stands gains wisdom. If the stand provides an effective resolution of the problem, so much the better for all concerned. If it does not, however, the wise executive analyzes the reasons for the failure and may learn even more than from a success. As Theodore Roosevelt wrote:

> The credit belongs to the man[4] who is actually in the arena—whose face is marred by dust and sweat and blood . . . who knows the great enthusiasms, the great devotions—and spends himself in a worthy cause—who, at best, if he wins, knows the thrills of high achievement—and if he fails, at least fails while daring greatly so that his place shall never be with those cold and timid souls who know neither victory nor defeat.

6. **In class: participate actively in support of your conclusions, but be open to new insights.** Of course, one can have a stand without the world being any wiser. To take a stand in case discussions means to participate actively in the discussion and to advocate your stand until new facts or analyses emerge to warrant a change.[5] Learning by the case method is not a spectator sport. A classic error many students make is to bring into the case-method classroom the habits of the lecture hall (i.e., passively absorbing what other people say). These habits fail miserably in the case-method classroom because they only guarantee that one absorbs the truths and fallacies uttered by others. The purpose of case study is to develop and exercise one's *own* skills and judgment. This takes practice and participation, just as in a sport. Here are two good general suggestions: (1) defer significant note-taking until after class and (2) strive to contribute to every case discussion.

7. **Immediately after class: jot down notes, corrections, and questions.** Don't overinvest in taking notes during class—that just cannibalizes "air time" in which you could be learning through discussing the case. But immediately after class, collect your learnings and questions in notes that will capture your thinking. Of course, ask a fellow student or your teacher questions to help clarify issues that still puzzle you.

---

[4]Today, a statement such as this would surely recognize women as well.

[5]There is a difference between taking a stand and pigheadedness. Nothing is served by clinging to your stand to the bitter end in the face of better analysis or common sense. Good managers recognize new facts and good arguments as they come to light and adapt.

8. **Once a week, flip through notes. Make a list of your questions, and pursue answers.** Take an hour each weekend to review your notes from class discussions during the past week. This will help build your grasp of the flow of the course. Studying a subject by the case method is like building a large picture with small mosaic tiles. It helps to step back to see the big picture. But the main objective should be to make an inventory of anything you are unclear about: terms, concepts, and calculations. Work your way through this inventory with classmates, learning teams, and, ultimately, the instructor. This kind of review and follow-up builds your self-confidence and prepares you to participate more effectively in future case discussions.

Conclusion: Focus on Process and Results Will Follow

View the case-method experience as a series of opportunities to test your mastery of techniques and your business judgment. If you seek a list of axioms to be etched in stone, you are bound to disappoint yourself. As in real life, there are virtually no "right" answers to these cases in the sense that a scientific or engineering problem has an exact solution. Jeff Milman has said, "The answers worth getting are never found in the back of the book." What matters is that you obtain a way of thinking about business situations that you can carry from one job (or career) to the next. In the case method, it is largely true that *how you learn is what you learn.*[6]

---

[6]In describing the work of case teachers, John H. McArthur has said, "How we teach is what we teach."

Ethics in Finance

The first thing is character, before money or anything else.
—J. P. Morgan (in testimony before the U.S. Congress)

The professional concerns himself with doing the right thing rather than making money, knowing that the profit takes care of itself if the other things are attended to.
—Edwin LeFevre, *Reminiscences of a Stock Operator*

Integrity is paramount for a successful career in finance and business, as practitioners remind us. One learns, rather than inherits, integrity. And the lessons are everywhere, even in case studies about finance. To some people, the world of finance is purely mechanical, devoid of ethical considerations. The reality is that ethical issues are pervasive in finance. **Exhibit 1** gives a list of prominent business scandals around the turn of the twenty-first century. One is struck by the wide variety of industrial settings and especially by the recurrent issues rooted in finance and accounting. Still, the disbelief that ethics matter in finance can take many forms.

"It's not my job," says one person, thinking that a concern for ethics belongs to a CEO, an ombudsperson, or a lawyer. But if you passively let someone else do your thinking, you expose yourself to complicity in the unethical decisions of others. Even worse is the possibility that if everyone assumes that someone else owns the job of ethical practice, then perhaps *no one* owns it and that therefore the enterprise has no moral compass at all.

Another person says, "When in Rome, do as the Romans do. It's a dog-eat-dog world. We have to play the game their way if we mean to do business there." Under that view, it is assumed that everybody acts ethically relative to his local environment so that it is inappropriate to challenge unethical behavior. This is moral relativism. The problem with this view is that it presupposes that you have no identity, that, like a chameleon, you are defined by the environment around you. Relativism is the enemy of personal identity and character. You *must* have a view, if you are rooted in any cultural system. Prepare to take a stand.

A third person says, "It's too complicated. Civilization has been arguing about ethics for 3,000 years. You expect me to master it in my lifetime?" The response must be that we use complicated systems dozens of times each day without a full mastery of their details. Perhaps the alternative would be to live in a cave, which is a simpler life but much less rewarding. Moreover, as courts have been telling the business world for centuries, ignorance of the law is no defense. If you want to succeed in the field of finance, you must grasp the norms of ethical behavior.

There is no escaping the fact that ethical reasoning is vital to the practice of business and finance. Tools and concepts of ethical reasoning belong in the financial toolkit alongside other valuable instruments of financial practice.

Ethics and economics were once tightly interwoven. The patriarch of economics, Adam Smith, was actually a scholar of moral philosophy. Although the two fields may have diverged in the last century, they remain strong complements.[1] Morality concerns norms and teachings. Ethics concerns the process of making morally *good* decisions or, as Andrew Wicks wrote, "Ethics has to do with pursuing—and achieving—laudable ends."[2] The *Oxford English Dictionary* defines moral as follows: "Of knowledge, opinions, judgments, etc.; relating to the nature and application of the distinction between right and wrong."[3] Ethics, however, is defined as the "science of morals."[4] To see how the decision-making processes in finance have ethical implications, consider the following case study.

Minicase: WorldCom Inc.[5]

The largest corporate fraud in history entailed the falsification of $11 billion in operating profits at WorldCom Inc. WorldCom was among the three largest long-distance telecommunications providers in the United States, the creation of a rollup acquisition strategy by its CEO, Bernard Ebbers. WorldCom's largest acquisition, MCI Communications in 1998, capped the momentum-growth story. This, combined with the buoyant stock market of the late 1990s, increased the firm's share price dramatically.

By early 2001, it dawned on analysts and investors that the United States was greatly oversupplied with long-distance telecommunications capacity. Much of that capacity had been put in place with unrealistic expectations of growth in Internet use. With the collapse of the Internet bubble, the future of telecom providers was suddenly in doubt.

---

[1] Sen (1987) and Werhane (1999) have argued that Smith's masterpiece, *Wealth of Nations,* is incorrectly construed as a justification for self-interest and that it speaks more broadly about virtues such as prudence, fairness, and cooperation.

[2] Wicks (2003), 5.

[3] *Oxford English Dictionary* (1989), vol. IX, 1068.

[4] *Oxford English Dictionary* (1989), vol. V, 421.

[5] This case is based on facts drawn from Pulliam (2003), Blumenstein and Pulliam (2003), Blumenstein and Solomon (2003), and Solomon (2003).

WorldCom had leased a significant portion of its capacity to both Internet service providers and telecom service providers. Many of those lessees declined and, starting in 2000, entered bankruptcy. In mid-2000, Ebbers and WorldCom's chief financial officer (CFO), Scott Sullivan, advised Wall Street that earnings would fall below expectations. WorldCom's costs were largely fixed—the firm had high operating leverage. With relatively small declines in revenue, earnings would decline sharply. In the third quarter of 2000, WorldCom was hit with $685 million in write-offs as its customers defaulted on capacity-lease commitments. In October 2000, Sullivan pressured three midlevel accounting managers at WorldCom to draw on reserve accounts set aside for other purposes to cover operating expenses, which reduced the reported operating expenses and increased profits. The transfer violated rules regarding the independence and purpose of reserve accounts. The three accounting managers acquiesced, but later regretted their action. They considered resigning, but were persuaded to remain with the firm through its earnings crisis. They hoped or believed that a turnaround in the firm's business would make their action an exception.

Conditions worsened in the first quarter of 2001. Revenue fell further, producing a profit shortfall of $771 million. Again, Sullivan prevailed on the three accounting managers to shift operating costs—this time, to capital-expenditure accounts. Again, the managers complied. This time, they backdated entries in the process. In the second, third, and fourth quarters of 2001, they transferred $560 million, $743 million, and $941 million, respectively. In the first quarter of 2002, they transferred $818 million.

The three accounting managers experienced deep emotional distress over their actions. In April 2002, when they discovered that WorldCom's financial plan for 2002 implied that the transfers would continue until the end of the year, the three managers vowed to cease making transfers and to look for new jobs. But inquiries by the U.S. Securities and Exchange Commission (SEC) into the firm's suspiciously positive financial performance triggered an investigation by the firm's head of internal auditing. Feeling the heat of the investigation, the three managers met with representatives from the SEC, the U.S. Federal Bureau of Investigation (FBI), and the U.S. attorney's office on June 24, 2002. The next day, WorldCom's internal auditor disclosed to the SEC the discovery of $3.8 billion in fraudulent accounting. On June 26, the SEC charged WorldCom with fraud.

But the scope of the fraud grew. In addition to the $3.8 billion reallocation of operating expenses to reserves and capital expenditures, WorldCom had shifted another $7.2 billion to its MCI subsidiary, which affected the tracking stock on that entity.

As news of the size of the fraud spread, WorldCom's stock price sank. From its peak in late 2000 until it filed for bankruptcy in July 2002, about $180 billion of WorldCom's equity-market value evaporated. In March 2003, WorldCom announced that it would write off $79.8 billion in assets following an impairment analysis: $45 billion of the write-off arose from the impairment of goodwill.

The three accounting managers had hoped that they would be viewed simply as witnesses. On August 1, they were named by the U.S. attorney's office as unindicted co-conspirators in the fraud. WorldCom fired them immediately. Unable to cope with the prospect of large legal bills for their defense, they pleaded guilty to securities fraud and conspiracy to commit fraud. The charges carried a maximum of 15 years in prison.

Bernard Ebbers and Scott Sullivan were charged with fraud. A study conducted by the bankruptcy examiner concluded that Ebbers had played a role in inflating the firm's revenues. One example cited in the report was the firm's announcement of the acquisition of Intermedia Communications Inc. in February 2001. Even before WorldCom's board had approved the deal, the firm's lawyers made it look as if the board had approved the deal by creating false minutes.

WorldCom emerged from bankruptcy in 2004 with a new name, MCI Communications. On March 2, 2004, Sullivan pleaded guilty to fraud. Ebbers continued to protest his innocence, arguing that the fraud was masterminded by Sullivan without Ebbers's knowledge. A jury found Ebbers guilty on March 15, 2005. In the summer of 2005, MCI agreed to be acquired by Verizon, a large regional telephone company in the United States.

This case illustrates how unethical behavior escalates over time. Such behavior is costly to companies, investors, and employees. It damages investor confidence and trust—and it is invariably uncovered. Fraud and earnings management share a common soil: a culture of aggressive growth. Although growth is one of the foremost aims in business, the mentality of growth at any price can warp the thinking of otherwise honorable people.

The shields against fraud are a culture of integrity, strong governance, and strong financial monitoring. Yet in some circumstances, such shields fail to forestall unethical behavior. Michael Jensen (2005) explored an important circumstance associated with managerial actions: when the stock price of a firm is inflated beyond its intrinsic (or true) value. Jensen pointed to the scandals that surfaced during and after a period of overvaluation in share prices between 1998 and 2001. He argued that "society seems to overvalue what is new." When a firm's equity becomes overvalued, it motivates behavior that poorly serves the interests of those investors on whose behalf the firm is managed. Managers whose compensation is tied to increases in share price are motivated to "game the system" by setting targets and managing earnings in ways that yield large bonuses. This behavior is a subset of problems originating from target-based corporate-budgeting systems.

Jensen argues that the market for corporate control solves the problem of *under*valued equity (i.e., firms operating at low rates of efficiency) with the instruments of hostile takeovers, proxy fights, leveraged buyouts, and so on. But he points out that there is little remedy for the opposite case, *over*valued equity. Equity-based compensation—in the form of stock options, shares of stock, stock-appreciation rights, and so on—merely adds fuel to the fire.

Paradoxically, a high stock price would seem to be desirable. But occasionally, stock prices become detached from the fundamental basis for their valuation—that is, when the price exceeds the intrinsic value of the shares. Jensen defines overvalued stock as occurring when the performance necessary to produce that price cannot be attained except by good fortune. The problem is that managers fail to face the facts and explain to investors the overvaluation of shares. Instead, they take actions that prolong, or even worsen, the overvaluation. Those actions destroy value in the long run, even though they may appear to create or preserve value in the short run—as was the case with WorldCom. A little of this behavior begins to stimulate more; soon, a sense of proportion is lost and the organization eventually turns to fraud. The hope is to postpone the inevitable correction in price until after the executive has moved on to another firm or retired. Telling the truth to investors about overvaluation is extremely painful. The firm's stock price falls, executive bonuses dwindle, and the directors listen to outraged investors.

What the tragedies of WorldCom and the other firms cited in **Exhibit 1** share is that, like Peter Pan, those companies refused to grow up. They refused to admit frankly to their shareholders and to themselves that their very high rates of growth were unsustainable.

Why One Should Care about Ethics in Finance

Managing in ethical ways is not merely about avoiding bad outcomes. There are at least five positive arguments for bringing ethics to bear on financial decision-making.

Sustainability. Unethical practices are not a foundation for enduring, sustainable enterprise. This first consideration focuses on the *legacy* one creates through one's financial transactions. What legacy do you want to leave? To incorporate ethics into our finance mind-set is to think about the kind of world that we would like to live in and that our children will inherit.

One might object that, in a totally anarchic world, unethical behavior might be the only path in life. But this view only begs the point: We don't live in such a world. Instead, our world of norms and laws ensures a corrective process against unethical behavior.

Ethical behavior builds trust. Trust rewards. The branding of products seeks to create a bond between producer and consumer: a signal of purity, performance, or other attributes of quality. This bond is built by trustworthy behavior. As markets reveal, successfully branded products command a premium price. Bonds of trust tend to pay. If the field of finance were purely a world of one-off transactions, it would seem ripe for opportunistic behavior. But in the case of repeated entry into financial markets and transactions by, for example, active buyers, intermediaries, and advisers, reputation can count for a great deal in shaping the expectations of counterparties. This implicit bond, trust, or reputation can translate into more effective and economically attractive financial transactions and policies.

Surely, ethical behavior should be an end in itself. If you are behaving ethically only to get rich, then you are hardly committed to that behavior. But it is a useful encouragement that ethical behavior need not entail pure sacrifice. Some might even see ethical behavior as an imperfect means by which justice expresses itself.

Ethical behavior builds teams and leadership, which underpin process excellence. Standards of global best-practice emphasize that good business processes drive good outcomes. Stronger teams and leaders result in more agile and creative responses to problems. Ethical behavior contributes to the strength of teams and leadership by aligning employees around shared values and by building confidence and loyalty.

An objection to this argument is that, in some settings, promoting ethical behavior is no guarantee of team-building. Indeed, teams might blow apart over disagreements about what is ethical or what action is appropriate to take. But typically, this is not the fault of ethics, but rather that of the teams' processes for handling disagreements.

Ethics sets a higher standard than laws and regulations. To a large extent, the law is a crude instrument. It tends to trail rather than anticipate behavior. It contains gaps that become recreational exploitation for the aggressive businessperson. Justice may be neither swift nor proportional to the crime; as Andrew Wicks said, it "puts you in an adversarial posture with respect to others, which may be counterproductive to other objectives in facing a crisis."[6] To use only the law as a basis for ethical thinking is to settle for the lowest common denominator of social norms. As Richard Breeden, the former SEC chair, said, "It is not an adequate ethical standard to want to get through the day without being indicted."[7]

Some might object to that line of thinking by claiming that, in a pluralistic society, the law is the only baseline of norms on which society can agree. Therefore, isn't the law a "good-enough" guide to ethical behavior? Lynn Paine argued that this view leads to a "compliance" mentality and that ethics takes one further. She wrote, "Attention to law, as an important source of managers' rights and responsibilities, is integral to, but not a substitute for, the ethical point of view—a point of view that is attentive to rights, responsibilities, relationships, opportunities to improve and enhance human well-being, and virtue and moral excellence."[8]

Reputation and conscience. Motivating ethical behavior only by trumpeting its financial benefits without discussing its costs is inappropriate. By some estimates, the average annual income for a lifetime of crime (even counting years spent in prison) is large—it seems that crime *does* pay. If income were all that mattered, most of us would switch to this lucrative field. The business world features enough cheats and scoundrels who illustrate that there are myriad opportunities for any professional to break promises—or worse—for money. Ethical professionals decline those opportunities for reasons having to do with the kind of people they want to be. Amar Bhide and Howard Stevenson wrote:

> The businesspeople we interviewed set great store on the regard of their family, friends, and the community at large. They valued their reputations, not for some nebulous financial gain but because they took pride in their good names. Even more important, since outsiders cannot easily judge trustworthiness, businesspeople seem guided by their inner voices, by their consciences. . . . We keep promises because it is right to do so, not because it is good business.[9]

---

[6]Wicks (2003), 11.

[7]K. V. Salwen, "SEC Chief's Criticism of Ex-Managers of Salomon Suggests Civil Action is Likely," *Wall Street Journal,* 20 November 1991, A10.

[8]Paine (1999), 194–195.

[9]Bhide and Stevenson (1990), 127–128.

For Whose Interests Are You Working?

Generally, the financial executive or deal designer is an agent acting on behalf of others. For whom are you the agent? Two classic schools of thought emerge.

- *Stockholders.* Some national legal frameworks require directors and managers to operate a company in the interests of its shareholders. This shareholder focus affords a clear objective: do what creates shareholder wealth. This approach would seem to limit charitable giving, "living-wage" programs, voluntary reduction of pollution, and enlargement of pension benefits for retirees, all of which can be loosely gathered under the umbrella of the social responsibility movement in business. Milton Friedman (1962), perhaps the most prominent exponent of the stockholder school of thought, has argued that the objective of business is to return value to its owners, and that to divert the objective to other ends is to expropriate shareholder value and threaten the survival of the enterprise. Also, the stockholder view would argue that, if all the companies deviated, the price system would cease to function well as a carrier of information about the allocation of resources in the economy. The stockholder view is perhaps dominant in the United States, the United Kingdom, and other countries in the Anglo-Saxon sphere.

- *Stakeholders.* The alternative view admits that stockholders are an important constituency of the firm, but that other groups such as employees, customers, suppliers, and the community also have a stake in the activities and the success of the firm. Edward Freeman (1984) argued that the firm should be managed in the interest of the broader spectrum of constituents. The manager would necessarily be obligated to account for the interests and concerns of the various constituent groups in arriving at business decisions. The aim would be to satisfy them all, or at least the most concerned stakeholders, on each issue. The complexity of that kind of decision-making can be daunting and slows the process. In addition, it is not always clear which stakeholder interests are relevant in making specific decisions. Such a definition seems to depend largely on the specific context, which would seem to challenge the ability to achieve equitable treatment of different stakeholder groups across time. But the important contribution of this view is to suggest a relational view of the firm and to stimulate the manager to consider the diversity of those relationships.

Adding complexity to the question of whose interests one serves is the fact that one often has many allegiances—not only to the firm or the client, but also to one's community, family, etc. One's obligations as an employee or as a professional are only a subset of one's total obligations.

What is "Good"? Consequences, Duties, Virtues

One confronts ethical issues when one must choose among alternatives on the basis of right versus wrong. The ethical choices may be stark where one alternative is truly right and the other truly wrong. But in professional life, the alternatives typically differ more subtly, as in choosing which alternative is *more* right or *less* wrong. Ernest Hemingway said that what is moral is what makes one feel good after and what is immoral is what makes one feel bad after. Because feelings about an action could vary tremendously from one person to the next, this simplistic test would seem to admit moral relativism as the only course, an ethical "I'm OK, you're OK" approach. Fortunately 3,000 years of moral reasoning provide frameworks for a better definition of what is right and wrong.

Right and wrong as defined by consequences. An easy point of departure is to focus on outcomes. An action might be weighed in terms of its utility[10] for society. Who is hurt or helped must be taken into consideration. Utility can be assessed in terms of the pleasure or pain for people. People choose to maximize utility. Therefore, the right action is that which produces the greatest good for the greatest number of people.

Utilitarianism has proven to be a controversial ideal. Some critics have argued that this approach might endorse gross violations of the norms that society holds dear, including the right to privacy, the sanctity of contracts, and property rights, when weighed against the consequences for all. And the calculation of utility might be subject to special circumstances or open to interpretation, making the assessment rather more situation-specific than some philosophers could accept.

Utilitarianism was the foundation for modern neoclassical economics. Utility has proved to be difficult to measure rigorously, and remains a largely theoretical idea. Yet utility-based theories are at the core of welfare economics, and underpin analyses of such widely varying phenomena as government policies, consumer preferences, and investor behavior.

Right and wrong as defined by duty or intentions. Immoral actions are ultimately self-defeating. The practice of writing bad checks, for instance, if practiced universally, would result in a world without check-writing and probably very little credit, too. Therefore, you should act on rules that you would be required to apply universally.[11] You should treat a person as an end, never as a means. It is vital to ask whether an action would show respect for others and whether that action was something a rational person would do: "If everyone behaved this way, what kind of world would we have?"

Critics of that perspective argue that its universal view is too demanding, indeed, even impossible for a businessperson to observe. For instance, the profit motive focuses on the manager's duty to just one company. But Norman Bowie responds, "Perhaps focusing on issues other than profits . . . will actually enhance the bottom line. . . . Perhaps we should view profits as a consequence of good business practices rather than as the goal of business."[12]

---

[10]The Utilitarian philosophers, Jeremy Bentham (1748–1832), James Mill (1773–1836), and John Stuart Mill (1806–1873), argued that the utility (or usefulness) of ideas, actions, and institutions could be measured in terms of their consequences.

[11]The philosopher Immanuel Kant (1724–1804) sought a foundation for ethics in the purity of one's motives.

[12]Bowie (1999), 13.

Right and wrong as defined by virtues. Finally, a third tradition[13] in philosophy argues that the debate over values is misplaced. The focus should instead, be on *virtues* and the qualities of the practitioner. The attention to consequences or duty is fundamentally a focus on *compliance*. Rather, one should consider whether an action is consistent with being a virtuous person. This view argues that personal happiness flowed from being virtuous and not merely from comfort (utility) or observance (duty). It acknowledges that vices are corrupting. And it focuses on personal pride: "If I take this action, would I be proud of what I see in the mirror? If it were reported tomorrow in the newspaper, would I be proud of myself?" Warren Buffett, chief executive officer (CEO) of Berkshire Hathaway, and one of the most successful investors in modern history, issued a letter to each of his operating managers every year emphasizing the importance of personal integrity. He said that Berkshire could afford financial losses, but not losses in reputation. He also wrote, "Make sure everything you do can be reported on the front page of your local newspaper written by an unfriendly, but intelligent reporter."[14]

Critics of virtue-based ethics raise two objections. First, a virtue to one person may be a vice to another. Solomon (1999) points out that Confucius and Friedrich Nietzsche, two other virtue ethicists, held radically different visions of virtue. Confucius extolled such virtues as respect and piety, whereas Nietzsche extolled risk-taking, war-making, and ingenuity. Thus, virtue ethics may be context-specific. Second, virtues can change over time. What may have been regarded as gentlemanly behavior in the nineteenth century might have been seen by feminists in the late twentieth century as insincere and manipulative.

A discrete definition of right and wrong remains the subject of ongoing discourse. But the practical person can abstract from those and other perspectives useful guidelines toward ethical conduct:

- How will my action affect others? What are the consequences?
- What are my motives? What is my duty here? How does this decision affect them?
- Does this action serve the best that I can be?

What Can *You* Do to Promote Ethical Behavior in Your Firm?

An important contributor to unethical business practices is the existence of a work environment that promotes such behavior. Leaders in corporate workplaces need to be proactive in shaping a high-performance culture that sets high ethical expectations. The leader can take a number of steps to shape an ethical culture.

Adopt a code of ethics. One dimension of ethical behavior is to acknowledge some code by which one intends to live. Corporations, too, can adopt codes of conduct that shape ethical expectations. Firms recognize the "problem of the commons" inherent in

---

[13]This view originated in ancient Greek philosophy, starting with Socrates, Plato, and Aristotle.

[14]Russ Banham, "The Warren Buffett School," *Chief Executive* (December 2002): http://www.robertpmiles.com/BuffettSchool.htm (accessed on 19 May 2003).

unethical behavior by one or a few employees. In 1909, the U.S. Supreme Court decided that a corporation could be held liable for the actions of its employees.[15] Since then, companies have sought to set corporate expectations for employee behavior, including codes of ethics.[16] **Exhibit 2** gives an example of one such code, from General Electric Company. Those norms are one page of a 35-page document outlining the code, to whom it applies, special responsibilities for employees and leaders, specific codes of conduct with respect to customers and suppliers, government business, competition, health, safety, employment, and the protection of GE's assets. Corporate codes are viewed by some critics as cynical efforts that seem merely to respond to executive liability that might arise from white-collar and other economic crimes. Companies and their executives may be held liable for an employee's behavior, even if the employee acted contrary to the company's instructions. Mere observance of guidelines in order to reduce liability is a legalistic approach to ethical behavior. Instead, Lynn Paine (1994) has urged firms to adopt an "integrity strategy" that uses ethics as the driving force within a corporation. Deeply held values would become the foundation for decision-making across the firm, and would yield a frame of reference that would integrate functions and businesses. By that view, ethics defines what a firm stands for.

In addition, an industry or a professional group can adopt a code of ethics. One example relevant to finance professionals is the Code of Ethics of the CFA Institute, the group that confers the Chartered Financial Analyst (CFA) designation on professional securities analysts and portfolio managers. Excerpts from the CFA Institute's Code of Ethics and Standards of Professional Conduct are given in **Exhibit 3.**

Talk about ethics within your team and firm. Many firms seek to reinforce a culture of integrity with a program of seminars and training in ethical reasoning. A leader can stimulate reflection through informal discussion of ethical developments (for example: indictments, convictions, civil lawsuits) in the industry or profession, or of ethical issues that the team may be facing. This kind of discussion (without preaching) signals that it is on the leader's mind and is a legitimate focus of discussion. One executive regularly raises issues such as those informally over lunch or morning coffee. Leaders believe that ethical matters are important enough to be the focus of team discussions.

Reflect on your dilemmas. The challenge for many finance practitioners is that ethical dilemmas do not readily lend themselves to the structured analysis that one would apply to valuing a firm or balancing the books. Nevertheless, one can harness the questions raised in the field of ethics to lend some rigor to one's reflections. Laura Nash (1981) abstracted a list of 12 questions on which the thoughtful practitioner might reflect in grappling with an ethical dilemma:

1. Have I defined the problem correctly and accurately?

2. If I stood on the other side of the problem, how would I define it?

---

[15]See *New York Central v. United States,* 212 U.S. 481.

[16]Murphy (1997) compiled 80 exemplary ethics statements.

3. What are the origins of this dilemma?

4. To whom and to what am I loyal, as a person and as a member of a firm?

5. What is my intention in making this decision?

6. How do the likely results compare with my intention?

7. Can my decision injure anyone? How?

8. Can I engage the affected parties in my decision before I decide or take action?

9. Am I confident that my decision will be as valid over a long period as it may seem at this moment?

10. If my boss, the CEO, the directors, my family, or the community learned about this decision, would I have misgivings about my actions?

11. What signals (or symbols) might my decision convey, if my decision were understood correctly? If misunderstood?

12. Are there exceptions to my position, perhaps special circumstances under which I might make a different decision?

Act on Your Reflections

This may be the toughest step of all. The field of ethics can lend structure to one's thinking, but has less to say about the action to be taken. When confronting a problem of ethics within a team or an organization, one can consider a hierarchy of responses, from questioning and coaching to whistle-blowing (either to an internal ombudsperson or, if necessary, to an outside entity) and, possibly, leaving the organization.

Conclusion

An analysis of finance's ethical issues is vital. The cases of WorldCom and other major business scandals show that ethical issues pervade the financial environment. Ethics is one of the pillars on which stands success in finance—it builds sustainable enterprise, trust, organizational strength, and personal satisfaction. Therefore, the financial decision-maker must learn to identify, analyze, and act on the ethical issues that may arise. Consequences, duties, and virtues stand out as three important benchmarks for ethical analysis. Nevertheless, the results of such analysis are rarely clear-cut. But real business leaders will take the time to sort through the ambiguities and do "the right thing" in the words of Edwin LeFevre. These and other ethical themes will appear throughout finance case studies and one's career.

References and Recommended Readings

Achampong, F., and W. Zemedkun. "An Empirical and Ethical Analysis of Factors Motivating Managers' Merger Decisions." *Journal of Business Ethics* 14 (1995): 855–865.

Bhide, A., and H. H. Stevenson. "Why be Honest if Honesty Doesn't Pay." *Harvard Business Review* (September–October 1990): 121–129.

Bloomenthal, Harold S. *Sarbanes-Oxley Act in Perspective*. (St. Paul, MN: West Group), 2002.

Blumenstein, R., and S. Pulliam. "WorldCom Report Finds Ebbers Played Role in Inflating Revenue." *Wall Street Journal*. 6 June 2003, downloaded from http://online.wsj.com/article_print/0,,SB105485251027721500,00.html.

Blumenstein, R., and D. Solomon. "MCI is Expected to Pay Massive Fine in SEC Deal." *Wall Street Journal*. 19 May 2003, downloaded from http://online.wsj .com/ article_print/0,,SB105329362774148600,00.html.

Boatright, J. R. *Ethics in Finance*. (Oxford: Blackwell Publishers), 1999.

Bowie, N. E. "A Kantian Approach to Business Ethics." in *A Companion to Business Ethics*. R. E. Frederick, ed. (Malden, MA: Blackwell), 1999, 3–16.

Carroll, A. B. "Ethics in Management." in *A Companion to Business Ethics*. R. E. Frederick, ed. (Malden, MA: Blackwell), 1999, 141–152.

Frederick, R. E. *A Companion to Business Ethics*. (Oxford: Blackwell Publishers).

Freeman, R. E. *Strategic Management: A Stakeholder Approach*. (Boston, MA: Pittman), 1984.

Friedman, M. *Capitalism and Freedom*. (Chicago, IL: University of Chicago Press), 1962.

General Electric Company. "Integrity: The Spirit and Letter of our Commitment." February 2004. http://www.ge.com/files/usa/en/commitment/social/integrity/downloads/english.pdf.

Jensen, M. "The Agency Costs of Overvalued Equity." *Financial Management* (Spring 2005): 5–19.

Kidder, R. "Ethics and the Bottom Line: Ten Reasons for Businesses to do Right." *Insights on Global Ethics* (Spring 1997): 7–9.

Murphy, P. E. "80 Exemplary Ethics Statements." in L. H. Newton, "A Passport for the Corporate Code: From Borg Warner to the Caux Principles." in R. E. Frederick, ed. *A Companion to Business Ethics*. (Malden, MA: Blackwell), 1999, 374–385.

Nash, L. L. "Ethics without the Sermon," *Harvard Business Review* (November–December 1981): 79–90.

Paine, L. S. "Managing for Organizational Integrity." *Harvard Business Review* (March–April 1994): 106–117.

———. "Law, Ethics, and Managerial Judgment," in R. E. Frederick, ed. *A Companion to Business Ethics*. (Malden, MA: Blackwell), 1999, 194–206.

Paine, L. S. *Value Shift: Why Companies Must Merger Social and Financial Imperatives to Achieve Superior Performance*. (New York: McGraw-Hill), 2003.

Pulliam, S. "A Staffer Ordered to Commit Fraud Balked, and then Caved." *Wall Street Journal*. 23 June 2003, A1.

Sen, A. *On Ethics and Economics*. (Oxford: Blackwell Publishers), 1987.

Shafer, W. "Effects of Materiality, Risk, and Ethical Perceptions on Fraudulent Reporting by Financial Executives." *Journal of Business Ethics* 38, 3 (2002): 243–263.

Solomon, R. "Business Ethics and Virtue." in R. E. Frederick, ed. *A Companion to Business Ethics*. (Malden, MA: Blackwell), 1999, 30–37.

Solomon, D. "WorldCom Moved Expenses to the Balance Sheet of MCI." *Wall Street Journal*. 31 March 2003, http://online.wsj.com/article_print/ 0,,SB104907054486790100,00.html.

Werhane, P. "Two Ethical Issues in Mergers and Acquisitions." *Journal of Business Ethics* 7 (1988): 41–45.

———. "Mergers, Acquisitions, and the Market for Corporate Control." *Public Affairs Quarterly* 4, 1 (1990): 81–96.

———. "A Note on Moral Imagination." Charlottesville, VA: University of Virginia Darden School of Business Case Collection (UVA-E-0114), 1997.

———. "Business Ethics and the Origins of Contemporary Capitalism: Economics and Ethics in the Work of Adam Smith and Herbert Spencer." in R. E. Frederick, ed. *A Companion to Business Ethics*. (Malden, MA: Blackwell), 1999, 325–341.

Wicks, A. "A Note on Ethical Decision Making." Charlottesville, VA: University of Virginia Darden School of Business Case Collection (UVA-E-0242), 2003.

EXHIBIT 1 | Prominent Business Scandals Revealed between 1998 and 2002

The companies and their alleged or admitted accounting issues are as follows:

- Adelphia (loans and looting)
- Bristol-Myers (improper inflation of revenues through sue of sales incentives)
- CMS Energy (overstatement of revenues through round-trip energy trades)
- Computer Associates (inflation of revenues)
- Dynegy (artificial increase of cash flow)
- Elan (use of off-balance-sheet entities)
- Enron (inflation of earnings and use of off-balance-sheet entities)
- Global Crossing (artificial inflation of revenues)
- Halliburton (improper revenue recognition)
- Kmart (accounting for vendor allowances)
- Lucent Technologies (revenue accounting and vendor financing)
- Merck (revenue recognition)
- MicroStrategy (backdating of sales contracts)
- Network Associates (revenue and expense recognition)
- PNC Financial Services (accounting for the transfer of loans)
- Qwest (revenue inflation)
- Reliance Resources (revenue inflation through round-trip energy trades)
- Rite Aid (inflation of earnings)
- Tyco International (improper use of "cookie jar" reserves and acquisition accounting)
- Vivendi Universal (withholding information about liquidity troubles)
- WorldCom (revenue and expense recognition)
- Xerox (revenue and earnings inflation)

These cases and their points of controversy are summarized in Bloomenthal (2002), Appendices E-1 and E-2.

EXHIBIT 2 | General Electric's (GE) Code of Conduct

- Obey the applicable laws and regulations governing our business conduct worldwide.
- Be honest, fair, and trustworthy in all your GE activities and relationships.
- Avoid all conflicts of interest between work and personal affairs.
- Foster an atmosphere in which fair employment practices extend to every member of the diverse GE community.
- Strive to create a safe workplace and to protect the environment.
- Through leadership at all levels, sustain a culture where ethical conduct is recognized, valued, and exemplified by all employees.

Source: General Electric Company, "Integrity: The Spirit and Letter of Our Commitment," February 2004, 5. A longer version of this resource is also available on the company's Web site at http://www.ge.com/files/usa/en/commitment/social/integrity/downloads/english.pdf.

EXHIBIT 3 | Excerpts from the CFA Institute's Code of Ethics and Standards of Professional Conduct: January 1, 2006

CFA Institute's Code of Ethics

- Act with integrity, competence, diligence, respect, and in an ethical manner with the public, clients, prospective clients, employers, employees, colleagues in the investment profession, and other participants in the global capital markets.
- Place the integrity of the investment profession and the interests of clients above their own personal interests.
- Use reasonable care and exercise independent professional judgment when conducting investment analysis, making investment recommendations, taking investment actions, and engaging in other professional activities.
- Practice and encourage others to practice in a professional and ethical manner that will reflect credit on themselves and the profession.
- Promote the integrity of, and uphold the rules governing, capital markets.
- Maintain and improve their professional competence and strive to maintain and improve the competence of other investment professionals.

CFA Institute's Standards of Professional Conduct (*excerpts that suggest the scope and detail of the complete standards*)

Members and candidates must:

- Understand and comply with all applicable laws, rules, and regulations . . .
- Use reasonable care and judgment to achieve and maintain independence and objectivity in their professional activities. Members and candidates must not offer, solicit, or accept any gift, benefit, compensation, or consideration that reasonably could be expected to compromise their own or another's independence and objectivity.
- Not knowingly make any misrepresentations relating to investment analysis, recommendations, actions, or other professional activities.
- Not engage in any professional conduct involving dishonesty, fraud, or deceit, or commit any act that reflects adversely on their professional reputation, integrity, or competence.
- Not act or cause others to act on the [material, nonpublic] information.
- Not engage in practices that distort prices or artificially inflate trading volume with the intent to mislead market participants.
- Have a duty of loyalty to their clients and must act with reasonable care and exercise prudent judgment. Members and candidates must act for the benefit of their clients and place their clients' interests before their employer's or their own interests. . . .
- Deal fairly and objectively with all clients. . . .
- Keep information about current, former, and prospective clients confidential. . . .
- Act for the benefit of their employer and not deprive their employer of the advantage of their skills and abilities, divulge confidential information, or otherwise cause harm to their employer.
- Not accept gifts, benefits, compensation, or consideration that competes with, or might reasonably be expected to create a conflict of interest with, their employer's interest. . . .
- Make reasonable efforts to detect and prevent violations of applicable laws, rules, regulations, and the Code and Standards by anyone subject to their supervision or authority.
- Disclose to clients and prospective clients the basic format and general principles of the investment processes used . . . Use reasonable judgment in identifying which factors are important to their investment analyses, recommendations, or actions and include those factors in communications with clients and prospective clients. . . . Distinguish between fact and opinion in the presentation of investment analysis and recommendations. . . .

Source: CFA Institute, *Code of Ethics and Standards of Professional Conduct* (Charlottesville, VA: CFA Institute), 2006, http://www.cfainstitute.org/cfacentre/pdf/English2006CodeandStandards.pdf.

Case Studies in Finance

Managing for
Corporate Value
Creation

## PART 1

Setting Some Themes

Warren E. Buffett, 2005

On May 24, 2005, Warren E. Buffett, the chairperson and chief executive officer (CEO) of Berkshire Hathaway Inc., announced that MidAmerican Energy Holdings Company, a subsidiary of Berkshire Hathaway, would acquire the electric utility PacifiCorp. In Buffett's largest deal since 1998, and the second largest of his entire career, MidAmerican would purchase PacifiCorp from its parent, Scottish Power plc, for $5.1 billion in cash and $4.3 billion in liabilities and preferred stock. "The energy sector has long interested us, and this is the right fit," Buffett said. At the announcement, Berkshire Hathaway's Class A shares closed up 2.4% for the day, for a gain in market value of $2.55 billion.[1] Scottish Power's share price also jumped 6.28% on the news;[2] the S&P 500 Composite Index closed up 0.02%. **Exhibit 1** illustrates the recent share price performance for Berkshire Hathaway, Scottish Power, and the S&P 500 Index.

The acquisition of PacifiCorp renewed public interest in its sponsor, Warren Buffett. In many ways, he was an anomaly. One of the richest individuals in the world (with an estimated net worth of about $44 billion), he was also respected and even beloved. Though he had accumulated perhaps the best investment record in history (a compound annual increase in wealth for Berkshire Hathaway of 24% from 1965 to 2004),[3] Berkshire paid him only $100,000 per year to serve as its CEO. While Buffett and other insiders controlled 41.8% of Berkshire Hathaway, he ran the company in the interests of all shareholders. "We will not take cash compensation, restricted stock, or option grants that would make our results superior to [those of Berkshire's investors]," Buffett said. "I will keep well over 99% of my net worth in Berkshire. My wife and I have never sold a share nor do we intend to."[4]

---

[1]The per-share change in Berkshire Hathaway's Class A share price at the date of the announcement was $2,010. The company had 1,268,783 Class A shares outstanding.

[2]The per-share change in Scottish Power's share price at the date of the announcement was (British pounds) GBP27.75. The company had 466,112,000 shares outstanding.

[3]In comparison, the annual average total return on all large stocks from 1965 to the end of 2004 was 10.5%. *Stocks, Bonds, Bills, and Inflation 2005 Yearbook* (Chicago: Ibbotson Associates, 2005), 217.

[4]Warren Buffett, Annual Letter to Shareholders, 2001.

Buffett was the subject of numerous laudatory articles and at least eight biographies, yet he remained an intensely private individual. Though acclaimed by many as an intellectual genius, he shunned the company of intellectuals and preferred to affect the manner of a down-home Nebraskan (he lived in Omaha) and a tough-minded investor. In contrast to investing's other "stars," Buffett acknowledged his investment failures both quickly and publicly. Although he held an MBA from Columbia University and credited his mentor, Professor Benjamin Graham, with developing the philosophy of value-based investing that had guided Buffett to his success, he chided business schools for the irrelevance of their finance and investing theories.

Numerous writers sought to distill the essence of Buffett's success. What were the key principles that guided Buffett? Could those principles be applied broadly in the 21st century, or were they unique to Buffett and his time? From an understanding of those principles, analysts hoped to illuminate the acquisition of PacifiCorp. What were Buffett's probable motives in the acquisition? What did Buffett's offer say about his valuation of PacifiCorp, and how would it compare with valuations for other regulated utilities? Would Berkshire's acquisition of PacifiCorp prove to be a success? How would Buffett define success?

Berkshire Hathaway Inc.

Berkshire Hathaway was incorporated in 1889 as Berkshire Cotton Manufacturing, and eventually grew to become one of New England's biggest textile producers, accounting for 25% of the United States' cotton textile production. In 1955, Berkshire merged with Hathaway Manufacturing and began a secular decline due to inflation, technological change, and intensifying competition from foreign competitors. In 1965, Buffett and some partners acquired control of Berkshire Hathaway, believing that its financial decline could be reversed.

Berkshire Hathaway "Class A" vs. S&P 500 Composite Index

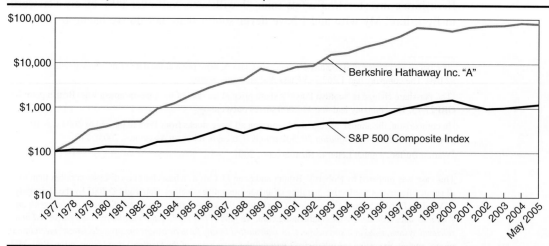

Over the next 20 years, it became apparent that large capital investments would be required to remain competitive and that even then the financial returns would be mediocre. Fortunately, the textile group generated enough cash in the initial years to permit the firm to purchase two insurance companies headquartered in Omaha: National Indemnity Company and National Fire & Marine Insurance Company. Acquisitions of other businesses followed in the 1970s and 1980s; Berkshire Hathaway exited the textile business in 1985.

The investment performance of a share in Berkshire Hathaway had astonished most observers. In 1977, the firm's year-end closing share price was $102; on May 24, 2005, the closing price on its Class A shares reached $85,500. Over the same period, the Standard & Poor's 500 Index grew from 96 to 1,194. Some observers called for Buffett to split[5] the firm's share price to make it more accessible to the individual investor. He steadfastly refused.[6]

In 2004, Berkshire Hathaway's annual report described the firm as "a holding company owning subsidiaries engaged in a number of diverse business activities."[7] Berkshire's portfolio of businesses included:

- **Insurance:** The largest component of Berkshire's portfolio focused on property and casualty insurance, on both a direct and a reinsurance basis (for example, GEICO, General Re).

- **Apparel:** Manufacturing and distribution of a variety of footwear and clothing products, including underwear, active-wear, children's clothes, and uniforms (for example, Fruit of the Loom, Garan, Fechheimer Brothers, H.H. Brown Shoe, Justin Brands).

- **Building products:** Manufacturing and distribution of a variety of building materials, and related products and services (for example, Acme Building Brands, Benjamin Moore, Johns Manville, MiTek).

- **Finance and financial products:** Proprietary investing, manufactured housing and related consumer financing, transportation equipment leasing, furniture leasing, life annuities and risk management products (for example, BH Finance, Clayton Homes, XTRA, CORT, Berkshire Hathaway Life, and General Re Securities).

- **Flight services:** Training to operators of aircraft and ships, and providing fractional ownership programs for general aviation aircraft (for example, FlightSafety, NetJets).

- **Retail:** Retail sales of home furnishings, appliances, electronics, fine jewelry, and gifts (for example, Nebraska Furniture Mart, R.C. Willey Home Furnishings, Star

---

[5]A split was an increase in the number of a firm's outstanding shares that did not cause a change in the shareholders' equity. A two-for-one split would entail a 50% reduction in the stock's price at the time of the split. Company directors authorized stock splits to make the company's shares affordable to a broader range of investors.

[6]In 1996, Berkshire Hathaway issued Class B shares, which had an economic interest equal to 1/30th and a voting interest equal to 1/200th that of the firm's Class A shares.

[7]Berkshire Hathaway Inc., 2004 Annual Report, 1.

Furniture Company, Jordan's Furniture, Borsheim's, Helzberg Diamond Shops, Ben Bridge Jeweler).

• **Grocery distribution:** Wholesale distributing of groceries and nonfood items (for example, McLane Company).

• **Carpet and floor coverings:** Manufacturing and distribution of carpet and floor coverings under a variety of brand names (for example, Shaw Industries).

Berkshire also owned an assortment of smaller businesses[8] generating about $3 billion in revenues. **Exhibit 2** gives a summary of revenues, operating profits, capital expenditures, depreciation, and assets for Berkshire's various business segments. The company's investment portfolio also included equity interests in numerous publicly traded companies, which are summarized in **Exhibit 3.** In addition, the company owned about $21.4 billion of foreign exchange contracts at year end, spread among 12 currencies. Prior to March 2002, neither Buffett nor Berkshire had ever traded in currencies, but Buffett had developed serious concerns about the United States' large current account deficits, and he hoped that his currency bets would offset the growing pressure on the dollar.

Buffett's Investment Philosophy

Warren Buffett was first exposed to formal training in investing at Columbia University where he studied under Professor Benjamin Graham. A coauthor of the classic text *Security Analysis,* Graham developed a method of identifying undervalued stocks (that is to say, stocks whose prices were less than their intrinsic value). This became the cornerstone of modern value investing. Graham's approach was to focus on the value of assets, such as cash, net working capital, and physical assets. Eventually, Buffett modified that approach to focus also on valuable franchises that were unrecognized by the market.

Over the years, Buffett had expounded his philosophy of investing in his chairperson's letter to the shareholders in Berkshire Hathaway's annual report. By 2005, those lengthy letters had accumulated a broad following because of their wisdom and their humorous, self-deprecating tone. The letters emphasized the following elements:

1. *Economic reality, not accounting reality.* Financial statements prepared by accountants conformed to rules that might not adequately represent the *economic* reality of a business. Buffett wrote:

   . . . because of the limitations of conventional accounting, consolidated reported earnings may reveal relatively little about our true economic performance. Charlie [Munger,

---

[8]These included Scott Fetzer, a diversified manufacturer and distributor of commercial and industrial products; Buffalo News, a newspaper publisher in western New York; International Dairy Queen, which licensed and serviced a system of 6,000 Dairy Queen stores; See's Candies, a manufacturer and distributor of boxed chocolates and other confectionery products; Larson-Juhl, which designed, manufactured, and distributed custom picture-framing products; CTB International, a manufacturer of equipment and systems for the poultry, hog, egg production, and grain industries; and the Pampered Chef, a direct seller of kitchen tools.

Buffett's business partner] and I, both as owners and managers, virtually ignore such consolidated numbers. . . . Accounting consequences do not influence our operating or capital-allocation process.[9]

Accounting reality was conservative, backward-looking, and governed by generally accepted accounting principles (GAAP). Investment decisions, on the other hand, should be based on the economic reality of a business. In economic reality, intangible assets, such as patents, trademarks, special managerial expertise, and reputation might be very valuable, yet under GAAP, they would be carried at little or no value. GAAP measured results in terms of net profit; in economic reality, the results of a business were its *flows of cash*.

A key feature to Buffett's approach defined economic reality at the level of the business itself, not the market, the economy, or the security—he was a *fundamental analyst* of the business. His analysis sought to judge the simplicity of the business, the consistency of its operating history, the attractiveness of its long-term prospects, the quality of management, and the firm's capacity to create value.

2. *The cost of the lost opportunity.* Buffett compared an investment opportunity against the next best alternative, the "lost opportunity." In his business decisions, he demonstrated a tendency to frame his choices as either/or decisions rather than yes/no decisions. Thus, an important standard of comparison in testing the attractiveness of an acquisition was the potential rate of return from investing in the common stocks of other companies. Buffett held that there was no fundamental difference between buying a business outright, and buying a few shares of that business in the equity market. Thus, for him, the comparison of an investment against other returns available in the market was an important benchmark of performance.

3. *Value creation: time is money.* Buffett assessed intrinsic value as the present value of future expected performance:

    [All other methods fall short in determining whether] an investor is indeed buying something for what it is worth and is therefore truly operating on the principle of obtaining value for his investments. . . . Irrespective of whether a business grows or doesn't, displays volatility or smoothness in earnings, or carries a high price or low in relation to its current earnings and book value, the investment shown by the discounted-flows-of-cash calculation to be the cheapest is the one that the investor should purchase.[10]

    Enlarging on his discussion of intrinsic value, Buffett used an educational example:

    We define intrinsic value as the discounted value of the cash that can be taken out of a business during its remaining life. Anyone calculating intrinsic value necessarily comes up with a highly subjective figure that will change both as estimates of future cash flows are revised and as interest rates move. Despite its fuzziness, however, intrinsic value is all important and is the only logical way to evaluate the relative attractiveness of investments and businesses.

---

[9]Berkshire Hathaway Inc., 2004 Annual Report, 2.

[10]Berkshire Hathaway Inc., 1992 Annual Report, 14.

To see how historical input (book value) and future output (intrinsic value) can diverge, let us look at another form of investment, a college education. Think of the education's cost as its "book value." If it is to be accurate, the cost should include the earnings that were foregone by the student because he chose college rather than a job. For this exercise, we will ignore the important non-economic benefits of an education and focus strictly on its economic value. First, we must estimate the earnings that the graduate will receive over his lifetime and subtract from that figure an estimate of what he would have earned had he lacked his education. That gives us an excess earnings figure, which must then be discounted, at an appropriate interest rate, back to graduation day. The dollar result equals the intrinsic economic value of the education. Some graduates will find that the book value of their education exceeds its intrinsic value, which means that whoever paid for the education didn't get his money's worth. In other cases, the intrinsic value of an education will far exceed its book value, a result that proves capital was wisely deployed. In all cases, what is clear is that book value is meaningless as an indicator of intrinsic value.[11]

To illustrate the mechanics of this example, consider the hypothetical case presented in **Exhibit 4.** Suppose an individual has the opportunity to invest $50 million in a business—this is its cost or book value. This business will throw off cash at the rate of 20% of its investment base each year. Suppose that instead of receiving any dividends, the owner decides to reinvest all cash flow back into the business—at this rate, the book value of the business will grow at 20% per year. Suppose that the investor plans to sell the business for its book value at the end of the fifth year. Does this investment create value for the individual? One determines this by discounting the future cash flows to the present at a cost of equity of 15%. Suppose that this is the investor's opportunity cost, the required return that could have been earned elsewhere at comparable risk. Dividing the present value of future cash flows (i.e., Buffett's intrinsic value) by the cost of the investment (i.e., Buffett's book value) indicates that every dollar invested buys securities worth $1.23. Value is created.

Consider an opposing case, summarized in **Exhibit 5.** The example is similar in all respects, except for one key difference: the annual return on the investment is 10%. The result is that every dollar invested buys securities worth $0.80. Value is destroyed.

Comparing the two cases in **Exhibits 4** and **5,** the difference in value creation and destruction is driven entirely by the relationship between the expected returns and the discount rate: in the first case, the spread is positive; in the second case, it is negative. Only in the instance where expected returns equal the discount rate will book value equal intrinsic value. In short, book value or the investment outlay may not reflect the economic reality. One needs to focus on the prospective rates of return, and how they compare to the required rate of return.

4. *Measure performance by gain in intrinsic value, not accounting profit.* Buffett wrote:

---

[11]Berkshire Hathaway Inc., 1994 Annual Report, 7.

Our long-term economic goal . . . is to maximize Berkshire's average annual rate of gain in intrinsic business value on a per-share basis. We do not measure the economic significance or performance of Berkshire by its size; we measure by per-share progress. We are certain that the rate of per-share progress will diminish in the future—a greatly enlarged capital base will see to that. But we will be disappointed if our rate does not exceed that of the average large American corporation.[12]

The gain in intrinsic value could be modeled as the value added by a business above and beyond the charge for the use of capital in that business. The gain in intrinsic value was analogous to the economic-profit and market-value-added measures used by analysts in leading corporations to assess financial performance. Those measures focus on the ability to earn returns in excess of the cost of capital.

5. *Risk and discount rates.* Conventional academic and practitioner thinking held that the more risk one took, the more one should get paid. Thus, discount rates used in determining intrinsic values should be determined by the risk of the cash flows being valued. The conventional model for estimating discount rates was the capital asset pricing model (CAPM), which added a risk premium to the long-term risk-free rate of return, such as the U.S. Treasury bond yield.

Buffett departed from conventional thinking by using the rate of return on the long-term (for example, 30 year) U.S. Treasury bond to discount cash flows.[13] Defending this practice, Buffett argued that he avoided risk, and therefore should use a "risk-free" discount rate. His firm used almost no debt financing. He focused on companies with predictable and stable earnings. He or his vice chair, Charlie Munger, sat on the boards of directors, where they obtained a candid, inside view of the company and could intervene in managements' decisions if necessary. Buffett once said, "I put a heavy weight on certainty. If you do that, the whole idea of a risk factor doesn't make sense to me. Risk comes from not knowing what you're doing."[14] He also wrote:

We define risk, using dictionary terms, as "the possibility of loss or injury." Academics, however, like to define "risk" differently, averring that it is the relative volatility of a stock or a portfolio of stocks—that is, the volatility as compared to that of a large universe of stocks. Employing databases and statistical skills, these academics compute with precision the "beta" of a stock—its relative volatility in the past—and then build arcane investment and capital allocation theories around this calculation. In their hunger for a single statistic to measure risk, however, they forget a fundamental principle: it is better to be approximately right than precisely wrong.[15]

---

[12]Berkshire Hathaway Inc., 2004 Annual Report, 74.

[13]The yield on the 30-year U.S. Treasury bond on May 24, 2005, was 5.76%. The beta of Berkshire Hathaway was 0.75.

[14]Quoted in Jim Rasmussen, "Buffett Talks Strategy with Students," *Omaha World-Herald,* 2 January 1994, 26.

[15]Berkshire Hathaway Inc., 1993 Annual Report. Republished in Andrew Kilpatrick, *Of Permanent Value: The Story of Warren Buffett* (Birmingham, AL: AKPE, 1994), 574.

6. *Diversification.* Buffett disagreed with conventional wisdom that investors should hold a broad portfolio of stocks in order to shed company-specific risk. In his view, investors typically purchased far too many stocks rather than waiting for one exceptional company. Buffett said,

> Figure businesses out that you understand and concentrate. Diversification is protection against ignorance, but if you don't feel ignorant, the need for it goes down drastically.[16]

7. *Investing behavior should be driven by information, analysis, and self-discipline, not by emotion or "hunch."* Buffett repeatedly emphasized awareness and information as the foundation for investing. He said, "Anyone not aware of the fool in the market probably is the fool in the market."[17] Buffett was fond of repeating a parable told to him by Benjamin Graham:

> There was a small private business and one of the owners was a man named Market. Every day, Mr. Market had a new opinion of what the business was worth, and at that price stood ready to buy your interest or sell you his. As excitable as he was opinionated, Mr. Market presented a constant distraction to his fellow owners. "What does he know?" they would wonder, as he bid them an extraordinarily high price or a depressingly low one. Actually, the gentleman knew little or nothing. You may be happy to sell out to him when he quotes you a ridiculously high price, and equally happy to buy from him when his price is low. But the rest of the time, you will be wiser to form your own ideas of the value of your holdings, based on full reports from the company about its operation and financial position.[18]

Buffett used this allegory to illustrate the irrationality of stock prices as compared to true intrinsic value. Graham believed that an investor's worst enemy was not the stock market, but oneself. Superior training could not compensate for the absence of the requisite temperament for investing. Over the long term, stock prices should have a strong relationship with the economic progress of the business. But daily market quotations were heavily influenced by momentary greed or fear, and were an unreliable measure of intrinsic value. Buffett said,

> As far as I am concerned, the stock market doesn't exist. It is there only as a reference to see if anybody is offering to do anything foolish. When we invest in stocks, we invest in businesses. You simply have to behave according to what is rational rather than according to what is fashionable.[19]

Accordingly, Buffett did not try to "time the market" (i.e., trade stocks based on expectations of changes in the market cycle)—his was a strategy of patient, long-term investing. As if in contrast to Mr. Market, Buffett expressed more

---

[16]Quoted in *Forbes* (19 October 1993). Republished in Andrew Kilpatrick, *Of Permanent Value,* 574.

[17]Quoted in Michael Lewis, *Liar's Poker* (New York: Norton, 1989), 35.

[18]Originally published in Berkshire Hathaway Inc., 1987 Annual Report. This quotation was paraphrased from James Grant, *Minding Mr. Market* (New York: Times Books, 1993), xxi.

[19]Peter Lynch, *One Up on Wall Street* (New York: Penguin Books, 1990), 78.

contrarian goals: "We simply attempt to be fearful when others are greedy and to be greedy only when others are fearful."[20] Buffett also said, "Lethargy bordering on sloth remains the cornerstone of our investment style,"[21] and "The market, like the Lord, helps those who help themselves. But unlike the Lord, the market does not forgive those who know not what they do."[22]

Buffett scorned the academic theory of capital market efficiency. The efficient markets hypothesis (EMH) held that publicly known information was rapidly impounded into share prices, and that as a result, stock prices were fair in reflecting what was known about the company. Under EMH, there were no bargains to be had and trying to outperform the market would be futile. "It has been helpful to me to have tens of thousands turned out of business schools taught that it didn't do any good to think," Buffett said.[23]

I think it's fascinating how the ruling orthodoxy can cause a lot of people to think the earth is flat. Investing in a market where people believe in efficiency is like playing bridge with someone who's been told it doesn't do any good to look at the cards.[24]

8. *Alignment of agents and owners.* Explaining his significant ownership interest in Berkshire Hathaway, Buffett said, "I am a better businessman because I am an investor. And I am a better investor because I am a businessman."[25]

As if to illustrate this sentiment, he said:

A managerial "wish list" will not be filled at shareholder expense. We will not diversify by purchasing entire businesses at control prices that ignore long-term economic consequences to our shareholders. We will only do with your money what we would do with our own, weighing fully the values you can obtain by diversifying your own portfolios through direct purchases in the stock market.[26]

For four of Berkshire's six directors, over 50% of their family net worth was represented by shares in Berkshire Hathaway. The senior managers of Berkshire Hathaway subsidiaries held shares in the company, or were compensated under incentive plans that imitated the potential returns from an equity interest in their business unit or both.[27]

---

[20]Berkshire Hathaway Inc., 1986 Annual Report, 16.

[21]Berkshire Hathaway Inc., 1990 Annual Report, 15.

[22]Berkshire Hathaway Inc., Letters to Shareholders, 1977–1983, 53.

[23]Quoted in Andrew Kilpatrick, *Of Permanent Value,* 353.

[24]Quoted in L. J. Davis, "Buffett Takes Stock," *New York Times,* 1 April 1990, 16.

[25]Quoted in *Forbes* (19 October 1993). Republished in Andrew Kilpatrick, *Of Permanent Value,* 574.

[26]"Owner-Related Business Principles," in Berkshire Hathaway's 2004 Annual Report, 75.

[27]In April 2005, the U.S. Securities and Exchange Commission interviewed Warren Buffett in connection with an investigation into the insurance giant AIG and its dealings with Berkshire Hathaway's General Re insurance unit. Buffett reported that he had questioned General Re's CEO about the transactions with AIG, but that he never learned any details.

MidAmerican Energy Holdings Company

MidAmerican Energy Holdings Company, a subsidiary of Berkshire Hathaway Inc., was a leader in the production of energy from diversified sources, including geothermal, natural gas, hydroelectric, nuclear power, and coal. Based in Des Moines, Iowa, the company was a major supplier and distributor of energy to over 5 million customers in the United States and Great Britain. Through its HomeServices of America division, MidAmerican also owned the second-largest full-service independent real-estate brokerage in the United States. **Exhibit 6** provides condensed, consolidated financial statements for MidAmerican for the years 2000 through 2004.

Berkshire Hathaway took a major stake in MidAmerican on March 14, 2000, with a $1.24 billion investment in common stock and a nondividend-paying convertible preferred stock.[28] This investment gave Berkshire about a 9.7% voting interest and a 76% economic interest in MidAmerican. "Though there are many regulatory constraints in the utility industry, it's possible that we will make additional commitments in the field," Buffett said, at the time. "If we do, the amounts could be large."[29] Subsequently, in March 2002, Berkshire acquired another 6.7 million shares of MidAmerican's convertible stock for $402 million, giving Berkshire a 9.9% voting interest and an 83.7% economic interest in the equity of MidAmerican (80.5% on a diluted basis).

At the time of Berkshire's initial investment in MidAmerican, Buffett explained that acquisitions in the electric utility industry were complicated by a variety of regulations, including the Public Utility Holding Company Act of 1935 (PUHCA), which was intended to prevent conglomerates from owning utilities and to impede the formation of massive national utilities that regulators could not control. This regulation made it necessary for Berkshire to structure its investment in MidAmerican such that it would not have voting control. Buffett had said he was eager to have PUHCA scaled back, and that if it were repealed he would invest $10 billion to $15 billion in the electric utility industry.[30]

PacifiCorp

For the past several years, Berkshire Hathaway had been unsuccessful in identifying attractive acquisition opportunities. In 2001, Buffett addressed the issue head-on in his annual letter to shareholders:

> Some years back, a good $10 million idea could do wonders for us (witness our investment in the *Washington Post* in 1973 or GEICO in 1976). Today, the combination of *ten* such

---

[28]Berkshire acquired 900,942 shares of common stock and 34,563,395 shares of convertible preferred stock of MidAmerican. Convertible preferred stock was preferred stock that carried the right to be exchanged by the investor for common stock. The exchange, or conversion, right was like a call option on the common stock of the issuer. The terms of the convertible preferred stated the price at which common shares could be acquired in exchange for the principal value of the convertible preferred stock.

[29]Berkshire Hathaway Inc., 1999 Annual Report, 11.

[30]Rebecca Smith and Karen Richardson, *Wall Street Journal,* 25 May 2005, A1.

ideas and a triple in the value of *each* would increase the net worth of Berkshire by only ¼ of 1%. We need "elephants" to make significant gains now—and they are hard to find.[31]

By 2004, Berkshire's fruitless search for "elephants" had begun to take its toll. In his annual letter that year, Buffett lamented his failure to make any multibillion-dollar acquisitions, and he bemoaned Berkshire's large cash balance that had been accumulating since 2002. "We don't enjoy sitting on $43 billion of cash equivalents that are earning paltry returns," Buffett said. "What Charlie [Munger] and I would like is a little action now."[32]

The announcement that Berkshire's wholly owned subsidiary, MidAmerican Energy Holdings Company, would acquire PacifiCorp seemed to indicate that Buffett had found an "elephant." PacifiCorp was a leading, low-cost energy producer and distributor that served 1.6 million customers in six states in the western United States. Based in Portland, Oregon, PacifiCorp generated power through company-owned coal, hydrothermal, renewable wind power, gas-fired combustion, and geothermal facilities. The company had merged with Scottish Power in 1999. **Exhibit 7** presents PacifiCorp's most recent financial statements.

The PacifiCorp announcement renewed general interest in Buffett's approach to acquisitions. **Exhibit 8** gives the formal statement of acquisition criteria contained in Berkshire Hathaway's 2004 Annual Report. In general, the policy expressed a tightly disciplined strategy that refused to reward others for actions that Berkshire Hathaway might just as easily take on its own. Analysts scrutinized the PacifiCorp deal for indications of how it fit Berkshire's criteria. Several noted that the timing of Berkshire Hathaway's bid closely followed Duke Energy's bid to acquire Cinergy for $9 billion. The PacifiCorp deal was expected to close after the federal and state regulatory reviews were completed, sometime in the next 12 to 18 months.

Exhibit 9 provides company descriptions and key financial data for comparable firms in the regulated electric utility business. **Exhibit 10** presents a range of enterprise values and equity market values for PacifiCorp implied by the multiples of comparable firms.

Conclusion

Conventional thinking held that it would be difficult for Warren Buffett to maintain his record of 24% annual growth in shareholder wealth. Buffett acknowledged that "a fat wallet is the enemy of superior investment results."[33] He stated that it was the firm's goal to meet a 15% annual growth rate in intrinsic value. Would the PacifiCorp acquisition serve the long-term goals of Berkshire Hathaway? Was the bid price appropriate? Because PacifiCorp was privately held by Scottish Power, how did Berkshire's offer measure up against the company's valuation implied by the multiples for comparable firms? What might account for the share price increase for Berkshire Hathaway at the announcement?

---

[31]Berkshire Hathaway Inc., 2001 Annual Report, 17.

[32]Berkshire Hathaway Inc., 2001 Annual Report, 17.

[33]Quoted in Garth Alexander, "Buffett Spends $2bn on Return to His Roots," *Times* (London), 17 August 1995.

EXHIBIT 1 | Relative Share Price Performance of Berkshire Hathaway "Class A" & Scottish Power plc vs. S&P 500 Index (January 3, 2005–May 23, 2005)

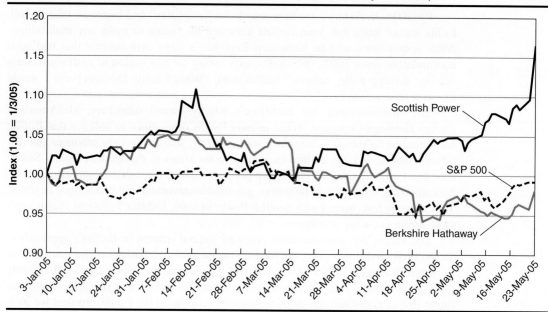

Source of data: Datastream.

EXHIBIT 2 | Business Segment Information for Berkshire Hathaway Inc. (dollars in millions)

Segment	Revenues		Earnings (loss) before Taxes		Capital Expenditures		Depreciation[1]		Identifiable Assets	
	2004	2003	2004	2003	2004	2003	2004	2003	2004	2003
Insurance	$23,927	$24,731	$4,375	$4,941	$ 52	$ 55	$ 52	$ 63	$114,759	$109,004
Apparel	2,200	2,075	325	289	51	71	52	51	1,582	1,523
Building products	4,337	3,846	643	559	219	170	172	174	2,803	2,593
Financial products	3,774	3,045	584	619	296	232	183	161	30,086	28,338
Flight services	3,244	2,431	191	72	155	150	146	136	2,823	2,875
Grocery distribution	23,373	13,743	228	150	136	51	107	59	2,349	2,243
Retail	2,601	2,311	163	165	126	106	56	51	1,669	1,495
Carpet & floor coverings	5,174	4,660	466	436	125	120	99	91	2,153	1,999
Other businesses	3,213	3,040	465	486	41	47	44	43	1,875	1,813
Total	$71,843	$59,882	$7,440	$7,717	$1,201	$1,002	$911	$829	$160,099	$151,883

[1]Excludes capital expenditures that were part of business acquisitions.

Source of data: Berkshire Hathaway Inc., 2004 Annual Report.

EXHIBIT 3 | Major Investees of Berkshire Hathaway (dollars in millions)

Company	Shares	% of Co. Owned	Cost[1] ($mm)	Market ($mm)	
American Express Company[2]	151,610,700	12.1	$1,470	$ 8,546	17%
The Coca-Cola Company[2]	200,000,000	8.3	1,299	8,328	16%
The Gillette Company[2]	96,000,000	9.7	600	4,299	14%
H&R Block, Inc.	14,350,600	8.1	223	703	32%
M&T Bank Corporation	6,708,760	5.8	103	723	14%
Moody's Corporation	24,000,000	16.2	499	2,084	24%
PetroChina "H" shares	2,338,961,000	1.3	488	1,249	39%
The Washington Post Company	1,727,765	18.1	11	1,698	1%
Wells Fargo & Company[2]	56,448,380	3.3	463	3,508	13%
White Mountain Insurance	1,724,200	16.0	369	1,114	33%
Others			3,531	5,465	65%
Total Common Stocks			$9,056	$37,717	

[1]This was both Berkshire's actual purchase price and tax basis; GAAP "cost" differed in a few cases because of write-ups or write-downs that had been required.

[2]Buffett referred to this group of companies as Berkshire Hathaway's "Big Four." Berkshire invested $3.83 billion in the four through multiple transactions between May 1988 and October 2003; on a composite basis, Berkshire's dollar-weighted purchase date was July 1992. By year-end 2004, Berkshire held these interests, on a weighted basis, for about 12.5 years.

Source of data: Berkshire Hathaway Inc., 2004 Annual Report, 16.

EXHIBIT 4 | Hypothetical Example of Value Creation

Assume:

- 5-year investment horizon, when you liquidate at "book" or accumulated investment value
- initial investment is $50 million
- no dividends are paid, all cash flows are reinvested
- return on equity = 20%
- cost of equity = 15%

Year	0	1	2	3	4	5
Investment or **book** equity value	50	60	72	86	104	124

Market value (or intrinsic value) = Present value @ 15% of 124 = $61.65

Market/book = $61.65/50.00 = $1.23

Value created: $1.00 invested becomes $1.23 in market value.

Source: Case writer analysis.

EXHIBIT 5 | Hypothetical Example of Value Destruction

Assume:

- 5-year investment horizon, when you liquidate at "book" or accumulated investment value
- initial investment of $50 million
- no dividends are paid, all cash flows are reinvested
- return on equity = 10%
- cost of equity = 15%

Year	0	1	2	3	4	5
Investment or **book** equity value	50	55	60	67	73	81

Market value (or intrinsic value) = Present value @ 15% of $81 = $40.30

Market/book = $40.30/50.00   = $0.80

Value destroyed: $1.00 invested becomes $0.80 in market value.

Source: Case writer analysis.

EXHIBIT 6 | MidAmerican Energy Holdings Co.: Condensed Consolidated Financial Statements (*dollars in millions*)

	2000	2001	2002	2003	2004
Balance sheets					
Assets:					
Properties, plants, and equipment, net	$ 5,349	$ 6,537	$10,285	$11,181	$11,607
Goodwill	3,673	3,639	4,258	4,306	4,307
Other assets	2,659	2,450	3,892	3,658	3,990
	$11,681	$12,626	$18,435	$19,145	$19,904
Liabilities and shareholders' equity:					
Debt, except debt owed to Berkshire	$ 5,919	$ 7,163	$10,286	$10,296	$10,528
Debt owed to Berkshire	1,032	455	1,728	1,578	1,478
Other liabilities and minority interest	3,154	3,300	4,127	4,500	4,927
	10,105	10,918	16,141	16,374	16,933
Shareholders' equity	1,576	1,708	2,294	2,771	2,971
	$11,681	$12,626	$18,435	$19,145	$19,904
Income statements					
Operating revenue and other income	$ 4,013	$ 4,973	$ 4,903	$ 6,143	$ 6,727
Costs and expenses:					
Cost of sales and operating expenses	3,100	3,522	3,092	3,913	4,390
Depreciation and amortization	383	539	530	603	638
Interest expense – debt held by Berkshire	40	50	118	184	170
Other interest expense	336	443	640	716	713
	3,859	4,554	4,380	5,416	5,911
Earnings before taxes	154	419	523	727	816
Income taxes and minority interests	73	276	126	284	278
Earnings from continuing operations	81	143	397	443	538
Loss on discontinued operations	—	—	(17)	(27)	(368)
Net earnings	$ 81	$ 143	$ 380	$ 416	$ 170

Source of data: Berkshire Hathaway regulatory filings.

EXHIBIT 7 | PacifiCorp Consolidated Financial Statements (*dollars in millions*)

	Year Ended March 31,	
	2004	**2005**
Balance sheets		
Assets:		
Current assets	$ 756.4	$ 1,214.3
Properties, plants, and equipment, net	9,036.5	9,490.6
Other assets	1,884.2	1,816.0
	$11,677.1	$12,520.9
Liabilities and shareholders' equity:		
Current liabilities	$ 1,074.3	$ 1,597.7
Deferred credits	$ 3,706.3	$ 3,868.3
Long-term debt and capital lease obligations	3,520.2	3,629.0
Preferred stock subject to mandatory redemption	56.3	48.8
	8,357.1	9,143.8
Shareholders' equity	3,320.0	3,377.1
	$11,677.1	$12,520.9
Income statements		
Operating revenue and other income	$ 3,194.5	$ 3,048.8
Costs and expenses:		
Operating expenses	2,147.8	1,955.5
Depreciation and amortization	428.8	436.9
Income from operations	617.9	656.4
Interest expense	224.4	236.2
Income from operations before income tax expense	393.5	420.2
Cumulative effect of accounting change	(0.9)	—
Income tax expense	144.5	168.5
Net income	$ 248.1	$ 251.7

Source of data: PacifiCorp 10-K regulatory filing.

EXHIBIT 8 | Berkshire Hathaway Acquisition Criteria

We are eager to hear *from principals or their representatives* about businesses that meet all of the following criteria:

1. Large purchases (at least $75 million of pretax earnings unless the business will fit into one of our existing units).
2. Demonstrated consistent earning power (Future projections are of no interest to us, nor are "turnaround" situations.)
3. Businesses earning good returns on equity while employing little or no debt.
4. Management in place (We can't supply it.)
5. Simple businesses (If there's lots of technology, we won't understand it.)
6. An offering price (We don't want to waste our time or that of the seller by talking, even preliminarily, about a transaction when price is unknown.)

   The larger the company, the greater will be our interest: We would like to make an acquisition in the $5 billion to $20 billion range. *We are not interested, however, in receiving suggestions about purchases we might make in the general stock market.*

   We will not engage in unfriendly takeovers. We can promise complete confidentiality and a very fast answer—customarily within five minutes—as to whether we're interested. We prefer to buy for cash, but will consider issuing stock when we receive as much in intrinsic business value as we give. *We don't participate in auctions.*

   Charlie and I frequently get approached about acquisitions that don't come close to meeting our tests: We've found that if you advertise an interest in buying collies, a lot of people will call hoping to sell you their cocker spaniels. A line from a country song expresses our feeling about new ventures, turnarounds, or auction-like sales: "When the phone don't ring, you'll know it's me."

Source: Berkshire Hathaway Inc., 2004 Annual Report, 28.

EXHIBIT 9 | Comparable Regulated Energy Firms

| | | | Price Per Share | | | | | (Dollars in Millions) | | | | | | | | | |
	Beta	Shares O/S (millions)	Low	High	Div. Per Share	S&P Rating	Total Assets	Total Liabilities	Cash and equiv.	ST Debt	LT Debt	Net Debt	Rev	EBITDA	EBIT	Net Income
Alliant Energy Corp.	0.85	115.74	$23.50	$28.80	$ 1.01	na	$ 8,275	$ 5,470	$276	$ 243	$2,300	$2,267	$2,959	$ 752	$ 420	$164
Cinergy Corp.	0.85	187.53	$34.90	$42.60	$ 1.88	BBB+	$14,982	$10,804	$165	$1,179	$4,228	$5,242	$4,688	$1,198	$ 738	$404
NSTAR	0.70	106.55	$22.70	$27.20	$ 1.13	A	$ 7,117	$ 5,633	$ 23	$ 311	$2,101	$2,389	$2,954	$ 702	$ 455	$190
SCANA Corp.	0.75	113.00	$32.80	$39.70	$ 1.46	na	$ 8,996	$ 6,430	$120	$ 415	$3,186	$3,481	$3,885	$ 861	$ 596	$264
Wisconsin Energy Corp.	0.70	116.99	$29.50	$34.60	$ 0.83	BBB+	$ 9,565	$ 7,043	$ 36	$ 439	$3,240	$3,643	$3,431	$ 857	$ 530	$306
PacifiCorp	na	312.18	na	na	na	na	$12,521	$ 9,144	$199	$ 270	$3,629	$3,700	$3,049	$1,093	$ 656	$252

ALLIANT: Alliant Energy's utilities, Interstate Power and Light (IPL), and Wisconsin Power and Light (WPL) provided electricity to more than 970,000 customers and natural gas to about 412,000 customers in four states.

CINERGY: Its traditional operating units generated, transmitted, and distributed electricity to more than 1.5 million customers and natural gas to 500,000 in Ohio, Indiana, and Kentucky. Cinergy had agreed to be acquired by utility behemoth, Duke Energy, in a $9 billion stock swap.

NSTAR: Utility holding company transmitted and distributed electricity to 1.4 million homes and businesses in Massachusetts; also served some 300,000 natural-gas customers. The company marketed wholesale electricity, operated liquefied natural-gas processing and storage facilities, provided district heating and cooling services, and offered fiber-optic telecommunications services.

SCANA: The holding company served more than 585,000 electricity customers and 690,000 gas customers in South and North Carolina and the neighboring states through utili-ties South Carolina Electric & Gas and Public Service Company of North Carolina.

WISCONSIN ENERGY: The company's utilities provided electricity to nearly 1.1 million customers and natural gas to 1 million customers in eastern and northern Wisconsin and Michigan's Upper Peninsula.

Sources of data: Value Line Investment Survey; Standard & Poor's (case writer's analysis).

EXHIBIT 10 | Valuation Multiples for Comparable Regulated Energy Firms

	(Dollars in Millions)				Enterprise Value as Multiple of:				MV Equity as Multiple of:	
	MV Equity	Enterprise Value	Book Value	EPS	Rev	EBIT	EBITDA	Net Income	EPS	Book Value
Alliant Energy Corp.	$3,333	$ 5,600	$2,805	$ 1.42	1.89x	13.33x	7.45x	34.15x	20.33x	1.19x
Cinergy Corp.	$7,989	$13,231	$4,178	$ 2.15	2.82x	17.93x	na	32.75x	19.77x	1.91x
NSTAR	$2,898	$ 5,287	$1,484	$ 1.78	1.79x	11.62x	7.53x	27.83x	15.25x	1.95x
SCANA Corp.	$4,486	$ 7,967	$2,566	$ 2.34	2.05x	13.37x	9.25x	30.18x	16.99x	1.75x
Wisconsin Energy Corp.	$4,048	$ 7,691	$2,522	$ 2.62	2.24x	14.51x	8.97x	25.13x	13.23x	1.61x
Median	$4,048	$ 7,691	$2,566	$ 2.15	2.05x	13.37x	8.25x	30.18x	16.99x	1.75x
Mean	$4,551	$ 7,955	$2,711	$ 2.06	2.16x	14.15x	8.30x	30.01x	17.11x	1.68x
Implied Value of PacifiCorp[1]			$3,377	$ 0.81	$6,252	$8,775	$9,023	$7,596	$4,277	$5,904
					$6,584	$9,289	$9,076	$7,553	$4,308	$5,678

[1] Implied values for PacifiCorp's enterprise value and market value of equity are derived using the median (top) and mean (bottom) multiples of the comparable firms.

Sources of data: Value Line Investment Survey; Standard & Poor's (case writer's analysis).

Bill Miller and Value Trust

Bill Miller's success is so far off the charts that you have to ask whether it is superhuman. Quite simply, fund managers are not supposed to be this good. Is it mortal genius, or is it celestial luck?[1]

By the middle of 2005, Value Trust, an \$11.2-billion mutual fund[2] managed by William H. (Bill) Miller III, had outperformed its benchmark index, the Standard & Poor's 500 Index (S&P 500), for an astonishing 14 years in a row. This record marked the longest streak of success for any manager in the mutual-fund industry; the next longest period of sustained performance was only half as long. For many fund managers, simply beating the S&P 500 in any *single* year would have been an accomplishment, yet Miller had achieved consistently better results during both the bull markets of the late 1990s and the bear markets of the early 2000s.

Over the previous 15 years, investors in Value Trust, one of a family of funds managed by the Baltimore, Maryland–based Legg Mason, Inc., could look back on the fund's remarkable returns: an average annual total return of 14.6%, which surpassed the S&P 500 by 3.67% per year. An investment of \$10,000 in Value Trust at its inception, in April 1982, would have grown to more than \$330,000 by March 2005. Unlike the fund's benchmark, which was a capitalization-weighted index composed of 500 widely held common stocks, Value Trust only had 36 holdings, 10 of which accounted for nearly 50% of the fund's assets. **Exhibit 1** presents a summary of Legg Mason Value Trust, Inc., as it stood in August 2005.

While Miller rarely had the best overall performance among fund managers in any given year, and while some managers had beaten his results over short-term periods, no one had ever matched his consistent index-beating record. Miller's results seemed to contradict conventional theories, which suggested that, in markets characterized by

---

[1] James K. Glassman, "More Than Pure Luck," *Washington Post,* 14 January 2004, F-01.

[2] A mutual fund was an investment vehicle that pooled the funds of individual investors to buy a portfolio of securities, stocks, bonds, and money-market instruments; investors owned a pro rata share of the overall investment portfolio.

high competition, easy entry, and informational efficiency, it would be extremely difficult to beat the market on a sustained basis. Observers wondered what might explain Miller's performance.

The U.S. Mutual-Fund Market[3]

The U.S. mutual-fund market was the largest in the world, accounting for half of the $16.2 trillion in mutual-fund assets reported worldwide. The aggregate figures somewhat masked the continual growth of mutual funds as an investment vehicle. Between 1995 and 2005, mutual-fund assets grew from $2.8 trillion to $8.1 trillion. Ninety-two million individuals, or nearly half of all households, owned mutual funds in 2004, compared with less than 6% in 1980. In 2004, individual investors held about 90% of all mutual-fund assets.

Mutual funds served several economic functions for investors. First, they afforded the individual investor the opportunity to diversify (own many different stocks) his or her portfolio efficiently without having to invest the sizable amount of capital usually necessary to achieve efficiency. Efficiency was also reflected in the ability of mutual funds to exploit scale economies in trading and transaction costs, economies unavailable to the typical individual investor. Second, in theory, mutual funds provided the individual investor with the professional expertise necessary to earn abnormal returns through successful analysis of securities. A third view was that the mutual-fund industry provided, according to one observer, "an insulating layer between the individual investor and the painful vicissitudes of the marketplace":

> This service, after all, allows individuals to go about their daily lives without spending too much time on the aggravating subject of what to buy and sell and when, and it spares them the even greater aggravation of kicking themselves for making the wrong decision. . . . Thus, the money management industry is really selling "more peace of mind" and "less worry," though it rarely bothers to say so.[4]

Between 1970 and 2005, the number of all mutual funds grew from 361 to 8,044. This total included many different kinds of funds; each one pursued a specific investment focus and was categorized into several acknowledged segments of the industry: aggressive growth (capital-appreciation-oriented), equity income, growth, growth and income, international, option, specialty, small company, balanced, and a variety of bond or fixed-income funds.[5] Funds whose principal focus of investing was common stocks comprised the largest sector of the industry.

---

[3]*Investment Company Fact Book,* 45th ed. (Investment Company Institute, 2005).

[4]Contrarious, "Good News and Bad News," *Personal Investing* (26 August 1987): 128.

[5]Aggressive growth funds sought to maximize capital gains, so current income was of little concern. Growth funds invested in better-known companies with steadier track records. Growth and income funds invested in companies with longer track records that were expected to increase in value and provide a steady income stream. International funds invested in foreign companies. Option funds sought to maximize current returns by investing in dividend-paying stocks on which call options were traded. Balanced funds attempted to conserve principal while earning both current income and capital gains.

U.S. Mutual Fund Industry: Total Number of Funds

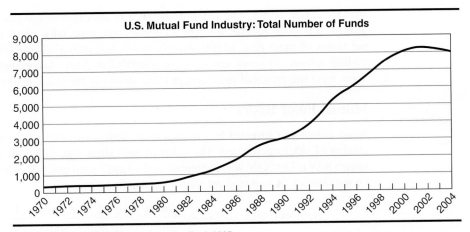

Source: Investment Company Institute Fact Book 2005.

To some extent, the growth in the number and types of mutual funds reflected the increased liquidity in the market and the demand by investors for equity. More importantly, it reflected the effort by mutual-fund organizations to segment the market (i.e., to identify the specialized and changing needs of investors, and to create products to meet those needs). One important result was a broader customer base for the mutual-fund industry as well as a deeper penetration of the total market for financial services.

Another important result of this development was that it added a degree of complexity to the marketplace that altered the investment behavior of some equity investors. In particular, the breadth of mutual-fund alternatives tended to encourage fund switching, especially from one type of fund to another within a family of funds. This reflected the greater range of mutual funds from which to choose, the increased volatility in the market, and the increased trend toward timing-oriented investment strategies. In short, as the mutual-fund industry grew, mutual-fund money became "hotter" (tended to turn over faster).

Institutional investors that managed mutual funds, pension funds, and hedge funds[6] on the behalf of individual investors dominated the market for common stocks in the United States in the mid 2000s. Indeed, at the end of 2004, mutual funds alone owned more than 20% of the outstanding stock of U.S. companies. The sheer dominance of those money managers appeared not only in the amount of assets held, but also in their trading muscle—their ability to move huge sums of money in and out of

---

[6]Hedge funds, like mutual funds, pooled investors' money and invested those funds in financial instruments to generate a positive return. Hedge-fund managers typically charged fees of 1% to 2% of the fund's assets plus a performance fee of 20% of profits. Participation in a fund was usually limited to a small number of high net-worth individuals, who were required to "lock up" their invested capital for a year or more. Worldwide growth in hedge funds had exploded in recent years, rising from approximately 600 funds with $38 billion in assets in 1990, to more than 8,000 funds with $1 trillion in assets in 2004. Many hedge funds took speculative, value-driven trading positions, believed to enhance market volatility and liquidity. Traditionally, hedge funds had been little known and unregulated, but their recent growth as an investment vehicle had brought about increasing regulatory scrutiny in the United States.

stocks on short notice. The rising dominance of institutional investors resulted in the growth of trading volume, average trade size, and, especially, block trading (individual trades of more than 10,000 shares), which had increased from about 15% of all trading volume 30 years ago to about one-third in 2004. Accordingly, money managers were the principal price-setters (lead steers) in the stock market.

Mutual-Fund Basics

When individuals invested in a mutual fund, their ownership was proportional to the number of shares purchased. The value of each share was called the fund's *net asset value* (NAV). The NAV was computed as the fund's total assets less liabilities, divided by the number of mutual-fund shares outstanding, or:

$$\text{Net asset value (NAV)} = \frac{\text{Market value of fund assets} - \text{Liabilities}}{\text{Fund shares outstanding}}$$

The performance of a mutual fund could thus be measured as the increase or decrease in net asset value plus the fund's income distributions (i.e., dividends and capital gains), expressed as a percentage of the fund's NAV at the beginning of the investment period, or:

$$\frac{\text{Annual}}{\text{total return}} = \frac{\text{Change in net asset value} + \text{Dividends} + \text{Capital-gain distributions}}{\text{NAV (at the beginning of the year)}}$$

Advisers, or managers, of mutual funds were compensated by investors through one-time transaction fees and annual payments. A fund's transaction fees, or loads, covered brokerage expenses and were rarely higher than 6% of an individual's investment in the fund. Annual payments were calculated as a percentage of the fund's total assets (called its *expense ratio*), and were charged to all shareholders proportionally. The expense ratio covered the fund's management fees, administrative costs, and advertising and promotion expenses. Expense ratios ranged from as low as 0.2% to as high as 2.0%. The average expense ratio was around 1.3% to 1.5%. Because the expense ratio was regularly deducted from the portfolio, it reduced the fund's NAV, thereby lowering the fund's gross returns. Depending on the magnitude of the fund's expense ratio, the net effect of loads and expense ratios on shareholder returns could be dramatic.[7]

Another drag on shareholders' returns was the fund's tendency to keep about 8% of its assets in cash to meet redemptions or to invest in unexpected bargains. One observer of the industry, economist Henry Kaufman, warned that a sudden economy-wide shock from interest rates or commodity prices could spook investors into panic-style redemptions from mutual funds, which themselves would liquidate investments and send security prices into a tailspin. Unlike the banking industry, which enjoyed the liquidity afforded by the U.S. Federal Reserve System to respond to the effects of panic by depositors, the mutual-fund industry enjoyed no such government-backed reserve.

---

[7]For instance, suppose that you invested $10,000 in a fund that would appreciate at 10% annually, which you then sold out after three years. Also, suppose that the advisory firm had an expense ratio of 2% and a front-end load of 4%. The fees would cut your pretax profit by 35%—from $3,310 to $2,162.

Performance of the Mutual-Fund Industry

The two most frequently used measures of performance were (1) the percentage of annual growth rate of NAV assuming reinvestment (the total return on investment) and (2) the absolute dollar value today of an investment made at some time in the past. Those measures were then compared with the performance of a benchmark portfolio such as the Russell 2000 Index or the S&P 500 Composite Index. **Exhibit 2** provides performance data on a range of mutual-fund categories and comparative indices. The Russell, S&P 500, Dow Jones, and Value Line indices offered benchmarks for the investment performance of hypothetical stock portfolios.[8]

Academicians criticized those performance measures because they failed to adjust for the relative risk of the mutual fund. Over long periods, as **Exhibit 3** shows, different types of securities yielded different levels of total return. **Exhibit 4** shows that each of those types of securities was associated with differing degrees of risk (measured as the standard deviation of returns). Thus, the relationship between risk and return was reliable both on average and over time. For instance, it should be expected that a conservatively managed mutual fund would yield a lower return—precisely because it took fewer risks.

After adjusting for the risk of the fund, academic studies reported that mutual funds were able to perform up to the market on a gross-returns basis; however, when expenses were factored in, they underperformed the market. For instance, Michael Jensen, in a paper published in 1968, reported that gross risk-adjusted returns were -0.4% and that net risk-adjusted returns (i.e., net of expenses) were -1.1%. In 1977, Main updated the study and found that, for a sample of 70 mutual funds, net risk-adjusted returns were essentially zero. Some analysts attributed this general result to the average 1.3% expense ratio of mutual funds and their desire to hold cash.

Most mutual-fund managers relied on some variation of the two classic schools of analysis:

Technical analysis: This involved the identification of profitable investment opportunities based on trends in stock prices, volume, market sentiment, Fibonacci numbers,[9] etc.

Fundamental analysis: This approach relied on insights afforded by an analysis of the economic fundamentals of a company and its industry: supply and demand costs, growth prospects, etc.

---

[8]The Dow Jones indices of industrial companies, transportation companies, and utilities reflected the stocks of a small number (e.g., 30) of large, blue-chip companies, all traded on the New York Stock Exchange (NYSE) and the NASDAQ. The S&P 500 was an index of shares of the 500 largest companies, traded on both the New York and American Stock Exchanges. The Value Line Index was an equal-weighted stock index containing 1,700 companies from the NYSE, American Stock Exchange, NASDAQ, and over-the-counter market; it was also known as the Value Line Investment Survey. The Russell 2000 measured the performance of 2,000 of the smallest companies in the Russell 3000 index of the biggest U.S. stocks. As any index sample became larger, it reflected a greater weighting of smaller, high-growth companies.

[9]The sequence, named for Leonard Fibonacci (1175-1240), consisted of the numbers 1, 1, 2, 3, 5, 8, 13 and so on. Each number after the first two equals the sum of the two numbers before it. No academic research associates this sequence with a consistent ability to earn supernormal returns from investing in the market.

While variations on those approaches often produced supernormal returns in certain years, there was no guarantee that they would produce such returns consistently over time.

Burton Malkiel, an academic researcher, concluded that a passive buy-and-hold strategy (of a large, diversified portfolio) would do as well for the investor as the average mutual fund:

> Even a dart-throwing chimpanzee can select a portfolio that performs as well as one carefully selected by the experts. This, in essence, is the practical application of the theory of efficient markets. . . . The theory holds that the market appears to adjust so quickly to information about individual stocks and the economy as a whole, that no technique of selecting a portfolio—neither technical nor fundamental analysis—can consistently outperform a strategy of simply buying and holding a diversified group of securities such as those that make up the popular market averages. . . . [o]ne has to be impressed with the substantial volume of evidence suggesting that stock prices display a remarkable degree of efficiency. . . . If some degree of mispricing exists, it does not persist for long. "True value will always out" in the stock market.[10]

Many scholars accepted that view. They argued that the stock market followed a "random walk," where the price movements of tomorrow were essentially uncorrelated with the price movements of today. In essence, this denied the possibility that there could be momentum in the movements of common stock prices. According to this view, technical analysis was the modern-day equivalent of alchemy. Fundamental analysis, too, had its academic detractors. They argued that capital markets' information was efficient, and that the insights available to any one fundamental analyst were bound to be impounded quickly into share prices.

The notion that capital markets incorporated all the relevant information into existing securities' prices was known as the *efficient market hypothesis* (EMH), and was widely, though not universally, accepted by financial economists. If EMH were correct and all current prices reflected the true value of the underlying securities, then arguably it would be impossible to beat the market with superior skill or intellect.

Economists defined three levels of market efficiency, which were distinguished by the degree of information believed to be reflected in current securities' prices. The *weak* form of efficiency maintained that all past prices for a stock were impounded into today's price; prices today simply followed a random walk with no correlation with past patterns. *Semistrong* efficiency held that today's prices reflected not only all past prices, but also all publicly available information. Finally, the *strong* form of market efficiency held that today's stock price reflected *all* the information that could be acquired through a close analysis of the company and the economy. "In such a market," as one economist said, "we would observe lucky and unlucky investors, but we wouldn't find any superior investment managers who can consistently beat the market."[11]

---

[10]Burton G. Malkiel, *A Random Walk Down Wall Street* (New York: Norton, 1990), 186, 211.

[11]Richard A. Brealey, Stewart C. Myers, and Franklin Allen, *Principles of Corporate Finance,* 8th ed. (New York: McGraw-Hill Irwin, 2006), 337.

By implication, proponents of those academic theories were highly critical of the services provided by active mutual-fund managers. Paul Samuelson, the Nobel Prize–winning economist, said:

> [E]xisting stock prices already have discounted in them an allowance for their future prospects. Hence . . . one stock [is] about as good or bad a buy as another. To [the] passive investor, chance alone would be as good a method of selection as anything else.[12]

Various popular tests of this thinking seemed to support that view. For instance, *Forbes* magazine chose 28 stocks by throwing darts in June 1967 and invested $1,000 in each. By 1984, the $28,000 investment was worth $131,697.61, for a 9.5% compound rate of return. This beat the broad market averages and almost all mutual funds. *Forbes* concluded, "It would seem that a combination of luck and sloth beats brains."[13]

Yet, the nagging problem remained that there were still some superstar money managers—like Bill Miller—who, over long periods, greatly outperformed the market. In reply, Malkiel suggested that beating the market was much like participating in a coin-tossing contest where those who consistently flip heads are the winners.[14] In a coin-tossing game with 1,000 contestants, half will be eliminated on the first flip. On the second flip, half of those surviving contestants are eliminated. And so on, until, on the seventh flip, only eight contestants remain. To the naïve observer, the ability to flip heads consistently looks like extraordinary skill. By analogy, Malkiel suggested that the success of a few superstar portfolio managers could be explained as luck.

As might be expected, the community of money managers received those scholarly theories with great hostility. And even in the ranks of academicians, dissension appeared in the form of the burgeoning field of "behavioral finance," which suggested that greed, fear, and panic were much more significant factors in the setting of stock prices than the mainstream theory would permit. For instance, to many observers, the Internet bubble of the late 1990s seemed to be totally inconsistent with the view of markets as fundamentally rational and efficient. Professor Robert Shiller of Yale University said:

> Evidence from behavioral finance helps us to understand . . . that the recent stock market boom, and then crash after 2000, had its origins in human foibles and arbitrary feedback relations and must have generated a real and substantial misallocation of resources. The challenge for economists is to make this reality a better part of their models.[15]

Similarly, the stock-market crash of October 1987 had also seemed to undermine the strength of the EMH. Professor Lawrence Summers of Harvard argued that the

---

[12]Malkiel, *Random Walk,* 182.

[13]Malkiel, *Random Walk,* 164.

[14]Malkiel, *Random Walk,* 175–176.

[15]Robert J. Shiller, "From Efficient Markets Theory to Behavioral Finance," *Journal of Economic Perspectives* (winter 2003): 102.

1987 crash was a "clear gap with the theory. If anyone did seriously believe that price movements are determined by changes in information about economic fundamentals, they've got to be disabused of that notion by [the] 500-point drop."[16] Shiller said, "The efficient market hypothesis is the most remarkable error in the history of economic theory. This is just another nail in its coffin."[17]

Academic research exposed other inconsistencies with the EMH. Those included apparently predictable stock-price patterns indicating reliable, abnormally positive returns in early January of each year (the "January effect"), and a "blue Monday" effect, where average stock returns were negative from the close of trading on Friday to the close of trading on Monday. Other evidence suggested that stocks with low price-to-earnings (P/E) multiples tended to outperform those with high P/E multiples. Finally, some evidence emerged for positive serial correlation (that is, momentum) in stock returns from week to week or from month to month. Those results were inconsistent with a random walk of prices and returns. Yet, despite the existence of those anomalies, the EMH remained the dominant paradigm in the academic community.

Bill Miller and Value Trust

Exhibit 5 presents a 10-year summary of the annual returns for Value Trust and eight other Legg Mason equity funds. Morningstar, the well-known statistical service for the investment community, gave Value Trust a five-star rating, its highest for investment performance. Some observers attributed this success to the fund manager's conscious strategy of staying fully invested at all times rather than attempting to time the extent of market investments. Another popular explanation for the fund's performance was the unusual skill of Bill Miller, the fund's portfolio manager.

Miller started investing when he was about 9 years old; he later bought his first stock, RCA, when he was 16. During the Vietnam War, Miller served in military intelligence, and afterward earned a doctorate in philosophy from Johns Hopkins University. He eventually joined Legg Mason, Inc., in 1981. Miller was an adherent of fundamental analysis, an approach to equity investing he had gleaned from a number of sources:

> I had read a bunch of stuff on investing ever since I had gotten interested: *Supermoney,* about Ben Graham and Warren Buffett; Graham's *Intelligent Investor; Security Analysis;* David Dreman's *Psychology in the Stock Market.* Combine those books and those approaches, and what you have is basically a contrarian, value-based methodology, which, psychologically, was very compatible with the way I tended to think about things. I tend to think stocks are more attractive at lower prices rather than higher prices.[18]

Miller's approach was research-intensive and highly concentrated. Nearly 50% of Value Trust's assets were invested in just 10 large-capitalization companies. While

---

[16]B. Donnelly, "Efficient-Market Theorists Are Puzzled by Recent Gyrations in Stock Market," *Wall Street Journal,* 23 October 1987, 7.

[17]B. Donnelly, "Efficient-Market Theorists."

[18]Jack Otter, "Meet Mr. Market," www.smartmoney.com, 5 May 2005, accessed 15 September 2005.

most of Miller's investments were value stocks, he was not averse to taking large positions in the stocks of growth companies.[19] Generally speaking, Miller's style was eclectic and difficult to distill. "He almost takes pleasure in having people think he's crazy," one industry veteran said of him. "It means he's doing well."[20] By the early 2000s, however, several key elements of Miller's contrarian strategy had begun to emerge:

- *Buy low-price, high intrinsic-value stocks:* "We want to know how stock prices depart from underlying value and why. That can be on the upside as we saw with the Internet, when most companies weren't worth anything like what the market thought they were worth. What we want is the reverse—tremendous pessimism, people believing that a business is broken, scandal, something everybody is fleeing."[21]

- *Take heart in pessimistic markets:* "Bargain prices do not occur when the consensus is cheery, the news is good, and investors are optimistic. Our research efforts are usually directed at precisely the area of the market the news media tells you has the least promising outlook, and we are typically selling those stocks that you are reading have the greatest opportunity for near-term gain."[22]

- *Remember that the lowest average cost wins:* "For most investors, if a stock starts behaving in a way that is different from what they think it ought to be doing—say, it falls 15%—they will probably sell. In our case, when a stock drops and we believe in the fundamentals, the case for future returns goes up. Think of it like this: If the underlying business is worth $40, and the stock is $20, my rate of return is 100%. The lower the shares go, the higher the future rate of return and the more money you should invest in them."[23]

- *Be wary of valuation illusions:* "I'll give you two historical valuation illusions: Wal-Mart stores and Microsoft. From the day they came public, they looked expensive. Nonetheless, if you bought Wal-Mart when it went public at an expensive-looking 20+ times earnings, you would have the returns of many thousands percent on that. The same goes for Microsoft. Until a couple of years ago, Microsoft went up an average 1% every week it was public, despite the fact that it looked expensive. Had we known the growth that was in front of it, we would have known it was actually a bargain."[24]

---

[19]The stock of a corporation that exhibited faster-than-average gains in earnings during recent periods was typically considered a growth stock. Growth stocks were generally riskier than the average stock, and they often had higher price-to-earnings ratios and paid little to no dividends. A value stock tended to trade at a lower price relative to its earnings, and it usually carried a high dividend yield and low price-to-book or price-to-earnings ratio.

[20]Christopher Davis, co-manager of the Davis Funds, quoted in Matthew Heimer, "Bill Miller," www.smartmoney.com, 1 July 2005.

[21]"Miller's Tale: Legg Mason's Revered Fund Steward Talks about Value, Metrics, and His Optimism," *Barron's* (3 February 2003).

[22]Ian McDonald, "Miller Finds Value in Dreary Places," *Wall Street Journal,* 16 May 2002.

[23]"Bill Miller: How to Profit from Falling Prices," *Fortune* (3 September 2003).

[24]"Miller's Tale."

- *Take the long view:* "Portfolio turnover is over 100% for the average mutual fund, implying a 10- or 11-month holding period even though the short term is pretty well reflected in stock prices. The biggest opportunity for investors is really thinking out longer term. [P]eople need to think long term. People tend to react and not anticipate. And what they react to is what they wish they'd done a year ago, or two years ago."[25, 26]

- *Look for cyclical* and *secular underpricing:* "Most value people tend to own stocks that are cyclically underpriced. Most growth people own stocks that are secularly underpriced: things that can grow for long periods of time. Our portfolios historically tended to be, though I wouldn't say they are now, better diversified along both cyclical and secular lines. And our portfolio tries to look at underpricing or mispricing along both of those dimensions so that we're not caught in one or the other."[27]

- *Buy low-expectation stocks:* "I think buying low-expectation stocks, buying higher dividend-yielding stocks, staying away from things with high expense ratios, and most important, the key thing would be—as Warren Buffett says—you need to be fearful when others are greedy, and greedy when others are fearful. So when the market's been down for a while, and it looks bad, then you should be more aggressive, and when it's been up for a while, then you should be less aggressive."[28]

- *Take risks:* "As Earl Weaver[29] used to say, you win more games on three-run homers than sacrifice bunts. That's the thing people in the markets don't understand as well as they should. A lot of people look to hit singles and sacrifice bunts and make small returns.[30] But statistically you are far better off with huge gains because you are going to make mistakes. And if you are playing small ball and you make a few mistakes, you can't recover."[31]

Value Trust had earned a cumulative return of more than 830% over the previous 14 years, more than double that of its average peer and the index, according to Morningstar. Even so, Miller remained modest about this record: "The evidence is pretty compelling that the market is pretty efficient and will beat most people most of the time."[32] He acknowledged that his much ballyhooed streak could just as easily have been an accident of the calendar. "If the year ended on different months, it wouldn't

---

[25]McDonald, "Bill Miller Dishes on His Streak and His Strategy," *Wall Street Journal,* 6 January 2005.

[26]Otter, "Meet Mr. Market."

[27]Otter, "Meet Mr. Market."

[28]Otter, "Meet Mr. Market."

[29]Earl Sidney Weaver was a long-time manager of the Baltimore Orioles, an American baseball team. During his tenure, the Orioles won six division titles, four league pennants, and the World Series championship. Bill Miller was widely known as an ardent Orioles fan.

[30]In American baseball, a homer (home run) was a hit that allowed a batter to circle all the bases and score a run. A bunt occurred when the batter hit the ball by positioning the bat in front of his body, rather than by swinging at it; a sacrifice bunt was a bunt that resulted in a base runner advancing and the batter being put out. A single was a batted ball that allowed a batter to reach first base only.

[31]"Bill Miller: How to Profit."

[32]McDonald, "Bill Miller Dishes."

be there, and at some point those mathematics will hit us," Miller said. "We've been lucky. Well, maybe it's not 100% luck. Maybe 95% luck."[33] According to Morningstar, Miller's fund lagged behind the S&P 500 in 32 12-month periods out of a total of 152 12-month periods, from the beginning of the streak through July 2004.

Conclusion

Judged from almost any perspective, Miller's investment success was remarkable. His long-run, market-beating performance defied conventional academic theories. Investors, scholars, and market observers wondered about the sources of Miller's superior performance and about its sustainability. As of the middle of 2005, was it rational for an equity investor to buy shares in Value Trust?

At 55, Bill Miller was hardly considered old. Warren Buffett was 74, and he remained an active and visible investor through his company, Berkshire Hathaway, Inc. (See UVA-F-1483, "Warren E. Buffett, 2005," for additional information on Warren Buffett and Berkshire Hathaway.) But investors and other observers had begun to wonder how long Miller would remain at the helm of Value Trust and whether his successor could sustain his exemplary record.

In addition to managing the $11.2-billion Value Trust, Miller also guided the $3.2-billion Legg Mason Opportunity Trust and the $3.2-billion Legg Mason Special Investment Trust. In addition, Miller served as the chief executive officer of Legg Mason Capital Management, which had about $40 billion in assets under its management.

---

[33]McDonald, "Bill Miller Dishes."

EXHIBIT 1 | Morningstar Report on Legg Mason Value Trust, Inc.

Legg Mason Value Prim

Governance and Management

Stewardship Grade B

Portfolio Manager(s)

Longtime manager Bill Miller has vastly outperformed his average peer and the index during his tenure. Assistant manager Nancy Dennin, who focused mostly on administrative tasks, recently stepped down. Some of her duties are being taken on by David Nelson, manager of American Leading Companies. The firm has hired a new research director. Ire Malis, and a chief strategist, Michael Mauboussin, along with a handful of new analysis.

Strategy

Bill Miller looks for companies that are trading cheaply relative to his estimates of what they're worth. This often leads him to beaten-down turnaround plays. Unlike many value managers, however, Miller is willing make fairly optimistic assumptions about growth, and he doesn't shy away from owning companies in traditional growth sectors. In this portfolio, pricey Internet stocks rub elbows with bargain-priced financials and turnaround plays. Miller will also let favored names run, allowing top positions to soak up a large percentage of assets.

Ticker	Load	NAV	Yield	Total Assets
LMVTX	12b-1only	$66.32	0.0%	$18,208 mil

Historical Profile

Return	High
Risk	High
Rating	★★★★★ Highest

89% 93% 99% 99% 99% 100% 98% 100% 100%

▼ Manager Change
▽ Partial Manager Change

50.6
43.6
32.4 **Growth of $10,000**
24.0 — Investment Values of Fund
17.0 — Investment Values of S&P 500
10.0

	1994	1995	1996	1997	1998	1999	2000	2001	2002	2003	2004	07-05	History
	19.04	25.19	32.99	42.74	61.58	75.27	55.44	50.06	40.59	58.26	65.23	66.32	NAV
	1.39	40.76	38.43	37.05	48.04	26.71	−7.14	−9.29	−18.92	43.53	11.96	1.67	Total Return %
	0.07	3.23	15.48	3.70	19.46	5.67	1.96	2.59	3.17	14.86	1.09	−1.21	+/−S&P 500
	1.00	2.99	15.98	4.20	21.02	5.80	0.65	3.16	2.73	13.64	0.56	−2.33	+/−Russ 1000
	0.27	0.93	0.66	0.11	0.00	0.00	0.00	0.00	0.00	0.00	0.00	0.00	Income Return %
	1.12	39.83	37.77	36.94	48.04	26.71	−7.14	−9.29	−18.92	43.53	11.96	1.67	Capital Return %
	21	3	2	4	1	20	52	25	23	2	24	82	Total Rtn % Rank Cat
	0.05	0.17	0.16	0.04	0.00	0.00	0.00	0.00	0.00	0.00	0.00	0.00	Income $
	0.04	1.24	1.53	2.32	1.41	2.46	14.47	0.26	0.00	0.00	0.00	0.00	Capital Gains $
	1.82	1.81	1.82	1.77	1.73	1.69	1.68	1.69	1.68	1.72	1.70	1.68	Expense Ratio %
	0.50	0.50	0.80	0.40	−0.10	−0.40	−0.60	−0.50	−0.50	−0.40	−0.60	0.77	Income Ratio %
	26	20	20	10	13	19	20	27	24	25	4	9	Turnover Rate %
	933	1,340	1,976	3,683	8,079	12,540	10,597	9,788	7,218	10,738	11,947	11,723	Net Assets $mil

Mstar Category
Large Blend

Investment Style
Equity
Stock%

Performance Quartile
(within Category)

Performance 07.31.05

	1st Qtr	2nd Qtr	3rd Qtr	4th Qtr	Total
2001	−3.08	7.33	−20.01	9.02	−9.29
2002	−3.66	−13.73	−13.96	13.38	−18.92
2003	−2.91	25.48	3.54	13.79	43.53
2004	−1.22	4.59	−5.80	15.04	11.96
2005	−5.95	3.52	—	—	—

Trailing	Total Return %	+/− S&P 500	+/− Russ 1000	% Rank Cat	Growth of $10,000
3 Mo	11.31	4.14	3.30	5	11,131
6 Mo	5.45	0.00	−1.24	45	10,545
1 Yr	19.54	5.50	3.34	10	11,954
3 Yr Avg	19.87	7.26	6.41	1	17,224
5 Yr Avg	2.93	4.28	3.73	12	11,553
10 Yr Avg	15.96	5.98	5.79	1	43,962
15 Yr Avg	14.88	3.94	3.62	2	80,106

Tax Analysis	Tax-Adj Rtn %	% Rank Cat	Tax-Cost Rat	% Rank Cat
3 Yr (estimated)	19.87	1	0.00	1
5 Yr (estimated)	2.39	11	0.52	29
10 Yr (estimated)	14.88	1	0.93	28

Potential Capital Gain Exposure: 31% of assets

Rating and Risk

Time Period	Load-Adj Return %	Morningstar Rtn vs Cat	Morningstar Risk vs Cat	Morningstar Risk-Adj Rating
1 Yr	19.54			
3 Yr	19.87	High	High	★★★★★
5 Yr	2.93	+Avg	High	★★★★
10 Yr	15.96	High	High	★★★★★
Incept	16.64			

Other Measures	Standard Index S&P 500	Best Fit Index Russ 1000
Alpha	3.6	2.4
Beta	1.31	1.33
R-Squared	88	89
Standard Deviation	18.25	
Mean	19.87	
Sharpe Ratio	1.00	

Portfolio Analysis 03-31-05

Share change since 12-04 Total Stocks:36

	Sector	PE	Tot Ret %	% Assets
Nextel Communications	Telecom	13.3	15.96	7.57
⊖ UnitedHealth Group	Health	24.8	18.86	7.22
Tyco International	Ind Mtrls	26.0	−14.20	6.96
AES	Utilities	24.7	17.41	5.16
⊕ Amazon.com	Consumer	36.1	1.94	4.88
⊕ IAC/InterActiveCorp	Consumer	NMF	−3.33	4.58
⊕ J.P. Morgan Chase & Co.	Financial	27.9	−7.32	3.98
Eastman Kodak	Goods	—	−16.31	3.35
⊖ Aetna	Financial	18.3	24.09	3.18
McKesson	Health	—	43.48	2.97
⊖ MGIC Investment	Financial	11.0	−0.11	2.80
⊕ eBay	Consumer	68.5	−28.18	2.71
⊖ Waste Management	Business	17.5	−4.80	2.69
⊖ Washington Mutual	Financial	13.8	3.92	2.56
Electronic Arts	Software	36.2	−6.61	2.54
⊕ Qwest Communications Int	Telecom	—	−13.96	2.49
Citigroup	Financial	13.2	−7.12	2.45
⊕ The Directv Group	Media	—	−8.00	2.44
WPP Grp	Business	—		2.34
Home Depot	Consumer	18.6	2.31	2.31

Morningstar's Take by Christopher Traulsen 08-01-05

Size isn't yet a big problem for this fund, but we're keeping an eye on the matter.

If you count all the money that manager Bill Miller and his team are running in this style, it totals $38 billion. That's a sizable sum, particularly when one considers that other large offerings spread their assets over many more names than Miller does here. Indeed, the typical actively managed domestic stock mutual fund with at least $35 billion in assets holds 265 stocks and stashed 22% of assets in its top 10 holdings. As of March 31, 2005, the fund held just 36 stocks and squeezed 50% of its assets into its top 10 holdings.

The worry is that as the fund grows, Miller will be forced to deviate from those ideas he thinks have the highest probability of success because he already owns too much of them. Miller discounts this as a real negative, noting that he can just buy highly correlated names if need be. However, doing so still runs the risk that those names wont be as strong as the best

opportunities identified by his research. It's worth noting, though, that other aspects of Miller's style make him well-suited to running such a large portfolio. First, he usually isn't competing for liquidity with the hordes of traders that a less contrarian manager might be. Miller also just doesn't trade much: The fund's turnover rate hasn't cracked 30% since 1992.

It's obvious that Miller is a brilliant portfolio manager—to glean that much, one just needs to look at his record and speak to him about how he thinks about investment opportunities. And we do not think the fund's current size is cause for concern. However, Legg Mason's recent deal with Citigroup means that a lot more brokers may suddenly be selling this fund (though it could also mean the share classes will be cheaper ongoing expenses may become available). Add to that the fact that as CEO of the fund advisor, Miller has little incentive to close this offering and slow the growth of his group's business, and we think the issue bears close watching.

Address:	100 Light St. Baltimore MD 21203 800-577-8589	Minimum Purchase:	$1000	Add: $100	IRA: $1000
		Min Auto Inv Plan:	$1000	Add: $50	
		Sales Fees:	0.70%B, 0.25%S		
Web Address:	www.leggmason.com	Management Fee:	0.7%		
Inception:	04-16-82	Actual Fees:	Mgt:0.66%	Dist:0.95%	
Advisor:	Legg Mason Funds Management Inc.	Expense Projections:	3Yr:$536	5Yr:$923	10Yr:$2009
Subadvisor:	None	Income Distrib:	Annually		

NTF Plans: DATALynx NTF, TD Waterhouse Ins NT

Current Investment Style

Value Blnd Growth

	Market cap	%
Giant		34.8
Large		54.2
Mid		11.0
Small		0.0
Micro		0.0

Avg $mil:
26,231

Value Measures		Rel Category
Price/Earnings	16.91	1.06
Price/Book	2.10	0.88
Price/Sales	1.01	0.72
Price/Cash Flow	9.92	1.27
Dividend Yield %	2.37	1.37

Growth Measures	%	Rel Category
Long-Term Erngs	13.08	1.16
Book Value	9.87	1.06
Sales	6.87	0.92
Cash Flow	27.70	2.89
Historical Erngs	0.46	0.03

Profitability	%	Rel Category
Return on Equity	12.99	0.72
Return on Assets	7.48	0.80
Net Margin	9.99	0.81

Sector Weightings	% of Stocks	Rel S&P 500	3 Year High	Low
⌖ Info	24.08	1.17		
Software	4.12	1.02	5	0
Hardware	3.70	0.37	4	2
Media	6.17	1.81	7	5
Telecom	10.09	3.36	12	10
⌖ Service	60.41	1.32		
Health	13.38	1.03	16	12
Consumer	18.93	1.99	23	19
Business	7.35	1.98	7	6
Financial	20.75	1.05	24	21
⌖ Mfg	15.51	0.46		
Goods	3.36	0.37	6	3
Ind Mtrls	6.98	0.58	7	5
Energy	0.00	0.00	0	0
Utilities	5.17	1.53	5	2

Composition

	%
● Cash	0.3
● Stocks	99.7
● Bonds	0.0
● Others	0.0
Foreign	2.3
(% of stock)	

EXHIBIT 2 | Morningstar Performance Comparison of Mutual-Fund Categories and Broad Market Indices (Performance Close-Ups)

Benchmark Performance

No. of Funds	Total Assets $Bil	Category	TR% YTD 10-14-05	Total Return % through 09-30-05				Annualized			Annual Return						
				1Mo	3Mo	6Mo	1Yr	3Yr	5Yr	10Yr	1998	1999	2000	2001	2002	2003	2004
7502	**2320**	**Domestic Stock**	**0.05**	**0.98**	**4.68**	**7.14**	**15.85**	**18.19**	**0.03**	**8.80**	**16.19**	**29.22**	**-0.03**	**-9.21**	**-22.05**	**33.39**	**12.40**
1190	0.0	Large Value	0.08	0.90	3.55	4.77	13.67	17.75	4.45	9.27	11.31	5.72	9.74	-3.08	-18.36	28.57	12.99
1683	860.9	Large Blend	-0.17	1.01	4.06	5.57	13.17	15.72	-1.17	8.23	21.33	20.43	-4.06	-11.42	-21.81	27.53	10.08
1482	654.0	Large Growth	-0.66	1.08	4.78	7.52	13.39	14.62	-7.28	6.94	33.00	38.92	-12.90	-21.12	-27.10	28.99	7.78
325	113.4	Mid-Cap Value	1.37	0.50	4.20	6.86	18.77	22.14	10.85	11.87	2.44	8.42	21.02	6.60	-12.80	36.29	18.55
423	121.8	Mid-Cap Blend	1.74	0.90	5.08	7.93	19.33	21.57	6.52	11.22	9.82	21.47	10.14	1.26	-16.30	36.77	16.23
850	191.7	Mid-Cap Growth	1.30	1.48	6.27	9.75	20.29	19.58	-4.36	8.17	17.95	59.61	-2.88	-18.62	-26.61	36.28	13.19
308	79.7	Small Value	0.19	0.27	4.46	7.49	18.61	24.23	14.59	13.04	-5.85	6.90	17.86	16.29	-10.05	43.95	20.81
505	160.9	Small Blend	0.26	0.63	5.25	8.69	19.24	23.25	10.07	11.77	-4.96	14.05	13.84	8.37	-15.68	42.81	18.72
736	137.7	Small Growth	-1.27	1.05	5.61	9.47	18.53	21.17	-1.45	8.13	6.19	62.84	-4.62	-8.45	-27.94	45.44	12.20
		S&P 500 Index	**-0.77**	**0.81**	**3.60**	**5.02**	**12.25**	**16.71**	**-1.49**	**9.48**	**28.58**	**21.04**	**-9.10**	**-11.88**	**-22.09**	**28.67**	**10.87**
		S&P MidCap 400	**3.56**	**0.77**	**4.88**	**9.35**	**22.14**	**22.09**	**7.04**	**14.13**	**19.11**	**14.72**	**17.49**	**-0.60**	**-14.53**	**35.59**	**16.47**
		Russell 2000	—	**0.31**	**4.69**	**9.21**	**17.95**	**24.12**	**6.45**	**9.37**	**-2.55**	**21.26**	**-3.02**	**2.49**	**-20.48**	**47.25**	**18.33**
1903	**771**	**International Stock**	**8.06**	**4.16**	**11.24**	**11.68**	**27.60**	**24.99**	**3.95**	**7.18**	**6.78**	**50.82**	**-15.34**	**-16.69**	**-14.55**	**39.91**	**18.57**
99	26.8	Europe Stock	7.64	1.89	9.82	9.25	27.79	26.94	6.45	10.09	15.25	33.81	-5.10	-16.46	-11.41	39.64	21.73
16	2.9	Latin Amer Stock	33.90	15.45	29.43	42.55	77.07	56.46	17.63	13.41	-37.07	60.18	-15.58	-5.91	-19.95	61.74	38.26
190	63.2	Div Emerging Mkts	16.31	8.58	17.33	21.77	44.04	36.80	14.08	6.70	-26.37	70.37	-29.86	-3.04	-5.72	55.51	23.80
21	2.2	Div Pac/Asia	11.71	7.78	14.73	14.81	29.60	23.03	3.63	4.47	-1.59	87.73	-30.50	-17.84	-10.74	41.05	17.39
87	9.3	Pac/Asia ex-Japan	9.73	4.85	9.65	12.99	28.48	26.57	9.31	4.34	-7.61	72.75	-23.59	-2.08	-9.32	52.82	13.22
42	10.9	Japan Stock	12.39	8.10	18.20	15.73	26.39	18.04	-3.45	1.15	6.29	111.88	-34.01	-30.52	-12.86	38.40	14.18
161	115.3	Foreign Large Value	6.77	3.65	10.04	8.99	26.39	25.34	7.76	9.24	10.77	25.71	-2.15	-13.52	-11.35	39.36	21.90
549	209.0	Foreign Large Blend	6.71	3.85	11.08	10.21	25.15	22.03	1.15	6.25	13.24	39.79	-15.86	-21.73	-16.86	33.38	17.31
204	83.7	Foreign Large Growth	6.21	3.86	11.27	10.86	24.73	21.46	-0.95	5.36	14.48	55.97	-19.86	-23.45	-18.91	34.86	15.90
54	33.9	Foreign Sm/Mid Val	9.61	2.92	9.86	9.45	28.59	29.43	12.74	10.86	5.07	33.86	-5.39	-8.30	-3.02	50.19	24.22
99	21.4	Foreign Sm Mid Grth	12.84	4.12	13.52	13.59	35.66	32.02	3.56	13.91	19.75	89.46	-15.83	-24.65	-14.73	54.13	23.73
381	192.6	World Stock	3.93	2.44	7.89	9.03	21.21	21.04	0.51	7.91	14.57	42.38	-8.24	-16.15	-19.12	24.98	15.24
		MSCI EAFE	—	**4.45**	**10.38**	**9.26**	**25.79**	**24.61**	**3.13**	**5.83**	**19.93**	**27.03**	**-14.19**	**-21.42**	**-15.94**	**38.59**	**20.25**
		MSCI Emerging Markets	—	**9.09**	**17.01**	**20.53**	**42.48**	**35.45**	**11.37**	**3.56**	**-27.67**	**64.09**	**-31.90**	**-4.68**	**-7.97**	**51.59**	**22.45**
1161	**221**	**Specialty Stock**	**4.76**	**2.47**	**8.15**	**14.62**	**22.82**	**23.97**	**1.63**	**10.56**	**8.40**	**32.02**	**12.80**	**-13.71**	**-17.84**	**40.80**	**15.67**
37	3.2	Communications	1.31	2.21	7.86	14.33	25.69	32.49	-11.13	7.18	42.58	58.01	-29.54	-28.73	-39.66	44.63	21.80
121	11.0	Financial	-3.13	0.61	1.48	5.21	9.40	16.65	7.40	12.85	6.35	-2.24	27.62	-2.70	-9.74	32.74	13.81
188	50.5	Health	4.42	0.50	7.02	14.35	15.93	16.43	-0.82	11.62	21.01	19.24	56.86	-11.24	-26.74	31.32	9.57
125	45.9	Natural Resources	28.86	5.72	21.88	24.59	48.39	37.78	17.33	15.07	-24.90	30.95	29.63	-10.79	-3.50	32.64	27.28
51	8.7	Precious Metals	7.96	16.62	20.65	19.54	13.78	23.41	27.49	4.01	-10.49	6.11	-16.71	18.84	62.93	58.49	-8.30
254	50.8	Real Estate	3.22	0.42	3.30	16.65	26.23	25.93	18.54	15.05	-15.86	-2.80	26.87	9.80	4.21	37.06	32.12
286	34.1	Technology	-3.07	2.12	7.70	11.30	17.85	24.67	-17.51	5.08	51.58	126.37	-31.73	-35.41	-42.22	57.04	4.32
99	16.8	Utilities	10.83	3.42	8.29	16.02	33.54	25.76	1.23	10.04	20.95	18.45	10.89	-20.66	-24.09	23.32	23.82

EXHIBIT 2 | Morningstar Performance Comparison of Mutual-Fund Categories and Broad Market Indices (Performance Close-Ups) *(continued)*

Benchmark Performance

No. of Funds	Total Assets $Bil	Category	TR% YTD 10-14-05	Total Return % through 09-30-05				Annualized			Annual Return						
				1Mo	3Mo	6Mo	1Yr	3Yr	5Yr	10Yr	1998	1999	2000	2001	2002	2003	2004
1752	713	**Hybrid**	0.70	0.49	2.73	4.50	9.57	11.56	2.69	7.59	12.16	11.25	2.68	-3.65	-9.02	18.86	8.11
516	103.3	Conservative Alloc	0.32	-0.04	1.37	3.13	5.95	7.90	3.44	6.56	10.59	5.63	4.37	0.02	-3.50	12.42	5.39
79	15.1	Convertible	-0.70	1.39	4.88	6.10	9.55	14.47	2.43	8.63	5.04	28.84	1.26	-6.36	-8.00	26.56	8.72
1084	499.3	Moderate Allocation	0.85	0.61	3.10	5.00	10.81	12.40	2.21	7.65	13.89	11.09	2.35	-4.58	-11.38	20.20	8.80
73	94.9	World Allocation	2.62	1.34	4.31	5.47	14.83	16.63	7.64	9.33	9.14	15.34	1.65	-3.08	-1.90	25.00	14.46
875	240	**Specialty Bond**	0.38	-0.48	1.14	2.92	6.37	12.36	7.03	6.57	1.12	4.84	-1.67	3.22	3.79	20.78	9.32
67	29.0	Bank Loan	3.44	0.39	1.65	2.23	4.81	6.73	4.70	5.10	6.28	5.91	5.33	1.63	0.75	10.32	5.09
464	125.1	High Yield Bond	0.34	-0.75	1.30	3.21	6.13	13.93	5.81	5.64	0.00	4.74	-6.96	2.40	-1.34	24.54	9.95
144	43.2	Multisector Bond	0.41	-0.43	0.74	2.92	6.06	10.60	7.49	6.72	0.80	3.26	1.06	3.67	6.89	17.05	8.28
149	31.9	World Bond	-2.99	-1.10	-0.20	-0.28	4.56	8.20	7.71	6.37	9.62	-2.52	3.37	2.06	13.83	13.57	8.91
51	10.5	Emerg Mkts Bd	6.50	2.08	4.13	11.48	16.96	22.35	15.58	14.57	-21.03	27.82	12.06	13.06	12.75	30.79	12.49
		CSFB High Yield	—	-0.97	-0.34	0.91	2.82	6.31	15.55	8.56	7.37	0.58	3.28	-5.21	5.78	3.11	27.93	11.96
1522	499	**General Bond**	0.84	-0.71	-0.34	1.81	2.26	3.61	5.48	5.50	6.88	-0.31	9.14	7.51	7.26	4.50	3.31
80	13.0	Long-Term Bond	0.73	-1.20	-0.91	2.33	4.04	7.27	7.61	6.77	5.85	-3.38	9.48	8.42	8.57	9.89	6.44
968	372.0	Interm-Term Bond	0.74	-0.97	-0.59	1.99	2.43	4.01	5.98	5.78	7.37	-1.32	9.77	7.71	8.17	5.06	3.92
366	82.5	Short-Term Bond	0.85	-0.29	0.06	1.31	1.31	2.13	4.14	4.80	6.16	2.20	7.76	7.23	5.52	2.67	1.64
108	31.3	Ultrashort Bond	1.79	0.16	0.67	1.45	2.25	1.78	3.05	4.42	5.06	4.48	6.74	5.77	2.74	1.56	1.25
		Lehman Bros Aggregate	—	-1.03	-0.67	2.31	2.80	3.96	6.62	6.55	8.69	-0.82	11.63	8.44	10.25	4.10	4.34
616	158	**Government Bond**	0.90	-0.70	-0.49	1.82	2.35	2.37	5.15	5.23	7.43	-0.93	10.75	6.79	9.09	2.09	3.15
85	24.5	Long Govt	1.68	-1.31	-1.25	3.20	5.45	5.11	8.35	7.04	10.55	-7.75	20.29	3.54	16.42	4.25	7.24
358	106.5	Interm Govt	0.85	-0.77	-0.53	1.81	2.28	2.47	5.34	5.41	7.51	-1.39	10.99	6.93	9.40	2.14	3.37
173	27.6	Short Govt	0.63	-0.37	-0.13	1.21	1.09	1.45	4.10	4.68	6.49	1.22	8.33	7.20	6.82	1.39	1.33
		Lehman Bros Govt	—	-1.18	-0.94	2.39	2.47	2.85	6.28	6.34	9.85	-2.23	13.24	7.23	11.50	2.36	3.48
1187	221	**Municipal Bond**	1.52	-0.62	-0.17	2.31	3.10	3.20	5.24	4.99	5.41	-3.70	10.23	4.20	8.01	4.41	3.32
89	37.3	High Yield Muni	4.53	-0.65	0.57	3.77	7.60	6.10	6.31	5.36	5.36	-4.65	5.63	4.98	6.09	6.91	6.48
263	70.9	Muni National Long	1.79	-0.74	-0.21	2.55	3.56	3.49	5.52	5.17	5.30	-4.76	11.27	3.86	8.45	4.84	3.72
211	53.0	Muni National Interm	0.82	-0.56	-0.31	2.05	2.01	2.74	5.02	4.85	5.53	-2.35	9.34	4.35	8.58	4.14	2.80
249	15.8	Muni Single ST Long	1.69	-0.67	-0.20	2.35	3.38	3.36	5.44	5.11	5.35	-4.76	11.19	4.24	8.14	4.65	3.65
260	16.4	Muni Single ST Intr	0.99	-0.63	-0.34	2.05	2.27	2.83	5.07	4.92	5.46	-3.05	9.86	4.29	8.44	4.13	2.89
115	28.0	Muni Short	0.70	0.04	0.24	1.16	1.06	1.59	3.30	3.62	4.55	0.69	5.73	4.80	5.03	2.37	1.16
		Lehman Bros Muni	—	-0.67	-0.12	2.80	4.05	4.18	6.34	6.06	6.48	-2.06	11.68	5.13	9.60	5.31	4.48
16518	5143	**Total Fund Average**	1.60	0.91	4.05	6.39	13.18	14.53	2.69	6.95	10.08	18.84	2.10	-5.07	-10.37	25.00	10.39

Source: Morningstar, Inc.

EXHIBIT 3 | Long-Term Cumulative Returns for Major
Asset Categories

Investments in the U.S. Capital Markets	Year-end 2004
Year-end 1925 = $1.00	
Small company stocks	$12,968.48
Large company stocks	$2,533.20
Long-term government bonds	$65.72
Treasury bills	$17.87
Inflation	$10.62

Source of data: *Stocks, Bonds, Bills, and Inflation 2005 Yearbook* (Chicago: Ibbotson Associates, 2005), 28.

EXHIBIT 4 | Mean Returns and Standard Deviation of Returns by Major
Asset Category

Series (from 1926 to 2004)	Geometric Mean	Arithmetic Mean	Standard Deviation
Large company stocks	10.4%	12.4%	20.3%
Small company stocks	12.7	17.5	33.1
Long-term corporate bonds	5.9	6.2	8.6
Long-term government	5.4	5.8	9.3
Intermediate-term government	5.4	5.5	5.7
U.S. Treasury bills	3.7	3.8	3.1
Inflation	3.0%	3.1%	4.3%

Source of data: *Stocks, Bonds, Bills, and Inflation 2005 Yearbook* (Chicago: Ibbotson Associates, 2005), 33.

EXHIBIT 5 | Average Annual Performance of Legg Mason Equity Funds

Fund Name	Average Annual Total Returns as of September 30, 2005 (%)					
	One Year	Three Year	Five Year	Seven Year	Ten Year	Since Inception
American Leading Companies Trust	17.87	19.75	4.22	6.93	9.83	9.37
Classic Valuation Fund	18.69	18.59	3.78	—	—	5.21
Value Trust, Inc.*	**14.25**	**21.86**	**2.07**	**9.41**	**15.04**	**16.39**
Growth Trust	12.81	27.39	4.51	8.93	11.44	11.74
Special Investment Trust*	18.95	27.31	9.24	16.06	14.62	13.75
U.S. Small-Capitalization Value Trust	15.02	22.23	16.24	12.11	—	8.01
Balanced Trust	9.31	10.15	1.94	2.97	—	4.34
Financial Services Fund	12.19	17.28	10.67	—	—	8.99
Opportunity Trust*	24.36	34.02	9.31	—	—	9.81

*Managed by Bill Miller.

Source of data: Company reports.

Ben & Jerry's Homemade

JERRY: What's interesting about me and my role in the company is I'm just this guy on the street. A person who's fairly conventional, mainstream, accepting of life as it is.

BEN: Salt of the earth. A man of the people.

JERRY: But then I've got this friend, Ben, who challenges everything. It's against his nature to do anything the same way anyone's ever done it before. To which my response is always, "I don't think that'll work."

BEN: To which my response is always, "How do we know until we try?"

JERRY: So I get to go through this leading-edge, risk-taking experience with Ben—even though I'm really just like everyone else.

BEN: The perfect duo. Ice cream and chunks. Business and social change. Ben and Jerry.

—*Ben & Jerry's Double-Dip*

As Henry Morgan's plane passed over the snow-covered hills of Vermont's dairy land, through his mind passed the events of the last few months. It was late January 2000. Morgan, the retired dean of Boston University's business school, knew well the trip to Burlington. As a member of the board of directors of Ben & Jerry's Homemade for the past 13 years, Morgan had seen the company grow both in financial and social stature. The company was now not only an industry leader in the super-premium ice cream market, but also commanded an important leadership position in a variety of social causes from the dairy farms of Vermont to the rainforests of South America.

Increased competitive pressure and Ben & Jerry's declining financial performance had triggered a number of takeover offers for the resolutely independent-minded company. Today's board meeting had been convened to consider the pending offers.

This case was prepared by Professor Michael J. Schill with research assistance from Daniel Burke, Vern Hines, Sangyeon Hwang, Wonsang Kim, Vincente Ladinez, and Tyrone Taylor. It was written as a basis for class discussion rather than to illustrate effective or ineffective handling of an administrative situation. Copyright © 2001 by the University of Virginia Darden School Foundation, Charlottesville, VA. All rights reserved. *To order copies, send an e-mail to* sales@dardenbusinesspublishing.com. *No part of this publication may be reproduced, stored in a retrieval system, used in a spreadsheet, or transmitted in any form or by any means—electronic, mechanical, photocopying, recording, or otherwise—without the permission of the Darden School Foundation.* Rev. 10/03.

Morgan expected a lively debate. Cofounders Ben Cohen and Jerry Greenfield knew the company's social orientation required corporate independence. In stark contrast, chief executive Perry Odak felt that Ben and Jerry's shareholders would be best served by selling out to the highest bidder.

Ben & Jerry's Homemade

Ben & Jerry's Homemade, a leading distributor of super-premium ice creams, frozen yogurts, and sorbets, was founded in 1978 in an old gas station in Burlington, Vermont. Cohen and Greenfield recounted their company's beginnings:

> One day in 1977, we [Cohen and Greenfield] found ourselves sitting on the front steps of Jerry's parents' house in Merrick, Long Island, talking about what kind of business to go into. Since eating was our greatest passion, it seemed logical to start with a restaurant. . . . We wanted to pick a product that was becoming popular in big cities and move it to a rural college town, because we wanted to live in that kind of environment. We wanted to have a lot of interaction with our customers and enjoy ourselves. And, of course, we wanted a product that we liked to eat. . . . We found an ad for a $5 ice-cream-making correspondence course offered through Penn State. Due to our extreme poverty, we decided to split one course between us, sent in our five bucks, read the material they sent back, and passed the open-book tests with flying colors. That settled it. We were going into the ice cream business.
>
> Once we'd decided on an ice cream parlor, the next step was to decide where to put it. We knew college students eat a lot of ice cream; we knew they eat more of it in warm weather. Determined to make an informed decision (but lacking in technological and financial resources), we developed our own low-budget "manual cross-correlation analysis." Ben sat at the kitchen table, leafing through a U.S. almanac to research towns that had the highest average temperatures. Jerry sat on the floor; reading a guide to American colleges, searching for the rural towns that had the most college kids. Then we merged our lists. When we investigated the towns that came up, we discovered that apparently someone had already done this work ahead of us. All the warm towns that had a decent number of college kids already had homemade ice-cream parlors. So we threw out the temperature criterion and ended up in Burlington, Vermont. Burlington had a young population, a significant college population, and virtually no competition. Later, we realized the reason why there was no competition. It's so cold in Burlington for so much of the year, and the summer season is so short, it was obvious (to everyone except us) that there was no way an ice cream parlor could succeed there. Or so it seemed.[1]

By January 2000, Cohen and Greenfield's ice cream operation in Burlington, Ben & Jerry's Homemade, had become a major premium ice cream producer with over 170 stores (scoop shops) across the United States and overseas, and had developed an important presence on supermarket shelves. Annual sales had grown to $237 million, and the company's equity was valued at $160 million (**Exhibits 1** and **2**). The

---

[1]Ben Cohen and Jerry Greenfield, *Ben & Jerry's Double-Dip* (New York: Simon & Schuster, 1997), 15–17.

company was known for such zany ice cream flavors as Chubby Hubby, Chunky Monkey, and Bovinity Divinity. **Exhibit 3** provides a selected list of flavors from its scoop-shop menu.

Ben & Jerry's Social Consciousness

Ben & Jerry's was also known for its emphasis on socially progressive causes and its strong commitment to the community. Although unique during the company's early years, Ben & Jerry's community orientation was no longer that uncommon. Companies such as Patagonia (clothing), Odwalla (juice), The Body Shop (body-care products), and Tom's of Maine (personal-care products) shared similar visions of what they termed "caring capitalism."

Ben & Jerry's social objective permeated every aspect of the business. One dimension was its tradition of generous donations of its corporate resources. Since 1985, Ben & Jerry's donated 7.5% of its pretax earnings to various social foundations and community-action groups. The company supported causes such as Greenpeace International and the Vietnam Veterans of America Foundation by signing petitions and recruiting volunteers from its staff and the public. The company expressed customer appreciation with an annual free cone day at all of its scoop shops. During the event, customers were welcome to enjoy free cones all day.

Although the level of community giving was truly exceptional, what really made Ben & Jerry's unique was its commitment to social objectives in its marketing, operations, and finance policies. Cohen and Greenfield emphasized that their approach was fundamentally different from the self-promotion-based motivation of social causes supported by most corporations.

> At its best, cause-related marketing is helpful in that it uses marketing dollars to help fund social programs and raise awareness of social ills. At its worst, it's "greenwashing"—using philanthropy to convince customers the company is aligned with good causes, so the company will be seen as good, too, whether it is or not. . . . They understand that if they dress themselves in that clothing, slap that image on, that's going to move product. But instead of just slapping the image on, wouldn't it be better if the company actually did care about its consumers and the community?[2]

An example of Ben & Jerry's social-value-led marketing included its development of an ice cream flavor to provide demand for harvestable tropical-rainforest products. The product's sidebar described the motivation:

> This flavor combines our super creamy vanilla ice cream with chunks of Rainforest Crunch, a cashew & Brazil nut buttercrunch made for us by our friends at Community Products in Montpelier, Vermont. The cashews & Brazil nuts in this ice cream are harvested in a sustainable way from tropical rainforests and represent an economically viable long-term alternative to cutting these trees down. Enjoy!
> —*Ben & Jerry*

---

[2]Ben Cohen and Jerry Greenfield, *Ben & Jerry's Double-Dip* (New York: Simon & Schuster, 1997), 33.

Financing decisions were also subject to community focus. In May of 1984, Ben & Jerry's initiated its first public equity financing. Rather than pursue a broad traditional public offering, the company issued 75,000 shares at $10.50 a share exclusively to Vermont residents. By restricting the offering to Vermonters, Cohen hoped to offer those who had first supported the company with the opportunity to profit from its success. To provide greater liquidity and capital, a traditional broad offering was later placed and the shares were then listed and traded on the NASDAQ. Despite Ben & Jerry's becoming a public company, Cohen and Greenfield did not always follow traditional investor-relations practices. "Chico" Lager, the general manager at the time, recalled the following Ben Cohen interview transcript that he received before its publication in the *Wall Street Transcript*:

> TWST: Do you believe you can attain a 15% increase in earnings each year over the next five years?
>
> COHEN: I got no idea.
>
> TWST: Umm-hmm. What do you believe your capital spending will be each year over the next five years?
>
> COHEN: I don't have any ideas as to that either.
>
> TWST: I see. How do you react to the way the stock market has been treating you in general and vis-à-vis other companies in your line?
>
> COHEN : I think the stock market goes up and down, unrelated to how a company is doing. I never expected it to be otherwise. I anticipate that it will continue to go up and down, based solely on rumor and whatever sort of manipulation those people who like to manipulate the market can accomplish.
>
> TWST : What do you have for hobbies?
>
> COHEN : Hobbies. Let me think. Eating, mostly. Ping-Pong.
>
> TWST : Huh?
>
> COHEN : Ping-Pong.[3]

Solutions to corporate operating decisions were also dictated by Ben & Jerry's interest in community welfare. The disposal of factory wastewater provided an example.

> In 1985, when we moved into our new plant in Waterbury, we were limited in the amount of wastewater that we could discharge into the municipal treatment plant. As sales and production skyrocketed, so did our liquid waste, most of which was milky water. [We] made a deal with Earl, a local pig farmer, to feed our milky water to his pigs. (They loved every flavor except Mint with Oreo Cookies, but Cherry Garcia was their favorite.) Earl's pigs alone couldn't handle our volume, so eventually we loaned Earl $10,000 to buy 200 piglets. As far as we could tell, this was a win-win solution to a tricky environmental

---

[3]Fred "Chico" Lager, *Ben & Jerry's: The Inside Scoop* (New York: Crown Publishers, 1994), 124–125.

problem. The pigs were happy. Earl was happy. We were happy. The community was happy.[4]

Ben & Jerry's social orientation was balanced with product and economic objectives. Its mission statement included all three dimensions, and stressed seeking new and creative ways of fulfilling each without compromising the others:

Product: To make, distribute, and sell the finest quality all-natural ice cream and related products in a wide variety of innovative flavors made from Vermont dairy products.

Economic: To operate the company on a sound financial basis of profitable growth, increasing value for our shareholders, and creating career opportunities and financial rewards for our employees.

Social: To operate the company in a way that actively recognizes the central role that business plays in the structure of society by initiating innovative ways to improve the quality of life of the broad community—local, national, and international.

Management discovered early on that the company's three objectives were not always in harmony. Cohen and Greenfield told of an early example:

One day we were talking [about our inability to make a profit] to Ben's dad, who was an accountant. He said, "Since you're gonna make such a high-quality product . . . why don't you raise your prices?" At the time, we were charging fifty-two cents a cone. Coming out of the '60s, our reason for going into business was that ours was going to be "ice cream for the people." It was going to be great quality products for everybody— not some elitist treat. . . . Eventually we said, Either we're going to raise our prices or we're going to go out of business. And then where will the people's ice cream be? They'll have to get their ice cream from somebody else. So we raised the prices. And we stayed in business.[5]

At other times, management chose to sacrifice short-term profits for social gains. Greenfield tells of one incident with a supplier:

Ben went to a Social Ventures Network meeting and met Bernie Glassman, a Jewish-Buddhist former nuclear-physicist monk. Bernie had a bakery called Greyston in inner-city Yonkers, New York. It was owned by a nonprofit religious institution; its purpose was to train and employ economically disenfranchised people [and] to fund low-income housing and other community-service activities. Ben said, "We're looking for someone who can bake these thin, chewy, fudgy brownies. If you could do that, we could give you some business, and you could make us the brownies we need, and that would be great for both of us." . . . The first order we gave Greyston was for a couple of tons. For us, that was a small order. For Greyston, it was a huge order. It caused their system to break down. The brownies were coming off the line so fast that they ended up getting packed hot. Then they needed to be

---

[4]*Ben & Jerry's Double-Dip,* 154.

[5]*Ben & Jerry's Double-Dip,* 154.

frozen. Pretty soon, the bakery freezer was filled up with these steaming 50-pound boxes of hot brownies. The freezer couldn't stay very cold, so it took days to freeze the brownies. By the time they were frozen, [they] had turned into 50-pound blocks of brownie. And that's what Greyston shipped to us. So we called up Bernie and we said, "Those two tons you shipped us were all stuck together. We're shipping them back." Bernie said, "I can't afford that. I need the money to meet my payroll tomorrow. Can't you unstick them?" And we said, "Bernie, this really gums up the works over here." We kept going back and forth with Greyston, trying to get the brownies right. Eventually we created a new flavor, Chocolate Fudge Brownie, so we could use the brownie blocks.[6]

Asset Control

The pursuit of a nonprofit-oriented policy required stringent restrictions on corporate control. For Ben & Jerry's, asset control was limited through elements of the company's corporate charter, differential stock-voting rights, and a supportive Vermont legislature.

Corporate Charter Restrictions

At the 1997 annual meeting, Ben & Jerry's shareholders approved amendments to the charter that gave the board greater power to perpetuate the mission of the firm. The amendments created a staggered board of directors, whereby the board was divided into three classes with one class of directors being elected each year for a three-year term. A director could only be removed with the approval of a two-thirds vote of all shareholders. Also, any vacancy resulting from the removal of a director could be filled by two-thirds vote of the directors who were then in office. Finally, the stockholders increased the number of votes required to alter, amend, repeal, or adopt any provision inconsistent with those amendments to at least two-thirds of shareholders. See **Exhibit 4** for a summary of the current board composition.

Differential Voting Rights

Ben & Jerry's had three equity classes: class A common, class B common, and class A preferred. The holders of class A common were entitled to one vote for each share held. The holders of class B common, reserved primarily for insiders, were entitled to 10 votes for each share held. Class B common was not transferable, but could be converted into class A common stock on a share-for-share basis and was transferable thereafter. The company's principals—Ben Cohen, Jerry Greenfield, and Jeffrey Furman—effectively held 47% of the aggregate voting power, with only 17% of the aggregate common equity outstanding. Nonboard members, however, still maintained 51% of the voting power (see **Exhibit 5**). The class A preferred stock was held exclusively by the Ben & Jerry's Foundation, a community-action group. The class A preferred gave the foundation a special voting right to act with respect to certain business combinations and the authority to limit the voting rights of common stockholders in

---

[6]*Ben & Jerry's Double-Dip,* 154.

certain transactions such as mergers and tender offers, even if the common stock-holders favored such transactions.

Vermont Legislature

In April 1998, the Vermont Legislature amended a provision of the Vermont Business Corporation Act, which gave the directors of any Vermont corporation the authority to consider the interests of the corporation's employees, suppliers, creditors, and customers when determining whether an acquisition offer or other matter was in the best interest of the corporation. The board could also consider the economy of the state in which the corporation was located and whether the best interests of the company could be served by the continued independence of the corporation.

Those and other defense mechanisms strengthened Ben & Jerry's ability to remain an independent, Vermont-based company, and to focus on carrying out the threefold corporate mission, which management believed was in the best interest of the company, its stockholders, employees, suppliers, customers, and the Vermont community at large.

The Offers

Morgan reviewed the offers on the table. Discussion with potential merger partners had been ongoing since the previous summer. In August 1999, Pillsbury (maker of the premium ice cream Haagen-Dazs) and Dreyer's announced the formation of an ice cream joint venture. Under past distribution agreements, Pillsbury-Dreyer's would become the largest distributor of Ben & Jerry's products. In response, the Ben & Jerry's board had authorized Odak to pursue joint-venture and merger discussions with Unilever and Dreyer's. By December, the joint-venture arrangements had broken down, but the discussions had resulted in takeover offers for Ben & Jerry's of between $33 and $35 a share from Unilever, and an offer of $31 a share from Dreyer's. Just yesterday, Unilever had raised its offer to $36, and two private investment houses, Meadowbrook Lane Capital and Chartwell Investments, had made two separate additional offers. The offer prices represented a substantial premium over the preoffer-announcement share price of $21.[7] See **Exhibit 6** for a comparison of investor-value measures for Ben & Jerry's and the select competitors.

Dreyer's Grand Ice Cream

Dreyer's Grand Ice Cream sold premium ice cream and other frozen desserts under the Dreyer's and Edy's brands and some under nonbranded labels. The Dreyer's and

---

[7]Recent food-company acquisitions included Kraft's $270-million acquisition of Balance Bar and Kellogg's $308-million acquisition of Worthington Foods. Balance Bar and Worthington—both health-food companies—sold at takeover premia of 76% and 88%, respectively. The mean acquisition premium offered by successful bidders in a large sample of U.S. multiple-bid contests was found to be 70%. See S. Betton and B. E. Eckbo, "Toeholds, Bid Jumps, and Expected Payoffs in Takeovers," *Review of Financial Studies* 13, 4 (winter 2000): 841–882.

Edy's lines were distributed through a direct store-delivery system. Total sales were over $1 billion, and company stock traded at a total capitalization of $450 million. Dreyer's was also involved in community-service activities. In 1987, the company established the Dreyer's Foundation to provide focused community support, particularly for youth and K–12 public education.

Unilever

Unilever manufactured branded consumer goods, including foods, detergents, and other home- and personal-care products. The company's ice cream division included the Good Humor, Breyers, Klondike, Dickie Dee, and Popsicle brands, and was the largest producer of ice cream in the world. Good Humor-Breyers was headquartered in Green Bay, Wisconsin, with plants and regional sales offices located throughout the United States. Unilever had a total market capitalization of $18 billion.

Meadowbrook Lane Capital

Meadowbrook Lane Capital was a private investment fund that portrayed itself as socially responsible. The firm was located in Northampton, Massachusetts. The Meadowbrook portfolio included holdings in Hain Foods, a producer of specialty health-oriented food products. Meadowbrook proposed acquiring a majority ownership interest through a tender offer to Ben & Jerry's shareholders.

Chartwell Investments

Chartwell Investments was a New York City private-equity firm that invested in growth financings and management buyouts of middle-market companies. Chartwell proposed investing between $30 million and $50 million in Ben & Jerry's in exchange for a convertible preferred-equity position that would allow Chartwell to obtain majority representation on the board of directors.

Morgan summarized the offers as follows:

Bidder	Offering Price	Main Proposal
Dreyer's Grand	$31 (stock)	• Maintain B&J management team • Operate B&J as a quasi-autonomous business unit • Encourage some social endeavors
Unilever	$36 (cash)	• Maintain select members of B&J management team • Integrate B&J into Unilever's frozen desserts division • Restrict social commitments and interests
Meadowbrook Lane	$32 (cash)	• Install new management team • Allow B&J to operate as an independent company controlled under the Meadowbrook umbrella • Maintain select social projects and interests
Chartwell	Minority interest	• Install new management team • Allow B&J to continue as an independent company

Conclusion

Henry Morgan doubted that the social mission of the company would survive a takeover by a large traditional company. Despite his concern for Ben & Jerry's social interests, Morgan recognized that, as a member of the board, he had been elected to represent the interests of the shareholders. A financial reporter, Richard McCaffrey, expressed the opinion of many shareholders:

> Let's jump right into the fire and suggest, depending upon the would-be acquiring company's track record at creating value, that it makes sense for the company [Ben & Jerry's] to sell. Why? At $21 a share, Ben & Jerry's stock has puttered around the same level, more or less, for years despite regular sales and earnings increases. For a company with a great brand name, about a 45% share of the super-premium ice cream market, successful new-product rollouts, and decent traction in its international expansion efforts, the returns should be better. Some of the reasons for underperformance, such as the high price of cream and milk, aren't factors the company can control. That's life in the ice cream business. But Ben & Jerry's average return on shareholders' equity, a measure of how well it's employing shareholders' money, stood at 7% last year, up from 5% in 1997. That's lousy by any measure, although it's improved this year and now stands at about 9%. This isn't helped by the company's charitable donations, of course, but if you're an investor in Ben & Jerry's you knew that going in—it's an ironclad part of corporate culture, and has served the company well. Still, Ben & Jerry's has to find ways to create value.[8]

The plane banked over icy Lake Champlain and began its descent into Burlington as Morgan collected his thoughts for what would undoubtedly be an emotional and spirited afternoon meeting.

---

[8]Richard McCaffrey, "In the Hunt for Ben & Jerry's," *Fool.com* (2 December 1999).

EXHIBIT 1 | Ben & Jerry's Homemade Financial Statements and Financial Ratios (in millions, except for per-share figures)

	1999	1998	1997	1996	1995	1994
1 Net sales	$237.0	$209.2	$174.2	$167.2	$155.3	$148.8
2 Cost of sales	145.3	136.2	114.3	115.2	109.1	109.8
3 Gross profit	91.8	73.0	59.9	51.9	46.2	39.0
4 Selling, general, & administrative expenses	82.9*	63.9	53.5	45.5	36.4	36.3
5 Earnings before interest and taxes	8.9*	9.1	6.4	6.4	9.8	2.8
6 Net income	8.0*	6.2	3.9	3.9	5.9	(1.9)
7 Working capital	$ 42.8	$ 48.4	$ 51.4	$ 50.1	$ 51.0	$ 37.5
8 Total assets	150.6	149.5	146.5	$136.7	131.1	120.3
9 Long-term debt and obligations	16.7	20.5	25.7	31.1	32.0	32.4
10 Stockholders' equity	89.4	90.9	86.9	82.7	78.5	72.5
Per-share figures:						
Sales	$31.34					
Earnings	$ 1.06*					
Book equity	$11.82					
Gross margin (3/1)	38.7%	34.9%	34.4%	31.0%	29.7%	26.2%
Operating margin (5/1)	3.8%*	4.3%	3.7%	3.8%	6.3%	1.9%
Net income margin (6/1)	3.4%*	3.0%	2.2%	2.3%	3.8%	−1.3%
Asset turnover (1/9)	1.6	1.4	1.2	1.2	1.2	1.2
Working capital turnover (1/8)	5.5	4.3	3.4	3.3	3.0	4.0
ROA (5 × [1 − 40%]/9)	3.5%*	3.7%	2.6%	2.8%	4.5%	1.4%
ROE (6/11)	8.9%*	6.8%	4.5%	4.7%	7.5%	−2.6%
Yield to maturity on 30-year U.S. Treasury bonds (DataStream)	6.5%	5.1%	5.9%	6.6%	6.0%	7.9%

*Adjusted by case writer for 50% of 1999 $8.6-million special charge for asset write-off and employee severance associated with frozen novelty manufacturing facility.

Source: SEC filings.

EXHIBIT 2 | Ben & Jerry's Homemade Stock-Price Performance

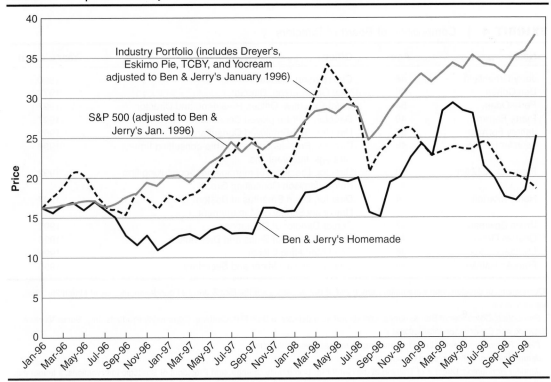

EXHIBIT 3 | Ben & Jerry's Selected List of Flavors (January 2000)

Bovinity Divinity	Milk-chocolate ice cream and white-chocolate cows swirled with white-chocolate ice cream and dark fudge cows
Cherry Garcia	Cherry ice cream with cherries and fudge flakes
Chocolate Chip Cookie Dough	Vanilla ice cream with gobs of chocolate-chip cookie dough
Chocolate Fudge Brownie	Chocolate ice cream with fudgy brownies
Chubby Hubby	Chocolate-covered, peanut-butter-filled pretzels in vanilla-malt ice cream with fudge and peanut-butter swirls
Chunky Monkey	Banana ice cream with walnuts and chocolate chunks
Coconut Almond Fudge Chip	Coconut ice cream with almonds and fudge chips
Coffee, Coffee, BuzzBuzzBuzz!	Coffee ice cream with espresso-fudge chunks
Deep Dark Chocolate	Very chocolaty ice cream
New York Super Fudge Chunk	Chocolate ice cream with white- and dark-chocolate chunks, pecans, walnuts, and chocolate-covered almonds
Peanut Butter Cup	Peanut-butter ice cream with peanut-butter cups
Phish Food	Milk-chocolate ice cream with marshmallow nougat, caramel swirls, and fudge fish
Pistachio Pistachio	Pistachio ice cream with pistachios
S'mores	Chocolate low-fat ice cream with marshmallow swirls and graham-cracker wedges
Southern Pecan Pie	Brown-sugar ice cream with roasted pecans, chunks of pecan-pie pieces, and a pecan-caramel swirl

EXHIBIT 4 | Composition of Board of Directors

Name	Age	Office	Year Elected
Jerry Greenfield	48	Chairperson, Director	1990
Ben Cohen	48	Vice Chairperson, Director	1977
Perry Odak	54	Chief Executive Officer, President, and Director	1997
Pierre Ferrari	49	Director, Self-Employed Consultant	1997
Jeffrey Furman	56	Director, Self-Employed Consultant	1982
Jennifer Henderson	46	Director, President of leadership-consulting firm– Strategic Interventions	1996
Frederick A. Miller	53	Director, President of management-consulting firm– Kaleel Jamison Consulting Group	1992
Henry Morgan	74	Director, Dean Emeritus of Boston University School of Management	1987
Bruce Bowman	47	Senior Director of Operations	1995
Charles Green	45	Senior Director of Sales and Distribution	1996
Michael Sands	35	Chief Marketing Officer	1999
Frances Rathke	39	Chief Financial Officer and Secretary	1990

*Occupations of directors who were neither employed at Ben & Jerry's nor the Ben & Jerry's Foundation, Inc., as of March 25, 1999, are as follows:

Ben Cohen: Cofounder of Ben & Jerry's, and served as a director at Blue Fish Clothing, Community Products, Inc., Social Venture Network, and Greenpeace International.

Pierre Ferrari: President of Lang International, a marketing-consulting firm.

Jeffrey Furman: Self-employed consultant.

Jennifer Henderson: Director of Training at the Center for Community Change, and President of Strategic Interventions, a leadership- and management-consulting firm.

Frederick A. Miller: President of Kaleel Jamison Consulting Group, a strategic-culture-change and management-consulting firm.

Henry Morgan: Dean Emeritus of the Boston University School of Management. Also served as a director at Cambridge Bancorporation, Southern Development Bancorporation, and Cleveland Development Bancorporation.

Source: SEC filings.

EXHIBIT 5 | Beneficial-Ownership Structure of Ben & Jerry's Homemade

	Class A Common Stock		Class B Common Stock		Preferred Stock	
	# Shares	% Outstanding Shares	# Shares	% Outstanding Shares	# Shares	% Outstanding Shares
Ben Cohen	413,173	6.1%	488,486	60.9%	—	—
Jerry Greenfield	130,000	1.9%	90,000	11.2%	—	—
Jeffrey Furman	17,000	*	30,300	3.8%	—	—
Perry Odak	368,521	5.5%	—	—	—	—
Pierre Ferrari	8,121	*	—	—	—	—
Jennifer Henderson	1,138	*	—	—	—	—
Frederick A. Miller	4,345	*	—	—	—	—
Henry Morgan	5,845	*	—	—	—	—
Bruce Bowman	46,064	*	—	—	—	—
Charles Green	17,809	*	—	—	—	—
Frances Rathke	51,459	*	—	—	—	—
Credit Suisse Asset Management	860,500	12.7%	—	—	—	—
Dimensional Fund Advisors	359,000	5.3%	—	—	—	—
All officers & directors as a group of 15 persons	1,115,554	16.5%	608,786	75.9%	—	—
Ben & Jerry's Foundation, Inc.	—	—	—	—	900	100.0%
Total shares outstanding (12/25/1999)	6,759,276		801,813		900	

*Less than 1%.

Source: SEC filings.

EXHIBIT 6 | Investor-Value Measures: Ben & Jerry's and Industry Comparables

	Price/Earnings	Price/Book
Dreyer's Grand	47.2	7.8
Eskimo Pie	30.7	1.1
TCBY Enterprises	12.5	1.2
Yocream International	9.4	1.8
Ben & Jerry's	19.8	1.8

Source: Case writer analysis.

The Battle for Value, 2004: FedEx Corp. vs. United Parcel Service, Inc.

FedEx will produce superior financial returns for shareowners by providing high value-added supply chain, transportation, business, and related information services through focused operating companies competing collectively, and managed collaboratively, under the respected FedEx brand.

FedEx Mission Statement (Excerpt)

We serve the evolving distribution, logistics, and commerce needs of our customers worldwide, offering excellence and value in all we do. We sustain a financially strong company, with broad employee ownership, that provides a long-term competitive return to our shareowners.

UPS Mission Statement (Excerpt)

On June 18, 2004, the United States and China reached a landmark air-transportation agreement that quintupled the number of commercial cargo flights between the two countries. The agreement also allowed for the establishment of air-cargo hubs in China and landing rights for commercial airlines at any available airport. The pact represented the most dramatic liberalization of air traffic in the history of the two nations, and FedEx Corporation and United Parcel Service, Inc. (UPS), the only U.S. all-cargo carriers then permitted to serve the vast Chinese market,[1] were certain to be the primary beneficiaries of this opportunity.

News of the transportation agreement did not come as a major surprise to most observers as U.S. and Chinese negotiators had been in talks since at least February. The stock prices of both companies had been rising steadily since those talks began,

---

[1] Northwest Airlines served China through both all-cargo and all-passenger services.

This case was prepared by Robert F. Bruner and Sean D. Carr as a basis for classroom discussion rather than to illustrate effective or ineffective management. The case complements "Battle for Value: Federal Express Corporation vs. United Parcel Service of America, Inc." (UVA-F-1115), prepared by Robert F. Bruner and Derick Bulkley. Copyright © 2005 by the University of Virginia Darden School Foundation, Charlottesville, VA. All rights reserved. *To order copies, send an e-mail to* sales@dardenbusinesspublishing.com. *No part of this publication may be reproduced, stored in a retrieval system, used in a spreadsheet, or transmitted in any form or by any means—electronic, mechanical, photocopying, recording, or otherwise—without the permission of the Darden School Foundation.* Rev 07/08

but FedEx's share price had rocketed at a rate nearly five times faster than UPS's.[2]
Exhibit 1 presents an illustration of recent stock-price patterns for the two firms
relative to the S&P 500 Index. FedEx had the largest foreign presence in China, with
11 weekly flights—almost twice as many as UPS. The company served 220 Chinese
cities, and flew directly to Beijing, Shenzhen, and Shanghai. FedEx's volumes in
China had grown by more than 50% between 2003 and 2004.

While UPS lagged behind FedEx in the Chinese market, it was still the world's
largest package-delivery company and the dominant parcel carrier in the United States.
UPS had been active in China since 1988 and was the first carrier in the industry to
offer nonstop service from the United States. By 2003, UPS had six weekly Boeing
747 flights to China, with direct flights to Beijing and Shanghai, serving nearly 200
cities. UPS reported a 60% growth in traffic on its principal U.S.–Shanghai route since
initiating that service in 2001, and it predicted that peak-season demand would exceed
its capacity.

As the U.S. package-delivery segment matured, the international markets—and especially China—became a battleground for the two package-delivery giants. FedEx had virtually invented customer logistical management, and was widely perceived as innovative,
entrepreneurial, and an operational leader. Historically, UPS had a reputation for being
big, bureaucratic, and an industry follower, but "Big Brown" was aggressively shedding its plodding image, as it too became an innovator and a tenacious adversary. UPS
had recently undergone a major overhaul of its image, and was repositioning itself as
a leading provider of logistics and supply-chain management services.

The 2004 air-transportation agreement between China and the United States was
a watershed moment for the international package-delivery business—more than 100
new weekly all-cargo flights were up for grabs with the United States' largest trading
partner. There was, however, no guarantee for exactly how those new cargo routes
would be allocated between UPS and FedEx, companies that had been battling each
other for dominance for more than 30 years. Moreover, the eventual assignment to
the region of other carriers would test each company's ability to fend off emerging
competitive threats.

Against this backdrop, industry observers wondered how the titanic struggle
between FedEx and UPS would develop, particularly for investors in the two firms.
Was the performance of the companies in recent years predictive of the future?
Success in China was widely seen as the litmus test for corporate survival in the new
millennium. Which company was better positioned to attract the capital necessary to
win this competitive battle?

FedEx Corporation

FedEx first took form as Fred Smith's undergraduate term paper for a Yale University
economics class. Smith's strategy dictated that FedEx would purchase the planes that
it required to transport packages, whereas all other competitors used the cargo space

---

[2]Between February 18 and June 18, 2004, FedEx's stock price rose 13.9%, whereas UPS's grew 3.1%.

available on passenger airlines. In addition to using his own planes, Smith's key innovation was a hub-and-spoke distribution pattern, which permitted cheaper and faster service to more locations than his competitors could offer. In 1971, Smith invested his $4-million inheritance, and raised $91 million in venture capital to launch the firm—the largest venture-capital start-up at the time.

In 1973, on the first night of continuous operation, 389 FedEx employees delivered 186 packages overnight to 25 U.S. cities. In those early years FedEx, then known as Federal Express Corporation, experienced severe losses, and Smith was nearly ousted from his chair position. By 1976, FedEx finally saw a modest profit of $3.6 million on an average daily volume of 19,000 packages. Through the rest of the 1970s, FedEx continued to grow by expanding services, acquiring more trucks and aircraft, and raising capital. The formula was successful. In 1981, FedEx generated more revenue than any other U.S. air-delivery company.

By 1981, competition in the industry had started to rise. Emery Air Freight began to imitate FedEx's hub system and to acquire airplanes, and UPS began to move into the overnight air market. The United States Postal Service (USPS) positioned its overnight letter at half the price of FedEx's, but quality problems and FedEx's "absolutely positively overnight" ad campaign quelled that potential threat. In 1983, FedEx reached $1 billion in revenues and seemed poised to own the market for express delivery.

During the 1990s, FedEx proved itself as an operational leader, even receiving the prestigious Malcolm Baldrige National Quality Award from the President of the United States. FedEx was the first company ever to win in the service category. Part of this success could be attributed to deregulation and to operational strategy, but credit could also be given to FedEx's philosophy of "People-Service-Profit," which reflected its emphasis on customer focus, total quality management, and employee participation. Extensive attitude surveying, a promote-from-within policy, effective grievance procedures that sometimes resulted in a chat with Fred Smith himself, and an emphasis on personal responsibility and initiative not only earned FedEx a reputation as a great place to work, but also helped to keep the firm largely free of unions.

FedEx's growth occurred within the context of fundamental change in the business environment. Deregulation of the domestic airline industry permitted larger planes to replace smaller ones, thereby permitting FedEx to purchase several Boeing 727s, which helped reduce its unit costs. Trucking industry deregulation also permitted FedEx to establish an integrated regional trucking system that lowered its unit costs on short-haul trips, enabling the company to compete more effectively with UPS. Rising inflation and global competitiveness compelled manufacturers to manage inventories more closely and to emulate the just-in-time (JIT) supply programs of the Japanese, creating a heightened demand for FedEx's rapid and carefully monitored movement of packages. And, finally, technological innovations enabled FedEx to achieve important advances in customer ordering, package tracking, and process monitoring.

By the end of 2003, FedEx had nearly $15.4 billion in assets and net income of $830 million on revenues of about $22.5 billion. **Exhibit 2** provides FedEx's financial and analytical ratios. The company had about 50,000 ground vehicles, 625 aircraft, 216,500 full- and part-time employees, and shipped more than 5.4 million packages daily.

United Parcel Service, Inc.

Founded in 1907, United Parcel Service, Inc., was the largest package-delivery company in the world. Consolidated parcel delivery, both on the ground and through the air, was the primary business of the company, although increasingly the company offered more specialized transportation and logistics services.

Known in the industry as Big Brown, UPS had its roots in Seattle, Washington, where 19-year-old Jim Casey started a bicycle-messenger service called American Messenger Company. After merging with a rival firm, Motorcycle Delivery Company, the company focused on department-store deliveries, and that remained true until the 1940s. Renamed United Parcel Service of America, UPS started an air-delivery service in 1929 by putting packages on commercial passenger planes. The company entered its strongest period of growth during the post–World War II economic boom and, by 1975, UPS had reached a milestone when it could promise package delivery to every address in the continental United States. That same year the company expanded outside the country with its first delivery to Ontario, Canada. The following year, UPS began service in West Germany with 120 of its trademark-brown delivery vans.

The key to the success of UPS, later headquartered in Atlanta, Georgia, was efficiency. According to *BusinessWeek*, "Every route is timed down to the traffic light. Each vehicle was engineered to exacting specifications. And the drivers . . . endure a daily routine calibrated down to the minute."[3] But this demand for machinelike precision met with resistance by UPS's heavily unionized labor force. Of those demands, UPS driver Mark Dray said:

> . . . drivers are expected to keep precise schedules (with hours broken down into hundredths) that do not allow for variables such as weather, traffic conditions, and package volume. If they're behind, they're reprimanded, and if they're ahead of schedule, their routes are lengthened.[4]

In its quest for efficiency, UPS experienced several major strikes resulting from changes in labor practices and driver requirements. In August 1997, the 190,000 teamsters employed at UPS went on strike for 15 days before agreeing to a new five-year contract. In addition to large wage increases, the new agreement called for the creation of 10,000 new full-time jobs and the shifting of 10,000 part-time workers into full-time positions. The strike cost UPS $700 million in lost revenue, resulting in less than 1% sales growth for the year (1996) and a decline in profits to $909 million from $1.15 billion.

---

[3]Todd Vogel and Chuck Hawkins, "Can UPS Deliver the Goods in a New World?" *BusinessWeek* (4 June 1990).

[4]Jill Hodges, "Driving Negotiations; Teamsters Survey Says UPS Drivers among Nation's Most Stressed Workers," *Star Tribune* (9 June 1993).

For most of the company's history, UPS stock was owned solely by UPS's managers, their families, former employees, or charitable foundations owned by UPS. The company acted as the market-maker in its own shares, buying or selling shares at a fair market value[5] determined by the board of directors each quarter. By the end of the millennium, however, having shrugged off the lingering effects of the strike and having emerged as a newly revitalized company with strong forward momentum, company executives determined that UPS needed the added flexibility of publicly traded stock in order to pursue a more aggressive acquisition strategy.

In November 1999, UPS initiated a two-for-one stock split, whereby the company exchanged each existing UPS share for two Class A shares. The company then sold 109.4 million newly created Class B shares on the New York Stock Exchange in an initial public offering (IPO) that raised $5.266 billion, net of issuance costs. UPS used the majority of these proceeds to repurchase 68 million shares of the Class A stock. Following a holding period after the IPO, Class A shares were convertible to Class B, and could be traded or sold accordingly. Although both shares of stock had the same economic interest in the company, Class A shares entitled holders to ten votes per share while the Class B shareowners were entitled to one vote.

Until the stock split and IPO in 1999, the financially and operationally conservative company had been perceived as slow and plodding. Although much larger than FedEx, UPS had not chosen to compete directly in the overnight delivery market until 1982, largely because of the enormous cost of building an air fleet. But after going public UPS initiated an aggressive series of acquisitions, beginning with a Miami-based freight carrier operating in Latin America and a franchise-based chain of stores providing packing, shipping, and mail services called Mail Boxes Etc. (later renamed the UPS Store) with more than 4,300 domestic and international locations.

More assertive than ever before, the UPS of the new millennium was the product of extensive reengineering efforts and a revitalized business focus. While the company had traditionally been the industry's low-cost provider, in recent years the company had been investing heavily in information technology, aircraft, and facilities to support service innovations, maintain quality, and reduce costs. In early 2003, the company revamped its logo for the first time since 1961, and emphasized its activities in the wider supply-chain industry. "The small-package market in the United States is about a $60-billion market. The worldwide supply-chain market is about a $3.2-trillion market," said Mike Eskew, UPS's chair and CEO. "It's everything from the moment something gets made until it gets delivered for final delivery, and then after market, it's parts replacement."[6]

---

[5]In setting its share price, the board considered a variety of factors, including past and current earnings, earnings estimates, the ratio of UPS's common stock to its debt, the business and outlook of UPS, and the general economic climate. The opinions of outside advisers were sometimes considered. The stock price had never decreased in value. The employee stock purchases were often financed with stock hypothecation loans from commercial banks. As the shares provided the collateral for those loans, the assessment made by the outside lenders provided some external validation for the share price.

[6]Harry R. Weber, "UPS, FedEx Rivalry: A Study in Contrasts," *Associated Press Newswires,* 21 May 2004.

By 2003, UPS offered package-delivery services throughout the United States and in more than 200 countries and territories, and moved more than 13 million packages and documents through its network every day. Domestic package operations accounted for 76% of revenues in 2002; international (15%); nonpackage (9%). In the United States, it was estimated that the company's delivery system carried goods having a value in excess of 6% of the U.S. gross domestic product.[7] The company employed 360,000 people (of whom 64% were unionized), and owned 88,000 ground vehicles and 583 aircraft.

At year-end 2003, UPS reported assets, revenues, and profits of $28.9 billion, $33.4 billion, and $2.9 billion, respectively. **Exhibit 3** provides UPS's financial and analytical ratios. The company's financial conservatism was reflected in its AAA bond rating.

Competition in the Express-Delivery Market

The $45-billion domestic U.S. package-delivery market could be segmented along at least three dimensions: weight, mode of transit, and timeliness of service. The weight categories consisted of letters (weighing 0–2.0 pounds), packages (2.0–70 pounds), and freight (over 70 pounds). The mode of transit categories were simply air and ground. Finally, time categories were overnight, deferred delivery (second-day), three-day delivery, and, lastly, regular delivery, which occurred four or more days after pickup.

The air-express segment was a $25-billion portion of the U.S. package-delivery industry, and was concentrated in letters and packages, overnight and deferred, and air or air-and-ground. While virtually all of FedEx's business activities were in the air-express segment of the package-delivery industry, only about 22% of UPS's revenues were derived from its next-day air business. FedEx and UPS's competition for dominance of the $25-billion domestic air-express delivery market foreshadowed an unusually challenging future.

Exhibit 4 provides a detailed summary of the major events marking the competitive rivalry between FedEx and UPS. Significant dimensions of this rivalry included the following:

- **Customer focus.** Both companies emphasized their focus on the customer. This meant listening carefully to the customer's needs, providing customized solutions rather than standardized products, and committing to service relationships.

- **Price competition.** UPS boldly entered the market by undercutting the price of FedEx's overnight letter by half. But by the late 1990s, both firms had settled into a predictable pattern of regular price increases. **Exhibit 5** provides a summary of recent rate increases.

- **Operational reengineering.** Given the intense price competition, the reduction of unit costs became a priority. Cost reduction was achieved through the exploitation

---

[7]"United Parcel Service, Inc.– SWOT Analysis," *Datamonitor Company Profiles* (16 July 2004).

of economies of scale, investment in technology, and business-process reengineering, which sought to squeeze unnecessary steps and costs out of the service process.

- **Information technology.** Information management became central to the operations of both UPS and FedEx. Every package handled by FedEx, for instance, was logged into COSMOS (Customer, Operations, Service, Master On-line System), which transmitted data from package movements, customer pickups, invoices, and deliveries to a central database at the Memphis, Tennessee, headquarters. UPS relied on DIADs (Delivery Information Acquisition Devices), which were handheld units that drivers used to scan package barcodes and record customer signatures.

- **Service expansion.** FedEx and UPS increasingly pecked at each other's service offerings. FedEx, armed with volume discounts and superb quality, went after the big clients that had previously used UPS without thought. UPS copied FedEx's customer interfaces by installing 11,500 drop-off boxes to compete with FedEx's 12,000 boxes, 165 drive-through stations, and 371 express-delivery stores. UPS also began Saturday pickups and deliveries to match FedEx's schedule. FedEx bought $200 million in ground vehicles to match UPS.

- **Logistics services.** The largest innovations entailed offering integrated logistics services to large corporate clients. These services were aimed at providing total inventory control to customers, including purchase orders, receipt of goods, order entry and warehousing, inventory accounting, shipping, and accounts receivable. The London design-company Laura Ashley, for instance, retained FedEx to store, track, and ship products quickly to individual stores worldwide. Similarly, Dell Computer retained UPS to manage its total inbound and outbound shipping.

The impact of the fierce one-upmanship occurring between FedEx and UPS was clearly reflected in their respective investment expenditures. Between 1992 and 2003, capital expenditures for FedEx and UPS rose at an annualized rate of 34.64% and 36.78%, respectively. During this period, the two companies matched each other's investments in capital almost exactly. (**Exhibit 6** provides a graphical representation of the firms' cumulative capital-investment expenditures.)

International Package-Delivery Market

By 2004, express cargo aircraft carried nearly 50% of all international trade, measured by value.[8] Yet throughout the 1990s, international delivery had remained only a small part of the revenues for UPS and FedEx. After making significant investments in developing European delivery capabilities, FedEx eventually relinquished its hub in Europe in 1992 by selling its Brussels, Belgium, operation to DHL. Analysts estimated that FedEx had lost $1 billion in Europe since its entry there in 1984. FedEx would continue to deliver to Europe, but relied on local partners. In 1995, FedEx expanded its routes in Latin America and the Caribbean, and later introduced FedEx AsiaOne, a

---

[8]Alexandara Harney and Dan Roberts, "Comment & Analysis," *Financial Times,* 9 August 2004.

next-business-day service between Asian countries and the United States via a hub in Subic Bay, Philippines.

UPS did not break into the European market in earnest until 1988, with the acquisition of 10 European courier services. To enhance its international delivery systems, UPS created a system that coded and tracked packages and automatically billed customers for customs' duties and taxes. UPS hoped that its international service would account for one-third of total revenue by 2000. In May 1995, it announced that it would spend more than $1 billion to expand its European operations during the next five years. **Exhibit 7** presents international and domestic (U.S.) segment data for FedEx and UPS.

According to economic and industry experts, China would become the world's second-largest economy within 11 years and the largest by 2039. It was already the world's largest market for mobile phones and a key center for the production of textiles, computer chips, and other high-tech products. According to recent economic projections, inter-Asia trade was projected to grow at a rate of 16.8% annually through 2005.[9]

The overall market for air cargo in China had been growing at 30% a year and was expected to increase at nearly that pace for the next five years.[10] FedEx and UPS focused primarily on the import/export package market and not the intra-China domestic market, using local partners to pick up and deliver parcels within the country (although, by December 2005, each company would be permitted to own completely package operations in China). One industry source believed the domestic parcel market was approximately $800 million, while China's export-import market was nearly $1 billion. "As it becomes the workshop of the world," one observer noted, "teeming factories along the Pearl and Yangtze river deltas represent both the start of the world's supply chain and the source of some of its biggest transport bottlenecks."[11]

The newly announced U.S.–China air-service agreement would allow an additional 195 weekly flights for each country—111 by all-cargo carriers and 84 by passenger airlines—resulting in a total of 249 weekly flights by the end of a six-year phase-in period. The two countries also agreed to allow their carriers to serve any city in the other country. Until that time, Chinese carriers were limited to twelve U.S. cities, and U.S. passenger carriers could fly to only five Chinese cities. The agreement also provided that when carriers established cargo hubs in the other country, they would be granted a high degree of operating flexibility. According to U.S. Transportation Secretary Norman Mineta, "This agreement represents a giant step forward in creating an international air-transportation system that meets the needs of the new global marketplace."

UPS and FedEx both welcomed the news. "This provides an extraordinary opportunity for strengthening commercial supply chains that support growing international trade between the United States and China and throughout the world," said Mike Eskew, UPS chair and CEO, who added that the hub provision in the agreement would

---

[9]UPS press release, 4 November 2004.

[10]Morgan Stanley, 6 April 2004.

[11]Alexandara Harney and Dan Roberts, "Comment & Analysis," *Financial Times,* 9 August 2004.

facilitate that process. Fred Smith, chair and CEO of FedEx, said, "We think China is a huge opportunity for the company. We have significant expansion plans in the country, reflecting its fantastic growth and unique position as one of the world's top manufacturing centers."[12]

Performance Assessment

Virtually all interested observers—customers, suppliers, investors, and employees—watched the competitive struggle between UPS and FedEx for hints about the next stage of the drama. The conventional wisdom was that if a firm were operationally excellent, strong financial performance would follow. Indeed, FedEx had set a goal of producing "superior financial returns," while UPS targeted "a long-term competitive return." Had the two firms achieved their goals? Moreover, did the trends in financial performance suggest whether strong performance could be achieved in the future? In pursuit of the answers to those questions, the following exhibits afford several possible avenues of analysis.

EPS, Market Values, and Returns

Exhibit 8 presents the share prices, earnings per share (EPS), and price-earnings ratios for the two firms. Also included is the annual total return from holding each share (percentage gain in share price plus dividend yield). Some analysts questioned the appropriateness of using UPS's fair market-value share price before the 1999 IPO, because it had been set by the board of directors rather than in an open market.

Ratio Analysis

Exhibits 2 and **3** present a variety of analytical ratios computed from the financial statements of each firm.

Economic Profit (Economic Value Added, or EVA™) Analysis

EVA reflects the value created or destroyed each year by deducting a charge for capital from the firm's net operating profit after taxes (NOPAT).

$$\text{EVA} = \text{Operating profits} - \text{Capital charge}$$
$$= \text{NOPAT} - (\text{K} \times \text{Capital})$$

The capital charge was determined by multiplying the cost of capital, K, by the capital employed in the business or operation. This computation could be done by either of two methods, both of which would yield the same answer; they are presented in the exhibits for the sake of illustration. The *operating approach* works with the asset side of the balance sheet, and computes NOPAT directly from the income statement. The *capital approach* works with the right-hand side of the balance sheet, and computes NOPAT indirectly (i.e., by adjusting net income).

---

[12]Dan Roberts, "FedEx Plans Expanded Services in China," *Financial Times,* 23 June 2004.

Estimating Capital   **Exhibits 9** and **10** calculate the actual amount of capital from both an operating and a capital approach. Included in capital are near-capital items that represent economic value employed on behalf of the firm, such as the present value of operating leases, amortized goodwill, and losses. The rationale for including losses and write-offs in continuing capital is that such losses represent unproductive assets or a failed investment. Were they excluded from the capital equation, the sum would only count successful efforts and would not accurately reflect the performance of the firm.

Estimating NOPAT   **Exhibits 9** and **10** calculate NOPAT with a similar regard for losses and write-offs. Here, the aim is to arrive at the actual cash generated by the concern. To do so, the exhibits add increases in deferred taxes back into income because it is not a cash expense, and calculate the interest expense of the leased operating assets as if they were leased capital assets.

Estimating Cost of Capital   The capital charge applied against NOPAT should be based on a blend of the costs of all the types of capital the firm employs, or the weighted-average cost of capital (WACC). The cost of debt (used for both debt and leases) is the annual rate consistent with each firm's bond rating (BBB for FedEx and AAA for UPS). The cost of equity may be estimated in a variety of ways. In the analysis here, the capital asset pricing model (CAPM)[13] was employed. FedEx's beta and cost of equity are used in estimating FedEx's cost of capital. Because UPS's beta was unobservable, the analysis that follows uses the average annual betas for UPS's publicly held peer firms: FedEx, Air Express, Airborne Freight, Roadway, Yellow Transport, and J.B. Hunt Transport.

Estimating EVA and MVA   In **Exhibits 9** and **10,** the stock of capital and the flow of cash are used to calculate the actual return and, with the introduction of the WACC, to calculate the EVA. These exhibits present the EVA calculated each year and cumulatively over time. The panel at the bottom of each exhibit estimates the market value created or destroyed (or the market value added [MVA]) over the observation period. MVA is calculated as the difference between the current market value of the company and its investment base. The market value created could be compared with cumulative EVA. In theory, the following relationships would hold:

$$\text{MVA} = \text{Present value of all future EVA}$$

$$\text{MVA} = \text{Market value of debt and equity} - \text{Capital}$$

Thus,

$$\text{Market value} = \text{Capital} + \text{Present value of all future EVA}$$

---

[13]The CAPM describes the cost of equity as the sum of the risk-free rate of return and a risk premium. The risk premium is the average risk premium for a large portfolio of stocks times the risk factor (beta) for the company. A beta equal to 1.0 suggests that the company is just as risky as the market portfolio; less than 1.0 suggests lower risk; greater than 1.0 implies greater risk.

In other words, maximizing the present value of EVA would amount to maximizing the market value of the firm.

Outlook for FedEx and UPS

About 70%[14] of FedEx's common shares were held by institutional investors that, it could be assumed, were instrumental in setting the prices for the company's shares. Typically, those investors absorbed the thinking of the several securities analysts who followed FedEx and UPS in 2004. **Exhibit 11** contains excerpts from various equity reports, which indicate the outlook held by those analysts.

Observers of the air-express package-delivery industry pondered the recent performance of the two leading firms and their prospects. What had been the impact of the intense competition between the two firms? Which firm was doing better? The companies faced a watershed moment with the dramatic liberalization of the opportunities in China. Might their past performance contain clues about the prospects for future competition?

---

[14]Officers, directors, and employees of FedEx owned 7% of the shares; the remainder, about 23%, was owned by individual investors not affiliated with the company.

EXHIBIT 1 | UPS and FedEx Price Patterns June 2003 to June 2004

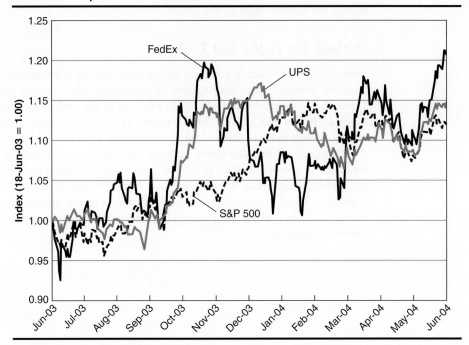

Source of data: Datastream (case writer's analysis).

EXHIBIT 2 | Financial and Analytical Ratios for FedEx

FEDEX CORP	1992	1993	1994	1995	1996	1997	1998	1999	2000	2001	2002	2003	
Activity Analysis													
Average days outstanding	44.10	42.60	41.82	41.79	42.67	44.11	39.74	44.57	46.98	46.98	44.25	41.54	365/receivables turnover
Working capital turnover	(42.21)	(817.85)	37.64	103.73	93.51	67.84	208.05	47.08	46.37	98.37	28.50	37.11	Sales/average net working capital
Fixed assets turnover	2.21	2.25	2.46	2.53	2.50	2.49	2.67	2.56	2.58	2.42	2.48	2.58	Sales/average net fixed assets
Total asset turnover	1.38	1.35	1.42	1.46	1.53	1.51	1.64	1.58	1.58	1.47	1.49	1.46	Sales/average total assets
Liquidity Analysis													
Current ratio	0.87	0.99	1.15	1.05	1.07	1.09	1.03	1.13	1.14	1.06	1.25	1.18	Current assets/current liab.
Cash ratio	0.06	0.11	0.26	0.20	0.06	0.06	0.08	0.12	0.02	0.04	0.11	0.16	(Cash + mkt. securities)/curr. liab.
Cash from operations ratio	0.38	0.50	0.50	0.58	0.58	0.51	0.61	0.64	0.56	0.63	0.76	0.56	Cash from operations/curr.liab.
Defensive interval	0.70	0.78	0.91	0.92	0.68	0.72	0.80	0.92	0.94	0.87	0.92	1.02	(Cash + AR + cash taxes)/(rents + gross CAPEX)
Long-Term Debt and Solvency Analysis													
Debt/equity ratio	1.24	1.21	0.95	0.70	0.52	0.51	0.41	0.29	0.37	0.36	0.28	0.28	Total debt/total equity
Times interest earned	1.36	1.82	2.92	3.73	4.31	5.06	6.42	7.78	7.83	6.58	6.98	10.51	EBIT/interest expense
Fixed-charge coverage ratio	0.34	0.46	0.64	0.65	0.61	0.57	0.74	0.75	0.72	0.65	0.61	0.83	EBIT/(rental exp. and int. exp.)
Capital expenditure ratio	0.15	0.21	0.22	0.28	0.23	0.22	0.29	0.27	0.23	0.25	0.27	0.22	Cash from operations/CAPEX
Cash from operations/debt ratio	0.27	0.36	0.42	0.65	0.71	0.66	1.04	1.29	0.91	0.96	1.23	0.93	Cash from operations/total debt
Profitability Analysis													
Margin before interest and tax	3.67%	4.67%	6.26%	6.29%	6.07%	5.94%	6.82%	6.93%	6.69%	6.09%	5.79%	6.54%	EBIT/sales
Net profit margin	(1.51%)	0.69%	2.41%	3.17%	3.00%	3.14%	3.17%	3.76%	3.77%	2.98%	3.45%	3.69%	Net income/sales
Return on assets	1.63%	4.38%	6.45%	7.09%	6.75%	6.51%	6.94%	7.33%	7.32%	5.74%	6.38%	6.30%	(NI + int. exp.)/avg. total assets
Return on total equity	(7.20%)	3.22%	10.62%	13.25%	11.95%	12.19%	12.70%	13.54%	14.38%	9.90%	10.85%	11.39%	Net income/average total equity
Financial leverage effect	(21.85%)	7.43%	26.64%	28.87%	32.51%	35.85%	29.48%	35.63%	42.35%	28.59%	31.87%	44.36%	Net income/operating income

Growth	'92–'93	'93–'94	'94–'95	'95–'96	'96–'97	'97–'98	'98–'99	'99–'00	'00–'01	'01–'02	'02–'03	CAGR	('92–'03)
Sales	3.42%	8.60%	10.76%	9.39%	12.13%	37.79%	5.67%	8.84%	7.52%	4.98%	9.12%	11.53%	(92–03)
Book assets	6.04%	3.44%	7.36%	4.13%	13.83%	27.02%	9.93%	8.25%	15.73%	3.54%	11.39%	9.81%	(92–03)
Net income bef unusual (gain) loss	(196.51%)	86.11%	45.61%	3.42%	17.37%	37.91%	26.73%	9.03%	(15.10%)	24.07%	14.48%	25.20%	(93–03)
Net income	(147.34%)	279.40%	45.61%	3.42%	17.37%	39.26%	25.51%	9.03%	(15.10%)	21.50%	16.90%	35.51%	(93–03)
Operating income	31.67%	45.51%	11.40%	5.53%	9.65%	58.27%	7.43%	4.99%	(2.14%)	(0.16%)	23.30%	13.64%	(92–03)

Source of data: DataStream (Thomson Financial).

EXHIBIT 3 | Financial and Analytical Ratios for UPS

UPS	1992	1993	1994	1995	1996	1997	1998	1999	2000	2001	2002	2003	
Activity Analysis													
Average days outstanding	23.13	23.11	25.66	30.50	34.81	38.57	37.68	39.67	44.79	53.16	54.92	51.60	365/receivables turnover
Working capital turnover	267.78	4,748.29	161.79	80.63	20.39	20.81	14.51	3.90	11.35	10.33	9.82	7.72	Sales/average net working capital
Fixed assets turnover	2.59	2.63	2.52	2.34	2.19	2.04	2.18	2.34	2.41	2.28	2.30	2.41	Sales/average net fixed assets
Total asset turnover	1.83	1.86	1.75	1.66	1.50	1.41	1.45	1.17	1.37	1.24	1.19	1.16	Sales/average total assets
Liquidity Analysis													
Current ratio	1.03	1.00	1.04	1.09	1.35	1.32	1.46	2.65	1.58	1.64	1.57	1.79	Current assets/current liab.
Cash ratio	0.06	0.12	0.09	0.07	0.12	0.14	0.44	1.50	0.43	0.35	0.54	0.72	(Cash + mkt. securities)/curr.liab.
Cash from operations ratio	0.69	0.74	0.56	0.66	0.60	0.73	0.77	0.53	0.61	0.84	1.01	0.84	Cash from operations/curr. liab.
Defensive interval	1.71	1.83	1.47	1.36	1.38	1.60	3.12	5.13	3.07	2.82	4.98	4.57	(Cash + AR + cash taxes)/ (rents + gross CAPEX)
Long-Term Debt and Solvency Analysis													
Debt/equity ratio	0.23	0.22	0.24	0.34	0.44	0.43	0.36	0.19	0.37	0.50	0.37	0.26	Total debt/total equity
Times interest earned	18.68	23.59	20.85	17.19	13.71	7.38	12.17	16.08	19.58	16.83	23.15	36.41	EBIT/interest expense
Fixed-charge coverage ratio	18.68	23.59	20.85	17.19	13.71	7.38	12.17	16.08	19.58	16.83	23.15	36.41	EBIT/(rental exp. and int.exp.)
Capital expenditure ratio	0.23	0.26	0.21	0.22	0.19	0.22	0.25	0.19	0.22	0.29	0.41	0.33	Cash from operations/CAPEX
Cash from operations/debt ratio	1.67	2.04	1.43	1.13	0.74	0.94	1.10	0.92	0.76	0.75	1.22	1.22	Cash from operations/total debt
Profitability Analysis													
Margin before interest and tax	7.74%	8.20%	7.95%	10.29%	9.07%	7.56%	12.47%	14.74%	15.19%	12.69%	12.81%	13.16%	EBIT/sales
Net profit margin	3.12%	4.55%	4.82%	4.96%	5.12%	4.05%	7.02%	3.26%	9.86%	7.83%	10.18%	8.65%	Net income/sales
Return on assets	6.47%	9.10%	9.10%	9.24%	8.65%	7.16%	11.69%	4.91%	14.61%	10.68%	12.73%	10.44%	(NI + int. exp.)/avg. total assets
Return on total equity	13.87%	20.53%	20.30%	20.25%	19.42%	14.93%	24.27%	7.08%	30.14%	23.41%	25.55%	19.51%	Net income/average total equity
Financial leverage effect	35.59%	46.16%	58.39%	53.41%	60.16%	36.82%	60.70%	39.72%	107.00%	61.51%	56.55%	62.38%	Net income/operating income

Growth	'92–'93	'93–'94	'94–'95	'95–'96	'96–'97	'97–'98	'98–'99	'99–'00	'00–'01	'01–'02	'02–'03	CAGR	
Sales	7.65%	10.08%	7.51%	6.29%	0.40%	10.37%	9.13%	10.05%	2.94%	2.04%	7.08%	7.32%	(92–'03)
Book assets	5.93%	16.80%	13.08%	18.26%	6.41%	7.26%	35.01%	(5.99%)	13.73%	6.99%	9.68%	8.12%	(92–'03)
Net income bef unusual (gain) loss	5.82%	16.51%	10.57%	9.88%	(20.68%)	91.53%	(49.28%)	232.28%	(17.35%)	34.19%	(10.94%)	14.25%	(92–'03)
Net income	56.86%	16.51%	10.57%	9.88%	(20.68%)	91.53%	(49.28%)	232.28%	(18.23%)	32.64%	(8.93%)	18.83%	(92–'03)
Operating income	14.08%	6.74%	39.21%	(6.33%)	(16.31%)	81.98%	29.06%	13.39%	(14.02%)	3.01%	10.01%	12.35%	(92–'03)

Source of data: DataStream (Thomson Financial).

EXHIBIT 4 | Timeline of Competitive Developments

FedEx Corp.		United Parcel Service, Inc.
• Offers 10:30 A.M. delivery	**1982**	• Establishes next-day air service
• Acquires Gelco Express and launches operations in Asia-Pacific	**1984**	
• Establishes European hub in Brussels	**1985**	• Begins intercontinental air service between United States and Europe
• Introduces handheld barcode scanner to capture detailed package information	**1986**	
• Offers warehouse services for IBM, National Semiconductor, Laura Ashley	**1987**	
	1988	• Establishes UPS's first air fleet • Offers automated customs service
• Acquires Tiger International to expand its international presence	**1989**	• Expands international air service to 180 countries
• Wins Malcolm Baldrige National Quality Award	**1990**	• Introduces 10:30 A.M. guarantee for next-day air
	1991	• Begins Saturday delivery • Offers electronic-signature tracking
• Offers two-day delivery	**1992**	• Expands delivery to over 200 countries
	1993	• Provides supply-chain solutions through UPS Logistics Group
• Launches Web site for package tracking	**1994**	• Launches Web site for package tracking
• Acquires air routes serving China • Establishes Latin American division	**1995**	• Offers guaranteed 8 A.M. overnight delivery
• Creates new hub at Roissy–Charles de Gaulle Airport in France	**1999**	• Makes UPS stock available through a public offering
• Launches business-to-consumer home-delivery service	**2000**	• Acquires all-cargo air service in Latin America
• Carries U.S. Postal Service packages • Acquires American Freightways Corp.	**2001**	• Acquires Mail Boxes Etc. retail franchise • Begins direct flights to China
• Expands home delivery to cover 100% of the U.S. population	**2002**	• Offers guaranteed next-day home delivery
• Acquires Kinko's retail franchise • Establishes Chinese headquarters	**2003**	• Contracts with Yangtze River Express for package delivery within China • Reduces domestic ground-delivery time

EXHIBIT 5 | Summary of Announced List-Rate Increases

UPS	1998	1999	2000	2001	2002	2003	2004	Average
Date implemented	2/8/02	2/9/03	2/8/04	2/6/05	1/8/06	1/7/07	1/6/08	
UPS ground	3.6%	2.5%	3.1%	3.1%	3.5%	3.9%	1.9%	3.1%
U.S. domestic air	3.3%	2.5%	3.5%	3.7%	4.0%	3.2%	2.9%	3.3%
U.S. export	0.0%	0.0%	2.9%	2.9%	3.9%	2.9%	2.9%	2.2%
Residential premium[1]	*$1.00*	*$1.00*	*$1.00*	*$1.05*	*$1.10*	*$1.15*	*$1.40*	
Commercial premium[2]	*N/A*	*N/A*	*N/A*	*N/A*	*N/A*	*N/A*	*$1.00*	
FedEx	**1998**	**1999**	**2000**	**2001**	**2002**	**2003**	**2004**	**Average**
Date implemented	2/16/02	2/9/03	2/2/04	2/2/05	1/8/06	1/7/07	1/6/08	
FedEx ground	3.6%	2.5%	3.1%	3.1%	3.5%	3.9%	1.9%	3.1%
U.S. domestic air	3.5%	2.8%	0.0%	4.9%	3.5%	3.5%	2.5%	3.0%
U.S. export	0.0%	0.0%	0.0%	2.9%	3.5%	3.5%	2.5%	1.8%
Residential premium-express[2]	*N/A*	*N/A*	*N/A*	*N/A*	*$1.35*	*$1.40*	*$1.75*	
Residential premium-ground[2]	*N/A*	*N/A*	*N/A*	*$1.30*	*$1.35*	*$1.40*	*$1.75*	
Residential premium-home delivery[2]	*N/A*	*N/A*	*N/A*	*$1.05*	*$1.10*	*$1.15*	*$1.40*	
Commercial premium-express[2]	*N/A*	*N/A*	*N/A*	*N/A*	*$1.50*	*$1.75*	*$1.00*	
Commercial premium-ground[2]	*N/A*	*N/A*	*N/A*	*N/A*	*N/A*	*N/A*	*$1.00*	

Sources of data: UPS, FedEx, and Morgan Stanley.

[1]The residential premium was an additional charge for deliveries of express letters and packages to residential addresses, a price distinction UPS had applied to residential ground deliveries for the previous 10 years to offset the higher cost of providing service to them.

[2]The commercial premium was applied to products shipped to remote locations and/or select zip codes.

EXHIBIT 6 | Cumulative Capital Expenditures for FedEx and UPS

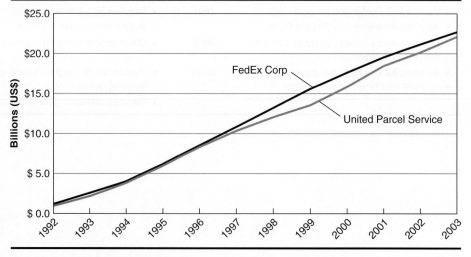

Sources of data: Company regulatory filings.

EXHIBIT 7 | Geographic Segment Information (values in millions of U.S. dollars)

FedEx Corp.	1992	1993	1994	1995	1996	1997	1998[a]	1999	2000	2001	2002	2003
U.S. domestic												
Revenue	5,195	5,668	5,195	6,839	7,466	8,322	9,665	12,910	13,805	14,858	15,968	17,277
Identifiable assets	3,941	4,433	4,884	5,322	5,449	6,123	6,873	6,506	7,224	8,637	8,627	9,908
International												
Revenue	2,355	2,140	2,280	2,553	2,807	3,198	3,589	3,863	4,452	4,771	4,639	5,210
Identifiable assets	1,522	1,360	1,109	1,112	1,250	1,503	1,503	1,001	1,018	1,254	1,520	1,536
Consolidated												
Revenue	7,550	7,808	7,474	9,392	10,274	11,520	13,255	16,773	18,257	19,629	20,607	22,487
Identifiable assets	5,463	5,793	5,992	6,433	6,699	7,625	8,376	7,507	8,242	9,891	10,147	11,444

United Parcel Service Inc.	1992	1993	1994	1995	1996	1997	1998[a]	1999	2000	2001	2002	2003
U.S. domestic												
Revenue	14,722	15,823	17,298	18,243	20,108	20,238	22,252	24,093	26,325	26,163	26,284	26,968
Identifiable assets	7,873	8,539	9,902	11,157	9,376	10,063	9,832	10,725	12,477	13,717	14,129	14,915
International												
Revenue	1,797	1,960	2,278	2,802	2,260	2,220	2,536	2,959	3,446	4,158	4,988	6,517
Identifiable assets	1,164	1,214	1,280	1,488	1,323	1,372	1,810	2,111	2,061	3,050	2,874	3,567
Consolidated												
Revenue	16,519	17,782	19,576	21,045	22,368	22,458	24,788	27,052	29,771	30,321	31,272	33,485
Identifiable assets	9,038	9,754	11,182	12,645	10,699	11,435	11,642	12,836	14,538	16,767	17,003	18,482

Sources of data: Company regulatory filings.

[a] FASB Statement No. 131 (Disclosures about Segments of an Enterprise and Related Information), established the standard to be used by enterprises to identify and report information about operating segments and for related disclosures about products and services, geographic areas, and major customers.

EXHIBIT 8 | Equity Prices and Returns for FedEx and UPS

United Parcel Service, Inc.	1992	1993	1994	1995	1996	1997	1998	1999	2000	2001	2002	2003
Stock price[1], December 31	$9.25	$10.38	$11.75	$13.13	$14.63	$15.38	$20.00	$69.00	$58.75	$54.50	$63.08	$74.55
Dividends per share[1]	$0.25	$0.25	$0.28	$0.32	$0.34	$0.35	$0.22	$0.58	$0.68	$0.76	$0.76	$0.92
EPS, basic incl. extra items[1]	$0.44	$0.70	$0.81	$0.92	$1.00	$0.82	$1.59	$0.79	$2.54	$2.13	$2.84	$2.57
P/E multiple	21.26	14.82	14.42	14.34	14.55	18.64	12.58	87.34	23.13	25.59	22.21	29.01
Capital appreciation		12.16%	13.25%	11.70%	11.43%	5.13%	30.08%	245.00%	(14.86%)	(7.23%)	15.74%	18.18%
Cumul. compound annual return[2]		12.16%	27.03%	41.89%	58.11%	66.22%	116.22%	645.95%	535.14%	489.19%	581.95%	705.95%

FedEx Corp.	1992	1993	1994	1995	1996	1997	1998	1999	2000	2001	2002	2003
Stock price, December 31	$10.19	$12.25	$19.13	$14.97	$19.16	$26.19	$32.06	$54.81	$35.50	$40.00	$53.95	$63.98
Dividends per share	$0.00	$0.00	$0.00	$0.00	$0.00	$0.00	$0.00	$0.00	$0.00	$0.00	$0.00	$0.20
EPS, basic incl. extra items	($0.53)	$0.25	$0.91	$1.32	$1.35	$1.56	$1.72	$2.13	$2.36	$2.02	$2.38	$2.79
P/E multiple	nmf	50.00	20.96	11.36	14.22	16.79	18.70	25.73	15.04	19.80	22.67	22.93
Capital appreciation		20.25%	56.12%	(21.73%)	27.97%	36.70%	22.43%	70.96%	(35.23%)	12.68%	34.88%	18.59%
Cumul. compound annual return[2]		20.25%	87.73%	46.93%	88.04%	157.06%	214.72%	438.04%	248.47%	292.64%	429.57%	528.02%

Standard & Poor's 500 Index	1992	1993	1994	1995	1996	1997	1998	1999	2000	2001	2002	2003
Index level	435.71	466.45	459.27	615.93	740.74	970.43	1,229.23	1,469.25	1,320.28	1,148.08	879.82	1,111.92
Annual return		7.06%	(1.54%)	34.11%	20.26%	31.01%	26.67%	19.53%	(10.14%)	(13.04%)	(23.37%)	26.38%
Cumul. compound annual return[2]		7.06%	5.41%	41.36%	70.01%	122.72%	182.12%	237.21%	203.02%	163.50%	101.93%	155.20%

Cumul. Market-Adjusted Returns	1993	1994	1995	1996	1997	1998	1999	2000	2001	2002	2003
UPS	5.11%	21.62%	0.53%	(11.90%)	(56.51%)	(65.90%)	408.74%	332.12%	325.69%	480.02%	550.75%
FedEx	13.19%	82.32%	5.57%	18.03%	34.33%	32.60%	200.83%	45.45%	129.14%	327.64%	372.83%

Source of data: Standard & Poor's *Research Insight*, annual reports.

[1]These data have been adjusted for the two-for-one stock split and initial public offering completed by UPS in November 1999. Prior to 1999, UPS shares were not publicly traded and the company acted as a market-maker for its own stock.

[2]Compound annual return calculation: (Current year price–Beginning year price)/Beginning year price.

EXHIBIT 9 | Economic Profit Analysis for FedEx

FedEx Corp.	1992	1993	1994	1995	1996	1997	1998	1999	2000	2001	2002	2003
Return on Net Assets (RONA)												
Net operating profit after tax ($mm)	$187	$176	$363	$405	$419	$499	$727	$726	$866	$750	$881	$1,418
Beginning capital ($mm)	$4,078	$4,344	$4,456	$4,655	$5,081	$5,663	$6,882	$7,863	$8,636	$10,090	$10,870	$12,050
RONA (NOPAT/beginning capital)	**4.59%**	**4.05%**	**8.16%**	**8.70%**	**8.25%**	**8.82%**	**10.56%**	**9.23%**	**10.03%**	**7.43%**	**8.10%**	**11.77%**
Weighted-Average Cost of Capital (WACC)												
Long-term debt ($mm)	$1,798	$1,882	$1,632	$1,325	$1,325	$1,398	$1,385	$1,360	$1,776	$1,900	$1,800	$1,709
Shares outstanding (mm)	216	219	224	225	228	230	295	298	284	297	298	299
Share price ($)	$10	$12	$19	$15	$19	$26	$32	$55	$36	$40	$54	$64
Market value of equity ($mm)	$2,205	$2,682	$4,274	$3,363	$4,359	$6,018	$9,453	$16,333	$10,098	$11,893	$16,087	$19,104
Tax rate (%)	23%	46%	46%	43%	43%	43%	45%	41%	39%	37%	38%	38%
Long-term U.S. gov't. bonds (%)	7.97%	6.80%	7.53%	7.01%	7.07%	6.89%	5.94%	5.79%	6.19%	5.65%	5.55%	4.76%
Senior Baa-rated debt (%)	9.20%	8.11%	8.71%	8.27%	8.46%	8.16%	7.33%	7.69%	8.87%	7.94%	7.96%	6.58%
Risk premium (%)	5.6%	5.6%	5.6%	5.6%	5.6%	5.6%	5.6%	5.6%	5.6%	5.6%	5.6%	5.6%
Beta	1.10	1.15	1.20	1.20	1.40	1.35	1.30	1.15	1.20	1.20	1.20	1.10
Cost of equity[1] (%)	14.13%	13.24%	14.25%	13.73%	14.91%	14.45%	13.22%	12.23%	12.91%	12.37%	12.27%	10.92%
WACC	**10.99%**	**9.72%**	**11.61%**	**11.18%**	**12.56%**	**12.61%**	**12.05%**	**11.64%**	**11.79%**	**11.35%**	**11.53%**	**10.36%**
Economic Value Added (EVA)												
RONA (NOPAT/beginning capital)	4.59%	4.05%	8.16%	8.70%	8.25%	8.82%	10.56%	9.23%	10.03%	7.43%	8.10%	11.77%
WACC	10.99%	9.72%	11.61%	11.18%	12.56%	12.61%	12.05%	11.64%	11.79%	11.35%	11.53%	10.36%
Spread	(6.39%)	(5.67%)	(3.46%)	(2.48%)	(4.30%)	(3.79%)	(1.48%)	(2.41%)	(1.75%)	(3.92%)	(3.43%)	1.41%
X beginning capital ($mm)	$4,078	$4,344	$4,456	$4,655	$5,081	$5,663	$6,882	$7,863	$8,636	$10,090	$10,870	$12,050
EVA (annual)	**($261)**	**($246)**	**($154)**	**($115)**	**($219)**	**($215)**	**($102)**	**($190)**	**($151)**	**($396)**	**($373)**	**$170**
EVA (cumulative)	**($261)**	**($507)**	**($661)**	**($777)**	**($995)**	**($1,210)**	**($1,312)**	**($1,502)**	**($1,653)**	**($2,049)**	**($2,422)**	**($2,252)**
Market Value Added (MVA)												
Market value of equity ($mm)	$2,205	$2,682	$4,274	$3,363	$4,359	$6,018	$9,453	$16,333	$10,098	$11,893	$16,087	$19,104
Long-term debt ($mm)	1,798	1,882	1,632	1,325	1,325	1,398	1,385	1,360	1,776	1,900	1,800	1,709
Capital (market value) ($mm)	4,002	4,565	5,907	4,687	5,684	7,416	10,838	17,693	11,874	13,793	17,887	20,813
Book value of equity ($mm)	1,580	1,671	1,925	2,246	2,576	2,963	3,961	4,664	4,785	5,900	6,545	7,288
Long-term debt ($mm)	1,798	1,882	1,632	1,325	1,325	1,398	1,385	1,360	1,776	1,900	1,800	1,709
Capital (book value) ($mm)	3,378	3,554	3,557	3,570	3,901	4,360	5,346	6,023	6,561	7,801	8,345	8,997
MVA (market value - book value)	**$625**	**$1,011**	**$2,350**	**$1,117**	**$1,783**	**$3,056**	**$5,492**	**$11,670**	**$5,313**	**$5,993**	**$9,542**	**$11,816**

Sources of data: *Value Line Investment Survey*, Standard & Poor's *Research Insight*, Bloomberg LP, Datastream.

[1]The cost of equity was derived using the capital asset pricing model (CAPM).

EXHIBIT 10 | Economic Profit Analysis for UPS

United Parcel Service, Inc.	1992	1993	1994	1995	1996	1997	1998	1999	2000	2001	2002	2003
Return on Net Assets (RONA)												
Net operating profit after tax ($mm)	$914	$888	$944	$1,448	$1,545	$1,379	$1,909	$3,215	$2,955	$2,846	$2,589	$3,309
Beginning capital ($mm)	$6,932	$7,195	$8,280	$9,679	$11,796	$12,514	$13,350	$18,845	$17,161	$20,007	$20,802	$23,391
RONA (NOPAT/beginning capital)	13.19%	12.34%	11.40%	14.96%	13.10%	11.02%	14.30%	17.06%	17.22%	14.23%	12.45%	14.15%
Weighted-Average Cost of Capital (WACC)												
Long-term debt ($mm)	$862	$852	$1,127	$1,729	$2,573	$2,583	$2,191	$1,912	$2,981	$4,648	$3,495	$3,149
Shares outstanding[1] (mm)	1,190	1,160	1,160	1,140	1,140	1,124	1,095	1,211	1,135	1,121	1,123	1,129
Share price[1] ($)	$9	$10	$12	$13	$15	$15	$20	$69	$59	$55	$63	$75
Market value of equity[1] ($mm)	$11,008	$12,035	$13,630	$14,963	$16,673	$17,282	$21,896	$83,538	$66,663	$61,068	$70,839	$84,167
Tax rate (%)	40%	43%	40%	39%	40%	41%	40%	58%	39%	38%	35%	34%
Long-term U.S. gov't. bonds (%)	7.97%	6.80%	7.53%	7.01%	7.07%	6.89%	5.94%	5.79%	6.19%	5.65%	5.55%	4.76%
Senior Baa-rated debt (%)	8.34%	7.36%	8.08%	7.71%	7.78%	7.53%	6.71%	6.90%	7.99%	7.16%	6.66%	5.47%
Risk premium (%)	5.6%	5.6%	5.6%	5.6%	5.6%	5.6%	5.6%	5.6%	5.6%	5.6%	5.6%	5.6%
Beta[2]	1.24	1.13	1.16	1.18	1.18	1.14	1.08	1.15	1.11	1.09	0.95	0.80
Cost of equity[3] (%)	14.92%	13.15%	14.02%	13.64%	13.68%	13.27%	11.99%	12.23%	12.41%	11.75%	10.87%	9.24%
WACC	14.20%	12.58%	13.32%	12.72%	12.47%	12.12%	11.26%	12.02%	12.09%	11.23%	10.56%	9.04%
Economic Value Added (EVA)												
RONA (NOPAT/beginning capital)	13.19%	12.34%	11.40%	14.96%	13.10%	11.02%	14.30%	17.06%	17.22%	14.23%	12.45%	14.15%
WACC	14.20%	12.58%	13.32%	12.72%	12.47%	12.12%	11.26%	12.02%	12.09%	11.23%	10.56%	9.04%
Spread	(1.01%)	(0.24%)	(1.91%)	2.24%	0.63%	(1.10%)	3.04%	5.04%	5.13%	2.99%	1.89%	5.11%
X beginning capital ($mm)	$6,932	$7,195	$8,280	$9,679	$11,796	$12,514	$13,350	$18,845	$17,161	$20,007	$20,802	$23,391
EVA (annual) ($mm)	($70)	($17)	($158)	$217	$74	($138)	$405	$949	$881	$599	$392	$1,195
EVA (cumulative) ($mm)	($70)	($87)	($246)	($28)	$45	($92)	$313	$1,262	$2,143	$2,741	$3,133	$4,328
Market Value Added (MVA)												
Market value of equity[1] ($mm)	$11,008	$12,035	$13,630	$14,963	$16,673	$17,282	$21,896	$83,538	$66,663	$61,068	$70,839	$84,167
Long-term debt ($mm)	862	852	1,127	1,729	2,573	2,583	2,191	1,912	2,981	4,648	3,495	3,149
Capital (market value) ($mm)	11,870	12,887	14,757	16,692	19,246	19,865	24,087	85,450	69,644	65,716	74,334	87,316
Book value of equity ($mm)	3,720	3,945	4,647	5,151	5,901	6,087	7,173	12,474	9,735	10,248	12,455	14,852
Long-term debt ($mm)	862	852	1,127	1,729	2,573	2,583	2,191	1,912	2,981	4,648	3,495	3,149
Capital (book value) ($mm)	4,583	4,797	5,775	6,880	8,474	8,670	9,364	14,386	12,716	14,896	15,950	18,001
MVA (market value - book value) ($mm)	$7,287	$8,090	$8,983	$9,812	$10,772	$11,195	$14,723	$71,064	$56,928	$50,820	$58,384	$69,315

Sources of data: *Value Line Investment Survey*, Standard & Poor's *Research Insight*, Bloomberg LP, DataStream.

[1]These data have been adjusted for the two-for-one stock split and initial public offering completed by UPS in November 1999. Prior to 1999, UPS shares were not publicly traded and the company acted as a market-maker for its own stock.

[2]For the period 1992–2001, this figure reflects the average betas for peer firms.

[3]The cost of equity was derived using the capital asset pricing model (CAPM).

EXHIBIT 11 | Equity Analysts' Outlook for FedEx and UPS

FedEx Corporation	
Analyst	**Comments**
Morgan Stanley's J.J. Valentine, April 6, 2004	It was refreshing to hear FedEx's management highlight some of the risks in China as we sense these issues are too often overlooked by the bulls. Some of these issues include:
	• lack of legal framework
	• different interpretations of laws by regional and local governments
	• nonperforming loans that put pressure on China's banking sector
	• liability by government for retirement program of state-owned enterprises
	• widening gap between the urban and the rural standard of living
	• government that often dictates commercial relationships
	One issue that's not as much a risk as it is a challenge is finding skilled, educated labor. This was a recurring theme that we heard during our visit to Asia, namely that China has a large unskilled workforce to produce cheap products, but it is becoming increasingly difficult to find skilled labor for the service industry, such as parcel delivery or logistics.
Value Line Investment Survey's W.R. Perkowitz Jr., Dec. 12, 2003	The international business should drive long-term growth. Unlike the domestic express business, which has reached maturity, the international market remains in the growth stage. Indeed, growth rates in this sector mirror the rate of domestic expansion in the late 1980s. Furthermore, demand for this service should rise going forward, as a greater amount of manufacturing capacity is outsourced to Asia. Finally, since a large portion of FedEx's cost structure is fixed, and it has ample capacity to serve additional business, any increases in volume should flow directly to the bottom line.
United Parcel Service Inc.	
Analyst	**Comments**
Value Line Investment Survey's D. Y. Fung, Dec. 12, 2003	United Parcel Service's third-quarter 2003 results were better than we expected. . . . This gain was driven by record-breaking results in the international and nonpackage segments. Indeed, both units experienced advances in volume and margins, which led to bottom-line increases of 171% and 61% respectively. Importantly, growth of these two businesses has resulted in greater earnings diversity at UPS. This has helped to protect investors from the cyclical downturn in the U.S. economy in the past two years. Going forward, we believe international and nonpackage will continue along their positive growth trajectory, while generating a higher portion of the company's net earnings.

Genzyme and Relational Investors: Science and Business Collide?

For Marblehead Neck, Massachusetts, it was an unusually warm morning in April 2009, so Henri Termeer decided to take a leisurely walk on the beach. Termeer had some serious issues to consider and often found that the fresh sea air and solitude did wonders for his thought process. For more than 20 years, Termeer had been the chairman and CEO of Genzyme Corporation, based in Cambridge, Massachusetts. Under his watch, Genzyme had grown from an entrepreneurial venture into one of the country's top-five biotechnology firms (**Exhibit 1** shows Genzyme's financial statements).

There were bumps along the way accompanying Termeer's achievements, and a recent event was one of them. The week before, Termeer had sat in a presentation by Ralph Whitworth, cofounder and principal of a large activist investment fund, Relational Investors (RI). Whitworth's company now had a 2.6% stake[1] in Genzyme (**Exhibit 2** shows Genzyme's top 10 shareholders). Whitworth had a history of engagements with the board of directors of numerous companies, and in several instances, the CEO had been forced to resign. In January, when RI had announced its initial 1% investment in Termeer's company, the two men had met for a meeting at the JP Morgan Healthcare Conference, and the discussion had been amicable. Whitworth and his team then traveled in April to Genzyme's headquarters and talked about Genzyme's core business, value creation, and the lack of transparency in some of the company's communications.

Termeer was proud of his company's accomplishments, shown by the number of people with rare diseases who had been successfully treated with Genzyme's products. He was also pleased with the long-term growth in the price of Genzyme's stock, which had easily outperformed the market over the last several years. In fact, the company had just

---

[1]Relational Investors Form 13F, March 31, 2009.

This case was prepared by Rick Green under the supervision of Professors Kenneth Eades and Pedro Matos. It was written as a basis for class discussion rather than to illustrate effective or ineffective handling of an administrative situation. Copyright 2011 by the University of Virginia Darden School Foundation, Charlottesville, VA. All rights reserved. *To order copies, send an e-mail to* sales@dardenbusinesspublishing.com. *No part of this publication may be reproduced, stored in a retrieval system, used in a spreadsheet, or transmitted in any form or by any means —electronic, mechanical, photocopying, recording, or otherwise— without the permission of the Darden School Foundation.*

posted record revenues of $4.6 billion for 2008. Although the 2007–08 financial crisis had affected the stock market overall, Genzyme, along with the biotechnology industry, was faring better than most (see **Exhibit 3** for charts on Genzyme's stock performance).

But a bigger blow came about a month after Termeer's first introduction to Whitworth. An operational problem surfaced in the company's plant in Allston, Massachusetts, followed by an official warning letter from the U.S. Food and Drug Administration (FDA) on February 27, 2009. The company responded to the FDA by publicly disclosing its manufacturing issues. Genzyme began conducting a quality assessment of its system, and Whitworth had expressed his confidence in the company's actions to address the issues. Recent news on the impending health care reform bill also hit companies in the health care sector hard. Genzyme's stock price, which had declined by 21% over five trading days, had yet to recover.

On top of handling Whitworth's demands, Termeer had to prepare for the shareholders' annual meeting scheduled for May 21. As Termeer mulled over the sequence of past events, the name of Whitworth's RI fund suggested to him that relationship building was its modus operandi and that perhaps Whitworth genuinely wanted to help Genzyme increase its performance. Up to this time, Termeer had not considered RI to be a threat, but if there were other corporate activists or hedge funds monitoring his company and looking to set its corporate policy, then maybe he should take note that Genzyme now had an "activist" investor. What should he do?

Biotechnology

Cheeses, beer, and wine have at least one thing in common: the application of biological science in the form of bacteria processing. The use of living organisms to stimulate chemical reactions had been taking place for thousands of years. But since the mid-20th century, when revolutionary research in genetics led to the description of the structure of DNA, molecular biology had been transformed into a thriving industry. Products among the 1,200-plus biotechnology companies in 2008 included innovations in the treatment of multiple sclerosis, rheumatoid arthritis, cancer, autoimmune disorders, and diabetes.

Biotechnology drugs were normally far more complex to produce than the chemical-based blockbuster drugs developed by Big Pharma companies. The U.S. Supreme Court recognized patent rights on genetically altered life forms in the early 1980s, and the U.S. Congress passed the Orphan Drug Act in 1983. Intended to attract investment for research and development (R&D) in the treatment of rare diseases (those affecting less than 200,000 people), the act gave companies that brought successful drugs to market a seven-year monopoly on sales.[2]

This exclusive sales incentive was not a free lunch, however; its purpose was to offset the numerous uncertainties in biotechnology development. Many of these uncertainties pertained to the U.S. drug approval process itself, one of the most rigorous in the world. In addition to the extremely high cost of R&D, a lengthy process was required to get new products to market. After a particular disease was targeted, its treatment went through a series of chemical tests to determine therapeutic effectiveness and

---

[2]Steven Silver, "Biotechnology," *Standard and Poor's Industry Surveys* (August 19, 2010): 9.

to uncover potential side effects. Preclinical studies were then done by testing animals over a period of years. Only then could the company submit an investigational new drug application to the FDA to begin clinical testing on humans.

Clinical trials on humans consisted of three phases: (1) testing the drug's safety by giving small doses to relatively healthy people; (2) administering the drug to patients suffering from the targeted disease or condition; and (3) employing random double-blind tests to eliminate bias in the process. Typically, one group of patients was given the potential drug, and the other group was given an inert substance or placebo. Due to the rigorous nature of the clinical trials, only about 5% to 10% of drugs that reached the testing stage ultimately received approval for marketing.[3] Not surprisingly, the biotechnology industry's R&D spending as a percentage of revenues was among the highest of any U.S. industry group.

The level of R&D expenditures made it crucial to get new drugs to market quickly. The FDA's Center for Drug Evaluation and Research was responsible for reviewing therapeutic biological products and chemical-based drugs. Unfortunately, inadequate funding and staffing of the FDA resulted in missed deadlines and a low level of final approvals. In 2008, the regulator approved 24 new drugs, out of which only six were biologic.[4] By 2009, it was estimated that, on average, new products took more than eight years to get through the clinical development and regulatory process.

The industry weathered the financial storms in 2007–08 relatively well, as demand for biotechnology products depended more on the population's health than the economy (see **Exhibit 4** for financial metrics for Genzyme and its major competitors). This was particularly true for large-cap companies with strong cash flows that did not need to access capital markets. Of more importance to some industry observers was that strong biotechnology companies might come under increased merger and acquisition (M&A) pressure from Big Pharma because these companies faced patent expirations on key blockbuster drugs in the coming years.[5]

Genzyme Corporation

Henry Blair, a Tufts University scientist, and Sheridan Snyder founded Genzyme in 1981 to develop products based on enzyme technologies.[6] Using venture capital funding, they purchased a small company, Whatman Biochemicals Ltd., which was absorbed into Genzyme. In 1983 (the same year that the Orphan Drug Act was passed), they recruited Henri Termeer to be president, joining the other 10 employees. Termeer had spent the previous 10 years with Baxter Travenol (later Baxter International), including several years running its German subsidiary. He left his lucrative position at Baxter to join the start-up. Shortly after Termeer became CEO, Genzyme raised $28.5 million in its 1986 IPO and began trading on the NASDAQ (ticker: GENZ).

---

[3]Silver, 6.

[4]Silver, 5.

[5]Silver, 9.

[6]An enzyme is basically one of a number of proteins produced by the body that functions as a catalyst for a biochemical process.

An accidental meeting between Termeer and a former Baxter colleague turned into a masterful acquisition for Genzyme. On a return flight from Chicago to Boston in 1989, Termeer and Robert Carpenter, chairman and CEO of Integrated Genetics (IG), based in Framingham, Massachusetts, discussed the businesses and finances of the two companies. Several months later, Genzyme purchased IG with its own stock for the equivalent of $31.5 million or less than $3 per share. Overnight Genzyme's expertise received a considerable boost in several areas of biotechnology: molecular biology, protein and nuclear acid chemistry, and enzymology.[7] Carpenter served as executive vice president of Genzyme for the next two years and was elected to the board of directors in 1994 (**Exhibit 5** lists Genzyme board members).

Avoiding the glamorous blockbuster drug industry, Termeer established Genzyme's footprint in the treatment of genetic disorders. His goal was to create targeted drugs to completely cure these diseases, despite the statistically small populations that were afflicted. In the company's formative years, Termeer focused R&D on lysosomal storage disorders (LSDs). Commonalities among LSD patients were inherited life-threatening enzyme deficiencies that allowed the buildup of harmful substances. Cures were aimed at creating the genetic material to generate the deficient enzymes naturally in these patients.

Genzyme's most rewarding product was the first effective long-term enzyme replacement therapy for patients with a confirmed diagnosis of Type I Gaucher's disease. This inherited disease was caused by deficiency of an enzyme necessary for the body to metabolize certain fatty substances. The deficiency produced several crippling conditions such as bone disease, enlarged liver or spleen, anemia, or thrombocytopenia (low blood platelet count).

Initially, the product was known as Ceredase and received a great deal of attention for its life-saving treatment. It was approved by the FDA in 1991 and protected by the Orphan Drug Act, but its success was not without controversy. The price for Ceredase was $150,000 per patient, per year, making it one of the most expensive drugs sold at the time. Genzyme argued that the price reflected the extraordinary expense of production; a year's supply for a single patient required enzyme extraction from approximately 20,000 protein-rich placentas drawn from a multitude of hospitals around the world.[8] By 1994, however, Genzyme's laboratories had developed Cerezyme, a genetically engineered replacement for Ceredase that was administered via intravenous infusion. Cerezyme was approved by the FDA in 1995 and also qualified for protection under the Orphan Drug Act.

Further successes against LSDs included Fabrazyme (to treat Fabry disease) and Myozyme (to treat Pompe disease). Fabry disease was caused by GL-3, a substance in cells lining the blood vessels of the kidney. Pompe disease shrank a patient's muscles, eventually affecting the lungs and heart. These two drugs, along with Cerezyme, formed the core business of the company and were developed and sold by its genetic disease segment (GD).

---

[7]Bruce P. Montgomery, updated by Steven Meyer and Jeffrey L. Covell, "Genzyme Corporation," *International Directory of Company Histories,* ed. Jay P. Pederson, 77 (Detroit: St. James Press), 165.

[8]Montgomery, 166.

Termeer was particularly proud of Genzyme's scientific team for developing Myozyme. Pompe disease was a debilitating illness that affected both infants and adults. The symptoms for adults included a gradual loss of muscle strength and ability to breathe. Depending on the individual, the rate of decline varied, but patients eventually needed a wheelchair and ultimately died prematurely most often because of respiratory failure. The symptoms were similar for infants, but progressed at a faster rate, so death from cardiac or respiratory failure occurred within the first year of life. The first human trials for Myozyme were conducted on a small sample of newborns and resulted in 100% of the infants surviving their first year. This success was so dramatic that the European regulators approved the drug for infants and for adults.

Concurrent with the company's focus on genetic disorders, it also invested in the development of hyaluronic acid-based drugs to reduce the formation of postoperative adhesions. Initially, it raised funds in 1989 through a secondary stock offering and an R&D limited partnership. The research the company conducted was significantly advanced by the acquisition of Biomatrix, Inc., in 2000, forming the biosurgery segment (BI).

Termeer also searched for nascent biotechnology research companies that had good products but limited capital or marketing capabilities. As a result, he created numerous alliances and joint ventures, providing funding in exchange for a share of future revenue streams. As one example, Genzyme formed a joint venture in 1997 with GelTex Pharmaceuticals, which specialized in the treatment of conditions in the gastrointestinal tract. GelTex's first drug, RenaGel, bound dietary phosphates in patients with chronic kidney dysfunction.

After 1997, Termeer completed a host of acquisitions. To some extent, the opportunity for these acquisitions resulted from the economic woes of other biotechnology firms whose clinical failures affected their funding abilities, resulting in research cuts and layoffs. Smaller start-up firms were vulnerable to economic stress if their flagship drug failed to succeed in time. These conditions suited Termeer, who had begun a broad strategy to diversify. But his strategy was not without risks because even drugs acquired in late-stage development had not yet been approved by the FDA.

Many of Genzyme's acquisitions were new drugs in various stages of development (**Exhibit 6** shows Genzyme's major acquisitions). They were generally considered to be incomplete biotechnologies that required additional research, development, and testing before reaching technological feasibility. Given the risk that eventual regulatory approval might not be obtained, the technology may not have been considered to have any alternative future use. In those cases, Genzyme calculated the fair value of the technology and expensed it on the acquisition date as in-process research and development (IPR&D).

Over time, Genzyme reorganized or added business segments based on its own R&D results and the addition of acquired firms. By December 2008, the company was organized into four major segments: GD, cardiometabolic and renal (CR), BI, and hematologic oncology (HO). (**Exhibit 7** displays segment product offerings and the fraction of 2008 revenues generated by each product).

In its presentation, RI had analyzed the performance of Genzyme's business segments using a metric called *cash flow return on investment* or CFROI. The idea was to quantify the profit generated with respect to the capital that was invested in each business line (**Exhibit 8** shows the CFROI estimates by RI for 2008). Termeer asked Genzyme's CFO to review the analysis. He believed the performance of the GD division was correct, but he was not sure about the low performance of the other segments.

The goal of Termeer's diversification strategy was to create solutions for curing more common diseases and to broaden the groups of patients who benefited.[9] Termeer was also a member of the board of directors of Project HOPE, an international non-profit health education and humanitarian assistance organization. Through a partnership with Project HOPE, Genzyme provided life-saving treatment at no cost to patients in developing countries, particularly those with inadequate health care services or medical plans.

Like most biotechnology firms, Genzyme did not pay dividends to its shareholders. As it stated, "We have never paid a cash dividend on our shares of stock. We currently intend to retain our earnings to finance future growth and do not anticipate paying any cash dividends on our stock in the foreseeable future."[10] The company had repurchased shares of its common stock amounting to $231.5 million in 2006 and $143 million in 2007, but these were offset by issuances of shares to honor option exercises. There was no open market share repurchase program.

In terms of operations, the $200 million manufacturing facility Genzyme had built in Allston produced the company's primary genetic drugs, Cerezyme, Fabrazyme, and Myozyme. A new facility was being constructed in Framingham, and major international facilities were located in England, Ireland, and Belgium. Administrative activities, sales, and marketing were all centered in Cambridge and Framingham. All was well until the first quarter of 2009, when Termeer received the FDA warning letter in February outlining deficiencies in the Allston plant. The "significant objectionable conditions" fell into four categories: maintenance of equipment, computerized systems, production controls, and failure to follow procedures regarding the prevention of microbiological contamination.[11] The problems in the Allston plant could be traced back to Termeer's decision to stretch the production capacity of the plant to meet an unanticipated demand for Myozyme. Production had increased, but the strain placed on the complex processes eventually led to the problems cited by the FDA. Anything that disrupted the production of the plant concerned Termeer because it produced Genzyme's best-selling products, and those medications were critical to the well-being of the patients who used them.

Relational Investors

If only one word were used to describe 52-year-old Ralph Whitworth, cofounder of Relational Investors, it would be "performance." While attending high school in Nevada, he raced his red 1965 Pontiac GTO against friends on the desert roads near

---

[9]Geoffrey Gagnon, "So This Is What a Biotech Tycoon Looks Like," *Boston Magazine,* June 2008.

[10]Genzyme Corporation, 10-K filing, 2009.

[11]David Armstrong, "FDA Warns Genzyme on Plant Conditions–Agency's Critique of Production Could Further Delay Biotech Company's Pompe Drug," *Wall Street Journal,* March 11, 2009.

his home town of Winnemucca, outperforming them all. After obtaining a JD from Georgetown University Law Center, Whitworth accepted a job with T. Boone Pickens, the famous "corporate raider" of the 1980s, and gained what he called "a PhD in capitalism" in the process.[12] He left Pickens in 1996 to found RI with David Batchelder whom he had met while working for Pickens. The largest initial investment was the $200 million that came from the California Public Employees' Retirement System (CalPERS). In recognition of RI's performance, CalPERS had invested a total of $1.3 billion in RI by 2008. (**Exhibit 9** illustrates RI's annual performance.)

RI was commonly classified by observers as an "activist" investment fund. The typical target firm was a company whose discounted cash flow analysis provided a higher valuation than the company's market price. Whitworth trained his executives to view the gap between a company's intrinsic value and its market price as the result of an entrenched management taking care of itself at the expense of its shareholders.[13] Specifically, Whitworth felt the value gap came primarily from two sources: (1) money not being spent efficiently enough to earn adequate returns, and/or (2) the company suffered from major corporate governance issues.[14] Common causes of underperformance were firm diversification strategies that were not providing an adequate return to shareholders, poor integration results with a merger partner or acquisition, or the misalignment of management incentives.

Once a firm was targeted, RI typically took a 1% to 10% stake in it and then engaged management with questions backed up by an RI detailed analysis. Depending upon the particular responses from executives and directors, Whitworth would follow one of several paths. For example, he might request certain changes or consider making criticisms public. Resistance might result in isolated pressure on one or more executives or board members. In other instances, Whitworth might request a seat on the board, suggest a change in executive management or board composition, or initiate a proxy fight.[15] Management and board compensation was a favorite target of RI criticism—one that was never well received by the target firm. Similar to most people's view of an athlete, Whitworth had no objections regarding high compensation for executives, so long as they performed. (**Exhibit 10** illustrates some of RI's major corporate governance engagements in the past.)

As one example, in late 2006, Whitworth and Batchelder contacted the board of Home Depot requesting changes in the company's strategy. By then, RI had purchased $1 billion of Home Depot stock. Specifically, they criticized CEO Robert Nardelli's decision to shift the company's focus to a lower-margin commercial supply business, which Nardelli considered a growth opportunity. This proved to be commercially unsuccessful. As a result, Nardelli had increased revenues, which was in keeping with his board-approved incentive contract, but earnings suffered. After the engagement of RI, Batchelder joined the board, and Nardelli was ousted.

---

[12]Francesco Guerrera and James Politi, "The Lone Ranger of Boardroom Battles," *Financial Times,* February 25, 2008.

[13]Jonathan R. Laing, "Insiders, Look Out!," *Barron's,* February 19, 2007.

[14]Aaron Bernstein and Jeffery M. Cunningham, "The Alchemist," *Directorship,* June/July 2007.

[15]Laing, "Insiders, Look Out!"

In another instance, this time with Sovereign Bancorp, corporate governance was the key issue. One director was found to have executed private transactions in branch offices. Another had an undisclosed ownership in a landscaping company that the bank hired. Instead of the more normal compensation of $80,000 paid to board members of similarly sized banks, Sovereign Bancorp's board members received $320,000 a year.[16] After uncovering these events and fighting with the board, Whitworth succeeded in being elected to it, and the CEO Jay Sidhu was ousted.

At its peak, RI's engagements comprised a total portfolio of $8.4 billion at the end of third quarter 2007. Given the drop in share prices following the financial crisis and the impact of several redemptions from investors, RI's portfolio value had been reduced to $4.3 billion by the end of March 2009. (**Exhibit 11** lists the amount of RI's engagements as of September 30 for each year since 2001 as well as the active engagements that RI had as of March 31, 2009.)

Which Path to Follow?

When Termeer finished his walk on the beach, he returned to the office, where he reviewed Whitworth's presentation slides. The main slide illustrated RI's calculation of the present value of each of Genzyme's divisions plus its R&D pipeline. The sum of these, representing RI's valuation of Genzyme, is compared to the company's current stock price (**Exhibit 12** shows RI's valuation analysis of Genzyme). It showed that Genzyme's share price was trading at $34 below its fundamental value—a significant discount. RI then offered recommendations as to how Genzyme could address this:

1. Improve capital allocation decision making to ensure that spending would be focused on the investment with the highest expected return.

2. Implement a share-buyback or dividend program.

3. Improve board composition by adding more members with financial expertise.

4. Focus executive compensation on the achievement of performance metrics.

Termeer reflected on the first two items on the RI list. During his presentation, Whitworth stated how impressed he was with Genzyme's growth and complemented Termeer on how well he had been able to create significant shareholder value. But Whitworth anticipated that the years of successful growth were about to lead to high positive cash flow for several years. (**Exhibit 13** shows how RI expected Genzyme to generate significant cash flow in the coming years.) That positive cash flow would create new challenges for Termeer. Whitworth explained that CEOs often failed to realize that value-adding investment opportunities were not available at the level of the cash flows being produced. As the CEOs continued to invest the large cash flows into lower-return investments, the market would eventually react negatively to the overinvestment problem and cause the share price to decline. Whitworth argued that

---

[16]Bernstein and Cunningham, 13.

it was better for management to distribute the newly found cash flow as part of a share repurchase program. Moreover, he thought Genzyme could leverage its share repurchases by obtaining external funding because Genzyme's balance sheet could support a significant increase in debt.

Termeer realized it would be difficult for him to change his conservative views about leverage, particularly in light of the fact that he had been so successful in building the company without relying on debt.[17] The thought of using debt to enhance a share repurchase program was doubly difficult for him to accept. But even more important was his opinion that one had to take a long-term view to succeed in biotechnology. Whitworth seemed to see investments as simply a use of cash, whereas Termeer saw investments as being critical to the business model and survival of Genzyme. In fact, the higher cash flow level would make it easier to fund the investments because it would reduce or eliminate the need to access capital markets. Termeer had always envisioned a future where diagnostics and therapeutics would be closer together, and now he recognized that this future would require Genzyme to pursue a variety of technologies on an on-going basis.

Then Termeer's eyes caught the third item on the list about adding board members with financial expertise. This brought to mind the earlier demands by another activist investor, Carl Icahn, who had purchased 1.5 million shares of Genzyme during third quarter 2007.[18] Termeer had strongly protested Icahn's involvement, and with the support of the board made a public plea to shareholders that ultimately led Icahn to sell his Genzyme shares and turn his attention to Biogen Idec, another major biotechnology company.[19]

In Termeer's mind, Icahn was more than just an activist investor. During his long career, Icahn had earned the title of "corporate raider" by taking large stakes in companies that often culminated in a takeover or, at a minimum, in a contentious proxy fight. Earlier in the year, Icahn had taken a large position in MedImmune, Inc., and helped arrange the sale of the company to AstraZeneca PLC. Were the current circumstances such that Icahn would see another opportunity to target Genzyme again? Where would Whitworth stand on this? "After all, at the end of the day, both Icahn and Whitworth are just after the cash flow," said Termeer.

Other recent events were on Termeer's mind as well. Genentech, the second-largest U.S. biotechnology firm and one of Genzyme's competitors, had just lost a bitterly contested hostile takeover from Roche Holding AG at the start of 2009. This takeover reminded Termeer of the possibility that some Big Pharma companies were looking to expand their operations into biotechnology.

As Termeer reflected on the last 26 years spent creating and building Genzyme, he realized that Whitworth's RI fund had been a shareholder for less than a year and held only 2.6% of the shares. It was no surprise these two men held such different viewpoints of what Genzyme had to offer to its owners and to society. Termeer, aware

---

[17]Geoffrey Gagnon, "So This Is What a Biotech Tycoon Looks Like."

[18]Capital IQ, "Genzyme Corporation," Public Ownership, Detailed, History—Carl Icahn LLC.

[19]Gagnon, "Biotech Tycoon."

that he needed a strategy for dealing with Whitworth, had identified three different approaches he could take:

1. Fight Whitworth as he had fought Icahn. To do this, he would need to enlist the board to join him in what would be a public relations battle for shareholder support.

2. Welcome Whitworth onto the board to reap the benefits of his experience in how to create shareholder value. In this regard, he could think of Whitworth as a free consultant.

3. Manage Whitworth by giving him some items on his list of demands but nothing that would compromise the core mission of Genzyme.

He had arranged for a phone call with Whitworth in the following week. Regardless of his approach, Termeer expected that Whitworth would probably request a hearing at the board meeting, which was scheduled two days before the annual shareholders' meeting on May 21. The prospect of such a meeting with the board only served to emphasize the importance of Termeer's having a strategy for the upcoming call with Whitworth and making decisions that would be in the best interest of his company.

EXHIBIT 1 | Income Statements

Amounts in $ thousands	2006	2007	2008
Revenue			
Net product sales	$2,887,409	$3,457,778	$4,196,907
Net service sales	282,118	326,326	366,091
Research & development revenue	17,486	29,415	42,041
Total revenues	3,187,013	3,813,519	4,605,039
Operating Costs			
Cost of products and services sold	735,671	927,330	1,148,562
Selling and administrative expenses	1,010,400	1,187,184	1,338,190
Research & development	649,951	737,685	1,308,330
Amortization of goodwill	209,355	201,105	226,442
Purchase of in-process R&D	552,900	106,350	0
Charges for impaired assets	219,245	0	2,036
Other operating expenses	3,377,522	3,159,654	4,023,560
Operating income (loss)	(190,509)	653,865	581,479
Investment income	56,001	70,196	51,260
Interest expense	(15,478)	(12,147)	(4,418)
Equity method investments	88,935	20,465	(3,139)
All other income (expense)	8,373	3,295	356
Total other income (expenses)	137,831	81,809	44,059
Income before income taxes	(52,678)	735,674	625,538
Provision for income taxes	35,881	(255,481)	(204,457)
Net income (loss)	($16,797)	$480,193	$421,081
Earnings per share			
Basic	($0.06)	$1.82	$1.57
Diluted	($0.06)	$1.74	$1.50

Data Source: Genzyme Corporation, 10-K filing, 2008.

EXHIBIT 1 | Balance Sheets (*Continued*)

Amounts in $ thousands	2006	2007	2008
Assets			
Cash and equivalents	$492,170	$867,012	$572,106
Short-term investments	119,894	80,445	57,507
Accounts receivable	746,746	904,101	1,036,940
Inventory	374,644	439,115	453,437
Other current assets	256,047	331,158	396,145
Total current assets	1,989,501	2,621,831	2,516,135
Property, plant & equipment—net	1,610,593	1,968,402	2,306,567
Investments—long term	740,103	602,118	427,403
Goodwill	1,298,781	1,403,828	1,401,074
Other intangibles	1,492,038	1,555,652	1,654,698
Other long-term assets	60,172	162,544	365,399
Total Assets	$7,191,188	$8,314,375	$8,671,276
Liabilities			
Accounts payable	$98,063	$128,380	$127,869
Accrued expenses payable	532,295	645,645	765,386
Current portion—long-term debt	6,226	696,625	7,566
Other short-term liabilities	14,855	13,277	13,462
Current Liabilities	651,439	1,483,927	914,283
Long-term debt	809,803	113,748	124,341
Other liabilities	69,235	103,763	326,659
Total Liabilities	1,530,477	1,701,438	1,365,283
Shareholders' Equity (a)			
Common stock and paid-in capital	5,108,904	5,387,814	5,783,460
Retained earnings	551,807	1,225,123	1,522,533
Total Equity	5,660,711	6,612,937	7,305,993
Total Liabilities and Shareholders' Equity	$7,191,188	$8,314,375	$8,671,276
Shares outstanding at December 31 (000)	263,026	266,008	270,704

Data Source: Genzyme Corporation, 10-K filings, 2007 and 2008.

EXHIBIT 1 | Statement of Cash Flows (*Continued*)

Amounts in $ thousands	2006	2007	2008
Cash from operations			
Net income	($16,797)	$480,193	$421,081
Depreciation & amortization	331,389	338,196	374,664
Stock-based compensation	208,614	190,070	187,596
Change in operating assets	(73,311)	(117,862)	(90,615)
Purchase of in-process R&D	552,900	106,350	0
Charge for impaired assets	219,243	0	2,036
Deferred income tax benefit	(279,795)	(106,140)	(195,200)
Other operating cash flows	(53,674)	27,865	59,613
Cash from operations	888,569	918,672	759,175
Cash from investing			
Capital expenditure	(333,675)	(412,872)	(597,562)
Acquisitions, net of acquired cash	(568,953)	(342,456)	(16,561)
Net sale (purchase) of investments	13,168	205,614	188,127
Net sale (purchase) of equity securities	132,588	(1,282)	(80,062)
Other investing activities	(79,540)	(40,060)	(75,482)
Cash from investing	(836,412)	(591,056)	(581,540)
Cash from financing			
Net long-term debt issued/repaid	(4,501)	(5,909)	(693,961)
Issuance of common stock	158,305	285,762	318,753
Repurchase of common stock	0	(231,576)	(143,012)
Other financing activities	(5,751)	(1,051)	45,679
Cash from financing	148,053	47,226	(472,541)
Net change in cash & equivalents	$200,210	$374,842	($294,906)

Data Source: Genzyme Corporation, 10-K filing, 2008.

EXHIBIT 2 | Top 10 Shareholders, March 31, 2009

	Shares Held	%
Clearbridge Advisors, LLC	15,103,597	5.7%
Barclays Global Investors, UK, Ltd.	11,974,523	4.5%
Wellington Management Co., LLP	10,790,760	4.0%
State Street Global Advisors, Inc.	9,326,639	3.5%
The Vanguard Group, Inc.	9,066,174	3.4%
Sands Capital Management, LLC	8,372,483	3.1%
UBS Global Asset Management	7,722,011	2.9%
Fidelity Investments	6,995,691	2.6%
Relational Investors LLC	6,942,506	2.6%
PRIMECAP Management Company	6,330,985	2.4%
SG Gestion	5,804,357	2.2%
Massachusetts Financial Services Company	5,522,034	2.1%
Total shares outstanding:	267,019,462	

Data Source: Forms 13F filed by investors.

EXHIBIT 3 | Genzyme (GENZ) vs. S&P 500 (S&P) and NASDAQ Biotechnology
Index (NBI), Weekly Close—Base = 1/1/20030

Data Source: Bloomberg.

EXHIBIT 4 | Biotechnology Financial Metrics as of December 2008

Amounts in $ millions	Genzyme	Amgen	Biogen Idec	Celgene	Cephalon	Genentech	Gilead Sci.
	GENZ	AMGN	BIIB	CELG	CEPH	DNA	GILD
Beta	0.70	0.65	0.75	0.80	0.70	n/a	0.65
Price as of 12/31/2008	$66.37	$57.75	$47.63	$55.28	$77.04	$82.91	$51.14
Market capitalization	$17,967	$60,464	$13,720	$25,381	$5,295	$87,304	$46,528
Revenues	$4,605	$15,003	$4,098	$2,255	$1,975	$10,531	$5,336
Return on Assets (ROA)	5.0	11.8	9.1	n/a	6.7	n/a	31.3
Return on Equity (ROE)	6.1	21.9	13.8	n/a	15.9	n/a	52.8
Net income	$421	$4,196	$783	($1,534)	$223	$3,427	$2,011
Net profit margin	9.1%	28.0%	19.1%	−68.0%	11.3%	32.5%	37.7%
EPS (weighted avg.)	$1.57	$3.92	$2.68	($3.47)	$3.28	$3.21	$2.18
P/E (trailing)	42.3	14.7	17.8	n/a	23.5	25.8	23.4
Dividends	$0	$0	$0	$0	$0	$0	$0
Share buybacks (a)	($143)	($2,268)	($739)	$0	($43)	($780)	($1,970)
Research & development	$1,308	$3,030	$1,072	$931	$362	$2,800	$722
R&D as % of revenues	28.4%	20.2%	26.2%	41.3%	18.3%	26.6%	13.5%
Cash flow—operations	$759	$5,988	$1,564	$182	($2)	$3,955	$2,204
Cash flow—investing	(582)	(3,165)	(366)	(522)	(108)	(1,667)	(178)
Cash flow—financing	(472)	(3,073)	(1,236)	214	(184)	(269)	(1,535)
Inc (Dec) in Cash Flow	($295)	($250)	($38)	($126)	($294)	$2,019	$491
Cash Flow / share	($1.10)	($0.23)	($0.13)	($0.28)	($4.32)	$1.89	$0.53
Book value	$7,306	$20,386	$5,806	$3,490	$1,503	$15,671	$4,152
Book value / share	$26.99	$19.47	$20.16	$7.60	$21.87	$14.88	$4.56
Price/book	2.5	3.0	2.4	7.3	3.5	5.6	11.2
Debt / Equity	1.8%	49.9%	19.2%	0.0%	68.8%	14.9%	31.4%
Debt / Debt & Equity	1.8%	33.3%	16.1%	0.0%	40.8%	12.9%	23.9%
Interest coverage ratio	144.1	17.6	22.7	n/a	7.3	67.2	228.8

Notes: (a) Share buybacks for Genzyme and Cephalon represent purchases to satisfy option exercises.

Data Sources: Company 10-K filings, 2008; Silver, "Biotechnology" exhibits.

EXHIBIT 5 | Board of Directors, March 31, 2009

Director	Committee	Experience
Henri A.Termeer (1983)		Chairman of Genzyme since 1988; deputy chairman of the Federal Reserve Bank of Boston; worked for Baxter laboratories for 10 years.
Charles L. Cooney (1983)	Compensation (Chairman); Corporate Governance	Distinguished professor of chemical and biochemical engineering at MIT (joined in 1970). Principal of BioInformation Associates, Inc., a consulting firm.
Douglas A. Berthiaume (1988)	Audit (Chairman); Compensation	Chairman, president, and CEO of Waters Corporation since 1994 (manufacturer of high-performance liquid chromatography instrumentation).
Robert J. Carpenter (1994)	Compensation	President of Boston Medical Investors, Inc. (invests in health care companies); chairman of Hydra Biosciences (ion-channel-based drugs); chairman of Peptimmune Inc. from 2002–07 (treatment of autoimmune diseases); cofounder of GelTex in 1991; CEO of Integrated Genetics until purchased by Genzyme in 1989.
Victor J. Dzau, MD (2000)	Corporate Governance; Compensation	Chancellor for Health Affairs and president and CEO of Duke University Health System.
Senator Connie Mack III (2001)	Corporate Governance (Chairman); Audit	Served as senior policy advisor at two law firms (King & Spalding LLP and Shaw Pittman); U.S. senator from Florida from 1989 to 2001.
Gail K. Boudreaux (2004)	Audit	EVP, United Healthcare Group (since May 2008). Former president of Blue Cross and Blue Shield of Illinois; held various positions over 20 years at Aetna Group Insurance.
Richard F. Syron (2006)	Corporate Governance; Audit	Chairman and CEO of FHLMC (Freddie Mac) from 2003 to 2008; held executive positions at Thermo Electron from 1999 to 2003 (developed technology instruments).

Note: Date in parentheses is the first year elected to the board.

Data Source: Genzyme Corporation, 14A filing, April 13, 2009.

EXHIBIT 6 | Acquisitions: 1997–2007 (in millions of dollars)

Date	Value	In-process R&D	Company Acquired	Drug or Business Acquired	Segment
1997	$112	$0	PharmaGenics, Inc.	Created Genzyme molecular oncology	HO
2000	1,284	118	GelTex	Obtained RenaGel (formerly a joint venture)	CR
2000	875	82	Biomatrix, Inc.	Became Genzyme Biosurgery division	BI
2001	17	17	Focal	Surgical biomaterials	BI
2003	596	158	SangStat Medical Corp.	Immune system treatment—Thymoglobulin	Other
2004	1,030	254	Ilex Oncology, Inc.	Cancer drugs—Campath and Clolar	HO
2005	659	12	Bone Care Int'l	Treatment of kidney disease—Hectorol	CR
2005	50	9	Verigen	Cartilage repair—MACI (launch in 2012)	BI
2005	12	7	Avigen	AV201—Parkinson's disease (launch in 2016)	GD
2006	589	553	AnorMED	Mozobil—stem cell transplant (approved 12/2008)	HO
2007	$350	$106	Bioenvision	Evoltra (launch 2010–13)	HO

Data Sources: LexisNexis, "Genzyme Corporation" Mergers and Acquisitions; Genzyme Corporation 10-K filings, 2000–07; Montgomery, 165.

EXHIBIT 7 | Main Products by Segment

Segment	Product	% of 2008 Total Revenues
Genetic Diseases (GD): The core business of the company focused on products to treat patients with genetic and other chronic debilitating diseases.	**Cerezyme:** Enzyme replacement therapy for Type 1 Gaucher's Disease; launched in 1995	29.5%
	Fabrazyme: intended to replace the missing enzyme alpha-Galactosidase in patients with the inherited Fabry disease; launched in 2001.	11.8%
	Myozyme: Lysosomal glycogen-specific enzyme for use in patients with infantile-onset of Pompe disease; launched in 2006.	7.1%
	Aldurazyme: for treatment of Mucopolysaccharidosis I (MPS I), a deficiency of a lysosomal enzyme, alpha-L-iduronidase; launched in 2003.	3.6%
	Other genetic diseases	1.1%
Cardiometabolic and Renal (CR): Treatment of renal, endocrine, and cardiovascular diseases.	**Renagel/ Renvela:** Used by patients with chronic kidney disease on dialysis for the control of serum phosphorus.	16.1%
	Hectorol: Treatment of secondary hyperparathyroidism in patients with stage 3 or 4 chronic kidney disease and on dialysis. Acquired via purchase of Bone Care in 2005.	3.1%
	Thyrogen: Treatment for thyroid cancer to allow patients to avoid traditional hypothyroidism treatment.	3.5%
	Other cardiometabolic and renal	0.0%
Biosurgery (BI): Orthopaedic products; formed via purchase of Biomatrix, Inc., in 2000.	**Synvisc:** a local therapy to reduce osteoporosis knee pain, facilitating increased mobility.	6.3%
	Sepra: a family of products used by to prevent adhesions after abdominal and pelvic open surgery, including a C-section, hysterectomy, myomectomy, colectomy, or hernia repair.	3.2%
	Other biosurgery	1.2%
Hematologic Oncology (HO): cancer treatment products		2.4%
Other product revenue (Other)		11.1%

Data Source: Genzyme Corporation, 10-K filings, 2008 and 2009.

EXHIBIT 8 | Genzyme—Estimates of CFROI by Segment (2008)

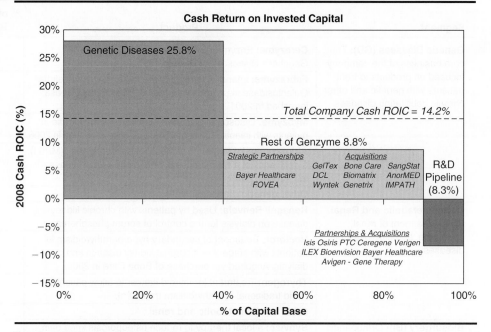

Note: Cash ROIC = Adjusted Cash Profits/Average Invested Capital.

Source: Relational Investors.

EXHIBIT 9 | Relational Investors—Calendar Year Performance (%)

	2002	2003	2004	2005	2006	2007	2008
Relational Investors	0.55%	40.77	16.49	9.89	9.29	−10.01	−40.01%
S&P	−22.12%	28.69	10.87	4.89	15.81	5.54	−37.01%
Alpha	22.67%	12.08	5.62	5.00	−6.52	−15.55	−4.00%

Note: RI was not required to disclose publicly its performance results. CalPERS disclosed its investment returns in RI's Corporate Governance Fund, and this serves as a good proxy for RI's performance.

Data Source: "Performance Analysis for the California Public Employers' Retirement System," Wilshire Consulting (Santa Monica, CA), September 30, 2010.

EXHIBIT 10 | Relational Investors—High-Profile Corporate Governance Engagements

Company	Engagement Period (a)	Max. % of company	MV (b) $ millions	Corporate Governance Issues	Actions/Results
Baxter	Q1/2004 to Q1/2009	5.1% in Q4/2007	$1,882	Ineffective board dynamics—emphasized growth at any cost. Poor capital allocation objectives.	Board hired new CEO in 2004, with 25 years experience at Abbott Labs. Revamped executive compensation
Home Depot	Q4/2006 to Q1/2009	2.2% in Q2/2008	$ 858	CEO moved from core franchise to invest in commercial building supply business. His incentive contract emphasized revenues and earnings, not returns on equity.	Batchelder placed on board in May 2007; resulted in CEO being ousted. Forced company to abandon commercial building supply business.
National Semiconductor	Q3/2001 to Q1/2009	15.3% in Q1/2008	$ 715	Analog chip maker investing in digital chips to compete with Intel—margins @ 45% compared with competitors' 60%	RI provided choice to stay with digital chips requiring 16% growth or stop spending and achieve 10.5%. Board chose the latter.
Sprint Nextel	Q1/2007 to Q4/2008	1.9% in Q4/2007	$ 697	Wanted to reverse the merger with Nextel and reduce focus on new subscribers.	Balance sheet was not stress-tested adequately, and reversal was abandoned.
Sovereign Bancorp	Q2/2004 to Q1/2009	8.9% in Q2/2008	$ 434	Related party transactions & other conflicts. Board members compensation of $320,000/year.	Whitworth joined board & ousted CEO, who sold part of bank without shareholder approval.
Waste Management	Q1/1998 to Q4/2004	1.3% in Q2/2004	$ 224	Questionable accounting practices; insider sales ahead of bad news.	Whitworth served on board from 1998 to 2004. He served as chairman from August to November 1999.

Notes: (a) Represents end-of-quarter periods until the time of the case (3/2009);

(b) Represents the MV when RI held its maximum % in the company. RI's position in $ may have been higher at another time.

Sources: Relational Investors, 13F filings to March 31, 2009.

Jonathan R. Laing, "Insider's Look Out," *Barron's*, February 19, 2007.

Aaron Bernstein and Jeffrey M. Cunningham, "Whitworth: The Alchemist in the Boardroom," *Directorship*, June/July 2007.

EXHIBIT 11 | Relational Investors—Portfolio Investments

Total market value of equity positions held by RI (as of Sept. 30 each year)	
	Total Invested ($ millions)
2001	$554
2002	$1,062
2003	$1,878
2004	$3,199
2005	$6,910
2006	$5,974
2007	$8,063
2008	$4,974
2009*	$4,282

* March 31, 2009.

Data source: Relational Investors, Form 13F.

List of RI's active engagements (as of 3/31/2009)			
Company	Value ($000) 3/31/2009	% of RI's Total	% Owned by RI
The Home Depot, Inc.	$856,826	22.1%	2.1%
Baxter International Inc.	568,012	14.6%	1.8%
Genzyme Corporation	412,315	10.6%	2.6%
Unum Group	398,879	10.3%	9.6%
Occidental Petroleum Corp.	292,752	7.5%	0.6%
Yahoo! Inc.	269,789	7.0%	1.5%
National Semiconductor Corp.	231,011	6.0%	9.8%
Burlington Northern	211,631	5.5%	1.0%
SPDR Trust Series 1	204,733	5.3%	0.3%
Freeport-McMoran	100,610	2.6%	0.6%
Others (under $100 million each)	334,000	8.6%	n/a
Total Investments	$3,880,558	100.0%	

Data Source: Relational Investors, Form 13F.

EXHIBIT 12 | Relational Investors' Fundamental Valuation of Genzyme

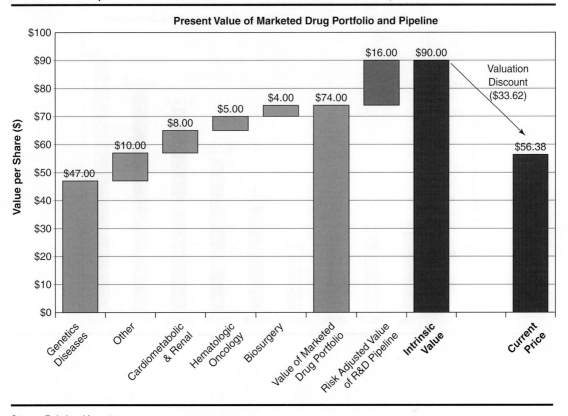

Source: Relational Investors.

EXHIBIT 13 | Relational Investors' Estimates of Genzyme's Free Cash Flow

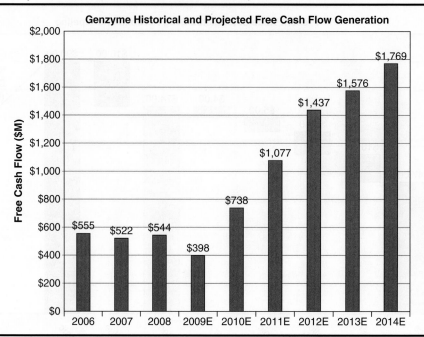

Source: Relational Investors.

## PART 2

Financial Analysis and Forecasting

The Thoughtful Forecaster

Every day, fortunes are won and lost on the backs of business-performance forecasts. Investors who successfully anticipate business development are rewarded handsomely. Investors who fail to anticipate such development pay the penalty. This note examines principles in the art and science of thoughtful financial forecasting. In particular, it reviews the importance of (1) understanding the financial relationships of a business enterprise, (2) grounding business forecasts in the reality of the industry and macroenvironment, (3) modeling a base-case forecast that incorporates the expectations for business strategy, and (4) recognizing the potential for cognitive bias in the forecasting process. Forecasting is not the same as fortune-telling; unanticipated events have a way of making certain that specific forecasts are never completely correct. This note purports, however, that thoughtful forecasts aid understanding of the key bets in any forecast and the odds associated with success. It closes with an example of financial forecasting based on the Maytag Corporation, a U.S. appliance manufacturer.

Understanding the Financial Relationships of the Business Enterprise

Financial statements provide information on the financial activities of an enterprise. Much like the performance statistics from an athletic contest, financial statements provide an array of identifying data on various historical strengths and weaknesses across a broad spectrum of business activities. The income statement, or profit-and-loss statement, measures *flows* of costs, revenue, and profits over a defined period of time. The balance sheet provides a *snapshot* of business investment and financing at a particular point in time. Both statements combine to provide a rich picture of a business's financial performance. Thorough analysis of financial statements is one important way of understanding the mechanics of the systems that make up business operations.

This technical note was prepared by Professor Michael J. Schill. Special thanks go to Vladimir Kolcin for data-collection assistance and to Lee Ann Long-Tyler and Ray Nedzel for technical assistance. Copyright © 2005 by the University of Virginia Darden School Foundation, Charlottesville, VA. All rights reserved. *To order copies, send an e-mail to* sales@dardenbusinesspublishing.com. *No part of this publication may be reproduced, stored in a retrieval system, used in a spreadsheet, or transmitted in any form or by any means— electronic, mechanical, photocopying, recording, or otherwise—without the permission of the Darden School Foundation.*

Interpreting Financial Ratios

Financial ratios provide a useful way to identify and compare relationships across financial-statement line items.[1] Trends in the relationships captured by financial ratios are particularly helpful in modeling a financial forecast. The comparison of ratios across time or with similar firms provides diagnostic tools for assessing the health of the various systems in the enterprise. We review below common financial ratios for examining business-operating performance. An understanding of the current condition of the business can be used to anticipate prospective performance.

Growth Rates   Growth rates capture the year-on-year percentage change in a particular line item. For example, if total revenue for a business increases from $1.8 million to $2.0 million, the total revenue growth for the business is said to be 11.1% [(2.0 − 1.8)/1.8]. Total revenue growth can be further decomposed into two other growth measures: unit growth (the growth in revenue due to an increase in units sold) and price growth (the growth in revenue due to an increase in the price of each unit). In the above example, if unit growth for the business is 5.0%, the remaining 6.1% of total growth can be attributed to price growth or price inflation.

Margins   Margin ratios capture the percentage of revenue accounted for by profit or, alternatively, the percentage of revenue not consumed by business costs. For example, if operating profit[2] is $0.2 million and total revenue is $2.0 million, the operating margin is 10% (0.2/2.0). Thus, for each revenue dollar, $0.90 is consumed by operating expenses and an operating profit of $0.10 is generated. The margin also measures the cost structure of the business. Common definitions of margin include the following:

$$\text{Gross margin} = \text{Gross profit/Total revenue}$$

$$\text{Operating margin} = \text{Operating profit/Total revenue}$$

$$\text{Net profit margin} = \text{Net income/Total revenue}$$

Turnover   Turnover ratios measure the productivity, or efficiency, of business assets. The turnover ratio is constructed by dividing a related measure of volume from the income statement by a measure of investment from the balance sheet. For example, if total revenue is $2.0 million and total assets are $2.5 million, the asset-turnover measure is 0.8 times (2.0/2.5). Thus, each dollar of total asset investment is producing $0.80 in revenue or, alternatively, total assets are turning over 0.8 times a year

---

[1]The analogy of athletic-performance statistics is again useful in understanding how ratios provide additional meaningful information. In measuring the effectiveness of a batter in baseball, the batting average (number of hits ÷ number of at-bats) may be more useful than simply knowing the number of hits. In measuring the success of a running back in football, the ratio of "rushing yards gained per carry" may be more useful than simply knowing the total rushing yards gained.

[2]Operating profit is also commonly referred to as earnings before interest and taxes (EBIT).

through the operations of the business. Productive or efficient assets produce high levels of asset turnover. Common measures of turnover include the following:

$$\text{Receivable turnover} = \text{Total revenue/Accounts receivable}$$

$$\text{Inventory turnover}[3] = \text{Cost of goods sold/Inventory}$$

$$\text{PPE turnover} = \text{Total revenue/Net property, plant, equipment}$$

$$\text{Asset turnover} = \text{Total revenue/Total assets}$$

$$\text{Total capital turnover} = \text{Total revenue/Total capital}$$

$$\text{Payable turnover}[3] = \text{Cost of goods sold/Accounts payable}$$

An alternative and equally informative measure of asset productivity is a "days" measure, which is computed as the investment amount divided by the volume amount multiplied by 365 days. This measure captures the average number of days in a year that an investment item is held by the business. For example, if total revenue is $2.0 million and accounts receivable is $0.22 million, the accounts-receivable days are calculated as 40.2 days (0.22/2.0 × 365). In other words, the average receivable is held by the business for 40.2 days before being collected. The lower the days measure, the more efficient is the investment item. The days measure does not actually provide any information not already contained in the respective turnover ratio, as it is simply the inverse of the turnover measure multiplied by 365 days. Common days measures include the following:

$$\text{Receivable days} = \text{Accounts receivable/Total revenue} \times 365 \text{ days}$$

$$\text{Inventory days} = \text{Inventory/Cost of goods sold} \times 365 \text{ days}$$

$$\text{Payable days} = \text{Accounts payable/Cost of goods sold} \times 365 \text{ days}$$

Return on Investment   Return on investment captures the profit generated per dollar of investment. For example, if operating profit is $0.2 million and total assets are $2.5 million, pretax return on assets is calculated as operating profit divided by total assets (0.2/2.5), or 8%. Thus, the total dollars invested in business assets are generating pretax operating-profit returns of 8%. Common measures of return on investment include the following:

$$\text{Pretax return on assets} = \text{Operating profit/Total assets}$$

$$\text{Return on capital (ROC)} = \text{Operating profit} \times (1 - \text{Tax rate})/\text{Total capital}$$

$$(\text{where Total capital} = \text{Total assets} - \text{Non-interest-bearing current liabilities})$$

$$\text{Return on equity (ROE)} = \text{Net income/Shareholders' equity}$$

It is worth observing that return on investment can be decomposed into a margin effect and a turnover effect. This relationship means that the same level of business profitability can be attained by a business with high margins and low turnover (e.g.,

---

[3]For inventory turnover and payable turnover, it is customary to use cost of sales as the volume measure because inventory and purchases are on the books at cost rather than at the expected selling price.

Nordstrom) as by a business with low margins and high turnover (e.g., Wal-Mart). This decomposition can be shown algebraically for pretax return on assets:

$$\text{Pretax ROA} = \text{Operating margin} \times \text{Asset turnover}$$

$$\frac{\text{Operating profit}}{\text{Total assets}} = \frac{\text{Operating profit}}{\text{Total revenue}} \times \frac{\text{Total revenue}}{\text{Total assets}}$$

Notice that the equality holds because the quantity for total revenue cancels out across the two right-hand ratios.

Using Financial Ratios in Financial Models

Financial ratios are particularly helpful when forecasting financial statements because financial ratios capture relationships across financial-statement line items that tend to be preserved over time. For example, rather than forecasting explicitly the gross-profit dollar amount for next year, it may be easier to forecast a revenue growth rate and a gross margin that, when applied to current-year revenue, give an implicit dollar forecast for gross profit. Thus, if we estimate revenue growth at 5% and operating margin at 24%, we can apply these ratios to last year's total revenue of $2.0 million to derive an implicit gross-profit forecast of $0.5 million [2.0 × (1 + 0.05) × 0.24]. Given some familiarity with the financial ratios of a business, the ratios are generally easier to forecast than the expected dollar values. In effect, we model the future financial statements based on assumptions about future financial ratios.

Financial models can be helpful in identifying the impact of particular assumptions on the forecast. For example, models easily allow us to see the financial impact on dollar profits of a difference of one percentage point in operating margin. To facilitate such a scenario analysis, financial models are commonly built in electronic-spreadsheet packages such as Excel. Good financial-forecast models make the forecast assumptions highly transparent. To achieve transparency, assumption cells for the forecast should be prominently displayed in the spreadsheet (e.g., total-revenue-growth-rate assumption cell, operating-margin assumption cell), and then those cells should be referenced in the generation of the forecast. In this way, it becomes easy not only to vary the assumptions for different forecast scenarios, but also to scrutinize the forecast assumptions.

Grounding Business Forecasts in the Reality of the Industry and Macroenvironment

Good financial forecasts recognize the impact of the business environment on the performance of the business. Financial forecasting should be grounded in an appreciation for industry- and economy-wide pressures. Because business performance tends to be correlated across the economy, information regarding macroeconomic business trends should be incorporated into a business's financial forecast. If, for example, price increases for a business are highly correlated with economy-wide inflation trends, the financial forecast should incorporate price-growth assumptions that capture the available information on expected inflation. If the economy is in recession, the forecast should be consistent with that economic reality.

Thoughtful forecasts should also recognize "industry reality." Business prospects are dependent on the structure of the industry in which the business operates. Some industries tend to be more profitable than others. Microeconomic theory provides some explanations for the variation in industry profitability. Profitability within an industry is likely to be greater if (1) barriers to entry discourage industry entrants, (2) ease of industry exit facilitates redeployment of assets for unprofitable players, (3) industry participants exert bargaining power over buyers and suppliers, or (4) industry consolidation reduces price competition.[4] **Table 1** shows the five most profitable industries and the five least profitable industries in the United States based on median pretax ROAs for all public firms from 1994 to 2004. Based on the evidence, firms operating in the apparel and accessory retail industry should have systematically generated more profitable financial forecasts over that period than did firms in the metal-mining industry. One explanation for the differences in industry profitability is the ease of industry exit. In the retail industry, unprofitable businesses are able to sell their assets easily for redeployment elsewhere. In the metal-mining industry, where asset redeployment is much more costly, industry capacity may have dragged down industry profitability.

Being within a profitable industry, however, does not ensure superior business performance. Business performance also depends on the competitive position of the firm within the industry. **Table 2** shows the variation of profitability for firms within the U.S. apparel and accessory industry from 1994 to 2004. Despite being the most profitable industry in **Table 1,** there is large variation in profitability within the industry; in fact, three firms generated median ROAs that were actually negative (Harold's, Syms, and Stage Stores). Good forecasting considers the ability of a business to sustain performance given the structure of its industry and its competitive position within that industry.

TABLE 1 | Most profitable and least profitable U.S. industries, 1994–2004. Ranking of two-digit SIC code industries based on median pretax ROAs for all public firms followed by Compustat from 1994 to 2004.

Most Profitable Industries	Median Firm ROA	Least Profitable Industries	Median Firm ROA
Apparel and accessory stores	12.1%	Metal mining	−1.4%
Building-construction contractors	11.0%	Chemicals and allied products	0.0%
Furniture and fixture manufacturers	10.7%	Business services	0.3%
Leather/leather-products manufacturers	10.5%	Banking	2.1%
Petroleum refining	10.0%	Insurance carriers	2.5%

[4]Michael E. Porter, "How Competitive Forces Shape Strategy," *Harvard Business Review* 57, no. 2 (March–April 1979): 137–45.

TABLE 2 | Most and least profitable firms within the apparel and accessory retail industry, 1994–2004. Ranking of firms based on median pretax ROAs for all public firms in the apparel and accessory retail industry followed by Compustat from 1994 to 2004.

Most Profitable Firms	Median Firm ROA	Least Profitable Firms	Median Firm ROA
Chico's	35.3%	Harold's	−9.7%
Abercrombie & Fitch	35.2%	Syms	−2.1%
Christopher & Banks	32.1%	Stage Stores	−1.2%
American Eagle Outfitters	28.0%	Guess	1.9%
Hot Topic	26.9%	United Retail	2.7%

Abnormal profitability is difficult to sustain over time. Competitive pressure tends to bring abnormal performance toward the mean. To show this effect, we sort all U.S. public companies for each year from 1994 to 2004 into five groups (Group 1 [low profits] through Group 5 [high profits]) based on their annual ROAs and sales growth. We then follow what happens to the composition of these groups over the next three years. The results of this exercise are captured in **Figure 1.** The ROA graph shows the mean group rankings for firms in subsequent years. For example, firms that rank in Group 5 (top ROA) at Year 0 tend to have a mean group ranking of 4.5 in Year 1,

FIGURE 1 | Firm-ranking transition matrix by profitability and sales growth. Firms are sorted for each year into five groups by either annual pretax ROA or sales growth. For example, in the ROA panel, Group 1 comprises the firms with the lowest 20% of ROA for the year; Group 5 comprises the firms with the highest 20% of ROA for the year. The figure plots the mean ranking number for all U.S. public firms followed by Compustat from 1994 to 2004.

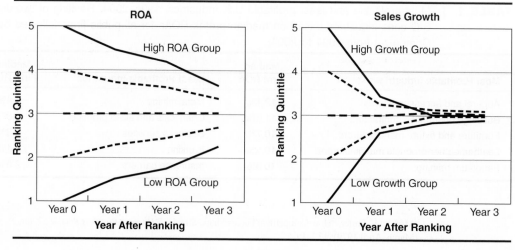

4.2 in Year 2, and 3.7 in Year 3. Firms that rank in Group 1 (bottom ROA) at Year 0 tend to have a mean group ranking of 1.5 in Year 1, 1.8 in Year 2, and 2.3 in Year 3. There is a systematic drift toward average performance (3.0) over time. The effect is even stronger vis-à-vis sales growth. **Figure 1** provides the transition matrix for average groups sorted by sales growth. Here we see that, by Year 2, the average sales-growth ranking for the high-growth group is virtually indistinguishable from that of the low-growth group.

Figure 1 illustrates that business is fiercely competitive. It is naïve to assume that superior business profitability or growth can continue unabated for an extended period of time. Abnormally high profits attract competitive responses that eventually return profits to normal levels.

Modeling a Base-Case Forecast That Incorporates Expectations for Business Strategy

With a solid understanding of the business's historical financial mechanics and of the environment in which the business operates, the forecaster can incorporate the firm's operating strategy into the forecast in a meaningful way. All initiatives to improve revenue growth, profit margin, and asset efficiency should be explicitly reflected in the financial forecast. The forecast should recognize, however, that business strategy does not play out in isolation. Competitors do not stand still. A good forecast recognizes that business strategy also begets competitive response. All modeling of the effects of business strategy should be tempered with an appreciation for the effects of aggressive competition.

One helpful way to temper the modeling of the effects of business strategy is to complement the traditional "bottom-up" approach to financial forecasting with a "top-down" approach. The top-down approach starts with a forecast of industry sales and then works back to the particular business of interest. The forecaster models firm sales by modeling market share within the industry. Such a forecast makes more explicit the challenge that sales growth must come from either overall industry growth or market-share gain. A forecast that explicit, demanding a market-share gain of, say, 20%–24%, is easier to scrutinize from a competitive perspective than a forecast that simply projects sales growth without any context (e.g., at an 8% rate).

Another helpful forecasting technique is to articulate business perspectives into a coherent qualitative "view" on business performance. This performance view encourages the forecaster to ground the forecast in a qualitative vision of how the future will play out. In blending qualitative and quantitative analyses into a coherent story, the forecaster develops a richer understanding of the relationships between the financial forecast and the qualitative trends and developments in the enterprise and its industry.

Forecasters can better understand their models by identifying the forecast's "value drivers," which are those assumptions that strongly affect the overall outcome. For example, for some businesses the operating-margin assumption may have a dramatic impact on overall business profitability, whereas the assumption for inventory turnover may make little difference. For other businesses, the inventory turnover may have a tremendous impact and thus be a value driver. In varying the assumptions, the forecaster can better appreciate which assumptions matter and thus channel resources to improve the forecast's precision by shoring up a particular assumption or altering business strategy to improve the performance of a particular line item.

Lastly, good forecasters understand that it is more useful to think of forecasts as ranges of possible outcomes than as precise predictions. A common term for forecast is "base case." A forecast represents the "best-guess" outcome or "expected value" of the forecast's line items. In generating forecasts, it is also important to have an unbiased appreciation for the range of possible outcomes, which is commonly done by estimating a high-side and a low-side scenario. In this way, the forecaster can bound the forecast with a relevant range of outcomes and can best appreciate the key bets in a financial forecast.

Recognizing the Potential for Cognitive Bias in the Forecasting Process

A substantial amount of research suggests that human decision making can be systematically biased. Bias in financial forecasts creates systematic problems in managing and investing in the business. Two elements of cognitive bias that play a role in financial forecasting are *optimism bias* and *overconfidence bias.* This note defines optimism bias as systematic positive error in the *expected value* of an unknown quantity, and defines overconfidence bias as systematic negative error in the *expected variance* of an unknown quantity. The definitions of these two terms are shown graphically in **Figure 2.** The dark curve shows the true distribution of the sales-growth rate. The realization of the growth rate is uncertain, with a higher probability of its being in the central part of the distribution. The expected value for the sales-growth rate is g*; thus,

FIGURE 2 | Optimism bias and overconfidence bias in forecasting sales-growth rate.

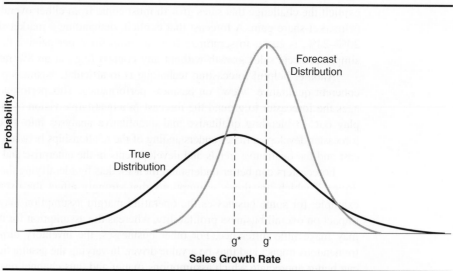

the proper base-case forecast for the sales-growth rate is precisely g*. The light curve shows the distribution expected by the average forecaster. This distribution is biased for two reasons. First, the expected value is too high. The forecaster expects the base-case sales-growth rate to be g', rather than g*. Such positive bias for expected value is termed optimistic. Second, the dispersion of the distribution is too tight. This dispersion is captured by the variance (or standard-deviation) statistic. Because the forecast dispersion is tighter than the true dispersion, the forecaster exhibits negative variance bias, or overconfidence—the forecaster believes that the forecast is more precise than it really is.

To test for forecasting bias among business-school forecasters, an experiment was performed in 2005 with the 300 first-year MBA students at the Darden Graduate School of Business Administration at the University of Virginia. Each student was randomly assigned both a U.S. public company and a year between 1980 and 2000[5]—that is, some students were assigned the same company, but no students were assigned the same company *and* the same year. The students were asked to forecast sales growth and operating margin for their assigned company for the subsequent three years. The students based their forecasts on the following information: industry name, firm sales growth and operating margin for the previous three years, historical and three-year prospective industry average growth and margins, and certain macroeconomic historical and three-year forecast data (real GNP growth, inflation rates, and the prevailing Treasury-bill yield). To avoid biasing the forecasts based on subsequent known outcomes, students were given the name of their firm's industry but not the firm's name. For the same reason, students were not given the identity of the current year. Responses were submitted electronically and anonymously. Forecast data from students who agreed to allow their responses to be used for research purposes were aggregated and analyzed. Summary statistics from the responses are presented in **Figure 3.**

The median values for the base-case forecast of expected sales growth and operating margin are plotted in **Figure 3.** The sales-growth panel suggests that students tended to expect growth to continue to improve over the forecast horizon (Years 1 through 3). The operating-margin panel suggests that students expected near-term performance to be constant, followed by later-term improvement. To benchmark the forecast, we compared the students' forecasts with the actual growth rates and operating margins realized by the companies. We expected that if students were unbiased in their forecasting, the distribution of the forecasts should be similar to the distribution of the actual results. **Figure 3** also plots the median value for the actual realizations. We observe that sales growth for these randomly selected firms did not improve but stayed fairly constant, whereas operating margins tended to decline over the extended term. The gap between

---

[5]More precisely, the population of sample firms was all U.S. firms followed by Compustat and the Value Line Investment Survey. To ensure meaningful industry forecast data, we required that each firm belong to a meaningful industry (i.e., multiform, industrial services, and diversified industries were not considered). We also required that Value Line report operating profit for each firm. To maintain consistency in the representation of firms over time, the sample began with a random identification of 25 firms per year. The forecast data were based on Value Line forecasts during the summer of the first year of the forecast. All historical financial data were from Compustat.

FIGURE 3 | Median expected and actual financial-forecast values for a random sample of U.S. companies. This figure plots the median forecast and actual company realization for sales growth and operating margin over the three-year historical period and the three-year forecast period based on the responses from MBA students in an experiment.

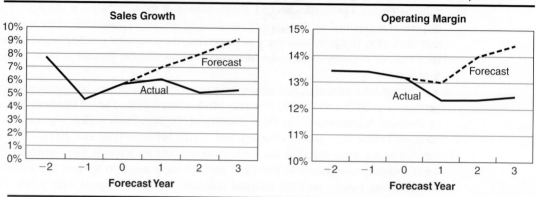

the two lines represents the systematic bias in the students' forecasts. Because the bias in both cases is positive, the results are consistent with systematic optimism in the students' forecasts. By the third year, the optimism bias is a large 4 percentage points for the sales-growth forecast and almost 2 percentage points for the margin forecast.

Although the average student tended to exhibit an optimistic bias, there was variation in the bias across groups of students. The forecast bias was further examined across two characteristics: gender and professional training. For both sales growth and operating margin, the test results revealed that males and those with professional backgrounds outside finance exhibited the most optimistic bias. For example, the bias in the third-year margin forecast was 0.7% for those with professional finance backgrounds and 1.9% for those outside finance; and 2.6% for the male students and just 0.8% for the female students.

In generating forecasts, it is also important to have an unbiased appreciation for the precision of the forecast, which is commonly done by estimating a high-side and a low-side scenario. To determine whether students were unbiased in appreciating the risk in forecast outcomes, they were asked to provide a high-side and a low-side scenario. The high-side scenario was defined explicitly as the 80th percentile level. The low-side scenario was defined as the 20th percentile level. **Figure 4** plots the median high-side and low-side scenarios, as well as the expected base-case forecast presented in **Figure 3.** For the three-year horizon, the median high-side forecast was 4 percentage points above the base case and the low-side forecast was 4 percentage points below the base case. The actual 80th percentile performance was 8 percentage points above the base case and the actual 20th percentile was 12 percentage points below the base case. The results suggest that the true variance in sales growth is substantially greater than that estimated by the students. The same is also true of the operating margin. The estimates provided by the students are consistent with strong overconfidence (negative variance bias) in the forecast.

FIGURE 4 | Median base-case, high-side, and low-side forecasts versus the actual 20th and 80th performance percentiles for sales growth and operating margin. This figure plots the median base-case, high-side, and low-side forecasts for sales growth and operating margin over the three-year forecast period based on the responses from MBA students in an experiment. The actual company 20th and 80th performance percentiles for sales growth and operating margin are also plotted. In the experiment, the low-side and high-side performance levels were defined as the students' belief in the 20th and 80th percentile levels.

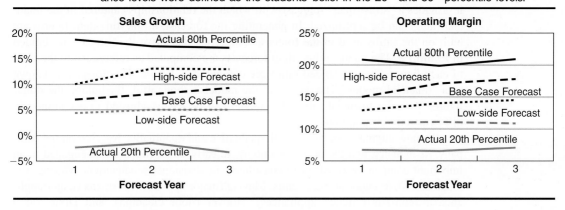

Maytag: An Example

The Maytag Corporation is a $4.7-billion home- and commercial-appliance company headquartered in Newton, Iowa. Suppose that in early 2004 we need to forecast the financial performance of the Maytag Corporation for the end of 2004. We suspect that one sensible place to start is to look at the company's performance over the past few years. The company's annual report provides information from its income statement and balance sheet (**Exhibit 1**).

One approach is to forecast each line item independently. Such an approach, however, ignores the important relationships among the different line items (e.g., costs and revenues tend to grow together). To gain an appreciation for these relationships, we calculate a variety of ratios, from sales growth to return on assets (**Exhibit 1**). In calculating the ratios, we notice some interesting patterns. First, sales growth declined sharply in 2003, from 11.5% to 2.7%. The sales decline was also accompanied by a decline in profitability margins; operating margin declined from 7.7% to 4.8%. Meanwhile, the asset ratios showed modest improvement; total asset turnover improved only slightly, from 1.5× to 1.6×. The steadiness of asset turnover was relatively constant across the various classes of assets (e.g., inventory days improved slightly in 2003, from 46.7 days to 43.5 days; PPE turnover also improved slightly, from 4.4× to 4.6×). The picture suggests that in 2003 Maytag experienced eroding sales growth and margins, while improvements in current asset efficiency kept asset turnover constant. Because return on assets comprises both a margin effect and an asset-productivity effect, we can attribute the 2003 decline in return on assets wholly to Maytag's margin decline. To be even more precise, because the operating expense as a percentage of sales actually declined, the margin (and ROA) decline is actually wholly due to a decline in gross margin. The historical-ratio analysis gives us some sense of the trends in business performance.

A common way to begin a financial forecast is to extrapolate current ratios into the future. For example, a simple starting point would be to assume that the 2003 financial ratios hold in 2004. If we make that simplifying assumption, we generate the financial forecast presented in **Exhibit 2.** We recognize this forecast as naïve, but it provides a "straw-man" forecast with which the relationships captured in the financial ratios can be scrutinized. In generating the forecast, all the line-item figures are built on the ratios used in the forecast. The ratios that drive the forecast are bolded in **Exhibit 2.** The financial line-item forecasts are computed as referenced to the right of each figure. The nonbolded ratios are computed as before. This forecast is known as a "financial model." The design of the model is thoughtful. By linking the dollar figures with the financial ratios, the model can be easily adjusted to accommodate different ratio assumptions.

We now augment our model with qualitative and quantitative research on the company, its industry, and the overall economy. In early 2004, Maytag was engaged in an important company-wide effort to consolidate its divisional headquarters. Maytag was made up of five major business units: Maytag (major appliances), Amana (major appliances), Jenn-Air (kitchen appliances), Hoover (floor cleaning), and Dixie-Narco (vending-machine equipment). The company expected this initiative to save $150 million in annual operating expenses. Maytag was also engaged in a plant-efficiency exercise. The company was introducing major new lines in its Maytag and Hoover units that it expected to compete with the best products in the industry.

The U.S. major-appliance industry had historically been made up of four primary players: General Electric, Whirlpool, Maytag, and Electrolux. Recently, these companies had experienced several challenges. First, the dramatic increase in steel prices, purportedly due to massive real investment in China, had increased industry production costs. Second, Asian manufacturers had begun to compete aggressively in their market. Third, products were becoming less easy to differentiate, leading to increased price competition. Tempering these effects, the buoyancy of the U.S. housing market had provided strong growth across the industry. Whirlpool had been particularly aggressive in its expansion efforts. In 2003, its sales growth was almost 11%, while operating margin was 6.8% and asset turnover was 1.7. In 2003, Whirlpool generated better ratios than Maytag across most dimensions.

Based on the business and environmental assessment, we take the view that Maytag will maintain its position in a deteriorating industry. We can adjust the naïve 2004 forecast (**Exhibit 3**) based on this assessment. We suspect that the increased entry by foreign competition and a stalling of the recent sales growth in the U.S. housing market will lead to zero sales growth for Maytag in 2004. We also expect the increased price competition and steel-price effect to lead to a further erosion of gross margins (to 16.0%). Although the company's efforts to reduce overhead costs are under way, we expect that Maytag will not see any benefits from these efforts until 2005. Consequently, we estimate that operating expenses will return to their 2002 percentage of sales (13.8%). These assumptions give us an operating-margin estimate of 2.2%. We expect the increased competition and housing-market decline to reduce Maytag's ability to work its current assets. We expect AR days to increase to 47.0, inventory turnover to decrease to 7.2×, and other-current-assets percentage to stay at 5%. Finally, we expect the productivity efforts to generate a small improvement in fixed-asset turnover. We project PPE turnover at 5.0× and other-noncurrent-asset turnover at 7.1×. These assumptions lead to an implied financial forecast. The resulting projected after-tax ROA is 2.2%. The forecast is thoughtful. It captures a coherent view of Maytag based on the company's historical financial relationships, a grounding in the macroeconomic and industry reality, and incorporation of Maytag's specific business strategy.

We recognize that we cannot anticipate all the events of 2004. Our forecast will inevitably be wrong. Nevertheless, we suspect that, by being thoughtful in our analysis, our forecast will provide a reasonable, unbiased expectation of future performance. **Exhibit 4** gives the actual 2004 results for Maytag. The big surprise was the substantial effect on sales growth and margin of an even more dramatic increase in steel prices. Maytag's realized sales growth was actually negative, and gross margin dropped from 22% and 18% in 2002 and 2003, respectively, to 14% in 2004. Our asset assumptions were fairly close to the outcome. Although we did not complete a high-side and a low-side scenario in this simple example, we can hope that, had we done so, we could have appropriately assessed the sources and level of uncertainty of our forecast.

EXHIBIT 1 | Financial Statements for Maytag Corporation (in millions of dollars)

	2002	2003
(1) Sales	4,666	4,792
(2) Cost of sales	3,661	3,932
(3) Gross profit	1,005	860
(4) Operating expenses	645	631
(5) Operating profit	360	229
(6) Accounts receivable	586	597
(7) Inventory	468	468
(8) Other current assets	268	239
(9) Net property, plant, & equipment	1,066	1,047
(10) Other noncurrent assets	715	673
(11) Total assets	3,104	3,024
Sales growth	11.5%	2.7%
Gross margin (3/1)	21.5%	17.9%
Operating exp/Sales (4/1)	13.8%	13.2%
Operating margin (5/1)	7.7%	4.8%
Receivable turnover (1/6)	8.0	8.0
Accounts receivable days (6/1*365 days)	45.9	45.5
Inventory turnover (2/7)	7.8	8.4
Inventory days (7/2*365 days)	46.7	43.5
Other current assets/Sales (8/1)	5.7%	5.0%
PPE turnover (1/9)	4.4	4.6
Other noncurrent asset turnover (1/10)	6.5	7.1
Total asset turnover (1/11)	1.5	1.6
Return on assets (5*(1−.35)/11)	7.5%	4.9%

Note: Although including both turnover and days ratios is redundant, doing so illustrates the two perspectives.

EXHIBIT 2 | Naïve Financial Forecast for Maytag Corporation (in millions of dollars)

	2002	2003	2004E	
(1) Sales	4,666	4,792	4,921	Sales03 * (1 + Sales growth)
(2) Cost of sales	3,661	3,932	4,038	Sales04 − Gross profit
(3) Gross profit	1,005	860	883	Sales04 * Gross margin
(4) Operating expenses	645	631	648	Sales04 * Operating exp/Sales
(5) Operating profit	360	229	235	Gross profit − Operating expenses
(6) Accounts receivable	586	597	613	Sales04 * AR days/365
(7) Inventory	468	468	585	Cost of sales/Inv turnover
(8) Other current assets	268	239	245	Sales04 * Other curr assets/Sales
(9) Net property, plant, & equipment	1,066	1,047	1,075	Sales04/PPE turnover
(10) Other noncurrent assets	715	673	691	Sales04/Other NC asset turnover
(11) Total assets	3,104	3,024	3,210	
Sales growth	11.5%	2.7%	**2.7%**	Estimate
Gross margin (3/1)	21.5%	17.9%	**17.9%**	Estimate
Operating exp/Sales (4/1)	13.8%	13.2%	**13.2%**	Estimate
Operating margin (5/1)	7.7%	4.8%	4.8%	
Receivable turnover (1/6)	8.0	8.0	8.0	
Accounts receivable days (6/1*365 days)	45.9	45.5	**45.5**	Estimate
Inventory turnover (2/7)	7.8	8.4	**6.9**	Estimate
Inventory days (7/2*365 days)	46.7	43.5	52.9	
Other current assets/ Sales (8/1)	5.7%	5.0%	**5.0%**	Estimate
PPE turnover (1/9)	4.4	4.6	**4.6**	Estimate
Other noncurrent asset turnover (1/10)	6.5	7.1	**7.1**	Estimate
Total asset turnover (1/11)	1.5	1.6	1.5	
Return on assets (5*(1−.35)/11)	7.5%	4.9%	4.8%	

EXHIBIT 3 | Revised Financial Forecast for Maytag Corporation (in millions of dollars)

	2002	2003	2004E	
(1) Sales	4,666	4,792	4,792	Sales03 * (1 + Sales growth)
(2) Cost of sales	3,661	3,932	4,025	Sales04 − Gross profit
(3) Gross profit	1,005	860	767	Sales04 * Gross margin
(4) Operating expenses	645	631	661	Sales04 * Operating exp/Sales
(5) Operating profit	360	229	105	Gross profit − Operating expenses
(6) Accounts receivable	586	597	617	Sales04 * AR days/365
(7) Inventory	468	468	559	Cost of sales/Inv turnover
(8) Other current assets	268	239	239	Sales04 * Other curr assets/Sales
(9) Net property, plant, & equipment	1,066	1,047	958	Sales04/PPE turnover
(10) Other noncurrent assets	715	673	675	Sales04/Other NC asset turnover
(11) Total assets	3,104	3,024	3,048	
Sales growth	11.5%	2.7%	**0.0%**	Estimate
Gross margin (3/1)	21.5%	17.9%	**16.0%**	Estimate
Operating exp/Sales (4/1)	13.8%	13.2%	**13.8%**	Estimate
Operating margin (5/1)	7.7%	4.8%	2.2%	
Receivable turnover (1/6)	8.0	8.0	7.8	
Accounts receivable days (6/1*365 days)	45.9	45.5	**47.0**	Estimate
Inventory turnover (2/7)	7.8	8.4	**7.2**	Estimate
Inventory days (7/2*365 days)	46.7	43.5	50.7	
Other current assets/ Sales (8/1)	5.7%	5.0%	**5.0%**	Estimate
PPE turnover (1/9)	4.4	4.6	**5.0**	Estimate
Other noncurrent asset turnover (1/10)	6.5	7.1	**7.1**	Estimate
Total asset turnover (1/11)	1.5	1.6	1.6	
Return on assets (5*(1 − .35)/11)	7.5%	4.9%	2.2%	

EXHIBIT 4 | Actual Financial Performance of Maytag Corporation
                (in millions of dollars)

	2002	2003	2004
(1) Sales	4,666	4,792	4,722
(2) Cost of sales	3,661	3,932	4,062
(3) Gross profit	1,005	860	660
(4) Operating expenses	645	631	625
(5) Operating profit	360	229	35
(6) Accounts receivable	586	597	630
(7) Inventory	468	468	515
(8) Other current assets	268	239	300
(9) Net property, plant, & equipment	1,066	1,047	921
(10) Other noncurrent assets	715	673	653
(11) Total assets	3,104	3,024	3,019
Sales growth	11.5%	2.7%	−1.5%
Gross margin (3/1)	21.5%	17.9%	14.0%
Operating exp/Sales (4/1)	13.8%	13.2%	13.2%
Operating margin (5/1)	7.7%	4.8%	0.7%
Receivable turnover (1/6)	8.0	8.0	7.5
Accounts receivable days (6/1*365 days)	45.9	45.5	48.7
Inventory turnover (2/7)	7.8	8.4	7.9
Inventory days (7/2*365 days)	46.7	43.5	46.3
Other current assets/Sales (8/1)	5.7%	5.0%	6.4%
PPE turnover (1/9)	4.4	4.6	5.1
Other noncurrent asset turnover (1/10)	6.5	7.1	7.2
Total asset turnover (1/11)	1.5	1.6	1.6
Return on assets (5*(1 − .35)/11)	7.5%	4.9%	0.8%

The Financial Detective, 2005

Financial characteristics of companies vary for many reasons. The two most prominent drivers are industry economics and firm strategy.

Each industry has a financial norm around which companies within the industry tend to operate. An airline, for example, would naturally be expected to have a high proportion of fixed assets (airplanes), while a consulting firm would not. A steel manufacturer would be expected to have a lower gross margin than a pharmaceutical manufacturer because commodities such as steel are subject to strong price competition, while highly differentiated products like patented drugs enjoy much more pricing freedom. Because of unique economic features of each industry, average financial statements will vary from one industry to the next.

Similarly, companies *within* industries have different financial characteristics, in part, because of the diverse strategies that can be employed. Executives choose strategies that will position their company favorably in the competitive jockeying within an industry. Strategies typically entail making important choices in how a product is made (e.g., capital intensive versus labor intensive), how it is marketed (e.g., direct sales versus the use of distributors), and how the company is financed (e.g., the use of debt or equity). Strategies among companies in the same industry can differ dramatically. Different strategies can produce striking differences in financial results for firms in the same industry.

The following paragraphs describe pairs of participants in a number of different industries. Their strategies and market niches provide clues as to the financial condition and performance that one would expect of them. The companies' common-sized financial statements and operating data, as of early 2005, are presented in a standardized format in **Exhibit 1.** It is up to you to match the financial data with the company descriptions. Also, try to explain the differences in financial results *across* industries.

Health Products

Companies A and B manufacture and market health-care products. One firm is the world's largest prescription-pharmaceutical company. This firm has a very broad and deep pipeline of ethical pharmaceuticals, supported by a robust research and development budget. In recent years, the company has divested several of its nonpharmaceutical businesses, and it has come to be seen as the partner of choice for licensing deals with other pharmaceutical and biotechnology firms.

The other company is a diversified health-products company that manufactures and mass markets a broad line of prescription pharmaceuticals, over-the-counter remedies (i.e., nonprescription drugs), consumer health and beauty products, and medical diagnostics and devices. For its consumer segment, brand development and management are a major element of this firm's mass-market-oriented strategy.

Beer

Of the beer companies, C and D, one is a national brewer of mass-market consumer beers sold under a variety of brand names. This company operates an extensive network of breweries and distribution systems. The firm also owns a number of beer-related businesses, such as snack and aluminum-container manufacturing, and several major theme parks.

The other company produces seasonal and year-round beers with smaller production volume and higher prices. This company outsources most of its brewing activity. The firm is financially conservative, and has recently undergone a major cost-savings initiative to counterbalance the recent surge in packaging and freight costs.

Computers

Companies E and F sell computers and related equipment. One company focuses exclusively on mail-order sales of built-to-order PCs, including desktops, laptops, notebooks, servers, workstations, printers, and handheld devices. The company is an assembler of PC components manufactured by its suppliers. The company allows its customers to design, price, and purchase through its Web site.

The other company sells a highly differentiable line of computers, consumer-oriented electronic devices, and a variety of proprietary software products. Led by its charismatic founder, the company has begun to recover from a dramatic decline in its market share. The firm has an aggressive retail strategy intended to drive traffic through its stores and to expand its installed base of customers by showcasing its products in a user-friendly retail atmosphere.

Books and Music

The book and music retailers are companies G and H. One focuses on selling primarily to customers through a vast retail-store presence. The company is the leader in traditional book retailing, which it fosters through its "community store" concept and regular discount policy. The firm also maintains an online presence and owns a publishing imprint.

The other company sells books, music, and videos solely through its Internet Web site. While more than three-quarters of its sales are media, it also sells electronics and other general merchandise. The firm has only recently become profitable, and it has followed an aggressive strategy of acquiring related online businesses in recent years.

Paper Products

Companies I and J are both paper manufacturers. One company is the world's largest maker of paper, paperboard, and packaging. This vertically integrated company owns timberland; numerous lumber, paper, paperboard, and packing-products facilities; and a paper-distribution network. The company has spent the last few years rationalizing capacity by closing inefficient mills, implementing cost-containment initiatives, and selling nonessential assets.

The other firm is a small producer of printing, writing, and technical specialty papers, as well as towel and tissue products. Most of the company's products are marketed under branded labels. The company purchases the wood fiber used in its paper-making process on the open market.

Hardware and Tools

Companies K and L manufacture and sell hardware and tools. One of the companies is a global manufacturer and marketer of power tools and power-tool accessories, hardware and home-improvement products, and fastening systems. The firm sells primarily to retailers, wholesalers, and distributors. Its products appear under a variety of well-known brand names and are geared for the end user.

The other tool company manufactures and markets high-quality precision tools and diagnostic-equipment systems for professional users. The firm offers a broad range of products, which it sells via its own technical representatives and mobile franchise dealers. The company also provides financing for franchisees and for customers' large purchases.

Retailing

Companies M and N are two large discount retailers. One firm carries a wide variety of nationally advertised general merchandise. The company is known for its low prices, breadth of merchandise, and volume-oriented strategy. Most of its stores are leased and are located near the company's expanding network of distribution centers. The company has begun to implement plans to expand both internationally and in large urban areas.

The other firm is a rapidly growing chain of upscale discount stores. The company competes by attempting to match other discounters' prices on similar merchandise and by offering deep discounts on its differentiated items. Additionally, the company has partnerships with several leading designers. Recently, the firm has divested several nondiscount department-store businesses. To support sales and earnings growth, this company offers credit to qualified customers.

Newspapers

Companies O and P own newspapers. One is a diversified media company that generates most of its revenues through newspapers sold around the country and around the world. Because the company is centered largely on one product, it has strong central controls. Competition for subscribers and advertising revenues in this firm's segment is fierce. The company has also recently built a large office building for its headquarters.

The other firm owns a number of newspapers in relatively small communities throughout the Midwest and the Southwest. Some analysts view this firm as holding a portfolio of small local monopolies in newspaper publishing. This company has a significant amount of goodwill on its balance sheet, stemming from acquisitions. Key to this firm's operating success is a strategy of decentralized decision making and administration.

EXHIBIT 1 | Common-Sized Financial Data and Ratios

	Health Prod.		Beer		Computers		Books & Music		Paper		Tools		Retail		Newspapers	
Assets	A	B	C	D	E	F	G	H	I	J	K	L	M	N	O	P
Cash & Short-Term Investments	24.2	16.1	1.4	55.6	42.2	67.9	54.8	16.2	7.6	5.9	9.3	6.5	4.6	7.0	0.6	1.1
Receivables	12.8	8.1	4.3	11.9	19.0	13.0	nmf	2.3	8.8	10.9	18.9	23.7	1.4	17.0	4.6	9.9
Inventories	7.0	5.4	4.3	11.7	2.0	1.3	14.8	38.6	7.9	14.4	17.8	14.9	24.5	16.7	0.8	0.8
Current Assets-Other	7.2	2.5	1.3	2.4	9.5	5.5	8.6	2.6	3.0	1.4	7.0	6.9	1.5	2.5	0.7	3.8
Current Assets-Total	51.2	32.1	11.2	81.7	72.8	87.6	78.2	59.7	27.2	32.6	52.9	52.1	32.0	43.1	6.6	15.5
Net Fixed Assets	19.6	14.9	54.7	16.0	7.3	8.8	7.6	24.4	50.8	62.5	13.6	13.7	57.0	52.2	14.1	34.6
Assets-Other	6.9	3.8	7.2	1.0	1.3	2.4	9.3	4.9	5.4	3.1	11.8	8.9	2.0	4.0	0.1	7.2
Intangibles	22.2	46.1	7.4	1.3	0.0	1.2	4.4	11.1	14.6	1.9	21.4	22.3	9.0	0.6	76.8	37.1
Investments & Advances	0.1	3.1	2.9	0.0	18.6	0.0	0.0	0.0	0.0	0.0	0.0	3.0	0.0	0.0	0.7	0.0
Assets-Total	100.0	100.0	100.0	100.0	100.0	100.0	100.0	100.0	100.0	100.0	100.0	100.0	100.0	100.0	100.0	100.0
Liabilities & Equity																
Accounts Payable	9.8	2.2	7.4	9.1	38.3	18.0	35.1	22.6	6.7	8.5	8.4	8.5	18.0	17.9	1.4	4.8
Debt in Current Liabilities	0.5	9.1	0.0	0.0	0.0	0.0	0.1	0.0	1.5	0.0	3.5	5.6	6.5	1.6	0.8	14.9
Income Taxes Payable	2.8	1.6	0.9	1.7	0.0	0.0	0.0	0.0	0.0	1.2	0.9	1.0	1.1	0.9	0.3	nmf
Current Liabilities-Other	13.0	8.5	3.8	13.7	22.6	15.3	14.7	17.6	6.1	7.1	19.5	14.4	10.1	5.1	5.1	8.7
Current Liabilities-Total	26.1	21.4	12.2	24.4	60.9	33.3	49.9	40.2	14.2	16.7	32.4	29.4	35.7	25.5	7.5	28.3
LT Debt	4.8	5.9	51.2	0.0	2.2	0.0	56.9	7.4	41.3	18.3	21.7	8.9	19.7	28.0	14.4	11.9
Deferred Taxes	0.8	10.2	10.7	1.9	0.0	0.0	nmf	5.9	5.0	12.0	3.1	3.3	nmf	3.0	15.0	3.3
Liabilities-Other	8.6	7.3	9.5	0.7	8.9	3.7	0.2	11.0	10.9	12.4	14.6	8.9	2.5	3.2	0.7	17.5
Liabilities-Total	40.3	44.8	83.5	27.1	72.1	36.9	107.0	64.7	75.9	59.5	71.8	51.5	58.9	59.7	37.5	64.5
Stockholders' Equity	59.7	55.2	16.5	72.9	27.9	63.1	(7.0)	35.3	24.1	40.5	28.2	48.5	41.1	40.3	62.5	35.5
Total Liabilities & Equity	100.0	100.0	100.0	100.0	100.0	100.0	100.0	100.0	100.0	100.0	100.0	100.0	100.0	100.0	100.0	100.0
Income/Expenses																
Sales-Net	100.0	100.0	100.0	100.0	100.0	100.0	100.0	100.0	100.0	100.0	100.0	100.0	100.0	100.0	100.0	100.0
Cost of Goods Sold	23.9	11.1	53.9	38.5	81.0	70.9	75.8	69.5	75.3	82.9	61.0	51.6	75.3	67.1	49.7	40.5
Gross Profit	76.1	88.9	46.1	61.5	19.0	29.1	24.2	30.5	24.7	17.1	39.0	48.4	24.7	32.9	50.3	59.5
SG&A Expense	44.5	46.7	17.3	50.5	9.7	23.1	16.9	21.8	12.0	7.3	24.8	38.9	17.9	22.5	23.0	39.7
Depreciation	4.5	9.7	6.2	2.0	0.7	1.8	1.1	3.7	6.1	5.8	2.6	2.5	1.5	2.7	7.0	4.1
Earnings Before Interest &Taxes	27.2	32.5	22.5	9.0	8.6	4.2	6.2	5.0	6.6	4.0	11.7	6.9	5.3	7.7	20.2	15.6
Nonoperating Income (Expense)	0.7	1.1	2.9	0.3	0.4	0.7	0.3	0.1	0.4	0.1	0.6	0.1	0.8	0.0	1.3	0.4
Interest Income (Expense)	(0.7)	0.7	2.9	0.0	0.0	0.0	1.5	0.3	3.3	1.0	1.1	1.0	0.5	1.0	1.9	1.6
Special Items-Income (Expense)	(0.0)	(6.3)	0.2	0.0	(0.3)	0.0	0.1	(0.3)	(0.8)	0.0	0.0	(1.0)	0.0	(0.2)	0.0	(0.1)
Pretax Income	27.1	26.7	22.8	9.2	9.0	4.6	5.1	4.5	2.9	3.1	11.2	5.1	5.6	6.5	19.7	14.4
Income Taxes-Total	9.1	5.1	7.8	3.5	2.8	1.3	(3.4)	1.9	0.8	1.2	3.0	1.6	2.0	2.4	7.1	5.6
Net Income (Loss)	18.0	21.6	15.0	5.8	6.2	3.3	8.5	2.9	(0.1)	2.0	8.4	3.4	3.6	6.8	12.6	8.9

123

EXHIBIT 1 | Common-Sized Financial Data and Ratios (Continued)

	Health Prod.		Beer		Computers		Books & Music		Paper		Tools		Retail		Newspapers	
Market Data	A	B	C	D	E	F	G	H	I	J	K	L	M	N	O	P
Beta	0.65	0.85	0.55	0.60	1.20	1.05	1.70	0.51	1.15	1.10	1.00	1.00	0.85	1.10	0.85	0.90
Price/Earnings	22.29	22.32	16.85	19.73	30.48	41.85	27.32	21.63	30.97	33.78	13.64	23.01	18.97	24.19	20.54	13.29
Price to Book	5.93	3.08	13.99	2.56	17.46	5.13	nmf	2.36	1.91	1.80	4.65	1.85	4.23	3.64	2.07	3.09
Dividend Payout	38.21	46.28	33.16	0.00	0.00	0.00	0.00	0.00	101.46	86.16	15.30	70.62	21.56	14.85	37.53	30.81
Liquidity																
Current Ratio	1.96	1.50	0.92	3.35	1.20	2.63	1.57	1.49	1.91	1.94	1.63	1.77	0.90	1.69	0.88	0.55
Quick Ratio	1.42	1.13	0.47	2.77	1.01	2.43	nmf	0.46	1.15	1.00	0.87	1.03	0.17	0.94	0.69	0.39
Asset Management																
Inventory Turnover	3.08	0.93	12.60	7.44	67.96	74.78	13.56	2.42	6.75	7.11	3.89	3.59	7.69	5.86	33.35	43.48
Receivables Turnover	7.06	5.47	21.87	18.68	12.23	8.28	nmf	72.11	8.68	11.64	5.82	4.42	192.73	8.31	10.98	8.50
Fixed Assets Turnover	4.67	2.86	1.72	12.67	30.68	12.03	29.42	6.54	1.43	1.86	7.63	7.50	4.50	2.77	3.43	2.59
Debt Management																
Total Debt/Total Assets	5.34	14.99	51.19	0.00	2.18	0.00	56.94	7.42	42.78	18.36	25.21	14.45	26.16	29.54	15.22	26.81
LT Debt/Shareholders' Equity	8.06	10.66	310.28	0.00	7.79	0.00	nmf	21.01	171.21	45.32	77.03	18.29	47.92	69.34	23.04	33.66
Interest Coverage After Tax	27.34	32.57	6.25	nmf	191.19	93.00	6.49	9.52	1.56	2.98	8.62	4.55	8.86	4.92	7.83	6.69
DuPont Analysis																
Net Profit Margin	17.97	21.58	15.00	5.76	6.18	3.33	8.50	2.53	1.87	1.96	8.17	3.39	3.59	4.02	12.65	8.86
Asset Turnover	0.93	0.44	0.97	2.23	2.31	1.11	2.56	1.43	0.73	1.20	1.11	1.09	2.54	1.47	0.48	0.85
Return on Equity	26.75	16.64	83.97	15.95	46.92	5.44	nmf	10.58	5.79	5.71	28.30	7.36	20.79	14.47	9.86	20.89

Sources of data: S&P's Research Insight; Value Line Investment Survey.

nmf = not a meaningful figure.

Krispy Kreme Doughnuts, Inc.

As the millennium began, the future for Krispy Kreme Doughnuts, Inc., smelled sweet. Not only could the company boast iconic status and a nearly cultlike following, it had quickly become a darling of Wall Street. Less than a year after its initial public offering, in April 2000, Krispy Kreme shares were selling for 62 times earnings and, by 2003, *Fortune* magazine had dubbed the company "the hottest brand in America." With ambitious plans to open 500 doughnut shops over the first half of the decade, the company's distinctive green-and-red vintage logo and unmistakable "Hot Doughnuts Now" neon sign had become ubiquitous.

At the end of 2004, however, the sweet story had begun to sour as the company made several accounting revelations, after which its stock price sank. From its peak in August 2003, Krispy Kreme's stock price plummeted more than 80% in the next 16 months. Investors and analysts began asking probing questions about the company's fundamentals, but even by the beginning of 2005, many of those questions remained unanswered. **Exhibits 1** and **2** provide Krispy Kreme's financial statements for fiscal-years 2000 through 2004. Was this a healthy company? What had happened to the company that some had thought would become the next Starbucks? If almost everyone loved the doughnuts, why were so many investors fleeing the popular doughnut maker?

Company Background

Krispy Kreme began as a single doughnut shop in Winston-Salem, North Carolina, in 1937, when Vernon Rudolph, who had acquired the company's special doughnut recipe from a French chef in New Orleans, started making and selling doughnuts wholesale to supermarkets. Within a short time, Rudolph's products became so popular that he cut a hole in his factory's wall to sell directly to customers—thus was born the central Krispy Kreme retail concept: the factory store. By the late 1950s, Krispy Kreme had 29 shops in 12 states, many of which were operated by franchisees.

This case was prepared by Sean Carr (MBA '03), under the direction of Robert F. Bruner of the Darden Graduate School of Business Administration. It was written as a basis for class discussion rather than to illustrate effective or ineffective handling of an administrative situation. Copyright © 2005 by the University of Virginia Darden School Foundation, Charlottesville, VA. All rights reserved. *To order copies, send an e-mail to sales@dardenbusinesspublishing.com. No part of this publication may be reproduced, stored in a retrieval system, used in a spreadsheet, or transmitted in any form or by any means—electronic, mechanical, photocopying, recording, or otherwise—without the permission of the Darden School Foundation.*

After Rudolph's death, in 1973, Beatrice Foods bought the company and quickly expanded it to more than 100 locations. Beatrice introduced other products, such as soups and sandwiches, and cut costs by changing the appearance of the stores and substituting cheaper ingredients in the doughnut mixture. The business languished, however, and by the early 1980s, Beatrice put the company up for sale.

A group of franchisees led by Joseph McAleer, who had been the first Krispy Kreme franchisee, completed a leveraged buyout of the company for $24 million in 1982. McAleer brought back the original doughnut formula and the company's traditional logo. It was also around this time that the company introduced the "Hot Doughnuts Now" neon sign, which told customers when fresh doughnuts were coming off the line. The company still struggled for a while, but by 1989, Krispy Kreme had become debt-free and had slowly begun to expand. The company focused on its signature doughnuts and added branded coffee in 1996. Scott Livengood, who became CEO in 1998 and chair the following year, took the company public in April 2000 in what was one of the largest initial public offerings (IPO) in recent years; one day after the offering, Krispy Kreme's share price was $40.63, giving the firm a market capitalization of nearly $500 million.

Krispy Kreme's Business

After the company's IPO, Krispy Kreme announced an aggressive strategy to expand the number of stores from 144 to 500 over the next five years. In addition, the company planned to grow internationally, with 32 locations planned for Canada and more for the United Kingdom, Mexico, and Australia. **Exhibit 3** provides an overview of the company's store openings.

Krispy Kreme Doughnuts generated revenues through four primary sources: on-premises retail sales at company-owned stores (accounting for 27% of revenues); off-premises sales to grocery and convenience stores (40%); manufacturing and distribution of product mix and machinery (29%); and franchisee royalties and fees (4%). In addition to the traditional domestic retail locations, the company sought growth through smaller "satellite concepts," which relied on factory stores to provide doughnuts for reheating, as well as the development of the international market.

- *On-premises sales:* Each factory store allowed consumers to see the production of doughnuts; Krispy Kreme's custom machinery and doughnut-viewing areas created what the company called a "doughnut theater." In that way, Krispy Kreme attempted to differentiate itself from its competition by offering customers an experience rather than simply a product. Each factory store could produce between 4,000-dozen and 10,000-dozen doughnuts a day, which were sold both on- and off-premises.

- *Off-premises sales:* About 60% of off-premises sales were to grocery stores, both in stand-alone cases and on store shelves. The remainder were sold to convenience stores (a small percentage were also sold as private label). The company maintained a fleet of delivery trucks for off-premises sales.

- *Manufacturing and distribution:* Krispy Kreme's Manufacturing and Distribution (KKM&D) division provided the proprietary doughnut mixes and doughnut-making equipment to every company-owned and franchised factory store. This vertical integration allowed the company to maintain quality control and product consistency throughout the system. The company maintained its own manufacturing facilities for its mixes and machines, and it provided quarterly service for all system units. All franchisees were required to buy mix and equipment from Krispy Kreme. KKM&D also included the company's coffee-roasting operation, which supplied branded drip coffee to both company-owned and franchised stores.

- *Franchise royalties and fees:* In exchange for an initial franchise fee and annual royalties, franchisees received assistance from Krispy Kreme with operations, advertising and marketing, accounting, and other information-management systems. Franchisees that had relationships with the company before the IPO in 2000 were called Associates, and they typically had locations in heritage markets in the southeastern United States. Associates were not responsible for opening new stores. New franchisees were called Area Developers, and they were responsible for developing new sites and building in markets with high potential. Area Developers typically paid $20,000 to $50,000 in initial franchise fees and between 4.5% and 6% in royalties. Franchisees also contributed 1% of their annual total sales to the corporate advertising fund.

Roughly 60% of sales at a Krispy Kreme store were derived from the company's signature product, the glazed doughnut. This differed from Dunkin' Donuts, the company's largest competitor, for which the majority of sales came from coffee.

Holes in the Krispy Kreme Story

On May 7, 2004, for the first time in its history as a public company, Krispy Kreme announced adverse results. The company told investors to expect earnings to be 10% lower than anticipated, claiming that the recent low-carbohydrate diet trend in the United States had hurt wholesale and retail sales. The company also said it planned to divest Montana Mills, a chain of 28 bakery cafés acquired in January 2003 for $40 million in stock, and would take a charge of $35 million to $40 million in the first quarter. In addition, Krispy Kreme indicated that its new Hot Doughnut and Coffee Shops were falling short of expectations and that it had plans to close three of them (resulting in a charge of $7 million to $8 million). Krispy Kreme's shares closed down 30%, at $22.51 a share.

Then, on May 25, the *Wall Street Journal* published a story describing aggressive accounting treatment for franchise acquisitions made by Krispy Kreme.[1] According to

---

[1]Mark Maremont and Rick Brooks, "Krispy Kreme Franchise Buybacks May Spur New Concerns," *Wall Street Journal,* 25 May 2004.

the article, in 2003, Krispy Kreme had begun negotiating to purchase a struggling seven-store Michigan franchise. The franchisee owed the company several million dollars for equipment, ingredients, and franchise fees and, as part of the deal, Krispy Kreme asked the franchisee to close two underperforming stores and to pay Krispy Kreme the accrued interest on past-due loans. In return for those moves, Krispy Kreme promised to raise its purchase price on the franchise.

According to the *Journal,* Krispy Kreme recorded the interest paid by the franchisee as interest income and, thus, as immediate profit; however, the company booked the purchase cost of the franchise as an intangible asset, under reacquired franchise rights, which the company did not amortize. Krispy Kreme also allowed the Michigan franchise's top executive to remain employed at the company after the deal, but shortly after the deal was completed, that executive left. In accordance with a severance agreement, this forced Krispy Kreme to pay the executive an additional $5 million, an expense the company also rolled into the unamortized-asset category as reacquired franchise rights.

The company denied any wrongdoing with this practice, maintaining it had accounted for its franchise acquisitions in accordance with generally accepted accounting principles (GAAP). On July 29, however, the company disclosed that the U.S. Securities and Exchange Commission (SEC) had launched an informal investigation related to "franchise reacquisitions and the company's previously announced reduction in earnings guidance." Observers remained skeptical. "Krispy Kreme's accounting for franchise acquisitions is the most aggressive we have found," said one analyst at the time. "We surveyed 18 publicly traded companies with franchise operations, four of which had reacquired franchises, and they had amortized them. That clearly seems like the right thing to do."[2] Over the previous three years, Krispy Kreme had recorded $174.5 million as intangible assets (reacquired franchise rights), which the company was not required to amortize. On the date of the SEC announcement, Krispy Kreme's shares fell another 15%, closing at $15.71 a share.

Analysts' Reactions

Since the heady days of 2001, when 80% of the equity analysts following Krispy Kreme were making buy recommendations for the company's shares, the conventional wisdom about the company had changed. By the time the *Wall Street Journal* published the article about Krispy Kreme's franchise-reacquisition accounting practices in May 2004, only 25% of the analysts following Krispy Kreme were recommending the company as a buy; another 50% had downgraded the stock to a hold. **Exhibits 4 and 5** provide tables of aggregate analysts' recommendations and EPS (earnings per share) estimates. As Krispy Kreme's troubles mounted during the second half of 2004, analysts became increasingly pessimistic about the stock:

---

[2]"Did Someone Say Doughnuts? Yes, the SEC," *New York Times,* 30 July 2004.

Analyst	Comment	Date
John Ivankoe, J.P. Morgan Securities, Inc.	In addition to the possibility of an earnings restatement, we believe many fundamental problems persist, exclusive of any "low-carb" impact. Declining new-store volumes are indicative of a worsening investment model, and we believe restructured store-development contracts, a smaller store format, and reduced fees charged for equipment and ingredients sold to franchises are necessary.	July 29, 2004
Jonathan M. Waite, KeyBanc Capital Markets	We believe that the challenges KKD faces, including margin compression, lower returns, an SEC investigation, and product saturation, currently outweigh the company's positive drivers. In addition, shares of KKD are trading at 16.6× CY05 earnings versus its 15% growth rate. As such, we rate KKD shares HOLD.	Oct. 12, 2004
John S. Glass, CIBC World Markets	Krispy Kreme's balance sheet became bloated over the past two years by acquisition goodwill that will likely need to be written down. As a result, KKD's return on invested capital has plunged to about 10% versus 18% two years ago prior to these acquisitions. We'd view a balance sheet write-down, including eliminating a significant portion of the $170+ million in "reacquired franchise rights," as a first step in the right direction.	Nov. 8, 2004
Glenn M. Guard, Legg Mason	In our opinion, management was not focused on operations the way it should have been. As a result, too many units were opened in poor locations as the company tripled its unit base since 2000. Additionally, we believe that franchisees were not trained properly as to how best to run their off-premises business. As a result, we believe many units are losing money off-premises, and franchisees are not motivated to grow that business. It also appears to us that basic blocking and tackling, execution, and cost discipline were seriously lacking in both the company and franchise systems, resulting in inefficiencies.	Nov. 23, 2004

As the headlines about the SEC investigation and Krispy Kreme's other management issues continued (e.g., Krispy Kreme's chief operating officer stepped down on August 16, 2004), observers looked more critically at the fundamentals of Krispy Kreme's business. In September, the *Wall Street Journal* published an article that focused attention on the company's growth:

> The biggest problem for Krispy Kreme may be that the company grew too quickly and diluted its cult status by selling its doughnuts in too many outlets, while trying to impress Wall Street. The number of Krispy Kreme shops has nearly tripled since early 2000, with 427 stores in 45 states and four foreign countries. Some 20,000 supermarkets, convenience stores, truck stops, and other outside locations also sell the company's doughnuts.
>
> Another issue is that Krispy Kreme has relied for a significant chunk of profits on high profit-margin equipment that it requires franchisees to buy for each new store. Its profits have also been tied to growth in the number of franchised stores, because of the upfront fee each must pay.[3]

---

[3]"Sticky Situation," *Wall Street Journal,* 3 September 2004.

In September 2004, Krispy Kreme announced that it would reduce its number of new stores for the year to about 60 from the previously announced 120.

Restatement Announced

On January 4, 2005, Krispy Kreme's board of directors announced that the company's previously issued financial statements for the fiscal year ended February 1, 2004 (FY2004) would be restated to "correct certain errors." The board determined that the adjustments, which principally related to the company's "accounting for the acquisitions of certain franchisees," would reduce pretax income for FY2004 by between $6.2 million and $8.1 million. The company also expected to restate its financial statements for the first and second quarters of FY2005.

Krispy Kreme also said it would delay the filing of its financial reports until the SEC's investigation had been resolved and the company's own internal inquiry was complete. However, the failure of the company to provide its lenders with financial statements by January 14, 2005, could constitute a default under the company's $150-million credit facility. In the event of such a default, Krispy Kreme's banks had the right to terminate the facility and to demand immediate payment for any outstanding amounts. Krispy Kreme's failure to file timely reports also placed the company at risk of having its stock delisted from the New York Stock Exchange (NYSE). By the end of the next day, Krispy Kreme's shares were trading at less than $10 a share.

Most analysts felt that Krispy Kreme's lenders would grant the company a waiver on its credit-facility default, and few felt the company was truly at risk of being delisted from the NYSE. The board's announcement, however, served only to raise more questions about the company. Since August 2003, the company had lost nearly $2.5 billion in its market value of equity. **Exhibit 6** illustrates the stock-price patterns for Krispy Kreme relative to the S&P 500 Composite Index. Were the revelations about the company's franchise accounting practices sufficient to drive that much value out of the stock? Were there deeper issues at Krispy Kreme that deserved scrutiny? **Exhibits 7, 8,** and **9** provide analytical financial ratios for Krispy Kreme and a group of comparable companies in the franchise food-service industry.

EXHIBIT 1 | Income Statements

Income Statement	($US thousands, except per-share amounts)					Three Months Ended		Three Months Ended	
	Jan. 30, 2000	Jan. 28, 2001	Feb. 3, 2002	Feb. 2, 2003	Feb. 1, 2004	May 5, 2003	May 2, 2004	Aug. 3, 2003	Aug. 1, 2004
Total revenues	220,243	300,715	394,354	491,549	665,592	148,660	184,356	159,176	177,448
Operating expenses	190,003	250,690	316,946	381,489	507,396	112,480	141,383	120,573	145,633
General and administrative expenses	14,856	20,061	27,562	28,897	36,912	8,902	10,664	9,060	11,845
Depreciation and amortization expenses	4,546	6,457	7,959	12,271	19,723	4,101	6,130	4,536	6,328
Arbitration award				9,075	(525)	(525)			
Provision for restructuring									
Impairment charges and closing costs							7,543		1,802
Income from operations	10,838	23,507	41,887	59,817	102,086	23,702	18,636	25,007	11,840
Interest income	293	2,325	2,980	1,966	921	227	176	205	226
Interest expense	(1,525)	(607)	(337)	(1,781)	(4,409)	(866)	(1,433)	(997)	(1,366)
Equity loss in joint ventures		(706)	(602)	(2,008)	(1,836)	(694)	(575)	(802)	(399)
Minority interest		(716)	(1,147)	(2,287)	(2,072)	(616)	(126)	(616)	267
Other expense, net		(20)	(235)	(934)	(13)	(25)	(156)	(343)	114
Income before income taxes	9,606	23,783	42,546	54,773	94,677	21,728	16,522	22,454	10,682
Provision for income taxes	3,650	9,058	16,168	21,295	37,590	8,588	6,675	9,014	4,438
Discontinued operations[1]							34,285	439	480
Net income	5,956	14,725	26,378	33,478	57,087	13,140	(24,438)	13,001	5,764
Diluted earnings per share	0.15	0.27	0.45	0.56	0.92	0.22	(0.38)	0.21	0.09
Share price (fiscal year close)		16.22	39.85	30.41	35.64				
Number of shares outstanding (millions)	39.7	54.5	58.6	59.8	62.1	60.7	63.6	62.1	63.4

[1]Resulting from divestiture of Montana Mills.

Source of data: Company filings with the Securities and Exchange Commission (SEC).

EXHIBIT 2 | Balance Sheets

(in thousands)	Fiscal Year Ended					Three Months Ended	
	Jan. 30, 2000	Jan. 28, 2001	Feb. 3, 2002	Feb. 2, 2003	Feb. 1, 2004	May 2, 2004	Aug. 1, 2004
ASSETS							
Current Assets:							
Cash and cash equivalents	3,183	7,026	21,904	32,203	20,300	13,715	19,309
Short-term investments	0	18,103	15,292	22,976			
Accounts receivable	17,965	19,855	26,894	34,373	45,283	47,434	44,329
Accounts receivable, affiliates	1,608	2,599	9,017	11,062	20,482	20,740	19,933
Other receivables	794	2,279	2,771	884	2,363	3,169	4,868
Notes receivable, affiliates	0	0	0	0	458	4,404	5,440
Inventories	9,979	12,031	16,159	24,365	28,573	32,974	33,076
Prepaid expenses	3,148	1,909	2,591	3,478	5,399	4,675	6,749
Income taxes refundable	861		2,534	1,963	7,946	7,449	8,139
Deferred income taxes	3,500	3,809	4,607	9,824	6,453	13,280	20,005
Assets held for sale					36,856	3,374	3,325
Total current assets	**41,038**	**67,611**	**101,769**	**141,128**	**174,113**	**151,214**	**165,173**
Property and equipment, net	60,584	78,340	112,577	202,558	281,103	301,160	297,154
Deferred income taxes	1,398	0	0	0	0		
Long-term investments	0	17,877	12,700	4,344	0		
Long-term notes receivable, affiliates	0	0	0	1,000	7,609	2,988	2,925
Investments in unconsolidated joint ventures		2,827	3,400	6,871	12,426	10,728	9,921
Reacquired franchise rights, goodwill, other intangibles	0	0	16,621	49,354	175,957	176,078	176,045
Other assets	1,938	4,838	8,309	5,232	9,456	12,315	10,390
Total assets	**104,958**	**171,493**	**255,376**	**410,487**	**660,664**	**654,483**	**661,608**

EXHIBIT 2 | Balance Sheets (*continued*)

	Fiscal Year Ended					Three Months Ended	
(in thousands)	Jan. 30, 2000	Jan. 28, 2001	Feb. 3, 2002	Feb. 2, 2003	Feb. 1, 2004	May 2, 2004	Aug. 1, 2004
LIABILITIES AND SHAREHOLDERS' EQUITY							
Current Liabilities:							
Accounts payable	13,106	8,211	12,095	14,055	18,784	18,866	18,817
Book overdraft	0	5,147	9,107	11,375	8,123	12,670	13,107
Accrued expenses	14,080	21,243	26,729	20,981	23,744	27,107	32,249
Arbitration award	0	0	0	9,075	0		
Revolving line of credit	0	3,526	3,871	0	0		
Current maturities of long-term debt	2,400	0	731	3,301	2,842	4,663	5,566
Short-term debt	0	0	0	900	0		
Income taxes payable	0	41	0	0	0		
Total current liabilities	**29,586**	**38,168**	**52,533**	**59,687**	**53,493**	**63,306**	**69,739**
Deferred income taxes	0	579	3,930	9,849	6,374	16,468	25,564
Compensation deferred (unpaid)	990	1,106	0	0	0		
Revolving lines of credit	0	0	0	7,288	87,000	72,000	62,000
Long-term debt, net of current portion	20,502	0	3,912	49,900	48,056	58,469	50,135
Accrued restructuring expenses	4,259	3,109	0	0	0		
Other long-term obligations	1,866	1,735	4,843	5,218	11,211	10,774	12,078
Total long-term liabilities	**27,617**	**6,529**	**12,685**	**72,255**	**152,641**	**157,711**	**149,777**
Minority interest		1,117	2,491	5,193	2,323	2,815	2,593
SHAREHOLDERS' EQUITY:							
Common stock, no par value, 300,000 shares authorized; issued and outstanding		85,060	121,052	173,112	294,477	296,812	299,865
Common stock, 10 par value, 1,000 shares authorized; issued and outstanding	4,670						
Paid-in capital	10,805						
Unearned compensation		(188)	(186)	(119)	(62)	(47)	(31)
Notes receivable, employees	(2,547)	(2,349)	(2,580)	(558)	(383)	(383)	(383)
Nonqualified employee benefit plan assets		(126)	(138)	(339)	(369)	(264)	(264)
Nonqualified employee benefit plan liability		126	138	339	369	264	264
Accumulated other comprehensive income (loss)		609	456	(1,486)	(1,315)	(783)	(768)
Retained earnings	34,827	42,547	68,925	102,403	159,490	135,052	140,816
Total shareholders' equity	**47,755**	**125,679**	**187,667**	**273,352**	**452,207**	**430,651**	**439,499**
Total liabilities and shareholders' equity	**104,958**	**171,493**	**255,376**	**410,487**	**660,664**	**654,483**	**661,608**

Source of data: Company filings with the Securities and Exchange Commission (SEC).

EXHIBIT 3 | Store Growth

Store growth	Jan. 30, 2000	Jan. 28, 2001	Feb. 3, 2002	Feb. 2, 2003	Feb. 1, 2004
Total company factory stores					
Beginning of period	61	58	63	75	99
Stores openings	2	8	7	14	28
Store closings	(5)	(3)	(2)	(3)	(2)
Stores acquired from franchisees	0	0	7	13	16
End of period	58	63	75	99	141
Net change	*(3)*	*5*	*12*	*24*	*42*
% year-over-year growth		*9%*	*19%*	*32%*	*42%*
Total franchised factory stores					
Beginning of period	70	86	111	143	177
Unit openings	19	28	41	49	58
Unit closings	(3)	(3)	(2)	(2)	(3)
Stores transferred to company	0	0	(7)	(13)	(16)
End of period	86	111	143	177	216
Net change	*16*	*25*	*32*	*34*	*39*
% year-over-year growth		*29%*	*29%*	*24%*	*22%*
Total factory stores					
Beginning of period	131	144	174	218	276
Store openings	21	36	48	63	86
Store closings	(8)	(6)	(4)	(5)	(5)
End of period	144	174	218	276	357
Net change	*13*	*30*	*44*	*58*	*81*
% year-over-year growth		*21%*	*25%*	*27%*	*29%*
% of total stores					
Company-owned	40.3%	36.2%	34.4%	35.9%	39.5%
Franchised	59.7%	63.8%	65.6%	64.1%	60.5%

Source of data: Company reports, case writer's analysis.

EXHIBIT 4 | Analysts' Recommendations

Period	Percentage Recommending:		
	Buy	**Sell**	**Hold**
14-Jun-01	80.0%	20.0%	0.0%
19-Jul-01	80.0%	20.0%	0.0%
16-Aug-01	80.0%	20.0%	0.0%
20-Sep-01	80.0%	20.0%	0.0%
18-Oct-01	80.0%	20.0%	0.0%
15-Nov-01	80.0%	20.0%	0.0%
20-Dec-01	80.0%	20.0%	0.0%
17-Jan-02	66.7%	33.3%	0.0%
14-Feb-02	57.1%	28.6%	14.3%
14-Mar-02	71.4%	28.6%	0.0%
18-Apr-02	66.7%	33.3%	0.0%
16-May-02	66.7%	33.3%	0.0%
20-Jun-02	71.4%	28.6%	0.0%
18-Jul-02	71.4%	28.6%	0.0%
15-Aug-02	71.4%	28.6%	0.0%
19-Sep-02	66.7%	33.3%	0.0%
17-Oct-02	57.1%	28.6%	14.3%
14-Nov-02	57.1%	28.6%	14.3%
19-Dec-02	50.0%	12.5%	37.5%
16-Jan-03	50.0%	12.5%	37.5%
20-Feb-03	62.5%	12.5%	25.0%
20-Mar-03	62.5%	12.5%	25.0%
17-Apr-03	62.5%	12.5%	25.0%
15-May-03	55.6%	11.1%	33.3%
19-Jun-03	66.7%	0.0%	33.3%
17-Jul-03	80.0%	0.0%	20.0%
14-Aug-03	83.3%	0.0%	16.7%
18-Sep-03	66.7%	16.7%	16.7%
16-Oct-03	66.7%	16.7%	16.7%
20-Nov-03	66.7%	16.7%	16.7%
18-Dec-03	42.9%	14.3%	42.9%
15-Jan-04	42.9%	14.3%	42.9%
19-Feb-04	28.6%	14.3%	57.1%
18-Mar-04	28.6%	14.3%	57.1%
15-Apr-04	37.5%	25.0%	37.5%
20-May-04	25.0%	25.0%	50.0%
17-Jun-04	25.0%	25.0%	50.0%
15-Jul-04	33.3%	11.1%	55.6%
19-Aug-04	28.6%	28.6%	42.9%
16-Sep-04	25.0%	37.5%	37.5%
14-Oct-04	14.3%	42.9%	42.9%
18-Nov-04	14.3%	42.9%	42.9%
16-Dec-04	14.3%	57.1%	28.6%
20-Jan-05	14.3%	57.1%	28.6%

Source of data: I/B/E/S (Thomson Financial/First Call).

EXHIBIT 5 | Consensus EPS Estimates

Estimate (Mean)	Estimate Date
$ 0.38	2-Jul-01
$ 0.43	24-Aug-01
$ 0.41	25-Oct-01
$ 0.44	16-Nov-01
$ 0.43	21-Dec-01
$ 0.62	8-Mar-02
$ 0.63	24-May-02
$ 0.63	3-Jun-02
$ 0.63	1-Jul-02
$ 0.64	29-Aug-02
$ 0.64	3-Sep-02
$ 0.63	8-Oct-02
$ 0.66	22-Nov-02
$ 0.65	10-Jan-03
$ 0.66	14-Feb-03
$ 0.87	20-Mar-03
$ 0.89	29-May-03
$ 0.90	30-Jul-03
$ 0.90	21-Aug-03
$ 0.91	15-Sep-03
$ 0.91	17-Dec-03
$ 0.92	27-Jan-04
$ 1.17	10-Mar-04
$ 1.00	7-May-04
$ 0.99	26-May-04
$ 0.98	24-Jun-04
$ 0.92	16-Aug-04
$ 0.59	27-Aug-04
$ 0.69	10-Sep-04
$ 0.65	13-Sep-04
$ 0.58	3-Nov-04
$ 0.45	23-Nov-04

Source of data: I/B/E/S (Thomson Financial/First Call).

EXHIBIT 6 | Stock-Price Patterns Relative to the S&P 500 Composite Index

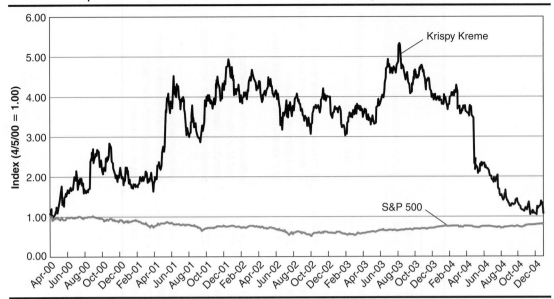

Source of data: Datastream.

EXHIBIT 7 | Analytical Financial Ratios for Krispy Kreme

	Fiscal Year Ended					
	Jan. 30, 2000	Jan. 28, 2001	Feb. 3, 2002	Feb. 2, 2003	Feb. 1, 2004	Ratio definitions
Liquidity ratios						
Quick (acid-test) ratio	1.05	1.46	1.63	1.96	2.72	(current assets-inventories)/curr.liab.
Current ratio	1.39	1.77	1.94	2.36	3.25	current assets/curr.liab.
Leverage ratios						
Debt-to equity (book)	47.96%	0.00%	2.47%	19.46%	11.26%	LT debt/shareholders' equity
Debt-to-capital	32.41%	0.00%	2.41%	16.29%	10.12%	LT debt/(shareholders' equity + debt)
Times interest earned	7.11	38.73	124.29	33.59	23.15	EBIT/interest expense
Assets to equity	2.20	1.36	1.36	1.50	1.46	total assets/shareholders' equity
Activity ratios						
Receivables turnover	10.81	12.16	10.19	10.61	9.70	sales/accounts receivables
Inventory turnover	19.04	20.84	19.61	15.66	17.76	cost of goods sold/inventory
Asset turnover	2.10	1.75	1.54	1.20	1.01	sales/total assets
Cash turnover	69.19	42.80	18.00	15.26	32.79	sales/cash and cash equivalents
Profitability ratios						
Return on assets	5.67%	8.59%	10.33%	8.16%	8.64%	net income/assets
Return on equity	12.47%	11.72%	14.06%	12.25%	12.62%	net income/shareholders' equity
Operating profit margin	4.92%	7.82%	10.62%	12.17%	15.34%	operating income/net sales
Net profit margin	2.70%	4.90%	6.69%	6.81%	8.58%	net income/sales

Source of data: Company filings with the Securities and Exchange Commission (SEC).

EXHIBIT 8 | Analytical Financial Ratios: Quick-Service Restaurants at End of FY2003

Company Name	Checkers	CKE	Domino's	Jack in the Box	Krispy Kreme	McDonald's	Panera Bread	Papa Johns	Sonic	Starbucks	Wendy's	Yum Brands
Sales-net (millions)	$190	$1,413	$1,333	$2,058	$666	$17,141	$356	$917	$447	$4,076	$3,149	$8,380
Liquidity ratios												
Quick ratio	0.96	0.47	0.60	0.23	2.72	0.49	1.34	0.33	0.77	0.76	0.61	0.26
Current ratio	1.42	0.76	0.99	0.63	3.25	0.76	1.58	0.77	0.92	1.52	0.88	0.55
Leverage ratios												
LT debt/equity (%)	33.97	262.97	(131.07)	61.82	11.26	77.97	0.00	38.30	62.53	0.21	39.39	183.57
Long-term debt/total capital(%)	25.36	72.45	421.90	38.20	10.12	43.81	0.00	26.98	38.11	0.21	28.26	64.74
Interest coverage before tax	6.99	(0.09)	2.05	5.44	23.15	6.93	1,014.10	8.93	14.09	nmf	9.25	5.79
Total assets/total equity	1.76	5.29	(0.62)	2.50	1.46	2.13	1.26	2.18	1.83	1.31	1.80	5.02
Activity ratios												
Receivables turnover	65.08	35.15	20.63	71.22	9.70	21.56	32.42	50.29	27.49	38.44	28.42	49.73
Inventory turnover	133.39	59.30	46.88	52.83	17.76	89.84	38.75	44.87	111.24	10.58	79.58	91.32
Total asset turnover	1.50	1.75	3.16	1.84	1.01	0.69	1.64	2.57	1.00	1.62	1.08	1.52
Cash turnover	12.00	38.83	40.90	147.12	32.79	41.64	8.74	110.73	40.31	10.84	17.12	46.04
Profitability ratios												
Return on assets (%)	12.23	(5.92)	8.66	6.26	8.64	5.91	12.46	9.79	10.75	9.83	7.46	11.00
Return on equity (%)	21.55	(31.30)	nmf	15.65	12.62	12.59	15.64	21.33	19.69	12.89	13.42	55.18
EBIT margin (%)	8.24	3.49	13.20	6.94	15.34	19.62	14.02	6.38	23.42	9.48	13.35	12.77
Net profit margin (%)	8.32	(3.24)	2.91	3.58	8.58	8.80	8.61	3.70	11.70	6.58	7.49	7.37

nmf = not a meaningful figure.

Source of data: Standard & Poor's *Research Insight.*

EXHIBIT 8 | Descriptions of Comparable Firms *(continued)*

Checkers Drive-in Restaurants, Inc.: Checkers is the #1 operator of drive-through fast-food restaurants, with more than 780 owned and franchised locations. Nearly 30% of its locations are company-owned.

CKE Restaurants, Inc.: CKE is a leading operator of quick-service food chains, with about 3,100 locations. CKE owns and operates more than a third of its restaurants; the rest are operated by franchisees.

Domino's Pizza, Inc.: Domino's is the world's #2 pizza chain, with more than 7,750 locations in more than 50 countries. Domino's stores are principally delivery locations and generally do not have any dine-in seating.

Jack in the Box Inc.: Jack in the Box operates and franchises over 2,000 of its flagship hamburger outlets in 17 states. More than 1,550 locations are company-owned, while the rest are franchised.

McDonald's Corp.: McDonald's is the world's #1 fast-food company by sales, with more than 31,000 flagship restaurants serving burgers and fries in more than 100 countries. Almost 30% of its locations are company-owned; the others are run by franchisees.

Panera Bread Company: Panera Bread is a leader in the quick-casual restaurant business, with more than 740 bakery cafés in about 35 states. Approximately 70% of its locations are operated by franchisees.

Papa John's International, Inc.: Papa John's is the #3 pizza chain, with 3,000 pizzerias across the United States and in 17 international markets. Papa John's owns and operates about 20% of its locations.

Sonic Corp.: The largest chain of quick-service drive-ins in the United States, Sonic operates about 535 restaurants and franchises more than 2,325 locations in 30 states.

Starbucks Corp.: The world's #1 specialty-coffee retailer, Starbucks operates and licenses more than 8,500 coffee shops in more than 30 countries. In addition, Starbucks markets its coffee through grocery stores, and licenses its brand for other food and beverage products.

Wendy's International, Inc.: Wendy's is the #3 hamburger chain by sales. There are almost 6,700 Wendy's restaurants worldwide; about 78% of them are franchised.

YUM! Brands, Inc.: YUM! Brands is one of the largest fast-food franchisers in the world, trailing only McDonald's in overall sales. It outnumbers the burger giant, however, in store locations, with more than 33,000 units in about 100 countries. (The company owns and operates almost a quarter of its stores and franchises most of the others.) The company's flagship brands include KFC, Pizza Hut, and Taco Bell. Yum! also owns A&W All-American Food Restaurants and Long John Silver's. Its long-term multibranding strategy (offering more than one of its brands at one site) has proven successful.

Source of data: Hoover's, Inc.

EXHIBIT 9 | Common-Sized Financial Statements: Limited-Service Restaurant Averages and Krispy Kreme (KKD)

	2001	2002	2003	KKD 2003
Balance Sheet: Assets (%)				
Cash & equivalents	12.8	12.4	13.7	3.1
Trade receivables (net)	1.6	0.9	1.4	10.4
Inventory	4.0	3.3	3.8	4.3
All other current	2.6	2.6	3.5	8.6
Total current	21.0	19.2	22.4	26.4
Fixed assets (net)	54.7	57.0	55.0	42.5
Intangibles (net)	13.3	14.2	12.6	26.6
All other noncurrent	11.0	9.6	10.0	4.5
Total assets	100.0	100.0	100.0	100.0
Balance Sheet: Liabilities & Equity (%)				
Notes payable, short-term	4.7	5.6	5.8	0.0
Current maturity, long-term debt	6.1	6.0	6.8	0.4
Trade payables	9.2	7.4	9.3	2.8
Income taxes payable	0.2	0.2	0.3	0.0
All other current	13.9	16.9	14.0	4.8
Total current	34.1	36.1	36.4	8.1
Long-term debt	40.2	45.6	41.9	7.3
Deferred taxes	0.1	0.2	0.1	1.0
All other non-current	4.7	8.3	8.7	14.9
Shareholders' equity	20.9	9.9	12.9	68.4
Total liabilities & equity	100.0	100.0	100.0	100.0
Income Statement (%)				
Net sales	100.0	100.0	100.0	100.0
Operating expenses	56.3	55.6	58.1	76.2
Operating profit	4.0	4.7	4.0	15.3
All other expenses (net)	1.3	1.6	1.5	1.1
Profit before taxes	2.7	3.0	2.5	14.2

Source of data: *Annual Statement Studies: 2004–2005*, The Risk Management Association.

The Body Shop International PLC 2001: An Introduction to Financial Modeling

Finance bored the pants off me. I fell asleep more times than not.[1]
　—Anita Roddick, founder,
　The Body Shop International

Roddick, as self-righteous as she is ambitious, professes to be unconcerned [with financial results]. . . . "Our business is about two things: social change and action, and skin care," she snaps. "Social change and action come first. You money-conscious people . . . just don't understand." Well, maybe we don't, but we sure know this: Roddick is one hell of a promoter. . . . She and her husband, Gordon, own shares worth just under $300 million. Now that's social action.[2]

One of our greatest frustrations at The Body Shop is that we're still judged by the media and the City by our profits, by the amount of product we sell, whereas we want and have always wanted to be judged by our actions in the larger world, by the positive difference we make.[3]
　—Anita Roddick

In the late 1990s, The Body Shop International PLC, previously one of the fastest growing manufacturer-retailers in the world, ran aground. Although the firm had an annual revenue growth rate of 20% in the early to middle 1990s, by the late 1990s, revenue growth slowed to around 8%. New retailers of the naturally based skin- and hair-care products entered the market, bringing intense competition for The Body

---

[1]Anita Roddick, *Body and Soul* (London: Ebury Press, 1991), 105.

[2]Jean Sherman Chatzky, "Changing the World," *Forbes* (2 March 1992): 87.

[3]Anita Roddick, *Business as Unusual* (London: Thorsons, 2000), 56.

This case was prepared by Susan Shank and John Vaccaro under the direction of Robert F. Bruner and Robert Conroy. It was written as a basis for class discussion rather than to illustrate effective or ineffective handling of an administrative situation. The financial support of the Batten Institute for case development is gratefully acknowledged. Copyright © 2001 by the University of Virginia Darden School Foundation, Charlottesville, VA. All rights reserved. *To order copies, send an e-mail to sales@dardenbusinesspublishing.com. No part of this publication may be reproduced, stored in a retrieval system, used in a spreadsheet, or transmitted in any form or by any means—electronic, mechanical, photocopying, recording, or otherwise—without the permission of the Darden School Foundation.*

Shop. Amidst the competition, The Body Shop failed to maintain its brand image by becoming something of a mass-market line as it expanded into "almost every mall in America, as well as virtually every corner on Britain's shopping streets."[4]

Anita Roddick, founder of The Body Shop, stepped down as chief executive officer (CEO) in 1998,[5] after numerous unsuccessful attempts to reinvent the company. Patrick Gournay, an executive from the French food giant Danone SA came on board as CEO. However, problems persisted despite the management change. In fiscal year 2001, revenue grew 13%, but pretax profit declined 21%. Gournay said of the results, "This is below our expectations, and we are disappointed with the outcome."[6]

Nonetheless, Gournay was confident that a newly implemented strategy would produce improved results. The strategy consisted of three principal objectives: "To enhance The Body Shop Brand through a focused product strategy and increased investment in stores; to achieve operational efficiencies in our supply chain by reducing product and inventory costs; and to reinforce our stakeholder culture."[7]

Suppose that Anita Roddick, the Shop's founder and cochair of the board of directors, and Patrick Gournay, CEO, came to you in the spring of 2001, looking for assistance in short- and long-term planning for The Body Shop. As a foundation for this work, you will need to estimate The Body Shop's future earnings and financial needs. The challenge of this advisory work should not be underestimated. Anita Roddick is a strong-willed decision-maker with little taste for finance or financial jargon. Your projections must not only be technically correct, but they must also yield practical insights and be straightforward. What you have to say and how you say it are equally important.

If you feel comfortable using **Exhibit 8** to prepare the next three years of financial statements and to demonstrate The Body Shop's debt financing needs, you might be better served by scanning the next few sections on basic financial modeling and concentrating on the last section of the case (Roddick Wants to Know). From experience, however, a vast number of students have found the following exercises to be invaluable in their early understanding of financial modeling.

An Overview of Financial Forecasting

In seeking to respond to Roddick's request, you can draw on at least two classic forecasting methods and a variety of hybrids that use some of each method. The two classic forecasting methods are as follows:

> *T-account forecasting:* This method starts with a base year of financial statements, such as last year's. Entries through double-entry bookkeeping determine how each account will change and what the resulting new balances will be. While

---

[4]Sarah Ellisan, "Body Shop Seeks a Makeover—U.K. Cosmetics Retailer Confirms Sale Talks with Mexico's Grupo Omnilife—A Long and Difficult Fall from Grace," *Wall Street Journal Europe,* 8 June 2001.

[5]Anita Roddick remained on the company's board of directors and, together with her husband Gordon Roddick, served as cochair.

[6]CEO report (The Body Shop International PLC's preliminary results for the 53 weeks to March 3, 2001).

[7]CEO report (3 March 2001).

exactly true to the mechanics of how funds flow through the firm, this method is cumbersome and may require a degree of forecast information about transactions that are unavailable to many analysts outside (and even inside) the firm.

Percentage-of-sales forecasting: This method starts with a forecast of sales and then estimates other financial statement accounts based on some presumed relationship between sales and that account. While simple to execute, this technique is easily misused. For instance, some naive analysts may assume that operational capacity can increase in fractional amounts parallel to increases in sales, but can an airline company really buy only half a jumbo jet? Operational capacity usually increases in lump amounts, rather than in smooth amounts. The lesson here is that when you use this technique, you should scrutinize the percentage-of-sales relationships to make sure they are reasonable.

The most widely used approach is a hybrid of these two. For instance, T-accounts are used to estimate shareholders' equity and fixed assets. Percentage-of-sales is used to estimate income statements, current assets, and current liabilities, because these latter items may credibly vary with sales. Other items will vary as a percentage of accounts other than sales. Tax expense will usually be a percentage of pretax income, while dividends will vary with after-tax income, and depreciation will usually vary with gross fixed assets.

A Pencil-and-Paper Forecast

As an introduction to financial modeling, we will walk through the construction of a forecasted income statement and balance sheet, first with pencil and paper (just visualizing the steps may suffice) and later with a spreadsheet. In either case, you are preparing a pro forma, or projected, income statement and balance sheet for The Body Shop for 2002 (income statement for the entire year and balance sheet for year-end). All values should be in British pounds (GBP). Use the following assumptions as a guide:

Sales:	GBP422.733 million (a 13% increase over 2001)
Cost of goods sold (COGS):	38% of sales
Operating expenses:	50% of sales
Interest expense:	6% of debt (about the current interest rate)
Profit before tax:	Sales − COGS − Depreciation and amortization (D&A) − Interest
Tax:	30% of profit before tax (the going corporate tax rate in Britain)
Dividends:	GBP10.9 million (same as the three previous years)
Earnings retained:	Profit after tax − Dividends
Current assets:	32% of sales
Fixed assets:	GBP110.6 million
Total assets:	Current assets + Fixed assets
Current liabilities:	28% of sales
Debt:	Total assets − Current liabilities + Shareholders' equity
Common equity:	GBP121.6 million + Retentions to earnings

Income statement: Begin with sales, and use it to estimate COGS and operating expenses. For the time being, leave interest expense at zero, since we do not yet know the amount of debt. Estimate profit before tax, tax expense, profit after tax, dividends, and earnings retained.

Balance sheet: Estimate current assets as 32% of sales and add that to GBP110.6 million to get an estimate for total assets. Next, estimate current liabilities as 28% of sales and common equity. Debt becomes the "plug" figure that makes the two sides of the balance sheet balance. This amount is your estimate of the external financing needed by The Body Shop by year-end 2002. Estimate the plug by subtracting the amounts for current liabilities and common equity from total assets.

Iterate: Initially, you entered an interest expense of zero on the income statement, but this cannot be correct if debt is outstanding or if excess cash is invested in interest-earning instruments. This is a classic finance problem arising from the income statement and balance sheet's dependence on each other. Interest expense is necessary to estimate retained earnings, which is necessary to estimate debt. Let's call this the problem of circularity. The way to deal with this problem is to insert your best estimate of interest expense in the income statement (using 6% × debt), then to re-estimate the plug figure, then re-estimate interest expense, and so on. By iterating through the two statements five or six times, you will come to estimates of interest expense and debt that do not change very much. Stop iterating when changes become small.

A Spreadsheet Model Forecast

Fortunately, the tedium of iterating can be eliminated with the aid of a computer and spreadsheet software such as Microsoft Excel. The specific commands reviewed here relate to Excel 2000. (These commands will appear in table form within the text.) The adaptation to other spreadsheet programs should be straightforward. Now, try the same forecast for The Body Shop using a computer spreadsheet.

Setup: Start with a clean spreadsheet. Set the recalculation mode to MANUAL so that the model will iterate only when you press CALC (F9). Also, set the number of iterations to **1** so that you will be able to see Excel re-estimate the plug figure and interest expense. You can set the number of iterations higher (Excel's default is 100), but Excel will converge on a solution after five or six iterations, so a setting of **1** is best to see the iterations in action. The commands are listed in **Table 1.**

TABLE 1 | Excel Spreadsheet Commands

Choose the <**Tools**> menu and then the <**Options**> menu item. Next, choose the <**Calculations**> tab; select the button next to <**Manual**>, and enter **1** in <**Maximum Iterations**>. Be sure the box next to <**Iterations**> is checked.

Saving: As you develop your model, be sure to save it every five minutes or so, just in case.

Format: Use the format in **Exhibit 1** as a guide to plan your worksheet. To facilitate sensitivity analysis, it is generally best to place the Input Data at the top of the worksheet. Next, develop the income statement just as you did on pencil and paper. Use **Exhibit 2** as your guide. Be sure to tie the cells to the proper percentage rate in the Input Data section. The first time through, enter **0** for the interest. (This is very important for the iteration to work properly.) We will return to it later.

Now do the balance sheet. Again, be sure to tie the balance sheet together by formulas. With the basic format laid out, go back and enter the formula to calculate interest as "Interest rate $\times$ Debt." Press the (F9) key, and you should see the worksheet change. You should be able to press the (F9) key several more times until the numbers stop changing, which means the model has converged to a solution. You should have interest as exactly 6% of long-term liabilities and a balance sheet that balances.

Once you have seen how this works, you may want to have the model converge without having to press <CALC> several times. In order to do that, you must set the number of iterations you wish the spreadsheet to perform. Set the number of iterations back to **100** (Excel's default), and allow the computer to recalculate automatically. See the Excel commands listed in **Table 2.**

TABLE 2 | Excel Spreadsheet Commands

Choose the <**Tools**> menu, and then the <**Options**> menu item. Next, choose the <**Calculations**> tab; click on <**Automatic**>, and enter **100** in <**Maximum Iterations**>. Be sure the box next to <**Iterations**> is checked.

Note: Changing your iterations setting, combined with the circularity of the debt plug and interest expense (later we'll add the circularity of data tables), can lead to some confusing situations. It is easy to forget where you have your iterations set (more data tables lead to more circularity). When comparing your work to someone else's, be sure that both of you have the same iterations setting and have hit (F9) the same number of times (be sure you either have no data tables or the same data tables). Your worksheet should now look like **Exhibit 3.**

Projecting Farther

So far, you have managed to project The Body Shop's financial statements through 2002. Now, extend your projection to years 2003 and 2004. See **Table 3** for Excel commands. A simple way to do this is to copy your model for two additional years. Before copying the formulas from column B to columns C and D, make sure that any references to your Input Data (cells B3 through B12) are absolute references as opposed to relative references. An absolute reference means that when you copy cells B16 through B35 to other parts of your spreadsheet, the cells are still linked back to the originals (i.e., B5). Otherwise, the program assumes that the cells should be linked to new cells, such as C5. To make a reference absolute, put in dollar signs— B3, instead of B3. Now you should be ready to copy:

TABLE 3 | Excel Spreadsheet Commands

Select the range of your data by highlighting it in the worksheet. Choose the <**Edit**> menu and then the <**Copy**> menu item. Highlight the cells where you want the copy to go. Choose the <**Edit**> menu and then the <**Paste**> menu item.

Note that you will have to change the equity formula for 2003 and 2004. For 2003, make the formula equal to 2002's equity plus 2003's additions to retained earnings. In addition, you should make sales grow by compounding. To do that, take 2002's sales × 2003's expected sales growth rate (say 13%). As you enter those changes, you should see the effect ripple through your model.

When Debt is Negative

Now modify the model to deal with the situation where the plug for debt is negative—this can happen routinely for firms with seasonal or cyclical sales patterns. Negative debt can be interpreted as excess cash. However, this is an odd way to show cash. A nonfinancial manager (like Anita Roddick) might not appreciate this type of presentation. The solution is to add a line for excess cash on the assets' side of the balance sheet and then to set up three new lines below the last entry in the balance sheet.

Name	Formula
Trial assets	Current assets + Fixed assets
Trial liabilities and equity	Current liabilities + equity
Plug	Trial assets − Trial liabilities

Now enter the formula for excess cash:

$$=IF(PLUG<0,-PLUG,0)$$

Instead of the word plug, you should use the cell address for the actual plug number. The formula for debt is the following.

$$=IF(PLUG>0,+PLUG,0)$$

See **Exhibit 4** for an example of how your spreadsheet should look. To see how these modifications really work, change your COGS/SALES assumption to 0.45 and press (F9).

With excess cash, you should generate interest income instead of interest expense. In the event of an excess cash balance, to have your model treat interest as income rather than expense, you need to modify your interest expense formula as follows.

$$= +(B6*B34)-(B6*B28)$$

An example of the finished results appears in **Exhibit 5.**

Explore Sensitivities

After your model replicates the exhibit, you are ready to conduct a sensitivity analysis on the pro forma years by seeing how variations in the forecast assumptions will affect the financing requirements. A financial analyst might want to try the following variations, or more than one in combination.

- Suppose sales in 2002 will be GBP500 million.
- Suppose COGS runs at 45% of sales.
- Suppose dividends are increased to 60% of net income.
- Suppose The Body Shop must double its manufacturing capacity by adding a new GBP100-million facility in 2002.
- Assume inventories run higher than expected (model this by increasing current assets to 40% of sales).
- Assume that accounts receivable collections improve so that current assets run at 28% of sales.
- Assume that operating expenses increase faster than sales.

What happens to the plug value (i.e., debt) under these different circumstances? In general, which assumptions in the Input Data section of your spreadsheet seem to have the biggest effect on future borrowing needs?

The data table is an invaluable tool for conducting a sensitivity analysis. It automatically calculates debt, or whatever else you want it to focus on, as it varies across different values for a particular assumption—for instance, growth rates. In Excel, you can create a data table using a two-step process illustrated in the following examples. Suppose you want to estimate The Body Shop's debt required and excess cash generated at COGS/SALES ratios of 0.35, 0.38, 0.40, 0.42, 0.44, 0.45, and 0.48.

1. **Set up the table.** Move to a clean part of the spreadsheet and type the COGS/SALES ratios (0.35, 0.38, 0.40, 0.42, 0.44, 0.45, and 0.48) in a column. At the top of the next column (one row above your first COGS/SALES ratio), enter the location of the value to be estimated, in this case, debt, or =B34. In the next column, type the cell location for excess cash, =B28. Your data table should be formatted as shown in **Exhibit 6.**

2. **Enter the data table commands. Table 4** gives the commands for setting up the data table.

TABLE 4 | Excel Spreadsheet Commands

Highlight the cells that contain your COGS/SALES ratios and your cell references to Debt and Excess Cash. The cells to the right of your COGS/SALES ratios and below your cell references to Debt and Excess Cash are the cells to be filled in and should also be highlighted.

Choose the <**Data**> menu and then the <**Table**> menu item.

In the <**Column Input Cell**> box, enter the cell where your COGS/SALES assumption is B4. The computer will fill in the table.

The additional circularity brought about by data tables can lead to some confusing results. To avoid this, be sure at this point to set the number of iterations to *at least* **10.** The result should look like **Exhibit 7.**

The data table in **Exhibit 7** reveals that at COGS/SALES ratios of 45%, the firm will need to borrow. This should trigger questions in your mind about what might cause that to happen, such as a price war or a surge in materials costs. Your spreadsheet format can tell you about some more sophisticated data-table formats. No financial analyst can afford to ignore that valuable tool. Armed with that tool, it is easy to go back and try the variations in other input assumptions listed previously.

Note: Remember that data tables add more calculations that need to be iterated in your worksheet. When comparing your work to that of a fellow student, make certain that your iterations are set the same and that you have roughly the same data tables in your files.

Roddick Wants to Know

Now that you have completed a simplified forecast, prepare a forecast based on the full range of accounts as actually reported by The Body Shop in 2001. **Exhibit 8** presents the results for the past three years. Please forecast all of the accounts individually for the next three years. You will see many familiar accounts, as well as some unusual accounts like minority interests.

For most accounts, you should extrapolate by using the same percentage of sales borne out by the preceding years' experience. You might use an average of the three historical years. You might want to use only the most recent year, or if you notice a significant upward or downward trend in an account, try growing or shrinking the percentage in the future years, according to your judgment. Whatever assumptions you decide upon, you should again isolate them at the top of your worksheet, so you can easily change an assumption and then have it flow through your worksheet. Additionally, this is very important for calculating sensitivities later, as you want to be able to point to one cell as the Column Input Cell in a data table.

Make overdrafts the plug figure and base interest expense (at 6%) on the overdrafts, current portion of long-term debt, and long-term liabilities. If you skipped to this section without doing the exercise above, you may differ from your fellow students in your treatment of the case where debt is negative.

Make your own assumptions regarding sales growth. Make other assumptions as needed. Be prepared to report to Roddick your answers to these questions.

1. How did you derive your forecast? Why did you choose the base case assumptions that you did?

2. Based on your pro forma projections, how much additional financing will The Body Shop need during this period?

3. What are the three or four most important assumptions or key drivers in this forecast? What is the effect on the financing need of varying each of these assumptions up or down from the base case? Intuitively, why are these assumptions so important?

4. Why are your findings relevant to a general manager like Roddick? What are the implications of these findings for her? What action should she take based on your analysis?

In discussing your analysis with Roddick, do not permit yourself to get mired in forecast technicalities or financial jargon. Focus your comments on your results. State them as simply and intuitively as you can. Do not be satisfied with simply presenting results. Link your findings to recommendations, such as key factors to manage, opportunities to enhance results, and issues warranting careful analysis. Remember that Roddick plainly admits she finds finance boring. Whenever possible, try to express your analysis in terms that she finds interesting, including people, customers, quality of natural products, and the health and dynamism of her business. Good luck!

EXHIBIT 1 | Format for Developing a Spreadsheet Model

	A	B
1	Input Data	
2		
3	SALES	422,733
4	COGS/SALES	0.38
5	OPERATING EXPENSES/SALES	0.50
6	INTEREST RATE	0.06
7	TAX RATE	0.30
8	DIVIDENDS (Thousand pounds)	10,900
9	CURR. ASSETS/SALES	0.32
10	CURR. LIABS./SALES	0.28
11	FIXED ASSETS	110,600
12	STARTING EQUITY	121,600
13		
14	INCOME STATEMENT	2002
15		
16	SALES	
17	COGS	
18	OPERATING EXPENSES	
19	INTEREST EXPENSE (INCOME)	
20	PROFIT BEFORE TAX	
21	TAX	
22	PROFIT AFTER TAX	
23	DIVIDENDS	
24	EARNINGS RETAINED	
25		
26	BALANCE SHEET	2002
27		
28	CURRENT ASSETS	
29	FIXED ASSETS	
30	TOTAL ASSETS	
31		
32	CURRENT LIABILITIES	
33	DEBT	
34	EQUITY	
35	TOTAL LIAB. & NET WORTH	

Case 9   The Body Shop International PLC 2001: An Introduction to Financial Modeling **153**

EXHIBIT 2 | Spreadsheet Formulas to Forecast 2002 Financials

	A	B
1	Input Data	
2		
3	SALES	422,733
4	COGS/SALES	0.38
5	OPERATING EXPENSES/SALES	0.50
6	INTEREST RATE	0.06
7	TAX RATE	0.30
8	DIVIDENDS (Thousand pounds)	10,900
9	CURR. ASSETS/SALES	0.32
10	CURR. LIABS./SALES	0.28
11	FIXED ASSETS	110,600
12	STARTING EQUITY	121,600
13		
14	INCOME STATEMENT	2002
15		
16	SALES	+B3
17	COGS	+B4*B16
18	OPERATING EXPENSES	+B5*B16
19	INTEREST EXPENSE (INCOME)	+B6*B33
20	PROFIT BEFORE TAX	+B16-B17-B18-B19
21	TAX	+B7*B20
22	PROFIT AFTER TAX	+B20-B21
23	DIVIDENDS	+B8
24	EARNINGS RETAINED	+B22-B23
25		
26	BALANCE SHEET	2002
27		
28	CURRENT ASSETS	+B9*B16
29	FIXED ASSETS	+B11
30	TOTAL ASSETS	+B28+B29
31		
32	CURRENT LIABILITIES	+B10*B16
33	DEBT	+B30-B32-B34
34	EQUITY	+B12+B24
35	TOTAL LIAB. & NET WORTH	+B32+B33+B34

EXHIBIT 3 | Basic Forecasting Results for 2002

	A	B
1	Input Data	
2		
3	SALES	422,733
4	COGS/SALES	0.38
5	OPERATING EXPENSES/SALES	0.50
6	INTEREST RATE	0.06
7	TAX RATE	0.30
8	DIVIDENDS (Thousand pounds)	10,900
9	CURR. ASSETS/SALES	0.32
10	CURR. LIABS./SALES	0.28
11	FIXED ASSETS	110,600
12	STARTING EQUITY	121,600
13		
14	INCOME STATEMENT	2002
15		
16	SALES	422,733
17	COGS	160,639
18	OPERATING EXPENSES	211,367
19	INTEREST EXPENSE (INCOME)	(1,171)
20	PROFIT BEFORE TAX	51,899
21	TAX	15,570
22	PROFIT AFTER TAX	36,329
23	DIVIDENDS	10,900
24	EARNINGS RETAINED	25,429
25		
26	BALANCE SHEET	2002
27		
28	CURRENT ASSETS	135,275
29	FIXED ASSETS	110,600
30	TOTAL ASSETS	245,875
31		
32	CURRENT LIABILITIES	118,365
33	DEBT	(19,520)
34	EQUITY	147,029
35	TOTAL LIAB. & NET WORTH	245,875

EXHIBIT 4 | Adjusting to Reflect Excess Cash

	A	B
1	Input Data	
2		
3	SALES	422,733
4	COGS/SALES	0.38
5	OPERATING EXPENSES/SALES	0.50
6	INTEREST RATE	0.06
7	TAX RATE	0.30
8	DIVIDENDS (Thousand pounds)	10,900
9	CURR. ASSETS/SALES	0.32
10	CURR. LIABS./SALES	0.28
11	FIXED ASSETS	110,600
12	STARTING EQUITY	121,600
13		
14	INCOME STATEMENT	2002
15		
16	SALES	422,733
17	COGS	160,639
18	OPERATING EXPENSES	211,367
19	INTEREST EXPENSE (INCOME)	+(B6*B34)-(B6*B28)
20	PROFIT BEFORE TAX	40,706
21	TAX	14,247
22	PROFIT AFTER TAX	26,459
23	DIVIDENDS	10,900
24	EARNINGS RETAINED	15,559
25		
26	BALANCE SHEET	2002
27		
28	EXCESS CASH	=IF(B40<0,-B40,0)
29	CURRENT ASSETS	135,275
30	FIXED ASSETS	110,600
31	TOTAL ASSETS	+B29+B30+B28
32		
33	CURRENT LIABILITIES	118,365
34	DEBT	=IF(B40>0,+B40,0)
35	EQUITY	137,159
36	TOTAL LIAB. & NET WORTH	+B33+B34+B35
37		
38	TRIAL ASSETS	+B29+B30
39	TRIAL LIABILITIES AND EQUITY	+B33+B35
40	PLUG: DEBT (EXCESS CASH)	+B38−B39

EXHIBIT 5 | Finished Results for 2002 Reflecting Excess Cash

	A	B
1	Input Data	
2		
3	SALES	422,733
4	COGS/SALES	0.38
5	OPERATING EXPENSES/SALES	0.50
6	INTEREST RATE	0.06
7	TAX RATE	0.30
8	DIVIDENDS (Thousand pounds)	10,900
9	CURR. ASSETS/SALES	0.32
10	CURR. LIABS./SALES	0.28
11	FIXED ASSETS	110,600
12	STARTING EQUITY	121,600
13		
14	INCOME STATEMENT	2002
15		
16	SALES	422,733
17	COGS	160,639
18	OPERATING EXPENSES	211,367
19	INTEREST EXPENSE (INCOME)	(1,171)
20	PROFIT BEFORE TAX	51,899
21	TAX	15,570
22	PROFIT AFTER TAX	36,329
23	DIVIDENDS	10,900
24	EARNINGS RETAINED	25,429
25		
26	BALANCE SHEET	2002
27		
28	EXCESS CASH	19,520
29	CURRENT ASSETS	135,275
30	FIXED ASSETS	110,600
31	TOTAL ASSETS	265,395
32		
33	CURRENT LIABILITIES	118,365
34	DEBT	0
35	EQUITY	147,029
36	TOTAL LIAB. & NET WORTH	265,395
37		
38	TRIAL ASSETS	245,875
39	TRIAL LIABILITIES AND EQUITY	265,395
40	PLUG: DEBT (EXCESS CASH)	(19,520)

EXHIBIT 6 | Setup for a Forecast with Data Table

	A	B	C	D	E	F
1	Input Data					
2						
3	SALES	422,733				
4	COGS/SALES	0.38				
5	OPERATING EXPENSES/SALES	0.50		Sensitivity Analysis		
6	INTEREST RATE	0.06		Of Debt and Excess Cash		
7	TAX RATE	0.30		To COGS/SALES Ratio		
8	DIVIDENDS (Thousand pounds)	10,900				
9	CURR. ASSETS/SALES	0.32		COGS/SALES	DEBT	Ex. CASH
10	CURR. LIABS./SALES	0.28			=B34	=B28
11	FIXED ASSETS	110,600		0.35		
12	STARTING EQUITY	121,600		0.38		
13				0.40		
14	INCOME STATEMENT	2002		0.42		
15				0.44		
16	SALES	422,733		0.45		
17	COGS	160,639		0.48		
18	OPERATING EXPENSES	211,367				
19	INTEREST EXPENSE (INCOME)	(1,171)				
20	PROFIT BEFORE TAX	51,899				
21	TAX	15,570				
22	PROFIT AFTER TAX	36,329				
23	DIVIDENDS	10,900				
24	EARNINGS RETAINED	25,429				
25						
26	BALANCE SHEET	2002				
27						
28	EXCESS CASH	19,520				
29	CURRENT ASSETS	135,275				
30	FIXED ASSETS	110,600				
31	TOTAL ASSETS	265,395				
32						
33	CURRENT LIABILITIES	118,365				
34	DEBT	-				
35	EQUITY	147,029				
36	TOTAL LIAB. & NET WORTH	265,395				
37						
38	TRIAL ASSETS	245,875				
39	TRIAL LIABILITIES AND EQUITY	265,395				
40	PLUG: DEBT (EXCESS CASH)	(19,520)				

EXHIBIT 7 | Finished Forecast with Data Table

	A	B	C	D	E	F
1	Input Data					
2						
3	SALES	422,733				
4	COGS/SALES	0.38				
5	OPERATING EXPENSES/SALES	0.50		Sensitivity Analysis		
6	INTEREST RATE	0.06		Debt and Excess Cash		
7	TAX RATE	0.30		By COGS/SALES		
8	DIVIDENDS (Thousand pounds)	10,900.00		COGS/SALES	DEBT	Ex. CASH
9	CURR. ASSETS/SALES	0.32			+B34	+B28
10	CURR. LIABS./SALES	0.28		0.35	0	28,787
11	FIXED ASSETS	110,600		0.38	0	19,520
12	STARTING EQUITY	121,600		0.40	0	13,342
13				0.42	0	7,165
14	INCOME STATEMENT	2002		0.44	0	987
15				0.45	2,102	0
16	SALES	422,733		0.48	11,369	0
17	COGS	160,639				
18	OPERATING EXPENSES	211,367				
19	INTEREST EXPENSE (INCOME)	(1,171)				
20	PROFIT BEFORE TAX	51,899				
21	TAX	15,570				
22	PROFIT AFTER TAX	36,329				
23	DIVIDENDS	10,900				
24	EARNINGS RETAINED	25,429				
25						
26	BALANCE SHEET	2002				
27						
28	EXCESS CASH	19,520				
29	CURRENT ASSETS	135,275				
30	FIXED ASSETS	110,600				
31	TOTAL ASSETS	265,395				
32						
33	CURRENT LIABILITIES	118,365				
34	DEBT	0				
35	EQUITY	147,029				
36	TOTAL LIAB. & NET WORTH	265,395				
37						
38	TRIAL ASSETS	245,875				
39	TRIAL LIABILITIES AND EQUITY	265,395				
40	PLUG: DEBT (EXCESS CASH)	(19,520)				

EXHIBIT 8 | Historical Financial Statements (GBP in millions)

	Fiscal Year Ended February 28					
	1999 (GBP)	1999 (% sales)	2000 (GBP)	2000 (% sales)	2001 (GBP)	2001 (% sales)
Income Statement						
Turnover	303.7	100.0	330.1	100.0	374.1	100.0
Cost of sales	127.7	42.0	130.9	39.7	149.0	39.8
Gross profit	176.0	58.0	199.2	60.3	225.1	60.2
Operating expenses:						
– excluding exceptional costs	151.4	49.9	166.2	50.3	195.7	52.3
– exceptional costs[1]	4.5	1.5	0.0	0.0	11.2	3.0
Restructuring costs[2]	16.6	5.5	2.7	0.8	1.0	0.3
Net interest expense	0.1	0.0	1.5	0.5	4.4	1.2
Profit before tax	3.4	1.1	28.8	8.7	12.8	3.4
Tax expense	8.0	2.6	10.4	3.2	3.5	0.9
Profit (loss) after tax	(4.6)	(1.5)	18.4	5.6	9.3	2.5
Ordinary dividends	10.9	3.6	10.9	3.3	10.9	2.9
Profit (loss) retained	(15.5)	(5.1)	7.5	2.3	(1.6)	(0.4)

EXHIBIT 8 | Historical Financial Statements (GBP in millions) (*continued*)

	Fiscal Year Ended February 28					
	1999 (GBP)	1999 (% sales)	2000 (GBP)	2000 (% sales)	2001 (GBP)	2001 (% sales)
Balance Sheet						
Assets						
Cash	34.0	11.2	19.2	5.8	13.7	3.7
Accounts receivable	27.8	9.2	30.3	9.2	30.3	8.1
Inventories	38.6	12.7	44.7	13.5	51.3	13.7
Other current assets	12.5	4.1	15.6	4.7	17.5	4.7
Net fixed assets	87.8	28.9	104.7	31.7	110.6	29.6
Other assets[3]	0.0	0.0	6.0	1.8	6.7	1.8
Total assets	200.7	66.1	220.5	66.8	230.1	61.5
Liabilities and equity						
Accounts payable	13.0	4.3	20.5	6.2	10.7	2.9
Taxes payable	11.3	3.7	11.7	3.5	7.1	1.9
Accruals	10.8	3.6	15.6	4.7	11.5	3.1
Overdrafts	0.0	0.0	0.3	0.1	0.7	0.2
Other current liabilities	21.6	7.1	13.3	4.0	16.9	4.5
Long-term liabilities	28.0	9.2	36.7	11.1	61.2	16.4
Other liabilities[4]	1.7	0.6	1.0	0.3	0.4	0.1
Shareholders' equity	114.3	37.6	121.4	36.8	121.6	32.5
Total liabilities and equity	200.7	66.1	220.5	66.8	230.1	61.5

[1]Exceptional costs in 2001 included redundancy costs ($4.6 million), costs of supply chain development ($2.4 million) and impairment of fixed assets and goodwill ($4.2 million). The exceptional costs of $4.5 million in 1999 were associated with closing unprofitable shops and an impairment review of the remaining shops in the United States.

[2]Restructuring costs in 2001 and 2000 relate to the sale of manufacturing plants in Littlehampton, England, and to associated reorganization costs. Restructuring costs in 1999 arose from the realignment of the management structure of the business in the United States and the United Kingdom.

[3]Other assets in 2001 and 2000 represented receivables related to the sale of the company's Littlehampton manufacturing plant.

[4]Other liabilities included mostly deferred taxes.

Value Line Publishing, October 2002

Competition between the two major players in the industry, Home Depot and Lowe's, has been heating up, especially now that they are operating in more of the same markets. Both companies are seeking new, but similar, ways to boost both their top and bottom lines, including initiatives aimed at bettering customer service, attracting professional customers, and creating a more favorable merchandise mix. Still, despite the growing competition between them, over the long term, we believe both companies are poised to benefit from additional market share freed up in this consolidating industry.

—**Carrie Galeotafiore**
Value Line analyst, July 2002

Slow but positive economic growth, low interest rates, a strong housing market, rising unemployment, uncertain consumer confidence, and concern over corporate misdeeds—such was the economic environment in early October 2002. Carrie Galeotafiore had followed the retail building-supply industry for nearly three years as an analyst for the investment-survey firm Value Line Publishing. Next week, Value Line would publish her quarterly report on the industry, including her five-year financial forecast for industry leaders Home Depot and Lowe's.

The Retail Building-Supply Industry

The Economist Intelligence Unit (EIU) estimated the size of the 2001 U.S. retail building- supply industry at $175 billion. The industry was traditionally divided among three retail formats: hardware stores, with 15% of sales; lumberyards, with 34% of sales; and the larger-format home centers, with 51% of sales. Annual growth

This case was prepared by Professor Michael J. Schill, with research assistance from Aimee Connolly and the cooperation of Carrie Galeotafiore of Value Line Publishing. It was written as a basis for class discussion rather than to illustrate effective or ineffective handling of an administrative situation. Copyright © 2003 by the University of Virginia Darden School Foundation, Charlottesville, VA. All rights reserved. *To order copies, send an e-mail to* sales@dardenbusinesspublishing.com. *No part of this publication may be reproduced, stored in a retrieval system, used in a spreadsheet, or transmitted in any form or by any means—electronic, mechanical, photocopying, recording, or otherwise—without the permission of the Darden School Foundation.* Rev. 11/07.

had declined from 7.7% in 1998 to 4.2% in 2001, yet was arguably still high considering the recessionary nature of the economic environment in 2001. Low interest rates and a robust housing-construction market provided ongoing strength to the industry. The EIU expected the industry to reach $194 billion by 2006. **Exhibit 1** provides the details of the EIU's forecast.

The industry was dominated by two companies: Home Depot and Lowe's. Together, the two players captured more than a third of the total industry sales. Both companies were viewed as fierce competitors whose rapid-expansion strategies had more than doubled own-store capacity in the past five years with the opening of 1,136 new stores. The penetration by the large Lowe's/Home Depot warehouse-format stores had had a profound impact on the industry. Independent hardware retailers were struggling to remain competitive. Some hardware stores had shifted their locations to high-rent shopping centers to attract more people or remained open for longer hours. Some of the smaller players were protected by segmentations in the market between the professional market that remained loyal to the lumberyards and do-it-yourself customers who were attracted to the discount chains. **Exhibit 2** provides selected company data and presents recent stock-market performances for the two companies.

Future Growth Opportunities for Home Depot and Lowe's

Galeotafiore expected that future growth for Home Depot and Lowe's would come from a variety of sources.

Acquisition/Consolidation

The industry had already experienced a substantial amount of consolidation. In 1999, Lowe's had acquired the 38-store, warehouse-format chain Eagle Hardware in a $1.3-billion transaction. In the past few years, Home Depot had acquired the plumbing wholesale distributor Apex Supply, the specialty-lighting company Georgia Lighting, the building-repair-and-replacement-products business N-E Thing Supply Company, and the specialty-plumbing-fixtures company Your "Other" Warehouse. Just last week, Home Depot had announced the purchase of three flooring companies that "when completed would instantly make Home Depot the largest turnkey supplier of flooring to the residential construction market."[1]

Professional Market

Both Home Depot and Lowe's had recently implemented important initiatives to attract professional customers more effectively, including stocking merchandise in larger quantities, training employees to deal with professionals, and carrying professional brands. Home Depot had developed Home Depot Supply and the "Pro Stores" to reach out to the small-professional market. The company was also on track to install professional-specific desks at 950 stores by the end of 2002.

---

[1]Press Release, Home Depot, 24 September 2002.

International Expansion

Home Depot had already developed some international presence with its acquisition of the Canadian home-improvement retailer Aikenhead in 1994, and it continued to expand its reach in that market with 11 new-store openings in 2001. More recently, the company had targeted the $12.5-billion home-improvement market in Mexico by acquiring the Mexican chains TotalHOME and Del Norte. By the end of 2001, 10% of Home Depot's stores were located outside the United States. In 2002, Lowe's did not yet have an international presence.

Alternative Retail Formats

Home Depot and Lowe's both maintained online stores. Lowe's specifically targeted the professional customer with a section of its Web site: "Accent & Style" offered decorating and design tips on such subjects as kitchens and baths. Home Depot was developing new retail formats for urban centers, showcased by its recently opened Brooklyn store, which offered convenient shopping to densely populated markets. These "urban" stores provided Home Depot products and services in a compact format. The acquisition of EXPO Design Centers provided an additional format for Home Depot and expansion beyond the traditional hardware and building-supply retailer. EXPO Design Centers were a one-stop design and decorating source, with eight showrooms in one location, highlighting kitchens, baths, carpets and rugs, lighting, patio and grills, tile and wood, window treatments, and appliances. Lowe's published *Creative Ideas, Garden Club,* and *Woodworker's Club* magazines to target customers with certain hobbies.

Alternative Products

Both Home Depot and Lowe's were expanding into installation services. The "at-home" business for Home Depot was currently at $3 billion. Home Depot expected its at-home business to grow at an annual rate of 30% in the near term.

Head-to-Head Competition

Home Depot had traditionally focused on large metropolitan areas, while Lowe's had concentrated on rural areas. To maintain its growth trajectory, Lowe's had begun systematic expansion into metropolitan markets. The investment community was becoming increasingly concerned about the eventuality of increased price competition. Aram Rubinson, of Bank of America Securities, had reported in August, "Since Lowe's comps [comparable store sales] have been outpacing Home Depot's, we have been growing increasingly concerned that Home Depot would fight back with increased promotions and more aggressive everyday pricing."

Financial Forecast for Home Depot and Lowe's

Home Depot's new CEO, Bob Nardelli, had expressed his intention to focus on enhancing store efficiency and inventory turnover through ongoing system investments. He expected to generate margin improvement through cost declines from product reviews, purchasing improvements, and an increase in the number of tool-rental centers. Recently, operating costs had increased owing to higher occupancy costs for new stores and increased energy costs. Home Depot had come under criticism for its declining customer service. Nardelli hoped to counter this trend with an initiative to help employees focus on customers during store hours and restocking shelves only after hours. Home Depot management expected revenue growth to be 15% to 18% through 2004. Some of the growth would be by acquisition, which necessitated the company's maintaining higher cash levels. Home Depot stock was trading at around $25 a share, implying a total equity capitalization of $59 billion.

Galeotafiore had been cautiously optimistic about the changes at Home Depot in her July report:

> Though the program [Service Performance Improvement] is still in the early stages, the do-it-yourself giant has already enjoyed labor productivity benefits, and received positive feedback from customers. . . . The Pro-Initiative program, which is currently in place at roughly 55% of Home Depot's stores, is aimed at providing services that accommodate the pro customer. Stores that provide these added services have generally outperformed strictly do-it-yourself units in productivity, operating margins, and inventory turnover. Home Depot shares offer compelling price-appreciation potential over the coming 3-to-5-year pull.

Other analysts did not seem to share her enthusiasm for Home Depot. Dan Wewer and Lisa Estabrooks observed,

> Home Depot's comp sales fell short of plan despite a step-up in promotional activity. In our view, this legitimizes our concerns that Home Depot is seeing diminishing returns from promotional efforts. . . . Our view that Lowe's is the most attractive investment opportunity in hard-line retailing is supported by key mileposts achieved during 2Q'02. Highlights include superior relative EPS momentum, robust comp sales, expanding operating margin, improving capital efficiency, and impressive new-store productivity. Importantly, Lowe's outstanding performance raises the hurdle Home Depot must reach if it is to return to favor with the investment community.[2]

Lowe's management had told analysts that it expected to maintain sales growth of 18% to 19% over the next two years. Lowe's planned to open 123 stores in 2002, 130 stores in 2003, and 140 stores in 2004, and to continue its emphasis on cities with populations greater than 500,000, such as New York, Boston, and Los Angeles. To date, the company's entry into metropolitan markets appeared to be successful. Lowe's planned to continue improving sales and margins through new merchandising, pricing strategies, and market-share gains, especially in the Northeast and West.[3] Lowe's stock was trading at around $37 a share, implying a total equity capitalization of $29 billion.

Donald Trott, an analyst at Jefferies, had recently downgraded Lowe's based on a forecast of a deflating housing-market bubble and a view that the company's stock

[2]Dan Wewer and Lisa Estabrooks, CIBC World Markets, 20 August 2002.
[3]Bear Stearns, 20 August 2002.

price was richly priced relative to Home Depot's. Galeotafiore countered that Lowe's had now shown that it could compete effectively with Home Depot. She justified the Lowe's valuation with an expectation of ongoing improvement in sales and gross margins.

> Lowe's is gaining market share in the appliance category, and its transition into major metropolitan areas (which will likely comprise the bulk of the company's expansion in the next years) is yielding solid results. Alongside the positive sales trends, the homebuilding supplier's bottom line is also being boosted by margin expansion, bolstered, in part, by lower inventory costs and product-mix improvements.

Galeotafiore's financial forecast for Home Depot and Lowe's would go to print next week. She based her forecasts on a review of historical performance, an analysis of trends and ongoing changes in the industry and the macroeconomy, and a detailed understanding of corporate strategy. She had completed a first-pass financial forecast for Home Depot, and was in the process of developing her forecast for Lowe's. She estimated the cost of capital for Home Depot and Lowe's to be 12.3% and 11.6%, respectively (see **Exhibit 3**). **Exhibits 4** and **5** provide historical financial statements for Home Depot and Lowe's. **Exhibit 6** details the historical and forecast values for Value Line's macroeconomic-indicator series. **Exhibits 7** and **8** feature Galeotafiore's first-pass historical ratio analysis and financial forecast for Home Depot.

EXHIBIT 1 | Sales Figures for Retail-Building-Supply Industry

Sales ($billions)	1997	1998	1999	2000	2001	2002E	2006E
Hardware	22.8				26.2	26.2	26.0
Home centers	64.5				89.0	91.9	102.0
Lumber	51.5				59.0	60.1	66.0
Total market	138.8	149.5	159.7	168.0	174.2	178.2	194.0
Share of Market					**2001**		
Home Depot, Inc.					22.9%		
Lowe's Companies					10.8%		
TruServe Corp.					2.9%		
Menard, Inc.					1.5%		

Source: Economist Intelligence Unit.

EXHIBIT 2 | Historical Company Performance

	Fiscal Year				
	1997	**1998**	**1999**	**2000**	**2001**
Home Depot					
Number of stores*	624	761	930	1,134	1,333
Sq. footage (millions)	66	81	100	123	146
Number of transactions (millions)	550	665	797	937	1,091
Number of employees	124,400	156,700	201,400	227,300	256,300
Lowe's					
Number of stores	477	520	576	650	744
Sq. footage (millions)	40	48	57	68	81
Number of transactions (millions)	231	268	299	342	395
Number of employees	64,070	72,715	86,160	94,601	108,317

*Excludes Apex Supply, Georgia Lighting, Maintenance Warehouse, Your "Other" Warehouse, and National Blinds.

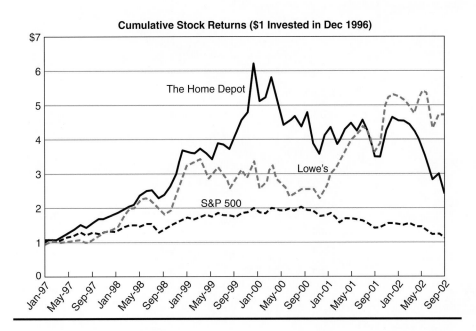

Cumulative Stock Returns ($1 Invested in Dec 1996)

EXHIBIT 3 | Cost-of-Capital Calculation

Current yield on long-term U.S. Treasuries	4.8%
Historical market-risk premium	5.5%
Home Depot	
Proportion of debt capital (market value)	2%
Cost of debt (current yields of Aaa-rated debt)	6.8%
Marginal tax rate	38.6%
Cost of equity (beta = 1.4)	12.5%
Weighted average cost of capital	12.3%
Lowe's	
Proportion of debt capital (market value)	12%
Cost of debt (current yields of Aa-rated debt)	7.3%
Marginal tax rate	37.0%
Cost of equity (beta = 1.4)	12.5%
Weighted average cost of capital	11.6%

EXHIBIT 4 | Financial Statements for Home Depot ($ millions)

	Fiscal Year				
	1997	1998	1999	2000	2001
INCOME STATEMENT					
Sales	24,156	30,219	38,434	45,738	53,553
Cost of sales	17,092	21,241	26,560	31,456	36,642
Gross profit	7,064	8,978	11,874	14,282	16,911
Cash operating expenses*	4,885	5,935	7,603	9,490	11,215
Depreciation & amortization	283	373	463	601	764
EBIT	1,896	2,670	3,808	4,191	4,932
Nonrecurring expenses	0	0	0	0	0
Net interest expense	(2)	16	4	(26)	(25)
EBT	1,898	2,654	3,804	4,217	4,957
Income taxes	738	1,040	1,484	1,636	1,913
Net earnings	1,160	1,614	2,320	2,581	3,044
BALANCE SHEET					
Cash and ST investments	174	62	170	177	2,546
Accounts receivable	556	469	587	835	920
Merchandise inventory	3,602	4,293	5,489	6,556	6,725
Other current assets	128	109	144	209	170
Total current assets	4,460	4,933	6,390	7,777	10,361
Net property and equipment	6,509	8,160	10,227	13,068	15,375
Other assets	260	372	464	540	658
Total assets	11,229	13,465	17,081	21,385	26,394
Accounts payable	1,358	1,586	1,993	1,976	3,436
Accrued salaries and wages	312	395	541	627	717
Short-term borrowings	0	0	0	0	0
Current maturities of long-term debt	8	14	29	4	5
Other current liabilities	778	862	1,093	1,778	2,343
Current liabilities	2,456	2,857	3,656	4,385	6,501
Long-term debt	1,303	1,566	750	1,545	1,250
Deferred income taxes	78	85	87	195	189
Other long-term liabilities	178	208	237	245	372
Minority interest	116	9	10	11	0
Shareholders' equity	7,098	8,740	12,341	15,004	18,082
Total liab. and owner's equity	11,229	13,465	17,081	21,385	26,394

*Includes operating-lease payments of $262 million in 1997, $321 million in 1998, $389 million in 1999, $479 million in 2000, and $522 million in 2001.

EXHIBIT 5 | Financial Statements for Lowe's ($ millions)

	Fiscal Year				
	1997	1998	1999	2000	2001
INCOME STATEMENT					
Sales	10,137	12,245	15,906	18,779	22,111
Cost of sales	7,447	8,950	11,525	13,488	15,743
Gross profit	2,690	3,295	4,381	5,291	6,368
Cash operating expenses*	1,825	2,189	2,870	3,479	4,036
Depreciation & amortization	241	272	338	410	534
EBIT	624	833	1,172	1,402	1,798
Nonrecurring expenses	0	0	24	0	0
Net interest expense	66	75	85	121	173
EBT	559	758	1,063	1,281	1,625
Income taxes	201	276	390	472	601
Net earnings	357	482	673	810	1,024
BALANCE SHEET					
Cash and ST investments	211	243	569	469	853
Accounts receivable	118	144	148	161	166
Merchandise inventory	1,715	2,105	2,812	3,285	3,611
Other current assets	65	94	164	243	291
Total current assets	2,110	2,586	3,693	4,157	4,920
Net property and equipment	3,005	3,637	5,177	7,035	8,653
Other assets	104	122	142	166	162
Total assets	5,219	6,345	9,012	11,358	13,736
Accounts payable	969	1,133	1,567	1,714	1,715
Accrued salaries and wages	83	113	164	166	221
Short-term borrowings	98	92	92	250	100
Current maturities of long-term debt	12	99	60	42	59
Other current liabilities	286	328	503	738	922
Current liabilities	1,449	1,765	2,386	2,911	3,017
Long-term debt	1,046	1,283	1,727	2,698	3,734
Deferred income taxes	124	160	200	251	305
Other long-term liabilities	0	0	4	3	6
Minority interest	0	0	0	0	0
Shareholders' equity	2,601	3,136	4,695	5,495	6,674
Total liab. and owner's equity	5,219	6,345	9,012	11,358	13,736

*Includes operating-lease payments of $59 million in 1997, $89 million in 1998, $144 million in 1999, $162 million in 2000, and $188 million in 2001.

EXHIBIT 6 | Value Line Economic Series

Annual Statistics	1997	1998	1999	2000	2001	2002*	2003*	2005–2007*
Gross domestic product ($ bill.)	8,318	8,782	9,274	9,825	10,082	10,440	10,984	13,255
Real GDP (1996 chained $ bill.)	8,159	8,509	8,859	9,191	9,215	9,428	9,728	10,827
Total consumption ($ bill.)	5,424	5,684	5,965	6,224	6,377	6,577	6,772	7,457
Nonresidential fixed investment ($ bill.)	1,009	1,136	1,228	1,324	1,255	1,190	1,266	1,625
Industrial prod. (% change, annualized)	6.9	5.1	3.7	4.5	−3.7	3.8	5.3	4.0
Housing starts (mill. units)	1.47	1.62	1.65	1.57	1.60	1.66	1.59	1.63
Unit car sales (mill. units)	8.3	8.1	8.7	8.9	8.4	8.2	8.3	8.0
Personal savings rate (%)	4.2	4.7	2.7	2.8	2.3	3.5	3.4	1.5
National unemployment rate (%)	4.9	4.5	4.2	4.0	4.8	5.9	5.9	5.0
AAA corp. bond rate (%)	7.3	6.5	7.0	7.6	7.1	6.4	6.4	7.3
10-Year Treasury note rate (%)	6.4	5.3	5.6	6.0	5.0	4.8	5.1	6.2
3-Month Treasury bill rate (%)	5.1	4.8	4.6	5.8	3.4	1.7	2.4	4.5
Annual Rates of Change								
Real GDP	4.4	4.3	4.1	3.8	0.3	2.3	3.2	3.8
GDP price index	1.9	1.2	1.4	2.1	2.4	1.7	2.5	2.6
Consumer price index	2.3	1.5	2.2	3.4	2.8	2.3	2.5	2.8

Quarterly Annualized Rates	2002				2003			
	1st	2nd*	3rd*	4th*	1st*	2nd*	3rd*	4th*
Gross domestic product ($ bill.)	10,313	10,307	10,475	10,600	10,756	10,901	11,060	11,270
Real GDP (1996 chained $ bill.)	9,363	9,388	9,446	9,516	9,598	9,681	9,770	9,861
Total consumption ($ bill.)	6,514	6,544	6,608	6,641	6,691	6,748	6,798	6,849
Nonresidential fixed investment ($ bill.)	1,188	1,184	1,190	1,199	1,222	1,249	1,279	1,315
Industrial production (% change, annualized)	2.6	4.6	3.0	5.0	5.5	5.5	5.0	5.0
Housing starts (mill. units)	1.73	1.66	1.65	1.60	1.57	1.58	1.60	1.60
Unit car sales (mill. units)	7.9	8.1	8.4	8.2	8.2	8.2	8.3	8.4

*Estimated.

Source: Value Line Publishing.

EXHIBIT 7 | Ratio Analysis for Home Depot

	Fiscal Year				
	1997	**1998**	**1999**	**2000**	**2001**
Working capital (CA–NIBCL*)	2,012	2,090	2,763	3,396	3,865
Fixed assets	6,769	8,532	10,691	13,608	16,033
Total capital	8,781	10,622	13,454	17,004	19,898
Tax rate	38.9%	39.2%	39.0%	38.8%	38.6%
NOPAT (EBIT $\times$ (1 – t))	1,158	1,623	2,323	2,565	3,028
PROFITABILITY					
Return on capital (NOPAT/total capital)	13.2%	15.3%	17.3%	15.1%	15.2%
Return on equity (net earnings/s. equity)	16.3%	18.5%	18.8%	17.2%	16.8%
MARGINS					
Gross margin (gross profit/sales)	29.2%	29.7%	30.9%	31.2%	31.6%
Cash operating expenses/sales	20.2%	19.6%	19.8%	20.7%	20.9%
Depreciation/sales	1.2%	1.2%	1.2%	1.3%	1.4%
Depreciation/P&E	4.3%	4.6%	4.5%	4.6%	5.0%
Operating margin (EBIT/sales)	7.8%	8.8%	9.9%	9.2%	9.2%
NOPAT margin (NOPAT/sales)	4.8%	5.4%	6.0%	5.6%	5.7%
TURNOVER					
Total capital turnover (sales/total capital)	2.8	2.8	2.9	2.7	2.7
P&E turnover (sales/P&E)	3.7	3.7	3.8	3.5	3.5
Working-capital turnover (sales/WC)	12.0	14.5	13.9	13.5	13.9
Receivable turnover (sales/AR)	43.4	64.4	65.5	54.8	58.2
Inventory turnover (COGS/m. inventory)	4.7	4.9	4.8	4.8	5.4
Sales per store ($ millions)	38.7	39.7	41.3	40.3	40.2
Sales per sq. foot ($)	366.0	373.1	384.3	371.9	366.8
Sales per transaction ($)	43.9	45.4	48.2	48.8	49.1
GROWTH					
Total sales growth		25.1%	27.2%	19.0%	17.1%
Sales growth for existing stores		2.6%	4.1%	–2.4%	–0.4%
Growth in new stores		22.0%	22.2%	21.9%	17.5%
Growth in sq. footage per store		0.6%	1.0%	0.9%	1.0%
LEVERAGE					
Total capital/equity	1.24	1.22	1.09	1.13	1.10

*Non-interest-bearing current liabilities.

EXHIBIT 8 | Financial Forecast for Home Depot

ASSUMPTIONS	Fiscal Year					
	2001	2002E	2003E	2004E	2005E	2006E
Growth in new stores	17.5%	15.0%	13.2%	9.0%	7.0%	5.5%
Sales growth for existing stores	−0.4%	3.0%	4.0%	8.3%	8.3%	8.3%
Total sales growth	17.1%	18.0%	17.2%	17.3%	15.3%	13.8%
Gross margin	31.6%	32.0%	32.3%	32.4%	32.5%	32.5%
Cash operating expenses/sales	20.9%	21.0%	20.7%	20.8%	20.5%	20.5%
Depreciation/sales	1.4%	1.4%	1.4%	1.4%	1.4%	1.4%
Income-tax rate	38.6%	37.6%	37.5%	37.5%	37.5%	37.5%
Cash & ST inv./sales	4.8%	5.0%	5.0%	5.1%	5.3%	5.3%
Receivable turnover	58.2	55.0	53.0	52.0	50.0	50.0
Inventory turnover	5.4	5.3	5.1	5.0	4.7	4.7
P&E turnover	3.5	3.3	3.3	3.3	3.3	3.3
Payables/COGS	9.4%	9.4%	9.4%	9.4%	9.4%	9.4%
Other curr. liab./sales	4.4%	4.4%	4.4%	4.4%	4.4%	4.4%
FORECAST						
Number of stores	1,333	1,533	1,735	1,891	2,024	2,135
Net sales	53,553	63,195	74,049	86,860	100,149	114,000
Cost of sales	36,642	42,972	50,131	58,717	67,601	76,950
Gross profit	16,911	20,222	23,918	28,143	32,549	37,050
Cash operating expenses	11,215	13,271	15,328	18,067	20,531	23,370
Depreciation & amortization	764	902	1,056	1,239	1,429	1,626
EBIT	4,932	6,050	7,533	8,837	10,589	12,054
NOPAT	3,028	3,775	4,708	5,523	6,618	7,534
Cash and ST investments	2,546	3,160	3,702	4,430	5,308	6,042
Accounts receivable	920	1,149	1,397	1,670	2,003	2,280
Merchandise inventory	6,725	8,170	9,868	11,743	14,383	16,372
Other current assets	170	170	170	170	170	170
Total current assets	10,361	12,648	15,138	18,014	21,864	24,864
Accounts payable	3,436	4,030	4,701	5,506	6,339	7,216
Accrued salaries and wages	717	717	717	717	717	717
Other current liabilities	2,348	2,765	3,240	3,800	4,382	4,988
Non-int.-bearing current liab.	6,501	7,511	8,658	10,023	11,438	12,920
Working capital	3,860	5,137	6,480	7,990	10,426	11,944
Net property and equipment	15,375	19,150	22,439	26,321	30,348	34,545
Other assets	658	658	658	658	658	658
Total capital	19,893	24,945	29,578	34,970	41,433	47,147
Return on capital	15.2%	15.1%	15.9%	15.8%	16.0%	16.0%

Horniman Horticulture

Bob Brown hummed along to a seasonal carol on the van radio as he made his way over the dark and icy roads of Amherst County, Virginia. He and his crew had just finished securing their nursery against some unexpected chilly weather. It was Christmas Eve 2005, and Bob, the father of four boys ranging in age from 5 to 10, was anxious to be home. Despite the late hour, he fully anticipated the hoopla that would greet him on his return and knew that it would be some time before even the youngest would be asleep. He regretted that the boys' holiday gifts would not be substantial; money was again tight this year. Nonetheless, Bob was delighted with what his company had accomplished. Business was booming. Revenue for 2005 was 15% ahead of 2004, and operating profits were up even more.

Bob had been brought up to value a strong work ethic. His father had worked his way up through the ranks to become foreman of a lumber mill in Southwest Virginia. At a young age, Bob began working for his father at the mill. After earning a degree in agricultural economics at Virginia Tech, he married Maggie Horniman in 1993. Upon his return to the mill, Bob was made a supervisor. He excelled at his job and was highly respected by everyone at the mill. In 2000, facing the financial needs of an expanding family, he and Maggie began exploring employment alternatives. In late 2002, Maggie's father offered to sell the couple his wholesale nursery business, Horniman Horticulture, near Lynchburg, Virginia. The business and the opportunity to be near Maggie's family appealed to both Maggie and Bob. Pooling their savings, the proceeds from the sale of their house, a minority-business-development grant, and a sizable personal loan from Maggie's father, the Browns purchased the business for $999,000. It was agreed that Bob would run the nursery's operations and Maggie would oversee its finances.

Bob thoroughly enjoyed running his own business and was proud of its growth over the previous three years. The nursery's operations filled 52 greenhouses and 40 acres of productive fields and employed 12 full-time and 15 seasonal employees. Sales were primarily to retail nurseries throughout the mid-Atlantic region. The company

This case was prepared by Michael J. Schill, Robert F. Vandell Research Associate Professor of Business Administration, as a basis for class discussion rather than to illustrate effective or ineffective handling of an administrative situation. Horniman Horticulture is a fictional company reflecting the issues facing actual firms. Copyright © 2006 by the University of Virginia Darden School Foundation, Charlottesville, VA. All rights reserved. *To order copies, send an e-mail to* sales@dardenbusinesspublishing.com. *No part of this publication may be reproduced, stored in a retrieval system, used in a spreadsheet, or transmitted in any form or by any means—electronic, mechanical, photocopying, recording, or otherwise—without the permission of the Darden School Foundation.* Rev. 04/11.

specialized in such woody shrubs as azaleas, camellias, hydrangeas, and rhododendrons, but also grew and sold a wide variety of annuals, perennials, and trees.[1] Over the previous two years, Bob had increased the number of plant species grown at the nursery by more than 40%.

Bob was a "people person." His warm personality had endeared him to customers and employees alike. With Maggie's help, he had kept a tight rein on costs. The effect on the business's profits was obvious, as its profit margin had increased from 3.1% in 2003 to an expected 5.8% in 2005. Bob was confident that the nursery's overall prospects were robust.

With Bob running the business full time, Maggie primarily focused on attending to the needs of her active family. With the help of two clerks, she oversaw the company's books. Bob knew that Maggie was concerned about the recent decline in the firm's cash balance to below $10,000. Such a cash level was well under her operating target of 8% of annual revenue. But Maggie had shown determination to maintain financial responsibility by avoiding bank borrowing and by paying suppliers early enough to obtain any trade discounts.[2] Her aversion to debt financing stemmed from her concern about inventory risk. She believed that interest payments might be impossible to meet if adverse weather wiped out their inventory.

Maggie was happy with the steady margin improvements the business had experienced. Some of the gains were due to Bob's response to a growing demand for more-mature plants. Nurseries were willing to pay premium prices for plants that delivered "instant landscape," and Bob was increasingly shifting the product mix to that line. Maggie had recently prepared what she expected to be the end-of-year financial summary (**Exhibit 1**).[3] To benchmark the company's performance, Maggie used available data for the few publicly traded horticultural producers (**Exhibit 2**).

Across almost any dimension of profitability and growth, Bob and Maggie agreed that the business appeared to be strong. They also knew that expectations could change quickly. Increases in interest rates, for example, could substantially slow market demand. The company's margins relied heavily on the hourly wage rate of $8.51, currently required for H2A-certified nonimmigrant foreign agricultural workers. There was some debate within the U.S. Congress about the merits of raising this rate.

Bob was optimistic about the coming year. Given the ongoing strength of the local economy, he expected to have plenty of demand to continue to grow the business. Because much of the inventory took two to five years to mature sufficiently to sell, his top-line expansion efforts had been in the works for some time. Bob was sure

---

[1]Over the past year, Horniman Horticulture had experienced a noticeable increase in business from small nurseries. Because the cost of carrying inventory was particularly burdensome for those customers, slight improvements in the credit terms had been accompanied by substantial increases in sales.

[2]Most of Horniman's suppliers provided 30-day payment terms, with a 2% discount for payments received within 10 days.

[3]As compensation for the Browns' services to the business, they had drawn an annual salary of $50,000 (itemized as an SG&A expense) for each of the past three years. This amount was effectively the family's entire income.

that 2006 would be a banner year, with expected revenue hitting a record 30% growth rate. In addition, he looked forward to ensuring long-term-growth opportunities with the expected closing next month on a neighboring 12-acre parcel of farmland.[4] But for now, it was Christmas Eve, and Bob was looking forward to taking off work for the entire week. He would enjoy spending time with Maggie and the boys. They had much to celebrate for 2005 and much to look forward to in 2006.

---

[4]With the acquisition of the additional property, Maggie expected 2006 capital expenditures to be $75,000. Although she was not planning to finance the purchase, prevailing mortgage rates were running at 6.5%. The expected depreciation expense for 2006 was $46,000.

EXHIBIT 1 | Projected Financial Summary for Horniman Horticulture (in thousands of dollars)

	2002	2003	2004	2005
Profit and loss statement				
Revenue	788.5	807.6	908.2	1048.8
Cost of goods sold	402.9	428.8	437.7	503.4
Gross profit	385.6	378.8	470.5	545.4
SG&A expense	301.2	302.0	356.0	404.5
Depreciation	34.2	38.4	36.3	40.9
Operating profit	50.2	38.4	78.2	100.0
Taxes	17.6	13.1	26.2	39.2
Net profit	32.6	25.3	52.0	60.8
Balance sheet				
Cash	120.1	105.2	66.8	9.4
Accounts receivable	90.6	99.5	119.5	146.4
Inventory[1]	468.3	507.6	523.4	656.9
Other current assets[2]	20.9	19.3	22.6	20.9
Current assets	699.9	731.6	732.3	833.6
Net fixed assets[3]	332.1	332.5	384.3	347.9
Total assets	1,032.0	1,064.1	1,116.6	1,181.5
Accounts payable	6.0	5.3	4.5	5.0
Wages payable	19.7	22.0	22.1	24.4
Other payables	10.2	15.4	16.6	17.9
Current liabilities	35.9	42.7	43.2	47.3
Net worth	996.1	1,021.4	1,073.4	1,134.2
Capital expenditure	22.0	38.8	88.1	4.5
Purchases[4]	140.8	145.2	161.2	185.1

[1]Inventory investment was valued at the lower of cost or market. The cost of inventory was determined by accumulating the costs associated with preparing the plants for sale. Costs that were typically capitalized as inventory included direct labor, materials (soil, water, containers, stakes, labels, chemicals), scrap, and overhead.

[2]Other current assets included consigned inventory, prepaid expenses, and assets held for sale.

[3]Net fixed assets included land, buildings and improvements, equipment, and software.

[4]Purchases represented the annual amount paid to suppliers.

EXHIBIT 2 | Financial Ratio Analysis and Benchmarking

	2002	2003	2004	2005	Benchmark[1]
Revenue growth	2.9%	2.4%	12.5%	15.5%	(1.8)%
Gross margin (gross profit/revenue)	48.9%	46.9%	51.8%	52.0%	48.9%
Operating margin (op. profit/revenue)	6.4%	4.8%	8.6%	9.5%	7.6%
Net profit margin (net profit/revenue)	4.1%	3.1%	5.7%	5.8%	2.8%
Return on assets (net profit/total assets)	3.2%	2.4%	4.7%	5.1%	2.9%
Return on capital (net profit/total capital)	3.3%	2.5%	4.8%	5.4%	4.0%
Receivable days (AR/revenue $\times$ 365)	41.9	45.0	48.0	50.9	21.8
Inventory days (inventory/COGS $\times$ 365)	424.2	432.1	436.5	476.3	386.3
Payable days (AP/purchases $\times$ 365)	15.6	13.3	10.2	9.9	26.9
NFA turnover (revenue/NFA)	2.4	2.4	2.4	3.0	2.7

[1]Benchmark figures were based on 2004 financial ratios of publicly traded horticultural producers.

Guna Fibres, Ltd.

Ms. Surabhi Kumar, the managing director and principal owner of Guna Fibres, Ltd., discovered the problem when she arrived at the parking lot of the company's plant one morning in early January 2012. Trucks filled with rolls of fiber yarns were being unloaded, but they had been loaded just the night before and had been ready to depart that morning. The fiber was intended for customers who had been badgering Kumar to fill their orders in a timely manner. The government tax inspector, who was stationed at the company's warehouse, would not clear the trucks for departure because the excise tax had not been paid. The tax inspector required a cash payment, but in seeking to draw funds for the excise tax that morning, Mr. Malik, the bookkeeper, discovered that the company had overdrawn its bank account again—the third time in as many weeks. The truck drivers were independent contractors who refused to wait while the company and government settled their accounts. They cursed loudly as they unloaded the trucks.

This shipment would not leave for at least another two days, and angry customers would no doubt require an explanation. Before granting a loan with which to pay the excise tax, the branch manager of the All-India Bank & Trust Company had requested a meeting with Kumar for the next day to discuss Guna's financial condition and its plans for restoring the firm's liquidity.

Kumar told Malik, "This cash problem is most vexing. I don't understand it. We're a very profitable enterprise, yet we seem to have to depend increasingly on the bank. Why do we need more loans just as our heavy selling season begins? We can't repeat this blunder."

Company Background

Guna Fibres, Ltd., was founded in 1972 to produce nylon fiber at its only plant in Guna, India, about 500 kilometers (km) south of New Delhi. By using new technology and domestic raw materials, the firm had developed a steady franchise among dozens of small, local textile weavers. It supplied synthetic fiber yarns used to weave colorful cloths for making saris, the traditional women's dress of India. On average,

This case was written by Thien T. Pham and professors Robert F. Bruner and Michael J. Schill as a basis for class discussion. The names and institutions in this case are fictitious. The financial support of the Batten Institute is gratefully acknowledged.

each sari required eight yards of cloth. An Indian woman typically would buy three saris a year. With India's female population at around 500 million, the demand for saris accounted for more than 12 billion yards of fabric. This demand was currently being supplied entirely from domestic textile mills that, in turn, filled their yarn requirements from suppliers such as Guna Fibres.

Synthetic-Textile Market

The demand for synthetic textiles was stable with year-to-year growth and predictable seasonal fluctuations. Unit demand increased with both population and national income. In addition, India's population celebrated hundreds of festivals each year, in deference to a host of deities, at which saris were traditionally worn. The most important festival, the Diwali celebration in mid-autumn, caused a seasonal peak in the demand for new saris, which in turn caused a seasonal peak in demand for nylon textiles in late summer and early fall. Thus, the seasonal demand for nylon yarn would peak in mid-summer. Unit growth in the industry was expected to be 15% per year.

Consumers purchased saris and textiles from cloth merchants located in the villages around the country. A cloth merchant was an important local figure usually well known to area residents; the merchant generally granted credit to support consumer purchases. Merchants maintained relatively low levels of inventory and built stocks of goods only shortly in advance of and during the peak selling season.

Competition among suppliers (the many small textile-weaving mills) to those merchants was keen and was affected by price, service, and the credit that the mills could grant to the merchants. The mills essentially produced to order, building their inventories of woven cloth shortly in advance of the peak selling season and keeping only maintenance stocks at other times of the year.

The yarn manufacturers competed for the business of the mills through responsive service and credit. The suppliers to the yarn manufacturers provided little or no trade credit. Being near the origin of the textile chain in India, the yarn manufacturers essentially banked the downstream activities of the industry.

Production and Distribution System

Thin profit margins had prompted Kumar to adopt policies against overproduction and overstocking, which would require Guna to carry inventories through the slack selling season. She had adopted a plan of seasonal production, which meant that the yarn plant would operate at peak capacity for two months of the year and at modest levels the rest of the year. That policy imposed an annual ritual of hirings and layoffs.

To help ensure prompt service, Guna Fibres maintained two distribution warehouses, but getting the finished yarn quickly from the factory in Guna to the customers was a challenge. The roads were narrow and mostly in poor repair. A truck was often delayed negotiating the trip between Calcutta and Guna, a distance of about 730 km. Journeys were slow and dangerous, and accidents were frequent.

Company Performance

Guna Fibres had experienced consistent growth and profitability (see **Exhibit 1** for recent financial statements for the firm). In 2011, sales had grown at an impressive rate of 18%. Recent profits were (Indian rupees) INR2.6 million, down from INR3.6 million in 2010. Kumar expected Guna's growth to continue with gross sales reaching INR90.9 million in 2012 (see **Exhibit 2**).[1]

Reassessment

After the episode in the parking lot, Kumar and her bookkeeper went to her office to analyze the situation. She pushed aside the several items on her desk to which she had intended to devote her morning: a message from the transportation manager regarding a possible change in the inventory policy (**Exhibit 3**), and a proposal from the operations manager for a scheme of level annual production (**Exhibit 4**).

To prepare a forecast on a business-as-usual basis, Kumar and Malik agreed on various parameters. Cost of goods sold would run at 73.7% of gross sales—a figure that was up from recent years because of increasing price competition. Annual operating expenses would be about 6% of gross annual sales—also up from recent years to include the addition of a quality-control department, two new sales agents, and three young nephews with whom she hoped to build an allegiance to the Kumar family business. The company's income tax rate was 30% and, although accrued monthly, positive balances were paid quarterly in March, June, September, and December. The excise tax (at 15% of sales) was different from the income tax and was collected at the factory gate as trucks left to make deliveries to customers and the regional warehouses. Kumar proposed to pay dividends of INR500,000 per quarter to the 11 members of her extended family who held the entire equity of the firm. For years Guna had paid high dividends. The Kumar family believed that excess funds left in the firm were at greater risk than if the funds were returned to shareholders.

Malik observed that accounts receivable collections in any given month had been running steadily at the rate of 48 days, comprised of 40% of the last month's gross sales plus 60% of the gross sales from the month before last. The cost of the raw materials for Guna's yarn production ran about 55% of the gross sale price. To ensure sufficient raw material on hand, it was Guna's practice to purchase each month the amount of raw materials expected to be sold in two months. The suppliers Guna used had little ability to provide credit such that accounts payable were generally paid within two weeks. Monthly direct labour and other direct costs associated with yarn manufacturing were equivalent to about 34% of purchases in the previous month.[2] Accounts payable ran at about half of the month's purchases. As a matter of policy, Kumar wanted to see a cash balance of at least INR750,000.

---

[1] At the time, the rupee exchange rate for U.S. dollars was roughly at the rate of INR50 per dollar.

[2] The 73.7% COGS rate assumption was determined based on these purchases and direct cost figures: $73.7\% = 55\% + 55\% \times 34\%$.

Guna Fibres had a line of credit at the All-India Bank & Trust Company, where it also maintained its cash balances. All-India's short-term interest rate was currently 14.5%, but Malik was worried that inflation and interest rates might rise in the coming year. By terms of the bank, the seasonal line of credit had to be reduced to a zero balance for at least 30 days each year. The usual cleanup month had been October,[3] but Guna Fibres had failed to make a full repayment at that time. Only after strong assurances by Kumar that she would clean up the loan in November or December had the bank lending officer reluctantly agreed to waive the cleanup requirement in October. Unfortunately, the credit needs of Guna Fibres did not abate as rapidly as expected in November and December, and although his protests increased each month, the lending officer agreed to meet Guna's cash requirements with loans. Now he was refusing to extend any more seasonal credit until Kumar presented a reasonable financial plan for the company that demonstrated its ability to clean up the loan by the end of 2012.

Financial Forecast

With some experience in financial modeling, Malik used the agreed upon assumptions to build out a monthly forecast of Guna's financial statements (see **Exhibit 5**). To summarize the seasonal pattern of the model, Malik handed Kumar a graph showing the projected monthly sales and key balance sheet accounts (**Exhibit 6**). After studying the forecasts for a few moments, Kumar expostulated:

> This is worse than I expected. The numbers show that we aren't even close to paying back All-India's loan by the end of December. The loan officer will never accept this forecast as a basis for more credit. We need a new plan, and fast. Maintaining this loan is critical for us to scale up for the most important part of our business season. Let's go over these assumptions in detail and look for any opportunities to improve our debt position.

Then, casting her gaze toward the two proposals she had pushed aside earlier, she muttered, "Perhaps these proposals will help."

---

[3] The selection of October as the loan-cleanup month was imposed by the bank on the grounds of tradition. Seasonal loans of any type made by the bank were to be cleaned up in October. Kumar had seen no reason previously to challenge the bank's tradition.

EXHIBIT 1 | Guna Fibres Annual Income
Statements (in 000s of Rupees)

	2010	2011
Gross Sales	64,487	75,867
Excise Tax	9,673	11,380
Net Sales	54,814	64,487
Cost of Goods	44,496	53,866
Gross Profits	10,318	10,621
Operating Expenses	3,497	4,829
Depreciation	769	909
Interest Expense	910	1,240
Profit Before Tax	5,142	3,644
Income Tax	1,545	1,093
Net Profit	3,597	2,551
Cash	895	762
Accounts Receivable	2,390	2,673
Inventory	2,974	3,450
Total Current Assets	6,259	6,885
Gross Plant, Property, and Equipment	8,868	10,096
Accumulated Depreciation	1,170	1,484
Net Plant, Property, and Equipment	7,698	8,612
Total Assets	13,957	15,497
Accounts Payable	603	822
Notes to Bank	0	798
Accrued Taxes	−62	−90
Total Current Liabilities	541	1,530
Owners' Equity	13,416	13,967
Total Liabilities and Equity	13,957	15,497

EXHIBIT 2 | Guna Fibres Actual and
Forecast of Monthly Sales (in 000s of Rupees)

	2011 (Actual)	2012 (Forecast)
January	2,012	2,616
February	2,314	2,892
March	3,421	4,447
April	7,043	8,804
May	12,074	13,885
June	15,294	17,588
July	14,187	16,315
August	7,144	8,576
September	4,025	5,031
October	3,421	4,447
November	2,717	3,531
December	2,214	2,767
Year	75,867	90,899

EXHIBIT 3 | Message from Transportation Manager

To: G. Kumar
From: R. Sikh

January 2, 2012

As you asked me to, I have been tracking our supply shipments over the past year. I have observed a substantial improvement in the reliability of the shipments. As a result, I would propose that we reduce our raw-material inventory requirement from 60 days to 30 days. This would reduce the amount of inventory we are carrying by one month, and should free up a lot of space in the warehouse. I am not sure if that will affect any other department since we will be buying the same amount of material, but it would make inventory tracking a lot easier for me. Please let me know so we can implement this in January such that I don't purchase any additional raw material this month.

EXHIBIT 4 | Message from Operations Manager

To: G. Kumar
From: L. Gupta

January 7, 2012

You asked me to estimate the production efficiencies arising from a scheme of level annual production. In order to provide for the estimated production needs in 2012 and 2013, I would recommend that purchases under level production be altered to INR5 million per month.

There are significant operating advantages to be gained under this operating scenario:

- Seasonal hirings and layoffs would no longer be necessary, permitting us to cultivate a stronger work force and, perhaps, to suppress labour unrest. You will recall that the unions have indicated that reducing seasonal layoffs will be one of their major negotiating objectives this year.
- Level production entails lower manufacturing risk. With the load spread throughout the year, we would suffer less from equipment breakdowns and could better match the routine maintenance with the demand on the plant and equipment.

With level production my team believes that direct labour and other direct manufacturing costs could be reduced from a forecasted 34% of purchases down to 29% of purchases.

EXHIBIT 5 | Monthly Financial Statement Forecast (in 000 of Rupees)

Assumptions

Excise Tax Rate	15%
Cost of Goods Sold / Gr Sales	73.7%
Annual Operating Expenses / Annual Gr Sales	6.0%
Depreciation / Gross PP&E	10%
Interest Rate on Borrowings (and Deposits)	14.5%
Income Tax Rate	30%
Dividends Paid (000s in March, June, Sep, Dec)	500

Minimum Cash Balance (000s)	750
Accounts Receivable Collection	
In One Month	40%
In Two Months	60%
Purchases / Gr Sales in Two Months	55%
Direct Labour / Purchases Last Month	34%
Capital Expenditures (every third month)	350
Accounts payable / Purchases	50%

	Nov-11	Dec-11	Jan-12	Feb-12	Mar-12	Apr-12	May-12	Jun-12	Jul-12	Aug-12	Sep-12	Oct-12	Nov-12	Dec-12	Full year 2012
Gross Sales (1)	2,717	2,214	2,616	2,892	4,447	8,804	13,885	17,588	16,315	8,576	5,031	4,447	3,531	2,767	90,899
Excise Taxes (2)			392	434	667	1,321	2,083	2,638	2,447	1,286	755	667	530	415	13,635
Net Sales			2,224	2,458	3,780	7,483	11,802	14,950	13,868	7,290	4,276	3,780	3,001	2,352	77,264
Cost of Goods Sold			1,928	2,131	3,277	6,489	10,233	12,962	12,024	6,321	3,708	3,277	2,602	2,039	66,993
Gross Profit			296	327	503	995	1,569	1,987	1,844	969	569	503	399	313	10,272
Operating Expenses (3)			454	454	454	454	454	454	454	454	454	454	454	454	5,454
Depreciation (4)			84	84	87	87	87	90	90	90	93	93	93	96	1,074
Interest Expense (5)			10	21	57	144	261	372	417	336	198	105	62	44	2,026
Profit Before Taxes			−253	−233	−96	309	767	1,071	882	88	−177	−150	−211	−281	1,717
Income Taxes			−76	−70	−29	93	230	321	265	26	−53	−45	−63	−84	515
Net Profit			−177	−163	−67	217	537	750	617	62	−124	−105	−147	−197	1,202
Dividend					500			500			500			500	

Notes:
(1) Follows forecast in Exhibit 2
(2) Gross Sales × Exercise Tax Rate
(3) Annual Operating Expenses / 12
(4) Gross PPE * Depreciation Rate / 12
(5) Notes Payable (t−1) * Interest Rate / 12

	Dec-11	Jan-12	Feb-12	Mar-12	Apr-12	May-12	Jun-12	Jul-12	Aug-12	Sep-12	Oct-12	Nov-12	Dec-12
Cash	762	750	750	750	750	750	750	750	750	750	750	750	750
Accounts Receivable (6)	2,673	2,773	3,291	5,011	10,301	17,996	24,748	25,697	17,194	9,006	6,295	5,028	3,715
Inventory	3,450	4,509	8,051	14,057	19,838	21,867	16,672	9,019	6,085	5,151	4,056	3,841	4,427
Total Current Assets	6,885	8,032	12,092	19,818	30,889	40,613	42,170	35,466	24,029	14,907	11,100	9,619	8,891
Gross Plant, Property, and Equip (7)	10,096	10,096	10,096	10,446	10,446	10,446	10,796	10,796	10,796	11,146	11,146	11,146	11,496
Accumulated Depreciation	1,484	1,568	1,652	1,739	1,826	1,913	2,003	2,093	2,183	2,276	2,369	2,462	2,558
Net Plant, Property, and Equipment	8,612	8,527	8,443	8,706	8,619	8,532	8,792	8,702	8,612	8,869	8,777	8,684	8,938
Total Assets	15,497	16,559	20,535	28,524	39,508	49,146	50,963	44,168	32,641	23,776	19,877	18,303	17,829
Accounts Payable (8)	822	1,223	2,421	3,818	4,837	4,487	2,358	1,384	1,223	971	761	935	994
Note Payable (9)	798	1,712	4,722	11,910	21,567	30,787	34,541	27,840	16,385	8,687	5,147	3,610	3,858
Accrued Taxes (10)	−90	−166	−236	−265	−172	58	0	265	291	0	−45	−108	−192
Total Current Liabilities	1,530	2,769	6,908	15,464	26,232	35,332	36,899	29,488	17,899	9,658	5,863	4,437	4,660
Shareholders' Equity (11)	13,967	13,790	13,627	13,060	13,277	13,813	14,063	14,680	14,742	14,118	14,013	13,866	13,169
Total Liabilities & Equity	15,497	16,559	20,535	28,524	39,508	49,146	50,963	44,168	32,641	23,776	19,877	18,303	17,829

Inventory Detail	Nov-11	Dec-11	Jan-12	Feb-12	Mar-12	Apr-12	May-12	Jun-12	Jul-12	Aug-12	Sep-12	Oct-12	Nov-12	Dec-12
Purchases (12)	1,439	1,591	2,446	4,842	7,637	9,673	8,973	4,717	2,767	2,446	1,942	1,522	1,871	1,989
Direct Labour & Other Mftg Costs (13)		489	541	832	1,646	2,596	3,289	3,051	1,604	941	832	660	517	636
Cost of Goods Sold			1,928	2,131	3,277	6,489	10,233	12,962	12,024	6,321	3,708	3,277	2,602	2,039
Inventory (14)		3,450	4,509	8,051	14,057	19,838	21,867	16,672	9,019	6,085	5,151	4,056	3,841	4,427

Notes:
(6) AR(t−1) + GSales(t) − 40% × GSales(t−2) − 60% × GSales(t−2)
(7) GPPE(t-1) + Capex(t)
(8) 50% × Purchases(t)
(9) Total Assets − AP − AccTax − ShrEquity
(10) AccTax(t−1) + IncTax(t) or 0 if postive balance and month of quarterly payment
(11) ShrEquity(t−1) + NetProfit(t) − Dividend(t)
(12) 55% × GSales(t+2)
(13) 35% × Purchases(t−1)
(14) Inventory(t−1) + Purchases(t) + Direct Labour(t) − COGS(t)

EXHIBIT 6 | Forecast of Accounts by Month

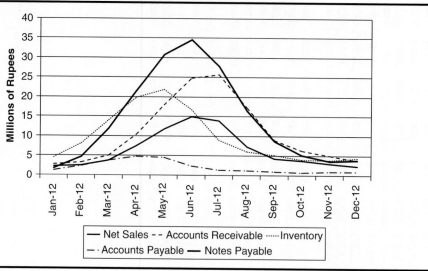

## PART 3

Estimating the Cost of Capital

Best Practices in Estimating the Cost of Capital: Survey and Synthesis

This paper presents the results of a cost-of-capital survey of 27 highly regarded corporations, ten leading financial advisers, and seven best selling textbooks and trade books. The results show close alignment among all these groups on the use of common theoretical frameworks and on many aspects of estimation. We find large variation, however, for the joint choices of the risk-free rate, beta, and the equity market risk premium, as well as for the adjustment of capital costs for specific investment risk. On these issues, we summarize arguments for different approaches and review responses in detail to glean tradeoffs faced by practitioners.

—Robert F. Bruner, Kenneth M. Eades, Robert S. Harris, and Robert C. Higgins

[JEL: G12, G20, G31]

In recent decades, theoretical breakthroughs in such areas as portfolio diversification, market efficiency, and asset pricing have converged into compelling recommendations about the cost of capital to a corporation. By the early 1990s, a consensus had emerged prompting such descriptions as "traditional . . . textbook . . . appropriate," "theoretically correct," and "a useful rule of thumb and a good vehicle."[1] Beneath this general agreement about cost-of-capital theory lies considerable ambiguity and confusion over how the theory can best be applied. The issues at stake are sufficiently important that differing choices on a few key elements can lead to wide disparities in estimated capital cost. The cost of capital is central to modern finance touching on investment and divestment decisions, measures of economic profit, performance appraisal, and

---

[1]The three sets of quotes come in order from Ehrhardt (1994), Copeland, Koller, and Murrin (1990), and Brealey and Myers (1993).

Robert F. Bruner, Kenneth M. Eades, and Robert S. Harris are Professors at the Darden Graduate School of Business Administration, University of Virginia, Charlottesville, VA 22906. Robert C. Higgins is a Professor at the University of Washington, Seattle, WA 98195.

The authors thank Todd Brotherson for excellent research assistance, and gratefully acknowledge the financial support of Coopers & Lybrand and the University of Virginia Darden School Foundation. The research would not have been possible without the cooperation of the 37 companies surveyed. These contributions notwithstanding, any errors remain the authors'.

incentive systems. Each year in the US, corporations undertake more than $500 billion in capital spending. Since a difference of a few percent in capital costs can mean a swing in billions of expenditures, how firms estimate the cost is no trivial matter.

The purpose of this paper is to present evidence on how some of the most financially sophisticated companies and financial advisers estimate capital costs. This evidence is valuable in several respects. First, it identifies the most important ambiguities in the application of cost-of-capital theory, setting the stage for productive debate and research on their resolution. Second, it helps interested companies benchmark their cost-of-capital estimation practices against best-practice peers. Third, the evidence sheds light on the accuracy with which capital costs can be reasonably estimated, enabling executives to use the estimates more wisely in their decision-making. Fourth, it enables teachers to answer the inevitable question, "How do companies really estimate their cost of capital?"

The paper is part of a lengthy tradition of surveys of industry practice. Among the more relevant predecessors, Gitman and Forrester (1977) explored "the level of sophistication in capital budgeting techniques" among 103 large, rapidly growing businesses, finding that the internal rate of return and the payback period were in common use. Although the authors inquired about the level of the firm's discount rate, they did not ask how the rate was determined. Gitman and Mercurio (1982) surveyed 177 *Fortune* 1000 firms about "current practice in cost of capital measurement and utilization," concluding that "the respondents' actions do not reflect the application of current financial theory." Moore and Reichert (1983) surveyed 298 Fortune 500 firms on the use of a broad array of financial techniques, concluding among other things, that 86% of firms surveyed use time-adjusted capital budgeting techniques. Bierman (1993) surveyed 74 *Fortune* 100 companies reporting that all use some form of discounting in their capital budgeting, and 93% use a weighted-average cost of capital. In a broad-ranging survey of 84 *Fortune* 500 large firms and *Forbes* 200 best small companies, Trahan and Gitman (1995) report that 30% of respondents use the capital-asset pricing model (CAPM).

This paper differs from its predecessors in several important respects. Existing published evidence is based on written, closed-end surveys sent to a large sample of firms, often covering a wide array of topics, and commonly using multiple-choice or fill-in-the-blank questions. Such an approach often yields response rates as low as 20% and provides no opportunity to explore subtleties of the topic. Instead, we report the result of a telephone survey of a carefully chosen group of leading corporations and financial advisers. Another important difference is that the intent of existing papers is most often to learn how well accepted modern financial techniques are among practitioners, while we are interested in those areas of cost-of-capital estimation where finance theory is silent or ambiguous, and practitioners are left to their own devices.

The following section gives a brief overview of the weighted-average cost of capital. The research approach and sample selection are discussed in Section II. Section III reports the general survey results. Key points of disparity are reviewed in Section IV. Section V discusses further survey results on risk adjustment to a baseline cost of capital, and Section VI offers conclusions and implications for the financial practitioner.

I. The Weighted-Average Cost of Capital

A key insight from finance theory is that any use of capital imposes an opportunity cost on investors; namely, funds are diverted from earning a return on the next best equal-risk investment. Since investors have access to a host of financial market opportunities, corporate uses of capital must be benchmarked against these capital market alternatives. The cost of capital provides this benchmark. Unless a firm can earn in excess of its cost of capital, it will not create economic profit or value for investors.

A standard means of expressing a company's cost of capital is the weighted-average of the cost of individual sources of capital employed. In symbols, a company's weighted-average cost of capital (or WACC) is

$$\text{WACC} = (W_{\text{debt}}(1 - t)K_{\text{debt}}) + (W_{\text{preferred}}K_{\text{preferred}}) + (W_{\text{equity}}K_{\text{equity}}) \tag{1}$$

where

$$K = \text{component cost of capital}$$
$$W = \text{weight of each component as percent of total capital}$$
$$t = \text{marginal corporate tax rate}$$

For simplicity, this formula includes only three sources of capital; it can be easily expanded to include other sources as well.

Finance theory offers several important observations when estimating a company's WACC. First, the capital costs appearing in the equation should be current costs reflecting current financial market conditions, not historical, sunk costs. In essence, the costs should equal the investors' anticipated internal rate of return on future cash flows associated with each form of capital. Second, the weights appearing in the equation should be market weights, not historical weights based on often arbitrary, out-of-date book values. Third, the cost of debt should be after corporate tax, reflecting the benefits of the tax deductibility of interest.

Despite the guidance provided by finance theory, use of the weighted-average expression to estimate a company's cost of capital still confronts the practitioner with a number of difficult choices.[2] As our survey results demonstrate, the most nettlesome component of WACC estimation is the cost of equity capital; for unlike readily available yields in bond markets, no observable counterpart exists for equities. This forces practitioners to rely on more abstract and indirect methods to estimate the cost of equity capital.

II. Sample Selection

This paper describes the results of a telephone survey of leading practitioners. Believing that the complexity of the subject does not lend itself to a written questionnaire, we wanted to solicit an explanation of each firm's approach told in the practitioner's

---

[2]Even at the theoretical level, Dixit and Pindyck (1994) point out that the use of standard net-present-value (NPV) decision rules (with, for instance, WACC as a discount rate) does not capture the option value of being able to delay an irreversible investment expenditure. As a result, a firm may find it better to delay an investment even if the current NPV is positive. Our survey does not explore the ways firms deal with this issue, rather, we focus on measuring capital costs.

own words. Though our interviews were guided by a series of questions, these were sufficiently open-ended to reveal many subtle differences in practice.

Since our focus is on the gaps between theory and application rather than on average or typical practice, we aimed to sample practitioners who were leaders in the field. We began by searching for a sample of corporations (rather than investors or financial advisers) in the belief that they had ample motivation to compute WACC carefully and to resolve many of the estimation issues themselves. Several publications offer lists of firms that are well-regarded in finance;[3] of these, we chose a research report, *Creating World-Class Financial Management: Strategies of 50 Leading Companies* (1992), which identified firms

> selected by their peers as being among those with the best financial management. Firms were chosen for excellence in strategic financial risk management, tax and accounting, performance evaluation and other areas of financial management . . . The companies included were those that were mentioned the greatest number of times by their peers.[4]

From the 50 companies identified in this report, we eliminated 18 headquartered outside North America.[5] Of those remaining, five declined to be interviewed, leaving a sample of 27 firms. The companies included in the sample are contained in **Exhibit 1.** We approached the most senior financial officer first with a letter explaining our research, and then with a telephone call. Our request was to interview the individual in charge of estimating the firm's WACC. We promised our interviewees that, in preparing a report on our findings, we would not identify the practices of any particular company by name—we have respected this promise in our presentation.

In the interest of assessing the practices of the broader community of finance practitioners, we surveyed two other samples:

- **Financial Advisers.** Using a "league table" of merger and acquisition advisers presented in *Institutional Investor* issues of April 1995, 1994, and 1993, we drew a sample of 10 of the most active[6] advisers. We applied approximately[7] the same set of questions to representatives of these firms' mergers and acquisitions departments. We wondered whether the financial advisers' interest in promoting deals

---

[3]For instance, *Institutional Investor* and *Euromoney* publish lists of firms with the best CFOs or with special competencies in certain areas. We elected not to use these lists because special competencies might not indicate a generally excellent finance department, nor might a stellar CFO.

[4]This survey was based upon a written questionnaire sent to CEOs, CFOs, controllers, and treasurers and was followed up by a telephone survey (Business International Corporation, 1992).

[5]Our reasons for excluding these firms were the increased difficulty of obtaining interviews, and possible difficulties in obtaining capital market information (such as betas and equity market premiums) that might preclude using American practices. The enlargement of this survey to firms from other countries is a subject worthy of future study.

[6]Activity in this case was defined as four-year aggregate deal volume in mergers and acquisitions. The sample was drawn from the top 12 advisers, using their *average* deal volume over the 1993-95 period. Of these 12, two firms chose not to participate in the survey.

[7]Specific questions differ, reflecting the facts that financial advisers infrequently deal with capital budgeting matters and that corporate financial officers infrequently value companies.

might lead them to lower WACC estimates than those estimated by operating companies. This proved not to be the case. If anything, the estimating techniques most often used by financial advisers yield higher, not lower, capital cost estimates.

- **Textbooks and Tradebooks.** From a leading textbook publisher, we obtained a list of the graduate-level textbooks in corporate finance having the greatest unit sales in 1994. From these, we selected the top four. In addition, we drew on three tradebooks that discuss the estimation of WACC in detail.

Names of advisers and books included in these two samples are shown in **Exhibit 1.**

III. Survey Findings

The detailed survey results appear in **Exhibit 2.** The estimation approaches are broadly similar across the three samples in several dimensions.

- Discounted Cash Flow (DCF) is the dominant investment-evaluation technique.
- WACC is the dominant discount rate used in DCF analyses.
- Weights are based on *market* not book value mixes of debt and equity.[8]
- The after-tax cost of debt is predominantly based on *marginal* pretax costs, and *marginal or statutory* tax rates.
- The CAPM is the dominant model for estimating the cost of equity. Some firms mentioned other multi-factor asset-pricing models (e.g., Arbitrage Pricing Theory) but these were in the small minority. No firms cited specific modifications of the CAPM to adjust for any empirical shortcomings of the model in explaining past returns.[9]

These practices differ sharply from those reported in earlier surveys.[10] First, the best-practice firms show much more alignment on most elements of practice. Second, they base their practice on financial economic models rather than on rules of thumb or arbitrary decision rules.

On the other hand, disagreements exist within and among groups on how to apply the CAPM to estimate cost of equity. The CAPM states that the required return (K) on any asset can be expressed as

$$K = R_f + \beta(R_m - R_f) \tag{2}$$

---

[8]The choice between target and actual proportions is not a simple one. Because debt and equity costs clearly depend on the proportions of each employed, it might appear that the actual proportions must be used. However, if the firm's target weights are publicly known, and if investors expect the firm soon to move to these weights, then observed costs of debt and equity may anticipate the target capital structure.

[9]For instance, even research supporting the CAPM has found that empirical data are better explained by an intercept higher than a risk-free rate and a price of beta risk less than the market risk premium. Ibbotson Associates (1994) offers such a modified CAPM in addition to the standard CAPM and other models, in its cost of capital service. Jagannathan and McGrattan (1995) provide a useful review of empirical evidence on the CAPM.

[10]See Gitman and Forrester (1977) and Gitman and Mercurio (1982).

where:

R_f = interest rate available on a risk-free bond.

R_m = return required to attract investors to hold the broad market portfolio of risky assests.

β = the relative risk of the particular asset.

According to CAPM then, the cost of equity, K_{equity}, for a company depends on three components: returns on risk-free bonds (R_f), the stock's equity beta which measures risk of the company's stock relative to other risky assets (β = 1.0 is average risk), and the market risk premium $(R_m - R_f)$ necessary to entice investors to hold risky assets generally versus risk-free bonds. In theory, each of these components must be a forward looking estimate. Our survey results show substantial disagreements on all three components.

A. The Risk-Free Rate of Return

As originally derived, the CAPM is a single-period model, so the question of which interest rate best represents the risk-free rate never arises. But in a many-period world typically characterized by upward-sloping yield curves, the practitioner must choose. Our results show the choice is typically between the 90-day Treasury bill yield and a long-term Treasury bond yield (see **Exhibit 3**). (Because the yield curve is ordinarily relatively flat beyond ten years, the choice of which particular long-term yield to use is not a critical one.)[11] The difference between realized returns on the 90-day T-bill and the ten-year T-bond has averaged 150 basis points over the long run; so choice of a risk-free rate can have a material effect on the cost of equity and WACC.[12]

The 90-day T-bill yields are more consistent with the CAPM as originally derived and reflect truly risk-free returns in the sense that T-bill investors avoid material loss in value from interest rate movements. However, long-term bond yields more closely reflect the default-free holding period returns available on long lived investments and thus more closely mirror the types of investments made by companies.

Our survey results reveal a strong preference on the part of practitioners for long-term bond yields. Of both corporations and financial advisers, 70% use Treasury bond yields maturities of ten years or greater. None of the financial advisers and only 4%

---

[11]In early January 1996, the differences between yields on the 10- and 30-year T-bonds were about 35 basis points. Some aficionados will argue that there *is* a difference between the ten- and 30-year yields. Ordinarily the yield curve declines just slightly as it reaches the 30-year maturity—this has been explained to us as the result of life insurance companies and other long-term buy-and-hold investors who are said to purchase the long bond in significant volume. It is said that these investors command a lower liquidity premium than the broader market, thus driving down yields. If this is true, then the yields at this point of the curve may be due not to some ordinary process of rational expectations, but rather to an anomalous supply-demand imbalance, which would render these yields less trustworthy. The counterargument is that life insurance companies could be presumed to be rational investors too. As buy-and-hold investors, they will surely suffer the consequences of any irrationality, and therefore have good motive to invest for yields "at the market."

[12]This was estimated as the difference in arithmetic mean returns on long-term government bonds and US Treasury bills over the years 1926 to 1994, given by Ibbotson Associates (1995).

of the corporations used the Treasury bill yield. Many corporations said they matched the term of the risk-free rate to the tenor of the investment. In contrast, 43% of the books advocated the T-bill yield, while only 29% used long-term Treasury yields.

B. Beta Estimates

Finance theory calls for a forward-looking beta, one reflecting investors' uncertainty about the future cash flows to equity. Because forward-looking betas are unobservable, practitioners are forced to rely on proxies of various kinds. Most often this involves using beta estimates derived from historical data and published by such sources as Bloomberg, Value Line, and Standard & Poor's.

The usual methodology is to estimate beta as the slope coefficient of the market model of returns.

$$R_{it} = \alpha_i + \beta_i(R_{mt}) \tag{3}$$

where

R_{it} = return on stock i in time period (e.g., day, week, month) t,

R_{mt} = return on the market portfolio in period t,

α_i = regression constant for stock i, and

β_i = beta for stock i.

In addition to relying on historical data, use of this equation to estimate beta requires a number of practical compromises, each of which can materially affect the results. For instance, increasing the number of time periods used in the estimation may improve the statistical reliability of the estimate but risks the inclusion of stale, irrelevant information. Similarly, shortening the observation period from monthly to weekly, or even daily, increases the size of the sample but may yield observations that are not normally distributed and may introduce unwanted random noise. A third compromise involves choice of the market index. Theory dictates that R_m is the return on the market portfolio, an unobservable portfolio consisting of *all* risky assets, including human capital and other nontraded assets, in proportion to their importance in world wealth. Beta providers use a variety of stock market indices as proxies for the market portfolio on the argument that stock markets trade claims on a sufficiently wide array of assets to be adequate surrogates for the unobservable market portfolio.

Exhibit 4 shows the compromises underlying the beta estimates of three prominent providers and their combined effect on the beta estimates of our sample companies. Note for example that the mean beta of our sample companies according to Bloomberg is 1.03, while the same number according to Value Line is 1.24. **Exhibit 5** provides a complete list of sample betas by publisher.

Over half of the corporations in our sample (item ten, **Exhibit 2**) rely on published sources for their beta estimates, although 30% calculate their own. Among financial advisers, 40% rely on published sources, 20% calculate their own, and another 40% use what might be called "fundamental" beta estimates. These are estimates which use multi-factor statistical models drawing on fundamental indices of firm and industry risk to estimate company betas. The best known provider of fundamental beta estimates is the consulting firm BARRA.

Within these broad categories, a number of survey participants indicated use of more pragmatic approaches, which combine published beta estimates or adjust published estimates in various heuristic ways. (See **Exhibit 6.**)

C. Equity Market Risk Premium

This topic prompted the greatest variety of responses among survey participants. Finance theory says the equity market risk premium should equal the excess return expected by investors on the market portfolio relative to riskless assets. How one measures expected future returns on the market portfolio and on riskless assets are problems left to practitioners. Because expected future returns are unobservable, all survey respondents extrapolated historical returns into the future on the presumption that past experience heavily conditions future expectations. Where respondents chiefly differed was in their use of *arithmetic* versus *geometric* average historical equity returns and in their choice of realized returns on T-bills versus T-bonds to proxy for the return on riskless assets.

The arithmetic mean return is the simple average of past returns. Assuming the distribution of returns is stable over time and that periodic returns are independent of one another, the arithmetic return is the best estimator of expected return.[13] The geometric mean return is the internal rate of return between a single outlay and one or more future receipts. It measures the compound rate of return investors earned over past periods. It accurately portrays historical investment experience. Unless returns are the same each time period, the geometric average will always be less than the arithmetic average, and the gap widens as returns become more volatile.[14]

Based on Ibbotson Associates' data (1995) from 1926 to 1995, **Exhibit 7** illustrates the possible range of equity market risk premiums depending on use of the geometric as opposed to the arithmetic mean equity return and on use of realized returns on T-bills as opposed to T-bonds.[15] Even wider variations in market risk premiums can arise when one changes the historical period for averaging. Extending US stock experience back to 1802, Siegel (1992) shows that historical market premia have changed over time and were typically lower in the pre-1926 period. Carleton and Lakonishok (1985) illustrate considerable variation in historical premia using different time periods and methods of calculation even with data since 1926.

---

[13]Several studies have documented significant negative autocorrelation in returns—this violates one of the essential tenets of the arithmetic calculation since, if returns are not serially independent, the simple arithmetic mean of a distribution will not be its expected value. The autocorrelation findings are reported by Fama and French (1986), Lo and MacKinlay (1988), and Poterba and Summers (1988).

[14]For large samples of returns, the geometric average can be approximated as the arithmetic average minus one half the variance of realized returns. Ignoring smaple size adjustments, the variance of returns in the current example is 0.09 yielding an estimate of $0.10 - 1/2(0.09) = 0.055 = 5.5\%$ versus the actual 5.8% figure. Kritzman (1994) provides an interesting comparison of the two types of averages.

[15]These figures are drawn from Table 2–1, Ibbotson Associates (1995), where the R_m was drawn from the "Large Company Stocks" series, and R_f drawn from the "Long-Term Government Bonds" and "US Treasury Bills" series.

Of the texts and tradebooks in our survey, 71% support use of the arithmetic mean return over T-bills as the best surrogate for the equity market risk premium. For long-term projects, Ehrhardt (1994) advocates forecasting the T-bill rate and using a different cost of equity for each future time period. Kaplan and Ruback (1995) studied the equity risk premium implied by the valuations in highly leveraged transactions and estimated a mean premium of 7.97%, which is most consistent with the arithmetic mean and T-bills. A minority view is that of Copeland, Koller, and Murrin (1990), "We believe that the geometric average represents a better estimate of investors' expected over long periods of time." Ehrhardt (1994) recommends use of the geometric mean return if one believes stockholders are buy-and-hold investors.

Half of the financial advisers queried use a premium consistent with the arithmetic mean and T-bill returns, and many specifically mentioned use of the arithmetic mean. Corporate respondents, on the other hand, evidenced more diversity of opinion and tend to favor a lower market premium: 37% use a premium of 5–6%, and another 11% use an even lower figure.

Comments in our interviews (see **Exhibit 8**) suggest the diversity among survey participants. While most of our 27 sample companies appear to use a 60+-year historical period to estimate returns, one cited a window of less than ten years, two cited windows of about ten years, one began averaging with 1960, and another with 1952 data.

This variety of practice should not come as a surprise since theory calls for a forward-looking risk premium, one that reflects current market sentiment and may change with market conditions. What is clear is that there is substantial variation as practitioners try to operationalize the theoretical call for a market risk premium. A glaring result is that few respondents specifically cited use of any forward-looking method to supplement or replace reading the tea leaves of past returns.[16]

IV. The Impact of Various Assumptions for Using CAPM

To illustrate the effect of these various practices, we estimated the hypothetical cost of equity and WACC for Black & Decker, which we identified as having a wide range in estimated betas, and for McDonald's, which has a relatively narrow range. Our estimates are "hypothetical" in that we do not adopt any information supplied to us by the companies but rather apply a range of approaches based on publicly available information as of late 1995. **Exhibit 9** gives Black & Decker's estimated costs of equity and WACCs under various combinations of risk-free rate, beta, and market risk premia. Three clusters of practice are illustrated, each in turn using three betas as provided by S & P, Value Line, and Bloomberg (unadjusted). The first approach, as suggested by some texts, marries a short-term risk-free rate (90-day T-bill yield) with

---

[16]Only two respondents (one adviser and one company) specifically cited forward-looking estimates although others cited use of data from outside sources (e.g., a company using an estimate from an investment bank) where we cannot identify whether forward-looking estimates were used. Some studies using financial analyst forecasts in dividend growth models suggest market risk premia average in the 6% to 6.5% range and change over time with higher premia when interest rates decline. See for instance, Harris and Marston (1992). Ibbotson Associates (1994) provides industry-specific cost-of-equity estimates using analysts' forecasts in a growth model.

Ibbotson's arithmetic mean (using T-bills) risk premium. The second, adopted by a number of financial advisers, uses a long-term risk-free rate (30-year T-bond yield) and a risk premium of 7.2% (the modal premium mentioned by financial advisers). The third approach also uses a long-term risk-free rate but adopts the modal premium mentioned by corporate respondents of 5.5%. We repeated these general procedures for McDonald's.

The resulting ranges of estimated WACCs for the two firms are

	Maximum WACC	Minimum WACC	Difference in Basis Points
Black & Decker	12.80%	8.50%	430
McDonald's	11.60%	9.30%	230

The range from minimum to maximum is large for both firms, and the economic impact is potentially stunning. To illustrate this, the present value of a level perpetual annual stream of $10 million would range between $78 million and $118 million for Black and Decker, and between $86 million and $108 million for McDonald's.

Given the positive but relatively flat slope of the yield curve in late 1995, most of the variation in our illustration is explained by beta and the equity market premium assumption. Variations can be even more dramatic, especially when the yield curve is inverted.

V. Risk Adjustments to WACC

Finance theory is clear that a single WACC is appropriate only for investments of broadly comparable risk: a firm's overall WACC is a suitable benchmark for a firm's average risk investments. Finance theory goes on to say that such a company-specific figure should be adjusted for departures from such an average risk profile. Attracting capital requires payment of a premium that depends on risk.

We probed whether firms use a discount rate appropriate to the risks of the flows being valued in questions on types of investment (strategic vs. operational), terminal values, synergies, and multidivisional companies. Responses to these questions displayed in **Exhibit 2** do not display much apparent alignment of practice. When financial advisers were asked how they value parts of multidivision firms, all ten firms surveyed reported that they use different discount rates for component parts (item 17). However, only 26% of companies always adjust the cost of capital to reflect the risk of individual investment opportunities (item 12). Earlier studies (summarized in Gitman and Mercurio, 1982) reported that between one-third and one-half of the firms surveyed did *not* adjust for risk differences among capital projects. These practices stand in stark contrast to the recommendations of textbooks and tradebooks: the books did not explicitly address all subjects, but when they did, they were uniform in their advocacy of risk-adjusted discount rates.

A closer look at specific responses reveals the tensions as theory based on traded financial assets is adapted to decisions on investments in real assets. Inevitably, a fine line is drawn between use of financial market data versus managerial judgments.

Responses from financial advisers illustrate this. As shown in **Exhibit 2,** all advisers use different capital costs for valuing parts (e.g., divisions) of a firm (item 17); only half ever select different rates for synergies or strategic opportunities (item 18); only one in ten state any inclination to use different discount rates for terminal values and interim cash flows (item 16). Two simplistic interpretations are that 1) advisers ignore important risk differences, or 2) material risk differences are rare in assessing factors such as terminal values. Neither of these fit; our conversations with advisers reveal that they recognize important risk differences but deal with them in a multitude of ways. Consider comments from two prominent investment banks who use different capital costs for valuing parts of multidivision firms. When asked about risk adjustments for prospective merger synergies, these same firms responded:

- "We make these adjustments in cash flows and multiples rather than in discount rates."

- "Risk factors may be different for realizations of synergies, but we make adjustments to cash flows rather than the discount rate."

While financial advisers typically value existing companies, corporations face further challenges. They routinely must evaluate investments in new products and technologies. Moreover, they deal in an administrative setting that melds centralized (e.g., calculating a WACC) and decentralized (e.g., specific project appraisal) processes. As **Exhibit 10** illustrates, these complexities lead to a blend of approaches for dealing with risk. A number of respondents mentioned specific rate adjustments to distinguish between divisional capital costs, international versus domestic investments and leasing versus nonleasing situations. In other instances, however, these same respondents favored cash flow adjustments to deal with risks.

Why do practitioners risk adjust discount rates in one case and work with cash flow adjustments in another? Our interpretation is that risk-adjusted discount rates are more likely used when the analyst can establish relatively objective financial market benchmarks for what rate adjustments should be. At the business (division) level, data on comparable companies provide cost-of-capital estimates. Debt markets provide surrogates for the risks in leasing cash flows. International financial markets shed insights on cross-country differences. When no such market benchmarks are available, practitioners look to other methods for dealing with risks. Lacking a good market analog from which to glean investor opinion (in the form of differing capital costs), the analyst is forced to rely more on internal focus. Practical implementation of risk-adjusted discount rates thus appears to depend on the ability to find traded financial assets that are comparable in risk to the cash flows being valued and then to have financial data on these traded assets.

The pragmatic bent of application also comes to the fore when companies are asked how often they reestimate capital costs (item 13, **Exhibit 2**). Even for those firms who reestimate relatively frequently, **Exhibit 11** shows that they draw an important distinction between estimating capital costs and policy changes about the capital cost figure used in the firm's decision making. Firms consider administrative costs in structuring their policies on capital costs. For a very large venture (e.g. an acquisition), capital costs may be revisited each time. On the other hand, only large material changes in costs may be fed into more formal project evaluation systems. Firms also recognize a certain ambiguity in any cost number and are willing to live with approximations. While the bond market reacts to minute basis point changes in investor return requirements, investments in real assets, where the decision process itself is time consuming and often decentralized, involve much less precision. To paraphrase one of our sample companies, we use capital costs as a rough yardstick rather than the last word in project evaluation.

Our interpretation is that the mixed responses to questions about risk adjusting and reestimating discount rates reflect an often sophisticated set of practical tradeoffs; these involve the size of risk differences, the quality of information from financial markets, and the realities of administrative costs and processes. In cases where there are material differences in perceived risk, a sufficient scale of investment to justify the effort, no large scale administrative complexities, and readily identifiable information from financial markets, practitioners employ risk adjustments to rates quite routinely. Acquisitions, valuing divisions of companies, analysis of foreign versus domestic investments, and leasing versus nonleasing decisions were frequently cited examples. In contrast, when one or more of these factors is not present, practitioners are more likely to employ other means to deal with risks.

VI. Conclusions

Our research sought to identify the "best practice" in cost-of-capital estimation through interviews of leading corporations and financial advisers. Given the huge annual expenditure on capital projects and corporate acquisitions each year, the wise selection of discount rates is of material importance to senior corporate managers.

The survey revealed broad acceptance of the WACC as the basis for setting discount rates. In addition, the survey revealed general alignment in many aspects of the estimation of WACC. The main area of notable disagreement was in the details of implementing CAPM to estimate the cost of equity. This paper outlined the varieties of practice in CAPM use, the arguments in favor of different approaches, and the practical implications.

In summary, we believe that the following elements represent best current practice in the estimation of WACC:

- Weights should be based on *market-value* mixes of debt and equity.

- The after-tax cost of debt should be estimated from *marginal* pretax costs, combined with *marginal or statutory* tax rates.

- CAPM is currently the preferred model for estimating the cost of equity.

- Betas are drawn substantially from published sources, preferring those betas using a long interval of equity returns. Where a number of statistical publishers disagree, best practice often involves judgment to estimate a beta.

- Risk-free rate should match the tenor of the cash flows being valued. For most capital projects and corporate acquisitions, the yield on the US government Treasury bond of ten or more years in maturity would be appropriate.

- Choice of an equity market risk premium is the subject of considerable controversy both as to its value and method of estimation. Most of our best-practice companies use a premium of 6% or lower while many texts and financial advisers use higher figures.

- Monitoring for changes in WACC should be keyed to major changes in financial market conditions, but should be done at least annually. Actually flowing a change through a corporate system of project valuation and compensation targets must be done gingerly and only when there are material changes.

- WACC should be risk adjusted to reflect substantive differences among different businesses in a corporation. For instance, financial advisers generally find the corporate WACC to be inappropriate for valuing different parts of a corporation. Given publicly traded companies in different businesses, such risk adjustment involves only modest revision in the WACC and CAPM approaches already used. Corporations also cite the need to adjust capital costs across national boundaries. In situations where market proxies for a particular type of risk class are not available, best practice involves finding other means to account for risk differences.

Best practice is largely consistent with finance theory. Despite broad agreement at the theoretical level, however, several problems in application remain that can lead to wide divergence in estimated capital costs. Based on these remaining problems, we believe that further applied research on two principal topics is warranted. First, practitioners need additional tools for sharpening their assessment of relative risk. The variation in company-specific beta estimates from different published sources can create large differences in capital-cost estimates. Moreover, use of risk-adjusted discount rates appears limited by lack of good market proxies for different risk profiles. We believe that appropriate use of averages across industry or other risk categories is an avenue worth exploration. Second, practitioners could benefit from further research on estimating equity market risk premia. Current practice displays large variations and focuses primarily on averaging past data. Use of expectational data appears to be a fruitful approach. As the next generation of theories gradually sharpen our insights, we feel that research attention to implementation of existing theory can make for real improvements in practice.

Finally our research is a reminder of the old saying that too often in business we measure with a micrometer, mark with a pencil, and cut with an ax. Despite the many advances in finance theory, the particular "ax" available for estimating company capital costs remains a blunt one. Best-practice companies can expect to estimate their weighted average cost of capital with an accuracy of no more than plus or minus 100 to 150 basis points. This has important implications for how managers use the cost of capital in decision making. First, do not mistake capital budgeting for bond pricing. Despite the tools available, effective capital appraisal continues to require thorough knowledge of the business and wise business judgment. Second, be careful not to throw out the baby with the bath water. Do not reject the cost of capital and attendant advances in financial management because your finance people are not able to give you a precise number. When in need, even a blunt ax is better than nothing.

References

Aggarwal, Raj, 1980, "Corporate Use of Sophisticated Capital Budgeting Techniques: A Strategic Perspective and A Critique of Survey Results," *Interfaces* 10 (No. 2, April), 31–34.

Bierman, Harold J., 1993, "Capital Budgeting in 1992: A Survey," *Financial Management* 22 (No. 3, Autumn), 24.

Brealey, Richard and Stewart Myers, 1991, *Principles of Corporate Finance,* 4th Ed., New York, NY, McGraw-Hill, 197.

Brigham, Eugene and Louis Gapenski, 1991, *Financial Management, Theory and Practice,* 6th Ed., Chicago, IL, Dryden Press.

Business International Corporation, 1992, *Creating World-Class Financial Management: Strategies of 50 Leading Companies,* Research Report 1-110, New York, NY, 7–8.

Carleton, Willard T. and Josef Lakonishok, 1985, "Risk and Return on Equity: The Use and Misuse of Historical Estimates," *Financial Analysts Journal* 4 (No. 1, January–February), 38–48.

Copeland, Tom, Tim Koller and Jack Murrin, 1994, *Valuation: Measuring and Managing the Value of Companies,* 2nd Ed., New York, NY, John Wiley & Sons.

Dixit, Avinash K. and Robert S. Pindyck, 1994, *Investment Under Uncertainty,* Princeton, NJ, Princeton University Press.

Dixit, Avinash K. and Robert S. Pindyck, 1995, "The Options Approach to Capital Investment," *Harvard Business Review* 73 (No. 3, May–June), 105–115.

Ehrhardt, Michael, 1994, *The Search for Value: Measuring the Company's Cost of Capital,* Boston, MA, HBS Press, Chapter One.

Fama, Eugene F. and Kenneth R. French, 1986, "Dividend Yields and Expected Stock Returns," *Journal of Financial Economics* 22 (No. 1, October), 3–25.

Gitman, Lawrence J., 1991, *Principles of Managerial Finance,* 6th Ed., New York, NY, HarperCollins.

Gitman, Lawrence J. and John R. Forrester, Jr., 1977, "A Survey of Capital Budgeting Techniques Used by Major U.S. Firms," *Financial Management* 6 (No. 3, Fall), 66–71.

Gitman, Lawrence J. and Vincent Mercurio, 1982, "Cost of Capital Techniques Used by Major U.S. Firms: Survey and Analysis of Fortune's 1000," *Financial Management* 11 (No. 4, Winter), 21–29.

Harris, Robert S. and Felicia C. Marston, 1992, "Estimating Shareholder Risk Premia Using Analysts' Growth Forecasts,"*Financial Management* 21 (No. 2, Summer), 63–70.

Ibbotson Associates, *1995 Yearbook: Stocks, Bonds, Bills, and Inflation,* 1995, Chicago, IL.

Ibbotson Associates, *1994 Yearbook: Cost of Capital Quarterly,* October 1994, Chicago, IL.

Jagannathan, Ravi and Ellen R. McGrattan, 1995, "The CAPM Debate," *The Federal Reserve Bank of Minneapolis Quarterly Review* 19 (No. 4, Fall), 2–17.

Kaplan, Steven N. and Richard S. Ruback, 1995, "The Valuation of Cash Flow Forecasts: An Empirical Analysis," *Journal of Finance* 50 (No. 4, September), 1059–1093.

Kritzman, Mark, 1994, "What Practitioners Need to Know . . . About Future Value," *Financial Analysts Journal* 50 (No. 3, May–June), 12–15.

Lo, Andrew W. and A. Craig MacKinlay, 1988, "Stock Market Prices Do Not Follow Random Walks: Evidence from a Simple Specification Test," *Review of Financial Studies* 1 (No. 1, Spring), 41–66.

Moore, James S. and Alan K. Reichert, 1983, "An Analysis of the Financial Management Techniques Currently Employed by Large U.S. Companies," *Journal of Business Finance and Accounting* 10 (No. 4, Winter), 623–645.

Poterba, James M. and Lawrence H. Summers, 1995, "A CEO Survey of U.S. Companies' Time Horizons and Hurdle Rates," *Sloan Management Review* 37 (No. 1, Fall), 43–53.

Poterba, James M. and Lawrence H. Summers, 1988, "Mean Reversion in Stock Prices: Evidence and Implications," *Journal of Financial Economics* 22 (No. 1, October), 27–59.

Ross, Stephen, Randolph Westerfield, and Jeffrey Jaffe, 1996, *Corporate Finance,* 4th Ed., Chicago, IL, Irwin.

Schall, Lawrence D., Gary L. Sundem, and William R. Geijsbeek, Jr., 1978, "Survey and Analysis of Capital Budgeting Methods," *Journal of Finance* 33 (No. 1, March), 281–292.

Siegel, Jeremy J., 1992, "The Equity Premium: Stock and Bond Returns Since 1802," *Financial Analysts Journal* 48 (No. 1, January–February), 28–46.

Trahan, Emery A. and Lawrence J. Gitman, 1995, "Bridging the Theory-Practice Gap in Corporate Finance: A Survey of Chief Financial Officers," *Quarterly Review of Economics & Finance* 35 (No. 1, Spring), 73–87.

EXHIBIT 1 | Three Survey Samples

Company Sample	Adviser Sample	Textbook/Tradebook Sample
Advanced Micro	CS First Boston	*Textbooks*
Allergan	Dillon, Read	Brealey and Myers
Black & Decker	Donaldson, Lufkin, Jenrette	Brigham and Gapenski
Cellular One	J. P. Morgan	Gitman
Chevron	Lehman Brothers	Ross, Westerfield & Jaffe
Colgate-Palmolive	Merrill Lynch	*Tradebooks*
Comdisco	Morgan Stanley	Copeland, Koller & Murrin
Compaq	Salomon Brothers	Ehrhardt
Eastman Kodak	Smith Barney	Ibbotson Associates
Gillette	Wasserstein Perella	
Guardian Industries		
Henkel		
Hewlett-Packard		
Kanthal		
Lawson Mardon		
McDonald's		
Merck		
Monsanto		
PepsiCo		
Quaker Oats		
Schering-Plough		
Tandem		
Union Carbide		
US West		
Walt Disney		
Weyerhauser		
Whirlpool		

EXHIBIT 2 | General Survey Results

	Corporations	Financial Advisers	Textbooks/Tradebooks
1. Do you use DCF techniques to evaluate investment opportunities?	89%—Yes, as a primary tool. 7%—Yes, only as secondary tool. 4%—No	100%—Rely on DCF, comparable companies multiples, comparable transactions multiples. Of these, 10%—DCF is a primary tool. 10%—DCF is used mainly as a check. 80%—Weight the three approaches depending on purpose and type of analysis.	100%—Yes
2. Do you use any form of a cost of capital as your discount rate in your DCF analysis?	89%—Yes 7%—Sometimes 4%—N/A	100%—Yes	100%—Yes
3. For your cost of capital, do you form any combination of capital cost to determine a WACC?	85%—Yes 4%—Sometimes 4%—No 7%—N/A	100%—Yes	100%—Yes
4. What weighting factors do you use? target vs. current debt/equity market vs. book weights	*Target/Current* *Market/Book* 52%—Target 59%—Market 15%—Current 15%—Book 26%—Uncertain 19%—Uncertain 7%—N/A 7%—N/A	*Target/Current* *Market/Book* 90%—Target 90%—Market 10%—Current 10%—Book	*Target/Current Market/Book* 86%—Target 100%—Market 14%—Current/Target
5. How do you estimate your before tax cost of debt?	52%—Marginal cost 37%—Current average 4%—Uncertain 7%—N/A	60%—Marginal cost 40%—Current average	71%—Marginal cost 29%—No explicit recommendation
6. What tax rate do you use?	52%—Marginal or statutory 37%—Historical average 4%—Uncertain 7%—N/A	60%—Marginal or statutory 30%—Historical average 10%—Uncertain	71%—Marginal or statutory 29%—No explicit recommendation
7. How do you estimate your cost of equity? (If you do not use CAPM, skip to question 12.)	81%—CAPM 4%—Modified CAPM 15%—N/A	80%—CAPM 20%—Other (including modified CAPM)	100%—Primarily CAPM Other methods mentioned: Dividend-Growth Model, Arbitrage-Pricing Model.
8. As usually written, the CAPM version of the cost of equity has three terms: a risk-free rate, a volatility or beta factor, and a market-risk premium. Is this consistent with your company's approach?	85%—Yes 0%—No 15%—N/A	90%—Yes 10%—N/A	100%—Yes

EXHIBIT 2 | *(continued)*

	Corporations	Financial Advisers	Textbooks/Tradebooks
9. What do you use for the risk-free rate?	4%—90-day T-Bill 7%—three- to seven-year Treasuries 33%—ten-year Treasuries 4%—20-year Treasuries 33%—ten- to 30-year Treasuries 4%—ten-years or 90-Day; Depends 15%—N/A (Many said they match the term of the risk-free rate to the tenor of the investment.)	10%—90-day T-Bill 10%—five- to ten-year Treasuries 30%—ten- to 30-year Treasuries 40%—30-year Treasuries 10%—N/A	43%—T-Bills 29%—LT Treasuries 14%—Match tenor of investment 14%—Don't say
10. What do you use as your volatility or beta factor?	52%—Published source 3%—Financial adviser's estimate 30%—Self calculated 15%—N/A	30%—Fundamental beta (e.g., BARRA) 40%—Published source 20%—Self calculated 10%—N/A	100%—Mention availability of published sources
11. What do you use as your market-risk premium?	11%—Use fixed rate of 4.0–4.5% 37%—Use fixed rate of 5.0–6% 4%—Use geometric mean 4%—Use arithmetic mean 4%—Use average of historical and implied 15%—Use financial adviser's estimate 7%—Use premium over treasuries 3%—Use Value Line estimate 15%—N/A	10%—Use fixed rate of 5.0% 50%—Use 7.0–7.4% (Similar to arithmetic) 10%—LT arithmetic mean 10%—Both LT arithmetic and geometric mean 10%—Spread above treasuries 10%—N/A	71%—Arithmetic historical mean 15%—Geometric historical mean 14%—Don't say
12. Having estimated your company's cost of capital, do you make any further adjustments to reflect the risk of individual investment opportunities?	26%—Yes 33%—Sometimes 41%—No	Not asked.	86%—Adjust beta for investment risk 14%—Don't say
13. How frequently do you re-estimate your company's cost of capital?	4%—Monthly 19%—Quarterly 11%—Semi-Annually 37%—Annually 7%—Continually/Every Investment 19%—Infrequently 4%—N/A (Generally, many said that in addition to scheduled reviews, they re-estimate as needed for significant events such as acquisitions and high-impact economic events.)	Not asked.	100%—No explicit recommendation

EXHIBIT 2 | *(concluded)*

	Corporations	Financial Advisers	Textbooks/Tradebooks
14. Is the cost of capital used for purposes other than project analysis in your company? (For example, to evaluate divisional performance?)	51%—Yes 44%—No 4%—N/A	Not asked.	100%—No explicit discussion
15. Do you distinguish between strategic and operational investments? Is cost of capital used differently in these two categories?	48%—Yes 48%—No 4%—N/A	Not asked.	29%—Yes 71%—No explicit discussion
16. What methods do you use to estimate terminal value? Do you use the same discount rate for the terminal value as for the interim cash flows?	Not asked.	30%—Exit multiples only 70%—Both multiples and perpetuity DCF model 70%—Use same WACC for TV 20%—No response 10%—Rarely change	71%—Perpetuity DCF model 29%—No explicit discussion 100%—No explicit discussion of separate WACC for terminal value
17. In valuing a multidivisional company, do you aggregate the values of the individual divisions, or just value the firm as a whole? If you value each division separately, do you use a different cost of capital for each one?	Not asked.	100%—Value the parts 100%—Use different WACCs for separate valuations	100%—Use distinct WACC for each division
18. In your valuations do you use any different methods to value synergies or strategic opportunities (e.g., higher or lower discount rates, options valuation)?	Not asked.	30%—Yes 50%—No 20%—Rarely	29%—Use distinct WACC for synergies 71%—No explicit discussion
19. Do you make any adjustments to the risk premium for changes in market conditions?	Not asked.	20%—Yes 70%—No 10%—N/A	14%—Yes 86%—No explicit discussion
20. How long have you been with the company? What is your job title?	10 years—Mean All senior, except one	7.3 years—Mean 4—MDs, 2 VPs, 4—Associates	N/A

EXHIBIT 3 | Choice of Bond Market Proxy

Some of our best-practice companies noted that their choice of a bond market proxy for a risk-free rate depended specifically on how they were proposing to spend funds. We asked, "What do you use for a risk-free rate?" and heard the following:

- "Ten-year Treasury bond or other duration Treasury bond if needed to better match project horizon."
- "We use a three- to five-year Treasury note yield, which is the typical length of our company's investment. We match our average investment horizon with maturity of debt."

EXHIBIT 4 | Compromises Underlying Beta Estimates and Their Effect on Estimated Betas of Sample Companies

	Bloomberg[a]	Value Line	Standard & Poor's
Number	102	260	60
Time Interval	wkly (2 yrs.)	wkly (5 yrs.)	mthly (5 yrs.)
Market Index Proxy	S&P 500	NYSE composite	S&P 500
Mean Beta	1.03	1.24	1.18
Median Beta	1.00	1.20	1.21

[a]With the Bloomberg service, it is possible to estimate a beta over many differing time periods, market indices, and as smoothed or unadjusted. The figures presented here represent the base-line or default-estimation approach used if other approaches are not specified.

EXHIBIT 5 | Betas for Corporate Survey Respondents

In this exhibit, Bloomberg's adjusted beta is $\beta_{adj} = (0.66)\beta_{raw} + (0.33)1.00$ and Value Line reported only Total Debt/Total Cap for these firms, except in the case of US West, in which LT Debt/Total Cap was reported.

	Bloomberg Betas		Value Line Betas	S&P Betas	Range
	Raw	Adjusted			Max.–Min.
Advanced Micro	1.20	1.13	1.70	1.47	0.57
Allergan	0.94	0.96	1.30	1.36	0.42
Black & Decker	1.06	1.04	1.65	1.78	0.74
Cellular One			Not Listed		
Chevron	0.70	0.80	0.70	0.68	0.12
Colgate-Palmolive	1.11	1.07	1.20	0.87	0.33
Comdisco	1.50	1.34	1.35	1.20	0.30
Compaq	1.26	1.18	1.50	1.55	0.37
Eastman Kodak	0.54	0.69	NMF	0.37	0.32
Gillette	0.93	0.95	1.25	1.30	0.37
Guardian Industries			Not Listed		
Henkel			Not Listed		
Hewlett-Packard	1.34	1.22	1.40	1.96	0.74
Kanthal			Not Listed		
Lawson Mardon			Not Listed		
McDonald's	0.93	0.96	1.05	1.09	0.16
Merck	0.73	0.82	1.10	1.15	0.42
Monsanto	0.89	0.93	1.10	1.36	0.47
PepsiCo	1.12	1.08	1.10	1.19	0.11
Quaker Oats	1.38	1.26	0.90	0.67	0.71
Schering-Plough	0.51	0.67	1.00	0.82	0.49
Tandem	1.35	1.23	1.75	1.59	0.52
Union Carbide	1.51	1.34	1.30	0.94	0.57
US West	0.61	0.74	0.75	0.53	0.22
Walt Disney	1.42	1.28	1.15	1.22	0.27
Weyerhauser	0.78	0.85	1.20	1.21	0.43
Whirlpool	0.90	0.93	1.55	1.58	0.68
Mean	1.03	1.02	1.24	1.18	0.42
Median	1.00	1.00	1.20	1.21	0.42
Standard Deviation	0.31	0.21	0.29	0.41	0.19

EXHIBIT 6 | Beta Factor

We asked our sample companies, "What do you use as your volatility or beta factor?" A sampling of responses shows the choice is not always a simple one.

- "We use adjusted betas reported by Bloomberg. At times, our stock has been extremely volatile. If at a particular time the factor is considered unreasonably high, we are apt to use a lower (more consistent) one."
- "We begin with the observed 60-month covariance between our stock and the market. We also consider, Value Line, Barra, S&P betas for comparison and may adjust the observed beta to match assessment of future risk."
- "We average Merrill Lynch and Value Line figures and use Bloomberg as a check."
- "We do not use betas estimated on our stock directly. Our company beta is built up as a weighted average of our business segment betas—the segment betas are estimated using pure-play firm betas of comparable companies."

EXHIBIT 7 | The Equity Market Risk Premium $(R_m - R_f)$

	T-Bill Returns	T-Bond Returns
Arithmetic Mean Return	8.5%	7.0%
Geometric Mean Return	6.5%	5.4%

EXHIBIT 8 | Market Risk Premium

"What do you use as your market risk premium?" A sampling of responses from our best-practice companies shows the choice can be a complicated one.

- "Our 400 basis point market premium is based on the historical relationship of returns on an actualized basis and/or investment bankers' estimated cost of equity based on analysts' earnings projections."
- "We use an Ibbotson arithmetic average starting in 1960. We have talked to investment banks and consulting firms with advice from 3–7%."
- "A 60-year average of about 5.7%. This number has been used for a long time in the company and is currently the subject of some debate and is under review. We may consider using a time horizon of less than 60 years to estimate this premium."
- "We are currently using 6%. In 1993, we polled various investment banks and academic studies on the issue as to the appropriate rate and got anywhere between 2% and 8%, but most were between 6% and 7.4%."

Comments from financial advisers also were revealing. While some simply responded that they use a published historical average, others presented a more complex picture.

- "We employ a self-estimated 5% (arithmetic average). A variety of techniques are used in estimation. We look at Ibbotson data and focus on more recent periods, around 30 years (but it is not a straight 30-year average). We use smoothing techniques, Monte Carlo simulation and a dividend discount model on the S&P 400 to estimate what the premium should be, given our risk-free rate of return."
- "We use a 7.4% arithmetic mean, after Ibbotson, Sinquefeld. We used to use the geometric mean following the then scholarly advice, but we changed to the arithmetic mean when we found later that our competitors were using the arithmetic mean and scholars' views were shifting."

EXHIBIT 9 | Variations in Cost of Capital (WACC) Estimates for Black and Decker Using Different Methods of Implementing the Capital-Asset Pricing Model

In this Exhibit, in all cases the CAPM is used to estimate the cost of equity, the cost of debt is assumed to be 7.81% based on a Beta rating, the tax rate is assumed to be 38%, and debt is assumed to represent 49% of capital.

Panel A. Short-Term Rate Plus Arithmetic Average Historical Risk Premium

(recommended by some texts)
$R_f = 5.36\%$, 90-day T-bills
$R_m - R_f = 8.50\%$, Ibbotson arithmetic average since 1926

	Cost of Equity	Cost of Capital
Beta Service	K_e	WACC
Bloomberg, $\beta = 1.06$	14.40%	9.70%
Value Line, $\beta = 1.65$	19.40%	12.20%
S&P, $\beta = 1.78$	20.25%	12.80%

Panel B. Long-Term Rate Plus Risk Premium of 7.20%

(modal practice of financial advisers surveyed)
$R_f = 6.26\%$, 30-year T-bonds
$R_m - R_f = 7.20\%$, modal response of financial advisers

	Cost of Equity	Cost of Capital
Beta Service	K_e	WACC
Bloomberg, $\beta = 1.06$	13.90%	9.40%
Value Line, $\beta = 1.65$	18.10%	11.60%
S&P, $\beta = 1.78$	19.10%	12.10%

Panel C. Long-Term Rate Plus Risk Premium of 5.50%

(modal practice of corporations surveyed)
$R_f = 6.26\%$, 30-year T-bonds
$R_m - R_f = 5.50\%$, modal response of corporations

	Cost of Equity	Cost of Capital
Beta Service	K_e	WACC
Bloomberg, $\beta = 1.06$	12.10%	8.50%
Value Line, $\beta = 1.65$	15.30%	10.20%
S&P, $\beta = 1.78$	16.10%	10.50%

EXHIBIT 10 | Adjustments for Project Risk

When asked whether they adjusted discount rates for project risk, companies provided a wide range of responses.

- "No, it's difficult to draw lines between the various businesses we invest in and we also try as best we can to make adjustments for risk in cash flow projections rather than in cost of capital factors . . . We advocate minimizing adjustments to cost of capital calculations and maximizing understanding of all relevant issues, e.g., commodity costs and international/political risks." At another point the same firm noted that "for lease analysis only the cost of debt is used."
- "No (we don't risk adjust cost of capital). We believe there are two basic components: 1) projected cash flows, which should incorporate investment risk, and 2) discount rate." The same firm noted, however: "For international investments, the discount rate is adjusted for country risk." and "For large acquisitions, the company takes significantly greater care to estimate an accurate cost of capital."
- "No, but use divisional costs of capital to calculate a weighted average company cost of capital . . . for comparison and possible adjustment."
- "Yes, we have calculated a cost of capital for divisions based on pure play betas and also suggest subjective adjustments based on each project. Our feeling is that use of divisional costs is the most frequent distinction in the company."
- "Rarely, but at least on one occasion we have for a whole new line of business."
- "We do sensitivity analysis on every project."
- "For the most part we make risk adjustments qualitatively, i.e., we use the corporate WACC to evaluate a project, but then interpret the result according to the risk of the proposal being studied. This could mean that a risky project will be rejected even though it meets the corporate hurdle rate objectives."
- "No domestically; yes internationally—we assess a risk premium per country and adjust the cost of capital accordingly."

EXHIBIT 11 | Cost-of-Capital Estimates

How frequently do you re-estimate your company's cost of capital? Here are responses from best-practice companies.

- "We usually review it quarterly but would review more frequently if market rates changed enough to warrant the review. We would only announce a change in the rate if the recomputed number was materially different than the one currently being used."
- "We reestimate it once or twice a year, but we rarely change the number that the business units use for decision and planning purposes. We expect the actual rate to vary over time, but we also expect that average to be fairly constant over the business cycle. Thus, we tend to maintain a steady discount rate within the company over time."
- "Usually every six months, except in cases of very large investments, in which it is reestimated for each analysis."
- "Whenever we need to, such as for an acquisition or big investment proposal."
- "Re-evaluate as needed e.g., for major tax changes, but unless the cost of capital change is significant (a jump to 21%, for instance), our cutoff rate is not changed; it is used as a *yardstick* rather than the last word in project evaluation."
- "Probably need 100 basis point change to publish a change. We report only to the nearest percent."

Roche Holding Ag: Funding The Genentech Acquisition

We are confident that we will have the financing available when the money is needed . . . The plan is to use as financing partly our own funds and then obviously bonds and then commercial paper and traditional bank financing. We will start by going to the bond market first.[1]
—Roche Chairman Franz Hume

In July 2008, Swiss pharmaceutical company Roche Holding AG (Roche) made an offer to acquire all remaining outstanding shares of U.S. biotechnology leader Genentech for (U.S. dollars) USD89.00 per share in cash. Six months later, with equity markets down 35%, Roche announced its recommitment to the deal with a discounted offer of USD86.50 in cash per share of Genentech stock.

To pay for the deal, Roche needed USD42 billion in cash. To meet that massive cash need, which was not fully available through bank debt, management planned to sell USD32 billion in bonds at various maturities from 1 year to 30 years and in three different currencies (U.S. dollar, euro, and British pound). The sale would begin with the dollar-denominated offering and followed up soon after with rounds of offerings in the other currencies.

In mid-February 2009, Roche was ready to move forward with what was anticipated to be the largest bond offering in history. With considerable ongoing turmoil in world financial markets and substantial uncertainty surrounding the willingness of

---

[1]Sam Cage, "Roche Goes Hostile, Cuts Genentech Bid to $42 Billion," *Reuters,* January 30, 2009.

This case, based on publicly available data, was prepared by Brett Durick (MBA'11), Drew Chambers (MBA'11), and Michael J. Schill, Robert F. Vandell Research Associate Professor of Business Administration. This case is dedicated to Courtney Turner Chambers, in recognition of the sacrifice and contribution of Darden partners. It was written as a basis for class discussion rather than to illustrate effective or ineffective handling of an administrative situation. Copyright © 2011 by the University of Virginia Darden School Foundation, Charlottesville, VA. All rights reserved. *To order copies, send an e-mail to sales@dardenbusinesspublishing.com. No part of this publication may be reproduced, stored in a retrieval system, used in a spreadsheet, or transmitted in any form or by any means—electronic, mechanical, photocopying, recording, or otherwise—without the permission of the Darden School Foundation.*

Genentech minority shareholders to actually sell their shares for the reduced offer of USD86.50, Roche's financing strategy was certainly bold.

Roche

In 1894, Swiss banker Fritz Hoffmann-La Roche, 26, joined Max Carl Traub to take over a small factory on Basel's Grenzacherstrasse from druggists Bohny, Hollinger & Co. Following a difficult first two years, Hoffmann-La Roche bought out his partner and entered F. Hoffmann-La Roche & Co. in the commercial register.

In the early years, the company's primary products included sleeping agents, antiseptics, and vitamins; by the late 1930s, the company had already expanded to 35 countries, an expansion that continued in the decades following the Second World War. In 1990, the company, by then known as Roche, acquired a majority stake in Genentech, a South San Francisco biotechnology company, for USD2.1 billion. Genentech's research focused primarily on developing products based on gene splicing or recombinant DNA to treat diseases such as cancer and AIDS. The acquisition gave Roche a strong foothold in the emerging biologics market as well as stronger presence in the U.S. market.

Since the 1990s, Roche had maintained focus on its two primary business units, pharmaceuticals and medical diagnostics; in 2004, Roche sold its over-the-counter consumer health business to Bayer AG for nearly USD3 billion. In 2008, Roche expanded its diagnostics business with the acquisition of Ventana Medical Systems for USD3.4 billion.

By the end of 2008, Roche's total revenue was just shy of (Swiss francs) CHF50 billion. The pharmaceutical division contributed 70% of the total Roche revenue and over 90% of the operating profit. Roche was clearly one of the leading pharmaceuticals in the world. **Exhibit 1** provides a revenue breakdown of Roche's 2008 revenue by geography and therapeutic area, as well as a detailed overview of Roche's top selling pharmaceutical products. Roche and Genentech's financial statements are detailed in **Exhibit 2** and **3**, respectively, and the stock performance of the two companies is shown in **Exhibit 4**.

Market Conditions

The past 18 months had been historic for global financial markets, which had undergone a sharp correction after dramatic declines in real estate prices and an overheated credit market. Since October 2007, world equity market prices had declined over 45%. Large numbers of commercial and investment banks had failed. The global labor market was shedding jobs, resulting in sharp increases in unemployment rates. Broad economic activity was also affected, with large declines in overall economic activity.

In response to what some feared would become the next Great Depression, world governments made massive investments in financial and industrial institutions. In an effort to stimulate liquidity, central banks had lowered interest rates. The market uncertainty was accompanied with a massive "flight to quality" as global investors moved capital to U.S. Treasury securities (particularly short-term T-bills), thereby driving down U.S. benchmark yields to historic lows. **Exhibit 5** shows the prevailing yield curve in U.S. dollars, euros, and British pounds. **Exhibit 6** contains the prevailing credit spreads over benchmark yields for U.S. industrial corporate bonds based on bond ratings from bond-rating agency Standard and Poor's. **Exhibit 7** plots historical trends in yields of bonds by various credit ratings over the past two years. **Exhibit 8** provides a definitional overview of Standard and Poor's credit ratings. Roche's current credit rating with Standard and Poor's was AA—and with Moody's was Aa1. **Exhibit 9** details median values for various financial ratios for companies rated within a particular category for 2007 and 2008. Despite the uncertainty in the credit markets, corporate transactions were reawakening in the pharmaceutical industry. Pfizer had recently agreed to acquire Wyeth for USD68 billion. In the deal, five banks had agreed to lend Pfizer USD22.5 billion to pay for the deal, and Pfizer was funding the remaining USD45.5 billion through issuance of a combination of cash and stock.

The Bond Offering Process

The issuance of publicly traded bonds, in addition to the pricing and marketing of the deal, required the satisfaction of certain legal requirements. Because of the complexity and importance of these two processes, corporations typically hired investment bankers to provide assistance. Given the size of the deal, Roche hired three banks as joint lead managers for the U.S. dollar deal (Banc of America Securities, Citigroup Global Markets, and JPMorgan) and four bankers for the euro and pound sterling deals (Barclays Capital, BNP Paribas, Deutsche Bank, and Banco Santander).

Because Roche's bonds would be publicly traded, it had to file with the appropriate regulatory agencies in the countries where the bonds would be issued. Simultaneous with the drafting of the documentation by legal teams, the underwriting banks' debt capital markets and syndication desks began the marketing process. The initial phase of this process was the "road show." During the road show, management teams for Roche and the banks held initial meetings with investors from all over the world. The Roche management team expected to meet with investors in many of the major investment centers in the United States and Europe.

Given the global nature of Roche's business, the banks determined that a mix of bonds at different maturities and in different currencies was the best option. By matching differing maturities and currencies to the company's operating cash flows in those currencies, Roche was able to reduce exchange rate risk. **Exhibit 10** provides an overview of the different currency and maturity tranches planned in the offering. The final amounts raised from each offering, along with the coupon rate, were not yet determined because pricing was expected to be highly influenced by investor demand. To ensure that the bond offering raised the targeted proceeds, the coupon rate was set to approximate the anticipated yield, such that the bond traded at par. Following market conventions, the U.S. dollar bonds would pay interest semiannually, and the euro and sterling issues would pay interest annually.

The coupon payments of the shorter durations were to be floating, and the interest to be paid was equivalent to the short-term interbank interest rate (LIBOR) plus a credit spread. The longer durations were to have fixed coupon payments for the duration of the bond. Investors typically referenced the "price" of bonds as the spread over the applicable risk-free rate. The risk-free rate was commonly established as the respective government borrowing rate and was referred to as the *benchmark, sovereign,* or *Treasury rate.* The spread was referred to as the *credit spread,* the logic being that the issuer had to offer a price over the risk-free rate to entice investors to buy the bonds.

During the road show, banks received feedback from investors on the demand for each tranche. Determining the final size and pricing of each issue was an iterative process between the investors, banks, and issuer. In the case of Roche, if investors showed strong demand for the four-year euro tranche, Roche could decide to either issue more at that price (thus reducing the amount of another tranche) or lower the coupon and pay a lower interest rate on the four-year euro issue. The banks' process of determining demand and receiving orders for each issue was known as *book-building.* Bond prices were set based on prevailing yields of bond issues by similar companies. **Exhibits 11** and **12** provide a sample of prevailing prices and terms of company bonds traded in the market, in addition to various equity market and accounting data.

The Genentech Deal

On July 21, 2008, Roche publicly announced an offer to acquire the 44.1% of Genentech's outstanding shares that it did not already own. The offer price of USD89.00 represented a 19% premium over the previous one-month share prices for Genentech. Roche management believed that economies justified the premium with an estimate that, following the transaction, the combined entity could realize USD750 million to USD850 million in operational efficiencies. Following the offer, Genentech's stock price shot up beyond the USD89.00 offer price with the anticipation that Roche would increase its offer.

On August 13, 2008, a special committee of Genentech's board of directors (those without direct ties to Roche) responded to Roche's offer. The committee stated that the offer "substantially undervalues the company." Without the support of Genentech's board of directors, Roche needed either to negotiate with the board or take the offer directly to shareholders with what was known as a *tender offer.* In that case, shareholders would receive a take-it-or-leave-it offer. If sufficient shareholders "tendered" their shares, the deal would go through regardless of the support of the board.

Over the next six months, the capital markets fell into disarray. As credit markets deteriorated, Genentech shareholders realized that Roche might not be able to finance an increased bid for the company, and the share price continued to decline through the end of the year. Contemporaneously with the deal, Genentech was awaiting the announcement of the clinical trial results for several of its next generation of potential drugs, including its promising cancer drug Avastin.

On January 30, 2009, Roche announced its intention to launch a tender offer for the remaining shares at a reduced price of USD86.50. The revised offer was contingent on Roche's ability to obtain sufficient financing to purchase the shares. The announcement was accompanied by a 4% price drop of Genentech's share price to USD80.82. Bill Tanner, analyst at Leerink Swann, warned Genentech shareholders that the stock was overvalued and that if upcoming Genentech drug trials showed mediocre results then the stock would fall into the USD60 range. He encouraged shareholders to take the sure USD86.50 offer claiming that "DNA's [the stock ticker symbol for Genentech] best days may be over."[2]

Jason Napadano, analyst at Zach's Investment Research, claimed that Roche was trying "to pull the wool over the eyes of Genentech shareholders." He continued, "Roche is trying to get this deal done before the adjuvant colon cancer data comes out and Genentech shareholders are well aware of that. I don't know why they would tender their shares for [USD]86.50, which is only 10% above today's price, when they can get closer to $95 to $100 a share if they wait."[3]

The Financing Proposal

Unlike Pfizer in its acquisition of Wyeth, Roche could not issue equity to Genentech shareholders. Roche was controlled by the remnants of its founder in the Oeri, Hoffman, and Sacher families. The company maintained two classes of shares, *bearer* and *Genussscheine* (profit-participation) shares. Both share classes had equal economic rights (i.e., same dividends, etc.) and traded on the Swiss Stock Exchange, but the bearer shares were the only shares with voting rights, and the founding family controlled just over 50% of the bearer shares. This dual-share structure existed before modern shareholder rights legislation in Switzerland and was grandfathered in. In the event Roche were to issue equity to Genentech shareholders, this dual-class share structure would have to be revisited, and the family might lose control. Given this ownership structure, Roche was forced to finance the deal entirely of debt and current cash on hand.

When Roche originally announced the transaction, the company had intended to finance the acquisition with a combination of bonds and loans from a variety of commercial banks. The collapse of the financial markets caused many of the commercial banks to demand a much higher interest rate on the loans than originally anticipated by Roche. As a result of the change in market conditions, Roche was limited to the bond market for the majority of its financing. Despite the magnitude of the debt-financing need, the investment banks assisting in the deal expected that Roche's cash flow was stable enough to manage the additional level of debt.

To ensure that Roche raised the necessary capital, it was important to correctly anticipate the required yield on each bond and set the coupon rate at the rate that would price the bond at par. This was done by simply setting the coupon rate equal to the anticipated yield. With such a substantial amount of money riding on the deal, it was critical that Roche correctly set the price, despite the immense uncertainty in capital markets.

---

[2] Bob O'Brien, "Analysts Debate Strategy Behind Sourer Offer," *Barron's*, January 30, 2009.
[3] O'Brien.

EXHIBIT 1 | 2008 Revenue Breakdown (sales in millions of Swiss francs)

By Geography	Share	Product (Indication)	Sales
North America	41%	MabThera/Rituxin (lymphoma, leukemia, rheumatoid arthritis)	5,923
Western Europe	29%	Avastin (colorectal, breast, lung, and kidney cancer)	5,207
CEMAI[1]	9%	Herceptin (breast cancer)	5,092
Japan	9%	CellCept (transplantation)	2,099
Latin America	6%	NeoRecormon/Epogin (anemia)	1,774
Asia-Pacific	5%	Peasys (hepatitis)	1,635
Others	1%	Tarceva (lung cancer, pancreatic cancer)	1,215
		Lucentis (macular degeneration)	960
By Therapeutic Category	**Share**	Tamiflu (influenza)	609
Oncology	55%	Xolair (asthma)	560
Inflammation and autoimmune diseases, transplantation	9%	Valcyte/Cymevene (herpes)	553
		Xenical (weight loss and control)	502
Central nervous system	3%	Pulmozyme (cystic fibrosis)	496
Respiratory	3%	Nutropin (growth hormone deficiency)	413
Metabolic diseases, bone diseases	8%	Neutrogin (neutropenia associated with chemotherapy)	404
Infectious diseases	1%	Rocephin (bacterial infections)	344
Cardiovascular diseases	3%	Activase, TNKase (heart attack)	342
Virology	9%	Madopar (Parkinson's disease)	311
Renal anemia	4%		
Ophthalmology	3%		
Others	2%		

Data Source: Roche 2008 annual report.

[1]CEMAI: Central and Eastern Europe, the Middle East, Africa, Central Asia, and the Indian Subcontinent. This acronym appears to be unique to Roche.

EXHIBIT 2 | Roche Financial Statements, Financial Years Ended December 31
(in millions of Swiss francs)

Income statement	2004	2005	2006	2007	2008
Revenue	31,092	36,958	43,432	48,376	47,904
COGS	7,718	9,270	13,096	13,738	13,605
Gross margin	23,374	27,688	30,336	34,638	34,299
Operating expense					
Sales and marketing	10,423	11,816	11,588	11,576	11,317
Research and development	5,154	5,672	7,286	8,327	8,720
Other operating	1,572	1,011	0	0	0
Operating income	6,225	9,189	11,462	14,735	14,262
Net interest expense (income)	311	(742)	(443)	(791)	(488)
Other non-operating expenses (income)	(677)	769	(682)	222	589
Income tax	1,865	2,284	3,436	3,867	3,317
Minority interest	−457	−943	−1,291	−1,676	−1,875
Net income	6,606	5,923	7,880	9,761	8,969
Balance sheet					
Total cash and ST investments	12,999	20,885	24,996	24,802	21,438
Total other current assets	16,680	14,741	15,899	18,032	17,166
Net PP&E	12,408	15,097	16,417	17,832	18,190
Other noncurrent assets	16,359	18,472	17,102	17,699	19,295
Total assets	58,446	69,195	74,414	78,365	76,089
Total current liabilities	10,134	9,492	12,692	14,454	12,104
Long-term debt	7,077	9,322	6,191	3,831	2,971
Unearned revenue	0	183	163	243	174
Other noncurrent liabilities	13,237	16,864	15,924	14,354	16,361
Total liabilities	30,448	35,861	34,970	32,882	31,610
Common stock	160	160	160	160	160
Retained earnings	35,960	38,624	44,251	50,922	52,081
Treasury stock	−4,326	−3,485	−2,102	−1,017	—
Comprehensive inc. and other	−3,796	−1,965	−2,865	−4,582	−7,762
Total shareholder equity	27,998	33,334	39,444	45,483	44,479
Total liabilities and SE	58,446	69,195	74,414	78,365	76,089

Data Source: Capital IQ.

EXHIBIT 3 | Genentech Financial Statements (in millions of U.S. dollars)

Income statement	2004	2005	2006	2007	2008
Revenue	4,621	6,633	9,284	11,724	13,418
COGS	805	1,155	1,366	1,767	1,971
Gross margin	3,816	5,478	7,918	9,957	11,447
Operating expense					
Sales and marketing	1,088	1,435	2,014	2,256	2,405
Research and development	816	1,118	1,588	2,250	2,573
Other operating	739	946	1,110	1,212	1,400
Operating income	1,173	1,979	3,206	4,239	5,069
Net interest expense (income)	(83)	(93)	(156)	(224)	(75)
Other non-operating expenses (income)	36	59	(35)	38	(286)
Income tax	435	734	1,290	1,657	2,004
Minority interest	0	0	0	0	0
Net income	785	1,279	2,107	2,768	3,426
Balance sheet					
Total cash and ST investments	1,665	2,365	2,493	3,975	6,198
Total other current assets	1,760	2,021	3,211	4,778	3,875
Net PP&E	2,091	3,349	4,173	4,986	5,404
Other noncurrent assets	3,887	4,412	4,965	5,201	6,310
Total assets	9,403	12,147	14,842	18,940	21,787
Total current liabilities	1,238	1,660	2,010	3,918	3,095
Long-term debt	412	2,083	2,204	2,402	2,329
Unearned revenue	268	220	199	418	444
Other noncurrent liabilities	703	714	951	297	248
Total liabilities	2,621	4,677	5,364	7,035	6,116
Common stock	21	21	21	21	21
Additional paid in capital	8,003	9,263	10,091	10,695	12,044
Retained earnings	(1,533)	(2,067)	(838)	992	3,482
Comprehensive inc. and other	291	253	204	197	124
Total shareholder equity	6,782	7,470	9,478	11,905	15,671
Total liabilities and SE	9,403	12,147	14,842	18,940	21,787

Data Source: Capital IQ.

EXHIBIT 4 | Stock Price Performance of Roche and Genentech, February 2007 to February 2009 (in Swiss francs and U.S. dollars, respectively)[1]

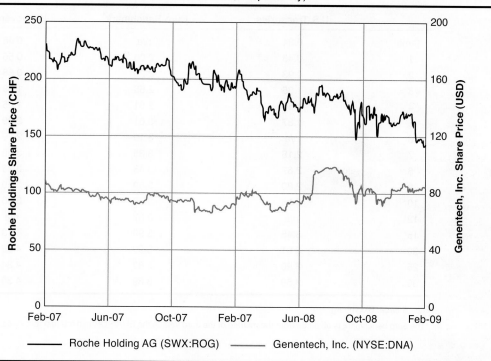

Data Source: Capital IQ.

[1]Correspondence of values between axes is approximate, based on exchange rates on February 28, 2007. The average rate for the period was USD1.13/CHF1.00.

EXHIBIT 5 | Annual Yield Rate to Maturity (U.S. Dollar, Euro, British Pound), February 2009 (in percent)

	U.S. Treasuries	Euro Benchmark[1]	UK Sovereign
6-mo	0.34	n/a	0.48
1	0.48	2.09	0.56
2	0.93	2.26	0.88
3	1.35	2.55	1.39
4	1.50	2.81	1.85
5	1.87	3.01	2.29
6	n/a	3.19	2.79
7	2.18	3.35	3.06
8	2.67	3.48	3.25
9	2.80	3.60	3.50
10	2.85	3.70	3.66
12	n/a	3.87	n/a
15	3.45	3.99	4.13
20	3.91	3.99	4.29
25	3.90	3.83	4.34
30	3.59	3.69	4.35

Data Source: Bloomberg.

[1]The euro benchmark is obtained from the midrate of the euro versus the EURIBOR mid-interest rate swap.

EXHIBIT 6 | U.S. Yield Spreads of U.S. Industrial Corporate Bonds over Comparable Maturity of U.S. Treasuries for S&P's Bond-Rating Categories, February 2009 (in basis points)

Rating	Years to maturity						
	1	2	3	5	7	10	30
AAA	90	82	77	90	136	114	170
AA	210	201	198	202	224	204	242
A+	211	201	217	226	243	226	242
A	279	261	278	277	290	275	263
A−	289	271	287	286	303	284	273
BBB+	406	387	409	406	412	406	394
BBB	417	398	422	424	435	418	411
BBB−	493	497	510	520	527	509	506

Data Source: Bloomberg.

EXHIBIT 7 | History of U.S. Bond Yields for 30-Year Maturities, February 2006 to February 2009 (in percent)

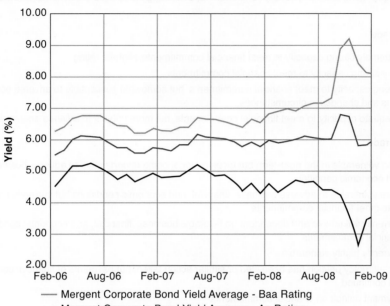

Mergent Corporate Bond Yield Average - Baa Rating
Mergent Corporate Bond Yield Average - Aa Rating
U.S. Treasuries 30-Year Yield

Data Source: Datastream, Mergent Bond Record.

EXHIBIT 8 | S&P Credit Ratings Overview

S&P's global bond-rating scale provides a benchmark for evaluating the relative credit risk of issuers and issues worldwide.

Investment grade

AAA	Extremely strong capacity to meet financial commitments. Highest rating
AA	Very strong capacity to meet financial commitments
A	Strong capacity to meet financial commitments, but somewhat susceptible to adverse economic conditions and changes in circumstances
BBB	Adequate capacity to meet financial commitments, but more subject to adverse economic conditions

Speculative grade

BB	Less vulnerable in the near-term but faces major ongoing uncertainties to adverse business, financial, and economic conditions
B	More vulnerable to adverse business, financial, and economic conditions but currently has the capacity to meet financial commitments
CCC	Currently vulnerable and dependent on favorable business, financial, and economic conditions to meet financial commitments
CC	Currently highly vulnerable
C	A bankruptcy petition has been filed or similar action taken, but payments of financial commitments are continued
D	Payment default on financial commitments

Ratings from "AA" to "CCC" may be modified by the addition of a plus (+) or minus (−) sign to show relative standing within the major rating categories. The Moody's bond-rating service had a similar rating scale but denoted an S&P "BBB" rating, for example, as "Baa."

Data Source: *Guide to Credit Rating Essentials,* Standard and Poor's, http://www2.standardandpoors.com/spf/pdf/fixedincome/SP_CreditRatingsGuide.pdf (accessed February 16, 2011).

EXHIBIT 9 | Median Financial Ratio Values for all U.S. Rated Industrial Companies, 2007 and 2008

	Number of companies	Debt/ (Debt + BookEq)	EBITDA/ Int. Expense	EBIT/ Int. Expense	Debt/ EBITDA
2007					
AAA	26	0.51	95.47	74.06	2.26
AA	189	0.30	35.92	31.05	0.85
A	539	0.41	12.45	9.86	1.63
BBB	924	0.50	8.20	6.11	2.66
BB	470	0.52	6.59	4.63	2.82
B	335	0.71	3.71	2.30	4.66
2008					
AAA	18	0.51	113.97	81.62	3.25
AA	182	0.26	43.97	31.21	0.81
A	559	0.43	12.78	9.89	1.81
BBB	924	0.50	8.23	6.42	2.47
BB	417	0.52	6.40	4.51	2.82
B	321	0.75	3.41	2.10	4.92

Data Source: Case writer analysis of Compustat data.

EXHIBIT 10 | Plan for Currency and Maturity of Roche Bond Offering Tranches[1]

U.S. dollar-denominated		
Maturity	**Amount (in billions of U.S. dollars)**	**Coupon**
1 year	3.00	Floating rate
2 years	1.25	Floating rate
3 years	2.50	Fixed rate
5 years	2.75	Fixed rate
10 years	4.50	Fixed rate
30 years	2.50	Fixed rate
Euro-denominated		
Maturity	**Amount (in billions of euros)**	**Coupon**
1 year	1.50	Floating rate
4 years	5.25	Fixed rate
7 years	2.75	Fixed rate
12 years	1.75	Fixed rate
Sterling-denominated		
Maturity	**Amount (in billions of British pounds)**	**Coupon**
6 years	1.25	Fixed rate

Data Source: Company documents.

[1]Prevailing exchange rates at the time were CHF1.67/GBP1.00, CHF1.18/USD1.00, and CHF1.48/EUR1.00.

EXHIBIT 11 | Prevailing Prices of Sample of Recently Rated Corporate Bonds (Mid-February 2009)

Company	Issue date	Maturity	Years remaining to maturity	S&P rating	Amount issued (millions)	Coupon	Price
U.S. dollar-denominated							
Altria	2/3/2009	2/6/2014	5	BBB	525	7.75	105.835
Altria	2/3/2009	2/6/2019	10	BBB	2,200	9.25	104.612
Altria	2/3/2009	2/6/2039	30	BBB	1,500	10.2	105.079
AT&T	1/29/2009	2/15/2014	5	A	1,000	4.85	99.790
AT&T	1/29/2009	2/15/2019	10	A	2,250	5.8	98.877
AT&T	1/29/2009	2/15/2039	30	A	2,250	6.55	96.626
Johnson & Johnson	6/23/2008	7/15/2038	29	AAA	700	5.85	111.000
McKesson	2/9/2009	2/15/2014	5	BBB+	350	6.5	103.372
McKesson	2/9/2009	2/15/2019	10	BBB+	350	7.5	106.156
Novartis	2/10/2009	2/10/2014	5	AA−	2,000	4.125	101.778
Novartis	2/10/2009	2/10/2019	10	AA−	3,000	5.125	100.746
Pfizer	2/3/2004	2/15/2014	5	AA	750	4.5	105.660
Schering-Plough	11/26/2003	12/1/2013	5	AA−	1,250	5.3	103.820
Schering-Plough	9/17/2007	9/15/2037	29	AA−	1,000	6.55	101.332
Verizon	11/4/2008	11/1/2018	10	A	2,000	8.75	118.582
Verizon	11/4/2008	3/31/2039	30	A	1,250	8.95	124.467
Warner Chilcott	2/1/2006	2/1/2015	6	BB-	600	8.75	95.000
Euro-denominated							
Anheuser-Busch InBev	2/9/2009	2/27/2014	5	BBB+	750	6.57	100.558
Imperial Tobacco	2/10/2009	2/17/2016	7	BBB	1,500	8.375	101.048
John Deere	1/19/2009	1/24/2014	5	A	600	7.5	105.801
Schering-Plough	10/1/2007	10/1/2014	6	AA−	1,500	5.375	99.710
Volkswagen	1/30/2009	2/9/2012	3	A−	2,500	5.625	100.332
Volkswagen	1/30/2009	2/9/2016	7	A−	1,000	7	100.238
Pound sterling-denominated							
Bayer AG	5/23/2006	5/23/2018	9	A−	350	5.625	100.817
Imperial Tobacco	2/10/2009	2/17/2022	13	BBB	1,000	9	107.062
Tesco	2/17/2009	2/24/2014	5	A−	600	5	100.284

Data Source: Case writer analysis using Bloomberg data.

EXHIBIT 12 | Selected Comparable Companies' Data for 2008 (in millions of U.S. dollars)[1]

	Shareholder equity	Total debt	Cash and equivalents	EBITDA	Interest expense	Current rating
Bayer AG	21,381	21,779	2,740	8,183	1,626	A−
Schering-Plough	10,529	8,176	3,373	2,917	536	AA−
Johnson & Johnson	46,100	11,852	10,768	19,001	435	AAA
Pfizer	57,556	17,290	2,122	20,929	516	AA
Wyeth	19,174	11,739	10,016	7,954	492	A+
GlaxoSmithKline	15,900	25,211	8,758	15,388	1,291	A+
Merck & Co	21,080	6,240	4,368	7,854	251	AA−
AstraZeneca	15,912	11,848	4,286	12,553	714	AA
Warner Chilcott	1,350	963	36	508	94	BB−
Roche Holding	41,569	4,051	4,870	16,751	213	AA−
Roche + Genentech (pro forma)	41,569	46,051	4,870	16,751	2,303	

Data Source: Capital IQ and case writer analysis.

[1] Because the Genentech financial figures are already consolidated in the Roche financial statements, only the debt and interest expense is expected to vary. The pro-forma interest expense is based on an arbitrary 5% interest rate.

Nike, Inc.: Cost of Capital

On July 5, 2001, Kimi Ford, a portfolio manager at NorthPoint Group, a mutual-fund management firm, pored over analysts' write-ups of Nike, Inc., the athletic-shoe manufacturer. Nike's share price had declined significantly from the beginning of the year. Ford was considering buying some shares for the fund she managed, the NorthPoint Large-Cap Fund, which invested mostly in Fortune 500 companies, with an emphasis on value investing. Its top holdings included ExxonMobil, General Motors, McDonald's, 3M, and other large-cap, generally old-economy stocks. While the stock market had declined over the last 18 months, the NorthPoint Large-Cap Fund had performed extremely well. In 2000, the fund earned a return of 20.7%, even as the S&P 500 fell 10.1%. At the end of June 2001, the fund's year-to-date returns stood at 6.4% versus −7.3% for the S&P 500.

Only a week earlier, on June 28, 2001, Nike had held an analysts' meeting to disclose its fiscal-year 2001 results.[1] The meeting, however, had another purpose: Nike management wanted to communicate a strategy for revitalizing the company. Since 1997, its revenues had plateaued at around $9 billion, while net income had fallen from almost $800 million to $580 million (see **Exhibit 1**). Nike's market share in U.S. athletic shoes had fallen from 48%, in 1997, to 42% in 2000.[2] In addition, recent supply-chain issues and the adverse effect of a strong dollar had negatively affected revenue.

At the meeting, management revealed plans to address both top-line growth and operating performance. To boost revenue, the company would develop more athletic-shoe products in the midpriced segment[3]—a segment that Nike had overlooked in recent years. Nike also planned to push its apparel line, which, under the recent leadership of

---

[1]Nike's fiscal year ended in May.

[2]Douglas Robson, "Just Do . . . Something: Nike's insularity and Foot-Dragging Have It Running in Place," *BusinessWeek,* (2 July 2001).

[3]Sneakers in this segment sold for $70–$90 a pair.

This case was prepared from publicly available information by Jessica Chan, under the supervision of Robert F. Bruner and with the assistance of Sean D. Carr. The financial support of the Batten Institute is gratefully acknowledged. It was written as a basis for class discussion rather than to illustrate effective or ineffective handling of an administrative situation. Copyright © 2001 by the University of Virginia Darden School Foundation, Charlottesville, VA. All rights reserved. *To order copies, send an e-mail to* sales@ dardenbusinesspublishing.com. *No part of this publication may be reproduced, stored in a retrieval system, used in a spreadsheet, or transmitted in any form or by any means—electronic, mechanical, photocopying, recording, or otherwise—without the permission of the Darden School Foundation.* Rev. 10/05.

industry veteran Mindy Grossman,[4] had performed extremely well. On the cost side, Nike would exert more effort on expense control. Finally, company executives reiterated their long-term revenue-growth targets of 8% to 10% and earnings-growth targets of above 15%.

Analysts' reactions were mixed. Some thought the financial targets were too aggressive; others saw significant growth opportunities in apparel and in Nike's international businesses.

Kimi Ford read all the analysts' reports that she could find about the June 28 meeting, but the reports gave her no clear guidance: a Lehman Brothers report recommended a strong buy, while UBS Warburg and CSFB analysts expressed misgivings about the company and recommended a hold. Ford decided instead to develop her own discounted cash flow forecast to come to a clearer conclusion.

Her forecast showed that, at a discount rate of 12%, Nike was overvalued at its current share price of $42.09 (**Exhibit 2**). However, she had done a quick sensitivity analysis that revealed Nike was *undervalued* at discount rates below 11.17%. Because she was about to go into a meeting, she asked her new assistant, Joanna Cohen, to estimate Nike's cost of capital.

Cohen immediately gathered all the data she thought she might need (**Exhibits 1** through **4**) and began to work on her analysis. At the end of the day, Cohen submitted her cost-of-capital estimate and a memo (**Exhibit 5**) explaining her assumptions to Ford.

---

[4]Mindy Grossman joined Nike in September 2000. She was the former president and chief executive of Jones Apparel Group's Polo Jeans division.

EXHIBIT 1 | Consolidated Income Statements

Year Ended May 31 (in millions of dollars except per-share data)	1995	1996	1997	1998	1999	2000	2001
Revenues	$4,760.8	$6,470.6	$9,186.5	$9,553.1	$8,776.9	$8,995.1	$9,488.8
Cost of goods sold	2,865.3	3,906.7	5,503.0	6,065.5	5,493.5	5,403.8	5,784.9
Gross profit	**1,895.6**	**2,563.9**	**3,683.5**	**3,487.6**	**3,283.4**	**3,591.3**	**3,703.9**
Selling and administrative	1,209.8	1,588.6	2,303.7	2,623.8	2,426.6	2,606.4	2,689.7
Operating income	**685.8**	**975.3**	**1,379.8**	**863.8**	**856.8**	**984.9**	**1,014.2**
Interest expense	24.2	39.5	52.3	60.0	44.1	45.0	58.7
Other expense, net	11.7	36.7	32.3	20.9	21.5	23.2	34.1
Restructuring charge, net	—	—	—	129.9	45.1	(2.5)	—
Income before income taxes	**649.9**	**899.1**	**1,295.2**	**653.0**	**746.1**	**919.2**	**921.4**
Income taxes	250.2	345.9	499.4	253.4	294.7	340.1	331.7
Net income	**$ 399.7**	**$ 553.2**	**$ 795.8**	**$ 399.6**	**$ 451.4**	**$ 579.1**	**$ 589.7**
Diluted earnings per common share	$1.36	$1.88	$2.68	$1.35	$1.57	$2.07	$2.16
Average shares outstanding (diluted)	294.0	293.6	297.0	296.0	287.5	279.8	273.3
Growth (%)							
Revenue		35.9	42.0	4.0	(8.1)	2.5	5.5
Operating income		42.2	41.5	(37.4)	(0.8)	15.0	3.0
Net income		38.4	43.9	(49.8)	13.0	28.3	1.8
Margins (%)							
Gross margin		39.6	40.1	36.5	37.4	39.9	39.0
Operating margin		15.1	15.0	9.0	9.8	10.9	10.7
Net margin		8.5	8.7	4.2	5.1	6.4	6.2
Effective tax rate (%)*		38.5	38.6	38.8	39.5	37.0	36.0

*The U.S. statutory tax rate was 35%. The state tax varied yearly from 2.5% to 3.5%.

Sources of data: Company filing with the Securities and Exchange Commission (SEC), UBS Warburg.

EXHIBIT 2 | Discounted Cash Flow Analysis

	2002	2003	2004	2005	2006	2007	2008	2009	2010	2011
Assumptions:										
Revenue growth (%)	7.0	6.5	6.5	6.5	6.0	6.0	6.0	6.0	6.0	6.0
COGS/sales (%)	60.0	60.0	59.5	59.5	59.0	59.0	58.5	58.5	58.0	58.0
SG&A/sales (%)	28.0	27.5	27.0	26.5	26.0	25.5	25.0	25.0	25.0	25.0
Tax rate (%)	38.0	38.0	38.0	38.0	38.0	38.0	38.0	38.0	38.0	38.0
Current assets/sales (%)	38.0	38.0	38.0	38.0	38.0	38.0	38.0	38.0	38.0	38.0
Current liabilities/sales (%)	11.5	11.5	11.5	11.5	11.5	11.5	11.5	11.5	11.5	11.5
Yearly depreciation and capex equal each other.										
Cost of capital (%)	12.00									
Terminal value growth rate (%)	3.00									

Discounted Cash Flow (in millions of dollars except per-share data)

	2002	2003	2004	2005	2006	2007	2008	2009	2010	2011
Operating income	$ 1,218.4	$1,351.6	$1,554.6	$1,717.0	$1,950.0	$2,135.9	$2,410.2	$2,554.8	$2,790.1	$2,957.5
Taxes	463.0	513.6	590.8	652.5	741.0	811.7	915.9	970.8	1,060.2	1,123.9
NOPAT	755.4	838.0	963.9	1,064.5	1,209.0	1,324.3	1,494.3	1,584.0	1,729.9	1,833.7
Capex, net of depreciation	—	—	—	—	—	—	—	—	—	—
Change in NWC	8.8	(174.9)	(186.3)	(198.4)	(195.0)	(206.7)	(219.1)	(232.3)	(246.2)	(261.0)
Free cash flow	764.1	663.1	777.6	866.2	1,014.0	1,117.6	1,275.2	1,351.7	1,483.7	1,572.7
Terminal value										17,998.3
Total flows	764.1	663.1	777.6	866.2	1,014.0	1,117.6	1,275.2	1,351.7	1,483.7	19,571.0
Present value of flows	$ 682.3	$ 528.6	$ 553.5	$ 550.5	$ 575.4	$ 566.2	$ 576.8	$ 545.9	$ 535.0	$6,301.2

Enterprise value	$11,415.4
Less: current outstanding debt	$ 1,296.6
Equity value	$10,118.8
Current shares outstanding	271.5
Equity value per share	$ 37.27

Current share price: $ 42.09

Sensitivity of equity value to discount rate:	
Discount rate	**Equity value**
8.00%	$ 75.80
8.50%	67.85
9.00%	61.25
9.50%	55.68
10.00%	50.92
10.50%	46.81
11.00%	43.22
11.17%	**42.09**
11.50%	40.07
12.00%	37.27

Source: Case writer's analysis.

EXHIBIT 3 | Consolidated Balance Sheets

(in millions of dollars)	As of May 31,	
	2000	2001
Assets		
Current assets:		
Cash and equivalents	$ 254.3	$ 304.0
Accounts receivable	1,569.4	1,621.4
Inventories	1,446.0	1,424.1
Deferred income taxes	111.5	113.3
Prepaid expenses	215.2	162.5
Total current assets	3,596.4	3,625.3
Property, plant and equipment, net	1,583.4	1,618.8
Identifiable intangible assets and goodwill, net	410.9	397.3
Deferred income taxes and other assets	266.2	178.2
Total assets	**$ 5,856.9**	**$ 5,819.6**
Liabilities and shareholders' equity		
Current liabilities:		
Current portion of long-term debt	$ 50.1	$ 5.4
Notes payable	924.2	855.3
Accounts payable	543.8	432.0
Accrued liabilities	621.9	472.1
Income taxes payable	—	21.9
Total current liabilities	2,140.0	1,786.7
Long-term debt	470.3	435.9
Deferred income taxes and other liabilities	110.3	102.2
Redeemable preferred stock	0.3	0.3
Shareholders' equity:		
Common stock, par	2.8	2.8
Capital in excess of stated value	369.0	459.4
Unearned stock compensation	(11.7)	(9.9)
Accumulated other comprehensive income	(111.1)	(152.1)
Retained earnings	2,887.0	3,194.3
Total shareholders' equity	3,136.0	3,494.5
Total liabilities and shareholders' equity	**$ 5,856.9**	**$ 5,819.6**

Source of data: Company filing with the Securities and Exchange Commission (SEC).

EXHIBIT 4 | Capital-Market and Financial Information On or Around July 5, 2001

Current Yields on U.S. Treasuries

3-month	3.59%
6-month	3.59%
1-year	3.59%
5-year	4.88%
10-year	5.39%
20-year	5.74%

Historical Equity Risk Premiums (1926-1999)

Geometric mean	5.90%
Arithmetic mean	7.50%

Current Yield on Publicly Traded Nike Debt*

Coupon	6.75% paid semi-annually
Issued	07/15/96
Maturity	07/15/21
Current Price	$95.60

Nike Historic Betas

1996	0.98
1997	0.84
1998	0.84
1999	0.63
2000	0.83
YTD 6/30/01	0.69
Average	0.80

Consensus EPS estimates:

FY 2002	FY 2003
$2.32	$2.67

Nike Share Price Performance Relative to S&P500:

January 2000 to July 5, 2001

Nike share price on July 5, 2001: $ 42.09

Dividend History and Forecasts

Payment Dates	31-Mar	30-Jun	30-Sep	31-Dec	Total
1997	0.10	0.10	0.10	0.10	0.40
1998	0.12	0.12	0.12	0.12	0.48
1999	0.12	0.12	0.12	0.12	0.48
2000	0.12	0.12	0.12	0.12	0.48
2001	0.12				

Value Line Forecast of Dividend Growth from '98-'00 to '04-'06: 5.50%

*Data have been modified for teaching purposes.

Sources of data: Bloomberg Financial Services, Ibbotson Associates Yearbook 1999, Value Line Investment Survey, IBES.

EXHIBIT 5 | Joanna Cohen's Analysis

TO:	Kimi Ford
FROM:	Joanna Cohen
DATE:	July 6, 2001
SUBJECT:	Nike's cost of capital

Based on the following assumptions, my estimate of Nike's cost of capital is 8.4%:

I. Single or Multiple Costs of Capital?

The first question that I considered was whether to use single or multiple costs of capital, given that Nike has multiple business segments. Aside from footwear, which makes up 62% of its revenue, Nike also sells apparel (30% of revenue) that complements its footwear products. In addition, Nike sells sport balls, timepieces, eyewear, skates, bats, and other equipment designed for sports activities. Equipment products account for 3.6% of its revenue. Finally, Nike also sells some non-Nike-branded products such as Cole Haan dress and casual footwear, and ice skates, skate blades, hockey sticks, hockey jerseys, and other products under the Bauer trademark. Non-Nike brands accounted for 4.5% of revenue.

I asked myself whether Nike's business segments had different enough risks from each other to warrant different costs of capital. Were their profiles really different? I concluded that it was only the Cole Haan line that was somewhat different; the rest were all sports-related businesses. Since Cole Haan makes up only a tiny fraction of revenues, however, I did not think that it was necessary to compute a separate cost of capital. As for the apparel and footwear lines, they are sold through the same marketing and distribution channels and are often marketed in other collections of similar designs. Since I believe they face the same risk factors, I decided to compute only one cost of capital for the whole company.

II. Methodology for Calculating the Cost of Capital: WACC

Since Nike is funded with both debt and equity, I used the WACC method (weighted-average cost of capital). Based on the latest available balance sheet, debt as a proportion of total capital makes up 27.0% and equity accounts for 73.0%:

Capital Sources	Book Values (in millions)	
Debt		
Current portion of long-term debt	$ 5.4	
Notes payable	855.3	
Long-term debt	435.9	
	$1,296.6	→ 27.0% of total capital
Equity	$3,494.5	→ 73.0% of total capital

III. Cost of Debt

My estimate of Nike's cost of debt is 4.3%. I arrived at this estimate by taking total interest expense for the year 2001 and dividing it by the company's average debt balance.[1] The rate is lower than Treasury yields, but that is because Nike raised a portion of its funding needs through Japanese yen notes, which carry rates between 2.0% and 4.3%.

After adjusting for tax, the cost of debt comes out to 2.7%. I used a tax rate of 38%, which I obtained by adding state taxes of 3% to the U.S. statutory tax rate. Historically, Nike's state taxes have ranged from 2.5% to 3.5%.

---

[1]Debt balances as of May 31, 2000 and 2001, were $1,444.6 million and $1,296.6 million, respectively.

EXHIBIT 5 | *(continued)*

IV. Cost of Equity

I estimated the cost of equity using the capital-asset-pricing model (CAPM). Other methods, such as the dividend-discount model (DDM) and the earnings-capitalization ratio, can be used to estimate the cost of equity. In my opinion, however, the CAPM is the superior method.

My estimate of Nike's cost of equity is 10.5%. I used the current yield on 20-year Treasury bonds as my risk-free rate, and the compound average premium of the market over Treasury bonds (5.9%) as my risk premium. For beta, I took the average of Nike's betas from 1996 to the present.

Putting it All Together

Inputting all my assumptions into the WACC formula, my estimate of Nike's cost of capital is 8.4%.

$$
\begin{aligned}
\text{WACC} &= K_d(l - t) \times D/(D + E) + K_e \times E/(D + E) \\
&= 2.7\% \times 27.0\% + 10.5\% \times 73.0\% \\
&= 8.4\%
\end{aligned}
$$

Teletech Corporation, 2005

Raider Dials Teletech

"Wake-Up Call Needed," Says Investor

New York—The reclusive billionaire Victor Yossarian has acquired a 10 percent stake in Teletech Corporation, a large regional telecommunications firm, and has demanded two seats on the firm's board of directors. The purchase was revealed yesterday in a filing with the Securities and Exchange Commission, and separately in a letter to Teletech's CEO, Maxwell Harper. "The firm is misusing its resources and not earning an adequate return," the letter said. "The company should abandon its misguided entry into computers, and sell its Products and Systems segment. Management must focus on creating value for shareholders." Teletech issued a brief statement emphasizing the virtues of a link between computer technology and telecommunications.

Wall Street Daily News, October 15 2005

Margaret Weston, Teletech Corporation's CFO, learned of Victor Yossarian's letter late one evening in early October 2005. Quickly, she organized a team of lawyers and finance staff to assess the threat. Maxwell Harper, the firm's CEO, scheduled a teleconference meeting of the firm's board of directors for the following afternoon. Harper and Weston agreed that before the meeting they needed to fashion a response to Yossarian's assertions about the firm's returns.

Ironically, returns had been the subject of debate within the firm's circle of senior managers in recent months. A number of issues had been raised about the hurdle rate used by the company when evaluating performance and setting the firm's annual capital budget. As the company was expected to invest nearly $2 billion in capital projects in the coming year, gaining closure and consensus on those issues had become an important priority for Weston. Now, Yossarian's letter lent urgency to the discussion.

In the short run, Weston needed to respond to Yossarian. In the long run, she needed to assess the competing viewpoints on Teletech's returns, and she had to

This case was written by Robert F. Bruner, with the assistance of Sean D. Carr. It is dedicated to the memory of Professor Robert F. Vandell, a scholar in corporate finance and investment analysis and the author of an antecedent case upon which the present case draws. Teletech Corporation is a fictional company, reflecting the issues facing actual firms, and is used as a basis for class discussion rather than to illustrate effective or ineffective handling of an administrative situation. The financial support of the Batten Institute is gratefully acknowledged. Copyright © 2005 by the University of Virginia Darden School Foundation, Charlottesville, VA. All rights reserved. *To order copies, send an e-mail to* sales@dardenbusinesspublishing.com. *No part of this publication may be reproduced, stored in a retrieval system, used in a spreadsheet, or transmitted in any form or by any means—electronic, mechanical, photocopying, recording, or otherwise—without the permission of the Darden School Foundation.* Rev. 10/10.

recommend new policies as necessary. What *should* the hurdle rates be for Teletech's two business segments, telecommunications services and its newer products and systems unit? Was the products and systems segment really paying its way?

The Company

The Teletech Corporation, headquartered in Dallas, Texas, defined itself as a "provider of integrated information movement and management." The firm had two main business segments: telecommunications services, which provided long-distance, local, and cellular telephone service to business and residential customers, and the products and systems segment, which engaged in the manufacture of computing and telecommunications equipment.

In 2004, telecommunications services had earned a return on capital (ROC)[1] of 9.10%; products and systems had earned 11%. The firm's current book value of net assets was $16 billion, consisting of $11.4 billion allocated to telecommunications services, and $4.6 billion allocated to products and systems. An internal analysis suggested that telecommunications services accounted for 75% of the market value (MV) of Teletech, while products and systems accounted for 25%. Overall, it appeared that the firm's prospective ROC would be 9.58%. Top management applied a hurdle rate of 9.30% to all capital projects and in the evaluation of the performance of business units.

Over the past 12 months, Teletech's shares had not kept pace with the overall stock market or with industry indexes for telephone, equipment, or computer stocks. Securities analysts had remarked on the firm's lackluster earnings growth, pointing especially to increasing competition in telecommunications, as well as disappointing performance in the Products and Systems segment. A prominent commentator on TV opined, "There's no precedent for a hostile takeover in this sector, but, in the case of Teletech, there is every reason to try."

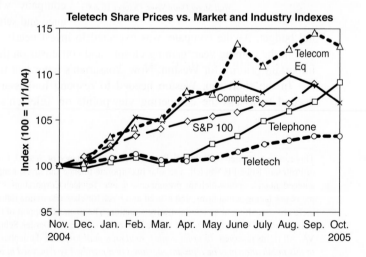

Teletech Share Prices vs. Market and Industry Indexes

---

[1]Return on capital was calculated as the ratio of net operating profits after tax (NOPAT) to capital.

Telecommunications Services

The telecommunications services segment provided long-distance, local, and cellular telephone service to more than 7 million customer lines throughout the Southwest and Midwest. Revenues in this segment grew at an average rate of 3% during 2000–04. In 2004, segment revenues, net operating profit after tax (NOPAT), and net assets were $11 billion, $1.18 billion, and $11.4 billion, respectively.

Since the court-ordered breakup of the Bell System telephone monopoly in 1983, Teletech had coped with the gradual deregulation of its industry through aggressive expansion into new services and geographical regions. Most recently, the firm had been a leading bidder for cellular telephone operations and for licenses to offer personal communications services (PCS). In addition, the firm had purchased a number of telephone-operating companies through privatization auctions in Latin America. Finally, the firm had invested aggressively in new technology—primarily, digital switches and optical-fiber cables—in an effort to enhance its service quality. All of those strategic moves had been costly: the capital budget in this segment had varied between $1.5 billion and $2 billion in each of the previous 10 years.

Unfortunately, profit margins in the telecommunications segment had been under pressure for several years. Government regulators had been slow to provide rate relief to Teletech for its capital investments. Other leading telecommunications providers had expanded into Teletech's geographical markets and invested in new technology and quality-enhancing assets. Teletech's management noted that large cable-TV companies had aggressively entered the telecommunications market and continued the pressure on profit margins.

Nevertheless, Teletech was the dominant service provider in its geographical markets and product segments. Customer surveys revealed that the company was the leader in product quality and customer satisfaction. Its management was confident that the company could command premium prices no matter how the industry might evolve.

Products and Systems

Before 2000, telecommunications had been the company's core business, supplemented by an equipment-manufacturing division that produced telecommunications components. In 2000, the company acquired a leading computer-workstation manufacturer with the goal of applying state-of-the-art computing technology to the design of telecommunications equipment. The explosive growth in the microcomputer market and the increased usage of telephone lines to connect home- and office-based computers with mainframes convinced Teletech's management of the potential value of marrying telecommunications equipment with computing technology. Using Teletech's capital base, borrowing ability, and distribution network to catapult growth, the products and systems segment increased its sales by nearly 40% in 2004. This segment's 2004 NOPAT and net assets were $480 million and $4.6 billion, respectively.

The products and systems segment was acknowledged as a technology leader in the industry. While this accounted for its rapid growth and pricing power, maintenance of that leadership position required sizable investments in research and development (R&D) and fixed assets. The rate of technological change was increasing, as witnessed by sudden major write-offs by Teletech on products that, until recently, management had thought were still competitive. Major computer manufacturers were entering the telecommunications-equipment industry. Foreign manufacturers were proving to be stiff competition for bidding on major supply contracts.

Focus on Value at Teletech

We will create value by pursuing business activities that earn premium rates of return.
    —Teletech Corporation mission statement (excerpt)

Translating Teletech's mission statement into practice had been a challenge for Margaret Weston. First, it had been necessary to help managers of the segments and business units understand what *creating value* meant. Because the segments and smaller business units did not issue securities in the capital markets, the only objective measure of value was the securities prices of the whole corporation—but the activities of any particular manager might not be significant enough to drive Teletech's securities prices. Therefore, the company had adopted a measure of value creation for use at the segment and business-unit level that would provide a proxy for the way investors would view each unit's performance. This measure, called economic profit, multiplied the excess rate of return of the business unit by the capital it used:

$$Economic\ profit = (ROC - Hurdle\ rate) \times Capital\ employed$$

Where:

$$ROC = Return\ on\ capital = \frac{NOPAT}{Capital}$$

$$NOPAT = Net\ operating\ profit\ after\ taxes$$

Each year, the segment and business-unit executives were evaluated based on economic profit. This measure was an important consideration in strategic decisions about capital allocation, manager promotion, and incentive compensation.

The second way in which the value-creation perspective influenced managers was in the assessment of capital-investment proposals. For each investment, projected cash flows were discounted to the present using the firm's hurdle rate to give a measure of the net present value (NPV) of each project. A positive (or negative) NPV indicated the amount by which the value of the firm would increase (or decrease) if the project were undertaken. The following shows how the hurdle rate was used in the familiar NPV equation:

$$Net\ present\ value = \sum_{t=1}^{n} \left[\frac{Free\ cash\ flow_t}{(1\ +\ Hurdle\ rate)^t} \right] - Initial\ investment$$

Hurdle Rates

The hurdle rate used in the assessments of economic profit and NPV had been the focus of considerable debate in recent months. This rate was based on an estimate of Teletech's weighted average cost of capital (WACC). Management was completely satisfied with the intellectual relevance of a hurdle rate as an expression of the opportunity cost of money. The notion that the WACC represented this opportunity cost had been hotly debated within the company, and while its measurement had never been considered wholly scientific, it was generally accepted.

Teletech was "split-rated" between A− and BBB+. An investment banker recently suggested that, at those ratings, new debt funds might cost Teletech 5.88% (about 3.53% after a 40% tax rate). With a beta of 1.15, the cost of equity might be about 10.95%. At market-value weights of 22% for debt and 78% for equity, the resulting WACC would be 9.30%. **Exhibit 1** summarizes the calculation. The hurdle rate of 9.30% was applied to all investment and performance-measurement analyses at the firm.

Arguments for Risk-Adjusted Hurdle Rates

How the rate should be used within the company in evaluating projects was another point of debate. Given the differing natures of the two businesses and the risks each one faced, differences of opinion arose at the segment level over the appropriateness of measuring all projects against the corporate hurdle rate of 9.30%. The chief advocate for multiple rates was Rick Phillips, executive vice president of telecommunications services, who presented his views as follows:

> Each phase of our business is different. They must compete differently and must draw on capital differently. Given the historically stable nature of this industry, many telecommunications companies can raise large quantities of capital from the debt markets. In operations comparable to telecommunications services, 50% of the necessary capital is raised in the debt markets at interest rates reflecting solid A quality, on average. This is better than Teletech's corporate bond rating of A−/BBB+.
>
> I also have to believe that the cost of equity for telecommunications services is lower than it is for products and systems. Although the products and systems segment's sales growth and profitability have been strong, its risks are high. Independent equipment manufacturers are financed with higher-yielding BB-rated debt and a greater proportion of equity.
>
> In my book, the hurdle rate for products and systems should reflect those higher costs of funds. Without the risk-adjusted system of hurdle rates, telecommunications services will gradually starve for capital, while products and systems will be force-fed—that's because our returns are less than the corporate hurdle rate, and theirs are greater. Telecommunications services lowers the risk of the whole corporation, and should not be penalized. Here's a rough graph of what I think is going on (**Figure 1**):
>
> Telecommunications services, which can earn 9.10% on capital, is actually profitable on a risk-adjusted basis, even though it is not profitable compared to the corporate hurdle rate. The triangle shape on the drawing shows about where telecommunications services is located. My hunch is that the reverse is true for products and systems [P&S], which promises to earn 11.0% on capital. P&S is located on the graph near the little circle. In deciding

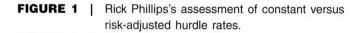

FIGURE 1 | Rick Phillips's assessment of constant versus risk-adjusted hurdle rates.

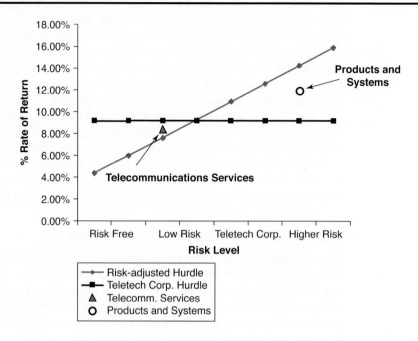

how much to loan us, lenders will consider the composition of risks. If money flows into safer investments, over time the cost of their loans to us will decrease.

Our stockholders are equally as concerned with risk. If they perceive our business as being more risky than other companies are, they will not pay as high a price for our earnings. Perhaps this is why our price-to-earnings ratio is below the industry average most of the time. It is not a question of whether we adjust for risk—we already do, informally. The only question in my mind is whether we make those adjustments systematically or not.

While multiple hurdle rates may not reflect capital-structure changes on a day-to-day basis, over time they will reflect prospects more realistically. At the moment, as I understand it, our real problem is an inadequate and very costly supply of equity funds. If we are really rationing equity capital, then we should be striving for the best returns on equity for the risk. Multiple hurdle rates achieve that objective.

Implicit in Phillips's argument, as Weston understood it, was the notion that if each segment in the company had a different hurdle rate, the costs of the various forms of capital would remain the same. The mix of capital used, however, would change in the calculation. Low-risk operations would use leverage more extensively, while the high-risk divisions would have little to no debt funds. This lower-risk segment would have a lower hurdle rate.

Opposition to Risk-Adjusted Hurdle Rates

While several others within Teletech supported Phillips's views, opposition was strong within the products and systems segment. Helen Buono, executive vice president of products and systems, expressed her opinion as follows:

> All money is green. Investors can't know as much about our operations as we do. To them the firm is a black box; they hire us to take care of what is inside the box, and judge us by the dividends coming out of the box. We can't say that one part of the box has a different hurdle rate than another part of the box if our investors don't think that way. Like I say, all money is green: all investments at Teletech should be judged against one hurdle rate.
>
> Multiple hurdle rates are illogical. Suppose that the hurdle rate for telecommunications services was much lower than the corporate-wide hurdle rate. If we undertook investments that met the *segment* hurdle rate, we would be destroying shareholder value because we weren't meeting the *corporate* hurdle rate.
>
> Our job as managers should be to put our money where the returns are best. A single hurdle rate may deprive an under profitable division of investments in order to channel more funds into a more profitable division, but isn't that the aim of the process? Our challenge today is simple: we must earn the highest absolute rates of return that we can get.
>
> In reality, we don't finance each division separately. The corporation raises capital based on its overall prospects and record. The diversification of the company probably helps keep our capital costs down and enables us to borrow more in total than the sum of the capabilities of the divisions separately. As a result, developing separate hurdle rates is both unrealistic and misleading. All our stockholders want is for us to invest our funds wisely in order to increase the value of their stock. This happens when we pick the most promising projects, irrespective of the source.

Margaret Weston's Concerns

As Weston listened to these arguments, presented over the course of several months, she became increasingly concerned about several related considerations. First, Teletech's corporate strategy had directed the company toward integrating the two segments. One effect of using multiple hurdle rates would be to make justifying high-technology research and application proposals more difficult, as the required rate of return would be increased. On the one hand, she thought, perhaps multiple hurdle rates were the right idea, but the notion that they should be based on capital costs rather than strategic considerations might be wrong. On the other hand, perhaps multiple rates based on capital costs should be used, but, in allocating funds, some qualitative adjustment should be made for unquantifiable strategic considerations. In Weston's mind, the theory was certainly not clear on how to achieve strategic objectives when allocating capital.

Second, using a single measure of the cost of money (the hurdle rate or discount factor) made the NPV results consistent, at least in economic terms. If Teletech adopted multiple rates for discounting cash flows, Weston was afraid that the NPV and economic-profit calculations would lose their meaning and comparability across business segments. To her, a performance criterion had to be consistent and understandable, or it would not be useful.

In addition, Weston was concerned about the problem of attributing capital structures to divisions. In the telecommunications services segment, a major new switching station might be financed by mortgage bonds. In products and systems, however, it was impossible for the division to borrow directly; indeed, any financing was only feasible because the corporation guaranteed the debt. Such projects were considered highly risky—at best, perhaps, warranting only a minimal debt structure. Also, Weston considered the debt-capacity decision difficult enough for the corporation as a whole, let alone for each division. Judgments could only be very crude.

In further discussions with others in the organization about the use of multiple hurdle rates, Weston discovered two predominant themes. One argument held that investment decisions should never be mixed with financing decisions. A firm should first decide what its investments should be and then determine how to finance them most efficiently. Adding leverage to a present-value calculation would distort the results. The use of multiple hurdle rates was simply a way of mixing financing with investment analysis. This argument also held that a single rate made the risk decision clear-cut. Management could simply adjust its standard (NPV or economic profit) as the risks increased.

The contrasting line of reasoning noted that the WACC tended to represent an average market reaction to a mixture of risks. Lower-than-average-risk projects should probably be accepted even when they did not meet the weighted-average criterion. Higher-than-normal-risk projects should provide a return premium. While the multiple-hurdle-rate system was a crude way to achieve this end, at least it was a step in the right direction. Moreover, some argued that Teletech's objective should be to maximize return on equity funds, and because equity funds were and would remain a comparatively scarce resource, a multiple-rate system would tend to maximize returns to stockholders better than a single-rate system would.

To help resolve these issues, Weston asked her assistant, Bernard Ingles, to summarize the scholarly thought regarding multiple hurdle rates. His memorandum is given in **Exhibit 2**. She also requested that Ingles obtain samples of firms comparable with the telecommunications services segment and the products and systems unit that might be used in deriving segment WACCs. A summary of the data is given in **Exhibit 3**. Information on capital-market conditions in October 2005 is given in **Exhibit 4**.

Conclusion

Weston could not realistically hope that all the issues before her would be resolved in time to influence Victor Yossarian's attack on management. But the attack did dictate the need for an objective assessment of the performance of Teletech's two segments—the choice of hurdle rates would be very important in the analysis. She did want to institute a pragmatic system of appropriate hurdle rates (or one rate), however, that would facilitate judgments in the changing circumstances faced by Teletech. What were the appropriate hurdle rates for the two segments? Was the products and systems segment underperforming, as suggested by Yossarian? How should Teletech respond to the raider?

EXHIBIT 1 | Summary of the WACC Calculation for Teletech Corporation and Segment
Worksheet

	Corporate	Telecommunications Services	Products and Systems
MV asset weights	100%	75%	25%
Bond rating	A−/BBB+	A	BB
Pretax cost of debt	5.88%	5.74%	7.47%
Tax rate	40%	40%	40%
After-tax cost of debt	3.53%	3.44%	4.48%
Equity beta	1.15		
R_f	4.62%		
R_M	10.12%		
$R_M - R_f$	5.50%		
Cost of equity	10.95%		
Weight of debt	22.2%		
Weight of equity	77.8%		
WACC	**9.30%**		

Data Source: Bloomberg LP, S&P Research Insight, and case writer analysis.

EXHIBIT 2 | Theoretical Overview of Multiple Hurdle Rates

To:	Margaret Weston
From:	Bernard Ingles
Subject:	Segment cost-of-capital theory
Date:	October 2005

You requested an overview of the theories on multiple hurdle rates. Without getting into the minutiae, the theories boil down to the following points:

1. The central idea is that required returns should be driven by risk. This is the dominant view in the field of investment management, and is based on a mountain of theory and empirical research stretching over several decades. The extension of this idea from investment management to corporate decision making is, at least in theory, straightforward.

2. An underlying assumption is that the firm is transparent (i.e., that investors can see through the corporate veil and evaluate the activities going on inside). No one believes firms are *completely* transparent, or that investors are perfectly informed. But financial accounting standards have evolved toward making the firm more transparent. And the investment community has grown tougher and sharper in its analysis. Teletech now has 36 analysts publishing both reports and forecasts on the firm. The reality is that for big publicly held firms, transparency is not a bad assumption.

3. Another underlying assumption is that the value of the whole enterprise is simply the sum of its parts—this is the concept of value additivity. We can define "parts" as either the business segments (on the left-hand side of the balance sheet) or the layers of the capital structure (on the right-hand side of the balance sheet). Market values have to balance.

$$MV_{Teletech} = (MV_{Telecommunication\ Services} + MV_{Products + Systems}) = (MV_{debt} + MV_{equity})$$

If those equalities did not hold, then a raider could come along and exploit the inequality by buying or selling the whole and the parts. This is arbitrage. By buying and selling, the actions of the raider would drive the MVs back into balance.

4. Investment theory tells us that the only risk that matters is nondiversifiable risk, which is measured by beta. Beta indicates the risk that an asset will add to a portfolio. Since we assume that an investor is diversified, we also assume she seeks a return for only the risk that she cannot shed, which is the nondiversifiable risk. The important point here is that the beta of a portfolio is equal to a weighted average of the betas of the portfolio components. Extending this to the corporate environment, the asset beta for the firm will equal a weighted average of the components of the firm—again, the components of the firm can be defined in terms of either the right-hand side or the left-hand side of the balance sheet.

$$\beta_{Teletech\ Assets} = (w_{Tel.Serv.}\ \beta_{Tel.Serv.} + w_{P+S}\beta_{P+S}) = (w_{debt}\beta_{debt} + w_{equity}\beta_{equity})$$

Where:

$$w = percentage\ weights\ based\ on\ market\ values.$$

$$\beta_{Tel.\ Serv.},\ \beta_{P+S} = Asset\ betas\ for\ business\ segments.$$

$$\beta_{debt} = \beta\ for\ the\ firm's\ debt\ securities.$$

$$\beta_{equity} = \beta\ of\ firm's\ common\ stock\ (given\ by\ Bloomberg,\ etc.)$$

This is a very handy way to model the risk of the firm, for it means that we can use the capital asset pricing model to estimate the cost of capital for a segment (i.e., using segment asset betas).

5. Given the foregoing, it follows that the weighted average of the various costs of capital (K) for the firm (WACC), which is the theoretically correct hurdle rate, is simply a weighted average of segment WACCs:

$$WACC_{Teletech} = (W_{Tel.Serv.}WACC_{Tel.Serv.}) + (W_{P+S}WACC_{P+S})$$

EXHIBIT 2 | Theoretical Overview of Multiple Hurdle Rates (*Continued*)

Where:

$$w = \text{percentage weights based on market values.}$$

$$WACC_{Tel.\ Serv.} = (w_{debt,\ Tel.\ Serv.}\ K_{debt,\ Tel.\ Serv.}) + (w_{equity,\ Tel.\ Serv.}\ K_{equity,\ Tel.\ Serv.})$$

$$WACC_{P+S} = (w_{debt,\ P+S}\ K_{debt,\ P+S}) + (w_{equity,\ P+S}\ K_{equity,\ P+S})$$

6. The notion in point number 5 may not hold exactly in practice. First, most of the components in the WACC formula are estimated with some error. Second, because of taxes, information asymmetries, or other market imperfections, assets may not be priced strictly in line with the model—for a company like Teletech, it is reasonable to assume that any mispricings are just temporary. Third, the simple two-segment characterization ignores a hidden third segment: the corporate treasury department that hedges and aims to finance the whole corporation optimally—this acts as a shock absorber for the financial policies of the segments. Modeling the WACC of the corporate treasury department is quite difficult. Most companies assume that the impact of corporate treasury is not very large, and simply assume it away. As a first cut, we could do this too, although it is an issue we should revisit.

Conclusions

- In theory, the corporate WACC for Teletech is appropriate *only* for evaluating an asset having the same risk as the whole company. It is not appropriate for assets having different risks than the whole company.
- Segment WACCs are computed similarly to corporate WACCs.
- In concept, the corporate WACC is a weighted average of the segment WACCs. In practice, the weighted average concept may not hold, due to imperfections in the market and/or estimation errors.
- If we start computing segment WACCs, we must use the cost of debt, cost of equity, and the weights *appropriate to that segment*. We need a lot of information to do this correctly, or else we really need to stretch to make assumptions.

EXHIBIT 3 | Samples of Comparable Firms

Company Name	2004 Revenues	Equity Beta	Bond Rating	Book Val. Debt/Total Capital	Price to Book	Mkt. Val. Debt/ Capital	Mkt. Val. Debt/ Equity	Price/ Earnings
Teletech Corporation	16,000	1.15	A−/BBB+	46%	3.0	22%	29%	12.9
Telecommunications Services Industry								
Alltel Corp.	8,246	1.00	A	42.3%	2.4	23.2%	30.1%	15.4
AT&T Corp.	30,537	1.10	BB+	53.9%	2.0	36.6%	57.7%	(2.4)
BellSouth Corp.	20,350	1.00	A	38.1%	2.1	22.9%	29.7%	16.7
Centurytel Corp.	2,411	1.05	BBB+	42.5%	1.3	37.0%	58.8%	13.3
Citizens Communications Co.	2,193	1.00	BB+	76.1%	3.5	47.7%	91.1%	65.0
IDT Corp.	2,217	1.05	NA	2.5%	1.2	2.1%	2.1%	(19.3)
SBC Communications Inc.	40,787	1.05	A	32.3%	1.9	20.0%	25.0%	19.6
Sprint Corp.	27,428	1.15	A−	50.8%	2.4	30.3%	43.4%	(43.1)
Verizon Communications Inc.	71,283	1.00	A+	45.0%	2.6	24.1%	31.8%	12.5
Average		1.04		42.6%	2.15	27.1%	41.1%	8.65
Telecommunications Equipment Industry								
Avaya Inc.	4,057	1.35	BB	14.0%	3.5	4.4%	4.6%	18.3
Belden CDT Inc.	966	1.45	NA	19.9%	1.2	17.5%	21.3%	38.7
Commscope Inc.	1,153	1.10	BB	36.9%	2.0	22.4%	28.9%	10.3
Corning Inc.	3,854	1.45	BBB−	41.9%	5.4	11.8%	13.4%	(11.1)
Harris Corp.	2,519	1.05	BBB−	24.5%	2.7	10.7%	11.9%	21.9
Lucent Technologies Inc.	9,045	1.75	B	109.8%	(26.0)	30.1%	43.0%	6.0
Nortel Networks Corp.	9,828	1.75	NA	43.9%	3.0	20.7%	26.0%	(51.8)
Plantronics Inc.	560	1.20	NA	0.7%	4.2	0.2%	0.2%	17.0
Scientific-Atlanta Inc.	1,708	1.45	NA	0.4%	2.6	0.1%	0.1%	20.7
Average		1.39		32.5%	(0.15)	13.1%	16.6%	7.77
Computer and Network Equipment Industry								
EMC Corp.	8,229	1.55	BBB	1.0%	2.9	0.4%	0.4%	34.3
Gateway Inc.	3,650	1.35	NA	42.3%	5.5	11.8%	13.4%	(4.2)
Hewlett-Packard Corp.	79,905	1.45	A−	12.7%	1.7	7.8%	8.5%	18.5
Int'l. Business Machines Corp.	96,293	1.10	A+	27.1%	4.1	8.4%	9.1%	15.2
Lexmark Int'l. Inc.	5,314	1.15	NA	5.5%	4.2	1.4%	1.4%	15.5
NCR Corp.	5,984	1.20	NA	13.7%	3.3	4.5%	4.8%	21.1
Seagate Technology	6,224	1.20	NA	33.0%	4.4	10.0%	11.1%	25.0
Storage Technology Corp.	2,224	1.15	NA	0.8%	2.4	0.3%	0.3%	18.2
Western Digital Corp.	3,047	1.80	NA	12.5%	4.8	2.9%	3.0%	16.7
Average		1.33		16.5%	3.70	5.3%	5.8%	17.81

EXHIBIT 4 | Debt-Capital-Market Conditions, October 2005

Corporate Bond Yields		U. S. Treasury Securities	
Industrials			
AAA	5.44%	3-month	3.56%
AA	5.51%	6-month	3.99%
A	5.74%	2-year	4.23%
		3-year	4.23%
BBB	6.23%	5-year	4.25%
BB	7.47%	10-year	4.39%
B	8.00%	30-year	4.62%
Phones			
A	6.17%		
BBB	6.28%		
Utilities			
A	5.69%		
BBB	6.09%		

Data Source: Bloomberg LP.

The Boeing 7E7

We still have a lot to get done as we move toward authority to offer the 7E7 to our customers. The team is making great progress—understanding what our customer wants, developing an airplane that meets their needs, and defining a case that will demonstrate the value of the program.

—Michael Bair, Boeing Senior Vice President[1]

In early 2003, Boeing announced plans to design and sell a new, "super-efficient" jet dubbed the 7E7, subsequently called the "Dreamliner." However, news over the next six months depressed the market for aircrafts, which were already in sharp contraction. The United States went to war against Iraq, spasms of global terrorism offered shocking headlines, and a deadly illness called SARS resulted in global travel warnings. For those and other reasons, airline profits were the worst seen in a generation. This seemed like an incredible environment in which to launch a major new airframe project. Nevertheless, on June 16, 2003, at the prestigious Paris Air Show, Michael Bair, the leader of the 7E7 project, announced that Boeing was making "excellent progress on the development of the 7E7 and continues to be on track to seek authority to offer the airplane."[2] In order to proceed with the project, Bair sought a firm commitment from Boeing's board of directors in early 2004. If the board approved the plan, he could start collecting orders from airlines and expect passengers to start flying on the new jets in 2008. Between now and his recommendation to the board, he would need to complete a valuation of the 7E7 project and gain the support of Boeing's CEO, Philip Condit, and the other senior managers. Would the financial analysis show that this project would be profitable for Boeing's shareholders?

---

[1]"Bair Provides Update on Boeing 7E7 Dreamliner," *Le Bourget*, 16 June 2003.

[2]"Bair Provides Update."

This case was prepared by Professors James Tompkins and Robert F. Bruner using public information. It was written as a basis for class discussion rather than to illustrate effective or ineffective handling of an administrative situation. Copyright © 2004 by the University of Virginia Darden School Foundation, Charlottesville, VA. All rights reserved. *To order copies, send an e-mail to* sales@dardenbusinesspublishing.com. *No part of this publication may be reproduced, stored in a retrieval system, used in a spreadsheet, or transmitted in any form or by any means—electronic, mechanical, photocopying, recording, or otherwise—without the permission of the Darden School Foundation.*

Origins of the 7E7 Project

Boeing had not introduced a new commercial aircraft since it rolled out the highly successful 777 in 1994. Later in the 1990s, however, Boeing announced and then cancelled two new commercial-aircraft programs. The most prominent of those was the "Sonic Cruiser," which promised to fly 15% to 20% faster than any commercial aircraft and bragged of a sleek and futuristic design. Unfortunately, after two years of developing the Sonic Cruiser, Boeing's potential customers were sending the message that passengers were not willing to pay a premium price for a faster ride. Boeing was now long overdue to develop a product that would pull it out of its financial slump, as well as help it regain the commercial-aircraft sales that the company had lost over the years to Airbus, its chief rival.

With the 7E7, an Airbus executive argued that Boeing seemed to be promising a "salesperson's dream and engineer's nightmare."[3] The 7E7, while carrying between 200 and 250 passengers, would be capable of both short, domestic flights as well as long, international hauls. It would use 20% less fuel than existing planes of its projected size and be 10% cheaper to operate than Airbus's A330-200. At a time when major airlines were struggling to turn a profit, less fuel, cheaper operating costs, and long or short distance flexibility would be a very attractive package at the right price.

Skeptics of the 7E7 were not in short supply and suggested that the name "Dreamliner" was appropriate. To make the plane more fuel efficient, the 7E7 would be the first commercial aircraft built primarily with carbon-reinforced material, which was both stronger and lighter than the traditional aluminum. In addition, Boeing promised greater fuel efficiency by using a more efficient engine. Boeing claimed that the use of composites would also reduce its manufacturing costs. The goal would be to design a plane with fewer components that could be assembled in 3 days as opposed to the current 20 days that it took to rivet together the Boeing 767. The use of composite materials, however, had its risks. Composite materials were suspected as a contributory cause to a 2001 plane crash in New York and, therefore, would have to overcome regulatory scrutiny. Boeing would also have to change its production methods radically. The last time Boeing made a major production change was in 1997 in an effort to cut costs. However, because the process was not smooth, it resulted in two production lines being shut down for 30 days and hundreds of missed airline deliveries.

The ability to produce a short and long distance aircraft would also have to overcome engineering obstructions. Analysts argued that building a plane that would do short hops in Asia and long trans-Atlantic flights would require two versions of the plane with different wingspans.[4] Boeing engineers considered the possibility of snap-on wing extensions. The question was whether this would be too costly, as well as being technically feasible.

Finally, there was the matter of Boeing's board. Two of the most powerful members of the 11-person board, Harry Stonecipher and John McDonnell, were rumored

---

[3]"Will Boeing's New Idea Really Fly?" *BusinessWeek*, 23 June 2003.

[4]Noted by Richard Aboulafia, a senior analyst at Teal Group consultant, in "Will Boeing's New Idea Really Fly?"

to have raised serious concerns regarding the cost of the 7E7. While the cost of developing the 7E7 project could be as high as $10 billion, there was an imminent veto threat if that number did not shrink by billions. More specifically the board wanted to keep 7E7 development costs down to only 40% of what it took to develop the 777. An additional pressure from the board was to keep the 7E7 per-copy costs to only 60% of the 777 costs. In response, Philip Condit, Boeing's CEO and chair, was quoted as saying that "Boeing has a responsibility to develop jetliners for less."[5] He knew, however, that if Boeing did not take bold risks in the commercial-aircraft industry that their days as a serious competitor to Airbus were numbered.

Commercial-Aircraft Industry

In 2002, two companies, Boeing and Airbus, dominated the large plane (100+ seats) commercial-aircraft industry. While Boeing historically held the lead in this market, through a number of measures Airbus became number one. In 2002, Airbus received 233 commercial orders compared to Boeing's 176 orders, representing a 57% unit market share and an estimated 53.5% dollar value market share.[6]

Airbus Industry

Airbus was understandably proud of its growth. Established in 1970, by a consortium of European companies, it took Airbus 23 years to deliver its first 1000 aircrafts, another six years to deliver the next 1000, and only another three years (by 2002) to pass the 3000 aircraft milestone.[7] In 1999, for the first time in its history, Airbus recorded more plane orders than its rival, Boeing.

Airbus's large plane commercial-aircraft products included the A300/310, A320, A330/340, and A380 families. Airbus touted the A300/310 family as having the flexibility to serve short-, medium-, and extended-range routes. The widebody, twin-engine aircraft was considered mid-size, with a typical passenger configuration of about 250 passengers. This family first flew passengers in 1983, and it was this aging fleet that provided a replacement opportunity for Boeing's 7E7. However, while Boeing was betting on the future demand for mid-size aircraft, Airbus announced its A380, superjumbo four-engine jet in 2000. The A380 was due to fly in 2006 with a 550-passenger configuration and long distance range of up to 8000 miles. It would be the largest passenger aircraft ever built.

The Boeing Company

Boeing was split into two primary segments: commercial airplanes and integrated defense systems. In 2002, it was awarded $16.6 billion in defense contracts, second

---

[5]"Losing Ground to Airbus, Boeing Faces a Key Choice," *Wall Street Journal,* 21 April 2003.

[6]"2002 Commercial Results," www.airbus.com.

[7]In 2001, Airbus formally became a single integrated entity through the transfer of Airbus related assets to the newly incorporated company. European Aeronautic Defense and Space Company (EADS) owned 80% of the new company, and BAE systems owned the remaining 20%.

only to Lockheed Martin with $17.0 billion. **Exhibit 1** shows that in 2002, each segment earned Boeing's revenues almost equally. In addition, while commercial-aircraft revenues had been falling, defense revenues had been rising. Analysts believed that Boeing was able to transfer significant amounts of technology from the defense R&D to the commercial-aircraft segment.

The commercial-aircraft segment produced and sold six main airframes designed to meet the needs of the short- to long-range markets: the 717, 737, and 757 standard-body models and the 747, 767, and 777 wide-body models. As of December 31, 2002, Boeing undelivered units under firm order of 1083 commercial aircraft and had a declining backlog of about $68 billion. For 2003, it projected 280 commercial-aircraft deliveries and expected between 275 and 300 in 2004. Boeing estimated that in 2003, the revenues for its commercial-airplane segment would be approximately $22 billion, down from $28 billion in 2002. Recognizing the negative impact of the September 11th attacks on commercial-aircraft demand, Boeing cut the production rates for 2002 in half in order to maintain profitability in that segment.

Exhibits 2 and **3** show Boeing's balance sheet and income statement respectively. While Boeing's earnings were down significantly from 2001 to 2002, most of this was the result of an accounting change (SFAS No. 142). However, a drop in commercial-airplane deliveries from 527 in 2001 to 381 in 2002 also contributed to the decline.

Demand for Commercial Aircraft

The long-term outlook for aircraft demand seemed positive.[8] Boeing's *Market Outlook* said the following:

> In the short term, air travel is influenced by business cycles, consumer confidence, and exogenous events. Over the long-term, cycles smooth out, and GDP, international trade, lower fares, and network service improvements become paramount. During the next 20 years, economies will grow annually by 3.2%, and air travel will continue its historic relationship with GDP by growing at an average annual rate of 5.1%.

As shown in **Exhibit 4,** Boeing's 20-year forecast from 2003 to 2022, was for 24,276 new commercial aircraft in 2002, valued at $1.9 trillion. The company predicted a composition of 4,303 smaller regional jets (fewer than 90 seats); 13,647 single-aisle airplanes; 5,437 intermediate twin-aisle airplanes; and 889 747-size or larger airplanes. This prediction reflected a world fleet that would more than double, with one-fourth of the market coming from aircraft replacement and three-fourths from projected passenger and cargo growth.

Exhibit 5 illustrates Airbus's 20-year predictions for the years 2000–2020. Although the report was dated 2002, because of the September 11 attacks, numbers included the year 2000, to serve as a benchmark year. For that period, Airbus predicted

---

[8]The primary sources for commercial-aircraft demand estimates include Boeing's *2003 Current Market Outlook* and Airbus's *2002 Global Market Forecast 2001–2020*. While both reports recognized the negative effects of "exogenous events" such as September 11, 2001, they both agreed on a healthy long-term outlook.

the delivery of 15,887 new commercial aircraft in 2002, with a value of (U.S. dollars) $1.5 trillion. This included 10,201 single-aisle aircraft; 3,842 twin-aisle aircraft; 1,138 very large aircraft, and 706 freighters. The 15,887-unit forecast did not include planes with less than 90 seats.

Although Boeing and Airbus's numbers are not directly comparable due to the slightly different time periods and aircraft classifications, it appeared that Airbus was more optimistic about the market for large aircraft than Boeing was. While Airbus predicted it to be a $270 billion market, including 1138 passenger units, Boeing projected only $214 billion with 653 passenger units. Boeing, however, estimated that the share of intermediate-size planes would increase from 18% to 22%. In its forecast, Boeing acknowledged that intermediate-size airplanes would economically allow airlines to fly the increased frequencies, city pairs, and nonstop flights requested by passengers. According to a recent study by Frost & Sullivan, they believed that the Airbus market projection for the A380 was "over-optimistic."[9]

Aircraft Development and Lifecycle

The development of a new airframe was characterized by huge initial cash outflows that might require between one and two decades to recoup. For example, the development costs for the Boeing 777 were rumored to be $7 billion. Any pricing would not only have to recoup the upfront development costs but also the production costs. In addition, pricing would be subject to rigorous, competitive pressures. In short, because of the financial strains a new product line might create, each new aircraft was a "bet the ranch" proposition. Over time, survival in the industry depended on introducing successful products and having the deep financial pockets with which to survive the initially gushing cash flow.

While aircraft sales were subject to short-term, cyclical deviations, there was some degree of predictability in sales. Sales would typically peak shortly after the introduction of the new aircraft, and then fall. Thereafter, sales would rise and fall as derivatives of the aircraft were offered. **Exhibit 6** shows the cycles for the first 20 years of the 757 and 767 sales.

The 7E7

The concept of the Boeing 7E7 was driven by customer requirements. Boeing originally announced in March 2001, its plans to build the Sonic Cruiser, a plane that would fly just below the speed of sound. The success of the Cruiser depended on whether passengers would pay a premium for a faster flight. However, potential airplane customers who had been interested in the Cruiser during a robust, commercial-air travel market were now focusing on survival. The events of September 11 and the bursting of the technology bubble led to a significant decline in airplane orders. As a result, Boeing solicited updated feedback from a number of potential customers who would soon need

---

[9]"An Ongoing Rivalry," *Avionics Today*, August 2003.

to replace their aging fleet of mid-range planes, such as the 757s, 767s, A300s, A310s, A321s, and A330s. Overwhelmingly, the revised message from customers was for a plane with lower operating costs.

Based on discussions with over 40 airlines throughout the world, Bair identified a fresh market to replace mid-size planes, based not only on lower operating costs, but also on the creation of a mid-size plane that could travel long distances, a feat previously viable by only large planes, such as the 747. Such flexibility would allow airlines to offer nonstop service on routes that required long-range planes but did not justify the subsequent larger size. Bair estimated there to be more than 400 city pairs (e.g., Atlanta–Athens) that could be served efficiently on a nonstop basis by the 7E7.

Boeing was considering two new members for the 7E7 family, a basic and a stretch version. **Exhibit 7** gives Boeing's description of the two configurations. Other improvements for passengers included wider aisles, lower cabin altitude, and increased cabin humidity. In addition, the planes would include systems that provided in-flight entertainment, Internet access, real-time airplane systems and structure health monitoring, and crew connectivity. Furthermore, Boeing claimed the 7E7 would have the smallest sound "footprint" with the quietest takeoff and landing in its class.

Boeing projected a demand for between 2000 and 3000 planes of the 7E7 type within 20 years of each one entering service. A study by Frost & Sullivan predicted the sale of "at least 2000 B7E7s."[10] However, the demand was highly dependent on whether Boeing could deliver the promised 20% cheaper fuel costs and the range flexibility in a mid-size aircraft. Furthermore, if the range flexibility did require snap-on wings, such a design may significantly increase the building costs of the aircraft. Not only did Boeing face the engineering uncertainty of being able to deliver such an aircraft, but also the risk of its duplication by Airbus. Airbus had already stated that if the fuel efficiency was primarily generated by new engine designs, then it would simply order the more efficient engines for its planes. Any uncertainty in the 7E7 plane specifications and risk of competition clearly put downward pressure on both the price Boeing could demand, as well as the number of units it would be able to sell.

Financial Forecast and Analysis

Exhibit 8 contains a 20-year forecast of free cash flows from the Boeing 7E7 project consistent with public information released by Boeing, Airbus, analysts, and other experts in the field. See the **Appendix** for detailed forecast assumptions. The primary implication of the forecast is that the 7E7 project would provide an internal rate of return (IRR) close to 16%. This assumes that Boeing would not only deliver the promised plane specifications, but that Airbus would be unable to replicate the 7E7 efficiencies.

Based on both analysts' and Boeing's expectations, the base case assumes that Boeing could sell 2500 units in the first 20 years of delivery. Pricing was estimated using 2002 prices for Boeing's 777 and 767. The 7E7 would be a hybrid of the two planes in terms of the number of passengers and range. By interpolating between the

---

[10]"An Ongoing Rivalry"

777 and 767 prices, it was possible to estimate the value placed on the range and number of passengers. Using this methodology, without any premium for the promised lower operating costs, the minimum price for the 7E7 and 7E7 Stretch was estimated to be $114.5 million and $144.5 million, respectively, in 2002. The forecast assumed that customers would be willing to pay a 5% price premium for the lower operating costs.

The IRR, which is consistent with "base case" assumptions, was 15.7%. But, the estimate of IRR was sensitive to variations in different assumptions. In particular, some obvious uncertainties would be the number of units that Boeing would be able to sell and at what price. For example, if Boeing only sold 1,500 units in the first 20 years, then, as shown in **Exhibit 9,** the IRR would drop to 11%. This might occur if air travel demand worsened, or if Airbus entered this segment with a new competing product.

Additional unknown variables were the development costs and the per-copy costs to build the 7E7. Boeing's board was anxious to minimize those costs. The forecast assumes $8 billion for development costs; however, analyst estimates were in the $6 billion to $10 billion range. The cost to manufacture the 7E7 was also subject to great uncertainty. On the one hand, engineers were challenged to build a mid-size aircraft with long-range capabilities. The engineering design to achieve this could push building costs up significantly. Conversely, if Boeing succeeded in using composite materials, which required a fraction of the normal assembly time, then construction costs would be lower. Consistent with Boeing's history, the base case assumes 80% as the percentage of cost of goods sold to sales. As shown in **Exhibit 9,** however, the IRR of the 7E7 was very sensitive to keeping production costs low.

Cost of Capital

Boeing's weighted-average cost of capital (WACC) could be estimated using the following well-known formula:

$$\text{WACC} = (\text{percent Debt})(r_d)(1 - t_c) + (\text{percent Equity})(r_e)$$

where:

$$r_d = \text{Pretax cost of debt capital}$$
$$t_c = \text{Marginal effective corporate tax rate}$$
$$\text{percent Debt} = \text{Proportion of debt in a market} - \text{value capital structure}$$
$$r_e = \text{Cost of equity capital}$$
$$\text{percent Equity} = \text{Proportion of equity in a market} - \text{value capital structure}$$

Exhibit 10 gives information about betas and debt/equity ratios for Boeing and comparable companies. **Exhibit 11** provides data about Boeing's outstanding debt issues. While Boeing's marginal effective tax rate had been smaller in the past, it currently was expected to be 35%. In June 2003, the yield on the three-month U.S. Treasury bill was 0.85%, and the yield on the 30-year Treasury bond was 4.56%. On June 16, 2003, Boeing's stock price closed at $36.41.

Analysts pointed out that Boeing actually consisted of two separate businesses: the relatively more stable defense business and the conversely more volatile commercial business. Defense corporations were the beneficiaries when the world became unstable due to the terrorist attacks on September 11, 2001. Furthermore, the United States, along with some of its allies, went to war against Iraq on March 20, 2003. While Bush declared an end to major Iraqi combat operations on May 1, 2003, as of June 16, the death toll in Iraq continued to rise on a daily basis. A different type of risk emanated with the outbreak of SARS. On February 1, 2003, China announced the discovery of the deadly and contagious illness that subsequently spread to Canada and Australia. As of June 16, travel warnings were still outstanding. Thus, the question arose of whether one should estimate Boeing's cost of capital to serve as a benchmark-required rate of return. Would a required return on a portfolio of those two businesses be appropriate for evaluating the 7E7 project? If necessary, how might it be possible to isolate a required return for commercial aircraft?

Conclusion

Within the aircraft-manufacturing industry, the magnitude of risk posed by the launching of a major new aircraft was accepted as a matter of course. With huge, upfront, capital costs in an environment of intense technology and price competition, there was no guarantee of success or major significant losses if the gamble did not pay off. At a time of great political and economic uncertainty, Michael Bair said:

> Clearly, we have to make a compelling business proposition. It could be [that] we'll still be in a terrible business climate in 2004. But you can't let what's happening today cause you to make bad decisions for this very long business cycle. This plane is very important to our future.[11]

Central to any recommendation that Bair would make to Boeing's board of directors was an assessment of the economic profitability of the 7E7 project. Would the project compensate the shareholders of Boeing for the risks and use of their capital? Were there other considerations that might mitigate the economic analysis? For instance, to what extent might organizational and strategic considerations influence the board? If Boeing did not undertake the 7E7, would it be conceding leadership of the commercial-aircraft business to Airbus?

---

[11]"New Team, Name for Boeing 'Super-Efficient' Jet," *Seattle Times,* 30 January 2003.

EXHIBIT 1 | Revenues, Operating Profits, and Identifiable Assets by Segment for the Boeing Company

	2002	2001	2000
Revenues			
Commercial airplanes	$28,387	$35,056	$31,171
Integrated defense systems	24,957	22,815	19,963
Accounting eliminations and other	725	1,047	187
Total	$54,069	$58,918	$51,321
Operating Profit			
Commercial airplanes	$2,847	$2,632	$2,736
Integrated defense systems	2,009	2,965	1,002
Accounting eliminations and other	(988)	(1,701)	(680)
Total	$3,868	$3,896	$3,058
Identifiable Assets			
Commercial airplanes	$9,726	$10,851	$10,367
Integrated defense systems	12,753	12,461	12,579
Unallocated and other	29,863	25,666	20,588
Total	$52,342	$48,978	$43,534

Source: Boeing Company, 2002 Annual Report.

EXHIBIT 2 | Boeing Balance Sheets ($ in millions)

	2002	2001
Assets		
Cash and cash equivalents	$2,333	$633
Accounts receivable	5,007	5,156
Inventories, net of advances, progress billings, and reserves	6,184	7,559
Other current assets	3,331	3,497
Total current assets	16,855	16,845
Customer and commercial financing–net	10,922	9,345
Property, plant, and equipment–net	8,765	8,459
Goodwill and other acquired intangibles–net	3,888	6,447
Prepaid pension expense	6,671	5,838
Deferred income taxes and other assets	5,241	2,044
Total assets	$52,342	$48,978
Liabilities and Shareholders' Equity		
Accounts payable and other liabilities	$13,739	$14,237
Short-term debt and current portion of long-term debt	1,814	1,399
Other current liabilities	4,257	4,930
Total current liabilities	19,810	20,566
Accrued retiree health-care and pension-plan liability	11,705	5,922
Long-term debt	12,589	10,866
Other liabilities	542	799
Shareholders' equity:		
Common shares	1,831	4,994
Retained earnings	14,262	14,340
Treasury shares	(8,397)	(8,509)
Total shareholders' equity	7,696	10,825
Total liabilities and shareholders' equity	$52,342	$48,978

Source: Boeing Company, 2002 Annual Report.

EXHIBIT 3 | Boeing Income Statements ($ in millions; except per-share data)

	2002	2001
Sales and other operating revenues	$54,069	$58,198
Cost of products and services	45,499	48,778
General and administrative expense	2,534	2,389
Research and development expense	1,639	1,936
Impact of September 11, 2001 charges/(recoveries)	(2)	935
Other operating expenses	531	264
Earnings from operations	3,868	3,896
Other income/(expense)	42	318
Interest and debt expense	(730)	(650)
Earnings before income taxes	3,180	3,564
Income taxes[1]	861	738
Net earnings before cumulative effect of accounting change	2,319	2,826
Cumulative effect of accounting change, net of tax	(1,827)	1
Net earnings	$492	$2,827
Earnings per share	$0.62	$3.46

Source: Boeing Company, 2002 Annual Report.

[1] Boeing's average tax rate consistent with reported financial performance for 2002 was 27%. Yet Boeing's marginal effective tax rate was 35%.

EXHIBIT 4 | Boeing Delivery Distribution Forecast 2003–2022

Seat Category	Models	2002 Dollars (billions)	Passenger Units Freighter Units Total Units
Single-aisle			
Small and intermediate regional jets	Fewer than 90 seats Regional jets	96.5	4,303 0
			4,303
90–170	717-200 737-600/-700/-800	575.5	11,249 58
	A318/A319/A320 Larger regional jets		11,307
171–240	737-900	170.0	2,307
	757		33
	A321		2,340
Twin-aisle			
230–310	767	370.7	2,521
(181–249)	A300		272
	A310 A330-200		2,793
311–399	777	488.3	2,482
(250–368)	A330-300		162
	A340		2,644
Large			
747 and larger	747-400	214.0	653
(>400)	A380		236
			889
Total		**1,915.0**	**23,515**
			761
			24,276

Source: Boeing Company.

EXHIBIT 5 | Airbus Delivery Distribution Forecast, 2000–2020

Seat Category (number of seats)	Examples of Models	2002 Dollars (billions)	Units
Single-aisle (passenger) (100–210)	A318, A319, A320, A321	609	10,201
Twin-aisle (passenger) (250–400)	A330, A340	524	3,842
Very large (passenger) (>400)	A380	270	1,138
Freighters		106	706
Total		**1,509**	**15,887**

Source: Boeing Company.

EXHIBIT 6 | Lifecycle of Unit Sales (Averaged across the Boeing 757 and 767)

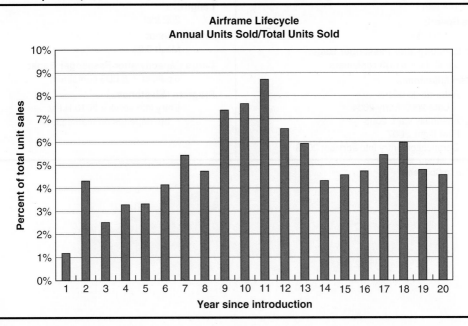

Source: Boeing Company Web site, www.boeing.com.

EXHIBIT 7 | Description of Product Configurations for the Baseline and Stretch Models of the 7E7

Boeing 7E7 Baseline Model	Boeing 7E7 Stretch
Brief Description: The Boeing 7E7 Baseline is a super-efficient airplane with new passenger-pleasing features. It will bring the economics of large jet transports to the middle of the market, using 20% less fuel than any other airplane its size.	**Brief Description:** The Boeing 7E7 Stretch is a slightly bigger version of the 7E7 Baseline. Both are super-efficient airplanes with new passenger-pleasing features. The Stretch will bring the economics of large jet transports to the middle of the market, using 20% less fuel than any other airplane its size.
Seating: 200 passengers in three-class configuration 300+ in single-class configuration	**Seating:** 250 passengers in three-class configuration 350+ in single-class configuration
Range: 6,600 nautical miles	**Range:** 8,000 nautical miles
Configuration: Twin-aisle	**Configuration:** Twin-aisle
Cross Section: 226 inches	**Cross Section:** 226 inches
Wing Span: 186 feet	**Wing Span:** 186 feet
Length: 182 feet	**Length:** 202 feet
Cruise Speed: Mach 0.85	**Cruise Speed:** Mach 0.85
Cargo Capacity after Passenger Bags: 5 pallets + 5 LD3 containers	**Cargo Capacity after Passenger Bags:** 6 pallets + 8 LD3 containers
Program Milestones: Authority to offer: Late 2003/Early 2004 Assembly start: 2005 First flight: 2007 Certification/entry into service: 2008	**Program Milestones:** Entry into service 2010 likely, but depends on marketplace

Source: Boeing Company.

EXHIBIT 8 | Forecast of Boeing 7E7 Free Cash Flows ($ in millions)

Assumptions	
Initial price of 7E7	$136.95
Initial price of 7E7 Stretch	$170.87
Cost of goods sold (% of sales)	80%
Working capital requirement (WCR) as a % of sales	6.7%
General, selling, and administrative (GS&A) as a % of sales	8%
R&D expense (% of sales)	2.3% (excluding 2004–2007)
Capital expenditure (% of sales)	0.16% (excluding 2004–2007)
Development costs (2004–2009)	$8,000
Total number of planes: yrs 1–20	2,500
Total number of planes: yrs 20–30	Same as year 20
Inflation	2%
Marginal effective tax rate	35%

	2004	2005	2006	2007	2008
Revenues					
Planes delivered					30
7E7 planes					30
7E7 Stretch planes					0
7E7 price					$136.95
7E7 Stretch price					
Total product revenues					4,108.64
Cost of goods sold					3,286.91
Gross profit					821.73
Depreciation	7.50	29.44	102.23	117.06	123.78
GS&A expense					308.15
Operating profit (before R&D)	(7.50)	(29.44)	(102.23)	(117.06)	389.80
R&D expense	300.00	900.00	3,000.00	900.00	694.50
Pretax profit	(307.50)	(929.44)	(3,102.23)	(1,017.06)	(304.69)
Taxes (or tax credit)	(107.63)	(325.30)	(1,085.78)	(355.97)	(106.64)
After-tax profit	(199.88)	(604.13)	(2,016.45)	(661.09)	(198.05)
Capital expenditure	100.00	300.00	1,000.00	300.00	206.57
Depreciation add-back	7.50	29.44	102.23	117.06	123.78
Change in WCR					275.28
Annual free cash flow	$(292.38)	$(874.70)	$(2,914.22)	$(844.03)	$(556.13)

EXHIBIT 8 | *(continued)*

	2009	2010	2011	2012	2013
Revenues					
Planes delivered	108	64	82	84	104
7E7 planes	108	51	41	42	52
7E7 Stretch planes	0	13	41	42	52
7E7 price	$139.69	$142.49	$145.34	$148.24	$151.21
7E7 Stretch price		170.87	174.28	177.77	181.33
Total product revenues	15,086.93	9,488.14	13,104.49	13,692.60	17,291.79
Cost of goods sold	12,069.55	7,590.51	10,483.59	10,954.08	13,833.44
Gross profit	3,017.39	1,897.63	2,620.90	2,738.52	3,458.36
Depreciation	123.80	115.66	108.67	102.83	99.64
GS&A expense	1,131.52	711.61	982.84	1,026.94	1,296.88
Operating profit (before R&D)	1,762.06	1,070.36	1,529.40	1,608.75	2,061.83
R&D expense	647.00	218.23	301.40	314.93	397.71
Pretax profit	1,115.06	852.13	1,227.99	1,293.82	1,664.12
Taxes (or tax credit)	390.27	298.25	429.80	452.84	582.44
After-tax profit	724.79	553.89	798.19	840.98	1,081.68
Capital expenditure	124.14	15.18	20.97	21.91	27.67
Depreciation add-back	123.80	115.66	108.67	102.83	99.64
Change in WCR	735.55	(375.12)	242.30	39.40	241.15
Annual free cash flow	$(11.09)	$1,029.48	$643.60	$882.50	$912.51

	2014	2015	2016	2017	2018
Revenues					
Planes delivered	136	119	185	192	219
7E7 planes	68	60	93	96	110
7E7 Stretch planes	68	59	92	96	109
7E7 price	$154.23	$157.32	$160.46	$163.67	$166.95
7E7 Stretch price	184.95	188.65	192.42	196.27	200.20
Total product revenues	23,064.59	20,569.48	32,626.19	34,554.82	40,185.75
Cost of goods sold	18,451.67	16,455.59	26,100.95	27,643.86	32,148.60
Gross profit	4,612.92	4,113.90	6,525.24	6,910.96	8,037.15
Depreciation	99.95	100.84	103.70	106.87	110.54
GS&A expense	1,729.84	1,542.71	2,446.96	2,591.61	3,013.93
Operating profit (before R&D)	2,783.12	2,470.35	3,974.57	4,212.48	4,912.68
R&D expense	530.49	473.10	750.40	794.76	924.27
Pretax profit	2,252.64	1,997.25	3,224.17	3,417.72	3,988.40
Taxes (or tax credit)	788.42	699.04	1,128.46	1,196.20	1,395.94
After-tax profit	1,464.21	1,298.21	2,095.71	2,221.52	2,592.46
Capital expenditure	36.90	32.91	52.20	55.29	64.30
Depreciation add-back	99.95	100.84	103.70	106.87	110.54
Change in WCR	386.78	(167.17)	807.80	129.22	377.27
Annual free cash flow	$1,140.48	$1,533.31	$1,339.41	$2,143.88	$2,261.44

EXHIBIT 8 | (continued)

	2019	2020	2021	2022	2023
Revenues					
Planes delivered	165	149	108	115	119
7E7 planes	83	75	54	58	60
7E7 Stretch planes	82	74	54	57	59
7E7 price	$170.29	$173.69	$177.17	$180.71	$184.32
7E7 Stretch price	204.20	208.29	212.45	216.70	221.03
Total product revenues	30,878.29	28,440.04	21,039.33	22,833.05	24,100.43
Cost of goods sold	24,702.63	22,752.03	16,831.46	18,266.44	19,280.34
Gross profit	6,175.66	5,688.01	4,207.87	4,566.61	4,820.09
Depreciation	112.89	114.85	115.88	117.16	118.63
GS&A expense	2,315.87	2,133.00	1,577.95	1,712.48	1,807.53
Operating profit (before R&D)	3,746.89	3,440.15	2,514.04	2,736.97	2,893.92
R&D expense	710.20	654.12	483.90	525.16	554.31
Pretax profit	3,036.69	2,786.03	2,030.13	2,211.81	2,339.61
Taxes (or tax credit)	1,062.84	975.11	710.55	774.13	818.86
After-tax profit	1,973.85	1,810.92	1,319.59	1,437.68	1,520.75
Capital expenditure	49.41	45.50	33.66	36.53	38.56
Depreciation add-back	112.89	114.85	115.88	117.16	118.63
Change in WCR	(623.60)	(163.36)	(495.85)	120.18	84.91
Annual free cash flow	$2,660.94	$2,043.63	$1,897.65	$1,398.13	$1,515.90

	2024	2025	2026	2027	2028
Revenues					
Planes delivered	136	150	120	115	115
7E7 planes	68	75	60	58	58
7E7 Stretch planes	68	75	60	57	57
7E7 price	$188.01	$191.77	$195.61	$199.52	$203.51
7E7 Stretch price	225.46	229.96	234.56	239.26	244.04
Total product revenues	28,115.61	31,630.06	25,810.13	25,209.53	25,713.72
Cost of goods sold	22,492.49	25,304.05	20,648.10	20,167.63	20,570.98
Gross profit	5,623.12	6,326.01	5,162.03	5,041.91	5,142.74
Depreciation	116.20	105.31	62.54	50.92	43.54
GS&A expense	2,108.67	2,372.25	1,935.76	1,890.72	1,928.53
Operating profit (before R&D)	3,398.25	3,848.45	3,163.73	3,100.27	3,170.68
R&D expense	646.66	727.49	593.63	579.82	591.42
Pretax profit	2,751.60	3,120.96	2,570.09	2,520.45	2,579.26
Taxes (or tax credit)	963.06	1,092.33	899.53	882.16	902.74
After-tax profit	1,788.54	2,028.62	1,670.56	1,638.29	1,676.52
Capital expenditure	44.98	50.61	41.30	40.34	41.14
Depreciation add-back	116.20	105.31	62.54	50.92	43.54
Change in WCR	269.02	235.47	(389.94)	(40.24)	33.78
Annual free cash flow	$1,590.73	$1,847.86	$2,081.74	$1,689.12	$1,645.13

EXHIBIT 8 | *(continued)*

	2029	2030	2031	2032	2033
Revenues					
Planes delivered	115	115	115	115	115
7E7 planes	58	58	58	58	58
7E7 Stretch planes	57	57	57	57	57
7E7 price	$207.58	$211.73	$215.96	$220.28	$224.69
7E7 Stretch price	248.92	253.90	258.98	264.16	269.44
Total product revenues	26,228.00	26,752.56	27,287.61	27,833.36	28,390.03
Cost of goods sold	20,982.40	21,402.05	21,830.09	22,266.69	22,712.02
Gross profit	5,245.60	5,350.51	5,457.52	5,566.67	5,678.01
Depreciation	39.86	41.10	42.13	43.19	44.07
GS&A expense	1,967.10	2,006.44	2,046.57	2,087.50	2,129.25
Operating profit (before R&D)	3,238.64	3,302.97	3,368.82	3,435.98	3,504.68
R&D expense	603.24	615.31	627.62	640.17	652.97
Pretax profit	2,635.39	2,687.66	2,741.21	2,795.81	2,851.71
Taxes (or tax credit)	922.39	940.68	959.42	978.53	998.10
After-tax profit	1,713.00	1,746.98	1,781.78	1,817.28	1,853.61
Capital expenditure	41.96	42.80	43.66	44.53	45.42
Depreciation add-back	39.86	41.10	42.13	43.19	44.07
Change in WCR	34.46	35.15	35.85	36.57	37.30
Annual free cash flow	$1,676.45	$1,710.13	$1,744.41	$1,779.37	$1,814.96

	2034	2035	2036	2037
Revenues				
Planes delivered	115	115	115	115
7E7 planes	58	58	58	58
7E7 Stretch planes	57	57	57	57
7E7 price	$229.18	$233.77	$238.44	$243.21
7E7 Stretch price	274.83	280.33	285.93	291.65
Total product revenues	28,957.83	29,536.99	30,127.73	30,730.28
Cost of goods sold	23,166.26	23,629.59	24,102.18	24,584.22
Gross profit	5,791.57	5,907.40	6,025.55	6,146.06
Depreciation	44.59	45.33	45.25	45.08
GS&A expense	2,171.84	2,215.27	2,259.58	2,304.77
Operating profit (before R&D)	3,575.14	3,646.80	3,720.72	3,796.21
R&D expense	666.03	679.35	692.94	706.80
Pretax profit	2,909.11	2,967.45	3,027.78	3,089.41
Taxes (or tax credit)	1,018.19	1,038.61	1,059.72	1,081.29
After-tax profit	1,890.92	1,928.84	1,968.06	2,008.12
Capital expenditure	46.33	47.26	48.20	49.17
Depreciation add-back	44.59	45.33	45.25	45.08
Change in WCR	38.04	38.80	39.58	40.37
Annual free cash flow	$1,851.14	$1,888.10	$1,925.52	$1,963.65

EXHIBIT 9 | Sensitivity Analysis of Project IRRs by Price, Volume, Development, and Production Costs

Unit Volume (First 20 Years)	Price Premium Above Expected Minimum Price			
	0%	5%	10%	15%
1,500	10.5%	10.9%	11.3%	11.7%
1,750	11.9%	12.3%	12.7%	13.1%
2,000	13.0%	13.5%	13.9%	14.4%
2,250	14.1%	14.6%	15.1%	15.5%
2,500	15.2%	*15.7%*	16.1%	16.6%
2,750	16.1%	16.6%	17.1%	17.6%
3,000	17.1%	17.6%	18.1%	18.6%

Development Costs	Cost of Goods Sold as a Percentage of Sales			
	78%	80%	82%	84%
$6,000,000,000	21.3%	18.7%	15.9%	12.6%
$7,000,000,000	19.4%	17.0%	14.4%	11.3%
$8,000,000,000	17.9%	*15.7%*	13.2%	10.3%
$9,000,000,000	16.6%	14.5%	12.1%	9.4%
$10,000,000,000	15.5%	13.5%	11.2%	8.6%

Note: The IRR consistent with "base case" assumptions is 15.7% and is indicated in italics in the table.

Source: Case writer's analysis.

EXHIBIT 10 | Information on Comparable Companies (Specially calculated betas estimated from daily stock and market returns over the periods indicated)

	Boeing	Lockheed Martin	Northrop Grumman	Raytheon
Percentage of revenues derived from government (defense and space)	46%	93%	91%	73%
Estimated betas				
1. Value Line[1]	1.05	0.60	0.70	0.80
2. Calculated against the S&P 500 index:[2]				
60 months	0.80	0.36	0.34	0.43
21 months	1.03	0.38	0.31	0.46
60 trading days	1.45	0.34	0.27	0.66
3. Calculated against the NYSE composite index:[2]				
60 months	1.00	0.49	0.44	0.59
21 months	1.17	0.44	0.36	0.53
60 trading days	1.62	0.37	0.30	0.73
Effective marginal tax rate	0.35	0.35	0.35	0.35
Market-value debt/equity ratios	0.525	0.410	0.640	0.624

Sources: Case writer's analysis and *Value Line Investment Survey.*

[1]Value Line betas are calculated from a regression analysis between the weekly percentage change in price of a stock and the weekly percentage changes of the New York Stock Exchange Composite Index. The beta is calculated using the last five years of data.

[2]Regression periods for the 60-day, 21-month, and 60-month begin on March 20, 2003, September 17, 2001, and June 16, 1998, respectively. Regression periods end on June 16, 2003.

EXHIBIT 11 | Outstanding Bonds of the Boeing Company as of June 2003 ($ values in millions)

Debt Amount	Debt Rating	Coupon	Maturity	Price	Yield To Maturity
$202	A-	7.625%	2/15/2005	106.175	3.911%
$298	A-	6.625%	6/1/2005	105.593	3.393%
$249	A-	6.875%	11/1/2006	110.614	3.475%
$175	A-	8.100%	11/15/2006	112.650	4.049%
$349	A-	9.750%	4/1/2012	129.424	5.470%
$597	A-	6.125%	2/15/2013	103.590	4.657%
$398	A-	8.750%	8/15/2021	127.000	6.239%
$300	A-	7.950%	8/15/2024	126.951	5.732%
$247	A-	7.250%	6/15/2025	114.506	6.047%
$249	A-	8.750%	9/15/2031	131.000	6.337%
$173	A-	8.625%	11/15/2031	138.974	5.805%
$393	A-	6.125%	2/15/2033	103.826	5.850%
$300	A-	6.625%	2/15/2038	106.715	6.153%
$100	A-	7.500%	8/15/2042	119.486	6.173%
$173	A-	7.825%	4/15/2043	132.520	5.777%
$125	A-	6.875%	10/15/2043	110.084	6.191%

Note: This table does not include the outstanding debt of Boeing's financing subsidiary, Boeing Capital Corporation.

Sources: Boeing Company 10-Q, Bloomberg Financial Services, and Mergent Online.

APPENDIX | Assumptions Underlying the Forecast of Cash Flows

Revenue Estimation

In order to project revenues for the project, several assumptions were made about the expected demand and timing for the units, their price, and price increases.

Demand: Boeing estimated that in the first 20 years they would sell 2,000–3,000 units.[1] Frost & Sullivan, aviation industry analysts, predicted at least 2,000 units.[2] Analysis assumes 2,500 units in years 1 through 20. Years 20–30 assume unit sales equal to year 20. First delivery of 7E7 expected in 2008 and 7E7 Stretch in 2010.

Timing of demand: Units sold per year is the percentage of the total units in the first 20 years as shown in **Exhibit 6. Exhibit 6** uses an historical average of the 757 and 767 unit sales during their first 20 years. The Boeing 7E7 is expected to be a replacement aircraft for the 757 and 767. Analysis assumes the 7E7 Stretch accounts for only 20% of unit sales in its first year of delivery and 50% thereafter. If the total number of unit sales per year is an odd number, the 7E7 units are rounded up and the 7E7 Stretch are rounded down.

Price: The expected price of the 7E7 and Stretch version is a function of the 767 and 777 prices in 2002. Using range and capacity as the primary variables, the 7E7 and 7E7 Stretch would be expected to have a minimum price of $114.5 million and $144.5 million respectively in 2002 dollars. This does not include a premium for the expected lower operating costs and flexibility of the 7E7. The analysis assumes a 5% price premium as a benchmark, resulting in expected prices of $120.2 million and $151.7 million in 2002.

Rate of price increases: Aircraft prices are assumed to increase at the rate of inflation. Inflation is assumed to be 2% per year until 2037.

Expense Estimation

Cost of goods sold: The average cost of goods sold for Boeing's commercial-aircraft division was 80% over the three-year period 2000–2002. The range was 77.9% to 81.1%. The analysis assumes 80% as the COGS.

General, selling, and administrative expense: The average general, selling, and administrative expense for Boeing was 7.5% over the three-year period 2000–2002. The range was 7.4% to 7.7%. The analysis assumes 7.5% as the general, selling, and administrative expense.

Depreciation: Boeing depreciated its assets on an accelerated basis. The forecast uses 150% declining balance depreciation with a 20-year asset life and zero salvage value as the base.

Research and development as a percentage of sales: The average research and development expense for Boeing's commercial-aircraft division as a percentage of commercial-aircraft sales was 2.3% over the three-year period 2000–2002. The range was 1.8% to 2.7%. During that period, Boeing did not have any extraordinary new commercial-aircraft development expenses. The analysis, therefore, assumes 2.3% as the estimated research and development expense. That does not include the initial research and development costs required to design and develop the 7E7.

Tax expense: Boeing's expected marginal effective tax rate was 35%.

Other Adjustments to Cash Flow

Capital expenditures: The 1998–2002 average for capital expenditures as a percentage of sales was 0.93%. During this period, Boeing did not have any extraordinary new commercial-aircraft development expenses. At the time, Boeing had six families of aircraft: the 717, 737, 747, 757, 767, and 777. The average capital expenditures per family line, as a percentage of sales, was therefore 0.16%. This does not include the initial capital expenditure costs required to develop and build the 7E7.

Change in working capital requirements (WCR): For the years 2000–2002, Boeing had negative working capital due to factors such as advance customer payments. The analysis assumes that the commercial segment of Boeing would require positive working capital. The years prior to 2000, Boeing had positive working capital. The 1997–1999, three-year average of working capital as a percentage of sales is 6.7% with a range from 3.5% to 11.2%. The analysis assumes this percentage.

---

[1]"New Team, Name for Boeing 'Super-Efficient' Jet," *Seattle Times,* 30 January 2003, 1.

[2]"An Ongoing Rivalry," *Aviation Today,* August 2003.

APPENDIX | (*continued*)

Initial development costs: Development costs include the research and capital requirements needed to design and build the 7E7. Analysts estimated between $6 billion and $10 billion.[3] The analysis assumes $8 billion. Assuming a launch in 2004, analysts expected spending to peak in 2006. Timing of the development costs are assumed to be 2004: 5%, 2005: 15%, 2006: 50%, 2007: 15%, 2008: 10%, and 2009: 5%. It is estimated that 75% of the initial development costs are research and development expenses, while the remaining 25% are capital expenditures.

[3]"Boeing Plays Defense," *Business Week,* 3 June 2003.

Source: Case writer's analysis.

## PART 4

Capital Budgeting and Resource Allocation

The Investment Detective

The essence of capital budgeting and resource allocation is a search for good investments to place the firm's capital. The process can be simple when viewed in purely mechanical terms, but a number of subtle issues can obscure the best investment choices. The capital-budgeting analyst, therefore, is necessarily a detective who must winnow bad evidence from good. Much of the challenge is in knowing what quantitative analysis to generate in the first place.

Suppose you are a new capital-budgeting analyst for a company considering investments in the eight projects listed in **Exhibit 1**. The chief financial officer of your company has asked you to rank the projects and recommend the "four best" that the company should accept.

In this assignment, only the quantitative considerations are relevant. No other project characteristics are deciding factors in the selection, except that management has determined that projects 7 and 8 are mutually exclusive.

All the projects require the same initial investment: $2 million. Moreover, all are believed to be of the same risk class. The firm's weighted average cost of capital has never been estimated. In the past, analysts have simply assumed that 10% was an appropriate discount rate (although certain officers of the company have recently asserted that the discount rate should be much higher).

To stimulate your analysis, consider the following questions:

1. Can you rank the projects simply by inspecting the cash flows?

2. What criteria might you use to rank the projects? Which quantitative ranking methods are better? Why?

3. What is the ranking you found by using quantitative methods? Does this ranking differ from the ranking obtained by simple inspection of the cash flows?

4. What kinds of real investment projects have cash flows similar to those in **Exhibit 1**?

This case was prepared by Robert F. Bruner, with the permission of Professor Gordon Donaldson, the author of an antecedent case. It was written as a basis for class discussion rather than to illustrate effective or ineffective handling of an administrative situation. Copyright © 1988 by the University of Virginia Darden School Foundation, Charlottesville, VA. All rights reserved. *To order copies, send an e-mail to* sales@dardenbusinesspublishing.com. *No part of this publication may be reproduced, stored in a retrieval system, used in a spreadsheet, or transmitted in any form or by any means—electronic, mechanical, photocopying, recording, or otherwise—without the permission of the Darden School Foundation.* Rev. 06/12.

EXHIBIT 1 | Projects' Free Cash Flows (dollars in thousands)

Project number: Initial investment	1 $(2,000)	2 $(2,000)	3 $(2,000)	4 $(2,000)	5 $(2,000)	6 $(2,000)	7 $(2,000)	8 $(2,000)
Year 1	$ 330	$1,666		$ 160	$ 280	$ 2,200*	$1,200	$ (350)
2	330	334*		200	280		900*	(60)
3	330	165		350	280		300	60
4	330			395	280		90	350
5	330			432	280		70	700
6	330			440*	280			1,200
7	330*			442	280			$ 2,250*
8	$1,000			444	280*			
9				446	280			
10				448	280			
11				450	280			
12				451	280			
13				451	280			
14				452	280			
15			$10,000*	$(2,000)	$ 280			
Sum of cash flow benefits	$3,310	$2,165	$10,000	$ 3,561	$4,200	$ 2,200	$2,560	$ 4,150
Excess of cash flow over initial investment	$1,310	$ 165	$ 8,000	$ 1,561	$2,200	$ 200	$ 560	$ 2,150

*Indicates year in which payback was accomplished.

Worldwide Paper Company

In December 2006, Bob Prescott, the controller for the Blue Ridge Mill, was considering the addition of a new on-site longwood woodyard. The addition would have two primary benefits: to eliminate the need to purchase shortwood from an outside supplier and create the opportunity to sell shortwood on the open market as a new market for Worldwide Paper Company (WPC). The new woodyard would allow the Blue Ridge Mill not only to reduce its operating costs but also to increase its revenues. The proposed woodyard utilized new technology that allowed tree-length logs, called longwood, to be processed directly, whereas the current process required shortwood, which had to be purchased from the Shenandoah Mill. This nearby mill, owned by a competitor, had excess capacity that allowed it to produce more shortwood than it needed for its own pulp production. The excess was sold to several different mills, including the Blue Ridge Mill. Thus adding the new longwood equipment would mean that Prescott would no longer need to use the Shenandoah Mill as a shortwood supplier and that the Blue Ridge Mill would instead compete with the Shenandoah Mill by selling on the shortwood market. The question for Prescott was whether these expected benefits were enough to justify the $18 million capital outlay plus the incremental investment in working capital over the six-year life of the investment.

Construction would start within a few months, and the investment outlay would be spent over two calendar years: $16 million in 2007 and the remaining $2 million in 2008. When the new woodyard began operating in 2008, it would significantly reduce the operating costs of the mill. These operating savings would come mostly from the difference in the cost of producing shortwood on-site versus buying it on the open market and were estimated to be $2.0 million for 2008 and $3.5 million per year thereafter.

Prescott also planned on taking advantage of the excess production capacity afforded by the new facility by selling shortwood on the open market as soon as possible. For 2008, he expected to show revenues of approximately $4 million, as the facility came on-line and began to break into the new market. He expected shortwood sales to reach $10 million in 2009 and continue at the $10 million level through 2013.

Prescott estimated that the cost of goods sold (before including depreciation expenses) would be 75% of revenues, and SG&A would be 5% of revenues.

In addition to the capital outlay of $18 million, the increased revenues would necessitate higher levels of inventories and accounts receivable. The total working capital would average 10% of annual revenues. Therefore the amount of working capital investment each year would equal 10% of incremental sales for the year. At the end of the life of the equipment, in 2013, all the net working capital on the books would be recoverable at cost, whereas only 10% or $1.8 million (before taxes) of the capital investment would be recoverable.

Taxes would be paid at a 40% rate, and depreciation was calculated on a straight-line basis over the six-year life, with zero salvage. WPC accountants had told Prescott that depreciation charges could not begin until 2008, when all the $18 million had been spent, and the machinery was in service.

Prescott was conflicted about how to treat inflation in his analysis. He was reasonably confident that his estimates of revenues and costs for 2008 and 2009 reflected the dollar amounts that WPC would most likely experience during those years. The capital outlays were mostly contracted costs and therefore were highly reliable estimates. The expected shortwood revenue figure of $4.0 million had been based on a careful analysis of the shortwood market that included a conservative estimate of the Blue Ridge Mill's share of the market plus the expected market price of shortwood, taking into account the impact of Blue Ridge Mill as a new competitor in the market. Because he was unsure of how the operating costs and the price of shortwood would be impacted by inflation after 2009, Prescott decided not to include it in his analysis. Therefore the dollar estimates for 2010 and beyond were based on the same costs and prices per ton used in 2009. Prescott did not consider the omission critical to the final decision because he expected the increase in operating costs caused by inflation would be mostly offset by the increase in revenues associated with the rise in the price of shortwood.

WPC had a company policy to use 15% as the hurdle rate for such investment opportunities. The hurdle rate was based on a study of the company's cost of capital conducted 10 years ago. Prescott was uneasy using an outdated figure for a discount rate, particularly because it was computed when 30-year Treasury bonds were yielding 10%, whereas currently they were yielding less than 5% (**Exhibit 1**).

EXHIBIT 1 | Cost-of-Capital Information

Interest Rates: December 2006

Bank loan rates (LIBOR)		**Market risk premium**	
1-year	5.38%	Historical average	6.0%

Government bonds		**Corporate bonds (10-year maturities):**	
1-year	4.96%	Aaa	5.37%
5-year	4.57%	Aa	5.53%
10-year	4.60%	A	5.78%
30-year	4.73%	Baa	6.25%

Worldwide Paper Financial Data

Balance-sheet accounts ($ millions)	
Bank loan payable (LIBOR + 1%)	500
Long-term debt	2,500
Common equity	500
Retained earnings	2,000

Per-share data	
Shares outstanding (millions)	500
Book value per share	$ 5.00
Recent market value per share	$24.00

Other	
Bond rating	A
Beta	1.10

Target Corporation

On November 14, 2006, Doug Scovanner, CFO of Target Corporation, was preparing for the November meeting of the Capital Expenditure Committee (CEC). Scovanner was one of five executive officers who were members of the CEC (**Exhibit 1**). On tap for the 8:00 a.m. meeting the next morning were 10 projects representing nearly $300 million in capital-expenditure requests. With the fiscal year's end approaching in January, there was a need to determine which projects best fit Target's future store growth and capital-expenditure plans, with the knowledge that those plans would be shared early in 2007, with both the board and investment community. In reviewing the 10 projects coming before the committee, it was clear to Scovanner that five of the projects, representing about $200 million in requested capital, would demand the greater part of the committee's attention and discussion time during the meeting.

The CEC was keenly aware that Target had been a strong performing company in part because of its successful investment decisions and continued growth. Moreover, Target management was committed to continuing the company's growth strategy of opening approximately 100 new stores a year. Each investment decision would have long-term implications for Target: an underperforming store would be a drag on earnings and difficult to turn around without significant investments of time and money, whereas a top-performing store would add value both financially and strategically for years to come.

Retail Industry

The retail industry included a myriad of different companies offering similar product lines (**Exhibit 2**). For example, Sears and JCPenney had extensive networks of stores that offered a broad line of products, many of which were similar to Target's product lines. Because each retailer had a different strategy and a different customer base, truly comparable stores were difficult to identify. Many investment analysts, however, focused on Wal-Mart and Costco as important competitors for Target, although for

This case was prepared by David Ding (MBA '08) and Saul Yeaton (MBA '08) under the supervision of Kenneth Eades, Professor of Business Administration. It was written as a basis for class discussion rather than to illustrate effective or ineffective handling of an administrative situation. Copyright © 2008 by the University of Virginia Darden School Foundation, Charlottesville, VA. All rights reserved. *To order copies, send an e-mail* sales@dardenbusinesspublishing.com. *No part of this publication may be reproduced, stored in a retrieval system, used in a spreadsheet, or transmitted in any form or by any means—electronic, mechanical, photocopying, recording, or otherwise—without the permission of the Darden School Foundation.* Rev. 07/12.

different reasons. Wal-Mart operated store formats similar to Target, and most Target stores operated in trade areas where one or more Wal-Mart stores were located. Wal-Mart and Target also carried merchandising assortments, which overlapped on many of the same items in such areas as food, commodities, electronics, toys, and sporting goods.

Costco, on the other hand, attracted a customer base that overlapped closely with Target's core customers, but there was less often overlap between Costco and Target with respect to trade area and merchandising assortment. Costco also differed from Target in that it used a membership-fee format.[1] Most of the sales of these companies were in the broad categories of general merchandise and food. General merchandise included electronics, entertainment, sporting goods, toys, apparel, accessories, home furnishing, and décor, and food items included consumables ranging from apples to zucchini.

Wal-Mart had become the dominant player in the industry, with operations located in the United States, Argentina, Brazil, Canada, Puerto Rico, United Kingdom, Central America, Japan, and Mexico. Much of Wal-Mart's success was attributed to its "everyday low price" pricing strategy that was greeted with delight by consumers but created severe challenges for local independent retailers who needed to remain competitive. Wal-Mart sales had reached $309 billion for 2005 for 6,141 stores and a market capitalization of $200 billion, compared with sales of $178 billion and 4,189 stores in 2000. In addition to growing its top line, Wal-Mart had been successful in creating efficiency within the company and branching into product lines that offered higher margins than many of its commodity type of products.

Costco provided discount pricing for its members in exchange for membership fees. For fiscal 2005, these fees comprised 2.0% of total revenue and 72.8% of operating income. Membership fees were such an important factor to Costco that an equity analyst had coined a new price-to-membership-fee-income ratio metric for valuing the company.[2] By 2005, Costco's sales had grown to $52.9 billion across its 433 warehouses, and its market capitalization had reached $21.8 billion. Over the previous five years, sales excluding membership fees had experienced compound growth of 10.4%, while membership fees had grown 14.6% making the fees a significant growth source and highly significant to operating income in a low-profit-margin business.

In order to attract shoppers, retailers tailored their product offerings, pricing, and branding to specific customer segments. Segmentation of the customer population had led to a variety of different strategies, ranging from price competition in Wal-Mart stores to Target's strategy of appealing to style-conscious consumers by offering unique assortments of home and apparel items, while also pricing competitively with Wal-Mart on items common to both stores. The intensity of competition among retailers had resulted in razor-thin margins making every line item on the income statement an important consideration for all retailers.

The effects of tight margins were felt throughout the supply chain as retailers constantly pressured their suppliers to accept lower prices. In addition, retailers used

---

[1] Sam's Club, which was owned by Wal-Mart, also employed a membership-fee format and represented 13% of Wal-Mart revenues.

[2] "Costco Wholesale Corp. Initiation Report" by Wachovia Capital Markets, September 18, 2006.

off-shore sources as low-cost substitutes for their products and implemented methods such as just-in-time inventory management, low-cost distribution networks, and high sales per square foot to achieve operational efficiency. Retailers had found that profit margins could also be enhanced by selling their own brands, or products with exclusive labels that could be marketed to attract the more affluent customers in search of a unique shopping experience.

Sales growth for retail companies stemmed from two main sources: creation of new stores and organic growth through existing stores. New stores were expensive to build, but were needed to access new markets and tap into a new pool of consumers that could potentially represent high profit potential depending upon the competitive landscape. Increasing the sales of existing stores was also an important source of growth and value. If an existing store was operating profitably, it could be considered for renovation or upgrading in order to increase sales volume. Or, if a store was not profitable, management would consider it a candidate for closure.

Target Corporation

The Dayton Company opened the doors of the first Target store in 1962, in Roseville, Minnesota. The Target name had intentionally been chosen to differentiate the new discount retailer from the Dayton Company's more upscale stores. The Target concept flourished. In 1995, the first SuperTarget store opened in Omaha, Nebraska, and in 1999, the Target.com Web site was launched. By 2000, the parent company, Dayton Hudson, officially changed its name to Target Corporation.[3]

By 2005, Target had become a major retailing powerhouse with $52.6 billion in revenues from 1,397 stores in 47 states (**Exhibits 3** and **4**). With sales of $30 billion in 2000, the company had realized a 12.1% sales growth over the past five years and had announced plans to continue its growth by opening approximately 100 stores per year in the United States in the foreseeable future. While Target Corporation had never committed to expanding internationally, analysts had been speculating that domestic growth alone would not be enough to sustain its historic success. If Target continued its domestic growth strategy, most analysts expected capital expenditures would continue at a level of 6–7% of revenues, which equated to about $3.5 billion for fiscal 2006.

In contrast with Wal-Mart's focus on low prices, Target's strategy was to consider the customer's shopping experience as a whole. Target referred to its customers as guests and consistently strived to support the slogan, "Expect more. Pay less." Target focused on creating a shopping experience that appealed to the profile of its "core guest": a college-educated woman with children at home who was more affluent than the typical Wal-Mart customer. This shopping experience was created by emphasizing a store décor that gave just the right shopping ambience. The company had been

---

[3] The Dayton Company merged with J. L. Hudson Company in 1969. After changing its name to Target, the company renamed the Dayton-Hudson stores as Marshall Field's. In 2004, Marshall Field's was sold to May Department Stores, which was acquired by Federated Department Stores in 2006; all May stores were given the Macy's name that same year.

highly successful at promoting its brand awareness with large advertising campaigns; its advertising expenses for fiscal 2005 were $1.0 billion or about 2.0% of sales and 26.6% of operating profit. In comparison, Wal-Mart's advertising dollars amounted to 0.5% of sales and 9.2% of operating income. Consistent advertising spending resulted in the Target bull's-eye logo's (**Exhibit 5**) being ranked among the most recognized corporate logos in the United States, ahead of the Nike "swoosh."

As an additional enhancement to the customer shopping experience, Target offered credit to qualified customers through its REDcards: Target Visa Credit Card and Target Credit Card. The credit-card business accounted for 14.9% of Target's operating earnings and was designed to be integrated with the company's overall strategy by focusing only on customers who visited Target stores.

Capital-Expenditure Approval Process

The Capital Expenditure Committee was composed of a team of top executives that met monthly to review all capital project requests (CPRs) in excess of $100,000. CPRs were either approved by the CEC, or in the case of projects larger than $50 million, required approval from the board of directors. Project proposals varied widely and included remodeling, relocating, rebuilding, and closing an existing store to building a new store.[4] A typical CEC meeting involved the review of 10 to 15 CPRs. All of the proposals were considered economically attractive, as any CPRs with questionable economics were normally rejected at the lower levels of review. In the rare instance when a project with a negative net present value (NPV) reached the CEC, the committee was asked to consider the project in light of its strategic importance to the company.

CEC meetings lasted several hours as each of the projects received careful scrutiny by the committee members. The process purposefully was designed to be rigorous because the CEC recognized that capital investment could have significant impact on the short-term and long-term profitability of the company. In addition to the large amount of capital at stake, approvals and denials also had the potential to set precedents that would affect future decisions. For example, the committee might choose to reject a remodeling proposal for a store with a positive NPV, if the investment amount requested was much higher than normal and therefore might create a troublesome precedent for all subsequent remodel requests for similar stores. Despite how much the projects differed, the committee was normally able to reach a consensus decision for the vast majority of them. Occasionally however, a project led to such a high degree of disagreement within the committee that the CEO made the final call.

Projects typically required 12 to 24 months of development prior to being forwarded to the CEC for consideration. In the case of new store proposals, which represented the majority of the CPRs, a real-estate manager assigned to that geographic region was responsible for the proposal from inception to completion and also for

---

[4] Target expected to allocate 65% of capital expenditures to new stores, 12% to remodels and expansions, and 23% to information technology, distribution, etc.

reviewing and presenting the proposal details. The pre-CPR work required a certain amount of expenditures that were not recoverable if the project were ultimately rejected by CEC. More important than these expenditures, however, were the "emotional sunk costs" for the real-estate managers who believed strongly in the merits of their proposals and felt significant disappointment if any project was not approved.

The committee considered several factors in determining whether to accept or reject a project. An overarching objective was to meet the corporate goal of adding about 100 stores a year while maintaining a positive brand image. Projects also needed to meet a variety of financial objectives, starting with providing a suitable financial return as measured by discounted cash-flow metrics: NPV and IRR (internal rate of return). Other financial considerations included projected profit and earnings per share impacts, total investment size, impact on sales of other nearby Target stores, and sensitivity of NPV and IRR to sales variations. Projected sales were determined based on economic trends and demographic shifts but also considered the risks involved with the entrance of new competitors and competition from online retailers. And lastly, the committee attempted to keep the project approvals within the capital budget for the year. If projects were approved in excess of the budgeted amount, Target would likely need to borrow money to fund the shortfall. Adding debt unexpectedly to the balance sheet could raise questions from equity analysts as to the increased risk to the shareholders as well as to the ability of management to accurately project the company's funding needs.

Other considerations included tax and real-estate incentives provided by local communities as well as area demographics. Target typically purchased the properties where it built stores, although leasing was considered on occasion. Population growth and affluent communities were attractive to Target, but these factors also invited competition from other retailers. In some cases, new Target stores were strategically located to block other retailers despite marginal short-term returns.

When deciding whether to open a new store, the CEC was often asked to consider alternative store formats. For example, the most widely used format was the 2004 version of a Target store prototype called P04, which occupied 125,000 square feet, whereas a SuperTarget format occupied an additional 50,000 square feet to accommodate a full grocery assortment. The desirability of one format over another often centered on whether a store was expected to eventually be upgraded. Smaller stores often offered a higher NPV; but the NPV estimate did not consider the effect of future upgrades or expansions that would be required if the surrounding communities grew, nor the advantage of opening a larger store in an area where it could serve the purpose of blocking competitors from opening stores nearby.

The committee members were provided with a capital-project request "dashboard" for each project that summarized the critical inputs and assumptions used for the NPV and IRR calculations. The template represented the summary sheet for an elaborate discounted cash flow model. For example, the analysis of a new store included incremental cash flow projections for 60 years over which time the model included a remodeling of the store every 10 years. **Exhibit 6** provides an example of a dashboard with a detailed explanation of the "Store Sensitivities" section. The example dashboard shows that incremental sales estimates, which were computed as the total sales expected for the new store less the sales cannibalized from Target stores already located in the general vicinity. Sales estimates were made by the Research and Planning group. The R&P group used demographic and other data to make site-specific forecasts. Incremental sales were computed as total sales less those cannibalized from other Target stores. The resulting NPV and IRR metrics were divided between value created by store sales and credit-card activity. NPV calculations used a 9.0% discount rate for cash flows related to the store cash flows and a 4.0% discount rate for credit-card cash flows. The different discount rates were chosen to represent the different costs of capital for funding store operations versus funding credit-card receivables.

The dashboards also presented a variety of demographic information, investment-cost details and sensitivity analyses. An important sensitivity feature was the comparison of the project's NPV and IRR to the prototype. For example, the P04 store had an NPV of about $10 million and an IRR of 13%.[5] The sensitivity calculations answered the question of how much a certain cost or revenue item needed to change in order for the project to achieve the same NPV or IRR that would be experienced for the typical P04 or SuperTarget store.

The November Meeting

Of the 10 projects under consideration for the November CEC meeting, Doug Scovanner recognized that five would be easily accepted, but that the remaining five CPRs were likely to be difficult choices for the committee. These projects included four new store openings (Gopher Place, Whalen Court, The Barn, and Goldie's Square) and one remodeling of an existing store into a SuperTarget format (Stadium Remodel). **Exhibit 7** contains a summary of the five projects, and **Exhibit 8** contains the CPR dashboards for the individual projects.

As was normally the case, all five of the CPRs had positive NPVs, but Scovanner wondered if the projected NPVs were high enough to justify the required investment. Further, with stiff competition from other large retailers looking to get footholds in major growth areas, how much consideration should be given to short-term versus long-term sales opportunities? For example, Whalen Court represented a massive investment with relatively uncertain sales returns. Should Scovanner take the stance that the CEC should worry less about Whalen Court's uncertain sales and focus more on the project as a means to increase Target's brand awareness in an area with dense foot traffic and high-fashion appeal? Goldie's Square represented a more typical investment level of $24 million for a SuperTarget. The NPV, however, was small at $317,000, well below the expected NPV of a SuperTarget prototype, and would be negative without the value contribution of credit-card sales.

As CFO, Scovanner was also aware that Target shareholders had experienced a lackluster year in 2006, given that Target's stock price had remained essentially flat (**Exhibit 9**). Stock analysts were generally pleased with Target's stated growth policy

---

[5] These NPV and IRR figures exclude the impact of the credit card.

and were looking for decisions from management regarding investments that were consistent with the company maintaining its growth trajectory. In that regard, Scovanner recognized that each of the projects represented a growth opportunity for Target. The question, however, was whether capital was better spent on one project or another to create the most value and the most growth for Target shareholders. Thus, Scovanner felt that he needed to rank the five projects in order to be able to recommend which ones to keep and which ones to reject during the CEC meeting the next day.

EXHIBIT 1 | Executive Officers and Capital Expenditure Committee Members

Timothy R. Baer	Executive Vice President, General Counsel, and Corporate Secretary	
Michael R. Francis	Executive Vice President, Marketing	
John D. Griffith	Executive Vice President, Property Development	CEC
Jodeen A. Kozlak	Executive Vice President, Human Resources	
Troy H. Risch	Executive Vice President, Stores	CEC
Janet M. Schalk	Executive Vice President, Technology Services and Chief Information Officer	
Douglas A. Scovanner	Executive Vice President and Chief Financial Officer	CEC
Terrence J. Scully	President, Target Financial Services	
Gregg W. Steinhafel	President	CEC
Robert J. Ulrich	Chairman and Chief Executive Officer	CEC

Chairman and CEO **Bob Ulrich,** 62. Ulrich began his career at Dayton-Hudson as a merchandising trainee in 1967. He advanced to the position of CEO of Target Stores in 1987 and to the position of Dayton-Hudson's CEO in 1994.

EVP and CFO **Doug Scovanner,** 49. Scovanner was named Target CFO in February 2000 after previously serving as CFO of Dayton-Hudson.

President of Target Stores **Gregg Steinhafel,** 50. Steinhafel began his career at Target as a merchandising trainee in 1979. He was named president in 1999.

EVP of Stores **Troy Risch,** 37. Risch was promoted to EVP in September 2006.

EVP of Property Development **John Griffith,** 44. Griffith was promoted to EVP in February 2005 from the position of senior vice president of Property Development he had held since February 2000.

Source: Target Corp.

EXHIBIT 2 | Retail Company Financial Information

	Revenue ($ billions)	Basic EPS	Debt ($ billions)	Debt Rating (S&P)	Beta	Fiscal Year Ended	Market Capitalization as of Oct 31, 2006 ($ billions)
Bed Bath & Beyond Inc.	$5.8	$1.95	$0.0	BBB	1.05	Feb-06	$11.4
Best Buy Co., Inc.	$30.8	$2.33	$0.6	BBB	1.25	Feb-06	$26.2
Costco Wholesale Corp.	$52.9	$2.24	$0.8	A	0.85	Aug-05	$24.1
Dick's Sporting Goods, Inc.	$2.6	$1.47	$0.2	Not Rated	1.15	Jan-06	$1.3
JCPenney Company, Inc.	$18.8	$4.30	$3.5	BB+	1.05	Jan-06	$16.6
Kohl's Corporation	$13.4	$2.45	$1.2	BBB	0.90	Jan-06	$23.1
Sears Holdings Corporation	$49.1	$5.63	$4.0	BB+	NMF	Jan-06	$26.9
Wal-Mart Stores, Inc.	$315.7	$2.68	$38.8	AA	0.80	Jan-06	$199.9
Target Corporation	**$52.6**	**$2.73**	**$9.9**	**A+**	**1.05**	**Jan-06**	**$50.1**

Data Source: Yahoo! Finance (www.finance.yahoo.com [accessed October 24, 2008]) and Value Line Investment Survey.

EXHIBIT 3 | Target Income Statements ($ millions)

Fiscal Year Ending	28 Jan 2006	29 Jan 2005
Net revenues	52,620	46,839
Cost of goods sold	34,927	31,445
Depreciation, depletion, and amortization	1,409	1,259
Gross income	16,284	14,135
Selling, general, and, admin expenses	11,961	10,534
Earnings before interest and taxes (EBIT)	4,323	3,601
Net interest expense	463	570
Pretax income	3,860	3,031
Income taxes	1,452	1,146
Net income before extra items	2,408	1,885
Gain (loss) sale of assets		1,313
Net income after extra items	2,408	3,198
Capital expenditures (net of disposals)	3,330	3,012
Capital expenditures/sales	6.3%	6.4%

Source: Target Corp. annual reports.

EXHIBIT 4 | Balance Sheet Statements ($ millions)

Fiscal Year Ending	28 Jan 2006	29 Jan 2005	31 Jan 2004
Assets			
Cash and cash equivalents	1,648	2,245	708
Accounts receivable (net)	5,666	5,069	4,621
Inventory	5,838	5,384	4,531
Other current assets	1,253	1,224	3,092
Total current assets	14,405	13,922	12,952
Property plant and equipment, net	19,038	16,860	15,153
Other assets	1,552	1,511	3,311
Total assets	**34,995**	**32,293**	**31,416**
Liabilities			
Accounts payable	6,268	5,779	4,956
Current portion of LT debt and notes payable	753	504	863
Income taxes payable	374	304	382
Other current liabilities	2,193	1,633	2,113
Total current liabilities	9,588	8,220	8,314
Long-term debt	9,119	9,034	10,155
Other liabilities	2,083	2,010	1,815
Total liabilities	**20,790**	**19,264**	**20,284**
Shareholders' equity			
Common equity	2,192	1,881	1,609
Retained earnings	12,013	11,148	9,523
Total liabilities and shareholders' equity	**34,995**	**32,293**	**31,416**

Source: Target Corp. annual reports.

EXHIBIT 5 | Target Logo

Source: Target Corp.

EXHIBIT 6 | Example of a Capital Project Request Dashboard

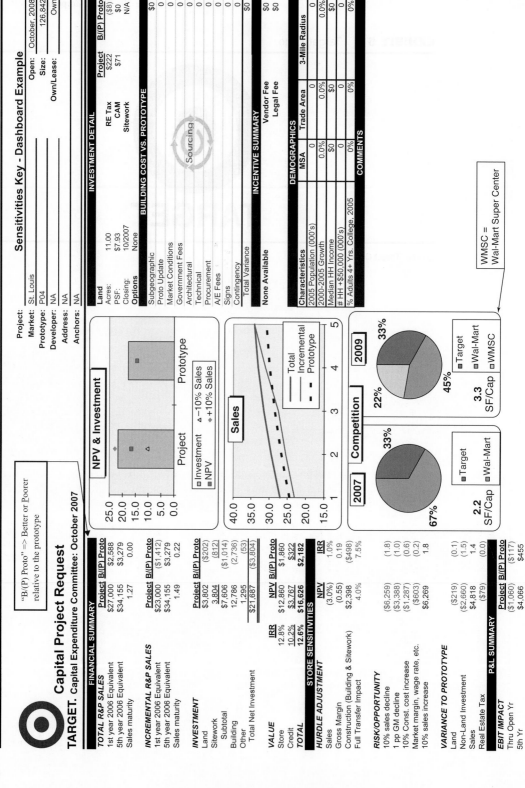

EXHIBIT 6 | Example of a Capital Project Request Dashboard (continued)

Dashboard Sensitivities Key (use with "Sensitivities Key-Dashboard Example")
Dashboard Example: P04; Store NPV: $12,860; Store IRR: 12.8%

HURDLE ADJUSTMENT (CPR Dashboard)

Sales
NPV (3.0%) Sales could decrease (3.0%) and still achieve Prototype Store NPV
IRR 1.0% Sales would have to increase 1.0% to achieve Prototype Store IRR

Gross Margin
NPV (0.55) Gross Margin could decrease (0.55) pp and still achieve Prototype Store NPV
IRR 0.19 Gross Margin would have to increase 0.19 pp to achieve Prototype Store IRR

Construction (Building & Sitework)
NPV $2,398 Construction costs could increase $2,398 and still achieve Prototype Store NPV
IRR ($498) Construction costs would have to decrease ($498) to achieve Prototype Store IRR

Full Transfer Impact Prototype Assumption: A nearby store transferring sales to a new store, fully recovers these sales by the 5th yr.
                          Sensitivity Assumption: If transfer sales are NOT fully recovered by the transferring store in year 5:
NPV 4.0% Sales would have to increase 4.0% to achieve Prototype Store NPV
IRR 7.5% Sales would have to increase 7.5% to achieve Prototype Store IRR

RISK/OPPORTUNITY

10% Sales Decline
NPV ($6,259) If sales decline by 10%, Store NPV would decline by ($6,259)
IRR (1.8) If sales decline by 10%, Store IRR would decline by (1.8) pp

1 pp GM Decline
NPV ($3,388) If margin decreased by 1 pp. Store NPV would decline by ($3,388)
IRR (1.0) If margin decreased by 1 pp. Store IRR would decline by (1.0) pp

10% Construction Cost Increase
NPV ($1,287) If construction costs increased by 10%, Store NPV would decline by ($1,287)
IRR (0.6) If construction costs increased by 10%, Store IRR would decline by (0.6) pp

Market Margin, Wage Rate, etc.
NPV ($603) If we applied market specific assumptions, Store NPV would decrease by ($603)
IRR (0.2) If we applied market specific assumptions, Store IRR would decrease by (0.2) pp

10% Sales Increase
NPV $6,269 If sales increased by 10%, Store NPV would increase by $6,269
IRR 1.8 If sales increased by 10%, Store IRR would increase by 1.8 pp

VARIANCE TO PROTOTYPE

The example dashboard with a Store NPV of $12,860 is $1,860K above Prototypical Store NPV. The following items contributed to the variance:

Land
NPV ($219) Land cost contributed a negative ($219) to the variance from Prototype
IRR (0.1) Land cost contributed a negative (0.1) pp to the variance from Prototype

Non-Land Investment
NPV ($2,660) Building/Sitework costs contributed a negative ($2,660) to the variance from Prototype
IRR (1.5) Building/Sitework costs contributed a negative (1.5) pp to the variance from Prototype

Sales
NPV $4,818 Sales contributed a positive $4,818 to the variance from Prototype
IRR 1.4 Sales contributed a positive 1.4 pp to the variance from Prototype

Real Estate Taxes
NPV ($79) Real Estate Taxes contributed a negative ($79) to the variance from Prototype
IRR (0.0) Real Estate Taxes contributed a negative (0.0) pp to the variance from Prototype

APPROX $ IMPACT ON STORE NPV			
	Cost	NPV	%
Land:	$100K	($110K)	110%
Sitework:	$100K	($70K)	70%
Building:	$100K	($85K)	85%
On-going Exp:	$100K	($1M)	x10
On-going Expense: eg. Real Estate Taxes, Operating Expense			
Assumes Store Opening occurs 1 year after closing.			

Source: Target Corp.

EXHIBIT 7 | Economic Analysis Summary of Project Proposals

	Investment ($000)	Net Present Value*				Population	Trade Area**		
		Base Case NPV ($000)	10% Sales Decline ($000)	IRR	Population		Population Increase 2000–2005	Median Income	% Adults 4+ yrs. college
Gopher Place	$23,000	$16,800	($4,722)	12.3%	70,000		27%	$56,400	12%
Whalen Court	$119,300	$25,900	($16,611)	9.8%	632,000		3%	$48,500	45%
The Barn	$13,000	$20,500	($4,066)	16.4%	151,000		3%	$38,200	17%
Goldie's Square	$23,900	$300	($4,073)	8.1%	222,000		16%	$56,000	24%
Stadium Remodel	$17,000	$15,700	($7,854)	10.8%	N. Ap.		N. Ap.	$65,931	42%

*NPV is computed using 9.0% as discount rate for store cash flows and 4.0% for credit-card cash flows.

**Trade area is the geographical area from which 70% of store sales will be realized.

Gopher Place was a request for $23.0 million to build a P04 store scheduled to open in October 2007. The prototype NPV would be achieved with sales of 5.3% below the R&P forecast level. This market was considered an important one, with five existing stores already in the area. Wal-Mart was expected to add two new supercenters in response to favorable population growth in the trade area, which was considered to have a very favorable median household income and growth rate. Because of the high density of Target stores, nearly 19% of sales included in the forecasts were expected to come from existing Target stores.

EXHIBIT 7 | Economic Analysis Summary of Project Proposals (*continued*)

Whalen Court was a request for $119.3 million to build a unique single-level store scheduled to open in October 2008. The prototype NPV could be achieved with sales of 1.9% above the R&P forecast level. Although Target currently operated 45 stores in this market, the Whalen Court market represented a rare opportunity for Target to enter the urban center of a major metropolitan area. Unlike other areas, this opportunity provided Target with major brand visibility and essentially free advertising for all passersby. Considering Target's larger advertising budget, the request for more than $100 million of capital investment could be balanced against the brand awareness benefits it would bring. Further, this opportunity was only available for a limited time. Unlike the majority of Target stores, this store would have to be leased. Thus, if it was not approved at the November meeting, the property would surely be leased by another retailer.

The Barn was a request for $13.0 million to build a P04 store scheduled to open in March 2007. The prototype NPV was achievable with sales of 18.1% below the R&P forecast level. This project was being resubmitted after initial development efforts failed because of a disagreement with the developer. This small rural area was an extreme contrast to Whalen Court. The small initial investment allowed for a large return on investment even if sales growth turned out to be less than expected. This investment represented a new market for Target as the two nearest Target stores were 80 and 90 miles away.

Goldie's Square was a request for $23.9 million to build a SuperTarget store scheduled to open in October 2007. The prototype NPV required sales 45.1% above the R&P forecast level. This area was considered a key strategic anchor for many retailers. The Goldie's Square center included Bed Bath & Beyond, JCPenney, Circuit City, and Borders. Target currently operated 12 stores in the area and was expected to have 24 eventually. Despite the relatively weak NPV figures, this was a hotly contested area with an affluent and fast-growing population, which could afford good brand awareness should the growth materialize.

Stadium Remodel was a request for $17.0 million to remodel a SuperTarget store opening March 2007. As a remodel, there was no prototype NPV for comparison. The recent sales decline and deteriorating facilities at this location could lead to tarnishing the brand image. This trade area had supported Target stores since 1972 and had already been remodeled twice previously. The $17 million investment would certainly give a lift to the lagging sales.

Source: Target Corp.

EXHIBIT 8 | Individual Capital Project Request Dashboards

Project:		"Gopher Place"		
Market:	Gopherville		Open:	October, 2007
Prototype:	P04.383-MSP		Size:	127,000
Developer:	Henderson Associates		Own/Lease:	Own
Address:	SWC of Hudson and Elk			
Anchors:	Freestanding			

Capital Project Request

TARGET. Capital Expenditure Committee: November 2006

INVESTMENT DETAIL

Land	Acres:	9.78	**Sitework**	Pro Rata, Maximum
	PSF:	$7.52	**RE Tax-Per Corp Tax**	$136
	Closing:	11/2006	B/(P) Proto	$62
	Garden Center, Seismic			

BUILDING COST VS. PROTOTYPE

Options		
Subgeographic		($1,238)
Proto Update		(117)
Market Conditions		(1,158)
Government Fees		(1,049)
Architectural		(485)
Technical		(615)
Procurement		(239)
A/E Fees		(81)
Signs		6
Contingency		(75)
Total Variance		($5,052)

INCENTIVE SUMMARY

None Available	Vendor Fee	$0
	Legal Fee	$0

DEMOGRAPHICS

Characteristics	MSA	Trade Area	3-Mile Radius
2005 Population (000's)	650	70	16
2000–2005 Growth	15.0%	27.0%	20.0%
Median HH Income	$46,700	$56,400	$59,400
# HH +$50,000 (000's)	97	11	3
% Adults 4+ Yrs. College, 2005	15%	12%	11%

COMMENTS

- Target currently operates 5 stores in the market.
- Transfer Sales: T-1526: 8% (7 miles E) derives 19% of sales from the proposed trade area.
- R&P Sales assume Wal-Mart relocates a store to a Supercenter in 2007; Wal-Mart adds an additional Supercenter in Badgerville in 2008.

FINANCIAL SUMMARY

TOTAL R&P SALES	Project	B/(P) Proto
1st year 2005 Equivalent	$26,000	$2,745
5th year 2005 Equivalent	$35,100	$5,688
Sales maturity	1.35	0.09

INCREMENTAL R&P SALES	Project	B/(P) Proto
1st year 2005 Equivalent	$22,800	($455)
5th year 2005 Equivalent	$35,100	$5,688
Sales maturity	1.54	0.27

INVESTMENT	Project	B/(P) Proto
Land	$3,205	$264
Sitework	3,164	(580)
Subtotal	$6,369	($315)
Building	15,420	(5,052)
Other	1,227	(96)
Total Net Investment	$23,016	($5,463)

VALUE	IRR	NPV	B/(P) Proto
Store	12.7%	$13,201	$2,493
Credit	8.1%	$3,554	$544
TOTAL	**12.3%**	**$16,755**	**$3,038**

HURDLE ADJUSTMENT

STORE SENSITIVITIES	NPV	IRR
Sales	(5.3%)	2.2%
Gross Margin	(0.72)	0.29
Construction (Building & Sitework)	$3,102	($751)
Full Transfer Impact	2.3%	9.3%

RISK/OPPORTUNITY

	NPV	
10% sales decline	($4,722)	(1.3)
1 pp GM decline	($3,481)	(0.9)
10% Const. cost increase	($1,494)	(0.6)
Market margin, wage rate, etc.	($5,434)	(1.5)
10% sales increase	$4,621	1.2

VARIANCE TO PROTOTYPE

P&L SUMMARY		
Land	$287	0.1
Non-Land Investment	($4,741)	(2.6)
Sales	$6,331	1.9
Real Estate Tax	$615	0.2

EBIT IMPACT	Project	B/(P) Proto
Thru Open Yr	($567)	($97)
5th Yr	$4,452	$886

NPV & Investment

Investment: NPV: ▲−10% Sales ◆+10% Sales

Project — Prototype

Sales

Total — Incremental ---- Prototype

Competition

2006 — 0.0 SF/Cap

2008 — 6.5 SF/Cap — 76% / 24%

■ Target ■ WMSC

EXHIBIT 8 | Individual Capital Project Request Dashboards (continued)

Capital Project Request
TARGET. Capital Expenditure Committee: November 2006

Project:	
Market:	"Whalen Court"
Prototype:	Unique Single Level
Developer:	Sawicky and Co.
Address:	NWQ of Gopher and High Investment Blvd.
Anchors:	Home Depot, Best Buy
Open:	October, 2008
Size:	173,585
Own/Lease:	Lease

FINANCIAL SUMMARY

TOTAL R&P SALES	Project	B/(P) Proto
1st year 2005 Equivalent	$86,000	$52,185
5th year 2005 Equivalent	$111,800	$69,031
Sales maturity	1.30	0.04

INCREMENTAL R&P SALES	Project	B/(P) Proto
1st year 2005 Equivalent	$79,600	$45,785
5th year 2005 Equivalent	$111,800	$69,031
Sales maturity	1.40	0.14

INVESTMENT	Project	B/(P) Proto
Lease	$87,309	($78,855)
Sitework	0	3,796
Subtotal	$87,309	($75,059)
Building	29,434	(15,128)
Other	2,520	93
Total Net Investment	$119,263	($90,094)

VALUE	IRR	NPV	B/(P) Proto
Store	9.9%	$14,225	($3,174)
Credit	8.2%	$11,650	$7,164
TOTAL	**9.8%**	**$25,875**	**$3,989**

STORE SENSITIVITIES

HURDLE ADJUSTMENT	NPV	IRR
Sales	1.9%	31.1%
Gross Margin	0.28	4.58
Construction (Building & Sitework)	($4,289)	($41,070)
Full Transfer Impact	7.7%	36.3%

RISK/OPPORTUNITY	
10% sales decline	(1.0)
1 pp GM decline	(0.7)
10% Const. cost increase	(0.1)
Market margin, wage rate, etc.	(1.1)
10% sales increase	1.0

VARIANCE TO PROTOTYPE		
Lease	($78,912)	(15.1)
Non-Land Investment	($10,168)	(7.9)
Sales	$99,963	22.9
Real Estate Tax	($637)	(0.2)

P&L SUMMARY

EBIT IMPACT	Project	B/(P) Proto
Thru Open Yr	($1,599)	($1,136)
5th Yr	$14,034	$8,509

NPV & Investment

140.0 / 120.0 / 100.0 / 80.0 / 60.0 / 40.0 / 20.0 / 0.0

Project — Prototype

■ Investment ■ NPV ▲ –10% Sales ◆ +10% Sales

Sales

135 / 115 / 95 / 75 / 55 / 35 / 15 — 1 2 3 4 5

Total — Incremental — Prototype

Competition

0.0 SF/Cap   0.5 SF/Cap

INVESTMENT DETAIL

Lease		Sitework	
Type:	Buildback	Building Lease	RE Tax (net of abatement) $358
Rent:	Prepay+$3.3K	B/(P) Proto	($60)
Closing:	10/2006		

L4: Unique Risk Security, District Office, 13k sf Exp. Stock, 2nd Lvl Stock

BUILDING COST VS. PROTOTYPE

Options	
Subgeographic	($1,200)
Proto Update	(124)
Market Conditions	0
Government Fees	0
Architectural	0
Technical	(7,927)
Procurement	(2,429)
A/E Fees	(428)
Signs	(18)
Contingency	(3,000)
Total Variance	($15,128)

INCENTIVE SUMMARY

Vendor Fee	$92
Legal Fee	$0

DEMOGRAPHICS

Characteristics	MSA	Trade Area	3-Mile Radius
2005 Population (000's)	18,768	632	1,248
2000-2005 Growth	2.0%	3.0%	2.0%
Median HH Income	$57,200	$48,500	$43,800
# HH +$50,000 (000's)	3,750	143	238
% Adults 4+ Yrs. College, 2005	30%	45%	37%

COMMENTS

See attached for additional information.

EXHIBIT 8 | Individual Capital Project Request Dashboards (*continued*)

Project:	Moose Land	Open:	March, 2007
Market:	P04 383-MSP	Size:	126,842
Prototype:	Hulbert Ventures		
Developer:		Own/Lease:	Own
Address:	NWQ of Badger and Wolverine		
Anchors:	Lowe's		

"The Barn"

Capital Project Request
TARGET. Capital Expenditure Committee: November 2006

FINANCIAL SUMMARY

TOTAL R&P SALES	Project	B/(P) Proto
1st year 2005 Equivalent	$24,000	$2,043
5th year 2005 Equivalent	$30,500	$2,729
Sales maturity	1.27	0.01

INVESTMENT	Project	B/(P) Proto
Land	$10	$3,390
Sitework	2,303	290
Subtotal	$2,313	$3,680
Building	9,705	(378)
Other	998	121
Total Net Investment	$13,017	$3,423

VALUE	IRR	NPV	B/(P) Proto
Store	17.5%	$17,406	$7,326
Credit	8.2%	$3,121	$279
TOTAL	16.4%	$20,527	$7,605

HURDLE ADJUSTMENT

STORE SENSITIVITIES	NPV	IRR
Sales	(18.1%)	(23.2%)
Gross Margin	(2.35)	(3.04)
Construction (Building & Sitework)	$8,908	$6,973

RISK/OPPORTUNITY	NPV	
10% sales decline	($4,066)	(1.9)
1 pp GM decline	($3,111)	(1.5)
10% Const. cost increase	($988)	(1.0)
Market margin, wage rate, etc.	($2,999)	(1.4)
10% sales increase	$4,096	1.9

VARIANCE TO PROTOTYPE		
Land	$3,675	3.2
Non-Land Investment	($570)	(0.3)
Sales	$3,603	1.4
Real Estate Tax	$617	0.2

NPV & Investment

Project — Prototype
Investment | NPV | ▲ –10% Sales | ◆ +10% Sales

(30.0, 25.0, 20.0, 15.0, 10.0, 5.0, 0.0)

Sales

Total — Incremental — Prototype

(1, 2, 3, 4, 5)
(33, 31, 29, 27, 25, 23, 21, 19, 17, 15)

Competition

2006
23% / 10% / 67%
WMSC | Sam's Club | Kmart
5.7 SF/Cap

2008
13% / 20% / 9% / 58%
Target | WMSC | Sam's Club | Kmart
6.4 SF/Cap

INVESTMENT DETAIL

Land		Sitework	Fixed Cost
Acres:	11.48	RE Tax-Per Corp. Tax	$136
PSF:	$0.02	B/(P) Proto	$62
Closing:	4/2006		
L3: Enhanced Risk Security			

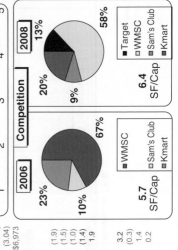

Options	BUILDING COST VS. PROTOTYPE
Subgeographic	$523
Proto Update	(22)
Market Conditions	(410)
Government Fees	0
Architectural	(95)
Technical	(122)
Procurement	(91)
A/E Fees	(76)
Signs	(9)
Contingency	(75)
Total Variance	($378)

INCENTIVE SUMMARY

None Available	Vendor Fee	$0
	Legal Fee	$0

DEMOGRAPHICS

Characteristics	MSA	Trade Area	3-Mile Radius
2005 Population (000's)	135	151	19
2000–2005 Growth	3.0%	3.0%	7.0%
Median HH Income	$36,600	$38,200	$47,300
# HH +$50,000 (000's)	20	22	4
% Adults 4+ Yrs. College, 2005	16%	17%	34%

COMMENTS

- Target is entering a new small market. The nearest Target stores are 80 miles NE, 80 miles S, 90 miles NW.
- R&P Sales assume Target is part of a major retail development of 600K sf.
- See attached Resubmission Summary.

EXHIBIT 8 | Individual Capital Project Request Dashboards (*continued*)

Project:	
Market:	Goldie Country
Prototype:	SUP04M
Developer:	Barsky Enterprises
Address:	SWQ of Ocean and Beach
Anchors:	JC Penney, Circuit City, Borders, Bed Bath & Beyond, Ross

"Goldie's Square"

Open:	October, 2007
Size:	173,770
Own/Lease:	Own

Capital Project Request

TARGET. Capital Expenditure Committee: November 2006

INVESTMENT DETAIL

Land		Sitework	Fixed Cost
Acres:	11.69		$539
PSF:	$7.10	RE Tax-Per Corp Tax	($269)
Closing:	8/2006	B/(P) Proto	
None			0

BUILDING COST VS. PROTOTYPE

Options	
Subgeographic	$829
Proto Update	(153)
Market Conditions	545
Government Fees	0
Architectural	(469)
Technical	(799)
Procurement	(170)
A/E Fees	(71)
Signs	50
Contingency	(75)
Total Variance	($313)

INCENTIVE SUMMARY

None Available	Vendor Fee	$0
	Legal Fee	$0

DEMOGRAPHICS

Characteristics	MSA	Trade Area	3-Mile Radius
2005 Population (000's)	1,415	222	67
2000-2005 Growth	13.0%	16.0%	4.0%
Median HH Income	$56,100	$56,000	$50,000
# HH +$50,000 (000's)	291	41	12
% Adults 4+ Yrs. College, 2005	36%	24%	26%

COMMENTS

- Target currently operates 12 stores in the market. Total Target buildout for this market is currently estimated at 24 of which 7 are active/near term opportunities. Build out will include 12 SuperTarget units, 50% of the total.
- Transfer Sales: 25% from a store located 2.1 miles NE; 4% from a store located 7 miles N; 25% of sales from a store 4 miles away.
- General Merchandise/Hardlines C Mix: 82/18.
- Alternatives to this buildback scenario:
  >Relo: T-683 closes when Goldie's Square opens: Total NPV: $6M; Total IRR: 9.3%.
  >T-683 closes 1 yr after Goldie's Square opens: Total NPV: $3.9M; Total IRR: 8.9%.
  >T-683 closes 2 yrs after Goldie's Square opens: Total NPV: $3.6M; Total IRR: 8.9%.

FINANCIAL SUMMARY

TOTAL R&P SALES	Project	B/(P) Proto
1st year 2005 Equivalent	$34,000	($10,304)
5th year 2005 Equivalent	$42,000	($14,036)
Sales maturity	1.24	(0.03)

INCREMENTAL R&P SALES	Project	B/(P) Proto
1st year 2005 Equivalent	$25,900	($18,404)
5th year 2005 Equivalent	$42,000	($14,036)
Sales maturity	1.62	0.36

INVESTMENT	Project	B/(P) Proto
Land	$3,615	$1,385
Sitework	3,695	(425)
Subtotal	$7,310	$960
Building	14,969	(313)
Other	1,660	48
Total Net Investment	$23,939	$694

VALUE	IRR		Proto
Store	8.1%		3,222
Credit	8.1%		(1,294)
TOTAL	**8.1%**		**3,516**

STORE SENSITIVITIE...

HURDLE ADJUSTMENT		IRR
Sales	45.1%	47.2%
Gross Margin	4.64	4.91
Construction (Building & Sitework)	($22,167)	($14,576)
Full Transfer Impact	62.5%	63.1%

RISK/OPPORTUNITY

10% sales decline	($4,073)	(1.1)
1 pp GM decline	($3,929)	(1.1)
10% Const. cost increase	($1,470)	(0.3)
Market margin, wage rate, etc.	$6,059	1.6
10% sales increase	$4,008	1.1

VARIANCE TO PROTOTYPE

Land	$1,501	0.3
Non-Land Investment	($581)	(0.1)
Sales	($16,455)	(4.4)
Real Estate Tax	($2,682)	(0.7)

P&L SUMMARY

EBIT IMPACT	Project	B/(P) Proto
Thru Open Yr	($1,921)	($654)
5th Yr	$2,951	($2,343)

NPV & Investment

Project | Prototype
Investment ■ NPV ■
△ −10% Sales ◆ +10% Sales

Sales

— Total — Incremental --- Prototype

Competition

2006: Target 20%, Wal-Mart 66%, WMSC 14% — 2.5 SF/Cap
2008: Target 17%, WMSC 83% — 3.0 SF/Cap
■ Target ■ Wal-Mart ■ WMSC

EXHIBIT 8 | Individual Capital Project Request Dashboards (*continued*)

Project:	
Market:	Boardwalk
Scope:	Interior Remodel
Prototype Before & After:	SUP1.1 / S04
Expansion Availability:	Not Site Constrained
Offsite Whse/Dist Office:	N/A

Remodel Cycle:	Cycle 3 2007
Last Remodel:	NA
Own/Lease:	Own
Sides Before & After:	484 / 455
POG Length:	24'/28'

"Stadium Remodel"

TARGET. Capital Expenditure Committee: November 2006

Capital Project Request

PROJECT DETAIL

Write Off	$1061 ($657 Bldg, $43 Roof, $361 Other)
RE Tax-Per Corp Tax	$332
B/(P) Proto	($62)

SQUARE FOOTAGE

	Total	Sales	Stock	Support
Original Sq Ft	203,300	153,019	35,245	15,036
Additional Sq Ft	–	(10,544)	12,870	(2,326)
Total Sq Ft After Remodel	203,300	142,475	48,115	12,710
SUP04 Prototype	177,376	136,616	27,500	13,260
B/(P) Prototype	25,924	5,859	20,615	(550)
B/(P) Guide 1st FY			20,615	

DEMOGRAPHICS

Characteristics	MSA	Trade Area	3-Mile Radius
2005 Population (000's)	806	113	84
2000-2005 Growth	5.0%	16.0%	15.0%
Median HH Income	$50,774	$65,931	$64,597
# HH +$50,000 (000's)	158	29	21
% Adults 4+ Yrs. College, 2005	28%	42%	44%

COMMENTS

- Entered market in 1972. Currently operate 8 stores in this market.
- A successful store at a strong long-term location serving an affluent family-oriented trade area.
- 2006 YTD Sales Trend: –0.9%.
- Post-remodel sales assume a 17% sales lift over R&P base case sales. Base case sales assume a (10%) impact from buildback (3.3 miles, October 2007); the store is also in the process of being impacted by Park Place South.
- Current Value of T-0530: $18.8M; R&P base case sales; Prototypical Interior Remodel in 2007; Tax benefit of depreciable property write-off: $0.4M; Rank: 783 of 1395.
- General Merchandise/Hardlines C Mix: 68/32; based on T-0530 historical trend.
- Options: New Entrance System, Relocate Pharmacy, Relocate Electrical Room.
- Scope: Refrigeration Replacement, 4 Phases of Grocery Staging, Flooring Replacement, Roof Replacement, Temp Pharmacy, New Food Avenue, New Starbucks, New Optical, New Portrait Studio, New Signage.

FINANCIAL SUMMARY

TOTAL R&P SALES

	Project	B/(P) Proto
1st year 2005 Equivalent	$64.000	$19,677
5th year 2005 Equivalent	$64.000	$7,940
Sales maturity	1.00	(0.26)

INCREMENTAL R&P SALES

	Project	
1st year 2005 Equivalent	$9,300	
5th year 2005 Equivalent	$9,300	
Sales maturity	1.00	

INVESTMENT

	Project	B/(P) Proto
Land	$0	$5,000
Sitework	1,173	2,097
Subtotal	$1,173	$7,097
Building	12,411	2,245
Other	3,271	(1,618)
Total Net Investment	$16,855	$7,724

STORE SENSITIVITIES

VALUE	IRR	NPV
Store	12.5%	$14,911
Credit	4.6%	$828
TOTAL	**10.8%**	**$15,739**

HURDLE ADJUSTMENT

	NPV	IRR
Sales		Remodel
Gross Margin		
Construction (Building & Sitework)		

RISK/OPPORTUNITY

10% sales decline	($7,854)	(1.8)
1 pp GM decline	($6,457)	(1.5)
10% Const. cost increase	($910)	(0.3)
Market margin, wage rate, etc.	($11,317)	(2.7)
10% sales increase	$6,216	1.5

P&L SUMMARY

EBIT IMPACT	Project	B/(P) Proto
Thru Open Yr	($6,103)	($4,812)
5th Yr	$1,272	($4,025)

NPV & Investment

Sales

Source: Target Corp.

EXHIBIT 9 | Stock Price Performance 2002–06

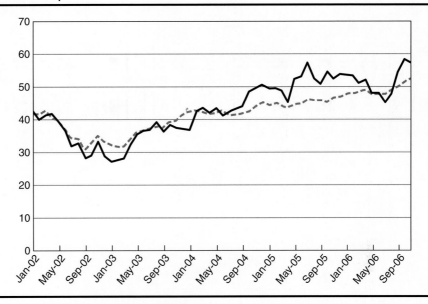

Data Source: Yahoo! Finance, http://finance.yahoo.com/.

Aurora Textile Company

In January 2003, Michael Pogonowski, the chief financial officer of Aurora Textile Company, was questioning whether the company should install a new ring-spinning machine, the Zinser[1] 351, in the Hunter production facility. A primary advantage of the new ring spinner was its ability to produce a finer-quality yarn that would be used for higher-quality and higher-margin products. The finer-quality yarn would be sold in a niche market that would command a 10% increase in the selling price of yarn, which was currently $1.0235 a pound. In addition, the Zinser would provide increased efficiency as well as greater reliability, which Aurora's operations management had been requesting for many years. The Zinser's efficiency would reduce operating costs, with lower power consumption and maintenance expenses. Sales volume, however, would be 5% lower than the current market, and the cost of customer returns would be higher, which, when combined with the $8.25 million installed cost, made the Zinser decision a difficult one.

Pogonowski believed that the decision to invest in the new technology was complicated by Aurora's lackluster financial performance as well as the difficult circumstances facing the U.S. textile industry. Aurora, however, was competing in a few select markets that were likely to continue to survive foreign competition, albeit at lower margins over the long run. He also recognized that there was unlikely to be a better time to upgrade to the Zinser as its price had been increasing 5% annually. Not every member of the management team, however, agreed with Pogonowski's logic. Some managers were arguing that it would be cheaper to continue with the current maintenance schedule, which should keep the current spinning machine running reliably and allow Aurora to postpone replacement indefinitely.

---

[1]The Zinser compact spinning technology was marketed under the trademark CompACT3.

Based on "Aurora Spinning Mills," an unpublished case by Robert Barnhardt (Dean Emeritus of the College of Textiles, North Carolina State University), this case was written by Lucas Doe (MBA/ME '04), under the supervision of Professor Kenneth Eades, as a basis for class discussion rather than to illustrate effective or ineffective handling of an administrative situation. Although the case is based on an actual company, many of the names and much of the data have been disguised for pedagogical purposes. Copyright © 2007 by the University of Virginia Darden School Foundation, Charlottesville, VA. All rights reserved. *To order copies, send an e-mail to* sales@dardenbusinesspublishing.com. *No part of this publication may be reproduced, stored in a retrieval system, used in a spreadsheet, or transmitted in any form or by any means— electronic, mechanical, photocopying, recording, or otherwise—without the permission of the Darden School Foundation.* Rev. 2/08.

The Company

Aurora Textile Company was a yarn manufacturer established in the early 1900s to service both the domestic and the international textile industry. Aurora's finished products were cotton and synthetic/cotton blend yarns that were sold to a variety of apparel and industrial-goods manufacturers that sold their products mainly in U.S. retail markets. Aurora serviced four major customer segments: hosiery, knitted outerwear, wovens, and industrial and specialty products. Although each of these markets had both domestic and international components, 90% of the company's revenue came from the domestic textile market.

Yarn sales for the hosiery market accounted for 43% of Aurora's revenue. The primary consumer products were athletic and dress socks, with white athletic socks accounting for the majority of sales. In fact, Aurora was the largest volume producer of all cotton yarns for white athletic socks in the United States, with nearly half the U.S. population owning socks made with Aurora yarns. Aurora had long enjoyed supplying the hosiery market for several reasons. First, as a leader in the market, Aurora was able to command attractive margins and maintain relationships with some of the largest and most profitable hosiery companies in the world. Second, hosiery was produced using bulky, heavy yarns. Aurora's plants were designed for this type of manufacturing operation, which allowed the company to process large quantities of yarn efficiently. Third, unlike other segments of the textile industry, the hosiery market had successfully defended itself against global competition. The heavy yarns and bulky products were costly to transport, making them less attractive for foreign producers. Moreover, this type of production was highly automated in the United States such that labor costs had been reduced to the point that Asian manufacturers did not have sufficient opportunity to provide significant cost savings over U.S. manufacturers.

The knitted-outerwear market was the second-largest revenue source for Aurora, accounting for 35% of sales. Aurora's customers within this market mainly produced knitted cotton and polyester/cotton dress shirts for a variety of major retailers. The yarns produced were medium- to fine-count yarns (14/1 to 22/1 ring and rotor).[2] This quality yarn, however, was easily produced by other market participants, leaving very little opportunity for suppliers to differentiate their products and creating an environment where there was constant price pressure on outerwear yarns.

Accounting for 13% of Aurora's business revenue, the wovens market was a relatively small but important segment for the company. Most of these yarns were used to produce denim for jeans. Although much of the production had shifted offshore to lower-cost producers, most weavers continued to purchase U.S. yarns in order to avoid the supply risks associated with sourcing yarns from other countries. In addition, the yarns produced for the wovens market were coarse (5/1 to 14/1 ring and rotor) and

---

[2]The coarseness of a yarn was measured by the amount of yarn it took to equal one pound: the more yarns per pound, the finer the yarn. One "hank" held 840 yards of yarn. A count of 22/1 specified that 22 hanks were needed to equal one pound. A count of 14/1 indicated a coarser yarn than a count of 22/1 in that one pound of 14/1 yarn required only 14 × 840 yards.

were cost efficient to produce in Aurora's manufacturing facilities. Aurora management believed that the company had an excellent opportunity for growth in this market.

Industrial and specialty products constituted the remaining 9% of Aurora's revenue. These yarns were used to produce medical supplies, industrial adhesives, rubber- and vinyl-coated fabrics, and protective clothing. Because the yarn component of many of these products was very small, it was not a high-volume business. Nevertheless, this segment provided the highest margins for Aurora, which made it an attractive opportunity for growth.

Aurora used rotor- and ring-spinning production processes, although rotor spinning, which was also called "open-end" spinning, had constituted the majority of the company's total revenue for many years. (**Exhibits 1** and **2** present Aurora's financial statements for 1999 through 2002.) The steady decline in sales had led to management's decision to close four manufacturing facilities in 2000 in an effort to rightsize Aurora's capacity to the shrinking textile market and reduce manufacturing costs. In January 2003, the company had four plants operating: Hunter, Rome, Barton, and Butler (see **Exhibit 3** for product mix, capacity, and process technology by plant).

The Textile-Mill Industry

The U.S. textile-mill industry had experienced dramatic changes over the years because of globalization, U.S. government trade policies, cheaper production costs overseas, and customer preferences and fads. The industry, which had started in New England, moved to the southern United States to take advantage of cheaper production costs. In more recent years, the search for cheaper production costs had begun to move the textile-mill industry to Asia. As more apparel makers moved their production abroad, the yarn makers followed suit. Thus, U.S. yarn manufacturers were declining in number while facing tougher and tougher competition from the influx of imported yarns. At the same time, the strong U.S. dollar had made it more appealing for some foreign textile manufacturers to export aggressively, flooding the U.S. market. Companies like Aurora, which had kept their manufacturing base exclusively in the United States, were frequently forced to cut costs and modernize their operations to remain competitive.

Consumer preferences and fads also shaped the market. The emphasis in the industry had shifted from mass production to flexible manufacturing as textile mills aimed to supply customized markets. Firms were concentrating on manufacturing systems that allowed small quantities of customized goods to be produced with minimal lead time. This change enabled apparel producers to bring goods to retailers and consumers in a significantly shorter time frame. Information technology allowed retailers to assess their merchandise needs rapidly and to communicate those needs through apparel manufacturers to textile firms. In general, consumer preferences had moved toward finer-quality yarn with minimum defects, and those preferences were even stronger in the high-end market.

Information technology also had a downside for yarn producers like Aurora because of the liability associated with customer returns. For example, a dress shirt that was sold at JCPenney for $25 might include $5 of Aurora yarn. If the yarn was defective and the defect could be traced back to Aurora, the company would be required to reimburse JCPenney for the full retail price of $25, five times the amount of revenue received by Aurora for the garment. In 2002, 1.5% of the Hunter plant's sales volume had been returned by its retailers. The percentage of volume returned had risen over the past few years owing to advancements in technology and information flow through the supply chain that made it easier to identify the yarn manufacturer associated with a particular garment. If Aurora began selling yarns for use in the high-end market, the company's dollar liability per garment would increase. For example, if Aurora supplied the yarn for a shirt that sold for $75 at Nordstrom, a customer return would make Aurora liable for paying $75 to Nordstrom despite the fact that Aurora would have received only $10 for the yarn used to make the shirt. Aurora's production engineers were confident that the Zinser would yield such high-quality yarn that the volume returned would drop to 1.0%.

The U.S. government's free-trade policies were implemented through the North American Free Trade Agreement (NAFTA) and the Caribbean Basin Initiative (CBI). These trade agreements had created a burden on the U.S. textile industry by encouraging trade with Canada, Mexico, and Caribbean countries, which lowered the prices of consumer goods in the U.S. market. This enriched trade also forced U.S. textile companies to compete against cheaper labor, lower environmental standards, and government-subsidized operations. The net effect was substantially lower-priced goods for U.S. consumers but a very difficult competitive environment for U.S.-based manufacturers.

For other parts of the world, the U.S. State Department had used textile quotas and tariffs as a political bargaining tool to obtain cooperation from foreign governments. The United States and other countries also used quotas and tariffs as a mechanism to prevent the dumping of foreign goods into local markets and to protect the domestic industry. Recently, however, the World Trade Organization (WTO)[3] had announced that, as the governing body for international trade, it would ban its members from using quotas, effective January 1, 2005. This move would further open the U.S. market to competition from countries beyond its immediate borders. Notwithstanding this outlook, most research analysts believed that the U.S. textile industry would grow around 2% in real terms, with prices and costs increasing at a 1% inflation rate for the foreseeable future.

Production Technology

The production of yarn involved the processes of cleaning and blending, carding, combining the slivers, spinning, and winding (**Exhibit 4**). Aurora used only rotor spinning and ring spinning in its yarn production. Ring spinning was a process of inserting twists by means of a rotating spindle. In ring spinning, twisting the yarn and winding it on a bobbin occurred simultaneously and continuously. Although ring spinning was more

---

[3]Established through agreements and negotiations signed by the bulk of the members of the General Agreement on Tariffs and Trade (GATT), the WTO replaced GATT in January 1995. The WTO was an international, multilateral organization that laid down rules for global trading systems and resolved disputes between member states. Of its 148 members, 76 were founding members, including the United States.

expensive than open spinning because of the former's slower speed, the yarn quality from ring spinning was better. The additional processes (roving and winding) required for ring spinning made the process more costly per pound produced.

Rotor spinning inserted twists by means of a rotating conical receptacle into which the fiber was admitted. In "open-end" spinning, air current and centrifugal force carried fibers to the perimeter of the rotor, where they were evenly distributed in a small group. The tails of the fibers were twisted together by the spinning action of the rotor as the yarn was continuously drawn from the center of the rotor. The process was very efficient and reduced the cost of spinning, in part, by eliminating the need for roving. At a speed of 60,000 rotations per minute, open-end rotors produced yarn at a rate three to five times higher than ring spinning. Moreover, the yarn from open-end spinning was much more uniform, but it was also considerably weaker and had a harsher feel.[4] Consequently, low-micronaire but stronger cottons were desirable for open-end spinning.

Financial Climate

Like many of its competitors, Aurora had been struggling financially. The company had not responded quickly to the deteriorating business environment, and had suffered consecutive losses for the past four years (**Exhibit 1**). Currently, the company had limited cash available and had trouble maintaining sufficient working capital. Since 1999, about 150 textile plants had been closed in the United States, and 200,000 industry jobs had been lost. Aurora had closed four inefficient manufacturing operations, and was evaluating the performance of its remaining facilities. Since 2000, the company had succeeded in cutting its SG&A spending by $3.9 million. These efforts had allowed the company to continue operations, but the difficult financial environment was expected to continue to present a challenge for Aurora.

The Zinser 351

The Zinser 351 would replace an older-generation spinning machine in the Hunter plant. The existing machine had been installed in 1997 and was carried on Aurora's books at a value of $2 million. If replaced, the existing machine could be sold for about $500,000 for use in Mexico. Management felt that by the time the machine was fully depreciated in 4 years, it would have no market value. Management also believed that, with proper maintenance, the existing machine could continue to operate for 10 more years, at which point the plant was expected to have grown from its current production level of 500,000 pounds a week to its capacity of 600,000 pounds a week.

---

[4]Micronaire was a quantification of fiber fineness as measured by air permeability of a fiber sample. A sample of fine fibers would have a high ratio of surface area to mass, allowing less airflow and resulting in a lower micronaire reading. Conversely, a sample of coarse fibers would exhibit a low ratio of surface area to mass, allowing more airflow and resulting in a higher micronaire reading.

To match the current production capacity of the Hunter plant would require the purchase of a machine with 35,000 spindles at a cost of $8.05 million. In addition, there would be an installation cost of $200,000, for a total capitalized cost of $8.25 million.[5] The new spinning machine would be fully depreciated (straight-line) in 10 years, at which point it would have zero book value, but was expected to realize $100,000 if sold on the open market. Aurora had already spent $15,000 on marketing research to gauge customer interest in its yarn as well as $5,000 on engineering tests concerning the suitability of Hunter's ventilation, materials-flow, and inventory systems.

The cost structure of a textile plant was primarily composed of a materials cost (the cost of cotton) and a conversion cost, which included the cost of labor, dyes and chemicals, power, maintenance, customer returns for defects, and various other production and overhead costs. In 2002, the Hunter plant's conversion cost was $0.43/lb. Most of the conversion costs would not be affected if the Zinser replaced the existing spinning machine. For example, there would be no change in the work force, although the current operators would need to be trained on the Zinser, at a one-time cost of $50,000, during the installation year. A significant benefit of the Zinser, however, was that it was expected to reduce power and maintenance costs equivalent to a savings of $0.03/lb. The cost of customer returns constituted $0.077/lb. of the conversion costs for 2002. Based on engineering and marketing projections, Pogonowski estimated that the cost of customer returns would rise to $0.084/lb. for the higher-quality yarn produced by the Zinser. As shown in **Exhibit 5,** the cost per pound was influenced by the return frequency (1.0%), the liability multiplier (7.5), and the expected increase in selling price per pound ($1.0235 $\times$ 110% = $1.126). Depreciation and SG&A expenses were not included as part of conversion costs. SG&A was estimated to remain at 7% of revenues for both the existing spinning machine and the Zinser.

Although the Zinser's reliability would reduce the inventory of unprocessed cotton, buffer stocks would be necessary to hedge against the uncertainties surrounding the cotton's timely delivery to the plant as well as slowdowns and shutdowns due to production problems with the spinning machine. The Zinser was becoming widely used by many U.S. yarn producers, and had proved itself a highly reliable machine, with very few production delays, compared with earlier-generation spinning machines. This dependability had allowed most manufacturers to reduce their cotton inventories to 20 days from the average of 30 days (see **Exhibit 6** for cotton spot prices).[6] When asked about this benefit, the Hunter plant manager responded:

> My job is making profits. I just happen to do it by spinning cotton yarn. A big part of those profits comes from controlling our cost of cotton. I do that by buying large quantities of cotton when the price is right. If you look at my cotton inventory over the year, you will see that it varies considerably, depending on whether I think it's a good time to buy cotton

---

[5]The installation cost included a building-modification cost of $115,000, an airflow-modification cost of $55,000, and freight and testing costs of $30,000.

[6]In addition to cotton inventories, plants often carried large finished-goods inventories. Textile manufacturers preferred to ship soon after completing production, but large buyers had increasingly been requiring producers to hold their finished-goods inventories to reduce the buyers' carrying costs.

or not. On average, I will have about three months of cotton at the plant, but that will fall as low as 20 days when the cotton market is running hot and as high as 120 days when cotton prices hit low points. Given my cost-minimizing strategy, I don't see where the Zinser would actually reduce the cotton inventory. I'm focused on the price of cotton much more than the rate at which we use it in the plant.

The Decision

Michael Pogonowski had to decide whether the company should purchase the Zinser or keep using the existing ring-spinning machine. Beyond this specific investment decision, he wondered whether it was in the shareholders' best interest to invest in Aurora when both the company and the industry were continuing to lose money. This was particularly troublesome when he considered that the U.S. textile market would likely experience intense competition when the WTO lifted the ban on quotas in January 2005, which would only worsen Aurora's financial condition and its credit rating of BB, already below investment grade (**Exhibit 7**). Pogonowski was also concerned about the higher liability risks associated with customer returns in the high-end market, where most of the new yarn would be sold. For example, if the frequency of customer returns remained at the current level of 1.5%, it would compromise Aurora's ability to realize the premium margins that had originally attracted the company to enter the segment.

Pogonowski was sensitive to the fact that, over the past four years, shareholders had seen the value of their Aurora holdings fall from about $30 a share to its current price of $12. In light of such poor performance, shareholders might prefer to see the institution of a dividend rather than see money spent on new assets for Aurora. Nevertheless, if buying the Zinser could reverse the downward trend of Aurora's stock price, then it would clearly be a welcome event for the owners. Aurora used a hurdle rate of 10% for this type of replacement decision. Pogonowski felt confident that the Zinser would return more than 10% over its expected life of 10 years, but he was less confident that Aurora would be able to remain in operation over that time span.

EXHIBIT 1 | Consolidated Income Statement for the Fiscal Years Ended
December 30, 1999–2002 (dollars in thousands)

	1999	2000	2001	2002
Pounds shipped (000s)	187,673	190,473	151,893	144,116
Average selling price/lb.	1.3103	1.2064	1.2045	1.0235
Conversion cost/lb.	0.4447	0.4421	0.4465	0.4296
Average raw-material cost/lb.	0.7077	0.6429	0.6487	0.4509
Net sales	**$245,908**	**$229,787**	**$182,955**	**$147,503**
Raw-material cost	132,812	122,461	98,536	64,982
Cost of conversion	83,454	84,212	67,822	61,912
Gross margin	29,641	23,114	16,597	20,609
SG&A expenses	14,603	14,218	11,635	10,305
Depreciation and amortization	15,241	13,005	11,196	9,859
Operating profit	**(203)**	**(4,109)**	**(6,234)**	**445**
Interest expense	6,777	6,773	5,130	3,440
Other income (expense)		1,143	(1,232)	(409)
Asset impairments[1]			4,758	7,564
Earnings before income-tax provision	(6,980)	(9,739)	(17,354)	(10,968)
Income-tax provision @ 36% tax rate	(2,513)	(3,506)	(6,247)	(3,949)
Net earnings	**($4,467)**	**($6,233)**	**($11,106)**	**($7,020)**

[1]Costs associated with the shutdown of plants.

EXHIBIT 2 | Consolidated Balance Sheets as of December 30, 1999–2002 (dollars in thousands)

	1999	2000	2001	2002
Assets				
Cash and cash equivalents	$1,144	$5,508	$2,192	$1,973
Accounts receivable, net	17,322	11,663	20,390	26,068
Inventories	34,778	33,155	31,313	33,278
Other current assets	2,774	1,922	712	2,378
Total current assets	$56,018	$52,247	$54,608	$63,697
Property and equipment				
Land	2,654	2,594	2,516	2,505
Buildings	32,729	31,859	30,308	30,427
Machinery and equipment	230,759	220,615	197,889	190,410
Gross PP&E	266,142	255,068	230,713	223,342
Less accumulated depreciation	(147,891)	(147,104)	(146,302)	(154,658)
Net PP&E	118,250	107,964	84,411	68,684
Goodwill	1,180	1,180	1,180	1,180
Other noncurrent assets	3,516	3,499	2,824	2,430
Total assets	**$178,965**	**$164,890**	**$143,023**	**$135,991**
Liabilities				
Accounts payable	12,236	7,693	9,667	10,835
Accrued compensation and benefits	4,148	3,712	4,176	4,730
Accrued interest	1,830	1,090	961	929
Other accrued expenses	4,083	3,914	3,881	3,657
Current portion of long-term debt	1,009	1,730	0	0
Total current liabilities	$23,306	$18,139	$18,685	$20,151
Long-term debt	66,991	66,991	58,000	58,000
Other long-term liabilities	16,566	14,081	11,776	10,297
Total liabilities	**$106,863**	**$99,211**	**$88,461**	**$88,448**
Shareholders' equity				
Common stock, par $0.01	50	50	50	50
Capital surplus	15,868	15,678	15,668	15,668
Retained earnings	56,184	49,951	38,845	31,825
Total shareholders' equity	$72,102	$65,679	$54,563	$47,543
Total liabilities and shareholders' equity	**$178,965**	**$164,890**	**$143,023**	**$135,991**

EXHIBIT 3 | Production Facilities

Plant	Technology	Product Mix	Count Range	Capacity (pounds/week)
Hunter	Ring	100% Cotton	5/1 to 22/1	600,000
Rome	Rotor	100% Cotton	5/1 to 22/1	1,200,000
Barton	Rotor	Heather and Poly/Cotton Blends	8/1 to 30/1	800,000
Butler	Rotor	100% Cotton	5/1 to 30/1	600,000

EXHIBIT 4 | Industrial Yarn Production

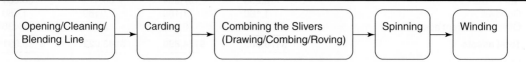

Opening/Cleaning/Blending Line
Cotton was shipped to the mills in bales and still contained vegetable matter. An automated process, designed to take small tufts of fibers from the tops of a series of 20 to 40 bales, opened or separated the fibers into small "clumps," removed any foreign particles in the tufts, and blended the tufts for a more homogeneous product. There was a continuous flow of fibers from the Opening Line to the Card.

Carding
The Card received the small tufts of fibers from the Opening Line and, through a series of metallic wire-covered cylinders, separated the tufts of fibers into individual fibers, which were parallelized, cleaned to remove smaller foreign particles, and formed into a strand of parallel fibers, called a sliver. The strand resembled a large, un-twisted rope.

Drawing
The Drawing Process combined six to eight slivers to allow greater uniformity of the drawn sliver.

Combing
The Combing Process was an optional process for ring-spun yarns. Combing removed short fibers (8%–12% of the weight of a sliver), eliminated practically all remaining foreign particles, and further blended the stock.

Roving
The Roving Process reduced the weight of a drawn sliver to the point that a small amount of twist was needed to provide the tensile strength required for ring spinning.

Ring Spinning
Ring Spinning further reduced the weight (linear density) of the strand of roving, added more twist, and created a small package weighing less than half a pound.

Winding
Winding was a process that simply took multiple packages of ring-spun yarn and "spliced" them together into one continuous strand, resulting in a package of yarn weighing three to four pounds.

EXHIBIT 5 | Cost of Customer Returns

	Existing Machine	Calculation
Price of yarn sold	$5.0	
Reimbursement cost	$25.0	
Liability multiplier	5.0	(25/5)
Returns as % of volume	1.50%	
Returns as % of revenue	7.50%	(5 × 1.5%)
Returns as cost/lb.	$0.077	(7.5% × $1.0235/lb.)

	Zinser	Calculation
Price of yarn sold	$10.0	
Reimbursement cost	$75.0	
Liability multiplier	7.5	(75/10)
Returns as % of volume	1.00%	
Returns as % of revenue	7.50%	(7.5 × 1.0%)
Returns as cost/lb.	$0.084	(7.5% × $1.0235/lb. × 110%)

EXHIBIT 6 | Cotton Spot Prices (1997–2002)[1]

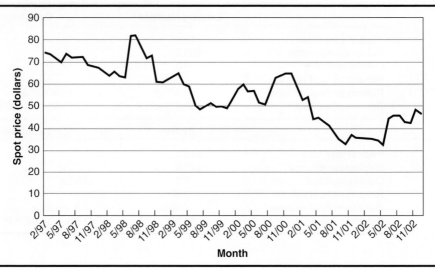

[1]Source: Bloomberg Database.

EXHIBIT 7 | Interest-Rate Yields: January 2003

U.S. Government (% yield)	
Treasury bill (1-year)	1.24
Treasury note (10-year)	3.98
Treasury bond (30-year)	4.83
Industrials (% yield)	
Prime rate[1]	4.25
AAA (10-year)	4.60
AA (10-year)	4.66
A (10-year)	4.87
BBB (10-year)	5.60
BB (10-year)	6.90

[1]The prime rate was the short-term interest rate charged by large U.S. banks for corporate clients with strong credit ratings.

Compass Records

Still bleary-eyed after an all-night drive from North Carolina, Alison Brown sat in the office below her recording studio near Nashville's famed "Music Row." It was late June 2005, and she had a moment to reflect on Compass Records, the artist-run record company that she and her husband, Garry West, had founded 10 years ago. The past few years had brought them great success, but managing the daily myriad decisions for the business remained a challenge. Foremost in her mind was whether to offer a recording contract to a talented new folk musician, Adair Roscommon, whose demo CD she was now listening to in her office.

Compass Records' tenth anniversary was a major milestone in the intense and unforgiving music business. With a roster of well-known and successful artists under contract, Compass had carved out a niche as an established player in the folk and roots musical genres. But unlike executives at the major record companies who typically had large budgets, every decision made by Brown and West regarding new musicians could have a major impact on their business. Compass could scarcely afford to squander resources on an artist in whom Brown and her husband did not believe strongly.

Brown was an acclaimed folk musician about whom the entertainment industry magazine *Billboard* once wrote: "In Brown's hands, the banjo is capable of fluid musical phrases of boundless beauty." Brown's assessment of another folk musician's artistic merit, therefore, had tremendous value, and she liked Adair Roscommon's work. Brown was also a former investment banker with an MBA who clearly understood Roscommon's potential as an investment for Compass. Intuitively, Brown grasped the implications of adding a risky asset, such as a new musician, to Compass Records' growing portfolio.

The central question for Brown, when contemplating any new musician, was whether to license that artist's music for a limited period of time or to produce and own the artist's master recording outright. In the short term, it was cheaper for Compass to license a recording, but it also limited the company's potential profit. If Compass

Records purchased a musician's master recording and the album failed to take off, however, the company risked owning a significantly impaired asset. This issue and a host of others gathered momentum in Brown's mind while the gentle melodies of Roscommon's demo filled the thick southern air in her office.

Alison Brown and Compass Records

Alison Brown grew up in a family of lawyers, and had she not been influenced by music at an early age, she might have ended up becoming a lawyer, too. After moving with her family to La Jolla, California, when she was 11, she immersed herself in banjo playing and developed a burgeoning talent. By the time she was 14, Brown was playing publicly, and by 15, she had won the Canadian National Five-String Banjo Championship. In 1980, Brown carried her passion for playing the banjo with her to Cambridge, Massachusetts, where she earned degrees in history and literature from Harvard University. She spent her extracurricular time traveling the bluegrass circuit in New England, and continued to develop herself as an artist.

Still thinking that music was an avocation and not a career, Brown enrolled at the University of California–Los Angeles, where she earned an MBA in 1986. Afterward, she accepted a position as an associate in the public-finance department at Smith Barney in San Francisco. During the next two years, Brown continued to kindle her passion for the banjo, even though playing publicly was incompatible with her new life as a banker. Brown eventually realized that she had a calling. "I knew people who would wake up in the morning and get in the shower and think about how they were going to refund a particular bond issue," Brown once said. "I would wake up in the morning and think about music." During a six-month hiatus from her office job, Brown was invited to play for the award-winning band Alison Krauss and Union Station. That job lasted three years and launched Brown into a new career.

By 1992, not only had Brown been named Banjo Player of the Year by the International Bluegrass Association, but she had also released her first album, which was nominated for a Grammy.[1] After leaving Alison Krauss, she accepted an invitation to join the world tour of folk-pop artist Michelle Shocked, where she met her future husband, Garry West. "About two months into [the tour] we realized there were a lot of things we wanted to do," West later said. "We were in Sweden, sitting around over strong coffee and pastries, wondering how we could encompass our vision of the good life: an outlet for our work, other recordings, publishing, and management." As Brown described it, they laid out their vision on the "proverbial napkin," and mapped out a plan for a business that would satisfy their needs.

In 1993, Brown and West started Small World Music and Video in Nashville, Tennessee, selling folk, world, and environmental records produced by a company they had discovered while on tour in Australia with Michelle Shocked. That same

---

[1]The Grammy Awards were presented by the Recording Academy, an association of recording-industry professionals, for outstanding achievement. The Grammies were awarded based on the votes of peers rather than on popular or commercial success. The awards were named for the trophy, a small, gilded statuette of a gramophone.

year, they were approached by a potential investor who had heard an interview that Brown had done on National Public Radio and who believed in what Brown and West wanted to do. With support from that investor, the two started producing their own projects and, in 1995, they launched the Compass Records label.[2]

By 2005, Brown and West's intuitive strategy was serving them well. Compass Records had grown to include nearly 50 artists under contract, and the company averaged about 20 releases a year. Their label was largely centered on roots music, and included marquee names like Victor Wooten, who was considered one of the best bass players in the world; Kate Rusby, a sensation among fans of traditional Anglo-Irish music; Colin Hay, the former front man and songwriter for the group Men At Work; Glenn Tilbrook, the former lead songwriter for the 1980s pop group Squeeze; Fairport Convention, one of the inventors of the folk-rock sound; and, of course, the dynamic bluegrass-jazz fusion of Alison Brown, who won a Grammy for her 2000 release, *Fair Weather*.

Compass Records in Context

Within the context of the global music business, Compass Records was tiny. The $32-billion music recording industry was dominated by a handful of large, multinational corporations, which accounted for 86% of the market for global recorded music. Those companies included Universal Music Group, with 29%; Sony/BMG, with 30%; Warner Music Group, with 16%; and EMI, with 11%. See **Figure 1** for a pie chart showing the percentages.

The major labels' dominance, deep pockets, and global distribution systems helped them to survive a turbulent and uncertain decade in the music industry. While the global market for recorded music had grown from $2 billion, in 1969, to $40 billion, in 1995, it had stagnated ever since. According to the Recording Industry Association of America (RIAA), the industry had registered no growth in any single year since 1995. By 2003, the recorded-music sector had shrunk to 1993 levels ($32 billion), and annual dollar sales were estimated to have declined at a compound annual growth rate of 5%.

As the major labels battled to preserve their slices of the shrinking pie, a number of new independent labels,[3] such as Compass Records, had begun to emerge. Smaller and more nimble, these companies saw opportunities in markets where the major record companies could ill-afford to go given the scale of their economies. "The trouble with those huge corporations is that they have to have enough sales volume on a

---

[2]A record label was a brand created by a company that specialized in manufacturing, distributing, and promoting audio and video recordings in various formats, including CDs, LPs, DVD-Audio, Super Audio CDs, and cassettes. The name was derived from the paper label at the center of the original gramophone record.

[3]Technically, an independent record label, or indie, operated without the funding or distribution network of one of the major record labels. In practice, the boundaries between majors and independents were ambiguous. Some independents, especially those with a successful roster of performing artists, received funding from major labels, and many independent labels relied on a major label for international licensing deals and distribution arrangements.

FIGURE 1 |

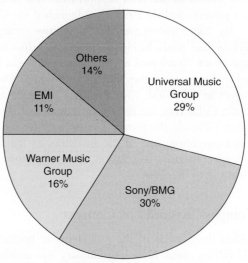

2004 U.S. Recorded Music Market Shares

Others
14%

Universal Music
Group
29%

EMI
11%

Warner Music
Group
16%

Sony/BMG
30%

Source: Nielsen *Soundscan*, Morgan Stanley Research.

release to feed this huge infrastructure," said Brown. "And yet something like 98% of all records sell fewer than 5,000 copies, so if your benchmark is a million, or even 100,000, you're obviously overlooking a lot of good music that sells well enough to deserve being out there."

Brown estimated that 40% of Compass Records' albums sold 5,000 units or more; only a few of her artists were popular enough to sell more than 20,000 units. "For a major label, 5,000 units is a failure," Brown said. "Only an indie can make this a success." Compass Records turned a profit on 80% of its titles in 2005 (versus a 10% success rate for the major labels). **Exhibits 1** and **2** provide Compass Records' balance sheet and income statement for the fiscal year ended December 31, 2004. **Exhibit 3** offers the company's historical income and expenses.

Music-Business Fundamentals

Recording Contracts

Recording contracts were agreements between a record label and an artist whereby the label had the right to promote and market recordings of the artist's music. Under such contracts, the record company could either license an artist's finished recordings for a limited period of time or produce the recordings and own them indefinitely. If the label negotiated to "produce and own," it was entitled to exploit the music through the sales of CDs and electronic downloads, as well as through licensing the music to other record companies or to firms that wished to use the music in other media, such as commercials, television, or film. When Compass Records opted to produce and own a master recording,[4] the artist received no payment up front.

Under a licensing contract, the record label licensed a work that had already been recorded and packaged. It had the right to exploit that recording only for a predetermined period of time, typically five to seven years. Unlike a contract to produce and own a master, a licensing contract obligated the label to pay the artist an up-front fee (advance), which was intended to defray some of the costs the artist had incurred in developing the album. Compass generally negotiated advances of $3,000 to $5,000. If the artist sought a very large advance (i.e., $20,000 or more), Brown believed that it made more sense to own the master recording instead. Under a licensing arrangement, additional costs included updates to the album's packaging (around $500) and touch-ups to the master itself, although generally not required. Marketing and promotional costs associated with the licensed recording were usually the same as those for the purchased master.

Certain recording contracts also gave the record company options on additional albums by the artist (with a purchased master, the label usually had three options, although it was not uncommon to have seven or eight options). Those options were particularly important with new artists because the label made significant up-front investments to launch a new act for which the company might not realize a return until three or four records down the road. Recording contracts customarily gave record companies the exclusive right to record an artist during the term of the agreement. If an artist failed to fulfill her obligations, most contracts permitted the company to suspend the contract. An artist could also request to be released from the contract, which the company might be willing to grant if it were repaid its recording costs and/or granted an override, or a percentage on the sales of the artist's records released by another company.

Royalties and Recoupment

Regardless of the type of recording contract, record labels paid royalties[5] to artists for the use and sale of their music. The two most common types of royalties were *mechanical royalties,* which were paid to songwriters and music publishers[6] for the use of their musical compositions, and *recording artist royalties,* which were paid to an artist for the recorded performance of those compositions. Each type of royalty worked somewhat differently.

In 2005 in the United States, mechanical royalties were fixed at a statutory rate of $0.085 per song. If the song were included on a CD, then the record company would pay the artist and/or the publisher that amount for each CD unit sold.

---

[4]A master recording, or master, was an original recording from which copies were made.

[5]A royalty was a payment to the owner for the use of the owner's property, especially patents, copyrighted works, and franchises.

[6]A music publisher was a company that worked with a songwriter to promote her musical compositions. Publishers negotiated partial or total ownership of an artist's copyright for her work, and she received a share of the mechanical royalties from the use of that work, typically about 50%.

Many record contracts, especially those with artists who were both the songwriter and the recording artist, included a *controlled composition*[7] *clause.* Because those artists received both mechanical and recording royalties, the clause allowed the label to limit its mechanical expense. Compass Records, for instance, often negotiated a 10-song per CD maximum for mechanicals, which capped the mechanical expense at $0.85 per CD sold.

Recording artist royalties were not determined statutorily, but were negotiated between the artist and the record label. The recording royalty varied widely, and often depended on the stature of the artist. It ranged between 8% and 25% of the suggested retail price of the album. Recording artist royalties also differed with the type of contract. At Compass Records, the average recording artist royalty for an owned master recording was $1.45 per unit sold, whereas the royalty for a licensed recording was around $1.75 per unit sold. Recording royalties were generally lower for produce-and-own contracts because the record label was underwriting the expense of album production.

The record label, however, did not pay any recording artist royalties until certain costs incurred in making and promoting the album had been recouped. All the costs of recording and preparing the music for manufacture were recoupable. About 50% of the marketing and promotional costs were recoupable. For licensing contracts, the advance was completely recoupable. An artist reimbursed the record label for those recoupable costs at her contracted royalty rate. For example, if the artist's royalty rate was $1.45, the record label reduced the amount of the total recoupable expense by $1.45 for every unit sold. When the label had recovered all recoupable expenses, the artist would begin to collect the recording artist royalties. (Mechanical royalties were not subject to the requirement that recoupable expenses be recovered first.)

Record companies' justification for the practice of recouping certain costs from an artist was that the label had invested its resources and had borne the financial risk of making and promoting the album. Some labels argued that this was similar to a joint venture in which production costs and overhead were repaid before the partners divided any profits. As an accounting matter, Compass Records recorded its recoupable costs as an asset on its balance sheet. On average, the company expensed those costs after two years.

Production and Manufacturing

If a record label negotiated a contract to produce and own an artist's master recording, the cost of producing that recording would depend on the size of the project, the complexity of the recording, and the level of perfection desired. The costs for producing an album would typically include fees for producers, arrangers, copyists, engineers, and background musicians, as well as the charges for studio and equipment rental, mixing, and editing. For relatively new artists signed by a major label, those costs could range between $80,000 and $150,000 for a single album, while established artists were known to run up production costs in excess of $500,000.

---

[7]A controlled composition was a piece of music that was written or owned by the recording artist.

As a small independent label, Compass Records incurred production costs that were significantly lower than the major labels'. Compass even had an advantage over some other indie labels because Brown and West had acquired a recording studio in May 2004. The wood-paneled, digital studio, which had cost Compass about $100,000 to equip, gave the label and its artists more flexibility in the creative process and saved the company about $500 a day, which it would otherwise have spent on studio rental. Compass Records might spend between $15,000 and $25,000 to produce an album.

Regardless of whether a record company opted to license or to produce and own an artist's album, the next major expense for the label was the manufacturing of the CDs. The manufacturing cost—which included pressing the CD, purchasing the standard jewel case, shrink-wrapping, and attaching a label to the top spine—was about $0.70 per unit. There was an additional unit cost of about $0.20 for printing the booklet and other materials contained inside the CD case. Compass had an arrangement with a CD manufacturer in Minneapolis, Minnesota, whereby the minimum initial order required was 1,000 units; thereafter, Compass could order in increments of 500. Because the manufacturer could turn around an order in three to five days, Brown and West tried to keep very tight control over their inventory.

Marketing and Distribution

For the major record labels, promoting an album depended on obtaining regular airplay on radio stations around the country. This process began with an album mail-out, which provided free copies of the recording to radio stations and music journalists. For a small independent label like Compass, promotional efforts were highly specialized and targeted. Compass focused on local radio programs and record stores in coordination with the performer's tour schedule. A typical album mail-out for Compass Records included 2,000 CD units. Compass usually negotiated a reduced rate of $0.50 per unit with its manufacturer for making the promotional CDs; the postage and collateral materials cost an additional $2.00 per unit. None of those costs were recoupable.

For Compass's artists, a major component of the marketing effort was venue sales at live concerts. Fans of folk, Celtic, and roots music were often known to postpone purchases of an album by a favorite artist until they could buy it at the concert, even if the album was locally available in stores. To encourage local fans to attend concerts by new artists, therefore, Compass usually paid for local print-advertising campaigns ($3,000), posters and press photos ($500), e-card mailings ($1,000), and the services of an independent radio promoter ($2,500).

With respect to CD distribution, major labels had divisions that handled the placement of millions of units worldwide. Independent labels such as Compass, however, secured deals with independent distributors to place their albums in regional retail outlets. Domestic distributors charged the label a fee; for Compass, this fee was 21% of the standard wholesale price of $11.45 per unit. The distribution of recorded music was also subject to a return privilege. All unsold CDs or cassettes were completely returnable by retailers. "This business is 100% consignment," Brown said. Compass was paid only for the CD units that sold, not for the number shipped. Retailers

FIGURE 2 |

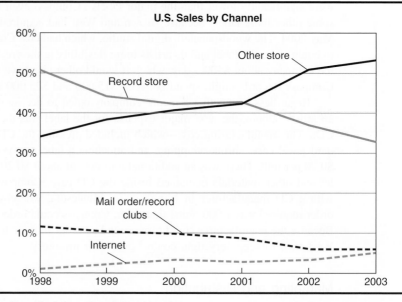

Source: Recording Industry Association of America.

returned unsold units to the distributor, which then returned them to the record company. Because of the return privilege, Compass typically manufactured about 30% more units than it estimated would actually sell at retail outlets; the company would usually write those units off after two years.

At the retail level, there had been a major shift from specialty record shops to mass- market and on-line retailers (see **Figure 2**). Record stores' share of U.S. music sales declined from 51%, in 1998, to 33%, in 2003, while the mass-market stores' share grew from 34% to 53% over the same period. Getting a record well placed with the large retailers was expensive. Brown estimated that Compass might spend around $5,000 for a new artist on in-store listening stations and other retail programs. The average retail list price for a Compass CD was $17.98 per unit.

Retailers gave an album only about 90 days from its release date to generate meaningful consumer demand; if that failed to occur, they exercised their return privilege. Therefore, in order to ensure high demand by an album's release date, sufficient publicity and promotion had to occur months in advance. "From a financial point of view," Brown said, "that means incurring all your recording, preproduction, and manufacturing costs six months or more before you will ever see any return." To keep an album available in the stores, a record label had to sell at least 50% of the total forecast sales in the first three months after the release date, and perhaps reach 75% in the first year. After that, sales might fall off quickly, with most of the remaining inventory sold the following year.

The Roscommon Decision

Adair Roscommon, an Irish singer who played fiddle, mandolin, and guitar, had been called "the Dublin folk scene's hottest up-and-comer" by one reviewer. She had begun her musical career as a teenager with the Irish traditional band Fairlea Brigham, and after reading history at Trinity University in Ireland, Roscommon started writing her own songs and touring with other artists in the United Kingdom and the United States. Her self-released 2003 album, *Swallows Fly,* did well—she sold 2,500 copies of the album from her van—and led to her being voted "Best New Artist of 2004" by the listeners of the influential Boston folk radio station WUMB. That local success caught the attention of Alison Brown. She liked how Roscommon combined the sophisticated, modern folk music of her native Ireland with the soulful strains of bluegrass; she had a sharp, accessible sound that was both classic and modern.

Brown and her husband believed strongly in Roscommon as an artist, but they were still undecided about whether Compass's contract with her should be to produce and own her next master or simply to license the finished recording. Purchasing her music would mean producing a master recording, which Compass Records would then own and from which it could potentially generate revenues indefinitely. Licensing the recording might be less expensive on the front end, but there was a finite life to the future cash flows associated with the recording. "If you fund a master, then it costs more than if you license [a finished recording]," Brown said, "but licensing means renting the material."

On the one hand, Brown believed she could negotiate a deal to produce Roscommon's next recording for $20,000, which included the standard options to produce and own three additional albums. As part of the deal, Compass would also negotiate a copublishing arrangement with Roscommon. Typically, an artist such as Roscommon, who wrote all her own songs, would split 50% of the mechanical royalties earned on an album with a music publisher, with which she would contract to promote her written compositions. Under this deal, however, Compass would be the publisher of the songs on the album. If Brown and her husband chose this alternative, therefore, Compass would effectively reduce their mechanical royalty expenses by half.

On the other hand, if Compass licensed Roscommon's finished recording, Brown thought the advance would be about $3,000, and Roscommon might be willing to include a performance-based option in the contract. With this option, if Compass achieved a sales target of 10,000 units, then it would earn the right to license her next album. "If we succeed with Roscommon under the license deal and make her a more well-known and viable act," Brown thought, "it's very possible that another label could swoop in with cash and promises of bigger things and reap the benefit of Compass's investment in her." Thus, having this additional clause in the licensing deal offered Brown some security. "We have a good feeling about her long-term potential," she said, "but we realize it may not show itself for a few albums."

Brown and West thought hard about their projections for Roscommon's album. "Only 1 in 20 albums will be the grand slam," Brown thought. For Compass, a grand slam might be 50,000 units, but success would depend on the up-front recording and marketing costs. They estimated that Compass could safely sell 5,000 units of

Roscommon's album in the United States through its domestic distributor. Because Roscommon already had a fan base overseas, they also believed they could generate international sales through distributors in other regions. Brown forecast sales of another 2,000 units in the United Kingdom, Ireland, and Europe; 1,000 units in Japan, New Zealand, and Australia; and 500 in Canada.[8] Roscommon herself could also probably sell at least 1,500 CDs from her van; she would pay Compass $6 per unit, and she would receive no artist or mechanical royalties on sales from her van. Brown used the industry's standard 12% discount rate for her analysis. Compass Records' marginal corporate tax rate was 40%.

At Compass, Brown had historically preferred to license rather than to own records. "It gives me the chance to wait and see," she said. But it wasn't always so simple. Compass's new distribution agreements in Europe and Asia created opportunities to sell an artist's CDs in new markets around the world, and Compass's recently built studio made producing an album easier and cheaper.

"We used to own only about 30% of the whole catalog for an artist, but with the studio we now own about half of them. The only rule of thumb is our experience," Brown said. She knew that an artist's success depended heavily on how active they were. A new artist that toured heavily and consistently could achieve 50% of their total sales at venues alone. "The rest just seems to come down to karma," Brown thought. "One thing we've learned is that you can't sell a record before its time; the hard part is guessing whether or not it's an artist's time."

---

[8]For sales in the United Kingdom, Ireland, and Europe, Compass typically received (euros) EUR7 per unit. For sales in Japan, Australia, and New Zealand, Compass received (U.S. dollars) USD6.50 per unit; for Canadian sales, Compass received USD7.00 per unit. Compass's international distributors did not charge an additional distribution fee. In mid June 2005, the USD/euro exchange rate was 1.224.

EXHIBIT 1 | Compass Records' Balance Sheet

	Dec. 31, 2004
Assets	
Current assets:	
Cash	$ 68,074
Accounts receivable	1,038,026
Other current assets	801,850
Total current assets	1,907,949
Fixed assets	433,608
Other assets:	
Accumulated amortization	(53,393)
Organizational costs	22,293
Start-up costs	3,510
Recoupable artist costs	908,226
Total other assets:	880,636
Total Assets	**$3,222,193**
LIABILITIES & EQUITY	
Liabilities	
Accounts payable	$ 280,907
Short-term debt	48,282
Other current liabilities:	
Accrued royalties payable	304,736
Royalty reserve account	322,737
Payroll tax payable	35,102
Sales tax payable	8,108
Credit card rec. issues	(567)
Franchise tax payable	(5,670)
Foreign taxes payable	6,105
Line of credit	1,024,216
Total other current liabilities	1,694,767
Total Liabilities	**$2,023,956**
Equity	
Paid-in capital	$270,000
Additional paid-in capital	530,053
Retained earnings	398,184
Total Equity	**$1,198,236**
Total Liabilities & Equity	**$3,222,193**

EXHIBIT 2 | Compass Records' Income Statement

	Jan–Dec 2004
Ordinary Income/Expense	
Income	
CDs	$4,634,967
Downloaded music	141
Consignment merchandise	1,625
Videos	2,225
DVDs	52,280
Studio rental income	14,128
Total Income	**$4,705,366**
Cost of Goods Sold	
Cassettes	$ 724
CDs	767,858
DVDs	7,006
Videos	805
Merchandise	210
Consignment	145
Total Cost of Goods Sold	**$ 776,748**
Gross Profit	**$3,928,618**
Expense	
Distribution expenses	$ 781,771
Royalty expense	570,565
Payroll expenses	466,542
General and administrative	576,583
Payroll tax expense	38,754
Other tax expense	15,786
Miscellaneous	36,167
Advertising	334,225
Promotion expense	71,116
Mailing expense	154,761
Travel & entertainment	48,558
Tour support	25,477
Graphic artist fees	33,064
Project expenses	24,244
Project costs not recouped	(3,375)
Total Expense	**$3,950,985**
Net Ordinary Income	**$ 754,381**
Other income	34,511
Net Income	**$ 788,892**

EXHIBIT 3 | Compass Records' Historical Income
and Expenses

	Total	
Year	Revenues	Expenses
2003	$2,702,840	$2,720,477
2002	2,734,773	2,755,426
2001	3,097,362	2,877,749
2000	2,898,315	3,075,899
1999	3,039,806	2,900,359
1998	1,343,050	1,389,010
1997	911,588	962,912
1996	770,094	906,439
1995	837,748	866,908

The Procter and Gamble Company: Investment in Crest Whitestrips Advanced Seal

It was May 2008, and Jackson Christopher, a financial analyst for the Procter and Gamble Company's (P&G) North America Oral Care (NAOC) group, hustled along a sunny downtown Cincinnati street on his way to work. NAOC's Crest teeth whitening group was considering the launch of an extension to its Whitestrips product, and the project had dominated most of his working hours. At least he avoided a long commute by living downtown.

The week before, the group had met to consider the merits of the proposed product, known as Crest Advanced Seal. Although openly intrigued by the concept, Angela Roman, the group's GM, was reserving judgment until she had a clearer picture of the idea and risks. She had tasked Christopher with putting together the economic perspective on Advanced Seal, an effort that had required a lot of work amalgamating all the different considerations and thinking through the financial implications. In the process, he had to manage a lot of different constituencies. In short, it had been an interesting week, and with the follow-up meeting the next day, Christopher knew he needed to present some conclusions.

The Procter and Gamble Company

P&G was one of the world's premier consumer goods companies. Its 2007 total revenue exceeded $72 billion and came from almost every corner of the globe. P&G's wide range of brands focused on beauty, grooming, and household care and delivered

This case was prepared by Daniel Lentz (Procter and Gamble) and Michael J. Schill, Robert F. Vandell Research Associate Professor of Business Administration. The individuals and figures in this case have been fictionalized. All narrative details and economics are purely fictional and are not intended to be used for a real assessment of the Crest Whitestrips business. Copyright © 2012 by the University of Virginia Darden School Foundation, Charlottesville, VA. All rights reserved. *To order copies, send an e-mail to sales@dardenbusinesspublishing.com. No part of this publication may be reproduced, stored in a retrieval system, used in a spreadsheet, or transmitted in any form or by any means—electronic, mechanical, photocopying, recording, or otherwise—without the permission of the Darden School Foundation.*

a broad array of products from fragrances to batteries and medication to toothpaste (**Exhibit 1**).

P&G was an aggressive competitor in its market, seeking to deliver total shareholder returns in the top one-third of its peer group (**Exhibit 2**). Management achieved these returns by following a strategy to reach more consumers (by extending category portfolios vertically into higher and lower value tiers) in more parts of the world (by expanding geographically into category whitespaces) more completely (by improving existing products and extending portfolios into adjacent categories).

NAOC's portfolio consisted of seven different product lines: toothpaste, manual toothbrushes, power toothbrushes, oral rinses, dental floss, denture adhesives and cleansers, and teeth whitening strips. Leveraging the collective benefit of multiple products enabled P&G to focus on more complete oral health solutions for consumers. NAOC followed the corporate strategy by, among other things, expanding the global toothpaste presence under the Oral B brand and to multiple adjacencies under the 3D White brand. At the heart of the portfolio, representing more than $5 billion in annual sales, was the Crest brand.

Crest Whitestrips and the Context for Advanced Seal

Crest Whitestrips, an at-home tooth enamel whitening treatment launched in 2001, allowed consumers to achieve whitening results that rivaled far more expensive dental office treatments. Existing whitening toothpastes had worked by polishing surface stains from the tooth enamel, but they were unable to change the fundamental color of teeth. Whitestrips worked through a strip applied temporarily to the teeth, binding the product to surface enamel and actually whitening the layer of dentin beneath the enamel itself. The intrinsic whitening results were unique to the category.

On its introduction, Crest Whitestrips saw nearly $300 million in annual sales but virtually no growth in sales or profits after the first year (**Exhibit 3**). Multiple attempts at line extensions had failed to significantly improve results, only managing to breed skepticism in major customers. Competitors that entered the category either left shortly thereafter or encountered the same stagnant sales as had P&G. (**Exhibit 4** documents the category history.)

The commercial team believed that, to turn around the business's lackluster performance and win back trust and merchandising support, something fundamental had to change. Advanced Seal, the extension under consideration, was based on a new technology that prevented the strips from slipping out of position during use. Because the new product binded with teeth more reliably, the active ingredient was delivered more effectively, improving both the usage experience and the whitening results, which were superior to any existing product on the market. **Exhibit 5** provides the proposed packaging for the product.

With an extremely strong market share position (**Figure 1**), the Whitestrips team had to manage any new launch carefully; future success had to be as much a function of P&L accretion as of increasing competitive share. The business rarely saw

FIGURE 1 | Market share of the teeth whitening category, 2008.

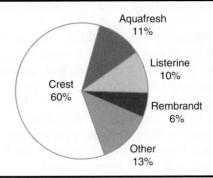

Source: Created by case writer.

household penetration figures any higher than 3%[1], so there were plenty of new consumers to target.

Last Week's Meeting

The previous week, NOAC members had gathered in a conference room to consider the proposed launch of Advanced Seal. As the meeting had progressed, the group strained to gauge the GM's reaction to the concept.

"I follow you so far," said Roman. "I have questions, but I don't want to derail you, Christina. Keep going."

Even among other brand managers, Christina Whitman was known for her energy and enthusiasm, which was saying something.

"Consumer research has been clear," Whitman asserted briskly. "The tendency of Whitestrips to slip off teeth is the number one barrier to repeat purchase and word-of-mouth recommendation. Advanced Seal's new technology will address this concern, providing a real jolt of energy to the whitening category and a strong sales lift in the process. "

"We see pricing this innovation at the high end of our range, which should drive up trade in our portfolio and improve market share. The product improvement gives us creative advertising and positioning opportunities to leverage as well. We definitely think we should move forward."

Roman sat back in her chair and exhaled thoughtfully. "What's the downside scenario here, everyone?"

Hector Toro, the account executive, cleared his throat. "I'm worried about whether we can count on getting the merchandising support we'll need to get this off to a good start. For the product to catch on, we'll need to get out of the gates

---

[1]*Household penetration* (HHP) tracked the percentage of a given market of households that had purchased a product within the last year. Whitestrips traditionally had very low HHP, whereas toothpaste had HHP of virtually 100%.

fast, and a lot of retailers are still frustrated about the mediocre velocity of our last line extension. If they don't get behind this, it won't be successful no matter what we do."

Whitman agreed immediately. "To show them we're committed to pulling consumers to the oral care aisle for this, we really need to adequately fund marketing. We also need to allow for strong trade margins[2] to get us display space and offset the high carrying cost of this inventory. It's a much higher price point than buyers are used to carrying in inventory."

Jackson Christopher, the data floating in his head from hours of study, saw an opportunity to bring up some of his concerns. "That may not be as straightforward as it sounds. Pricing this at a premium is one thing, but can we price it high enough to cover the costs of the improvements?"

This was the first Roman had heard of this potential issue. "Say more about that. I agree with Christina in principle, but what are the preliminary economics we're looking at here?"

"Oh, we'll be able to price this up, for sure," he replied. "We could charge a 25% premium without having a precipitous drop in volume. The problem is that this product improvement will drive up our costs by almost 75%. That could easily dilute our margins. We could end up making less gross profit on this product than on our current Premium product line. If we're not careful, the more this product takes off, the worse off we'll be."

"But even so," Whitman interjected, "we're confident that we'll pick up so much incremental volume that we'll be net better off anyway." Whitman knew Christopher's concerns were valid but didn't want them to kill the idea prematurely.

"What do you think, Margaret?" asked Roman, turning to Margaret Tan, a market researcher.

"I think the real answer is probably somewhere in the middle," Tan replied. "I don't think we'll be able to price this high enough to offset the costs, but we probably will pick up a lot of new volume. Whether we'll be net better off depends on bringing in enough new users to the category to offset profit dilution from the cost structure."

Everyone was silent as Roman took a few moments to think it over. "Alright then," she said. "I'm OK to proceed at this point. I like the idea. We need to be looking for ways to delight our consumers. This product improvement really is huge for this consumer; we know that she's been complaining about Whitestrips slipping off her teeth for quite some time. We need to find ways to meet her needs while preserving our core structural economics."

She turned to Christopher. "I'm going to need you to set our baseline here. There are a lot of moving pieces, and I need you to paint the picture on how this comes together. Does this pay out for our business? Are we financially better off launching this product or not, what are the risks, what do we need to be thinking about as we

---

[2]*Trade margins* were the gross profit margins retailers made on any product they sold, the difference between the shelf price and the list price paid to product manufacturers. In general, the higher the shelf price (determined by the retailer), the higher the trade margin requirement to retailers.

design this? Work with marketing, sales, manufacturing, and market research to pull together the overall picture in the next week or so. We'll get back together and decide where to go from here."

Christopher agreed, and the meeting wrapped up.

Establishing a Base Case

Christopher's initial analysis established the expected price point for retailers at $22 per unit for Advanced Seal, compared to $18 and $13 per unit for P&G's Premium and Basic offering, respectively. Christopher had worked with his supply chain leaders to estimate the cost structure. The new technology would run at a cost of $5 per unit cost more than the current Premium product offering, such that the gross profit would be lower than premium. **Exhibit 6** provides the summary assessments that had coalesced regarding the unit price and cost for the Crest Whitestrips products.

The forecasting models suggested a base case annual forecast of 2 million units for Advanced Seal. The analysis also suggested that cannibalization of existing Crest Whitestrips products would be high, on the order of 50 to 60 percent for Premium units and 15% for Basic units. Such cannibalization rates meant that 65 to 75 percent of Advanced Seal's 2 million units was coming straight out of existing P&G sales.

Preliminary discussions around advertising spending indicated an expected launch budget of $6 million per year. He estimated that the cannibalized Premium and Basic products already received $4 million per year in advertising support that would no longer be required after the launch. This meant the group would have to spend an incremental $2 million in advertising to support the launch. He also needed to include $1 million per year for incremental selling, general, and administrative expenses.

Based on the amount of time R&D felt it would take a competitor to match the product innovation, Christopher expected a project life of four years, over which time annual unit sales were expected to be relatively constant. For this type of decision, P&G used an 8% discount rate and a 40% tax rate. Manufacturing partners expected to spend $4 million in capital expenditures and incur $1.5 million in one-time development expenses to get the project going. The accountants he conferred with regarding capital expenditure depreciations recommended the five-year accelerated schedule for tax purposes and the straight-line schedule for reporting purposes.[3] Engineering indicated that the equipment would likely need to be replaced at the end of the project life, and they did not expect it to have any residual value.

Christopher also knew that he had to factor in any incremental working capital required to support the project. For the Whitestrips business, net working capital typically ran at a rate of between 8 and 10 times.[4] The project would require that at least

---

[3] Five-year accelerated depreciation specified by the U.S. tax authority (IRS) was calculated by multiplying the amount of investment by the following percentages for each respective year, 20% in Year 1, 32% in Year 2, 19.2% in Year 3, 11.52% in Year 4, 11.52% in Year 5, and 5.76% in Year 6.

[4] The net working capital turnover ratio was defined as Revenue divided by Net Working Capital, where Net Working Capital was equal to Current Assets less Non-Interest-Bearing Current Liabilities.

this amount be on hand prior to the market launch date. It was P&G's policy to model the recovery of any working capital investment at the end of the project life.

Proposal to Drive Revenue

Later that week, as Christopher rubbed his eyes to remove the imprint of a spreadsheet from his vision, Whitman popped her head into his cube. "I came to see where the steam was coming from. I guess from your ears."

Christopher chuckled. "The math isn't really complicated, but the results all depend on what you assume. I just need to make sure I think through everything the right way." He was getting close to wrapping up his work, but he knew that when she came by unannounced and excited, it meant her creative wheels were turning and that she was looking for more advertising dollars.

"I had some great buzz-creation ideas that I think we can use for the launch," she said, her voice lowering. "I'm thinking through some digital campaigns that I think can go viral, and I'm also interested in expanding our initial media plan. We have such low household penetration numbers that if we drive a change in launch plans we could focus a great deal more on driving trial. One problem with trial according to Margaret is that we're really at the high end of the price range. She thinks a small drop in price could really accelerate sales."

"That makes sense. What kind of numbers are we talking about?"

"Good. I'm going to need my starting advertising budget to go from $6 million to $7.5 million in year one. I can then go back to $6 million per year after that. Next, we reduce price by $1 to $21 for Advanced Seal. Margaret thinks those two effects will drive annual unit sales up 1.25 million to 3.25 million units per year."

"Sounds impressive. Let me take a look, and I'll let you know where we land."

"Thanks! We all know that Roman is looking for bigger revenue dollars from Whitestrips and my calculations suggest this will certainly deliver big revenue gains for the group."

Proposal to Minimize Cannibalization

The next day Christopher thought he had figured out what he would recommend to Roman, and he had a good risk profile built for the team to design and sell against. Just as he was starting to relax, Tam entered his cube.

"This can't be good," Christopher said preemptively.

Tam sighed. "Yes and no. I've gone back and reworked the volume forecast for Christina's initiative. We may have a more severe cannibalization problem than we thought. It's not certain, but there is greater likelihood that we end up sourcing more of the incremental volume from our current Premium products."

"How much of an increase are we talking about here?"

"I expect that the price reduction and extra advertising expands the range of cannibalization rates on Premium to between 50 percent and 65 percent."

"Alright, that might not be so bad."

"Well, in case it is, we've worked up an alternative strategy." Tam continued. "Strategy B is to pivot to a more conservative position to minimize cannibalization by reducing the launch advertising splash and focusing the marketing on untapped customers. In doing so we'll have less of a broad appeal than we thought. More of a niche. We'd be prioritizing cannibalization over trial. Our thought was to also offset the gross profit differential by raising price to $23, giving Advanced Seal an $11 gross profit. It's clearly not what Christina was hoping for."

Together, they agreed on the final assumptions. The advertising budget would be reduced by $1 million each year, to $5 million. The sales model predicted that the effect on Advanced Seal units would be strong with unit sales declining to just 1 million per year. The changes would also reduce the cannibalization rate for Premium to a more certain rate of 45 percent.

The Recommendation

Christopher still needed to figure out how to convert all this data into a realistic P&L for the initiative and find the baseline net present value. Beyond that, he needed to determine what the team needed to do to mold this opportunity into a winning proposition for P&G shareholders. He agreed with Whitman that this was an exciting technology, but he had to make sure that any decision would give investors something to smile about.

EXHIBIT 1 | Procter and Gamble Brands

Beauty and Grooming		
Always	Anna Sui	Aussie
Braun	Camay	Christina Aguilera Perfumes
Clairol Professional	CoverGirl	Crest
DDF	Dolce & Gabbana Cosmetics	Dolce & Gabbana Fragrances
Dunhill Fragrances	Escada Fragrances	Fekkai
Fusion	Ghost	Gillette
Gucci Fragrances	Hugo Boss Fragrances	Head & Shoulders
Herbal Essences	Ivory	Lacoste Fragrances
MACH3	Naomi Campbell	Natural Instincts
Nice 'n Easy	Nioxin	Olay
Old Spice	Oral-B	Pantene
Pert	Prestobarba/Blue	Puma
Rejoice	SK-II	Safeguard
Scope	Sebastian Professional	Secret
Tampax	Venus	Vidal Sassoon
Wella		

Household Care		
Ace	Align	Ariel
Bold	Bounce	Bounty
Cascade	Charmin	Cheer
Comet	Dash	Dawn
Downy	Dreft Laundry	Duracell
Era	Eukanuba	Febreze
Gain	Iams	Joy
Luvs	Metamucil	Mr. Clean
Pampers	Pepto-Bismol	Prilosec OTC
Pringles	Puffs	Swiffer
Tide	Vicks	

EXHIBIT 2 | Value of $1 Invested in P&G Stock and the S&P 500 Index, 2001 to 2008

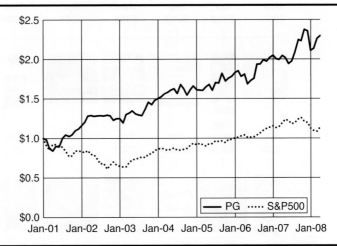

Data Source: Yahoo! Finance.

EXHIBIT 3 | Crest Whitestrips' Revenue and After-Tax Profit Since 2001 Launch (in millions of dollars)

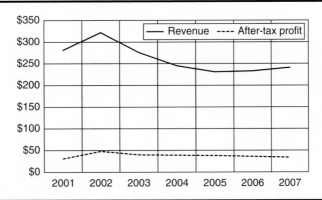

Note: Data is disguised.

EXHIBIT 4 | Whitening Category History

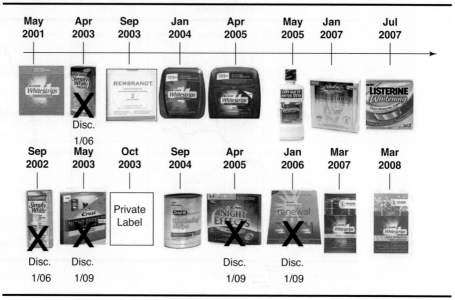

Image Source: Procter and Gamble Company. Used with permission.

EXHIBIT 5 | Crest Whitestrips' Advanced Seal Packaging

Image Source: Procter and Gamble Company. Used with permission.

EXHIBIT 6 | Gross Profit Comparison

	Advanced Seal	Premium Product	Basic Product
Per-unit revenue and costs			
Revenue	$22	$18	$13
Cost of goods sold expenses	$12	$7	$6
Gross profit	$10	$11	$7

Note: Case writer has disguised these figures.

Victoria Chemicals plc (A): The Merseyside Project

Late one afternoon in January 2008, Frank Greystock told Lucy Morris, "No one seems satisfied with the analysis so far, but the suggested changes could kill the project. If solid projects like this can't swim past the corporate piranhas, the company will never modernize."

Morris was plant manager of Victoria Chemicals' Merseyside Works in Liverpool, England. Her controller, Frank Greystock, was discussing a capital project that Morris wanted to propose to senior management. The project consisted of a (British pounds) GBP12 million expenditure to renovate and rationalize the polypropylene production line at the Merseyside plant in order to make up for deferred maintenance and to exploit opportunities to achieve increased production efficiency.

Victoria Chemicals was under pressure from investors to improve its financial performance because of the accumulation of the firm's common shares by a well-known corporate raider, Sir David Benjamin. Earnings had fallen to 180 pence per share at the end of 2007 from around 250 pence per share at the end of 2006. Morris thus believed that the time was ripe to obtain funding from corporate headquarters for a modernization program for the Merseyside Works—at least she had believed this until Greystock presented her with several questions that had only recently surfaced.

Victoria Chemicals and Polypropylene

Victoria Chemicals, a major competitor in the worldwide chemicals industry, was a leading producer of polypropylene, a polymer used in an extremely wide variety of products (ranging from medical products to packaging film, carpet fibers, and automobile

This case was prepared by Robert F. Bruner as a basis for class discussion rather than to illustrate effective or ineffective handling of an administrative situation. Victoria Chemicals is a fictional company reflecting the issues facing actual firms. The author wishes to acknowledge the helpful comments of Dr. Frank H. McTigue, the literary color of Anthony Trollope, and the financial support of the Citicorp Global Scholars Program.

components) and known for its strength and malleability. Polypropylene was essentially priced as a commodity.

The production of polypropylene pellets at Merseyside Works began with propylene, a refined gas received in tank cars. Propylene was purchased from four refineries in England that produced it in the course of refining crude oil into gasoline. In the first stage of the production process, polymerization, the propylene gas was combined with a diluent (or solvent) in a large pressure vessel. In a catalytic reaction, the polypropylene precipitated to the bottom of the tank and was then concentrated in a centrifuge.

The second stage of the production process compounded the basic polypropylene with stabilizers, modifiers, fillers, and pigments to achieve the desired attributes for a particular customer. The finished plastic was extruded into pellets for shipment to the customer.

The Merseyside Works production process was old, semicontinuous at best, and, therefore, higher in labor content than its competitors' newer plants. The Merseyside Works plant was constructed in 1967.

Victoria Chemicals produced polypropylene at Merseyside Works and in Rotterdam, Holland. The two plants were of identical scale, age, and design. The managers of both plants reported to James Fawn, executive vice president and manager of the Intermediate Chemicals Group (ICG) of Victoria Chemicals. The company positioned itself as a supplier to customers in Europe and the Middle East. The strategic-analysis staff estimated that, in addition to numerous small producers, seven major competitors manufactured polypropylene in Victoria Chemicals' market region. Their plants operated at various cost levels. **Exhibit 1** presents a comparison of plant sizes and indexed costs.

The Proposed Capital Program

Morris had assumed responsibility for the Merseyside Works only 12 months previously, following a rapid rise from the entry position of shift engineer nine years before. When she assumed responsibility, she undertook a detailed review of the operations and discovered significant opportunities for improvement in polypropylene production. Some of those opportunities stemmed from the deferral of maintenance over the preceding five years. In an effort to enhance the operating results of Merseyside Works, the previous manager had limited capital expenditures to only the most essential. Now what previously had been routine and deferrable was becoming essential. Other opportunities stemmed from correcting the antiquated plant design in ways that would save energy and improve the process flow: (1) relocating and modernizing tank-car unloading areas, which would enable the process flow to be streamlined; (2) refurbishing the polymerization tank to achieve higher pressures and thus greater throughput; and (3) renovating the compounding plant to increase extrusion throughput and obtain energy savings.

Morris proposed an expenditure of GBP12 million on this program. The entire polymerization line would need to be shut down for 45 days, however, and because the Rotterdam plant was operating near capacity, Merseyside Works' customers would buy from competitors. Greystock believed the loss of customers would not be permanent.

The benefits would be a lower energy requirement[1] as well as a 7% greater manufacturing throughput. In addition, the project was expected to improve gross margin (before depreciation and energy savings) from 11.5% to 12.5%. The engineering group at Merseyside Works was highly confident that the efficiencies would be realized.

Merseyside Works currently produced 250,000 metric tons of polypropylene pellets a year. Currently, the price of polypropylene averaged GBP675 per ton for Victoria Chemicals' product mix. The tax rate required in capital-expenditure analyses was 30%. Greystock discovered that any plant facilities to be replaced had been completely depreciated. New assets could be depreciated on an accelerated basis[2] over 15 years, the expected life of the assets. The increased throughput would necessitate an increase of work-in-process inventory equal in value to 3.0% of cost of goods. Greystock included in the first year of his forecast preliminary engineering costs of GBP500,000 spent over the preceding nine months on efficiency and design studies of the renovation. Finally, the corporate manual stipulated that overhead costs be reflected in project analyses at the rate of 3.5% times the book value of assets acquired in the project per year.[3]

Greystock had produced the discounted-cash-flow (DCF) summary given in **Exhibit 2**. It suggested that the capital program would easily hurdle Victoria Chemicals' required return of 10% for engineering projects.

Concerns of the Transport Division

Victoria Chemicals owned the tank cars with which Merseyside Works received propylene gas from four petroleum refineries in England. The Transport Division, a cost center, oversaw the movement of all raw, intermediate, and finished materials throughout the company and was responsible for managing the tank cars. Because of the project's

---

[1]Greystock characterized the energy savings as a percentage of sales and assumed that the savings would be equal to 1.25% of sales in the first five years and 0.75% in years 6-10. Thereafter, without added aggressive green spending, the energy efficiency of the plant would revert to its old level, and the savings would be zero. He believed that the decision to make further environmentally oriented investments was a separate choice (and one that should be made much later) and, therefore, that to include such benefits (of a presumably later investment decision) in the project being considered today would be inappropriate.

[2]The company's capital-expenditure manual suggested the use of double-declining-balance (DDB) depreciation, even though other more aggressive procedures might be permitted by the tax code. The reason for this policy was to discourage jockeying for corporate approvals based on tax provisions that could apply differently for different projects and divisions. Prior to senior-management's approval, the controller's staff would present an independent analysis of special tax effects that might apply. Division managers, however, were discouraged from relying heavily on those effects. In applying the DDB approach, accelerated depreciation was used until the straight-line calculation gave a higher number at which point depreciation was calculated on a straight-line basis. The conversion to straight line was commonly done so that the asset would depreciate fully within its economic life.

[3]The corporate-policy manual stated that new projects should be able to sustain a reasonable proportion of corporate overhead expense. Projects that were so marginal as to be unable to sustain those expenses and also meet the other criteria of investment attractiveness should not be undertaken. Thus, all new capital projects should reflect an annual pretax charge amounting to 3.5% of the value of the initial asset investment for the project.

increased throughput, the Transport Division would have to increase its allocation of tank cars to Merseyside Works. Currently, the Transport Division could make this allocation out of excess capacity, although doing so would accelerate from 2012 to 2010 the need to purchase new rolling stock to support the anticipated growth of the firm in other areas. The purchase was estimated to be GBP2 million in 2010. The rolling stock would have a depreciable life of 10 years,[4] but with proper maintenance, the cars could operate much longer. The rolling stock could not be used outside Britain because of differences in track gauge.

A memorandum from the controller of the Transport Division suggested that the cost of the tank cars should be included in the initial outlay of Merseyside Works' capital program. But Greystock disagreed. He told Morris:

> The Transport Division isn't paying one pence of actual cash because of what we're doing at Merseyside. In fact, we're doing the company a favor in using its excess capacity. Even *if* an allocation has to be made somewhere, it should go on the Transport Division's books. The way we've always evaluated projects in this company has been with the philosophy of "every tub on its own bottom"—every division has to fend for itself. The Transport Division isn't part of our own Intermediate Chemicals Group, so they should carry the allocation of rolling stock.

Accordingly, Greystock had not reflected any charge for the use of excess rolling stock in his preliminary DCF analysis, given in **Exhibit 2**.

The Transport Division and Intermediate Chemicals Group reported to separate executive vice presidents, who reported to the chairman and chief executive officer of the company. The executive vice presidents received an annual incentive bonus pegged to the performance of their divisions.

Concerns of the ICG Sales and Marketing Department

Greystock's analysis had led to questions from the director of sales. In a recent meeting, the director had told Greystock:

> Your analysis assumes that we can sell the added output and thus obtain the full efficiencies from the project, but as you know, the market for polypropylene is extremely competitive. Right now, the industry is in a downturn and it looks like an oversupply is in the works. This means that we will probably have to shift capacity away from Rotterdam toward Merseyside in order to move the added volume. Is this really a gain for Victoria Chemicals? Why spend money just so one plant can cannibalize another?

The vice president of marketing was less skeptical. He said that with lower costs at Merseyside Works, Victoria Chemicals might be able to take business from the plants of competitors such as Saône-Poulet or Vaysol. In the current severe recession, competitors would fight hard to keep customers, but sooner or later the market would

---

[4]The transport division depreciated rolling stock using DDB depreciation for the first eight years and straight-line depreciation for the last two years.

revive, and it would be reasonable to assume that any lost business volume would return at that time.

Greystock had listened to both the director and the vice president and chose to reflect no charge for a loss of business at Rotterdam in his preliminary analysis of the Merseyside project. He told Morris:

> Cannibalization really isn't a cash flow; there is no check written in this instance. Anyway, if the company starts burdening its cost-reduction projects with fictitious charges like this, we'll never maintain our cost competitiveness. A cannibalization charge is rubbish!

Concerns of the Assistant Plant Manager

Griffin Tewitt, the assistant plant manager and Morris's direct subordinate, proposed an unusual modification to Greystock's analysis during a late-afternoon meeting with Greystock and Morris. Over the past few months, Tewitt had been absorbed with the development of a proposal to modernize a separate and independent part of the Merseyside Works, the production line for ethylene-propylene-copolymer rubber (EPC). This product, a variety of synthetic rubber, had been pioneered by Victoria Chemicals in the early 1960s and was sold in bulk to European tire manufacturers. Despite hopes that this oxidation-resistant rubber would dominate the market in synthetics, EPC remained a relatively small product in the European chemical industry. Victoria Chemicals, the largest supplier of EPC, produced the entire volume at Merseyside Works. EPC had been only marginally profitable to Victoria Chemicals because of the entry by competitors and the development of competing synthetic-rubber compounds over the past five years.

Tewitt had proposed a renovation of the EPC production line at a cost of GBP1 million. The renovation would give Victoria Chemicals the lowest EPC cost base in the world and would improve cash flows by GBP25,000 ad infinitum. Even so, at current prices and volumes, the net present value (NPV) of this project was −GBP750,000. Tewitt and the EPC product manager had argued strenuously to the company's executive committee that the negative NPV ignored strategic advantages from the project and increases in volume and prices when the recession ended. Nevertheless, the executive committee had rejected the project, basing its rejection mainly on economic grounds.

In a hushed voice, Tewitt said to Morris and Greystock:

> Why don't you include the EPC project as part of the polypropylene line renovations? The positive NPV of the poly renovations can easily sustain the negative NPV of the EPC project. This is an extremely important project to the company, a point that senior management doesn't seem to get. If we invest now, we'll be ready to exploit the market when the recession ends. If we don't invest now, you can expect that we will have to exit the business altogether in three years. Do you look forward to more layoffs? Do you want to manage a shrinking plant? Recall that our annual bonuses are pegged to the size of this operation. Also remember that, in the last 20 years, no one from corporate has monitored renovation projects once the investment decision was made.

Concerns of the Treasury Staff

After a meeting on a different matter, Greystock described his dilemmas to Andrew Gowan, who worked as an analyst on Victoria Chemicals' treasury staff. Gowan scanned Greystock's analysis and pointed out:

> Cash flows and discount rate need to be consistent in their assumptions about inflation. The 10% hurdle rate you're using is a nominal target rate of return. The Treasury staff thinks this impounds a long-term inflation expectation of 3% per year. Thus, Victoria Chemicals' real (that is, zero inflation) target rate of return is 7%.

The conversation was interrupted before Greystock could gain full understanding of Gowan's comment. For the time being, Greystock decided to continue to use a discount rate of 10% because it was the figure promoted in the latest edition of Victoria Chemicals' capital-budgeting manual.

Evaluating Capital-Expenditure Proposals at Victoria Chemicals

In submitting a project for senior management's approval, the project's initiators had to identify it as belonging to one of four possible categories: (1) new product or market, (2) product or market extension, (3) engineering efficiency, or (4) safety or environment. The first three categories of proposals were subject to a system of four performance "hurdles," of which at least three had to be met for the proposal to be considered. The Merseyside project would be in the engineering-efficiency category.

1. *Impact on earnings per share:* For engineering-efficiency projects, the contribution to net income from contemplated projects had to be positive. This criterion was calculated as the average annual earnings per share (EPS) contribution of the project over its entire economic life, using the number of outstanding shares at the most recent fiscal year-end (FYE) as the basis for the calculation. (At FYE2007, Victoria Chemicals had 92,891,240 shares outstanding.)

2. *Payback:* This criterion was defined as the number of years necessary for free cash flow of the project to amortize the initial project outlay completely. For engineering-efficiency projects, the maximum payback period was six years.

3. *Discounted cash flow:* DCF was defined as the present value of future cash flows of the project (at the hurdle rate of 10% for engineering-efficiency proposals) less the initial investment outlay. This net present value of free cash flows had to be positive.

4. *Internal rate of return:* IRR was defined as being the discount rate at which the present value of future free cash flows just equaled the initial outlay—in other words, the rate at which the NPV was zero. The IRR of engineering-efficiency projects had to be greater than 10%.

Conclusion

Morris wanted to review Greystock's analysis in detail and settle the questions surrounding the tank cars and the potential loss of business volume at Rotterdam. As

Greystock's analysis now stood, the Merseyside project met all four investment criteria:

1. Average annual addition to EPS = GBP0.022
2. Payback period = 3.8 years
3. Net present value = GBP10.6 million
4. Internal rate of return = 24.3%

Morris was concerned that further tinkering might seriously weaken the attractiveness of the project.

EXHIBIT 1 | Comparative Information on the Seven Largest Polypropylene Plants in Europe

	Plant Location	Year Plant Built	Plant Annual Output (in metric tons)	Production Cost per Ton (indexed to low-cost producer)
CBTG A.G	Saarbrün	1981	350,000	1.00
Victoria Chemicals	Liverpool	1967	250,000	1.09
Victoria Chemicals	Rotterdam	1967	250,000	1.09
Hosche A.G.	Hamburg	1977	300,000	1.02
Montecassino SpA	Genoa	1961	120,000	1.11
Saône-Poulet S.A.	Marseille	1972	175,000	1.07
Vaysol S.A.	Antwerp	1976	220,000	1.06
Next 10 largest plants			450,000	1.19

Source: Case writer analysis.

EXHIBIT 2 | Greystock's DCF Analysis of the Merseyside Project (financial values in millions of GBP)

Assumptions

Annual Output (metric tons)	250,000	Discount rate	10.0%
Output Gain/Original Output	7.0%	Tax Rate	30%
Price/ton (pounds sterling)	675	Investment Outlay (mill.)	12.0
Inflation Rate (prices and costs)	0.0%	Depreciable Life (years)	15
Gross Margin (ex. Deprec.)	12.50%	Salvage Value	0
Old Gross Margin	11.5%	WIP Inventory/Cost of Goods	3.0%
Energy savings/Sales Yr. 1-5	1.25%	Months Downtime, Construction	1.5
Yr. 6-10	0.75%	Preliminary Engineering Costs	0.5
Yr. 11-15	0.0%	Overhead/Investment	3.5%

Year	Now	1 2008	2 2009	3 2010	4 2011	5 2012	6 2013	7 2014	8 2015	9 2016	10 2017	11 2018	12 2019	13 2020	14 2021	15 2022
1. Estimate of Incremental Gross Profit																
New Output (tons)		267,500	267,500	267,500	267,500	267,500	267,500	267,500	267,500	267,500	267,500	267,500	267,500	267,500	267,500	267,500
Lost Output—Construction		(33,438)														
New Sales (Millions)		157.99	180.56	180.56	180.56	180.56	180.56	180.56	180.56	180.56	180.56	180.56	180.56	180.56	180.56	180.56
New Gross Margin		13.8%	13.8%	13.8%	13.8%	13.8%	13.3%	13.3%	13.3%	13.3%	13.3%	12.5%	12.5%	12.5%	12.5%	12.5%
New Gross Profit		21.72	24.83	24.83	24.83	24.83	23.92	23.92	23.92	23.92	23.92	22.57	22.57	22.57	22.57	22.57
Old Output		250,000	250,000	250,000	250,000	250,000	250,000	250,000	250,000	250,000	250,000	250,000	250,000	250,000	250,000	250,000
Old Sales		168.75	168.75	168.75	168.75	168.75	168.75	168.75	168.75	168.75	168.75	168.75	168.75	168.75	168.75	168.75
Old Gross Profit		19.41	19.41	19.41	19.41	19.41	19.41	19.41	19.41	19.41	19.41	19.41	19.41	19.41	19.41	19.41
Incremental gross profit		2.32	5.42	5.42	5.42	5.42	4.52	4.52	4.52	4.52	4.52	3.16	3.16	3.16	3.16	3.16
2. Estimate of Incremental WIP inventory																
New WIP inventory		4.09	4.67	4.67	4.67	4.67	4.70	4.70	4.70	4.70	4.70	4.74	4.74	4.74	4.74	4.74
Old WIP inventory		4.48	4.48	4.48	4.48	4.48	4.48	4.48	4.48	4.48	4.48	4.48	4.48	4.48	4.48	4.48
Incremental WIP inventory		−0.39	0.19	0.19	0.19	0.19	0.22	0.22	0.22	0.22	0.22	0.26	0.26	0.26	0.26	0.26
3. Estimate of Incremental Depreciation																
New Depreciation		1.60	1.39	1.20	1.04	0.90	0.78	0.68	0.59	0.55	0.55	0.55	0.55	0.55	0.55	0.55
4. Overhead		0.42	0.42	0.42	0.42	0.42	0.42	0.42	0.42	0.42	0.42	0.42	0.42	0.42	0.42	0.42
5. Prelim. Engineering Costs		0.50														
Pretax Incremental Profit		−0.20	3.61	3.80	3.96	4.10	3.32	3.42	3.51	3.55	3.55	2.20	2.20	2.20	2.20	2.20
6. Cash Flow Adjustments																
Less Capital Expenditures	−12.00															
Add back Depreciation		1.60	1.39	1.20	1.04	0.90	0.78	0.68	0.59	0.55	0.55	0.55	0.55	0.55	0.55	0.55
Less Added WIP inventory		0.39	−0.58	0.00	0.00	0.00	−0.03	0.00	0.00	0.00	0.00	−0.04	0.00	0.00	0.00	0.00
7. Free Cash Flow	−12.00	1.85	3.33	3.86	3.81	3.77	3.08	3.07	3.05	3.03	3.03	2.04	2.08	2.08	2.08	2.34

NPV = £10.57
IRR = 24.3%

Source: Created by case writer using fictitious data.

Victoria Chemicals Plc (B): The Merseyside and Rotterdam Projects

James Fawn, executive vice president of the Intermediate Chemicals Group (ICG) of Victoria Chemicals, planned to meet with his financial analyst, John Camperdown, to review two mutually exclusive capital-expenditure proposals. The firm's capital budget would be submitted for approval to the board of directors in early February 2008, and any projects Fawn proposed for the ICG had to be forwarded to the CEO of Victoria Chemicals soon for his review. Plant managers in Liverpool and Rotterdam had independently submitted expenditure proposals, each of which would expand the polypropylene output of their respective plants by 7% or 17,500 tons per year.[1] Victoria Chemicals' strategic-analysis staff argued strenuously that a company-wide increase in polypropylene output of 35,000 tons made no sense but half that amount did. Thus, Fawn could not accept *both* projects; he could sponsor only one for approval by the board.

Corporate policy was to evaluate projects based on four criteria: (1) net present value (NPV) computed at the appropriate cost of capital, (2) internal rate of return (IRR), (3) payback, and (4) growth in earnings per share. In addition, the board of directors was receptive to "strategic factors"—considerations that might be difficult to quantify. The manager of the Rotterdam plant, Elizabeth Eustace, argued vociferously that her project easily surpassed all the relevant quantitative standards and that

---

[1] Background information on Victoria Chemicals and the polypropylene business is given in "Victoria Chemicals PLC (A): The Merseyside Project," (UVA-F-1543).

This case was prepared by Robert F. Bruner as a basis for class discussion rather than to illustrate effective or ineffective handling of an administrative situation. Victoria Chemicals is a fictional company, reflecting the issues facing actual firms. The author wishes to acknowledge the helpful comments of Dr. Frank H. McTigue, the literary color of Anthony Trollope, and the financial support of the Citicorp Global Scholars Program.

it had important strategic benefits. Indeed, Eustace had interjected those points in two recent meetings with senior management and at a cocktail reception for the board of directors. Fawn expected to review the proposal from Lucy Morris, manager of Merseyside Works, the Liverpool plant, at the meeting with Camperdown, but he suspected that neither proposal dominated the other on all four criteria. Fawn's choice would apparently not be straightforward.

The Proposal from Merseyside, Liverpool

The project for the Merseyside plant entailed enhancing the existing facilities and the production process. Based on the type of project and the engineering studies, the potential benefits of the project were quite certain. To date, Morris had limited her discussions about the project to conversations with Fawn and Camperdown. Camperdown had raised exploratory questions about the project and had presented preliminary analyses to managers in marketing and transportation for their comments. The revised analysis emerging from those discussions would be the focus of Fawn's discussion with Camperdown in the forthcoming meeting.

Camperdown had indicated that Morris's final memo on the project was only three pages long. Fawn wondered whether this memo would satisfy his remaining questions.

The Rotterdam Project

Elizabeth Eustace's proposal consisted of a 90-page document replete with detailed schematics, engineering comments, strategic analyses, and financial projections. The basic discounted cash flow (DCF) analysis presented in **Exhibit 1** shows that the project had an NPV of (British pounds) GBP15.5 million and an IRR of 18.0%. Accounting for a worst-case scenario, which assumed erosion of Merseyside's volume equal to the gain in Rotterdam's volume, the NPV was GBP12.45 million.

In essence, Eustace's proposal called for the expenditure of GBP10.5 million over three years to convert the plant's polymerization line from batch to continuous-flow technology and to install sophisticated state-of-the-art process controls throughout the polymerization and compounding operations. The heart of the new system would be an analog computer driven by advanced software written by a team of engineering professors at an institute in Japan. The three-year-old process-control technology had been installed in several polypropylene production facilities in Japan, and although the improvements in cost and output had been positive on average, the efficiency gains had varied considerably across each of the production facilities. Other major producers were known to be evaluating this system for use in their plants.

Eustace explained that installing the sophisticated new system would not be feasible without also obtaining a continuous supply of propylene gas. She proposed obtaining this gas by pipeline from a refinery five kilometers away (rather than by railroad tank cars sourced from three refineries). Victoria Chemicals had an option to purchase a pipeline and its right-of-way for GBP3.5 million, which Eustace had included in her GBP10.5 million estimate for the project; then, for relatively little cost, the pipeline could be extended to the Rotterdam plant and refinery at the other end. The option had been purchased several years earlier. A consultant had informed Eustace that to purchase a right-of-way at current prices and to lay a comparable pipeline would cost approximately GBP6 million, a value the consultant believed was roughly equal to what it could be sold for at auction in case the plan didn't work out. The consultant also forecasted that the value of the right-of-way would be GBP40 million in 15 years.[2] This option was set to expire in six months.

Some senior Victoria Chemicals executives firmly believed that if the Rotterdam project were not undertaken, the option on the right-of-way should be allowed to expire unexercised. The reasoning was summarized by Jeffrey Palliser, chairman of the executive committee:

> Our business is chemicals, not land speculation. Simply buying the right-of-way with the intention of reselling it for a profit takes us beyond our expertise. Who knows when we could sell it, and for how much? How distracting would this little side venture be for Elizabeth Eustace?

Younger members of senior management were more willing to consider a potential investment arbitrage on the right-of-way.

Eustace expected to realize the benefit of this investment (i.e., a 7% increase in output) gradually over time, as the new technology was installed and shaken down and as the learning-curve effects were realized. She advocated a phased-investment program (as opposed to all at once) in order to minimize disruption to plant operations and to allow the new technology to be calibrated and fine-tuned. Admittedly, there was a chance that the technology would not work as well as hoped, but due to the complexity of the technology and the extent to which it would permeate the plant, there would be no going back once the decision had been made to install the new controls. Yet it was possible that the technology could deliver more efficiencies than estimated in the cash flows, if the controls reached the potential boasted by the Japanese engineering team.

Fawn recalled that the strategic factors to which Eustace referred had to do with the obvious cost and output improvements expected from the new system, as well as from the advantage of being the first major European producer to implement the new technology. Being the first to implement the technology probably meant a head start

---

[2] The right-of-way had several commercial uses. Most prominently, the Dutch government had expressed an interest in using the right-of-way for a new high-speed railroad line. The planning for this line had barely begun, however, which suggested that land-acquisition efforts were years away. Moreover, government budget deficits threatened the timely implementation of the rail project. Another potential user was Medusa Communications, an international telecom company that was looking for pathways along which to bury its new optical-fiber cables. Power companies and other chemical companies or refineries might also be interested in acquiring the right-of-way.

in moving down the learning curve toward reducing costs as the organization became familiar with the technology. Eustace argued:

> The Japanese, and now the Americans, exploit the learning-curve phenomenon aggressively. Fortunately, they aren't major players in European polypropylene, at least for now. This is a once-in-a-generation opportunity for Victoria Chemicals to leapfrog its competition through the exploitation of new technology.

In an oblique reference to the Merseyside proposal, Eustace went on to say:

> There are two alternatives to implementation of the analog process-control technology. One is a series of myopic enhancements to existing facilities, but this is nothing more than sticking one's head in the sand, for it leaves us at the mercy of our competitors who *are* making choices for the long term. The other alternative is to exit the polypropylene business, but this amounts to walking away from the considerable know-how we've accumulated in this business and from what is basically a valuable activity. Our commitment to analog controls makes it the right choice at the right time.

Fawn wondered how to take the technology into account in making his decision. Even if he recommended the Merseyside project over the Rotterdam project, it would still be possible to add the new controls to Merseyside at some point in the future. Practically speaking, Fawn believed the controls could be added in 2010, which would allow sufficient time to complete all the proposed capital improvements before embarking on the new undertaking. As with the Rotterdam project, it was expected that the controls would raise Merseyside's margin by 0.5% a year, to a maximum of 15%. The controls would not result in an incremental volume gain, however, as Merseyside would already be operating at its capacity of 267,500 tons. To obtain a supply of propylene gas at Merseyside, it would be necessary to enter into a 15-year contract with a local supplier. Although the contract would cost GBP0.4 million a year, it would obviate the need to build the proposed pipeline for Rotterdam, resulting in an investment at Merseyside of GBP7.0 million spread over three years.[3]

Lucy Morris, the plant manager at Merseyside, told James Fawn that she preferred to "wait and see" before entertaining a technology upgrade at her plant because there was considerable uncertainty in her mind as to how valuable, if at all, the analog technology would prove to be. Fawn agreed that the Japanese technology had not been tested with much of the machinery that was currently being used at Rotterdam and Merseyside. Moreover, he knew that reported efficiency gains had varied substantially across the early adopters.[4]

---

[3] If the Merseyside project were to begin two years later, the cost of the contract and the investment costs were expected to rise by the rate of inflation. Gas contracts were quoted in terms of the first-year cost but carried an inflation clause that raised the cost for each subsequent year by the inflation rate.

[4] Using Monte Carlo simulation, Morris had estimated that the cash returns from the Japanese technology had a standard deviation of 35%. The nominal risk-free rate of return was about 5.5%.

Conclusion

Fawn wanted to give this choice careful thought because the plant managers at Merseyside and Rotterdam seemed to have so much invested in their own proposals. He wished that the capital-budgeting criteria would give a straightforward indication of the relative attractiveness of the two mutually exclusive projects. He wondered by what rational analytical process he could extricate himself from the ambiguities of the present measures of investment attractiveness. Moreover, he wished he had a way to evaluate the primary technological difference between the two proposals: (1) the Rotterdam project, which firmly committed Victoria Chemicals to the new-process technology, or (2) the Merseyside project, which retained the flexibility to add the technology in the future.

EXHIBIT 1 | Analysis of Rotterdam Project (financial values in GBP millions)

Assumptions

Annual Output (metric tons)	250,000	Discount rate	10.0%
Output Gain Per Year/Prior Year	2.0%	Depreciable Life (years)	15
Maximum Possible Output	267,500	Overhead/Investment	0.0%
Price/ton (pounds sterling)	675	Salvage Value	0
Inflation (prices and costs)	0.0%	WIP Inventory/Cost of Goods Sold	3.0%
Gross Margin Growth Rate/Year	0.50%	Terminal Value of Right-of-way	40
Maximum Possible Gross Margin	15.0%	Months Downtime, Construction	
Gross Margin	11.5%	2008	5
Tax Rate	30.0%	2009	4
Investment Outlay (millions) Now	3.5	2010	3
2008	5	2011	0
2009	1		
2010	1		

Year	0	1	2	3	4	5	6	7	8	9	10	11	12	13	14	15
	Now	2008	2009	2010	2011	2012	2013	2014	2015	2016	2017	2018	2019	2020	2021	2022
1. Estimate of Incremental Gross Profit																
New Output		255,000	260,100	265,302	267,500	267,500	267,500	267,500	267,500	267,500	267,500	267,500	267,500	267,500	267,500	267,500
Lost Output—Construction		(106,250)	(86,700)	(66,326)												
New Sales (Millions)		100.41	117.05	134.31	180.56	180.56	180.56	180.56	180.56	180.56	180.56	180.56	180.56	180.56	180.56	180.56
New Gross Margin		11.5%	12.0%	12.5%	13.0%	13.5%	14.0%	14.5%	15.0%	15.0%	15.0%	15.0%	15.0%	15.0%	15.0%	15.0%
New Gross Profit		11.55	14.05	16.79	23.47	24.38	25.28	26.18	27.08	27.08	27.08	27.08	27.08	27.08	27.08	27.08
Old Output		250,000	250,000	250,000	250,000	250,000	250,000	250,000	250,000	250,000	250,000	250,000	250,000	250,000	250,000	250,000
Old Sales		168.75	168.75	168.75	168.75	168.75	168.75	168.75	168.75	168.75	168.75	168.75	168.75	168.75	168.75	168.75
Old Gross Profit		19.41	19.41	19.41	19.41	19.41	19.41	19.41	19.41	19.41	19.41	19.41	19.41	19.41	19.41	19.41
Incremental Gross Profit		(7.86)	(5.36)	(2.62)	4.07	4.97	5.87	6.78	7.68	7.68	7.68	7.68	7.68	7.68	7.68	7.68
2. Estimate of Incremental Depreciation																
Yr. 1 Outlays	0.67	0.58	0.50	0.43	0.38	0.33	0.28	0.24	0.23	0.23	0.23	0.23	0.23	0.23	0.23	
Yr. 2 Outlays		0.14	0.12	0.10	0.09	0.08	0.07	0.06	0.06	0.05	0.05	0.05	0.05	0.05	0.05	
Yr. 3 Outlays			0.15	0.13	0.11	0.09	0.08	0.07	0.06	0.05	0.05	0.05	0.05	0.05	0.05	
Total, New Depreciation	0.67	0.72	0.78	0.78	0.67	0.58	0.50	0.43	0.37	0.33	0.33	0.33	0.33	0.33	0.33	0.33
3. Overhead	0	0	0	0	0	0	0	0	0	0	0	0	0	0	0	0
4. Pretax Incremental Profit		(8.53)	(6.08)	(3.39)	3.40	4.39	5.38	6.35	7.31	7.35	7.35	7.35	7.35	7.35	7.35	7.35
5. Tax Expense		(2.56)	(1.82)	(1.02)	1.02	1.32	1.61	1.90	2.19	2.20	2.21	2.21	2.21	2.21	2.21	2.21
6. After-tax Profit		(5.97)	(4.26)	(2.38)	2.38	3.08	3.76	4.44	5.12	5.14	5.15	5.15	5.15	5.15	5.15	5.15
7. Cash Flow Adjustments																
Add back Depreciation	0.67	0.72	0.78	0.78	0.67	0.58	0.50	0.43	0.37	0.33	0.33	0.33	0.33	0.33	0.33	0.33
Less added WIP inventory		1.81	(0.42)	(0.44)	(1.19)	0.03	0.03	0.03	0.03	—	—	—	—	—	—	0.12
Less Capital Spending	(3.50)	(5.00)	(1.00)	(1.00)	—	—	—	—	—	—	—	—	—	—	—	—
Terminal Value, land																40.00
8. Free Cash Flow	(3.50)	(8.49)	(4.96)	(3.03)	1.86	3.68	4.29	4.90	5.51	5.47	5.47	5.47	5.47	5.47	5.47	45.60

DCF, Rotterdam = 15.50
IRR, Rotterdam = 18.0%

Year	0 Now	1 2001	2 2002	3 2003	4 2004	5 2005	6 2006	7 2007	8 2008	9 2009	10 2010	11 2011	12 2012	13 2013	14 2014	15 2015
9. Adjustment for erosion in Merseyside volume:																
Lost Merseyside Output		—	—	—	17,500	17,500	17,500	17,500	17,500	17,500	17,500	17,500	17,500	17,500	17,500	17,500
Lost Merseyside Revenue		—	—	—	11.81	11.81	11.81	11.81	11.81	11.81	11.81	11.81	11.81	11.81	11.81	11.81
Lost Merseyside Gross Profits		—	—	—	1.36	1.36	1.36	1.36	1.36	1.36	1.36	1.36	1.36	1.36	1.36	1.36
Lost Gross Profits after Taxes		—	—	—	0.95	0.95	0.95	0.95	0.95	0.95	0.95	0.95	0.95	0.95	0.95	0.95
Change in Merseyside Inventory		—	—	—	0.35	0.35	0.35	0.35	0.35	0.35	0.35	0.35	0.35	0.35	0.35	0.35
Total Effect on Free Cash Flow		—	—	—	(0.60)	(0.60)	(0.60)	(0.60)	(0.60)	(0.60)	(0.60)	(0.60)	(0.60)	(0.60)	(0.60)	(0.60)
DCF, Erosion Merseyside	3.05															
Cash flows after erosion	(3.50)	(8.49)	(4.96)	(3.03)	1.26	3.08	3.69	4.30	4.92	4.88	4.88	4.88	4.88	4.88	4.88	45.00
DCF, Rotterdam Adjusted for Full Erosion at Merseyside =	**12.45**															
IRR	16.5%															

Star River 星河 Electronics Ltd.

On July 5, 2001, her first day as CEO of Star River Electronics Ltd., Adeline Koh confronted a host of management problems. One week earlier, Star River's president and CEO had suddenly resigned to accept a CEO position with another firm. Koh had been appointed to fill the position—starting immediately. Several items in her in-box that first day were financial in nature, either requiring a financial decision or with outcomes that would have major financial implications for the firm. That evening, Koh asked to meet with her assistant, Andy Chin, to begin addressing the most prominent issues.

Star River Electronics and the Optical-Disc-Manufacturing Industry

Star River Electronics had been founded as a joint venture between Starlight Electronics Ltd., United Kingdom, and an Asian venture-capital firm, New Era Partners. Based in Singapore, Star River had a single business mission: to manufacture CD-ROMs as a supplier to major software companies. In no time, Star River gained fame in the industry for producing high-quality discs.

The popularity of optical and multimedia products created rapid growth for CD-ROM manufacturers in the mid-1990s. Accordingly, small manufacturers proliferated, creating an oversupply that pushed prices down by as much as 40%. Consolidation followed as less efficient producers began to feel the pinch.

Star River Electronics survived the shakeout, thanks to its sterling reputation. While other CD-ROM manufacturers floundered, volume sales at the company had grown at a robust rate in the past two years. Unit prices, however, had declined because of price competition and the growing popularity of substitute storage devices, particularly digital video discs (DVDs). The latter had 14 times more storage capacity and threatened to displace CD-ROMs. Although CD-ROM *disc drives* composed 93% of

---

This case is derived from materials originally prepared by Robert F. Bruner, Dean and Charles C. Abbott Professor of Business Administration, Robert Conroy, Paul M. Hammaker Research Professor of Business Administration, and Kenneth Eades, Professor of Business Administration. The firms and individuals in the case are fictitious. The financial support of the Batten Institute is gratefully acknowledged. It was written as a basis for class discussion rather than to illustrate effective or ineffective handling of an administrative situation. Copyright © 2001 by the University of Virginia Darden School Foundation, Charlottesville, VA. All rights reserved. *To order copies, send an e-mail to* sales@dardenbusinesspublishing.com. *No part of this publication may be reproduced, stored in a retrieval system, used in a spreadsheet, or transmitted in any form or by any means—electronic, mechanical, photocopying, recording, or otherwise—without the permission of the Darden School Foundation.* Rev. 12/05.

all optical-disc-drive shipments in 1999, a study predicted that this number would fall to 41% by 2005, while the share of DVD drives would rise to 59%.[1] Star River had begun to experiment with DVD manufacturing, but DVDs still accounted for less than 5% of its sales at fiscal year-end 2001. With newly installed capacity, however, the company hoped to increase the proportion of revenue from DVDs.

Financial Questions Facing Adeline Koh

That evening, Koh met with Andy Chin, a promising new associate whom she had brought along from New Era Partners. Koh's brief discussion with Chin went as follows:

KOH: Back at New Era, we looked at Star River as one of our most promising venture-capital investments. Now it seems that such optimism may not be warranted—at least until we get a solid understanding of the firm's past perform-ance and its forecast performance. Did you have any success on this?

CHIN: Yes, the bookkeeper gave me these: the historical income statements [**Exhibit 1**] and balance sheets [**Exhibit 2**] for the last four years. The accounting system here is still pretty primitive. However, I checked a number of the accounts, and they look orderly. So I suspect that we can work with these figures. From these statements, I calculated a set of diagnostic ratios [**Exhibit 3**].

KOH: I see you have been busy. Unfortunately, I can't study these right now. I need you to review the historical performance of Star River for me, and to give me any positive or negative insights that you think are significant.

CHIN: When do you need this?

KOH: At 7:00 a.m. tomorrow. I want to call on our banker tomorrow morning and get an extension on Star River's loan.

CHIN: The banker, Mr. Tan, said that Star River was "growing beyond its financial capabilities." What does that mean?

KOH: It probably means that he doesn't think we can repay the loan within a reasonable period. I would like you to build a simple financial forecast of our performance for the next two years (ignore seasonal effects), and show me what our debt requirements will be at the fiscal years ending 2002 and 2003. I think it is reasonable to expect that Star River's sales will grow at 15% each year. Also, you should assume capital expenditures of SGD54.6 million[2] for DVD manufacturing equipment, spread out over the next two years and depreciated over seven years. Use whatever other assumptions seem appropriate to you, based on your historical analysis of results. For this forecast, you should assume that any external funding is in the form of debt.

CHIN: But what if the forecasts show that Star River cannot repay the loan?

---

[1]Global Industry Analysts, Inc., "TEAC—Facts, Figures and Forecasts," 5.

[2]SGD = Singaporean dollars.

KOH: Then we'll have to go back to Star River's owners, New Era Partners and Star River Electronics United Kingdom, for an injection of equity. Of course, New Era Partners would rather not invest more funds unless we can show that the returns on such an investment would be very attractive and/or that the survival of the company depends on it. Thus, my third request is for you to examine what returns on book assets and book equity Star River will offer in the next two years and to identify the "key-driver" assumptions of those returns. Finally, let me have your recommendations about operating and financial changes I should make based on the historical analysis and the forecasts.

CHIN: The plant manager revised his request for a new packaging machine and thinks these are the right numbers [see the plant manager's memorandum in **Exhibit 4**]. Essentially, the issue is whether to invest now or wait three years to buy the new packaging equipment. The new equipment can save significantly on labor costs but carries a price tag of SGD1.82 million. My hunch is that our preference between investing now versus waiting three years will hinge on the discount rate.

KOH: [laughing] The joke in business school was that the discount rate was always 10%.

CHIN: That's not what my business school taught me! New Era always uses a 40% discount rate to value equity investments in risky start-up companies. But Star River is reasonably well established now and shouldn't require such a high-risk premium. I managed to pull together some data on other Singaporean electronics companies with which to estimate the required rate of return on equity [see **Exhibit 5**].

KOH: Fine. Please estimate Star River's weighted average cost of capital and assess the packaging-machine investment. I would like the results of your analysis tomorrow morning at 7:00.

EXHIBIT 1 | Historical Income Statements for Fiscal Year Ended June 30 (SGD 000)

	1998	1999	2000	2001
Sales	71,924	80,115	92,613	106,042
Operating expenses:				
Production costs and expenses	33,703	38,393	46,492	53,445
Admin. and selling expenses	16,733	17,787	21,301	24,177
Depreciation	8,076	9,028	10,392	11,360
Total operating expenses	58,512	65,208	78,185	88,983
Operating profit	13,412	14,908	14,429	17,059
Interest expense	5,464	6,010	7,938	7,818
Earnings before taxes	7,949	8,897	6,491	9,241
Income taxes*	2,221	2,322	1,601	2,093
Net earnings	5,728	6,576	4,889	7,148
Dividends to all common shares	2,000	2,000	2,000	2,000
Retentions of earnings	3,728	4,576	2,889	5,148

*The expected corporate tax rate was 24.5%.

EXHIBIT 2 | Historical Balance Sheets for Fiscal Year Ended June 30
(SGD 000)

	1998	1999	2000	2001
Assets:				
Cash	4,816	5,670	6,090	5,795
Accounts receivable	22,148	25,364	28,078	35,486
Inventories	23,301	27,662	53,828	63,778
Total current assets	50,265	58,697	87,996	105,059
Gross property, plant & equipment	64,611	80,153	97,899	115,153
Accumulated depreciation	(4,559)	(13,587)	(23,979)	(35,339)
Net property, plant & equipment	60,052	66,566	73,920	79,814
Total assets	110,317	125,262	161,916	184,873
Liabilities and Stockholders' Equity:				
Short-term borrowings (bank)[1]	29,002	37,160	73,089	84,981
Accounts payable	12,315	12,806	11,890	13,370
Other accrued liabilities	24,608	26,330	25,081	21,318
Total current liabilities	65,926	76,296	110,060	119,669
Long-term debt[2]	10,000	10,000	10,000	18,200
Shareholders' equity	34,391	38,967	41,856	47,004
Total liabilities and stockholders' equity	110,317	125,263	161,916	184,873

[1]Short-term debt was borrowed from City Bank at an interest rate equal to Singaporean prime lending rates + 1.5%. Current prime lending rates were 5.2%. The benchmark 10-year Singapore treasury bond currently yielded 3.6%.

[2]Two components made up the company's long term debt. One was a SGD10 million loan that had been issued privately in 1996 to New Era Partners and to Star River Electronics Ltd., U.K. This debt was subordinate to any bank debt outstanding. The second component was a SGD8.2 million from a 5-year bond issued on a private placement basis last July 1, 2000, at a price of SGD97 and a coupon of 5.75% paid semiannually.

EXHIBIT 3 | Ratio Analyses of Historical Financial Statements

	1998	1999	2000	2001
Profitability				
Operating margin (%)	18.6%	18.6%	15.6%	16.1%
Tax rate (%)	27.9%	26.1%	24.7%	22.6%
Return on sales (%)	8.0%	8.2%	5.3%	6.7%
Return on equity (%)	16.7%	16.9%	11.7%	15.2%
Return on assets (%)	5.2%	5.2%	3.0%	3.9%
Leverage				
Debt/equity ratio	1.13	1.21	1.99	2.20
Debt/total capital (%)	0.53	0.55	0.67	0.69
EBIT/interest (x)	2.45	2.48	1.82	2.18
Asset Utilization				
Sales/assets	65.2%	64.0%	57.2%	57.4%
Sales growth rate (%)	15.0%	11.4%	15.6%	14.5%
Assets growth rate (%)	8.0%	13.5%	29.3%	14.2%
Days in receivables	112.4	115.6	110.7	122.1
Payables to COGS	36.5%	33.4%	25.6%	25.0%
Inventories to COGS	69.1%	72.1%	115.8%	119.3%
Liquidity				
Current ratio	0.76	0.77	0.80	0.88
Quick ratio	0.41	0.41	0.31	0.34

EXHIBIT 4 | Lim's Memo Regarding New Packaging Equipment

MEMORANDUM

TO: Adeline Koh, President and CEO, Star River Electronics
FROM: Esmond Lim, Plant Manager
DATE: June 30, 2001
SUBJECT: New Packaging Equipment

Although our CD packaging equipment is adequate at current production levels, it is terribly inefficient. The new machinery on the market can give us significant labor savings as well as increased flexibility with respect to the type of packaging used. I recommend that we go with the new technology. Should we decide to do so, the new machine can be acquired immediately. The considerations relevant to the decision are included in this memo.

Our current packaging equipment was purchased five years ago as used equipment in a liquidation sale of a small company. Although the equipment was inexpensive, it is slow, requires constant monitoring and is frequently shut down for repairs. Since the packaging equipment is significantly slower than the production equipment, we routinely have to use overtime labor to allow packaging to catch up with production. When the packager is down for repairs, the problem is exacerbated and we may spend several two-shift days catching up with production. I cannot say that we have missed any deadlines because of packaging problems, but it is a constant concern around here and things would run a lot smoother with more reliable equipment. In 2002, we will pay about SGD15,470 per year for maintenance costs. The operator is paid SGD63,700 per year for his regular time, but he has been averaging SGD81,900 per year because of the overtime he has been working. The equipment is on the tax and reporting books at SGD218,400 and will be fully depreciated in three years' time (we are currently using the straight-line depreciation method for both tax and reporting purposes and will continue to do so). Because of changes in packaging technology, the equipment has no market value other than its worth as scrap metal. But its scrap value is about equal to the cost of having it removed. In short, we believe the equipment has no salvage value at all.

The new packager offers many advantages over the current equipment. It is faster, more reliable, more flexible with respect to the types of packaging it can perform, and will provide enough capacity to cover all our packaging needs in the foreseeable future. With suitable maintenance, we believe the packager will operate indefinitely. Thus, for the purposes of our analysis, we can assume that this will be the last packaging equipment we will ever have to purchase. Because of the anticipated growth at Star River, the current equipment will not be able to handle our packaging needs by the end of 2004. Thus, if we do not buy new packaging equipment by this year's end, we will have to buy it after three years' time anyway. Since the speed, capacity, and reliability of the new equipment will eliminate the need for overtime labor, we feel strongly that we should buy now rather than wait another three years.

The new equipment currently costs SGD1.82 million, which we would depreciate over 10 years at SGD182,000 per year. It comes with a lifetime factory maintenance contract that covers all routine maintenance and repairs at a price of SGD3,640 for the initial year. The contract stipulates that the price after the first year will be increased by the same percentage as the rate of increase of the price of new equipment. Thus if the manufacturer continues to increase the price of new packaging equipment at 5% per annum as it has in the past, our maintenance costs will rise by 5% also. We believe that this sort of regular maintenance should insure that the new equipment will keep operating in the foreseeable future without the need for a major overhaul.

Star River's labor and maintenance costs will continue to rise due to inflation at approximately 1.5% per year over the long term. Because the manufacturer of the packaging equipment has been increasing its prices at about 5% per year, we can expect to save SGD286,878 in the purchase price by buying now rather than waiting three years. The marginal tax rate for this investment would be 24.5%.

EXHIBIT 5 | Data on Comparable Companies and Capital-Market Conditions

Name	% of Sales from CD-ROM and/or DVD Production	Price/ Earnings Ratio	Beta	Book D/E	Book Value per Share	Market Price per Share	Number of Shares Outstanding (millions)	Last Annual Dividend	5-Year Earnings Growth Forecast
Sing Studios, Inc.	20%	9.0	1.07	0.23	1.24	1.37	9.3	1.82	4.0%
Wintronics, Inc.	95%	NMF	1.56	1.70	1.46	6.39	177.2	0.15	15.7%
STOR-Max Corp.	90%	18.2	1.67	1.30	7.06	27.48	89.3	none	21.3%
Digital Media Corp.	30%	34.6	1.18	0.00	17.75	75.22	48.3	none	38.2%
Wymax, Inc.	60%	NMF	1.52	0.40	6.95	22.19	371.2	1.57	11.3%

Note: NMF means not a meaningful figure. This arises when a company's earnings or projected earnings are negative.

Singapore's equity market risk premium could be assumed to be close to the global equity market premium of 6%, given Singapore's high rate of integration into global markets.

Descriptions of Companies

Sing Studios, Inc.
This company was founded 50 years ago. Its major business activities historically had been production of original-artist recordings, management and production of rock-and-roll road tours, and personal management of artists. It entered the CD-production market in the 1980s, and only recently branched out into the manufacture of CD-ROMs. Most of its business, however, related to the manufacture and sale of MIDI (Music Instrument Digital Interface) CDs.

Wintronics, Inc.
This company was a spin-off from a large technology-holding corporation in 1981. Although the company was a leader in the production of CD-ROMs and DVDs, it has recently suffered a decline in sales. Infighting among the principal owners has fed concerns about the firm's prospects.

STOR-Max Corp.
This company, founded only two years ago, had emerged as a very aggressive competitor in the area of CD-ROM and DVD production. It was Star River's major competitor and its sales level was about the same.

Digital Media Corp.
This company had recently been an innovator in the production of DVDs. Although DVD manufacturing was not a majority of its business (film production and digital animation were its main focus), the company was projected to be a major competitor within the next three years.

Wymax, Inc.
This company was an early pioneer in the CD-ROM and DVD industries. Recently, however, it had begun to invest in software programming and had been moving away from disc production as its main focus of business.

The Jacobs Division 2010

Richard Soderberg, financial analyst for the Jacobs Division of MacFadden Chemical Company, was reviewing several complex issues related to possible investment in a new product for the following year, 2011. The product was a specialty coating material, which qualified for investment according to company guidelines. But Mark Reynolds, the Jacobs Division manager, was fearful that it might be too risky. While regarding the project as an attractive opportunity, Soderberg believed that the only practical way to sell the product in the short run would place it in a weak competitive position over the long run. He was also concerned that the estimates used in the probability analysis were little better than educated guesses.

Company Background

MacFadden Chemical Company was one of the larger chemical firms in the world whose annual sales were in excess of $10 billion. Its volume had grown steadily at the rate of 10% per year throughout the 1980s until 1993; sales and earnings had grown more rapidly. Beginning in 1993, the chemical industry began to experience overcapacity, particularly in basic materials, which led to price cutting. Also, for firms to remain competitive, more funds had to be spent in marketing and research. As a consequence of the industry problems, MacFadden achieved only modest growth of 4% in sales in the 1990s and experienced an overall decline in profits. Certain shortages began developing in the economy in 2002, however, and by 2009, sales had risen 60% and profits over 100%, as a result of price increases and near-capacity operations. Most observers believed that the "shortage boom" would be only a short respite from the intensely competitive conditions of the last decade.

The 11 operating divisions of MacFadden were organized into three groups. Most divisions had a number of products centered on one chemical, such as fluoride, sulfur, or petroleum. The Jacobs Division was an exception.

It was the newest and—with sales of $100 million—the smallest division. Its products were specialty industrial products with various chemical bases, such as dyes,

This revised and updated case, based on "The Jacobs Division" by Professors Diana Harrington and Robert Vandell, was prepared by Professor Robert M. Conroy. It was written as a basis for class discussion rather than to illustrate effective or ineffective handling of an administrative situation. Copyright © 2003 by the University of Virginia Darden School Foundation, Charlottesville, VA. All rights reserved. *To order copies, send an e-mail to* sales@dardenbusinesspublishing.com. *No part of this publication may be reproduced, stored in a retrieval system, used in a spreadsheet, or transmitted in any form or by any means—electronic, mechanical, photocopying, recording, or otherwise—without the permission of the Darden School Foundation.*

adhesives, and finishes, which were sold in relatively small lots to diverse industrial customers. No single product had sales over $5 million, and many had sales of only $500,000. There were 150 basic products in the division, each of which had several minor variations. Jacobs was one of MacFadden's more rapidly growing divisions—12% per year prior to 2009—with a 13% return on total net assets.

Capital Budgeting for New Projects

Corporate-wide guidelines were used for analyzing new investment opportunities. In the current environment, the long-term, risk-free rate was about 6%. At the firm level, the return criteria were 8% for cost-reduction projects, 12% for expansion of facilities, and 16% for new products or processes. Returns were measured in terms of discounted cash flows after taxes. Soderberg believed that these rates and methods were typical of those used throughout the chemical industry.

Reynolds tended, however, to demand higher returns for projects in his division, even though its earnings–growth stability in the past marked it as one of MacFadden's more reliable operations. Reynolds had three reasons for wanting better returns than corporate required. First, one of the key variables used in appraising management performance and compensation at MacFadden was the growth of residual income, although such aspects as market share and profit margins were also considered.[1] Reynolds did not like the idea of investing in projects that were close to the target rate of earnings embedded in the residual-income calculation.

Second, many new projects had high start-up costs. Even though they might achieve attractive returns over the long run, such projects hurt earnings performance in the short run. "Don't tell me what a project's discount rate of return is. Tell me whether we're going to improve our return on total net assets within three years," Reynolds would say. Third, Reynolds was skeptical of estimates. "I don't know what's going to happen here on this project, but I'll bet we overstate returns by 2% to 5%, on average," was a typical comment. He therefore tended to look for at least 4% more than the company standard before becoming enthusiastic about a project. "You've got to be hard-nosed about taking risk," he said. "By demanding a decent return for riskier opportunities, we have a better chance to grow and prosper."

Soderberg knew that Reynolds's views were reflected in decisions throughout the division. Projects that did not have promising returns, according to Reynolds's standards, were often dropped or shelved early in the decision process. Soderberg guessed that, at Jacobs Division, almost as many projects with returns meeting the company hurdle rates were abandoned as were ultimately approved. In fact, the projects that were finally submitted to Reynolds were usually so promising that he rarely rejected them. Capital projects from his division were accepted virtually unchanged, unless top management happened to be unusually pessimistic about prospects for business and financing in general.

---

[1] Residual income was the division's profit after allocated taxes minus a 10% capital charge on total assets after depreciation.

The Silicone-X Project

A new product was often under study for several years after research had developed a "test-tube" idea. The product had to be evaluated relative to market needs and competition. The large number of possible applications of any product complicated this analysis. At the same time, technological studies were undertaken to examine such factors as material sources, plant location, manufacturing-process alternatives, and economies of scale. While a myriad of feasible alternatives existed, only a few could be actively explored, and they often required outlays of several hundred thousand dollars before the potential of the project could be ascertained. "For every dollar of new capital approved, I bet we spend $0.30 on the opportunities," said Soderberg, "and that doesn't count the money we spend on research."

The project that concerned Soderberg at the moment was called Silicone-X, a special-purpose coating that added slipperiness to a surface. The coating could be used on a variety of products to reduce friction, particularly where other lubricants might imperfectly eliminate friction between moving parts. Its uniqueness lay in its hardness, adhesiveness to the applied surface, and durability. The product was likely to have a large number of buyers, but most of them could use only small quantities: Only a few firms were likely to buy amounts greater than 5,000 pounds per year.

Test-tube batches of Silicone-X had been tested both inside and outside the Jacobs Division. Comments were universally favorable, although $2.00 per pound seemed to be the maximum price that would be acceptable. Lower prices were considered unlikely to produce larger volume. For planning purposes, a price of $1.90 per pound had been used.

Demand was difficult to estimate because of the variety of possible applications. The division's market research group had estimated a first-year demand of 1 to 2 million pounds with 1.2 million pounds was cited as most likely. Soderberg said:

> They could spend another year studying it and be more confident, but we wouldn't find
> them more believable. The estimates are educated guesses by smart people. But they are
> also pretty wild stabs in the dark. They won't rule out the possibility of demand as low as
> 500,000 pounds, and 2 million pounds is not the ceiling.

Soderberg empathized with the problem facing the market-research group. "They tried to do a systematic job of looking at the most probable applications, but the data were not good." The market researchers believed that, once the product became established, average demand would probably grow at a healthy rate, perhaps 10% per year. But the industries served were likely to be cyclical with volume requirements swinging 20% depending on market conditions. The market researchers concluded, "We think demand should level off after 8 to 10 years, but the odds are very much against someone developing a cheaper or markedly superior substitute."

On the other hand, there was no patent protection on Silicone-X, and the technological know-how involved in the manufacturing process could be duplicated by others in perhaps as little as 12 months. "This product is essentially a commodity, and someone is certainly going to get interested in it when sales volume reaches $3 million," said Soderberg.

The cost estimates looked solid. Soderberg continued, "Basic chemicals, of course, fluctuate in purchase price, but we have a captive source with stable manufacturing costs. We can probably negotiate a long-term transfer price with Wilson [another MacFadden division], although this is not the time to do so."

Project Analysis

In his preliminary analysis, Soderberg used a discount rate of 20% and a project life of 15 years, because most equipment for the project was likely to wear out and need replacement during that time frame. He said:

> We also work with most likely estimates. Until we get down to the bitter end, there are too many alternatives to consider, and we can't afford probabilistic measures or fancy simulations. A conservative definition of most likely values is good enough for most of the subsidiary analyses. We've probably made over 200 present value calculations using our computer programs just to get to this decision point, and heaven knows how many quick-and-dirty paybacks.
>
> We've made a raft of important decisions that affect the attractiveness of this project. Some of them are bound to be wrong. I hope not critically so. In any case, these decisions are behind us. They're buried so deep in the assumptions, no one can find them, and top management wouldn't have time to look at them anyway.

With Silicone-X, Soderberg was down to a labor-intensive, limited-capacity approach and a capital-intensive method. "The analyses all point in one direction," he said, "but I have the feeling it's going to be the worst one for the long run."

The labor-intensive method involved an initial plant and equipment outlay of $900,000. It could produce 1.5 million pounds per year.

According to Soderberg:

> Even if the project bombs out, we won't lose much. The equipment is very adaptable. We could probably sell the equipment for $381,000 net of taxes. We should salvage the working-capital part without any trouble. The start-up costs and losses are our real risks. We'll spend $50,000 debugging the process, and we'll be lucky to satisfy half the possible demand. But I believe we can get this project on stream in one year's time.

Exhibit 1 shows Soderberg's analysis of the labor-intensive alternative. His calculations showed a small net present value when discounted at 20% and a sizable net present value at 8%. When the positive present values were compared with the negative present values, the project looked particularly attractive.

The capital-intensive method involved a much larger outlay for plant and equipment: $3.3 million. Manufacturing costs would, however, be reduced by $0.35 per unit and fixed costs by $100,000, excluding depreciation. The capital-intensive plant was designed to handle 2.0 million pounds, the lowest volume for which appropriate equipment could be acquired. Since the equipment was more specialized, the after-tax salvage value is $1.384 million. It would take two years to get the plant on line, and the first year's operating volume was likely to be low—perhaps 700,000 pounds at the most. Debugging costs were estimated to be $100,000.

Exhibit 2 presents Soderberg's analysis of the capital-intensive method. At a 20% discount rate, the capital-intensive project had a large negative present value and thus appeared much worse than the labor-intensive alternative. But at an 8% discount rate, it looked significantly better than the labor-intensive alternative.

Problems in the Analysis

Several things concerned Soderberg about the analysis. Reynolds would only look at the total return. Thus, the capital-intensive project would not be acceptable. Yet, on the basis of the breakeven analysis, the capital-intensive alternative seemed the safest way to start. It needed sales of just 369,333 pounds to break even, while the labor-intensive method required 540,000 pounds (**Exhibit 3**).

Soderberg was concerned that future competition might result in price-cutting. If the price per pound fell by $0.20, the labor-intensive method would not break even unless 900,000 pounds were sold. Competitors could, once the market was established, build a capital-intensive plant that would put them in a good position to cut prices by $0.20 or more. In short, there was a risk, given the labor-intensive solution, that Silicone-X might not remain competitive. The better the demand proved to be, the more serious this risk would become. Of course, once the market was established, Jacobs could build a capital-intensive facility, but almost none of the labor-intensive equipment would be useful in such a new plant. The new plant would still cost $3.3 million, and Jacobs would have to write off losses on the labor-intensive facility.

The labor-intensive facility would be difficult to expand economically. It would cost $125,000 for each 200,000 pounds of additional capacity. It was only practical in 200,000-pound increments). In contrast, an additional 100,000 pounds of capacity in the capital-intensive unit could be added for $75,000.

The need to expand, however, would depend on sales. If demand remained low, the project would probably return a higher rate under the labor-intensive method. If demand developed, the capital-intensive method would clearly be superior. This analysis led Soderberg to believe that his breakeven calculations were somehow wrong.

Pricing strategy was another important element in the analysis. At $1.90 per pound, Jacobs could be inviting competition. Competitors would be satisfied with a low rate of return, perhaps 12%, in an established market. At a price lower than $1.90, Jacobs might discourage competition. Even the labor-intensive alternative would not provide a rate of return of 20% at any lower price. It began to appear to Soderberg that using a high discount rate was forcing the company to make a riskier decision than would a lower rate; it was also increasing the chance of realizing a lower rate of return than had been forecast.

Soderberg was not sure how to incorporate pricing into his analysis. He knew he could determine what level of demand would be necessary to encourage a competitor, expecting a 50% share and needing a 12% return on a capital-intensive investment, to enter the market at a price of $1.70, or $1.90, but this analysis did not seem to be enough.

Finally, Soderberg was concerned about the volatility of demand estimates on which he had based the analysis. He reviewed some analysts' reports and found some information on firms that were in businesses similar to Silicone-X. Based on those firms' stock market returns he estimated that the volatility of returns for this line of business was around 0.35.

Soderberg's job was to analyze the alternatives fully and to recommend one of them to Reynolds. On the simplest analysis, the labor-intensive approach seemed best. Even at 20%, its present value was positive. That analysis, however, did not take other factors into consideration.

EXHIBIT 1 | Analysis of Labor-Intensive Alternative for Silicone-X
(dollars in thousands, except per-unit data)

			Year			
	0	1	2	3	4	5–15
Investments						
Plant and equipment	$ 900					
Change in Net Working Capital		$ 140	$ 14	$ 15	$ 17	$ 20
Demand (thousands of pounds)		1,200	1,320	1,452	1,597	N.A.
Capacity (thousands of pounds)		600	1,500	1,500	1,500	1,500
Sales (thousands of pounds)		600	1,320	1,452	1,500	1,500
Sales price/unit		$1.90	$1.90	$1.90	$1.90	$1.90
Variable costs/unit						
Manufacturing		1.30	1.30	1.30	1.30	1.30
Marketing		0.10	0.10	0.10	0.10	0.10
Total variable costs/unit		1.40	1.40	1.40	1.40	1.40
Fixed costs						
Overhead		210	210	210	210	210
Depreciation		60	60	60	60	60
Start-up costs		50	0	0	0	0
Total fixed costs		320	270	270	270	270
Sales Revenue		$1,140	$2,508	$2,759	$2,850	$2,850
−Total Variable Costs		840	1,848	2,033	2,100	2,100
−Total Fixed Costs		320	270	270	270	270
Profit before taxes		(20)	390	456	480	480
−Taxes (tax rate = 50%)		10	(195)	(228)	(240)	(240)
Net Operating Profit after taxes		(10)	195	228	240	240
Cash flow from operations						
+Profit after taxes + depreciation		50	255	288	300	300
−Capital Expenditures	(900)	0	0	0	0	0
−Change in NWC		(140)	(14)	(15)	(17)	(20)
Free cash flow	$(900)	$ (90)	$ 241	$ 273	$ 283	280
Terminal value (year 15)						$ 381

N.A. = not available.

EXHIBIT 2 | Analysis of Capital-Intensive Alternative for Silicone-X
(dollars in thousands, except per-unit data)

					Year			
	0	1	2	3	4	5	6	7–15
Investments								
Plant and equipment	$ 1,900	$ 1,400						
Working capital			$ 160	$ 11	$ 17	$ 20	$ 24	$ 30
Demand (thousands of pounds)			1,320	1,452	1,597	1,757	1,933	2,125
Capacity (thousands of pounds)			700	2,000	2,000	2,000	2,000	2,000
Sales (thousands of pounds)			700	1,452	1,597	1,757	1,933	2,000
Sales price/unit			$1.90	$1.90	$1.90	$1.90	$1.90	$1.90
Variable costs/unit								
Manufacturing			1.05	1.05	1.05	1.05	1.05	1.05
Selling			0.10	0.10	0.10	0.10	0.10	0.10
Total variable costs/unit			1.15	1.15	1.15	1.15	1.15	1.15
Fixed costs								
Overhead			110	110	110	110	110	110
Depreciation			167	167	167	167	167	167
Start-up costs			100	0	0	0	0	0
Total fixed costs								
Sales Revenue			1,330	2,759	3,034	3,338	3,673	3,800
–Total Variable Costs			805	1,670	1,837	2,021	2,223	2,300
–Total Fixed Costs			377	277	277	277	277	277
Profit before taxes			148	812	921	1,041	1,173	1,223
–Taxes (50%)			(74)	(406)	(460)	(520)	(586)	(612)
Net Operating Profit after taxes (NOPAT)			74	406	460	520	586	612
Cash flow from operations								
(NOPAT + depreciation)			241	573	627	687	753	779
–Capital Expenditures	(1,900)	(1,400)	0	0	0	0	0	0
–Change in NWC			(160)	(11)	(17)	(20)	(24)	(30)
Free cash flow	$(1,900)	$(1,400)	$401	$584	$644	$707	$777	$809
Terminal value (year 15)								$1,384

EXHIBIT 3 | Breakeven Analysis for Silicone-X

	Labor-Intensive	Capital-Intensive
Fixed costs		
Operations	$210,000	$110,000
Depreciation	60,000	167,000
Total	$270,000	$277,000
Sales price per unit	$1.90	$1.90
Variable Cost per unit	$1.40	$1.15
Contribution per unit	$0.50	$0.75
Units to breakeven	540,000	369,333
Sales price per unit	$1.70	$1.70
Variable cost per unit	$1.40	$1.15
Contribution per unit	$0.30	$0.55
Units to breakeven	900,000	503,636

University of Virginia Health System: The Long-Term Acute Care Hospital Project

On the morning of March 2, 2006, Larry Fitzgerald knew he had to complete all the last-minute details for the board meeting the following day. Fitzgerald, the vice president for business development and finance for the University of Virginia Health System (U.Va. Health System), was eager to see the board's reaction to his proposal for a new long-term acute care (LTAC) hospital. His excitement was somewhat tempered that the board had rejected the LTAC hospital concept when Fitzgerald had first joined the U.Va. Health System in 1999. Since that time, however, the regulations regarding LTAC facilities had changed, which gave Fitzgerald reason to give the project another chance. The bottom line was that Fitzgerald thought that a LTAC hospital would improve patient care and, at the same time, bring more money into the U.Va. Health System.

As he looked at the memo on his desk from his analyst Karen Mulroney regarding the LTAC facility, Fitzgerald began to consider what guidance he could give her that would lead to the best possible proposal to present to the hospital's board of directors.

The U.Va. Health System

The University of Virginia (U.Va.) opened its first hospital in 1901, with a tripartite mission of service, education, and research. At its inception, the hospital had only 25 beds and 3 operating rooms, but by 2005, it had expanded to more than 570 beds and 24 operating rooms, with 28,000 admissions and 65,000 surgeries per year. This first hospital was the only Level 1 trauma center in the area and provided care for Charlottesville residents as well as patients from across the state of Virginia and the Southeast.[1]

---

[1]Trauma centers were designated Level 1, 2, or 3. Level 1 centers provided the highest level of surgical care to patients.

This case was prepared by Nili Mehta (MBA '12) and Kenneth Eades, the Paul Tudor Jones Research Professor of Business Administration. It was written as a basis for class discussion rather than to illustrate effective or ineffective handling of an administrative situation. Copyright © 2012 by the University of Virginia Darden School Foundation, Charlottesville, VA. All rights reserved. *To order copies, send an e-mail to* sales @dardenbusinesspublishing.com. *No part of this publication may be reproduced, stored in a retrieval system, used in a spreadsheet, or transmitted in any form or by any means—electronic, mechanical, photocopying, recording, or otherwise—without the permission of the Darden School Foundation.*

For each patient admitted, the hospital was reimbursed a predetermined amount by a private or public insurance company. For an open-heart surgery, for example, the hospital typically received $25,000 regardless of how many days a patient stayed in the hospital or which medications or interventions the patient needed during that time. But the cost to the hospital varied considerably based on length of stay and level of care received, which gave the hospital the incentive to help the patient recover and be discharged as quickly as possible.

Numerous studies showed that it was also in the patient's best interest to have a short stay in the hospital; longer stays put patients at risk for infections, morbidity, and mortality because there were more infectious diseases in hospitals than in patients' homes or other facilities. Lengthier hospital stays also compromised patient morale, which, in turn, was counterproductive to healing.

Like many hospital systems, U.Va.'s faced capacity issues due to its inadequate number of patient beds. The sooner it was able to discharge a patient, the sooner its staff could start caring for another; therefore, efficient patient turnover was beneficial to both patients and U.Va.

Before coming to the U.Va. Health System, Fitzgerald had been the CFO of American Medical International, a hospital ownership company that later became known as Tenet. His experience in the for-profit sector had convinced him that LTAC facilities brought value to a hospital system. Even though the idea of LTAC hospitals was relatively new in the nonprofit sector, Fitzgerald had pitched the idea for opening one when he first arrived at the U.Va. Health System in 1999. At that time, however, the regulatory system required a LTAC facility to be built within the original hospital structure. The project was rejected by the board partly because of anticipated disputes from medical service units within the hospital that would be asked to forfeit some beds to make room for the LTAC hospital. But in 2006, Fitzgerald still saw the advantages of having a LTAC facility and was certain he could justify building one within the U.Va. Hospital.

Fitzgerald knew it was critical to gain approval for adding an LTAC facility at the following day's board meeting, because the Centers for Medicare & Medicaid Services (CMS) had recently decided that, because LTAC hospitals were making so much money, they were partly responsible for driving up health care costs.[2] Reacting to this finding, the CMS had decided to put a moratorium on the establishment of new LTAC facilities beginning January 2007. For Fitzgerald, this meant that it was now or never to make his case for establishing an LTAC as part of the U.Va. Health System.

The Advantages of LTAC Hospitals

LTAC hospitals were designed to service patients who required hospital stays of 25 days or more and at least some acute care during that time. LTACs especially benefited patients who were diagnosed with infectious diseases and who needed to be

---

[2]CMS was a federal agency within the U.S. Department of Health and Human Services that had a number of health care–related responsibilities, including the determination of quality standards for long-term care facilities.

weaned off ventilators, required pulmonary care or wound care, and who had critical care issues. It was often elderly patients who required these complex treatments, which were difficult to perform in a normal hospital setting.

LTAC hospitals were financially attractive to medical centers, because having one increased the amount of money available for patient care. Insurance companies reimbursed hospitals set amounts of money for each patient in its facility based on the patient's diagnosis, regardless of the time involved the patient's treatment and hospital stay. Yet if the patient was transferred to a LTAC facility, the hospital could bill insurance for the patient's stay in the hospital as well as for time spent in the LTAC. The LTAC facility also reduced patient care costs as the average daily hospital stay per patient cost more than $3,000 compared to only $1,500 per day for an LTAC.

Another advantage of an LTAC facility was that it helped address the capacity issues that the U.Va. Health System and most other hospital systems faced. By adding an LTAC facility, a hospital gained an additional 25 bed days for each patient transferred to the LTAC hospital. The average patient stay was five days in the hospital, compared to the average patient stay of 25 days in an LTAC facility. Therefore, by adding an LTAC facility, a hospital gained an additional 25 bed days for each patient transferred to the LTAC hospital. Thus, the hospital could take five more admissions for each patient transferred to an LTAC facility.

A stay in an LTAC facility had a number of advantages from the patient's perspective as well. The typical hospital setting was loud, the food could quickly become boring, and patients usually had to share rooms. Because the LTAC facility was essentially an extended-stay hospital, each patient had a private room, and the extended stay also helped a patient become more familiar with the caregivers. Fitzgerald remembered how, at one LTAC facility he had helped set up, a patient who was an avid bird watcher missed not seeing birds outside his window. To fix the problem, the staff climbed the tree outside his room and set up a bird feeder to allow him to enjoy his favorite pastime. This experience was not feasible within a regular hospital setting that often suffered from overcrowding of patients, understaffing, and an impersonal atmosphere. By contrast, patients were generally delighted with the atmosphere of an LTAC hospital with its attractive facilities, single rooms, fewer beds, and general lack of overcrowding. Higher patient morale meant a better rate of recovery and a lower rate of infection than in a typical hospital.

The U.Va. Health System comprised a large primary care network, a large hospital center, a community hospital in nearby Culpepper, a home health agency, a rehabilitation hospital, several nursing homes, an imaging center, and a physical therapy network. The LTAC facility would be another important part of the U.Va. Health System's network of care. Having all their medical care provided by U.Va. was advantageous for patients because it facilitated better communication between physicians through its electronic medical-records system.

Capital Investments at U.Va.

The U.Va. Health System's mission was to provide the highest quality health care service to the surrounding community while reinvesting in teaching and research.

Unlike the for-profit hospitals that ultimately had to earn a return for shareholders, nonprofits such as the U.Va. Health System had to strike a balance across its various objectives. A typical for-profit hospital required a pretax profit margin of 15% to justify a capital investment, whereas a nonprofit could require a lower margin and still meet its objective of providing excellent clinical care.

During Fitzgerald's tenure, the U.Va. Health System had maintained an average net profit margin of 4.9%. The board of directors considered a margin of 3.0% to be the minimum needed to sustain the system. In order to be able to grow and develop the system, however, the board wanted a 5.0% profit margin as the minimum for new projects. The board reinvested any profits beyond the 5.0% level in the School of Medicine to support the U.Va. Health System's teaching and research missions.

When an investment proposal was brought forward, the board generally considered three distinct sources of funding: cash, debt, and leasing. When analyzing a project, a primary consideration for the board was to maintain an AA bond rating for the hospital. This was the highest rating a hospital could receive due to associated business risk. Maintaining the credit rating kept borrowing costs low and allowed the hospital to effectively compete for debt dollars in the future. On the other hand, the desire for an AA rating limited the total amount of debt the hospital could carry. Based on discussions with several banks about the LTAC project, Fitzgerald was confident that he could obtain the $15 million loan needed and that the added debt on the balance sheet would not jeopardize the U.Va. Health System's AA bond rating.

LTAC Project Analysis

Larry Fitzgerald looked at the memo and financial projections from his analyst (**Exhibits 1** and **2**) and realized that much work needed to be done before the board meeting the next day. But before he began to prepare his answers for Mulroney, he notified his assistant that she should expect a late addition to the paperwork for the board by early the next morning.

Fitzgerald was pleased that Mulroney had gathered working capital data and financial data from the for-profit hospital sector. But he was disappointed to see so many omissions in her projections on the eve of the board meeting. Fitzgerald was convinced that the LTAC facility would be profitable for the U.Va. Health System, but to get board approval, he would need to present an analysis that justified such a large undertaking. Because of the size and risk of the project, the LTAC hospital would need to have a profit margin well above the 5.0% level, and if it was to be debt-financed, he would need to show an adequate coverage of the interest expense. Finally, he would have to be ready to defend each of the assumptions used to create the financial projections, because the financial acumen varied significantly across the board members.

EXHIBIT 1 | Memo from Karen Mulroney

MEMO: Long-Term Acute Care Facility

Date: March 3, 2006

To: Larry Fitzgerald, Vice President of Business Development and Finance

From: Karen Mulroney, Analyst

Dear Mr. Fitzgerald,

After our meeting last week, I have developed the attached spreadsheet for the LTAC facility project. As you can see, I have most of the necessary assumptions in place to generate an operating profit, but more work needs to be done, and I have a few questions. What follows are my explanations about the key parts of the analysis.

VOLUME Metrics

We are assuming a 50-bed facility, which equals a capacity of 18,250 patient days. As with all LTAC facilities, the initial year is expected to have a low utilization rate (26%) until it is granted Medicare certification. Medicare will only provide certification if the facility can demonstrate that the average length of stay for patients is at least 25 days. If the facility is not certified, it will not be able to bill the LTAC rate for its patients on Medicare. Therefore, in the first year, we assume LTAC will be very selective by only admitting patients who are certain to stay for more than 25 days, which is why I have assumed 30 days as the average length of stay for Year 1. After the first year, I used 27 days, which is the national average length of stay for an LTAC facility patient.

For Year 2, I raised the utilization estimate to 60%, although a worst-case estimate is closer to 45%. For subsequent years, the utilization rate should increase 3% to 5% each year but will not be able to exceed 90% utilization. The utilization of the facility will be based on a number of factors including whether the facility is well received by the community, support from referring physicians, and hiring of hospitalists and nurses to ensure the facility runs smoothly and that patients receive exceptional care. Note that this version uses a 4% annual increase in the utilization, but we can easily reduce that if you want to see a more conservative scenario.

Total patient days for each year are computed as the utilization rate multiplied by the patient day capacity of 18,250 days. The next metric is the average patient census per day. Patient census measures how many patients the LTAC facility expects to serve on the average day. The average patient census is an important number because it is used to estimate how many full-time employees (FTEs) are needed to care for the patients. Due to the inefficiencies of the first year and based on the experiences of comparable LTAC facilities, we assume 4.8 FTEs are needed per occupied bed in the first year of operation. For subsequent years, we assume 3.5 FTEs will be needed as a reflection of operating at the efficiency level of an average LTAC facility.

EXHIBIT 1 | Memo from Karen Mulroney (*Continued*)

PAYER MIX metrics

Based on national trends and the local population demographics, we are confident that Medicare, Medicaid, and Indigent patients will represent 36%, 29%, and 2%, respectively, of our patient population. The "Commercial Payer Pool" and "Other"[1] were more difficult to estimate. The only information on this data is from for-profit hospital systems, and I am unsure if these numbers can be applied to a nonprofit organization such as U.Va. The data I found suggested commercial payers ranged from 20% to 28% of the mix with "Other" ranging from 5% to 13%.

NET REVENUE

Revenues for the LTAC facility are determined by patients' insurance policies. Medicare, Medicaid, Other, and Indigent categories are billed and paid per case. Those figures range from $28,000 to $38,000 per case. Commercial payers, however, pay based on the number days spent in the facility. Using current contracts and taking into account the mix of major commercial insurance carriers, we estimated an average billing rate of $2,800 per day.

I have also used historical data to estimate the annual billing rate increases for each of the payer categories, with commercial payers' rates increasing about 5% annually. Per our standard practice, net revenue is computed as total revenue less 1% to reflect noncollectable billings.

EXPENSES

Salaries, wages, and benefits for FTEs are estimated at $60,250 per employee with an increase of 3% per year, based on university and other local salary data. Supplies, drugs, and food for patient care are estimated as 16.3% of net revenues. Per your suggestion, I have included 8% of net revenues as the fees paid for managing the LTAC facility, which includes management salaries, billing, and overhead.

Operating expenses include utilities, minor equipment purchases and repairs, and legal and professional expenses. These costs were estimated to have a fixed component of $1.2 million and a variable component. The variable portion is estimated to range from 7% to 10% of net revenues.

The land for the LTAC facility will be leased for $200,000 per year. We have several bids from construction companies, all of which are close to an all-in cost of $15 million to build the facility. About half the construction will occur prior to the first operating year, and the balance will be spent in the first half of Year 1.

---

[1]The "Other" category included out-of-pocket and foreign patients, who were always difficult to estimate.

EXHIBIT 1 | Memo from Karen Mulroney (*Continued*)

Per your request, my final objective of the analysis is to compute a net present value and internal rate of return for the cash flows of the project. I recognize that in order to compute the cash flows, I will need to convert the above assumptions into revenues and costs, but first, I have a few questions:

1. It looks like we can get bank financing on the facility at 8.0%. This will be structured as a 30-year mortgage with monthly payments that include both principal and interest, which on an annual basis sum to $1.33 million. To calculate net profit, should I include the full amount as "interest expense," or should I segregate the interest and principal and only report the interest portion? When I worked in the for-profit world, we omitted interest expense because we wanted an "unlevered" cash flow (i.e., without financing cash flows). I assume that I should also compute an unlevered cash flow here for the NPV and IRR calculations, but I need to include interest expense to calculate a net profit, which I know the board wants to see.

2. Should I include depreciation of the facility as an expense? In my previous positions in manufacturing companies, we always viewed depreciation as a noncash flow, except for its impact upon taxes. Since this is a nonprofit entity that pays no taxes, would it be easier for me to just ignore depreciation?

3. You had instructed me to use 10 years as the time frame for the analysis, but the facility will last much longer, albeit with the benefit of significant renovations along the way. What should I show for cash flows after 10 years?

4. Are there any balance sheet effects for me to consider such as changes in working capital? Based on other LTAC facilities and the hospital, I would assume accounts receivable of 30 days, inventory of supplies, drugs, and food of 60 days, and accounts payable of 30 days. Would you be comfortable with these numbers?

5. What should I use as the discount rate to compute the NPV and to assess the IRR? I have compiled financial information for comparable publicly traded health care companies (**Exhibit 3**). I have also collected data about current yields on government and corporate bonds (**Exhibit 4**). Should I rely on these data to estimate a "market-based" cost of capital to use as the discount rate?

My notes from our January meeting indicate that you wanted this analysis completed by the end of February. I apologize for being late with this, but I have been busy analyzing the behavior of our receivables and payables balances for the hospital.

Any feedback you have on the attached projections would be greatly appreciated.

Sincerely,

Karen Mulroney
Analyst

EXHIBIT 2 | Karen Mulroney's LTAC Hospital Financial Projections

Assumptions

Number of Beds	50
Year 1 Utilization	26%
Year 2 Utilization	60%
Utilization Increase after Year 2	4%
Commercial Payer Mix	24%
Commercial Payer Billing per Day	$2,800
Operating Variable Expense	7.0%

VOLUME

	Year 1	Year 2	Year 3	Year 4	Year 5	Year 6	Year 7	Year 8	Year 9	Year 10
Patient Day Capacity	18,250	18,250	18,250	18,250	18,250	18,250	18,250	18,250	18,250	18,250
Utilization	26%	60%	64%	68%	72%	76%	80%	84%	88%	90%
Patient Days Used	4,745	10,950	11,680	12,410	13,140	13,870	14,600	15,330	16,060	16,425
Average Patient Census per Day	13	30	32	34	36	38	40	42	44	45
Average Length of Stay	30	27	27	27	27	27	27	27	27	27
Number of Patients per Year	158	406	433	460	487	514	541	568	595	608
Full-Time Employees/Census	4.8	3.5	3.5	3.5	3.5	3.5	3.5	3.5	3.5	3.5
Full-Time Employees	62	105	112	119	126	133	140	147	154	158

INSURANCE PAYERS

	MIX	Billing Rate		Annual Increase
Medicare	36%	$27,795	per case	0.0%
Medicaid	29%	$35,000	per case	1.3%
Commercial Payers	24%	$2,800	per day	5.0%
Other	9%	$38,500	per case	1.3%
Indigent	2%	$35,000	per case	1.3%

Total Revenue		
Net Revenues		
Annual Increase		

EXPENSES

Salary, Wage, Benefits	$60,250	per FTE	3%
Supplies, Drugs, Food	16.3%	of net rev	N.Ap.
Management Fees	8.0%	of net rev	N.Ap.
Operating Expenses (fixed)	$1,200,000		N.Ap.
Operating Expenses (variable)	7%	of net rev	N.Ap.
Land Lease (annual rate)	$200,000		3%
Construction	$15,000,000		N.Ap.

Total Operating Expenses	
–Interest Expense	
Net Profit	

Source: Created by case writer.

EXHIBIT 3 | Financial Data of For-Profit Health Care Companies

	HCA Inc	Community Health	Health Management Associates	Manor Care	Triad Hospitals	Universal Health Services
Revenues (millions)	$24,475	$3,720	$3,580	$3,375	$4,805	$4,030
Assets (millions)	$5,222	$961	$997	$693	$1,458	$775
Total debt (millions)	$9,278	$1,810	$1,014	$857	$1,703	$532
Stock price ($/share)	$52.12	$39.73	$23.25	$39.49	$41.46	$49.03
Shares outstanding (millions)	452.7	88.5	247.2	78.7	84.8	54.6
Market cap (millions)	$23,593	$3,517	$5,747	$3,108	$3,517	$2,676
Bond rating	A	B	BB	BB	B	BB
Beta	0.60	0.60	0.70	0.80	0.60	0.60

- HCA Inc.—hospital management company; manages hospitals mainly in the Southeast and Texas.

- Community Health—operates general acute care hospitals in nonurban communities.

- Health Management Associates, Inc.—provides a range of general an acute care health services in nonurban communities.

- Manor Care—provider of health services with broad capabilities; operates skilled nursing facilities, subacute medical and rehabilitation units, outpatient rehab clinics, assisted living facilities, and acute care hospitals.

- Triad Hospitals—owns and manages health care facilities including hospitals and ambulatory surgery centers.

- Universal Health Services—owns and operates acute care and surgical hospitals, behavioral health centers, and surgery and radiation oncology centers.

Data Source: Value Line, December 2005.

EXHIBIT 4 | U.S. Treasury and Corporate Bond Yields for March 2, 2006

U.S. Treasury Yields*	
1-year	4.77%
5-year	4.72%
10-year	4.72%
30-year	4.73%

Corporate Bond Yields**	
AAA	5.31%
AA	5.38%
A	5.45%
BBB	5.88%
BB	6.79%
B	7.57%

*Data Source: http://federalreserve.gov/releases/h15/data.htm (accessed March 2006).

**Data Source: Bloomberg, "Fair Market Curve Analysis," 10-Year Corporate Bonds, March 2, 2006.

## PART 5

Management of the Firm's Equity: Dividends and Repurchases

Gainesboro Machine Tools Corporation

In mid-September 2005, Ashley Swenson, chief financial officer (CFO) of Gainesboro Machine Tools Corporation, paced the floor of her Minnesota office. She needed to submit a recommendation to Gainesboro's board of directors regarding the company's dividend policy, which had been the subject of an ongoing debate among the firm's senior managers. Compounding her problem was the uncertainty surrounding the recent impact of Hurricane Katrina, which had caused untold destruction across the southeastern United States. In the weeks after the storm, the stock market had spiraled downward and, along with it, Gainesboro's stock, which had fallen 18%, to $22.15. In response to the market shock, a spate of companies had announced plans to buy back stock. While some were motivated by a desire to signal confidence in their companies as well as in the U.S. financial markets, still others had opportunistic reasons. Now, Ashley Swenson's dividend-decision problem was compounded by the dilemma of whether to use company funds to pay shareholder dividends or to buy back stock.

Background on the Dividend Question

After years of traditionally strong earnings and predictable dividend growth, Gainesboro had faltered in the past five years. In response, management implemented two extensive restructuring programs, both of which were accompanied by net losses. For three years in a row since 2000, dividends had exceeded earnings. Then, in 2003, dividends were decreased to a level below earnings. Despite extraordinary losses in 2004, the board of directors declared a small dividend. For the first two quarters of 2005, the board declared no dividend. But in a special letter to shareholders, the board committed itself to resuming payment of the dividend as soon as possible—ideally, sometime in 2005.

This case was written by Robert F. Bruner and Sean Carr, and is dedicated to Professors Robert F. Vandell and Pearson Hunt, the authors of an antecedent case, long out of print, that provided the model for the economic problem in this case. "Gainesboro" is a fictional firm, though it draws on dilemmas of contemporary companies. The financial support of the Batten Institute is gratefully acknowledged. Copyright © 2005 by the University of Virginia Darden School Foundation, Charlottesville, VA. All rights reserved. *To order copies, send an e-mail to sales@dardenbusinesspublishing.com. No part of this publication may be reproduced, stored in a retrieval system, used in a spreadsheet, or transmitted in any form or by any means—electronic, mechanical, photocopying, recording, or otherwise—without the permission of the Darden School Foundation.*

In a related matter, senior management considered embarking on a campaign of corporate-image advertising, together with changing the name of the corporation to "Gainesboro Advanced Systems International, Inc." Management believed that the name change would help improve the investment community's perception of the company.

Overall, management's view was that Gainesboro was a resurgent company that demonstrated great potential for growth and profitability. The restructurings had revitalized the company's operating divisions. In addition, the newly developed machine tools designed on state-of-the-art computers showed signs of being well received in the market, and promised to render the competitors' products obsolete. Many within the company viewed 2005 as the dawning of a new era, which, in spite of the company's recent performance, would turn Gainesboro into a growth stock. The company had no Moody's or Standard & Poor's rating because it had no bonds outstanding, but Value Line rated it an "A" company.[1]

Out of this combination of a troubled past and a bright future arose Swenson's dilemma. Did the market view Gainesboro as a company on the wane, a blue-chip stock, or a potential growth stock? How, if at all, could Gainesboro affect that perception? Would a change of name help to positively frame investors' views of the firm? Did the company's investors expect capital growth or steady dividends? Would a stock buyback instead of a dividend affect investors' perceptions of Gainesboro in any way? And, if those questions could be answered, what were the implications for Gainesboro's future dividend policy?

The Company

Gainesboro Corporation was founded in 1923 in Concord, New Hampshire, by two mechanical engineers, James Gaines and David Scarboro. The two men had gone to school together and were disenchanted with their prospects as mechanics at a farm-equipment manufacturer.

In its early years, Gainesboro had designed and manufactured a number of machinery parts, including metal presses, dies, and molds. In the 1940s, the company's large manufacturing plant produced armored-vehicle and tank parts and miscellaneous equipment for the war effort, including riveters and welders. After the war, the company concentrated on the production of industrial presses and molds, for plastics as well as metals. By 1975, the company had developed a reputation as an innovative producer of industrial machinery and machine tools.

In the early 1980s, Gainesboro entered the new field of computer-aided design and computer-aided manufacturing (CAD/CAM). Working with a small software company, it developed a line of presses that could manufacture metal parts by responding to computer commands. Gainesboro merged the software company into its operations and, over the next several years, perfected the CAM equipment. At the same time, it developed a superior line of CAD software and equipment that would allow an engineer to

---

[1]Value Line's financial-strength ratings, from A++ to C, were a measure of a company's ability to withstand adverse business conditions and were based on leverage, liquidity, business risk, company size, and stock-price variability, as well as analysts' judgments.

design a part to exacting specifications on a computer. The design could then be entered into the company's CAM equipment, and the parts could be manufactured without the use of blueprints or human interference. By the end of 2004, CAD/CAM equipment and software were responsible for about 45% of sales; presses, dies, and molds made up 40% of sales; and miscellaneous machine tools were 15% of sales.

Most press and mold companies were small local or regional firms with limited clientele. For that reason, Gainesboro stood out as a true industry leader. Within the CAD/CAM industry, however, a number of larger firms, including Autodesk, Inc., Cadence Design, and Synopsys, Inc., competed for dominance of the growing market.

Throughout the 1990s, Gainesboro helped set the standard for CAD/CAM, but the aggressive entry of large foreign firms into CAD/CAM and the rise of the U.S. dollar dampened sales. In the late 1990s and early 2000s, technological advances and aggressive venture capitalism fueled the entry of highly specialized, state-of-the-art CAD/CAM firms. Gainesboro fell behind some of its competition in the development of user-friendly software and the integration of design and manufacturing. As a result, revenues slipped from a high of $911 million, in 1998, to $757 million, in 2004.

To combat the decline in revenues and to improve weak profit margins, Gainesboro took a two-pronged approach. First, it devoted a greater share of its research-and-development budget to CAD/CAM in an effort to reestablish its leadership in the field. Second, the company underwent two massive restructurings. In 2002, it sold two unprofitable lines of business with revenues of $51 million, sold two plants, eliminated five leased facilities, and reduced personnel. Restructuring costs totaled $65 million. Then, in 2004, the company began a second round of restructuring by altering its manufacturing strategy, refocusing its sales and marketing approach, and adopting administrative procedures that allowed for a further reduction in staff and facilities. The total cost of the operational restructuring in 2004 was $89 million.

The company's recent consolidated income statements and balance sheets are provided in **Exhibits 1** and **2.** Although the two restructurings produced losses totaling $202 million in 2002 and 2004, by 2005 the restructurings and the increased emphasis on CAD/CAM research appeared to have launched a turnaround. Not only was the company leaner, but also the research led to the development of a system that Gainesboro's management believed would redefine the industry. Known as the Artificial Workforce, the system was an array of advanced control hardware, software, and applications that could distribute information throughout a plant.

Essentially, the Artificial Workforce allowed an engineer to design a part on CAD software and input the data into CAM equipment that could control the mixing of chemicals or the molding of parts from any number of different materials on different machines. The system could also assemble and can, box, or shrink-wrap the finished product. The Artificial Workforce ran on complex circuitry and highly advanced software that allowed the machines to communicate with each other electronically. Thus, a product could be designed, manufactured, and packaged solely by computer no matter how intricate it was.

Gainesboro had developed applications of the product for the chemicals industry and for the oil- and gas-refining industries in 2004 and, by the next year, it had created applications for the trucking, automobile-parts, and airline industries.

By October 2004, when the first Artificial Workforce was shipped, Gainesboro had orders totaling $75 million. By year end, the backlog was $100 million. The future for the product looked bright. Several securities analysts were optimistic about the product's impact on the company. The following comments paraphrase their thoughts:

> The Artificial Workforce products have compelling advantages over competing entries, which will enable Gainesboro to increase its share of a market that, ignoring periodic growth spurts, will expand at a real annual rate of about 5% over the next several years.

> The company is producing the Artificial Workforce in a new automated facility, which, when in full swing, will help restore margins to levels not seen in years.

> The important question now is how quickly Gainesboro will be able to ship in volume. Manufacturing mishaps and missing components delayed production growth through May 2005, putting it about six months beyond the original target date. And start-up costs, which were a significant factor in last year's deficits, have continued to penalize earnings. Our estimates assume that production will proceed smoothly from now on and that it will approach the optimum level by year's end.

Gainesboro's management expected domestic revenues from the Artificial Workforce series to total $90 million in 2005 and $150 million in 2006. Thereafter, growth in sales would depend on the development of more system applications and the creation of system improvements and add-on features. International sales through Gainesboro's existing offices in Frankfurt, Germany; London, England; Milan, Italy; and Paris, France; and new offices in Hong Kong, China; Seoul, Korea; Manila, Philippines; and Tokyo, Japan, were expected to provide additional revenues of $150 million by as early as 2007. Currently, international sales accounted for approximately 15% of total corporate revenues.

Two factors that could affect sales were of some concern to Gainesboro. First, although the company had successfully patented several of the processes used by the Artificial Workforce system, management had received hints through industry observers that two strong competitors were developing comparable products and would probably introduce them within the next 12 months. Second, sales of molds, presses, machine tools, and CAD/CAM equipment and software were highly cyclical, and current predictions about the strength of the U.S. economy were not encouraging. As shown in **Exhibit 3,** real GDP (gross domestic product) growth was expected to hover at a steady but unimpressive 3.0% over the next few years. Industrial production, which had improved significantly since 2001, would likely indicate a trend slightly downward next year and the year after that. Despite the macroeconomic environment, Gainesboro's management remained optimistic about the company's prospects because of the successful introduction of the Artificial Workforce series.

Corporate Goals

A number of corporate objectives had grown out of the restructurings and recent technological advances. First and foremost, management wanted and expected the firm to grow at an average annual compound rate of 15%. A great deal of corporate planning had been devoted to that goal over the past three years and, indeed, second-quarter financial data suggested that Gainesboro would achieve revenues of about $870 million in 2005, as shown in **Exhibit 1.** If Gainesboro achieved a 15% compound rate of growth through 2011, the company could reach $2.0 billion in sales and $160 million in net income.

In order to achieve that growth goal, Gainesboro management proposed a strategy relying on three key points. First, the mix of production would shift substantially. CAD/CAM and peripheral products on the cutting edge of industrial technology would account for three-quarters of sales, while the company's traditional presses and molds would account for the remainder. Second, the company would expand aggressively in the international arena, whence it hoped to obtain half of its sales and profits by 2011. This expansion would be achieved through opening new field sales offices around the world. Third, the company would expand through joint ventures and acquisitions of small software companies, which would provide half of the new products through 2011; in-house research would provide the other half.

The company had had an aversion to debt since its inception. Management believed that small amounts of debt, primarily to meet working-capital needs, had their place, but that anything beyond a 40% debt-to-equity ratio was, in the oft-quoted words of Gainesboro cofounder David Scarboro, "unthinkable, indicative of sloppy management, and flirting with trouble." Senior management was aware that equity was typically more costly than debt, but took great satisfaction in the company's "doing it on its own." Gainesboro's highest debt-to-capital ratio in the past 25 years (22%) had occurred in 2004, and was still the subject of conversations among senior managers.

Although eleven members of the Gaines and the Scarboro families owned 13% of the company's stock and three were on the board of directors, management placed the interests of the outside shareholders first. (Shareholder data are provided in **Exhibit 4.**) Stephen Gaines, board chair and grandson of the cofounder, sought to maximize growth in the market value of the company's stock over time.

At 61, Gaines was actively involved in all aspects of the company's growth. He dealt fluently with a range of technical details of Gainesboro's products, and was especially interested in finding ways to improve the company's domestic market share. His retirement was no more than four years away, and he wanted to leave a legacy of corporate financial strength and technological achievement. The Artificial Workforce, a project that he had taken under his wing four years earlier, was finally beginning to bear fruit. Gaines now wanted to ensure that the firm would also soon be able to pay a dividend to its shareholders.

Gaines took particular pride in selecting and developing promising young managers. Ashley Swenson had a bachelor's degree in electrical engineering and had been a systems analyst for Motorola before attending graduate school. She had been hired in 1995, fresh out of a well-known MBA program. By 2004, she had risen to the position of CFO.

Dividend Policy

Gainesboro's dividend and stock-price histories are presented in **Exhibit 5.** Before 1999, both earnings and dividends per share had grown at a relatively steady pace, but Gainesboro's troubles in the early 2000s had taken their toll on earnings. Consequently, dividends were pared back in 2003 to $0.25 a share—the lowest dividend since 1990. In 2004, the board of directors declared a payout of $0.25 a share, despite reporting the largest per-share earnings loss in the firm's history and despite, in effect, having to borrow to pay that dividend. In the first two quarters of 2005, the directors did not declare a dividend. In a special letter to shareholders, however, the directors declared their intention to continue the annual payout later in 2005.

In August 2005, Swenson contemplated her choices from among the three possible dividend policies to decide which one she should recommend:

- *Zero-dividend payout:* This option could be justified in light of the firm's strategic emphasis on advanced technologies and CAD/CAM, and reflected the huge cash requirements of such a move. The proponents of this policy argued that it would signal that the firm now belonged in a class of high-growth and high-technology firms. Some securities analysts wondered whether the market still considered Gainesboro a traditional electrical-equipment manufacturer or a more technologically advanced CAD/CAM company. The latter category would imply that the market expected strong capital appreciation, but perhaps little in the way of dividends. Others cited Gainesboro's recent performance problems. One questioned the "wisdom of ignoring the financial statements in favor of acting like a blue chip." Was a high dividend in the long-term interests of the company and its stockholders, or would the strategy backfire and make investors skittish?

    Swenson recalled a recently published study that found that firms were displaying a lower propensity to pay dividends. The study found that the percentage of firms paying cash dividends had dropped from 66.5%, in 1978, to 20.8%, in 1999.[2] In that light, perhaps the market would react favorably, if Gainesboro adopted a zero dividend-payout policy.

- *40% dividend payout or a dividend of around $0.20 a share:* This option would restore the firm to an implied annual dividend payment of $0.80 a share, the highest since 2001. Proponents of this policy argued that such an announcement was justified by expected increases in orders and sales. Gainesboro's investment banker suggested that the market might reward a strong dividend that would bring the firm's payout back in line with the 36% average within the electrical-industrial-equipment industry and with the 26% average in the machine-tool industry. Still others believed that it was important to send a strong signal to shareholders, and that a large dividend (on the order of a 40% payout) would suggest that the company had conquered its problems and that its directors were confident of its future earnings. Supporters of this view argued that borrowing to pay dividends was consistent with the behavior of most firms. Finally, some older managers opined that a growth rate in the range of 10% to 20% should accompany a dividend payout of between 30% and 50%.

- *Residual-dividend payout:* A few members of the finance department argued that Gainesboro should pay dividends only after it had funded all the projects that

---

[2]Eugene Fama and Kenneth French, "Changing Firm Characteristics or Lower Propensity to Pay," *Journal of Financial Economics* 60 (April 2001): 3–43.

offered positive net present values (NPV). Their view was that investors paid managers to deploy their funds at returns better than they could otherwise achieve, and that, by definition, such investments would yield positive NPVs. By deploying funds into those projects and returning otherwise unused funds to investors in the form of dividends, the firm would build trust with investors and be rewarded through higher valuation multiples.

Another argument in support of that view was that the particular dividend policy was "irrelevant" in a growing firm: any dividend paid today would be offset by dilution at some future date by the issuance of shares needed to make up for the dividend. This argument reflected the theory of dividends in a perfect market advanced by two finance professors, Merton Miller and Franco Modigliani.[3] To Ashley Swenson, the main disadvantage of this policy was that dividend payments would be unpredictable. In some years, dividends could even be cut to zero, possibly imposing negative pressure on the firm's share price. Swenson was all too aware of Gainesboro's own share-price collapse following its dividend cut. She recalled a study by another finance professor, John Lintner,[4] which found that firms' dividend payments tended to be "sticky" upward—that is, dividends would rise over time and rarely fall, and that mature, slower-growth firms paid higher dividends, while high-growth firms paid lower dividends.

In response to the internal debate, Swenson's staff pulled together **Exhibits 6** and **7,** which present comparative information on companies in three industries—CAD/CAM, machine tools, and electrical-industrial equipment—and a sample of high- and low-payout companies. To test the feasibility of a 40% dividend-payout rate, Swenson developed the projected sources-and-uses of cash statement provided in **Exhibit 8.** She took the boldest approach by assuming that the company would grow at a 15% compound rate, that margins would improve over the next few years to historical levels, and that the firm would pay a dividend of 40% of earnings every year. In particular, the forecast assumed that the firm's net margin would hover between 4% and 6% over the next six years, and then increase to 8% in 2011. The firm's operating executives believed that this increase in profitability was consistent with economies of scale to be achieved upon the attainment of higher operating output through the Artificial Workforce series.

Image Advertising and Name Change

As part of a general review of the firm's standing in the financial markets, Gainesboro's director of Investor Relations, Cathy Williams, had concluded that investors misperceived the firm's prospects and that the firm's current name was more consistent with its historical product mix and markets than with those projected for the future.

---

[3]M. H. Miller and F. Modigliani, "Dividend Policy, Growth, and the Valuation of Shares," *Journal of Business* 34 (October 1961): 411–433.

[4]J. Lintner, "Distribution of Incomes of Corporations among Dividends, Retained Earnings, and Taxes," *American Economic Review* 46 (May 1956): 97–113.

Williams commissioned surveys of readers of financial magazines, which revealed a relatively low awareness of Gainesboro and its business. Surveys of stockbrokers revealed a higher awareness of the firm, but a low or mediocre outlook on Gainesboro's likely returns to shareholders and its growth prospects. Williams retained a consulting firm that recommended a program of corporate-image advertising targeted toward guiding the opinions of institutional and individual investors. The objective was to enhance the firm's visibility and image. Through focus groups, the image consultants identified a new name that appeared to suggest the firm's promising new strategy: Gainesboro Advanced Systems International, Inc. Williams estimated that the image-advertising campaign and name change would cost approximately $10 million.

Stephen Gaines was mildly skeptical. He said, "Do you mean to raise our stock price by 'marketing' our shares? This is a novel approach. Can you sell claims on a company the way Procter & Gamble markets soap?" The consultants could give no empirical evidence that stock prices responded positively to corporate-image campaigns or name changes, though they did offer some favorable anecdotes.

Conclusion

Swenson was in a difficult position. Board members and management disagreed on the very nature of Gainesboro's future. Some managers saw the company as entering a new stage of rapid growth and thought that a large (or, in the minds of some, any) dividend would be inappropriate. Others thought that it was important to make a strong public gesture showing that management believed that Gainesboro had turned the corner and was about to return to the levels of growth and profitability seen in the 1980s and '90s. This action could only be accomplished through a dividend. Then there was the confounding question about the stock buyback. Should Gainesboro use its funds to repurchase stocks instead of paying out a dividend? As Swenson wrestled with the different points of view, she wondered whether Gainesboro's management might be representative of the company's shareholders. Did the majority of public shareholders own stock for the same reason, or were their reasons just as diverse as those of management?

EXHIBIT 1 | Consolidated Income Statements (dollars in thousands, except per-share data)

	For the Years Ended December 31			Projected 2005
	2002	2003	2004	
Net sales	$858,263	$815,979	$756,638	$870,000
Cost of sales	540,747	501,458	498,879	549,750
Gross profit	317,516	314,522	257,759	320,250
Research & development	77,678	70,545	75,417	77,250
Selling, general, & administrative	229,971	223,634	231,008	211,500
Restructuring costs	65,448	0	89,411	0
Operating profit (loss)	(55,581)	20,343	(138,077)	31,500
Other income (expense)	(4,500)	1,065	(3,458)	(4,200)
Income (loss) before taxes	(60,081)	21,408	(141,534)	27,300
Income taxes (benefit)	1,241	8,415	(750)	9,282
Net income (loss)	($61,322)	$ 12,993	($140,784)	$ 18,018
Earnings (loss) per share	($3.25)	$ 0.69	($7.57)	$ 0.98
Dividends per share	$ 0.77	$ 0.25	$ 0.25	$ 0.39

Note: The dividends in 2005 assume a payout ratio of 40%.

EXHIBIT 2 | Consolidated Balance Sheets (dollars in thousands)

	For the Years Ended December 31		Projected 2005
	2003	2004	
Cash & equivalents	$ 13,917	$ 22,230	$ 25,665
Accounts receivable	208,541	187,235	217,510
Inventories	230,342	203,888	217,221
Prepaid expenses	14,259	13,016	15,011
Other	22,184	20,714	21,000
Total current assets	489,242	447,082	496,407
Property, plant, & equipment	327,603	358,841	410,988
Less depreciation	167,414	183,486	205,530
Net property, plant, & equipment	160,190	175,355	205,458
Intangible assets	9,429	2,099	1,515
Other assets	15,723	17,688	17,969
Total assets	**$674,583**	**$642,223**	**$721,350**
Bank loans	$ 34,196	$ 71,345	$ 74,981
Accounts payable	36,449	34,239	37,527
Current portion of long-term debt	300	150	1,515
Accruals and other	129,374	161,633	183,014
Total current liabilities	200,318	267,367	297,037
Deferred taxes	16,986	13,769	16,526
Long-term debt	9,000	8,775	30,021
Deferred pension costs	44,790	64,329	70,134
Other liabilities	2,318	5,444	7,505
Total liabilities	273,411	359,683	421,224
Common stock, $1 par value	18,855	18,855	18,835
Capital in excess of par	107,874	107,907	107,889
Cumulative translation adjustment	(6,566)	20,208	26,990
Retained earnings	291,498	146,065	156,875
Less treasury stock at cost:			
1990–256,151; 1991–255,506	(10,490)	(10,494)	(10,464)
Total shareholders' equity	401,172	282,541	300,126
Total liabilities & equity	**$674,583**	**$642,223**	**$721,350**

Note: Projections assume a dividend-payout ratio of 40%.

EXHIBIT 3 | Economic Indicators and Projections (all numbers are percentages)

	2001	2002	2003	2004	Projected 2005	Projected 2006	Projected 2007
Three-month Treasury bill rate (at auction)	3.4	1.6	1.0	1.4	3.2	4.2	4.7
Ten-year Treasury note yield	5.0	4.6	4.0	4.3	4.3	4.8	5.7
AAA corporate bond rate	7.1	6.5	5.7	5.6	5.3	5.9	6.8
Percentage change in:							
Real gross domestic product	0.8	1.9	3.0	4.3	3.3	2.9	3.2
Producer prices, finished goods	2.0	(1.3)	3.2	3.5	1.2	(0.2)	0.1
Industrial production	(3.4)	(0.6)	0.3	4.5	3.7	3.4	4.8
Consumption of durable goods	4.3	6.5	7.4	6.0	2.4	4.2	4.5
Consumer spending	2.5	3.1	3.3	3.5	2.9	2.9	2.8
GDP deflator	2.4	1.7	1.8	2.1	1.9	1.7	1.9

Sources of data: *Value Line Investment Survey,* 26 August 2005; *U.S. Economic Outlook,* Global Insight, September 2004.

EXHIBIT 4 | Comparative Stockholder Data, 1994 and 2004 (in thousands of shares)

	1994 Shares	1994 Percentage	2004 Shares	2004 Percentage
Founders' families	2,390	13%	2,421	13%
Employees and families	3,677	20%	3,155	17%
Institutional investors				
Growth-oriented	2,390	13%	1,138	6%
Value-oriented	1,471	8%	2,421	13%
Individual investors				
Long-term retirement	6,803	37%	4,806	26%
Short-term; trading-oriented	919	5%	2,421	13%
Other; unknown	735	4%	2,239	12%
Total	18,385	100%	18,600	100%

Note: The investor-relations department identified these categories from company records. The type of institutional investor was identified from promotional materials stating the investment goals of the institutions. The type of individual investor was identified from a survey of subsamples of investors.

EXHIBIT 5 | Per-Share Financial and Stock Data[1]

Year	Sales/ Share[2]	EPS[2]	DPS[2]	CPS[2]	Stock Price High	Stock Price Low	Stock Price Avg.	Avg. P/E	Payout Ratio	Avg. Yield	Shares Outstanding (millions)
1989	$14.52	$0.45	$0.18	$0.97	$20.37	$9.69	$14.48	32.4	40%	1.2%	15.49
1990	16.00	0.74	0.22	1.29	21.11	10.18	14.85	20.2	30%	1.5%	15.58
1991	22.25	0.89	0.27	1.43	21.23	8.20	13.50	15.1	30%	2.0%	16.04
1992	25.64	1.59	0.31	2.05	18.50	10.18	13.35	8.4	19%	2.3%	17.87
1993	27.19	2.29	0.40	2.83	22.48	12.17	18.36	8.0	17%	2.2%	18.08
1994	30.06	2.59	0.57	3.25	23.84	18.01	21.00	8.1	22%	2.7%	18.39
1995	31.66	2.61	0.72	3.34	26.70	18.25	22.73	8.7	27%	3.1%	18.76
1996	37.71	2.69	0.81	3.60	29.43	19.50	24.23	9.0	30%	3.4%	18.76
1997	40.69	2.56	0.86	3.62	39.74	20.12	29.48	11.5	34%	2.9%	18.78
1998	48.23	3.58	0.92	4.81	40.98	27.32	33.98	9.5	26%	2.7%	18.88
1999	43.59	2.79	1.03	4.25	38.74	21.36	31.82	11.4	37%	3.2%	18.66
2000	42.87	0.65	1.03	2.23	47.19	29.55	36.81	57.0	160%	2.8%	18.66
2001	41.48	0.35	1.03	2.00	40.23	26.82	31.26	89.9	297%	3.3%	18.66
2002	45.52	(3.25)	0.77	2.86	30.75	22.13	26.45	nmf	nmf	2.9%	18.85
2003	43.28	0.69	0.25	1.99	71.88	50.74	61.33	88.2	35%	0.4%	18.85
2004	$40.68	($7.57)	$0.25	($0.97)	$39.88	$18.38	$29.15	nmf	nmf	0.9%	18.60

nmf = not a meaningful figure.

[1]Adjusted for a 3-for-2 stock split in January 1995 and a 50% stock dividend in June 1997.

[2]EPS: earnings per share; CPS: cash earnings per share; DPS: dividend per share.

EXHIBIT 6 | Comparative Industry Data, August 2005

	Sales ($mm)	Annual Growth Rate of Cash Flow (%)		Current Payout Ratio (%)	Current Dividend Yield (%)	Debt/ Equity (%)[1]	Insider Ownership (%)	P/E Ratio (x)
		Last 5 Years	Next 3–5 Years					
Gainesboro Machine Tools Corp.	504	(1.5)	15.0	0.0	0.0	28.0	30.0	nmf
CAD/CAM companies (software and hardware)								
Autodesk, Inc.	1,234	4.5	10.5	6.0	0.3	0.0	3.2	25.3
Ansys, Inc.	135	16.5	13.0	0.0	0.0	0.0	4.4	23.3
Cadence Design	1,198	(1.5)	6.0	0.0	0.0	24.7	3.5	21.4
Intergraph Corp.	551	(8.0)	12.0	0.0	0.0	0.2	3.1	25.7
Mentor Graphics	711	4.5	2.0	0.0	0.0	65.5	5.9	21.9
Moldflow Corp.	49	nmf	11.5	0.0	0.0	0.0	15.4	36.2
Parametric Technology Corp.	660	(6.5)	6.0	0.0	0.0	0.0	5.4	33.4
Synopsys, Inc.	1,092	6.5	6.0	0.0	0.0	0.0	5.6	26.5
Electrical-industrial equipment manufacturers								
Cooper Industries, Inc.	4,463	1.5	3.0	39.0	2.4	30.6	1.0	16.4
Emerson Electric Company	15,615	2.5	3.5	54.0	2.6	43.3	0.8	20.5
Hubbell Inc.	1,993	5.0	6.0	52.0	3.0	21.1	2.9	17.6
Thomas & Betts Corp.	1,516	(10.0)	5.0	0.0	0.0	60.2	2.4	17.7
Machine tool manufacturers								
Actuant Corp.	976	(21.5)	12.5	0.0	0.0	180.8	5.9	19.1
Lincoln Electric Holdings, Inc.	1,334	2.5	10.0	32.0	2.2	28.4	5.2	15.0
Milacron, Inc.	774	(15.5)	(2.5)	0.0	0.0	468.1	4.6	nmf
Snap-on Inc.	2,407	5.0	3.5	71.0	3.1	18.3	3.0	22.9

nmf = not a meaningful figure.

[1] Based on book values.

Source of data: *Value Line Investment Survey,* August 2005.

EXHIBIT 7 | Selected Healthy Companies with High and Zero Dividend-Payouts, August 2005

	Industry	Expected Return on Total Capital (next 3–5 years)	Expected Growth Rate of Dividends (next 3–5 years)	Current Dividend Payout	Current Dividend Yield	Expected Growth Rate of Sales (next 3–5 years)	Current P/E Ratio
High-Payout Companies							
Crescent Real Estate Equities Co.	Real estate investment trust	5.0	nmf	123.0	8.9	nmf	12.4
Equity Office Properties Trust	Real estate investment trust	5.5	nmf	96.6	7.2	nmf	nmf
Frontline, Ltd.	Oil transport	20.0	9.0	115.0	35.3	(5.0)	3.2
Scudder High Income Trust	Investment management	nmf	nmf	96.4	9.2	nmf	nmf
TEPPCO Partners, LP	Pipeline operations	12.0	3.5	104.0	6.7	5.0	24.3
UIL Holdings	Electric utility	4.5	0.0	112.0	6.0	5.5	18.7
Zero-Payout Companies							
Amgen Inc.	Biotechnology	17.5	0.0	0.0	0.0	18.5	26.5
Cisco Systems, Inc.	Network systems	49.0	0.0	0.0	0.0	16.0	21.6
Coach, Inc.	Luxury retail	22.5	0.0	0.0	0.0	20.5	25.8
eBay Inc.	Internet auction	26.0	0.0	0.0	0.0	32.0	74.7
Oracle Corporation	Software	31.0	0.0	0.0	0.0	14.5	17.9
Research in Motion Limited	Telecommunications	13.5	0.0	0.0	0.0	30.0	nmf
Yahoo! Inc.	Internet/media	14.5	0.0	0.0	0.0	31.0	nmf

Source of data: *Value Line Investment Survey*, August 2005.

EXHIBIT 8 | Projected Sources-and-Uses Statement Assuming a 40% Payout Ratio[1] (dollars in millions)

Assumptions:	2005	2006	2007	2008	2009	2010	2011	
1. Sales Growth Rate:	15%	15%	15%	15%	15%	15%	15%	
2. Net Income as % of Sales	2.1%	4.0%	5.0%	5.5%	6.0%	5.6%	8.0%	
3. Dividend-Payout Ratio	40.0%	40.0%	40.0%	40.0%	40.0%	40.0%	40.0%	

Projections:	2005	2006	2007	2008	2009	2010	2011	Total 2005–11
Sales	$870.1	$1,000.7	$1,150.8	$1,323.4	$1,521.9	$1,750.1	$2,012.7	$9,629.6
Sources:								
Net income	$ 18.1	$ 40.0	$ 57.5	$ 72.8	$ 91.3	$ 98.0	$ 160.0	$ 537.8
Depreciation	$ 22.5	$ 25.5	$ 30.0	$ 34.5	$ 40.5	$ 46.5	$ 52.5	$ 252.0
Total	$ 40.6	$ 65.5	$ 87.5	$ 107.3	$ 131.8	$ 144.5	$ 212.5	$ 789.8
Uses:								
Capital expenditures	$ 43.8	$ 50.4	$ 57.5	$ 66.2	$ 68.5	$ 78.8	$ 90.6	$ 455.7
Change in working capital	$ 19.5	$ 22.4	$ 25.8	$ 29.6	$ 34.0	$ 38.5	$ 44.3	$ 214.1
Total	$ 63.3	$ 72.8	$ 83.3	$ 95.8	$ 102.4	$ 117.3	$ 134.9	$ 669.8
Excess cash/(borrowing needs)	$ (22.7)	$ (7.3)	$ 4.2	$ 11.5	$ 29.4	$ 27.2	$ 77.6	$ 120.0
Dividend	$ 7.2	$ 16.0	$ 23.0	$ 29.1	$ 36.5	$ 39.2	$ 64.0	$ 215.1
After dividend								
Excess cash/(borrowing needs)	$ (29.9)	$ (23.3)	$ (18.8)	$ (17.6)	$ (7.2)	$ (12.0)	$ 13.6	$ (95.1)

Note: Dividend calculated as 40% of net income.

[1]This analysis ignores the effects of borrowing on interest and amortization. It includes all increases in long-term liabilities and equity items other than retained earnings.

Autozone, Inc.

On February 1, 2012, Mark Johnson, portfolio manager at Johnson & Associates, an asset management company, was in the process of reviewing his largest holdings, which included AutoZone, an aftermarket auto-parts retailer. AutoZone shareholders had enjoyed strong price appreciation since 1997, with an average annual return of 11.5% (**Exhibit 1**). The stock price stood at $348, but Johnson was concerned about the recent news that Edward Lampert, AutoZone's main shareholder, was rapidly liquidating his stake in the company.

Since 2004, AutoZone shareholders had received large distributions of the company's cash flows in the form of share repurchases. When a company repurchased its own shares, it enhanced earnings per share by reducing the shares outstanding, and it also served to reduce the book value of shareholders' equity (see AutoZone financial statements in **Exhibits 2, 3, 4,** and **5**). Johnson felt that Lampert was likely a driving force behind AutoZone's repurchase strategy because the repurchases started around the time Lampert acquired his stake and accelerated as he built up his position. Now that Lampert was reducing his stake, however, Johnson wondered if AutoZone would continue to repurchase shares or if the company would change its strategy and use its cash flows for initiating a cash dividend or reinvesting the cash in the company to grow its core business. In addition, given its large debt burden (**Exhibit 6**), AutoZone could choose to repay debt to improve its credit rating and increase its financial flexibility.

With AutoZone potentially changing its strategy for the use of its cash flows, Johnson needed to assess the impact of the change on the company's stock price and then decide whether he should alter his position in the stock.

The Auto Parts Business

Aftermarket auto-parts sales were split into the Do-It-Yourself (DIY) and Do-It-For-Me (DIFM) segments. In the DIY segment, automobile parts were sold directly to vehicle

This case was prepared by Justin Brenner (MBA '12) under the supervision of Kenneth Eades, Paul Tudor Jones Research Professor of Business Administration. It was written as a basis for class discussion rather than to illustrate effective or ineffective handling of an administrative situation. The character of Mark Johnson and the Johnson & Associates company are fictional. Copyright © 2012 by the University of Virginia Darden School Foundation, Charlottesville, VA. All rights reserved. *To order copies, send an e-mail to* sales @dardenbusinesspublishing.com. *No part of this publication may be reproduced, stored in a retrieval system, used in a spreadsheet, or transmitted in any form or by any means—electronic, mechanical, photocopying, recording, or otherwise—without the permission of the Darden School Foundation.*

owners who wanted to fix or improve their vehicles on their own. In the DIFM segment, automobile repair shops provided the parts for vehicles left in their care for repair. DIY customers were serviced primarily through local retail storefronts where they could speak with a knowledgeable sales associate who located the necessary part. DIFM service providers, because of their expertise in repairing vehicles, generally did not require storefront access or the expertise of a sales associate. DIFM customers, however, were concerned with pricing, product availability, and efficient product delivery.

Sales in both segments were strongly related to the number of miles a vehicle had been driven. For the DIY segment, the number of late-model cars needing repair was also a strong predictor of auto-parts sales. As the age of a car increased, more repairs were required, and the owners of older cars were more likely to repair these senior vehicles themselves (**Exhibit 7**).

The number of miles a car was driven was affected by several economic fundamentals, the most important of which was the cost of gasoline. The number of older cars on the road increased during those times when fewer consumers bought new cars. New car purchases were subject to the same general economic trends applicable to most durable goods. As a result, in periods of strong economic growth and low unemployment, new car sales increased. Conversely, when the economy struggled and unemployment was high, fewer new cars were purchased and older cars were kept on the road longer, requiring more frequent repairs.

Overall, when the economy was doing well, gas prices and new car sales both increased, decreasing both the number of older cars on the road and the amount of additional mileage accumulated. When the economy did poorly, gas prices and new car sales were more likely to be depressed, increasing the utilization of older cars and their mileage. Because of these dynamics, auto-parts sales, especially in the DIY segment, were somewhat counter-cyclical.

The auto-parts business consisted of a large number of small, local operations as well as a few large, national retailers, such as AutoZone, O'Reilly Auto Parts, Advance Auto Parts, and Pep Boys. The national chains had sophisticated supply-chain operations to ensure that an appropriate level of inventory was maintained at each store while managing the tradeoff between minimizing inventory stock outs and maximizing the number of stock-keeping units (SKUs). This gave the large, national retailers an advantage because customers were more likely to find the parts they wanted at one of these stores. Counterbalancing the inventory advantage, however, was the expertise of sales associates, which allowed the smaller, local stores to enhance the customer service experience in DIY sales.

Recent Trends

In 2008, the U.S. economy had gone through the worst recession since the Great Depression, and the recovery that followed had been unusually slow. As a result, the auto-parts retail business enjoyed strong top-line growth. The future path of the U.S. economy was still highly uncertain as was the potential for a disconnect between GDP growth and gas price increases and between gas prices and miles driven. Furthermore, as auto-parts retailers operated with high-gross margins and significant fixed costs, profits varied widely with the level of sales, making the near-term earnings in the auto-parts retail segment particularly difficult to predict.

The auto-parts retail business experienced more competition as national retailers continued to expand their operations. Most of their expansion was at the expense of local retailers, but competition between major national retailers was heating up. If the economy strengthened and the auto-parts retail business was negatively affected by the replacement of older cars with new ones, competition between large, national retailers could make a bad situation worse.

Linked to high levels of industry competition and the expansion of the major retailers was the possibility that growth would eventually hit a wall if the market became oversaturated with auto-parts stores. Despite this concern, by 2012, AutoZone[1] management had stated that it was not seeing any signs of oversaturation, implying that expansion opportunities still remained.

The industry was also seeing an increase in sales via online channels as consumers enjoyed the flexibility of purchasing online and either picking up at the most convenient location or having their order delivered to their doorstep. Given the high operating leverage provided by selling through online channels, especially given the preexisting supply chains that already were built for storefront operations, as well as the growth in this channel, the national retail chains continued to invest in their online solutions and looked at that channel for future earnings growth.

Finally, another trend was the expansion of the large, U.S. auto-parts retailers into adjacent foreign markets, such as Mexico, Canada, and Puerto Rico. Thus far, the national retail companies were successful using this strategy, but their ability to continue to succeed and prosper in these markets, as well as in new, attractive locations such as Brazil, was not yet a reality.

AutoZone

AutoZone's first store opened in 1979 under the name Auto Shack in Forrest City, Arizona. In 1987, the name was changed to AutoZone, and the company implemented the first electronic auto-parts catalog for the retail industry. Then, in 1991, after four years of steady growth, AutoZone went public and was listed on the New York Stock Exchange under the ticker symbol AZO.

By 2012, AutoZone had become the leading retailer of automotive replacement parts and accessories in the United States, with more than 65,000 employees and 4,813 stores located in every state in the contiguous United States, Puerto Rico, and Mexico. AutoZone also distributed parts to commercial repair shops. In addition, a small but growing portion of AutoZone sales came through its online channel.

From the beginning, AutoZone had invested heavily in expanding its retail footprint via both organic and inorganic growth. It had also developed a sophisticated hub-and-feeder inventory system that kept the inventories of individual stores low as well as reduced the likelihood of stock outs. The expansion of its retail footprint had driven top-line revenue growth. AutoZone's success in developing category-leading distribution capabilities had resulted in both the highest operating margin for its industry and strong customer service backed by the ability of its distribution network to supply stores with nearly all of the AutoZone products on a same-day basis (**Exhibit 8**).

---

[1] AutoZone Q1 2012 Earnings Call—"I haven't seen a market yet that was so saturated yet that we were challenged economically," Bill Rhodes, AutoZone chairman, president, and CEO.

AutoZone's management focused on after-tax return on invested capital (ROIC) as the primary way to measure value creation for the company's capital providers. As a result, while AutoZone management invested in opportunities that led to top-line revenue growth and increased margins, it also focused on capital stewardship. What resulted was an aggressively managed working capital at the store level through the efficient use of inventory as well as attractive terms from suppliers.

Starting in 1998, AutoZone had returned capital to its equity investors through share repurchases. Although share-repurchase programs were common among U.S. companies, the typical result was a modest impact on shares outstanding. AutoZone's consistent use of share repurchases, however, had resulted in a significant reduction of both the shares outstanding and the equity capital. In particular, shares outstanding had dropped 39% from 2007 to 2011, and shareholders' equity had been reduced to a negative $1.2 billion in 2011. The repurchases had been funded by strong operating cash flows and by debt issuance. The net result was that AutoZone's invested capital had remained fairly constant since 2007, which, combined with increased earnings, created attractive ROIC levels (**Exhibit 9**).

Operating Cash Flow Options

While AutoZone had historically repurchased shares with operating cash flow, Mark Johnson felt that Edward Lampert's reduced stake in the company could prompt management to abandon repurchases and use the cash flows for other purposes. For example, AutoZone could distribute cash flows through cash dividends, reinvest the cash flows back into the core business, or use the funds to acquire stores. The company could also invest further in its operational capabilities to stay on the leading edge of the retail auto-parts industry. Finally, given a negative book-equity position and a continually growing debt load, AutoZone might consider using its cash flows to pay down debt to increase its future financial flexibility.

Dividends versus Share Repurchases

Assuming that AutoZone decided to distribute some of its operating cash flows to shareholders, the company had the choice of distributing the cash through dividends, share repurchases, or some combination of the two. Dividends were seen as a way to provide cash to existing shareholders, whereas only those shareholders who happened to be selling their shares would receive cash from a share-repurchase program. On the other hand, dividends were taxed at the shareholder level in the year received, whereas if a share-repurchase program succeeded in increasing the share price, the nonselling shareholders could defer paying taxes until they sold the stock.[2]

Dividends were also generally considered to be "sticky," meaning that the market expected a company to either keep its dividend steady or raise it each year.

---

[2] Current tax laws did allow for most dividends to be taxed at the same long-term capital gains rates, although this was not always the case, and the tax law regarding dividends was not certain going forward.

Because of this mindset, the implementation of a dividend or an increase of the dividend was usually interpreted by the market as a positive signal of the firm's ability to earn enough to continue paying the dividend far into the future. Conversely, any decrease in the dividend was normally viewed by the market as a very negative signal. Therefore, the stock price tended to change according to the dividend news released by the firm, which would be favorable for AutoZone shareholders so long as management was able to continue or increase the dividend each year.

Share repurchases were not viewed as sticky by the market because the amount of the repurchase often varied each year. The variance in the shares purchased might be caused by economic headwinds or tailwinds or differences in the quantity and size of investment opportunities that management believed would create shareholder value. Also, share repurchases were seen by some as a way to signal management's belief that the stock was undervalued and thus represented a good investment for the company.

Some companies chose to return shareholder capital through both dividends and share repurchases. In most of these cases, the company provided a stable but relatively small cash dividend and then repurchased shares at varying levels according to the circumstances each year. The benefit of this approach was to give shareholders the benefit of a sticky dividend while also receiving the price support of share repurchases.

Organic Growth

AutoZone could consider using its operating cash flow to increase the number of new stores it opened each year. Although the retail auto-parts industry was competitive and relatively mature, AutoZone's CEO had recently indicated that he did not see oversaturation of retail auto-parts stores in any of the company's markets.[3] Therefore, AutoZone could seize the opportunity to expand more rapidly, and perhaps preempt competition from gaining a foothold in those markets.

Rapid expansion came with a number of risks. First, Johnson was not sure that AutoZone had the managerial capacity to expand that swiftly. The company's growth in recent years had been substantial, as were the returns on investment, but it was not apparent if further growth would necessarily continue to create value. In addition, Johnson reasoned that the best retail locations were already covered, and that remaining areas would have lower profitability. This could be exacerbated if AutoZone expanded into areas that were less well served by its distribution network.

Johnson thought that there were some very attractive overseas investment opportunities, as evidenced by successful store openings in Mexico and Puerto Rico. AutoZone's 2011 annual report indicated work was underway to expand into Brazil over the next several years.[4] The company could increase its global presence by aggressively opening multiple stores in Brazil and other international locations. Hasty expansion into foreign markets, however, brought with it not only the risks of rapid store expansion, but also the difficulties inherent in transferring and translating the domestically successful supply model.

---

[3]See footnote 1.

[4]AutoZone annual report, 2011.

Growth by Acquisition

Johnson noted that in 1998 AutoZone had acquired over 800 stores from competitors and reasoned that another way to swiftly increase revenues would be for AutoZone to acquire other auto-parts retail stores. While this strategy would require some postmerger integration investment, such stores would be productive much more quickly than greenfield stores and shorten the return time on AutoZone's investment. This was an interesting strategy, but Johnson also knew that industry consolidation (**Exhibit 10**) had removed most of the viable takeover targets from the market; therefore it was unclear whether a merger of two of the large players would be allowed by the U.S. Department of Justice.

Debt Retirement

A final consideration was whether AutoZone might use part or all of its operating cash flows to retire some of the debt that the company had accumulated over the years. Much of the debt had been used to fund the share repurchases, but with a negative book-equity position and such a large debt position, Johnson wondered whether it was prudent to continue adding debt to the balance sheet. If AutoZone ran into trouble, it could struggle under the strain of making the interest payments and rolling over maturing debt. At some point, it was conceivable that AutoZone could lose its investment-grade credit rating,[5] which would only make future debt financing more difficult to secure and more expensive.

The Decision

Johnson had to decide what to do with his AutoZone investment. He was impressed with the company's history of strong shareholder returns and its leading position in the industry. Still, he wondered if Lampert's reduced influence and the potential for less favorable economic trends for auto-parts retailers were enough uncertainty for him to consider selling some or all of his position in the stock. As an analyst, Johnson's first consideration regarding the value of a company was to determine how well management was using the operating cash flow to maximize value for shareholders. Based on the ROIC (**Exhibit 9**), AutoZone was earning high returns on the capital invested in the company, which was undoubtedly the primary driver of stock returns. The extent to which share repurchases had contributed to the stock's performance, however, was less clear.

How would the market react to the news that AutoZone was reducing or eliminating its share repurchases after years of consistently following that strategy? Did the market view AutoZone's share repurchases as a cash dividend or was it indifferent about whether cash flows were distributed by repurchasing shares or paying a cash dividend? In any case, Johnson wondered if any move away from repurchasing shares after so many years might cause the stock price to fall, regardless of how the cash flows were ultimately spent. Or would AutoZone's stock price continue to appreciate as it had in the past so long as it continued to produce strong cash flows?

---

[5]Moody's and S&P had consistently assigned investment-grade ratings of Baa and BBB, respectively, for AutoZone's senior unsecured debt.

EXHIBIT 1 | Edward Lampert's Position in AutoZone

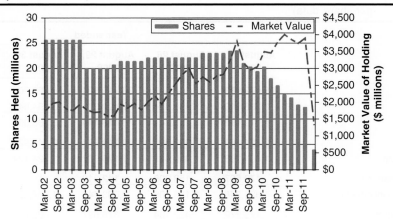

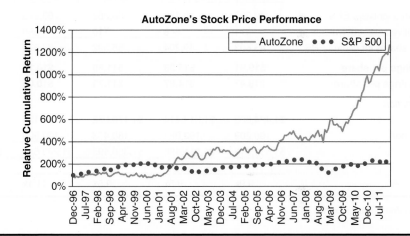

Data Source: Bloomberg.

EXHIBIT 2 | AutoZone Income Statement (August FY, in thousands of dollars, except ratios and per-share data)

	Year ended				
	August 27, 2011	August 28, 2010	August 29, 2009	August 30, 2008	August 25, 2007
Net sales	$8,072,973	$7,362,618	$6,816,824	$6,522,706	$6,169,804
Cost of sales	3,953,510	3,650,874	3,400,375	3,254,645	3,105,554
Gross profit	4,119,463	3,711,744	3,416,449	3,268,061	3,064,250
SG&A	2,624,660	2,392,330	2,240,387	2,143,927	2,008,984
Operating profit	1,494,803	1,319,414	1,176,062	1,124,134	1,055,266
Interest expense, net	170,557	158,909	142,316	116,745	119,116
Income before income taxes	1,324,246	1,160,505	1,033,746	1,007,389	936,150
Income tax expense	475,272	422,194	376,697	365,783	340,478
Net income	**$848,974**	**$738,311**	**$657,049**	**$641,606**	**$595,672**
Wt. avg. shares for basic EPS	42,632	48,488	55,282	63,295	69,101
Effect of dilutive stock equivalents	971	816	710	580	743
Adj. wt. avg. shares for diluted EPS	43,603	49,304	55,992	63,875	69,844
Basic earnings per share	**$19.91**	**$15.23**	**$11.89**	**$10.14**	**$8.62**
Diluted earnings per share	**$19.47**	**$14.97**	**$11.73**	**$10.04**	**$8.53**
Other information:					
EBIT	$1,494,803	$1,319,414	$1,176,062	$1,124,134	$1,055,266
Depr. & Amort.	196,209	192,084	180,433	169,509	159,411
EBITDA	$1,691,012	$1,511,498	$1,356,495	$1,293,643	$1,214,677
EBITDA/Interest	9.9x	9.5x	9.5x	11.1x	10.2x

Data Source: AutoZone annual reports.

EXHIBIT 3 | AutoZone Balance Sheet (August FY, in thousands of dollars)

	August 27, 2011	August 28, 2010	August 29, 2009	August 30, 2008	August 25, 2007
Assets					
Current assets:					
Cash and cash equivalents	$97,606	$98,280	$92,706	$242,461	$86,654
Accounts receivable	140,690	125,802	126,514	71,241	59,876
Merchandise inventories	2,466,107	2,304,579	2,207,497	2,150,109	2,007,430
Other current assets	88,022	83,160	135,013	122,490	116,495
Deferred income taxes	—	—	—	—	—
Total current assets	2,792,425	2,611,821	2,561,730	2,586,301	2,270,455
Property and equipment:					
Land	740,276	690,098	656,516	643,699	625,992
Buildings and improvements	2,177,476	2,013,301	1,900,610	1,814,668	1,720,172
Equipment	994,369	923,595	887,521	850,679	780,199
Leasehold improvements	275,299	247,748	219,606	202,098	183,601
Construction in progress	184,452	192,519	145,161	128,133	85,581
Gross property and equipment	4,371,872	4,067,261	3,809,414	3,639,277	3,395,545
Less: Accumulated depreciation and amortization	1,702,997	1,547,315	1,455,057	1,349,621	1,217,703
Net property and equipment	2,668,875	2,519,946	2,354,357	2,289,656	2,177,842
Goodwill	302,645	302,645	302,645	302,645	302,645
Deferred income taxes	10,661	46,223	59,067	38,283	21,331
Other long-term assets	94,996	90,959	40,606	40,227	32,436
Total assets	**$5,869,602**	**$5,571,594**	**$5,318,405**	**$5,257,112**	**$4,804,709**
Liabilities and Stockholders' Deficit					
Current liabilities:					
Accounts payable	$2,755,853	$2,433,050	$2,118,746	$2,043,271	$1,870,668
Accrued expenses and other	449,327	432,368	381,271	327,664	307,633
Income taxes payable	25,185	25,385	35,145	11,582	25,442
Deferred income taxes	166,449	146,971	171,590	136,803	82,152
Short-term borrowings	34,082	26,186	—	—	—
Total current liabilities	3,430,896	3,063,960	2,706,752	2,519,320	2,285,895
Long-term debt	3,317,600	2,882,300	2,726,900	2,250,000	1,935,618
Other long-term liabilities	375,338	364,099	317,827	258,105	179,996
Stockholders' deficit:					
Common stock, par: $0.01/share	441	501	579	636	713
Additional paid-in capital	591,384	557,955	549,326	537,005	545,404
Retained earnings	(643,998)	(245,344)	136,935	206,099	546,049
Accumulated other comprehensive loss	(119,691)	(106,468)	(92,035)	(4,135)	(9,550)
Treasury stock, at cost	(1,082,368)	(945,409)	(1,027,879)	(509,918)	(679,416)
Total stockholders' equity	(1,254,232)	(738,765)	(433,074)	229,687	403,200
Total liabilities and stockholders' equity	**$5,869,602**	**$5,571,594**	**$5,318,405**	**$5,257,112**	**$4,804,709**
Shares issued	44,084	50,061	57,881	63,600	71,250
Shares outstanding	40,109	45,107	50,801	59,608	65,960
Other information:					
Capital lease obligations	86,656	88,280	54,764	64,061	55,088

Data Source: AutoZone annual reports.

EXHIBIT 4 | AutoZone Statement of Cash Flows (August FY, in thousands of dollars)

	Year ended				
	August 27, 2011	August 28, 2010	August 29, 2009	August 30, 2008	August 25, 2007
Cash flows from operating activities:					
Net income	$848,974	$738,311	$657,049	$641,606	$595,672
Adjustments to reconcile net income to net cash provided by operating activities:					
Depreciation and amortization of property and equipment	196,209	192,084	180,433	169,509	159,411
Amortization of debt origination fees	8,962	6,495	3,644	1,837	1,719
Income tax benefit from exercise of stock options	(34,945)	(22,251)	(8,407)	(10,142)	(16,523)
Deferred income taxes	44,667	(9,023)	46,318	67,474	24,844
Share-based compensation expense	26,625	19,120	19,135	18,388	18,462
Other	—	—	—	—	—
Changes in operating assets and liabilities:					
Accounts receivable	(14,605)	782	(56,823)	(11,145)	20,487
Merchandise inventories	(155,421)	(96,077)	(76,337)	(137,841)	(160,780)
Accounts payable and accrued expenses	342,826	349,122	137,158	175,733	186,228
Income taxes payable	34,319	12,474	32,264	(3,861)	17,587
Other, net	(6,073)	5,215	(10,626)	9,542	(1,913)
Net cash provided by operating activities	1,291,538	1,196,252	923,808	921,100	845,194
Cash flows from investing activities:					
Capital expenditures	(321,604)	(315,400)	(272,247)	(243,594)	(224,474)
Purchase of marketable securities	(43,772)	(56,156)	(48,444)	(54,282)	(94,615)
Proceeds from sale of marketable securities	43,081	52,620	46,306	50,712	86,921
Acquisitions	—	—	—	—	—
Disposal of capital assets	3,301	11,489	10,663	4,014	3,453
Net cash used in investing activities	(318,994)	(307,447)	(263,722)	(243,150)	(228,715)
Cash flows from financing activities:					
Net proceeds from commercial paper	134,600	155,400	277,600	(206,700)	84,300
Net proceeds from short-term borrowings	6,901	26,186	—	—	—
Proceeds from issuance of debt	500,000	—	500,000	750,000	—
Repayment of debt	(199,300)	—	(300,700)	(229,827)	(5,839)
Net proceeds from sale of common stock	55,846	52,922	39,855	27,065	58,952
Purchase of treasury stock	(1,466,802)	(1,123,655)	(1,300,002)	(849,196)	(761,887)
Income tax benefit from exercise of stock options	34,945	22,251	8,407	10,142	16,523
Payments of capital lease obligations	(22,781)	(16,597)	(17,040)	(15,880)	(11,360)
Other	(17,180)	—	(15,016)	(8,286)	(2,072)
Net cash used in financing activities	(973,771)	(883,493)	(806,896)	(522,682)	(621,383)
Effect of exchange rate changes on cash	553	262	(2,945)	539	—
Net (decrease) increase in cash and cash equivalents	(674)	5,574	(149,755)	155,807	(4,904)
Cash and cash equivalents at beginning of year	98,280	92,706	242,461	86,654	91,558
Cash and cash equivalents at end of year	$97,606	$98,280	$92,706	$242,461	$86,654
Supplemental cash flow information:					
Interest paid, net of interest cost capitalized	$155,531	$150,745	$132,905	$107,477	$116,580
Income taxes paid	$405,654	$420,575	$299,021	$313,875	$299,566
Assets acquired through capital lease	$32,301	$75,881	$16,880	$61,572	$69,325

Data Source: AutoZone annual reports.

EXHIBIT 5 | AutoZone 2011 Statement of Stockholders' Equity (dollars in thousands)

(in thousands)	Common Shares Issued	Common Stock	Additional Paid-in Capital	Retained (Deficit) Earnings	Accumulated Other Comprehensive Loss	Treasury Stock	Total
Balance at August 28, 2010	50,061	501	$557,955	($245,344)	($106,468)	($945,409)	($738,765)
Net income				848,974			848,974
Pension liability adjustments, net of taxes of ($3,998)					(17,346)		(17,346)
Foreign currency translation adjustment					8,347		8,347
Unrealized loss adjustment on marketable securities, net of taxes of ($91)					(171)		(171)
Net losses on terminated derivatives					(5,453)		(5,453)
Reclassification of net losses on derivatives into earnings					1,400		1,400
Comprehensive income							835,751
Purchase of 5,598 shares of treasury stock						(1,466,802)	(1,466,802)
Retirement of treasury shares	(6,577)	(66)	(82,150)	(1,247,627)		1,329,843	—
Sale of common stock under stock options and stock purchase plan	600	6	55,840				55,846
Share-based compensation expense			24,794				24,794
Income tax benefit from exercise of stock options			34,945				34,945
Other				(1)			(1)
Balance at August 27, 2011	44,084	441	$591,384	($643,998)	($119,691)	($1,082,368)	($1,254,232)

Data Source: AutoZone annual reports.

EXHIBIT 6 | AutoZone Capital Structure and Coverage Ratio

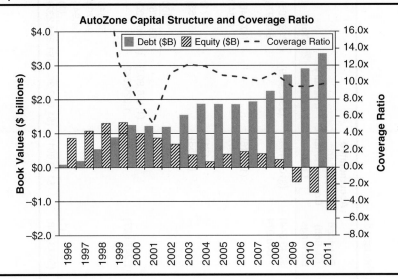

Note: Coverage ratio is defined as EBITDA divided by interest expense.

Data Source: AutoZone annual reports.

EXHIBIT 7 | Miles Driven and Average Vehicle Age

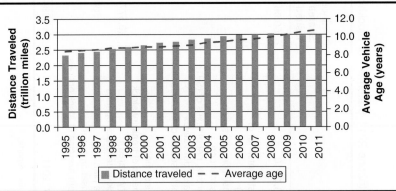

Data Source: U.S. Department of Transportation (miles driven) and, Polk Research (vehicle age).

EXHIBIT 8 | Merchandise Listing (as of October 17, 2011)

Failure	Maintenance	Discretionary
A/C Compressors	Antifreeze & Windshield Washer Fluid	Air Fresheners
Batteries & Accessories	Brake Drums, Rotors, Shoes & Pads	Cell Phone Accessories
Belts & Hoses	Chemicals, including Brake & Power	Drinks & Snacks
Carburetors	Steering Fluid, Oil & Fuel Additives	Floor Mats & Seat Covers
Chassis	Oil & Transmission Fluid	Mirrors
Clutches	Oil, Air, Fuel & Transmission Filters	Performance Products
CV Axles	Oxygen Sensors	Protectants & Cleaners
Engines	Paint & Accessories	Seat Covers
Fuel Pumps	Refrigerant & Accessories	Sealants & Adhesives
Fuses	Shock Absorbers & Struts	Steering Wheel Covers
Ignition	Spark Plugs & Wires	Stereos & Radios
Lighting	Windshield Wipers	Tools
Mufflers		Wash & Wax
Starters & Alternators		
Water Pumps		
Radiators		
Thermostats		

Data Source: AutoZone annual report.

EXHIBIT 9 | Share Repurchases and ROIC 1996–2011

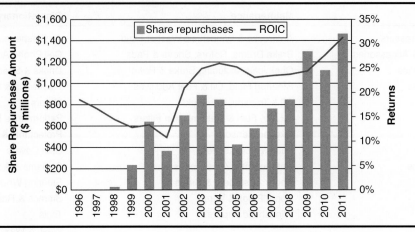

Note: ROIC is calculated as the sum of net income and tax-adjusted interest and rent expenses divided by the sum of average debt, average equity, six times rent expense (to approximate capitalizing rent), and average capital lease obligations.

Data Source: AutoZone annual reports.

EXHIBIT 10 | Aftermarket Auto Parts Industry Structure

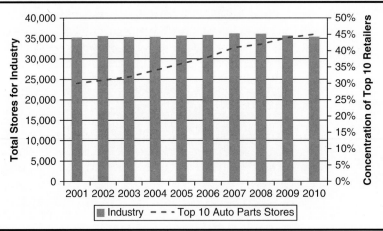

Note: The top 10 companies (stores) as of August 2010: AutoZone (4,728), O'Reilly Auto Parts (3,657), Advance Auto Parts (3,627), General Parts/CARQUEST (1,500), Genuine Parts/NAPA (1,035), Pep Boys (630), Fisher Auto Parts (406), Uni-Select (273), Replacement Parts (155), and Auto-Wares Group (128).

Data Source: *AAIA Factbook* and SEC filings.

## PART 6

Management of the Corporate Capital Structure

An Introduction to Debt Policy and Value

Many factors determine how much debt a firm takes on. Chief among them ought to be the effect of the debt on the value of the firm. Does borrowing create value? If so, for whom? If not, then why do so many executives concern themselves with leverage?

If leverage affects value, then it should cause changes in either the discount rate of the firm (that is, its weighted-average cost of capital) or the cash flows of the firm.

1. Please fill in the following:

	0% Debt/ 100% Equity	25% Debt/ 75% Equity	50% Debt/ 50% Equity
Book Value of Debt	—	$2,500	$5,000
Book Value of Equity	$10,000	$7,500	$5,000
Market Value of Debt	—	$2,500	$5,000
Market Value of Equity	$10,000	$8,350	$6,700
Pretax Cost of Debt	5.00%	5.00%	5.00%
After-Tax Cost of Debt	3.30%	3.30%	3.30%
Market Value Weights of			
Debt	0%	_____	_____
Equity	100%	_____	_____
Levered Beta	0.80	_____	
Risk-Free Rate	5.0%	5.0%	5.0%
Market Premium	6.0%	6.0%	6.0%
Cost of Equity	_____		
Weighted-Average Cost of Capital	_____		
EBIT	$1,485	$1,485	$1,485
Taxes (@ 34%)	_____		

(Continued)

(Continued)

	0% Debt/ 100% Equity	25% Debt/ 75% Equity	50% Debt/ 50% Equity
EBIAT			
+ Depreciation	$500	$500	$500
− Capital exp.	($500)	($500)	($500)
+ Change in net working capital	—	—	—
Free Cash Flow			
Value of Assets (FCF/WACC)			

Why does the value of assets change? Where, specifically, do those changes occur?

2. In finance, as in accounting, the two sides of the balance sheet must be equal. In the previous problem, we valued the asset side of the balance sheet. To value the other side, we must value the debt and the equity, and then add them together.

	0% Debt/ 100% Equity	25% Debt/ 75% Equity	50% Debt/ 50% Equity
Cash flow to creditors:			
Interest	—	$125	$250
Pretax cost of debt	5.0%	5.0%	5.0%
Value of debt:			
(Int/K_d)			
Cash flow to shareholders:			
EBIT	$1,485	$1,485	$1,485
Interest	—	$125	$250
Pretax profit			
Taxes (@ 34%)			
Net income			
+ Depreciation	$500	$500	$500
− Capital exp.	($500)	($500)	($500)
+ Change in net working capital	—	—	—
− Debt amortization	—	—	—
Residual cash flow			
Cost of equity			
Value of equity (RCF/K_e)			
Value of equity plus value of debt			

As the firm levers up, how does the increase in value get apportioned between the creditors and the shareholders?

3. In the preceding problem, we divided the value of all the assets between two classes of investors: creditors and shareholders. This process tells us where the change in value is *going*, but it sheds little light on where the change is *coming from*. Let's divide the free cash flows of the firm into *pure business flows* and cash flows resulting from *financing effects*. Now, an axiom in finance is that you should discount cash flows at a rate consistent with the risk of those cash flows. Pure business flows should be discounted at the unlevered cost of equity (i.e., the cost of capital for the unlevered firm). Financing flows should be discounted at the rate of return required by the providers of debt.

	0% Debt/ 100% Equity	25% Debt/ 75% Equity	50% Debt/ 50% Equity
Pure Business Cash Flows:			
EBIT	$1,485	$1,485	$1,485
Taxes (@ 34%)	$505	$505	$505
EBIAT	$980	$980	$980
+ Depreciation	$500	$500	$500
− Capital exp.	($500)	($500)	($500)
+ Change in net working capital	—	—	—
Free Cash Flow	$980	$980	$980
Unlevered Beta	0.8	0.8	0.8
Risk-Free Rate	5.0%	5.0%	5.0%
Market Premium	6.0%	6.0%	6.0%
Unlevered WACC			
Value of Pure Business Flows: (FCF/Unlevered WACC)			
Financing Cash Flows			
Interest			
Tax Reduction			
Pretax Cost of Debt	5.0%	5.0%	5.0%
Value of Financing Effect: (Tax Reduction/Pretax Cost of Debt)			
Total Value (Sum of Values of Pure Business Flows and Financing Effects)			

The first three problems illustrate one of the most important theories in finance. This theory, developed by two professors, Franco Modigliani and Merton Miller, revolutionized the way we think about capital structure policies.

The M&M theory says:

$$
\underbrace{\begin{array}{c} \text{Value of} \\ \text{assets} \end{array}}_{\text{Problem 1}} = \underbrace{\begin{array}{c} \text{Value of} \\ \text{debt} \end{array} + \begin{array}{c} \text{Value of} \\ \text{equity} \end{array}}_{\text{Problem 2}} = \underbrace{\begin{array}{c} \text{Value of} \\ \text{unlevered} \\ \text{firm} \end{array} + \begin{array}{c} \text{Value of} \\ \text{debt tax} \\ \text{shields}^{1} \end{array}}_{\text{Problem 3}}
$$

4. What remains to be seen, however, is whether shareholders are better or worse off with more leverage. Problem 2 does not tell us because there we computed total value of equity, and shareholders care about value *per* share. Ordinarily, total value will be a good proxy for what is happening to the price per share, but in the case of a relevering firm, that may not be true. Implicitly, we assumed that, as our firm in problems 1–3 levered up, it was repurchasing stock on the open market (you will note that EBIT did not change, so management was clearly not investing the proceeds from the loans into cash-generating assets). We held EBIT constant so that we could see clearly the effect of financial changes without getting them mixed up in the effects of investments. The point is that, as the firm borrows and repurchases shares, the total value of equity may decline, but the price per share may *rise*.

   Now, solving for the price per share may seem impossible because we are dealing with two unknowns—share price and the change in the number of shares:

$$
\text{Share price} = \frac{\text{Market value of equity}}{\text{Original shares} - \text{Repurchased shares}}
$$

   But by rewriting the equation, we can put it in a form that can be solved:

$$
\text{Share price} = \frac{\text{Original market value of equity} + \text{Value of financing effect}}{\text{Number of original shares}}
$$

   Referring to the results of problem 2, let's assume that all the new debt is equal to the cash paid to repurchase shares. Please complete the following table:

	0% Debt/ 100% Equity	25% Debt/ 75% Equity	50% Debt/ 50% Equity
Total Market Value of Equity			
Cash Paid Out			
# Original Shares	1,000	1,000	1,000
Total Value Per Share			

---

[1]Debt tax shields can be valued by discounting the future annual tax savings at the pretax cost of debt. For debt, that is assumed to be outstanding in perpetuity, the tax savings is the tax rate, t, times the interest payment, $k \times D$. The present value of this perpetual savings is $tkD/k = tD$.

5. In this set of problems, is leverage good for shareholders? Why? Is levering/ unlevering the firm something that shareholders can do for themselves? In what sense should shareholders pay a premium for shares of levered companies?

6. From a macroeconomic point of view, is society better off if firms use more than zero debt (up to some prudent limit)?

7. As a way of illustrating the usefulness of the M&M theory and consolidating your grasp of the mechanics, consider the following case and complete the worksheet. On March 3, 1988, Beazer PLC (a British construction company) and Shearson Lehman Hutton, Inc. (an investment-banking firm) commenced a hostile tender offer to purchase all the outstanding stock of Koppers Company, Inc., a producer of construction materials, chemicals, and building products. Originally, the raiders offered $45 a share; subsequently, the offer was raised to $56 and then finally to $61 a share. The Koppers board asserted that the offers were inadequate and its management was reviewing the possibility of a major recapitalization.

   To test the valuation effects of the recapitalization alternative, assume that Koppers could borrow a maximum of $1,738,095,000 at a pretax cost of debt of 10.5% and that the aggregate amount of debt will remain constant in perpetuity. Thus, Koppers will take on additional debt of $1,565,686,000 (that is, $1,738,095,000 minus $172,409,000). Also assume that the proceeds of the loan would be paid as an extraordinary dividend to shareholders. **Exhibit 1** presents Koppers' book- and market-value balance sheets, assuming the capital structure before recapitalization. Please complete the worksheet for the recapitalization alternative.

EXHIBIT 1 | Koppers Company, Inc. (values in thousands)

	Before Recapitalization	After Recapitalization
Book-Value Balance Sheets		
Net working capital	$ 212,453	_____
Fixed assets	601,446	_____
Total assets	813,899	_____
Long-term debt	172,409	_____
Deferred taxes, etc.	195,616	_____
Preferred stock	15,000	_____
Common equity	430,874	_____
Total capital	$ 813,899	_____
Market-Value Balance Sheets		
Net working capital	$ 212,453	_____
Fixed assets	1,618,081	_____
PV debt tax shield	58,619	_____
Total assets	1,889,153	_____
Long-term debt	172,409	_____
Deferred taxes, etc.	—	_____
Preferred stock	15,000	_____
Common equity	1,701,744	_____
Total capital	$1,889,153	_____
Number of shares	28,128	_____
Price per share	$ 60.50	_____
Value to Public Shareholders		
Cash received	$ —	_____
Value of shares	$1,701,744	_____
Total	$1,701,744	_____
Total per share	$ 60.50	_____

Structuring Corporate Financial Policy: Diagnosis of Problems and Evaluation of Strategies

This note outlines a diagnostic and prescriptive way of thinking about corporate financial policy. Successful diagnosis and prescription depend heavily on thoughtful creativity and careful judgment, so the note presents no cookie-cutter solutions. Rather, it discusses the elements of good *process* and offers three basic stages in that process:

Description: The ability to describe a firm's financial policies (which have been chosen either explicitly or by default) is an essential foundation of diagnosis and prescription. Part I of this note defines "financial structure" and discusses the design elements by which a senior financial officer must make choices. This section illustrates the complexity of a firm's financial policies.

Diagnosis: One derives a "good" financial structure by triangulating from benchmark perspectives. Then one compares the idealized and actual financial structures, looking for opportunities for improvement. Part II of this note is an overview of three benchmarks by which the analyst can diagnose problems and opportunities: (1) the expectations of investors, (2) the policies and behavior of competitors, and (3) the internal goals and motivations of corporate management itself. Other perspectives may also exist. Parts III, IV, and V discuss in detail the estimation and application of the three benchmarks. These sections emphasize artful homework and economy of effort by focusing on key considerations, questions, and information. The goal is to derive insights unique to each benchmark, rather than to churn data endlessly.

Prescription: Action recommendations should spring from the insights gained in description and diagnosis. Rarely, however, do unique solutions or ideas exist; rather, the typical chief financial officer (CFO) must have a *view* about competing suggestions. Part VI addresses the task of comparing competing proposals. Part VII presents the conclusion.

Part I: Identifying Corporate Financial Policy: The Elements of Its Design

You can observe a lot just by watching.
　—Yogi Berra

The first task for financial advisers and decision makers is to understand the firm's *current* financial policy. Doing so is a necessary foundation for diagnosing problems and prescribing remedies. This section presents an approach for identifying the firm's financial policy, based on a careful analysis of the *tactics* by which that policy is implemented.

The Concept of Corporate Financial Policy

The notion that firms *have* a distinct financial policy is startling to some analysts and executives. Occasionally, a chief financial officer will say, "All I do is get the best deal I can whenever we need funds." Almost no CFO would admit otherwise. In all probability, however, the firm has a more substantive policy than the CFO admits to. Even a management style of myopia or opportunism is, after all, a policy.

Some executives will argue that calling financing a "policy" is too fancy. They say that financing is reactive: it happens after all investment and operational decisions have been made. How can reaction be a policy? At other times, one hears an executive say, "Our financial policy is simple." Attempts to characterize a financial structure as reactive or simplistic overlook the considerable richness of choice that confronts the financial manager.

Finally, some analysts make the mistake of "one-size-fits-all" thinking; that is, they assume that financial policy is mainly driven by the economics of a certain industry and they overlook the firm-specific nature of financial policy. Firms in the same, well-defined industry can have very different financial policies. The reason is that financial policy is a matter of *managerial choice.*

"Corporate financial policy" is a set of broad *guidelines* or a preferred *style* to guide the raising of capital and the distribution of value. Policies should be set to support the mission and strategy of the firm. As the environment changes, policies should adapt.

The analyst of financial policy must come to terms with its ambiguity. Policies are guidelines; they are imprecise. Policies are products of managerial choice rather than the dictates of an economic model. Policies change over time. Nevertheless, the framework in this note can help the analyst define a firm's corporate financial policy with enough focus to identify potential problems, prescribe remedies, and make decisions.

The Elements of Financial Policy

Every financial structure reveals underlying financial policies through the following seven elements of financial-structure design:[1]

---

[1]For economy, this note will restrict its scope to these seven items. One can, however, imagine dimensions other than the ones listed here.

1. *Mix* of classes of capital (such as debt versus equity, or common stock versus re-tained earnings): *How heavily does the firm rely on different classes of capital? Is the reliance on debt reasonable in light of the risks the firm faces and the nature of its industry and technology?* Mix may be analyzed through capitalization ratios, debt-service coverage ratios, and the firm's sources-and-uses-of-funds statement (where the analyst should look for the origins of the new additions to capital in the recent past). Many firms exhibit a pecking order of financing: they seek to fulfill their funding needs through the retention of profits, then through debt, and, finally, through the issuance of new shares. *Does the firm observe a particular pecking order in its acquisition of new capital?*

2. *Maturity structure of the firm's capital:* To describe the choices made about the maturity of outstanding securities is to be able to infer the judgments the firm made about its priorities—for example, future financing requirements and opportunities or relative preference for refinancing risk[2] versus reinvestment risk.[3] A risk-neutral position with respect to maturity would be where the life of the firm's assets equals the life of the firm's liabilities. Most firms accept an inequality in one direction or the other. This might be due to ignorance or to sophistication: managers might have a strong internal "view" about their ability to reinvest or refinance. Ultimately, we want managers to maximize value, not minimize risk. The absence of a perfect maturity hedge might reflect managers' better-informed bets about the future of the firm and markets. Measuring the maturity structure of the firm's capital can yield insights into the bets that the firm's managers are appar-ently making. The standard measures of maturity are term to maturity, average life, and duration. *Are the lives of the firm's assets and liabilities roughly matched? If not, what gamble is the firm taking (i.e., is it showing an appetite for refunding risk or interest-rate risk)?*

3. *Basis of the firm's coupon and dividend payments:* In simplest terms, basis addresses the firm's preference for fixed or floating rates of payment and is a useful tool in fathoming management's judgment regarding the future course of interest rates. Interest-rate derivatives provide the financial officer with choices conditioned by caps, floors, and other structured options. Understanding manage-ment's basis choices can reveal some of the fundamental bets management is placing, even when it has decided to "do nothing." *What is the firm's relative preference for fixed or floating interest rates? Are the firm's operating returns fixed or floating?*

---

[2]Refinancing risk exists where the life of the firm's assets is *more* than the life of the firm's liabilities. In other words, the firm will need to replace (or "roll over") the capital originally obtained to buy the asset. The refinancing risk is the chance that the firm will be unable to obtain funds on advantageous terms (or at all) at the rollover date.

[3]Reinvestment risk exists where the life of the firm's assets is *less* than the life of the firm's liabilities. In other words, the firm will need to replace, or roll over, the investment that the capital originally financed. Reinvestment risk is the chance that the firm will be unable to reinvest the capital on advantageous terms at the rollover date.

4. *Currency* addresses the global aspect of a firm's financial opportunities: These opportunities are expressed in two ways: (a) management of the firm's exposure to foreign exchange-rate fluctuations, and (b) the exploitation of unusual financing possibilities in global capital markets. Exchange-rate exposure arises when a firm earns income (or pays expenses) in a variety of currencies. Whether and how a firm hedges this exposure can reveal the "bets" that management is making regarding the future movement of exchange rates and the future currency mix of the firm's cash flows. The financial-policy analyst should look for foreign-denominated securities in the firm's capital and for swap, option, futures, and forward contracts—all of which can be used to manage the firm's foreign-exchange exposure. The other way that currency matters to the financial-policy analyst is as an indication of the management's willingness to source its capital "offshore." This is an indication of sophistication and of having a view about the parity of exchange rates with security returns around the world. In a perfectly integrated global capital market, the theory of interest rate parity would posit the futility of finding bargain financing offshore. But global capital markets are not perfectly integrated, and interest rate parity rarely holds true everywhere. Experience suggests that financing bargains may exist temporarily. Offshore financing may suggest an interest in finding and exploiting such bargains. *Is the currency denomination of the firm's capital consistent with the currency denomination of the firm's operating cash flows? Do the balance sheet footnotes show evidence of foreign-exchange hedging? Also, is the company, in effect, sourcing capital on a global basis or is it focusing narrowly on the domestic capital markets?*

5. *Exotica:* Every firm faces a spectrum of financing alternatives, ranging from plain-vanilla bonds and stocks to hybrids and one-of-a-kind, highly tailored securities.[4] This element considers management's relative preference for financial innovation. Where a firm positions itself on this spectrum can shed light on management's openness to new ideas, intellectual originality and, possibly, opportunistic tendencies. As a general matter, option-linked securities often appear in corporate finance where there is some disagreement between issuers and investors about a firm's prospects. For instance, managers of high-growth firms will foresee rapid expansion and vaulting stock prices. Bond investors, not having the benefit of inside information, might see only high risk—issuing a convertible bond might be a way to allow the bond investors to capitalize the risk[5] and to enjoy the creation of value through growth in return for accepting a lower current yield. Also, the circumstances under which exotic securities were issued are often fascinating episodes in a company's history. *Based on past financings, what is the firm's appetite for issuing exotic securities? Why have the firm's exotic securities been tailored as they are?*

---

[4]Examples of highly tailored securities include exchangeable and convertible bonds, hybrid classes of common stock, and contingent securities, such as a dividend-paying equity issued in connection with an acquisition.

[5]In general, the call options embedded in a convertible bond will be more valuable depending on the greater the volatility of the underlying asset.

6. *External control:* Any management team probably prefers little outside control. One must recognize that, in any financial structure, management has made choices about subtle control trade-offs, including *who* might exercise control (for example, creditors, existing shareholders, new shareholders, or a raider) and the control *trigger* (for example, default on a loan covenant, passing a preferred stock dividend, or a shareholder vote). How management structures control triggers (for example, the tightness of loan covenants) or forestalls discipline (perhaps through the adoption of poison pills and other takeover defenses) can reveal insights into management's fears and expectations. Clues about external control choices may be found in credit covenants, collateral pledges, the terms of preferred shares, the profile of the firm's equity holders, the voting rights of common stock, corporate bylaws, and antitakeover defenses. *In what ways has management defended against or yielded to external control?*

7. *Distribution:* seeks to determine any patterns in (a) the way the firm markets its securities (i.e., acquires capital), and (b) the way the firm delivers value to its investors (i.e., returns capital). Regarding marketing, insights emerge from knowing where a firm's securities are listed for trading, how often the shares are sold, and who advises the sale of securities (the adviser that a firm attracts is one indication of its sophistication). Regarding the delivery of value, the two generic strategies involve dividends or capital gains. Some companies will pay low or no dividends and force their shareholders to take returns in the form of capital gains. Other companies will pay material dividends, even borrowing to do so. Still others will repurchase shares, split shares, and declare extraordinary dividends. Managers' choices about delivering value yield clues about management's beliefs regarding investors and the company's ability to satisfy investors' needs. *How have managers chosen to deliver value to shareholders, and with whose assistance have they issued securities?*

A Comparative Illustration

The value of looking at a firm's financial structure through these seven design elements is that the insights they provide can become a basis for developing a broad, detailed picture of the firm's financial policies. Also, the seven elements become an organizational framework for the wealth of financial information on publicly owned companies.

Consider the examples of Eli Lilly and Company, a leading manufacturer and marketer of pharmaceuticals and animal-health products, and Genentech, Inc., a biotechnology company focused on developing products in oncology, immunology, and pulmonary medicine. Sources such as the *Mergent Industrial Manual* and the *Value Line Investment Survey* distill information from annual reports and regulatory filings and permit the analyst to draw conclusions about the seven elements of each firm's financial policy. Drawing on the financial results for 2004, analysts may glean the following insights about the policies of Eli Lilly and Genentech from **Table 1.**

As **Table 1** shows, standard information available on public companies yields important contrasts in their financial policies. Note that the insights are *informed*

TABLE 1 | Financial Policies for Eli Lilly and Genentech.

Elements of Financial Policy	Eli Lilly and Company	Genentech, Inc.
Mix	**Moderate debt** • Debt/assets = 19% • Debt/capital = 30% • Sold equity in 1972, 1973, 1978 • S&P credit rating: AA • Acquisitions financed with combinations of cash and stock	**Equity orientation** • Debt/assets = 4% • Debt/capital = 6% • Sold equity in 1980, 1985, 1999, 2000 • S&P credit rating: A+ • Acquisitions financed with cash
Maturity	**Medium to long** • Average life = 16.3 years • 64% @ 5 to 15 years • 36% @ 30 years	**Short-term** • Maintains a single 2-year issue
Basis	**Fixed rates** • 91% of debt is at a fixed rate	**Floating rates** • Variable interest, with minimum 1.2% rate
Currency	**Exclusively U.S. dollars**	**Exclusively U.S. dollars**
Exotica	**No exotics** • Modest use of leases	**No exotics**
Control	**Favors large stockholders** • Debt unsecured and callable • Lilly Foundation owned 13.4% of the stock	**Significant investor** • Roche Holdings Inc. owned 56.1% of outstanding common stock • Increased authorized shares from 300 million in 2000 to 3 billion in 2004
Distribution	**Steady dividends** • Average payout: 47% • Numerous stock splits • Participating preferred available	**Capital gains** • Rapid growth and high returns • No dividends • Stock splits in 1999, 2000, 2004
	Various advisers • Morgan Stanley & Co.; Goldman, Sachs & Co.; J.P. Morgan; Deutsche Banc; Merrill Lynch & Co., among others	**Single adviser** • Hambrecht & Quist
	Broadly international • Subsidiaries and affiliates in over 40 major countries	**Some international** • Subsidiaries in Canada, Switzerland, Japan, Germany, United Kingdom, and the Netherlands

guesses: neither of those firms explicitly describes its financial policies. Nonetheless, with practice and good information, the validity of the guesses can be high.

Eli Lilly and Genentech present distinctly different policy profiles. While Genentech's policy is conservative in almost every dimension, Lilly's is somewhat more aggressive. Two such firms would warrant very different sets of questions by a director or an outside financial adviser. The key idea is that financial policies can be characterized by the tracks they leave. Good strategic assessment begins with good tracking of current or past policy.

Part II: General Framework for Diagnosing Financial-Policy Opportunities and Problems

Having parsed the choices embedded in the firm's financial structure, one must ask, "Were these the *right* choices?" What is "right" is a matter of the context and the clientele to which management must respond. A firm has many potential claimants.[6] The discussion that follows will focus on the perspectives of competitors, investors, and senior corporate managers.

1. *Does the financial policy create value?*

From the standpoint of investors, the best financial structure will (a) maximize shareholder wealth, (b) maximize the value of the entire firm (i.e., the market value of assets), and (c) minimize the firm's weighted-average cost of capital (WACC). When those conditions occur, the firm makes the best trade-offs among the choices on each of the seven dimensions of financial policy. This analysis is all within the context of the *market* conditions.

2. *Does the financial policy create a competitive advantage?*

Competitors should matter in the design of corporate financial policy. Financial structure can enhance or constrain competitive advantage mainly by opening or foreclosing avenues of competitive response over time. Thus, a manager should critically assess the strategic options created or destroyed by a particular financial structure. Also, assuming that they are reasonably well managed, competitors' financial structures are probably an indicator of good financial policy in a particular industry. Thus, a manager should want to know how his or her firm's financial structure compares with the peer group. In short, this line of thinking seeks to evaluate the relative position of the firm in its competitive environment on the basis of financial structure.

3. *Does the financial policy sustain senior management's vision?*

The internal perspective tests the appropriateness of a capital structure from the standpoint of the expectations and capacities of the corporate organization itself. The analyst begins with an assessment of corporate strategy and the resulting stream of cash requirements and resources anticipated in the future. The realism

---

[6]With a moment's reflection, the analyst will call up a number of claimants (stakeholders or clientele), whose interests the company might serve. Managers, customers, and investors are often the first to come to mind. Creditors (for example, bankers) often have interests that differ from those of the equity investors. Workers (and unions) often make tangible claims on the firm. Governments, through their taxing and regulatory powers, do so as well. One might extend the list to environmentalists and other social activists. The possibilities are almost limitless. For economy, this discussion treats only the three perspectives that yield the most insight about financial policy.

of the plan should be tested against expected macroeconomic variations, as well as against possible but unexpected financial strains. A good financial structure meets the classic maxim of corporate finance, "Don't run out of cash": in other words, the ideal financial structure adequately funds the growth goals and dividend payouts of the firm without severely diluting the firm's current equity owners. The concept of self-sustainable growth provides a straightforward test of this ideal.

The next three sections will discuss these perspectives in more detail. All three perspectives are unlikely to offer a completely congruent assessment of financial structure. The investor's view looks at the *economic* consequences of a financial structure; the competitor's view considers *strategic* consequences; the internal view addresses the firm's *survival and ambitions*. The three views ask entirely different questions. An analyst should not be surprised when the answers diverge.

Rather like estimating the height of a distant mountain through the haze, the analyst develops a concept of the best financial structure by a process of *triangulation*. Triangulation involves weighing the importance of each of the perspectives as each one *complements* the other rather than as it substitutes for the other, identifying points of consistency, and making artful judgments where the perspectives diverge.

The goal of this analysis should be to articulate concretely the design of the firm's financial structure, preferably in terms of the seven elements discussed in Part I. This exercise entails developing notes, comments, and calculations for every one of the cells of this analytical grid:

Elements of Financial Structure	Current Structure	Investor View	Competitor View	Internal View	Evaluation/ Comments
1. Mix					
2. Maturity					
3. Basis					
4. Currency					
5. Exotica					
6. External Control					
7. Distribution					

No chart can completely anticipate the difficulties, quirks, and exceptions that the analyst will undoubtedly encounter. What matters most, however, is the way of thinking about the financial-structure design problem that encourages both critical thinking and organized, efficient digestion of information.

Figure 1 summarizes the approach presented in this section. Good financial-structure analysis develops three complementary perspectives on financial structure, and then blends those perspectives into a prescription.

FIGURE 1 | Overview of Financial-Structure Analysis

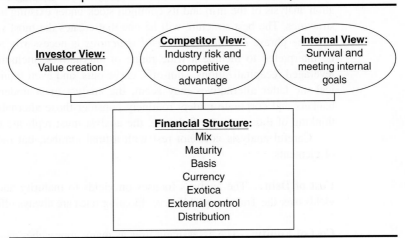

Investor View:
Value creation

Competitor View:
Industry risk and
competitive
advantage

Internal View:
Survival and
meeting internal
goals

Financial Structure:
Mix
Maturity
Basis
Currency
Exotica
External control
Distribution

Part III: Analyzing Financial Policy from the Investors' Viewpoint[7]

In finance theory, the investors' expectations should influence all managerial decisions. This theory follows the legal doctrine that firms should be managed in the interests of their owners. It also recognizes the economic idea that if investors' needs are satisfied after all other claims on the firm are settled, then the firm must be healthy. The investors' view also confronts the reality of capital market discipline. The best defense against a hostile takeover (or another type of intrusion) is a high stock price. In recent years, the threat of capital market discipline has done more than any academic theory to rivet the management's attention to *value creation*.

Academic theory, however, is extremely useful in identifying value-creating strategies. Economic value is held to be the present value of expected future cash flows discounted at a rate consistent with the risk of those cash flows. Considerable care must be given to the estimation of cash flows and discount rates (a review of discounted cash flow [DCF] valuation is beyond the scope of this note). Theory suggests that leverage can create value through the *benefits of debt tax shields* and can destroy value through the *costs of financial distress*. The balance of those costs and benefits depends upon specific capital market conditions, which are conveyed by the debt and equity costs that capital providers impose on the firm. Academic theory's bottom line is as follows:

> An efficient (i.e., value-optimizing) financial structure is one that simultaneously minimizes the weighted-average cost of capital and maximizes the share price and value of the enterprise.

---

[7]Excellent summaries of the investors' orientation are found in Tom Copeland, Tim Koller, and Jack Murrin, *Valuation: Measuring and Managing the Value of Companies,* 2nd ed. (New York: Wiley, 1994); and Alfred Rappaport, *Creating Shareholder Value,* 2nd ed. (New York: Free Press, 1997).

The investors' perspective is a rigorous approach to evaluating financial structures: valuation analysis of the firm and its common stock under existing and alternative financial structures. The best structure will be one that creates the most value.

The phrase *alternative financial structures* is necessarily ambiguous, but should be interpreted to include a wide range of alternatives, including leveraged buyouts, leveraged recapitalizations, spin-offs, carve-outs, and even liquidations. However radical the latter alternatives may seem, the analyst must understand that investment bankers and corporate raiders routinely consider those alternatives. To anticipate the thinking of those agents of change, the analyst must replicate their homework.

Careful analysis does not rest with a final number, but rather considers a range of elements:

Cost of Debt: The analysis focuses on yields to maturity and the spreads of those yields over the Treasury yield curve. Floating rates are always effective rates of interest.

Cost of Equity: The assessment uses as many approaches as possible, including the capital asset pricing model, the dividend discount model, the financial leverage equation, the earnings/price model, and any other avenues that seem appropriate. Although it is fallible, the capital asset pricing model has the most rigor.

Debt/Equity Mix: The relative proportions of types of capital in the capital structure are important factors in computing the weighted-average cost of capital. All capital should be estimated on a *market value* basis.

Price/Earnings Ratio, Market/Book Ratio, Earnings before Interest and Taxes (EBIT) Multiple: Comparing those values to the average levels of the entire capital market or to an industry group can provide an alternative check on the valuation of the firm.

Bond Rating: The creditors' view of the firm is important. S&P and Moody's publish average financial ratios for bond-rating groups. Even for a firm with no publicly rated debt outstanding, a simple ratio analysis can reveal a firm's likely rating category and its current cost of debt.

Ownership: The relative mix of individual and institutional owners and the presence of block holders with potentially hostile intentions can help shed light on the current pricing of a firm's securities.

Short Position: A large, short-sale position on the firm's stock can indicate that some traders believe a decline in share price is imminent.

To conclude, the first rule of financial-policy analysis is: *Think like an investor.* The investors' view assesses the value of a firm's shares under alternative financial structures and the existence of any strongly positive or negative perceptions in the capital markets about the firm's securities.

Part IV: Analyzing Financial Policy from a Competitive Perspective

The competitive perspective matters to senior executives for two important reasons. First, it gives an indication about (1) standard practice in the industry, and (2) the strategic position of the firm relative to the competition. Second, it implies rightly that finance can be a strategic competitive instrument.[8]

The competitive perspective may be the hardest of the three benchmarks to assess. There are few clear signposts in industry dynamics, and, as most industries become increasingly global, the comparisons become even more difficult to make. Despite the difficulty of this analysis, however, senior executives typically give an inordinate amount of attention to it. The well-versed analyst must be able to assess the ability of the current policy (and its alternatives) to maintain or improve its competitive position.

This analysis does not proceed scientifically, but rather evolves iteratively toward an accurate assessment of the situation.[9] The steps might be defined as follows:

1. Define the universe of competitors.

2. Spread the data and financial ratios on the firm and its competitors in comparative fashion.

3. Identify similarities and, more importantly, differences. Probe into anomalies. Question the data and the peer sample.

4. Add needed information, such as a foreign competitor, another ratio, historical normalization, etc.

5. Discuss or clarify the information with the CFO or industry expert.

As the information grows, the questions will become more probing. What is the historical growth pattern? Why did the XYZ company suddenly increase its leverage or keep a large cash balance? Did the acquisition of a new line actually provide access to new markets? Are the changes in debt mix and maturity or in the dividend policy related to the new products and markets?

Economy of effort demands that the analyst begin with a few ratios and data that can be easily obtained (from Value Line, 10-Ks, etc.). If a company is in several industries and does not have pure competitors, choose group-divisional competitors and, to the extent possible, use segment information to devise ratios that will be valid, which is to say, operating income to sales, rather than an after-tax equivalent). Do not forget information that may be outside the financial statements and may be critical to competitive survival, such as geographic diversification, research and

---

[8]For a discussion of finance as a competitive instrument, see the classic work by William E. Fruhan Jr., *Financial Strategy: Studies in the Creation, Transfer, and Destruction of Shareholder Value* (Homewood, IL: Irwin, 1979).

[9]A good overview of industry and competitor analysis may be found in Michael Porter, *Competitive Analysis* (New York: Free Press, 1979). An excellent survey of possible information sources on firms is in Leonard M. Fuld, *Competitor Intelligence* (New York: Wiley, 1985).

development expenditures, and union activity. For some industries, other key ratios are available through trade groups, such as same-store sales and capacity analyses. Whatever the inadequacy of the data, the comparisons will provide direction for subsequent analysis.

The ratios and data to be used will depend on the course of analysis. An analyst could start with the following general types of measures with which to compare a competitor group:

1. *Size:* sales, market value, number of employees or countries, market share

2. *Asset productivity:* return on assets (ROA), return on invested capital, market to book value

3. *Shareholder wealth:* price/earnings (P/E), return on market value

4. *Predictability:* Beta, historical trends

5. *Growth:* 1- to 10-year compound growth of sales, profits, assets, and market value of equity

6. *Financial flexibility:* debt-to-capital, debt ratings, cash flow coverage, estimates of the cost of capital

7. *Other significant industry issues:* unfunded pension liabilities, postretirement medical benefit obligations, environmental liabilities, capacity, research and development expense to sales, percentage of insider control, etc.

One of the key issues to resolve in analyzing the comparative data is whether all the peer-group members display the same results and trends. Inevitably, they will not—which begs the question, why not? Trends in asset productivity and globalization have affected the competitors differently and elicited an assortment of strategic responses. These phenomena should stimulate further research.

The analyst should augment personal research efforts with the work of industry analysts. Securities analysts, consultants, academicians, and journalists—both through their written work and via telephone conversations—can provide valuable insights based on their extensive, personal contacts in the industry.[10]

Analyzing competitors develops insights into the range of financial structures in the industry and the appropriateness of your firm's structure in comparison. Developing those insights is more a matter of qualitative judgment than of letting the numbers speak for themselves. For instance:

1. Suppose your firm is a highly leveraged computer manufacturer with an uneven record of financial performance. Should it unlever? You discover that the peer group of computer manufacturers is substantially equity financed, owing largely to the rapid rate of technological innovation and the predation of a few large players in the industry. The *strategic rationale* for low leverage is to survive the business and short product lifecycles. Yes, it might be good to unlever.

---

[10]See, for example, *Nelson's Guide to Securities Research* for a directory of securities analysts. The Frost & Sullivan *Predicast* and the indexes to the *Wall Street Journal* can give quick overviews of industry trends.

2. Suppose your firm is an airline that finances its equipment purchases with flotations of commercial paper. The average life of the firm's liabilities is 4 years, while the average life of the firm's assets is 15 years. Should the airline refinance its debt using securities with longer maturity? You discover that the peer group of airlines finances its assets with leases, equipment-trust certificates, and project-finance deals that almost exactly match the economic lives of assets and liabilities. The *strategic rationale* for lengthening the maturity structure of liabilities is to hedge against yield-curve changes that might adversely affect your firm's ability to refinance, yet still leave its peer competitors relatively unaffected.

3. Here is a trickier example. Your firm is the last nationwide supermarket chain that is publicly held. All other major supermarket chains have gone private in leveraged buyouts (LBO). Should your firm lever up through a leveraged share repurchase? Competitor analysis reveals that other firms are struggling to meet debt service payments on already thin margins and that a major shift in customer patronage may be under way. You conclude that price competition in selected markets would trigger realignment in market shares in your firm's favor, because the competitors have little pricing flexibility. In that case, adjusting to the industry-average leverage would not be appropriate.

Part V: Diagnosing Financial Policy from an Internal Perspective[11]

Internal analysis is the third major screen of a firm's financial structure. It accounts for the expected cash requirements and resources of a firm, and tests the consistency of a firm's financial structure with the profitability, growth, and dividend goals of the firm. The classic tools of internal analysis are the forecast cash flow, financial statements, and sources-and-uses of funds statements. The standard banker's credit analysis is consistent with this approach.

The essence of this approach is a concern for (1) the preservation of the firm's *financial flexibility,* (2) the *sustainability* of the firm's financial policies, and (3) the *feasibility* of the firm's strategic goals. For example, the firm's long-term goals may call for a doubling of sales in five years. The business plan for achieving that goal may call for the construction of a greenfield plant in year one, and then regional distribution systems in years two and three. Substantial working capital investments will be necessary in years two through five. How this growth is to be financed has huge implications for your firm's financial structure *today*. Typically, an analyst addresses this problem by forecasting the financial performance of the firm, experimenting with different financing sequences and choosing the best one, then determining the structure that makes the best foundation for that financing sequence. This analysis implies the need to maintain future financial flexibility.

---

[11]An excellent overview of the "in-house" view of a firm's financial policies may be found in Gordon Donaldson, *Managing Corporate Wealth: The Operation of a Comprehensive Financial Goals System* (New York: Praeger, 1984).

Financial Flexibility

Financial flexibility is easily measured as the excess cash and unused debt capacity on which the firm might call. In addition, there may be other reserves, such as unused land or excess stocks of raw materials, that could be liquidated. All reserves that could be mobilized should be reflected in an analysis of financial flexibility. Illustrating with the narrower definition (cash and unused debt capacity), one can measure financial flexibility as follows:

1. Select a target minimum debt rating that is acceptable to the firm. Many CFOs will have a target minimum in mind, such as the BBB/Baa rating.

2. Determine the book value[12] debt/equity mix consistent with the minimum rating. Standard & Poor's, for instance, publishes average financial ratios, including debt/equity, that are associated with each debt-rating category.[13]

3. Determine the book value of debt consistent with the debt/equity ratio from step 2. This gives the amount of debt that would be outstanding, if the firm moved to the minimum acceptable bond rating.

4. Estimate financial flexibility using the following formula:

   Financial flexibility
   $$= \text{Excess cash} + (\text{Debt at minimum rating} - \text{Current debt outstanding}).$$

The amount estimated by this formula indicates the financial reserves on which the firm can call to exploit unusual or surprising opportunities (for example, the chance to acquire a competitor) or to defend against unusual threats (for example, a price war, sudden product obsolescence, or a labor strike).

Self-Sustainable Growth

A shorthand test for sustainability and internal consistency is the self-sustainable growth model. This model is based on one key assumption: over the forecast period, the firm sells no new shares of stock (this assumption is entirely consistent with the actual behavior of firms over the long run).[14] As long as the firm does not change its mix of debt and equity, the self-sustainable model implies that assets can grow only as fast as equity grows. Thus, the issue of sustainability is significantly determined by the firm's return on equity (ROE) and dividend payout ratio (DPO):

$$\text{Self-sustainable growth rate of assets} = \text{ROE} \times (1 - \text{DPO})$$

---

[12]Ideally, one would work with market values rather than book values, but the rating agencies compute their financial ratios only on a book value basis. Because this analysis, in effect, mimics the perspective of the rating agencies, the analyst must work with book values.

[13]See *CreditWeek,* published by Standard & Poor's.

[14]From 1950 to 1989, only 5% of the growth of the U.S. economy's business sector was financed by the sale of new common stock. The most significant sources were short-term liabilities, long-term liabilities, and retained earnings, in that order.

The test of feasibility of any long-term plan involves comparing the growth rate implied by this formula and the *targeted* growth rate dictated by management's plan. If the targeted growth rate equals the implied rate, then the firm's financial policies are in balance. If the implied rate exceeds the targeted rate, the firm will gradually become more liquid, creating an asset deployment opportunity. If the targeted rate exceeds the implied rate, the firm must raise more capital by selling stock, levering up, or reducing the dividend payout.

Management policies can be modeled finely by recognizing that ROE can be decomposed into various factors using two classic formulas:

DuPont system of ratios: $ROE = P/S \times S/A \times A/E$

P/S = profit divided by sales or net margin; a measure of profitability
S/A = sales divided by assets; a measure of asset productivity
A/E = assets divided by equity; a measure of financial leverage

Financial-leverage equation:[15] $ROE = ROTC + [(ROTC - K_d) \times (D/E)]$

$ROTC$ = return on total capital
K_d = cost of debt
D/E = debt divided by equity; a measure of leverage

Inserting either of those formulas into the equation for the self-sustainable growth rate gives a richer model of the drivers of self-sustainability. One sees, in particular, the importance of internal operations. The self-sustainable growth model can be expanded to reflect explicitly measures of a firm's operating and financial policies.

The self-sustainable growth model tests the internal consistency of a firm's operating and financial policies. *This model, however, provides no guarantee that a strategy will maximize value.* Value creation does not begin with growth targets; growth per se does not necessarily lead to value creation, as the growth-by-acquisition strategies of the 1960s and '70s abundantly illustrated. Also, the adoption of growth targets may foreclose other, more profitable strategies. Those targets may invite managers to undertake investments yielding less than the cost of capital. Meeting sales or asset growth targets can destroy value. Thus, any sustainable growth analysis must be augmented by questions about the value-creation potential of a given set of corporate policies. These questions include (1) What are the magnitude and duration of investment returns as compared with the firm's cost of capital? and (2) With what alternative set of policies is the firm's share price maximized? With questions such as those, the investor orientation discussed in Part III is turned inward to double-check the appropriateness of any inferences drawn from financial forecasts of the sources-and-uses of funds statements and from the analysis of the self-sustainable growth model.

---

[15]This is the classic expression for the cost of equity, as originally presented in the work of the Nobel Prize winners, Franco Modigliani and Merton Miller.

Part VI: What Is Best?

Any financial structure evaluated against the perspectives of investors, competitors, and internal goals will probably show opportunities for improvement. Most often, CFOs choose to make changes at the margin rather than tinkering radically with a financial structure. For changes large and small, however, the analyst must develop a framework for judgment and prescription.

The following framework is a way of identifying the trade-offs among "good" and "bad," rather than finding the right answer. Having identified the trade-offs implicit in any alternative structure, it remains for the CFO and the adviser to choose the structure with the most attractive trade-offs.

The key elements of evaluation are as follows:

Flexibility: the ability to meet unforeseen financing requirements as they arise—
those requirements may be favorable (for example, a sudden acquisition opportunity) or unfavorable (such as the Source Perrier and the benzene scare). Flexibility may involve liquidating assets or tapping the capital markets in adverse market environments or both. Flexibility can be measured by bond ratings, coverage ratios, capitalization ratios, liquidity ratios, and the identification of salable assets.

Risk: the predictable variability in the firm's business. Such variability may be
due to both macroeconomic factors (such as consumer demand) and industry- or firm-specific factors (such as product life cycles, or strikes before wage negotiations). To some extent, past experience may indicate the future range of variability in EBIT and cash flow. High leverage tends to amplify those predictable business swings. The risk associated with any given financial structure can be assessed by EBIT–EPS (earnings per share) analysis, break-even analysis, the standard deviation of EBIT, and beta. In theory, beta should vary directly with leverage.[16]

Income: this compares financial structures on the basis of value creation. Measures
such as DCF value, projected ROE, EPS, and the cost of capital indicate the comparative value effects of alternative financial structures.

Control: alternative financial structures may imply changes in control or different
control constraints on the firm as indicated by the percentage distribution of share ownership and by the structure of debt covenants.

Timing: asks the question whether the current capital-market environment is
the right moment to implement any alternative financial structure, and what the implications for future financing will be if the proposed structure is

---

[16]This relationship is illustrated by the formula for estimating a firm's levered beta:

$$B_l = B_u \times [1 + (1 - t) \times D/E]$$

where: B_l = levered beta; B_u = unlevered beta; t = firm's marginal tax rate; and D/E = the firm's market value, debt-to-equity ratio.

adopted. The current market environment can be assessed by examining the Treasury yield curve, the trend in the movement of interest rates, the existence of any windows in the market for new issues of securities, P/E multiple trends, etc. Sequencing considerations are implicitly captured in the assumptions underlying the alternative DCF value estimates, and can be explicitly examined by looking at annual EPS and ROE streams under alternative financing sequences.

This framework of flexibility, risk, income, control, and timing (FRICT) can be used to assess the relative strengths and weaknesses of alternative financing plans. To use a simple example, suppose that your firm is considering two financial structures: (1) 60% debt and 40% equity (i.e., debt will be issued), and (2) 40% debt and 60% equity (i.e., equity will be issued). Also, suppose that your analysis of the two structures under the investor, competitor, and internal-analysis screens leads you to make this basic comparison:

	60% Debt	**40% Debt**
Flexibility	A little low, not bad	High
	BBB debt rating	AA debt rating
	$50 million in reserves	$300 million in reserves
Risk	High	Medium
	EBIT coverage = 1.5	EBIT coverage = 3.0
Income	Good-to-high	Mediocre
	DCF value = $20/share	DCF value = $12/share (dilutive)
Control	Covenants tight	Covenants not restrictive
	No voting dilution	10% voting dilution
Timing	Interest rates low today	Equity multiples low today
	Risky sequence	Low-risk sequence for future

The 60% debt structure is favored on the grounds of income, control, and today's market conditions. The 40% debt structure is favored on the grounds of flexibility, risk, and the long-term financial sequencing. This example boils down to a decision between "eating well" and "sleeping well." It remains up to senior management to make the difficult choice between the two alternatives, while giving careful attention to the views of the investors, competitors, and managers.

Part VII: Conclusion

Description, diagnosis, and prescription in financial structuring form an iterative process. It is quite likely that the CFO in the eat-well/sleep-well example would send the analyst back for more research and testing of alternative structures. **Figure 2** presents an expanded view of the basic cycle of analysis and suggests more about the complexity of the financial-structuring problem. With time and experience, the analyst develops an intuition for efficient information sources and modes of analysis. In the long run, this intuition makes the cycle of analysis manageable.

FIGURE 2 | An Expanded Illustration of the Process of Developing a Financial Policy

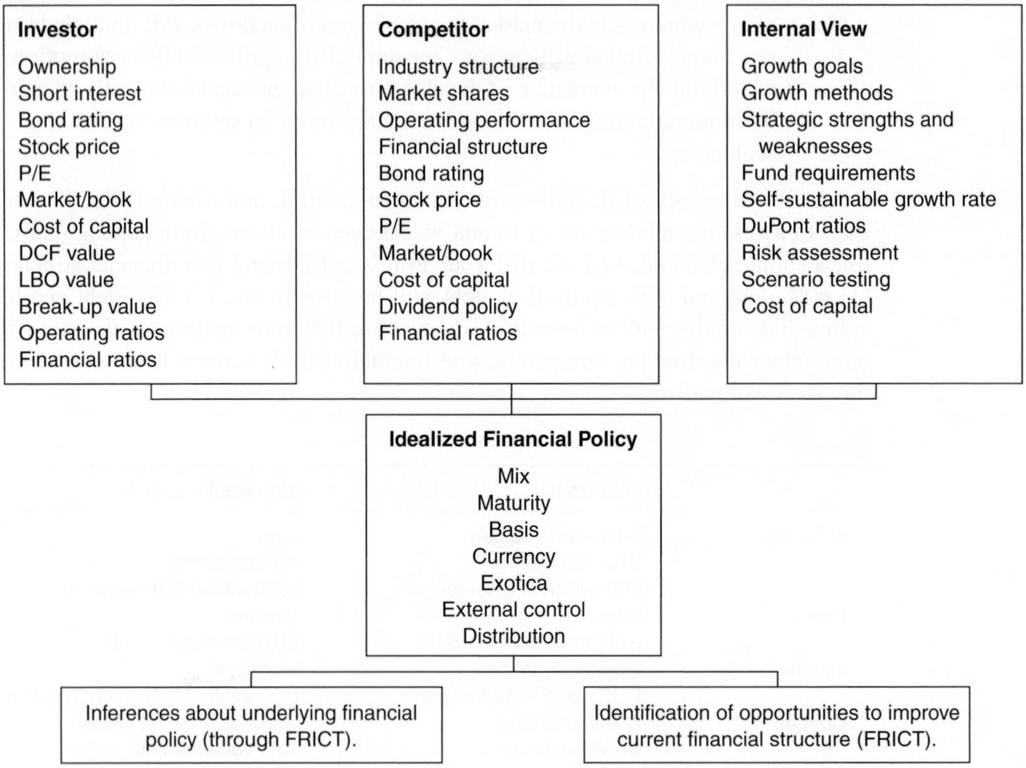

Investor

Ownership
Short interest
Bond rating
Stock price
P/E
Market/book
Cost of capital
DCF value
LBO value
Break-up value
Operating ratios
Financial ratios

Competitor

Industry structure
Market shares
Operating performance
Financial structure
Bond rating
Stock price
P/E
Market/book
Cost of capital
Dividend policy
Financial ratios

Internal View

Growth goals
Growth methods
Strategic strengths and
    weaknesses
Fund requirements
Self-sustainable growth rate
DuPont ratios
Risk assessment
Scenario testing
Cost of capital

Idealized Financial Policy

Mix
Maturity
Basis
Currency
Exotica
External control
Distribution

Inferences about underlying financial
policy (through FRICT).

Identification of opportunities to improve
current financial structure (FRICT).

California Pizza Kitchen

Everyone knows that 95% of restaurants fail in the first two years, and a lot of people think it's "location, location, location." It could be, but my experience is you have to have the financial staying power. You could have the greatest idea, but many restaurants do not start out making money—they build over time. So it's really about having the capital and the staying power.

> Rick Rosenfield, Co-CEO, California Pizza Kitchen[1]

In early July 2007, the financial team at California Pizza Kitchen (CPK), led by Chief Financial Officer Susan Collyns, was compiling the preliminary results for the second quarter of 2007. Despite industry challenges of rising commodity, labor, and energy costs, CPK was about to announce near-record quarterly profits of over $6 million. CPK's profit expansion was explained by strong revenue growth with comparable restaurant sales up over 5%. The announced numbers were fully in line with the company's forecasted guidance to investors.

The company's results were particularly impressive when contrasted with many other casual dining firms, which had experienced sharp declines in customer traffic. Despite the strong performance, industry difficulties were such that CPK's share price had declined 10% during the month of June to a current value of $22.10. Given the price drop, the management team had discussed repurchasing company shares. With little money in excess cash, however, a large share repurchase program would require debt financing. Since going public in 2000, CPK's management had avoided putting any debt on the balance sheet. Financial policy was conservative to preserve what co-CEO Rick Rosenfeld referred to as staying power. The view was that a strong balance sheet would maintain the borrowing ability needed to support CPK's expected growth trajectory. Yet with interest rates on the rise from historical lows, Collyns was aware of the benefits of moderately levering up CPK's equity.

---

[1]Richard M. Smith, "Rolling in Dough; For the Creators of California Pizza Kitchen, Having Enough Capital Was the Key Ingredient to Success," *Newsweek,* 25 June 2007.

California Pizza Kitchen

Inspired by the gourmet pizza offerings at Wolfgang Puck's celebrity-filled restaurant, Spago, and eager to flee their careers as white-collar criminal defense attorneys, Larry Flax and Rick Rosenfield created the first California Pizza Kitchen in 1985 in Beverly Hills, California. Known for its hearth-baked barbecue-chicken pizza, the "designer pizza at off-the-rack prices" concept flourished. Expansion across the state, country, and globe followed in the subsequent two decades. At the end of the second quarter of 2007, the company had 213 locations in 28 states and 6 foreign countries. While still very California-centric (approximately 41% of the U.S. stores were in California), the casual dining model had done well throughout all U.S. regions with its family-friendly surroundings, excellent ingredients, and inventive offerings.

California Pizza Kitchen derived its revenues from three sources: sales at company-owned restaurants, royalties from franchised restaurants, and royalties from a partnership with Kraft Foods to sell CPK-branded frozen pizzas in grocery stores. While the company had expanded beyond its original concept with two other restaurant brands, its main focus remained on operating company-owned full-service CPK restaurants, of which there were 170 units.

Analysts conservatively estimated the potential for full-service company-owned CPK units at 500. Both the investment community and management were less certain about the potential for the company's chief attempt at brand extension, its ASAP restaurant concept. In 1996, the company first developed the ASAP concept in a franchise agreement with HMSHost. The franchised ASAPs were located in airports and featured a limited selection of pizzas and "grab-n-go" salads and sandwiches. While not a huge revenue source, management was pleased with the success of the airport ASAP locations, which currently numbered 16. In early 2007, HMSHost and CPK agreed to extend their partnership through 2012. But the sentiment was more mixed regarding its company-owned ASAP locations. First opened in 2000 to capitalize on the growth of fast casual dining, the company-owned ASAP units offered CPK's most-popular pizzas, salads, soups, and sandwiches with in-restaurant seating. Sales and operations at the company-owned ASAP units never met management's expectations. Even after retooling the concept and restaurant prototype in 2003, management decided to halt indefinitely all ASAP development in 2007 and planned to record roughly $770,000 in expenses in the second quarter to terminate the planned opening of one ASAP location.

Although they had doubts associated with the company-owned ASAP restaurant chain, the company and investment community were upbeat about CPK's success and prospects with franchising full-service restaurants internationally. At the beginning of July 2007, the company had 15 franchised international locations, with more openings planned for the second half of 2007. Management sought out knowledgeable franchise partners who would protect the company's brand and were capable of growing the number of international units. Franchising agreements typically gave CPK an initial payment of $50,000 to $65,000 for each location opened and then an estimated 5% of gross sales. With locations already in China (including Hong Kong), Indonesia, Japan, Malaysia, the Philippines, and Singapore, the company planned to expand its global reach to Mexico and South Korea in the second half of 2007.

Management saw its Kraft partnership as another initiative in its pursuit of building a global brand. In 1997, the company entered into a licensing agreement with Kraft Foods to distribute CPK-branded frozen pizzas. Although representing less than 1% of current revenues, the Kraft royalties had a 95% pretax margin, one equity analyst estimated.[2] In addition to the high-margin impact on the company's bottom line, management also highlighted the marketing requirement in its Kraft partnership. Kraft was obligated to spend 5% of gross sales on marketing the CPK frozen pizza brand, more than the company often spent on its own marketing.

Management believed its success in growing both domestically and internationally, and through ventures like the Kraft partnership, was due in large part to its "dedication to guest satisfaction and menu innovation and sustainable culture of service."[3] A creative menu with high-quality ingredients was a top priority at CPK, with the two co-founders still heading the menu-development team. **Exhibit 1** contains a selection of CPK menu offerings. "Its menu items offer customers distinctive, compelling flavors to commonly recognized foods," a Morgan Keegan analyst wrote.[4] While the company had a narrower, more-focused menu than some of its peers, the chain prided itself on creating craved items, such as Singapore Shrimp Rolls, that distinguished its menu and could not be found at its casual dining peers. This strategy was successful, and internal research indicated a specific menu craving that could not be satisfied elsewhere prompted many patron visits. To maintain the menu's originality, management reviewed detailed sales reports twice a year and replaced slow-selling offerings with new items. Some of the company's most recent menu additions in 2007 had been developed and tested at the company's newest restaurant concept, the LA Food Show. Created by Flax and Rosenfield in 2003, the LA Food Show offered a more upscale experience and expansive menu than CPK. CPK increased its minority interest to full ownership of the LA Food Show in 2005 and planned to open a second location in early 2008.

In addition to crediting its inventive menu, analysts also pointed out that its average check of $13.30 was below that of many of its upscale dining casual peers, such as P.F. Chang's and the Cheesecake Factory. Analysts from RBC Capital Markets labeled the chain a "Price–Value–Experience" leader in its sector.[5]

CPK spent 1% of its sales on advertising, far less than the 3% to 4% of sales that casual dining competitors, such as Chili's, Red Lobster, Olive Garden, and Outback Steakhouse, spent annually. Management felt careful execution of its company model resulted in devoted patrons who created free, but far more-valuable word-of-mouth marketing for the company. Of the actual dollars spent on marketing, roughly 50% was spent on menu-development costs, with the other half consumed by more typical

---

[2]Jeffrey D. Farmer, CIBC World Markets Equity Research Earnings Update, "California Pizza Kitchen, Inc.; Notes from West Coast Investor Meetings: Shares Remain Compelling," April 12, 2007.

[3]Company press release, February 15, 2007.

[4]Destin M. Tompkins, Robert M. Derrington, and S. Brandon Couillard, Morgan Keegan Equity Research, "California Pizza Kitchen, Inc.," April 19, 2007.

[5]Larry Miller, Daniel Lewis, and Robert Sanders, RBC Capital Markets Research Comment, "California Pizza Kitchen: Back on Trend with Old Management," September 14, 2006.

marketing strategies, such as public relations efforts, direct mail offerings, outdoor media, and online marketing.

CPK's clientele was not only attractive for its endorsements of the chain, but also because of its demographics. Management frequently highlighted that its core customer had an average household income of more than $75,000, according to a 2005 guest satisfaction survey. CPK contended that its customer base's relative affluence sheltered the company from macroeconomic pressures, such as high gas prices, that might lower sales at competitors with fewer well-off patrons.

Restaurant Industry

The restaurant industry could be divided into two main sectors: full service and limited service. Some of the most popular subsectors within full service included casual dining and fine dining, with fast casual and fast food being the two prevalent limited-service subsectors. Restaurant consulting firm Technomic Information Services projected the limited-service restaurant segment to maintain a five-year compound annual growth rate (CAGR) of 5.5%, compared with 5.1% for the full-service restaurant segment.[6] The five-year CAGR for CPK's subsector of the full-service segment was projected to grow even more at 6.5%. In recent years, a number of forces had challenged restaurant industry executives, including:

- Increasing commodity prices;
- Higher labor costs;
- Softening demand due to high gas prices;
- Deteriorating housing wealth;
- Intense interest in the industry by activist shareholders.

High gas prices not only affected demand for dining out, but also indirectly pushed a dramatic rise in food commodity prices. Moreover, a national call for the creation of more biofuels, primarily corn-produced ethanol, played an additional role in driving up food costs for the restaurant industry. Restaurant companies responded by raising menu prices in varying degrees. The restaurants believed that the price increases would have little impact on restaurant traffic given that consumers experienced higher price increases in their main alternative to dining out—purchasing food at grocery stores to consume at home.

Restaurants not only had to deal with rising commodity costs, but also rising labor costs. In May 2007, President Bush signed legislation increasing the U.S. minimum wage rate over a three-year period beginning in July 2007 from $5.15 to $7.25 an hour. While restaurant management teams had time to prepare for the ramifications of this gradual increase, they were ill-equipped to deal with the nearly 20 states in late 2006 that passed anticipatory wage increases at rates higher than those proposed by Congress.

---

[6]Destin M. Tompkins, Robert M. Derrington, and S. Brandon Couillard, Morgan Keegan Equity Research, "California Pizza Kitchen, Inc.," April 19, 2007.

In addition to contending with the rising cost of goods sold (COGS), restaurants faced gross margins that were under pressure from the softening demand for dining out. A recent AAA Mid-Atlantic survey asked travelers how they might reduce spending to make up for the elevated gas prices, and 52% answered that food expenses would be the first area to be cut.[7] Despite that news, a Deutsche Bank analyst remarked, "Two important indicators of consumer health—disposable income and employment—are both holding up well. As long as people have jobs and incomes are rising, they are likely to continue to eat out."[8]

The current environment of elevated food and labor costs and consumer concerns highlighted the differences between the limited-service and full-service segments of the restaurant industry. Franchising was more popular in the limited-service segment and provided some buffer against rising food and labor costs because franchisors received a percentage of gross sales. Royalties on gross sales also benefited from any pricing increases that were made to address higher costs. Restaurant companies with large franchising operations also did not have the huge amount of capital invested in locations or potentially heavy lease obligations associated with company-owned units. Some analysts included operating lease requirements when considering a restaurant company's leverage.[9] Analysts also believed limited-service restaurants would benefit from any consumers trading down from the casual dining sub-sector of the full-service sector.[10] The growth of the fast-casual subsector and the food-quality improvements in fast food made trading down an increasing likelihood in an economic slowdown.

The longer-term outlook for overall restaurant demand looked much stronger. A study by the National Restaurant Association projected that consumers would increase the percentage of their food dollars spent on dining out from the 45% in recent years to 53% by 2010.[11] That long-term positive trend may have helped explain the extensive interest in the restaurant industry by activist shareholders, often the executives of private equity firms and hedge funds. Activist investor William Ackman with Pershing Square Capital Management initiated the current round of activist investors forcing change at major restaurant chains. Roughly one week after Ackman vociferously criticized the McDonald's corporate organization at a New York investment conference in late 2005, the company declared it would divest 1,500 restaurants, repurchase $1 billion of its stock, and disclose more restaurant-level performance details. Ackman advocated all those changes and was able to leverage the power of his 4.5% stake in McDonald's by using the media. His success did not go unnoticed, and other vocal minority investors aggressively pressed for changes at numerous chains including

[7]Amy G. Vinson and Ted Hillard, Avondale Partners, LLC, "Restaurant Industry Weekly Update," June 11, 2007.

[8]Jason West, Marc Greenberg, and Andrew Kieley, Deutsche Bank Global Markets Research, "Transferring Coverage–Reservations Available," June 7, 2007.

[9]As of July 1, 2007, CPK had $154.3 million in minimum lease payments required over the next five years with $129.6 million due in more than five years.

[10]Jeff Omohundro, Katie H. Willett, and Jason Belcher, Wachovia Capital Markets, LLC Equity Research, "The Restaurant Watch," July 3, 2007.

[11]Destin M. Tompkins, Robert M. Derrington, and S. Brandon Couillard, Morgan Keegan Equity Research, "California Pizza Kitchen, Inc.," April 19, 2007.

Applebee's, Wendy's, and Friendly's. These changes included the outright sale of the company, sales of noncore divisions, and closure of poor-performing locations.

In response, other chains embarked on shareholder-friendly plans including initiating share repurchase programs; increasing dividends; decreasing corporate expenditures; and divesting secondary assets. Doug Brooks, chief executive of Brinker International Inc., which owned Chili's, noted at a recent conference:

> There is no shortage of interest in our industry these days, and much of the recent news has centered on the participation of activist shareholders . . . but it is my job as CEO to act as our internal activist.[12]

In April 2007, Brinker announced it had secured a new $400 million unsecured, committed credit-facility to fund an accelerated share repurchase transaction in which approximately $300 million of its common stock would be repurchased. That followed a tender offer recapitalization in 2006 in which the company repurchased $50 million worth of common shares.

Recent Developments

CPK's positive second-quarter results would affirm many analysts' conclusions that the company was a safe haven in the casual dining sector. **Exhibits 2** and **3** contain CPK's financial statements through July 1, 2007. **Exhibit 4** presents comparable store sales trends for CPK and peers. **Exhibit 5** contains selected analysts' forecasts for CPK, all of which anticipated revenue and earnings growth. A Morgan Keegan analyst commented in May:

> Despite increased market pressures on consumer spending, California Pizza Kitchen's concept continues to post impressive customer traffic gains. Traditionally appealing to a more discriminating, higher-income clientele, CPK's creative fare, low check average, and high service standards have uniquely positioned the concept for success in a tough consumer macroeconomic environment.[13]

While other restaurant companies experienced weakening sales and earnings growth, CPK's revenues increased more than 16% to $159 million for the second quarter of 2007. Notably, royalties from the Kraft partnership and international franchises were up 37% and 21%, respectively, for the second quarter. Development plans for opening a total of 16 to 18 new locations remained on schedule for 2007. Funding CPK's 2007 growth plan was anticipated to require $85 million in capital expenditures.

The company was successfully managing its two largest expense items in an environment of rising labor and food costs. Labor costs had actually declined from 36.6% to 36.3% of total revenues from the second quarter of 2006 to the second quarter of 2007. Food, beverage, and paper-supply costs remained constant at roughly 24.5% of

---

[12]Sarah E. Lockyer, "Who's the Boss? Activist Investors Drive Changes at Major Chains: Companies Pursue 'Shareholder-Friendly' Strategies in Response to Public Pressure," *Nation's Restaurant News,* 23 April 2007.

[13]Destin M. Tompkins and Robert M. Derrington, Morgan Keegan Equity Research, "California Pizza Kitchen, Inc.," May 11, 2007.

total revenue in both the second quarter of 2006 and 2007. The company was implementing a number of taskforce initiatives to deal with the commodity price pressures, especially as cheese prices increased from $1.37 per pound in April to almost $2.00 a pound by the first week of July. Management felt that much of the cost improvements had been achieved through enhancements in restaurant operations.

Capital Structure Decision

CPK's book equity was expected to be around $226 million at the end of the second quarter. With a share price in the low 20s, CPK's market capitalization stood at $644 million. The company had recently issued a 50% stock dividend, which had effectively split CPK shares on a 3-for-2 shares basis. CPK investors received one additional share for every two shares of common stock held. Adjusted for the stock dividend, **Exhibit 6** shows the performance of CPK stock relative to that of industry peers.

Despite the challenges of growing the number of restaurants by 38% over the last five years, CPK consistently generated strong operating returns. CPK's return on equity (ROE), which was 10.1% for 2006, did not benefit from financial leverage.[14] Financial policy varied across the industry, with some firms remaining all equity capitalized and others levering up to half debt financing. **Exhibit 7** depicts selected financial data for peer firms. Because CPK used the proceeds from its 2000 initial public offering (IPO) to pay off its outstanding debt, the company completely avoided debt financing. CPK maintained borrowing capacity available under an existing $75 million line of credit. Interest on the line of credit was calculated at LIBOR plus 0.80%. With LIBOR currently at 5.36%, the line of credit's interest rate was 6.16% (see **Exhibit 8**).

The recent 10% share price decline seemed to raise the question of whether this was an ideal time to repurchase shares and potentially leverage the company's balance sheet with ample borrowings available on its existing line of credit. One gain from the leverage would be to reduce the corporate income-tax liability, which had been almost $10 million in 2006. **Exhibit 9** provides pro forma financial summaries of CPK's tax shield under alternative capital structures. Still, CPK needed to preserve its ability to fund the strong expansion outlined for the company. Any use of financing to return capital to shareholders needed to be balanced with management's goal of growing the business.

---

[14]By a familiar decomposition equation, a firm's ROE could be decomposed into three components: operating margin, capital turnover, and leverage. More specifically, the algebra of the decomposition was as follows:

ROE = Profit ÷ Equity = (Profit ÷ Revenue) × (Revenue ÷ Capital) × (Capital ÷ Equity).

EXHIBIT 1 | Selected Menu Offerings

Appetizers

Avocado Club Egg Rolls: A fusion of East and West with fresh avocado, chicken, tomato, Monterey Jack cheese, and applewood smoked bacon, wrapped in a crispy wonton roll. Served with ranchito sauce and herb ranch dressing.

Singapore Shrimp Rolls: Shrimp, baby broccoli, soy-glazed shiitake mushrooms, romaine, carrots, noodles, bean sprouts, green onion, and cilantro wrapped in rice paper. Served chilled with a sesame ginger dipping sauce and Szechuan slaw.

Pizzas

The Original BBQ Chicken: CPK's most-popular pizza, introduced in their first restaurant in Beverly Hills in 1985. Barbecue sauce, smoked gouda and mozzarella cheeses, BBQ chicken, sliced red onions, and cilantro.

Carne Asada: Grilled steak, fire-roasted mild chilies, onions, cilantro pesto, Monterey Jack, and mozzarella cheeses. Topped with fresh tomato salsa and cilantro. Served with a side of tomatillo salsa.

Thai Chicken: This is the original! Pieces of chicken breast marinated in a spicy peanut ginger and sesame sauce, mozzarella cheese, green onions, bean sprouts, julienne carrots, cilantro, and roasted peanuts.

Milan: A combination of grilled spicy Italian sausage and sweet Italian sausage with sautéed wild mushrooms, caramelized onions, fontina, mozzarella, and parmesan cheeses. Topped with fresh herbs.

Pasta

Shanghai Garlic Noodles: Chinese noodles wok-stirred in a garlic ginger sauce with snow peas, shiitake mushrooms, mild onions, red and yellow peppers, baby broccoli, and green onions. Also available with chicken and/or shrimp.

Chicken Tequila Fettuccine: The original! Spinach fettuccine with chicken, red, green, and yellow peppers, red onions, and fresh cilantro in a tequila, lime, and jalapeño cream sauce.

Source: California Pizza Kitchen Web site, http://www.cpk.com/menu (accessed on 12 August 2008).

EXHIBIT 2 | Consolidated Balance Sheets (in thousands of dollars)

	As of		
	1/1/06	12/31/06	7/1/07
Assets			
Current assets			
Cash and cash equivalents	$ 11,272	$ 8,187	$ 7,178
Investments in marketable securities	11,408		
Other receivables	4,109	7,876	10,709
Inventories	3,776	4,745	4,596
Current deferred tax asset, net	8,437	11,721	11,834
Prepaid income tax	1,428		8,769
Other prepaid expenses & other current assets	5,492	5,388	6,444
Total current assets	45,922	37,917	49,530
Property and equipment, net	213,408	255,382	271,867
Noncurrent deferred tax asset, net	4,513	5,867	6,328
Goodwill and other intangibles	5,967	5,825	5,754
Other assets	4,444	5,522	6,300
Total assets	$274,254	$310,513	$339,779
Liabilities and Shareholders' Equity			
Current liabilities			
Accounts payable	$ 7,054	$ 15,044	$ 14,115
Accrued compensation and benefits	13,068	15,042	15,572
Accrued rent	13,253	14,532	14,979
Deferred rent credits	4,056	4,494	5,135
Other accrued liabilities	9,294	13,275	13,980
Accrued income tax		3,614	9,012
Total current liabilities	46,725	66,001	72,793
Other liabilities	5,383	8,683	8,662
Deferred rent credits, net of current portion	24,810	27,486	32,436
Shareholders' equity:			
Common stock	197	193	291
Additional paid-in-capital	231,159	221,163	228,647
Accumulated deficit	(34,013)	(13,013)	(3,050)
Accumulated comprehensive loss	(7)		
Total shareholders' equity	197,336	208,343	225,888
Total liabilities & Shareholders' Equity	$274,254	$310,513	$339,779

Sources of data: Company annual and quarterly reports.

EXHIBIT 3 | Consolidated Income Statements (in thousands of dollars, except per-share data)

	Fiscal Year[1]				Three Months Ended	
	2003	2004	2005	2006	7/2/06	7/1/07
Restaurant sales	$356,260	$418,799	$474,738	$547,968	$134,604	$156,592
Franchise and other revenues	3,627	3,653	4,861	6,633	1,564	1,989
Total revenues	359,887	422,452	479,599	554,601	136,168	158,581
Food, beverage and paper supplies	87,806	103,813	118,480	135,848	33,090	38,426
Labor	129,702	152,949	173,751	199,744	49,272	56,912
Direct operating and occupancy	70,273	83,054	92,827	108,558	26,214	30,773
Cost of Sales	287,781	339,816	385,058	444,150	108,576	126,111
General and administrative	21,488	28,794	36,298	43,320	11,035	12,206
Depreciation and amortization	20,714	23,975	25,440	29,489	7,070	9,022
Pre-opening costs	4,147	737	4,051	6,964	800	852
Severance charges[2]	1,221					
Loss on impairment of PP&E	18,984		1,160			
Store closure costs		2,700	152	707		768
Legal settlement reserve		1,333	600			
Operating income	5,552	25,097	26,840	29,971	8,687	9,622
Interest income	317	571	739	718	287	91
Other income			1,105			
Equity in loss of unconsolidated JV	(349)	(143)	(22)			
Total other income (expense)	(32)	428	1,822	718	287	91
Income before income tax provision	5,520	25,525	28,662	30,689	8,974	9,713
Income tax provision (benefit)	(82)	7,709	9,172	9,689	2,961	3,393
Net income	$ 5,602	$ 17,816	$ 19,490	$ 21,000	$ 6,013	$ 6,320
Net income per common share:						
Basic	$ 0.30	$ 0.93	$ 1.01	$ 1.08	$ 0.20	$ 0.22
Diluted	$ 0.29	$ 0.92	$ 0.99	$ 1.06	$ 0.20	$ 0.21
Selected Operating Data:						
Restaurants open at end of period	168	171	188	205	193	213
Company-owned open at end of period[3]	137	141	157	176	162	182
Avg weekly full service rest. sales[3]	$ 54,896	$ 57,509	$ 62,383	$ 65,406	$ 65,427	$ 68,535
18-mo. comparable rest. sales growth[3]	3.4%	8.0%	7.5%	5.9%	4.8%	5.4%

Notes:

[1]For the years ended December 31, 2006, January 1, 2006, and January 2, 2005, December 28, 2003.

[2]Severance charges represent payments to former president/CEO and former senior vice president/senior development officer under the terms of their separation agreements.

[3]Data for company-owned restaurants.

Sources of data: Company annual and quarterly reports and quarterly company earnings conference calls.

EXHIBIT 4 | Selected Historical Comparable Store Sales (calendarized)

	CY03	CY04	CY05	Q1	CY06 Q2	Q3	Q4	CY07 Q1
California Pizza Kitchen	3.4%	9.3%	6.4%	4.8%	5.9%	5.6%	6.9%	4.7%
Applebee's International, Inc.	4.1%	4.8%	1.8%	2.6%	−1.8%	−2.3%	−1.1%	−4.0%
BJ's Restaurants, Inc.	3.3%	4.0%	4.6%	6.8%	5.9%	5.3%	5.5%	6.9%
Brinker International[1]	2.1%	1.9%	3.2%	2.7%	−2.0%	−2.1%	−2.1%	−4.4%
The Cheesecake Factory, Inc.	0.7%	3.9%	1.7%	−1.3%	−0.8%	−1.6%	0.8%	0.4%
Chipotle Mexican Grill, Inc.	24.4%	13.3%	10.2%	19.7%	14.5%	11.6%	10.1%	8.3%
Darden Restaurants, Inc.—Red Lobster	0.0%	−3.9%	4.2%	1.6%	9.4%	−2.1%	0.7%	4.6%
Darden Restaurants, Inc.—Olive Garden	2.2%	4.7%	8.6%	5.7%	2.5%	2.9%	2.9%	1.0%
McCormick & Schmick's Seafood Restaurants, Inc.	1.1%	3.8%	3.0%	4.1%	2.8%	2.9%	2.0%	2.8%
Panera Bread Company	0.2%	2.7%	7.8%	9.0%	3.2%	2.8%	2.0%	0.0%
P. F. Chang's China Bistro	5.1%	3.0%	1.2%	1.3%	−1.0%	−0.5%	−0.9%	−2.5%
RARE—Longhorn Steakhouse	4.6%	5.0%	2.8%	3.7%	−0.4%	−0.3%	1.5%	−1.0%
Red Robin Gourmet Burgers	4.1%	7.5%	3.8%	4.8%	3.3%	0.8%	0.2%	−0.5%
Ruth's Chris Steak House, Inc.	1.4%	11.6%	10.4%	6.8%	6.0%	4.3%	7.4%	1.9%
Sonic Corporation	1.6%	7.0%	5.4%	5.5%	4.3%	4.0%	3.4%	2.0%
Texas Roadhouse, Inc.	3.5%	7.6%	5.6%	6.4%	1.2%	2.3%	3.3%	0.9%

Note:

[1]Brinker's comparable store sales were a blended rate for its various brands.

Source of data: KeyBanc Capital Markets equity research.

EXHIBIT 5 | Selected Forecasts for California Pizza Kitchen

Firm	Date of Report	Price Target	2007E Revenues	2007E EPS	2008E Revenues	2008E EPS	2009E Revenues	2009E EPS
Oppenheimer and Co. Inc.	4/9/07	$40	$652.9	$1.33	NA	NA	NA	NA
CIBC World Markets	4/12/07	37	647.5	1.29	755.1	1.57	NA	NA
KeyBanc Capital Markets	5/11/07	NA	NA	1.28	NA	1.55	NA	NA
RBC Capital Markets	5/11/07	37	650.7	1.31	753.1	1.59	878.2	1.90
Morgan Keegan & Co., Inc.	5/11/07	NA	644.2	1.33	742.1	1.58	NA	NA
MKM Partners	5/11/07	39	647.5	1.34	754.3	1.69	NA	NA

Source of data: Selected firms' equity research.

EXHIBIT 6 | Stock Price Comparison

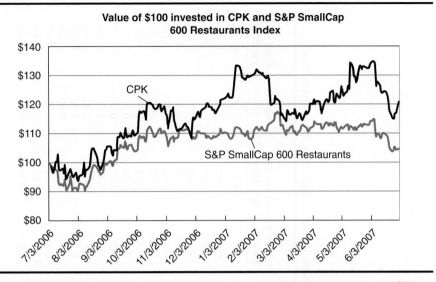

Value of $100 invested in CPK and S&P SmallCap
600 Restaurants Index

Note: Adjusted for the June 2007 50% stock dividend. With such a dividend, an owner of two shares of CPK stock was given an additional share. The effect was to increase CPK shares by one-third, yet maintain the overall capitalization of the equity.

Sources of data: Yahoo! Finance and Datastream.

EXHIBIT 7 | Comparative Restaurant Financial Data, 2006 Fiscal Year (in millions of dollars, except per-share data)

	Fiscal Year End Month	7/2/2007 Share Price	Revenue	EBITDA Margin	Net Profit Margin	Earnings per Share	Dividends per Share	Book Value per Share	Beta
California Pizza Kitchen	Dec.	$22.10	$55	10.7%	3.8%	$0.71	$ 0.00	$7.20	0.85
Applebee's International, Inc.	Dec.	24.28	1,338	15.9%	6.5%	1.17	0.20	6.49	0.80
BJ's Restaurants, Inc.	Dec.	20.05	239	9.6%	4.1%	0.41	0.00	7.78	1.05
Brinker International[1]	June	29.37	4,151	12.0%	4.7%	1.49	0.20	8.59	0.90
Buffalo Wild Wings, Inc.	Dec.	41.78	278	13.3%	5.8%	0.93	0.00	6.61	1.10
The Cheesecake Factory, Inc.	Dec.	24.57	1,315	12.2%	6.2%	1.02	0.00	9.09	1.00
Chipotle Mexican Grill, Inc.	Dec.	86.00	823	13.0%	5.0%	1.28	0.00	14.56	NA
Darden Restaurants, Inc.[2]	May	44.14	5,721	13.2%	5.9%	2.16	0.40	8.37	1.00
Frisch's Restaurants, Inc.	May	30.54	291	31.6%	3.1%	1.78	0.44	19.84	0.60
McCormick & Schmick's	Dec.	25.66	308	9.7%	4.3%	0.92	0.00	11.20	1.10
Panera Bread Company	Dec.	46.02	829	16.3%	7.2%	1.87	0.00	12.53	1.25
P.F. Chang's China Bistro	Dec.	35.37	938	10.5%	3.6%	1.24	0.00	11.41	1.10
RARE Hospitality Int'l Inc.[3]	Dec.	26.76	987	11.6%	5.1%	1.45	0.00	11.17	0.57
Red Robin Gourmet Burgers	Dec.	40.19	619	13.7%	4.9%	1.82	0.00	14.68	1.05
Ruth's Chris Steak House, Inc.	Dec.	16.80	272	15.6%	8.7%	1.01	0.00	2.93	NA
Sonic Corporation	Aug.	22.00	693	24.9%	11.4%	0.88	0.00	4.66	0.90
Texas Roadhouse, Inc.	Dec.	12.81	597	12.5%	5.7%	0.44	0.00	4.30	0.90

EXHIBIT 7 | Comparative Restaurant Financial Data, 2006 Fiscal Year (in millions of dollars, except per-share data) *(continued)*

	Current Assets	Current Liabilities	Total Debt	Share Equity	Debt/ Capital	Interest Coverage	Total Capital Turnover	Return on	
								Capital	Equity
California Pizza Kitchen	$38	$66	$ 0	$ 208	0.0%	NMF	2.7	10.1%	10.1%
Applebee's International, Inc.	105	187	175	487	26.5%	11.7	2.0	14.0%	18.0%
BJ's Restaurants, Inc.	96	36	0	203	0.0%	NMF	1.2	4.9%	4.9%
Brinker International[1]	242	497	502	1,076	31.8%	14.4	2.6	13.2%	18.0%
Buffalo Wild Wings, Inc.	75	26	0	116	0.0%	NMF	2.4	14.0%	14.0%
The Cheesecake Factory, Inc.	203	163	0	712	0.0%	NMF	1.8	11.4%	11.4%
Chipotle Mexican Grill, Inc.	179	61	0	474	0.0%	NMF	1.7	8.8%	8.7%
Darden Restaurants, Inc.[2]	378	1,026	645	1,230	34.4%	10.9	3.1	20.6%	27.5%
Frisch's Restaurants, Inc.	12	31	43	101	30.1%	5.9	2.0	7.9%	9.1%
McCormick & Schmick's	30	40	0	160	0.2%	NMF	1.9	8.3%	8.3%
Panera Bread Company	128	110	0	398	0.0%	NMF	2.1	15.1%	15.1%
P.F. Chang's China Bistro	65	104	19	290	6.2%	NMF	3.0	11.1%	11.5%
RARE Hospitality Int'l Inc.[3]	125	134	166	360	31.6%	29.2	1.9	9.8%	13.9%
Red Robin Gourmet Burgers	29	70	114	244	31.9%	7.7	1.7	9.3%	12.5%
Ruth's Chris Steak House, Inc.	26	59	68	68	50.0%	12.8	2.0	18.6%	34.9%
Sonic Corporation	43	78	159	392	28.9%	15.0	1.3	15.3%	20.1%
Texas Roadhouse, Inc.	53	78	36	319	10.2%	19.9	1.7	9.7%	10.7%

Notes:

[1] For the years ended December 31, 2006, January 1, 2006 and January 2, 2005, December 28, 2003.

[2] Severance charges represent payments to former president/CEO and former senior vice president/senior development officer under the terms of their separation agreements.

[3] Data for company-owned restaurants.

Sources of data: Company annual and quarterly reports and conference calls.

EXHIBIT 8 | Interest Rates and Yields

| | U.S. Treasury Securities | | | | | Corporate bonds (Moody's) | | Average Prime Lending | Average LIBOR 3-month |
| | Bills | | Notes & Bonds | | | | | | |
	3-month	6-month	3-year	10-year	30-year	Aaa 3	Baa		
2000	5.85%	5.92%	6.22%	6.03%	5.94%	7.62%	8.36%	9.23%	6.55%
2001	3.45%	3.39%	4.09%	5.02%	5.49%	7.08%	7.95%	6.91%	3.63%
2002	1.62%	1.69%	3.10%	4.61%	—	6.49%	7.80%	4.67%	1.79%
2003	1.02%	1.06%	2.10%	4.01%	—	5.67%	6.77%	4.12%	1.22%
2004	1.38%	1.58%	2.78%	4.27%	—	5.63%	6.39%	4.34%	1.67%
2005	3.16%	3.40%	3.93%	4.29%	—	5.24%	6.06%	6.19%	3.63%
2006: Jan.	4.20%	4.30%	4.35%	4.42%	—	5.29%	6.24%	7.38%	4.68%
Feb.	4.41%	4.51%	4.64%	4.57%	4.54%	5.35%	6.27%	7.50%	4.82%
Mar.	4.51%	4.61%	4.74%	4.72%	4.73%	5.53%	6.41%	7.63%	4.99%
Apr.	4.59%	4.72%	4.89%	4.99%	5.06%	5.84%	6.68%	7.75%	5.15%
May	4.72%	4.81%	4.97%	5.11%	5.20%	5.95%	6.75%	7.88%	5.23%
June	4.79%	4.95%	5.09%	5.11%	5.15%	5.89%	6.78%	7.13%	5.51%
July	4.96%	5.09%	5.07%	5.09%	5.13%	5.85%	6.76%	8.25%	5.49%
Aug.	4.98%	4.99%	4.85%	4.88%	5.00%	5.68%	6.59%	8.25%	5.40%
Sept.	4.82%	4.90%	4.69%	4.72%	4.85%	5.51%	6.43%	8.25%	5.37%
Oct.	4.89%	4.91%	4.72%	4.73%	4.85%	5.51%	6.42%	8.25%	5.37%
Nov.	4.95%	4.96%	4.64%	4.60%	4.69%	5.33%	6.20%	8.25%	5.37%
Dec.	4.85%	4.88%	4.58%	4.56%	4.68%	5.32%	6.22%	8.25%	5.36%
2007: Jan.	4.96%	4.94%	4.79%	4.76%	4.85%	5.40%	6.34%	8.25%	5.36%
Feb.	5.02%	4.97%	4.75%	4.72%	4.82%	5.39%	6.28%	8.25%	5.36%
Mar.	4.97%	4.90%	4.51%	4.56%	4.72%	5.30%	6.27%	8.25%	5.35%
Apr.	4.88%	4.87%	4.60%	4.69%	4.87%	5.47%	6.39%	8.25%	5.36%
May	4.77%	4.80%	4.69%	4.75%	4.90%	5.47%	6.39%	8.25%	5.36%
June	4.63%	4.77%	5.00%	5.10%	5.20%	5.79%	6.70%	8.25%	5.36%

Sources of data: *Economic Report of the President* and Fannie Mae Web site.

EXHIBIT 9 | Pro Forma Tax Shield Effect of Recapitalization Scenarios (dollars in thousands, except share data; figures based on end of June 2007)

	Actual	Debt/Total Capital		
		10%	20%	30%
Interest rate[1]	6.16%	6.16%	6.16%	6.16%
Tax rate	32.5%	32.5%	32.5%	32.5%
Earnings before income taxes and interest[2]	30,054	30,054	30,054	30,054
Interest expense	0	1,391	2,783	4,174
Earnings before taxes	30,054	28,663	27,271	25,880
Income taxes	9,755	9,303	8,852	8,400
Net income	20,299	19,359	18,419	17,480
Book value:				
Debt	0	22,589	45,178	67,766
Equity	225,888	203,299	180,710	158,122
Total capital	225,888	225,888	225,888	225,888
Market value:				
Debt[3]	0	22,589	45,178	67,766
Equity[4]	643,773	628,516	613,259	598,002
Market value of capital	643,773	651,105	658,437	665,769

Notes:

[1]Interest rate of CPK's credit facility with Bank of America: LIBOR + 0.80%.

[2]Earnings before interest and taxes (EBIT) include interest income.

[3]Market values of debt equal book values.

[4]Actual market value of equity equals the share price ($22.10) multiplied by the current number of shares outstanding (29.13 million).

Source: Case writer analysis based on CPK financial data.

The Wm. Wrigley Jr. Company: Capital Structure, Valuation, and Cost of Capital

Interest rates are at their lowest point in 50 years. Yet the use of debt financing by corporations is declining—this happens anyway in a recession. And some deleveraging is due to strategic changes in an industry, such as technological innovation or other developments that increase business risk. But corporate deleveraging seems to have gone too far. CEOs are missing valuable opportunities to create value for their shareholders. In the extreme case, you have mature firms who use no debt at all! Take William Wrigley Jr. Company, for instance. It has a leading market share in a stable low-technology business—it makes chewing gum—and yet has no debt. I bet that if we could persuade Wrigley's board to do a leveraged recapitalization through a dividend or major share repurchase, we could create significant new value. Susan, please run some numbers on the potential change in value. And get me the names and phone numbers of all of Wrigley's directors.

With those words, Blanka Dobrynin, managing partner of Aurora Borealis LLC, asked Susan Chandler, an associate, to initiate the research for a potential investment in Wrigley. Aurora Borealis was a hedge fund with about $3 billion under management and an investment strategy that focused on distressed companies, merger arbitrage, change-of-control transactions, and recapitalizations. Dobrynin had immigrated to the United States from Russia in 1991, and had risen quickly to become partner at a major Wall Street firm. In 2000, she founded Aurora Borealis to pursue an "active-investor" strategy. Her typical mode of operation was to identify opportunities for a corporation to restructure, invest significantly in the stock of the target firm, and then undertake a process of persuading management and directors to restructure. Now, in June 2002, Dobrynin could look back on the large returns from the use of that strategy.

467

Chandler noted that Wrigley's market value of common equity was about $13.1 billion. Dobrynin and Chandler discussed the current capital-market conditions and decided to focus on the assumption that Wrigley could borrow $3 billion at a credit rating between BB and B, to yield 13%. Chandler agreed to return soon to discuss the results of her research.

The William Wrigley Jr. Company

Wrigley was the world's largest manufacturer and distributor of chewing gum. The firm's industry, branded consumer foods and candy, was intensely competitive and was dominated by a few large players. **Exhibit 1** gives product profiles of Wrigley and its peers. Over the preceding two years, revenues had grown at an annual compound rate of 10% (earnings at 9%), reflecting the introduction of new products and foreign expansion (**Exhibit 2**). Historically, the firm had been conservatively financed. At the end of 2001, it had total assets of $1.76 billion and no debt (**Exhibit 3**). As **Exhibit 4** shows, Wrigley's stock price had significantly outperformed the S&P 500 Composite Index, and was running slightly ahead of its industry index.

Estimating the Effect of a Leveraged Recapitalization

Under the proposed leveraged recapitalization, Wrigley would borrow $3 billion and use it either to pay an equivalent dividend or to repurchase an equivalent value of shares. Chandler knew that this combination of actions could affect the firm's share value, cost of capital, debt coverage, earnings per share, and voting control. Accordingly, she sought to evaluate the effect of the recapitalization on those areas. She gathered financial data on Wrigley and its peer companies (**Exhibit 5**).

Impact on Share Value

Chandler recalled that the effect of leverage on a firm could be modeled by using the adjusted present-value formula, which hypothesized that debt increased the value of a firm by means of shielding cash flows from taxes. Thus, the present value of debt tax shields could be added to the value of the unlevered firm to yield the value of the levered enterprise. The marginal tax rate Chandler proposed to use was 40%, reflecting the sum of federal, state, and local taxes.

Impact on Debt Rating

A key assumption in the analysis would be the debt rating for Wrigley, after assuming $3 billion in debt, and whether the firm could cover the resulting interest payments. Dobrynin had suggested that Chandler should assume Wrigley would borrow $3 billion at a rating between BB and B. Was a rating of BB/B likely? In that regard, Chandler gathered information on the average financial ratios associated with different debt-rating categories (**Exhibit 6**). Dobrynin thought that Wrigley's pretax cost of debt would be around 13%. Chandler sought to check that assumption against the capital-market information given in **Exhibit 7.**

Impact on Cost of Capital

Chandler knew that the maximum value of the firm was achieved when the weighted average cost of capital (WACC) was minimized. Thus, she intended to estimate what the cost of equity and the WACC might be, if Wrigley pursued this capital-structure change. The projected cost of debt would depend on her assessment of Wrigley's debt rating after recapitalization and on current capital-market rates (summarized in **Exhibit 7**).

The cost of equity (K_E) could be estimated by using the capital asset pricing model. **Exhibit 7** gives yields on U.S. Treasury instruments, which afforded possible estimates of the risk-free rate of return. The practice at Aurora Borealis was to use an equity-market risk premium of 7.0%. Wrigley's beta would also need to be relevered to reflect the projected recapitalization.

Chandler wondered whether her analysis covered everything. Where, for instance, should she take into account potential costs of bankruptcy and distress or the effects of leverage as a signal about future operations? More leverage would also create certain constraints and incentives for management. Where should those be reflected in her analysis?

Impact on Reported Earnings Per Share

Chandler intended to estimate the expected effect on earnings per share (EPS) that would occur at different levels of operating income (EBIT) with a change in leverage. The beginnings of an EBIT/EPS analysis are presented in **Exhibit 8.**

Impact on Voting Control

The William Wrigley Jr. Company had 232.441 million shares outstanding. A repurchase of shares would alter that amount. The Wrigley family controlled 21% of the common shares outstanding and 58% of Class B common stock, which had superior voting rights to the common stock.[1] Assuming the Wrigley family did not sell any shares, how would the share-repurchase alternative affect the family's voting-control position in the company?

Conclusion

Although Susan Chandler's analysis followed a familiar path, each company that she had analyzed differed in important respects from previous firms. Blanka Dobrynin paid her to run numbers and, more importantly, to find the differences wherein hidden threats and opportunities lay. Running the numbers was easy for Chandler; drawing profitable insights from them was not.

---

[1]Shares of Class B common stock had 10 votes each; ordinary common shares had one vote each. Class B shares were restricted in their sale or transfer and could be converted into ordinary common shares on a 1:1 basis. Thus, for purposes of computing per-share values, the total number of shares outstanding for Wrigley consisted of the sum of common shares (189.8 million) and Class B shares (42.641 million), a total of 232.441 million shares.

EXHIBIT 1 | Description of Industry Peer Firms

Company	Description
Cadbury Schweppes plc	Cadbury Schweppes plc made and distributed confectionary and beverage products worldwide. Sold 51% stake in Coca-Cola and Schweppes Beverages Ltd. in 1997; beverage brands in 160 international markets in 1999. In 1998, owned 40% of American Bottling. Licensed Cadbury to Hershey in U.S. Acquired Dr. Pepper/7Up in '95; Hawaiian Punch in '99; and Snapple in '00. Segment sales/operating profits in '01: beverages, 43%/61%; confectionary, 57%/39%. Sales by region: U.K., 21%; U.S., 42%; Australia, 10%; other (including Europe), 27%. Had 36,460 employees. Bond rating: BBB/Baa2.
Hershey Foods Corp.	Hershey Foods Corp. was the largest U.S. producer of chocolate and nonchocolate confectionary products (major brands: Hershey's, Reese's, Cadbury, Kit Kat, Sweet Escapes, TasteTations, Jolly Rancher, Good & Plenty, and Milk Duds). Sold majority of pasta operations in 1/99. Acquired Cadbury U.S. in 9/88; Henry Heide in 12/95; and Leaf North America in 12/96. Advertising costs: 4.2% of '01 sales. '01 depreciation rate: 6.6%. Had 14,400 employees; 40,300 shareholders. Hershey Trust Co. owns 11.5% of common stock and 99.6% of Class B. Bond rating: A+/A1.
Kraft Foods Inc.	Kraft Foods Inc. was the largest branded food and beverage company headquartered in the U.S. and second largest worldwide. The company marketed many of the world's leading food brands, including Kraft cheese, Maxwell House coffee, Nabisco cookies and crackers, Philadelphia cream cheese, Oscar Mayer meats, and Post cereals. Its products were sold in more than 145 countries. North American sales accounted for 74% of '01 sales; international, 26%. Acquired Nabisco in 12/00. Had about 14,000 employees. Philip Morris owns 84% of its common stock(3/02 proxy). Bond rating: BBB+/A3.
Tootsie Roll Industries, Inc.	Tootsie Roll Industries, Inc., produced candy. Products include Tootsie Roll, Tootsie Pop, Tootsie Bubble Pop, and Mason Dots. Acquired Brach's Confections' Andes Candies in 5/00; Warner-Lambert's former chocolate/caramel brands (Junior Mints, Sugar Daddy, Charleston Chew, and Pom Poms) in 9/88; Cella Confections in 7/85. Five plants in U.S., one in Mexico. Int'l ops. (Mexico and Canada): 7% of '01 sales. Had about 1,950 employees. M. J. & E. R. Gordon control 74% of voting power. Bond rating: N/A.
The Wm. Wrigley Jr. Company	The Wm. Wrigley Jr. Company was the world's largest manufacturer and seller of chewing gums, specialty gums, and gum base. Principal brands: Doublemint, Spearmint, Juicy Fruit, Big Red, WinterFresh, Extra, Orbit, Freedent. Amurol Products subsidiary made novelty gums, including Bubble Tape, Big League Chew; markets Hubba Bubba bubble gum. Foreign sales: 58% of 2001 total, 58% of pretax profit. Had 10,800 employees; 38,701 common shareholders. William Wrigley Jr. owned 21% of common stock and 58% of Class B. Bond rating: N/A.

Sources of information: Value Line Investment Survey; Bloomberg LP.

EXHIBIT 2 | Income Statements for the Wm. Wrigley Jr. Company

	Year Ended December 31		
(in thousands, except per-share amounts)	2001	2000	1999
Earnings			
Net sales	$ 2,429,646	$ 2,145,706	$ 2,061,602
Cost of sales	997,054	904,266	904,183
Gross profit	1,432,592	1,241,440	1,157,419
Selling, general and administrative expenses	919,236	778,197	721,813
Operating income	513,356	463,243	435,606
Investment income	18,553	19,185	17,636
Other expense	(4,543)	(3,116)	(8,812)
Earnings before income taxes	527,366	479,312	444,430
Income taxes	164,380	150,370	136,247
Net earnings	$ 362,986	$ 328,942	$ 308,183
Per-share amounts			
Net earnings per share of common stock	$ 1.61	$ 1.45	$ 1.33
Dividends paid per share of common stock	$ 0.745	$ 0.70	$ 0.66

Source of data: Company regulatory filings.

EXHIBIT 3 | Consolidated Balance Sheets for the Wm. Wrigley Jr. Company

(in thousands of dollars)	2001	2000
ASSETS		
Current assets:		
Cash and equivalents	$ 307,785	$ 300,599
Short-term investments, at amortized cost	25,450	29,301
Accounts receivable	239,885	191,570
Inventories		
Finished goods	75,693	64,676
Raw materials and supplies	203,288	188,615
	278,981	253,291
Other current assets	46,896	39,728
Deferred income taxes - current	14,846	14,226
Total current assets	913,843	828,715
Marketable equity securities, at fair value	25,300	28,535
Deferred charges and other assets	115,745	83,713
Deferred income taxes - noncurrent	26,381	26,743
Property, plant, and equipment (at cost)		
Land	39,933	39,125
Buildings and building equipment	359,109	344,457
Machinery and equipment	857,044	756,050
	1,256,086	1,139,632
Less accumulated depreciation	571,717	532,598
Net property, plant and equipment	684,379	607,034
TOTAL ASSETS	$1,765,648	$1,574,740
LIABILITIES AND STOCKHOLDERS' EQUITY		
Current liabilities:		
Accounts payable	$ 91,225	$ 73,129
Accrued expenses	128,406	113,779
Dividends payable	42,711	39,467
Income and other taxes payable	68,437	60,976
Deferred income taxes - current	1,455	859
Total current liabilities	332,234	288,210
Deferred income taxes - noncurrent	43,206	40,144
Other non-current liabilities	113,921	113,489
Common stock	12,646	12,558
Class B convertible stock	2,850	2,938
Additional paid-in capital	1,153	346
Retained earnings	1,684,337	1,492,547
Treasury stock	(289,799)	(256,478)
Accumulated other comprehensive income	(134,900)	(119,014)
Total stockholders' equity	1,276,287	1,132,897
TOTAL LIABILITIES AND STOCKHOLDERS' EQUITY	$1,765,648	$1,574,740

Source of data: Company regulatory filings.

EXHIBIT 4 | Stock-Price Performance of the Wm. Wrigley Jr. Company (value of $1,000 investment: June 1, 2000, to June 7, 2002)

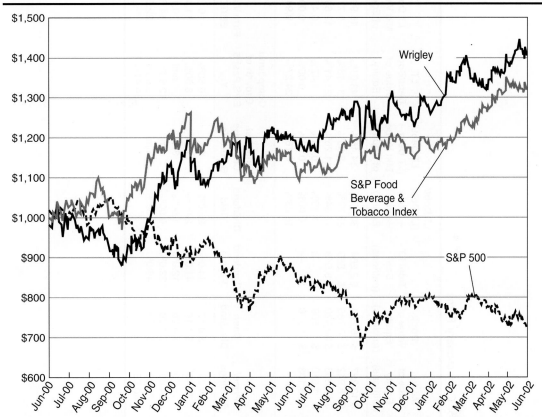

Source of data: Datastream, with casewriter's analysis.

EXHIBIT 5 | Financial Characteristics of Major Confectionary Firms

Company Name	Recent Price	Common Shares Outstanding (millions)	Market Value of Equity (millions)	Book Value of Equity (millions)	Total LT Debt (millions)	LT Debt/ (LT Debt + Book Value of Equity)	LT Debt/ (LT Debt + Mkt Value of Equity)	LT Debt/Book Value of Equity	LT Debt/ Mkt Value of Equity
Cadbury Schweppes plc	$ 26.66	502.50	$ 13,397	$ 5,264	$ 2,264	30.07%	14.46%	43.01%	16.90%
Hershey Foods Corp.	$ 65.45	136.63	$ 8,942	$ 2,785	$ 869	23.77%	8.85%	31.18%	9.71%
Kraft Foods	$ 38.82	1,735.00	$ 67,353	$ 39,920	$ 8,548	17.64%	11.26%	21.41%	12.69%
Tootsie Roll Industries Inc.	$ 31.17	51.66	$ 1,610	$ 509	$ 8	1.45%	0.46%	1.47%	0.47%
Wm. Wrigley Jr. Co.	$ 56.37	232.44	$ 13,103	$ 1,276	$ —	0.00%	0.00%	0.00%	0.00%
S&P 500 Composite	$ 1,148.08					18.23%	8.76%	24.27%	9.94%

Company Name	Beta	EPS	Price/ Earnings	Cash Dividend	Dividend Payout	Dividend Yield	Interest Coverage Before Tax	Compound Growth of EPS Past 5 Yrs	Firm Value/ EBITDA
Cadbury Schweppes plc	0.60	1.39	15.20	$ 0.67	44.0%	2.50%	4.6x	6.50%	10.3
Hershey Foods Corp.	0.60	2.74	20.40	$ 1.16	41.0%	2.00%	11.1x	6.50%	11.4
Kraft Foods	nmf	1.17	18.70	$ 0.26	12.0%	1.50%	3.4x	nmf	10.1
Tootsie Roll Industries Inc.	0.65	1.30	24.00	$ 0.28	22.0%	0.90%	nmf	12.50%	14.6
Wm. Wrigley Jr. Co.	0.75	1.61	29.30	$ 0.75	46.0%	1.50%	nmf	9.00%	22.6
S&P 500 Composite	1.00	18.78	40.55					-49.57%	

Note: nmf = not a meaningful figure.

Source of data: *Value Line Investment Survey.*

EXHIBIT 6 | Key Industrial Financial Ratios by Credit Rating

	Investment Grade				Non-Investment Grade	
	AAA	AA	A	BBB	BB	B
EBIT interest coverage (x)	23.4	13.3	6.3	3.9	2.2	1.0
Funds from operations/total debt (%)	214.2	65.7	42.2	30.6	19.7	10.4
Free operating cash flow/total debt (%)	156.6	33.6	22.3	12.8	7.3	1.5
Return on capital (%)	35.0	26.6	18.1	13.1	11.5	8.0
Operating income/sales (%)	23.4	24.0	18.1	15.5	15.4	14.7
Long-term debt/capital (%)	(1.1)	21.1	33.8	40.3	53.6	72.6
Total debt/capital, incl. short-term debt (%)	5.0	35.9	42.6	47.0	57.7	75.1

Source of data: Standard & Poor's *CreditStats*, September 8, 2003.

Definitions:

EBIT interest coverage divides earnings before interest and taxes (EBIT) by gross interest expense (before subtracting capitalized interest and interest income).

FFO/total debt divides funds from operations (FFO) by total debt. FFO is defined as net income from continuing operations, depreciation and amortization, deferred income taxes, and other noncash items/Long-term debt + current maturities + commercial paper, and other short-term borrowings.

Free operating cash flow/total debt. Free operating cash flow is defined as FFO − capital expenditures − (+) increase (decrease) in working capital (excluding changes in cash, marketable securities, and short-term debt)/Long-term debt + current maturities, commercial paper, and other short-term borrowings.

Total debt/EBITDA. Long-term debt + current maturities, commercial paper, and other short-term borrowing/Adjusted earnings from continuing operations before interest, taxes, and depreciation and amortization.

Return on capital. EBIT/Average of beginning of year and end of year capital, including short-term debt, current maturities, long-term debt, noncurrent deferred taxes, minority interest, and equity (common and preferred stock).

Total debt/capital. Long-term debt + current maturities, commercial paper, and other short-term borrowings/Long-term debt + current maturities, commercial paper, and other short-term borrowings + shareholders' equity (including preferred stock) + minority interest.

Source of data: Standard & Poor's *Corporate Ratings Criteria* (New York: Standard & Poor's, 2005), 42.

EXHIBIT 7 | Capital-Market Conditions as of June 7, 2002

U.S. Treasury Obligations	Yield
3 mos.	1.670%
6 mos.	1.710%
1 yr.	2.310%
2 yr.	3.160%
3 yr.	3.660%
5 yr.	4.090%
7 yr.	4.520%
10 yr.	4.860%
20 yr.	5.650%

Other Instruments	
U.S. Federal Reserve Bank discount rate	1.730%
LIBOR (1 month)	1.840%
Certificates of deposit (6 month)	1.980%
Prime interest rates	4.750%

Corporate Debt Obligations (10 year)	Yield
AAA	9.307%
AA	9.786%
A	10.083%
BBB	10.894%
BB	12.753%
B	14.663%

U.S. Treasury Yield Curve

June 7, 2002

Source of data: Bloomberg LP; Federal Reserve Bank Reports.

EXHIBIT 8 | EPS versus EBIT Analysis

Assumptions

Interest rate on debt

Pre-recap debt

Tax rate

Before recapitalization

	Worst case	Most likely	Best case
Operating income (EBIT)			
Interest expense			
Taxable income			
Taxes			
Net income			
Shares outstanding			
Earnings per share			

Assumptions

Interest rate on debt

Pre-recap debt

Tax rate

After recapitalization

	Worst case	Most likely	Best case
Operating income (EBIT)			
Interest expense			
Taxable income			
Taxes			
Net income			
Shares outstanding			
Earnings per share			

Deluxe Corporation

In the late summer of 2002, Rajat Singh, a managing director at Hudson Bancorp, was reflecting on the financial policies of Deluxe Corporation, the largest printer of paper checks in the United States. Earlier in the year, Deluxe had retired all of its long-term debt, and the company had not had a major bond issue in more than 10 years. Simultaneously, the company had been pursuing an aggressive program of share repurchases, the latest of which was nearly complete. So far, those actions had proven successful; investors had responded well to the share repurchases, and the company's stock was at its highest level in nearly 10 years. But Singh, who had been retained by Deluxe's board of directors to provide guidance on the company's financial strategy, saw dangers looming for Deluxe that would require the company's managers to do more.

Deluxe Corporation was the dominant player in the highly concentrated and competitive check-printing industry. Deluxe's sales and earnings growth, however, had been in a slow decline as the company struggled to fight a relentless wave of technological change. Since the advent of online payment methods and the rising popularity of credit and debit cards, consumers' usage of paper checks had fallen steadily. In response, Deluxe's chair and chief executive officer (CEO), Lawrence J. Mosner, had led a major restructuring of the firm whereby he rationalized its operations, reduced its labor force, and divested several noncore businesses. Singh sensed that those measures would only carry the company so far and that the board was looking for other alternatives.

Singh surmised that there would eventually be a tipping point at which the demand for paper checks would fall precipitously. In this challenging operating environment, Singh was convinced that Deluxe would need continued financial flexibility to fend off the eventual disintegration of its core business. Singh had already told the board that the company had probably gone as far as it could with share repurchases. The time for a new round of debt financing was at hand. The board had asked Singh for a detailed plan in five days, and had insisted that, as part of the plan, he undertake

This case was prepared from public data by Sean D. Carr, under the supervision of Robert F. Bruner and Professor Susan Chaplinsky. Hudson Bancorp and Rajat Singh are fictional; the case is intended solely as a basis for class discussion rather than to illustrate effective or ineffective handling of an administrative situation. Copyright © 2005 by the University of Virginia Darden School Foundation, Charlottesville, VA. All rights reserved. *To order copies, send an e-mail to* sales@dardenbusinesspublishing.com. *No part of this publication may be reproduced, stored in a retrieval system, used in a spreadsheet, or transmitted in any form or by any means—electronic, mechanical, photocopying, recording, or otherwise—without the permission of the Darden School Foundation.*

a complete assessment of the firm's overall debt policy, focusing primarily on the appropriate mix of debt and equity. In the not-too-distant future, Deluxe's financial and strategic choices would be severely constrained, and Singh believed it was essential that the company's financial policies afford it the necessary funding and flexibility to steer a path to survivability.

Modest Beginnings

Deluxe Corporation was founded in 1915 by a chicken-farmer-turned-printer in a one-room print shop in St. Paul, Minnesota. Then known as Deluxe Check Printers, the company was a pioneer in the emerging check printing business, and specialized in imprinting personalized information on checks and checkbooks. Deluxe became a publicly traded company in 1965, and traded on the New York Stock Exchange in 1980 under the name Deluxe Corporation. The company was the largest provider of checks in the United States, serving customers through more than 10,000 financial institutions. Deluxe processed more than 100 million check orders each year—nearly half of the U.S. market. American consumers wrote more than 42 billion checks annually, although check usage had declined in recent years.

Between 1975 and 1995, the peak years of check usage in the United States, Deluxe Corporation's revenues grew at a compound annual rate of 12%. This rate, however, had declined over the past decade as checks lost share to the electronic forms of payment, such as ATMs, credit cards, debit cards, and Internet bill-paying systems. As those new forms of payment created a highly fragmented payment industry, check printing itself remained highly concentrated, with only a few firms controlling 90% of the market. Deluxe competed primarily with two other companies, John Harland and Clarke American, a subsidiary of U.K.-based Novar (**Figure 1**). With a proliferation of alternative payment systems, the check-printing business faced an annual decline of 1%–3% in check demand, a trend that most industry analysts expected to continue.

FIGURE 1 | U.S. Check-printing market share

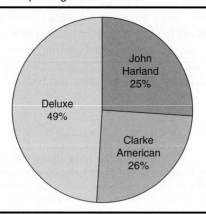

Source of data: D.A. Davidson & Co.

Recent Financial Performance

With the prospect of a precipitous decline in demand for paper checks emerging in the late 1990s, Deluxe undertook a major reorganization during which it divested non-strategic businesses and dramatically reduced the number of its employees and facilities. The company went from 62 printing plants to 13, reduced its labor force from 15,000 to 7,000, outsourced information technology functions, improved manufacturing efficiencies, and divested nearly 20 separate businesses. The resulting reductions in operating expenses helped reverse Deluxe's earnings slump in 1998, despite the continued softening in revenue growth.

In 2000, Deluxe announced a major strategic shift with the spinoff of its technology-related subsidiaries, eFunds and iDLX Technology Partners, in an initial public offering. The subsidiary eFunds provided electronic-payment products and services (e.g., electronic transaction processing, electronic funds transfer, and payment protection services) to the financial and retail industries; iDLX offered technology-related consulting services to financial services companies. Deluxe's CEO, Mosner, believed that Deluxe offered more value to shareholders as a pure-play company. While he admitted that the eventual demise of the paper-check business was a certainty, he insisted that there were still growth opportunities for the company:

> We don't want to abandon the core business too soon. Instead, you mine all you can out of the core business before [moving on]. We have a very good business, a very solid business with high levels of profitability. We feel we can generate revenues and profits on our core business not only today but over the next five years.[1]

With the spinoff of eFunds and iDLX, management abandoned its plan for Deluxe to offer products and services targeting the electronic-transfer market and refocused on its core business. Repositioning the firm as a pure-play check-printing company made sense to investors, and the company's stock price rose on the news.

Following the spinoff, Mosner reorganized Deluxe's remaining paper-payments segment around three primary business units. Financial Services sold checks to consumers through financial institutions, with institutional clients typically entering into three-to-five-year supplier contracts. Direct Checks sold to consumers through direct mail and the Internet. The Business Services segment sold checks, forms, and related products through financial institutions and directly to small businesses, targeting firms with no more than 20 employees. See **Figure 2** for data on Deluxe's 2001 sales by segment.

According to some analysts, the Business Services segment ultimately held the most promise for Deluxe because it could allow the company to bundle or cross-sell a variety of products and services to the growing small-business sector. Rather than simply grow its number of individual customers, as it had done in the past with its check business, Business Services could generate growth in the number of products or services it sold *per* customer. Furthermore, there were several regional companies active in this sector that had the potential to be strategic partners for Deluxe.

---

[1] Dee DePass, "Cashing Out: Even Deluxe Corp. Admits That Paper Checks Are Headed for the Dust Heap of History," *Star-Tribune Newspapers of the Twin Cities,* 17 January 2002.

FIGURE 2 | Deluxe Corp. Sales by Segment, 2001

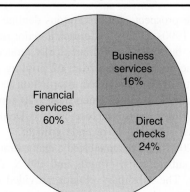

Source of data: Company reports.

By year-end 2001, the market had responded favorably to the spinoff and restructuring efforts—the firm's share price had grown by more than 65% over the year, outperforming the S&P 500 Index, which had fallen nearly 20%. Over the preceding decade, however, the firm's share price growth had lagged the broad market indexes. **Exhibit 1** gives a 10-year summary of the financial characteristics of the firm, including share prices and data on comparable market performance. From 1998 to 2001, Deluxe Corporation's compound annual rate of sales growth was −4.0%, which reflected the growing maturity of the market for paper checks in the United States. Consistent with the perceived maturity of the market segment, Deluxe's 2001 price earnings ratio (P/E) of 11.0× hovered well below the broader market's P/E of 29.5×.

Concerns about revenue growth and declining demand for printed checks were echoed in the comments of analysts who followed the firm. Despite a positive assessment of the firm's recent ability to improve margins, one analyst covering Deluxe was guarded:

> [W]e remain cautious concerning Deluxe's long-term prospects for earnings growth, until the company can improve profitability in its core [Financial Services] check printing segment. At present, this seems like a tough proposition, given a relatively mature market, intense price competition, the growth in electronic payments, and consolidation in the banking sector.[2]

Rajat Singh knew that Deluxe's board members had many of the same concerns, but also knew that they believed the analyst community had taken a shortsighted view of the company's potential. In fact, Deluxe's most recent annual report stated, "While the check printing industry is mature, our existing leadership position in the market

---

[2]David Gallen, *Value Line Investment Survey,* 24 May 2002.

place contributes to our financial strength."[3] The U.S. Federal Reserve Board's 2001 *Bank Payment Study* indicated that checks still remained consumers' most preferred method of noncash payment, representing 60% of all retail noncash payments. The company's management believed that it was well positioned to extract value from this business and to explore noncheck offerings that would closely leverage Deluxe's core competencies. **Exhibits 2** and **3** give the latest years' income statements and balance sheets for Deluxe Corporation.

Current and Future Financing

Against this backdrop, Singh assessed the current and future financing requirements of the firm. From time to time, Deluxe required additional financing for such general corporate purposes as working capital, capital asset purchases, possible acquisitions, repayment of outstanding debts, dividend payments, and repurchasing the firm's securities. To meet those short-term financing needs, Deluxe could draw upon the following debt instruments:

- **Commercial paper:**[4] Deluxe maintained a $300-million commercial-paper program, which carried a credit rating of A1/P1. "The risk of a downgrade of Deluxe's short-term credit rating is low," Singh thought. "If for any reason, they were unable to access the commercial paper markets, they would rely on their line of credit for liquidity." Deluxe had $150 million in commercial paper outstanding, at a weighted-average interest rate of 1.85%.

- **Line of credit:** Deluxe also had $350 million available under a committed line of credit, which would expire in August 2002, and $50 million under an uncommitted line of credit. During 2001, the company drew no amounts on its committed line of credit. The average amount drawn on the uncommitted line during 2001 was $1.3 million, at a weighted-average interest rate of 4.26%. At year-end, no amount was outstanding on this line of credit.

- **Medium-term notes:** Deluxe had a shelf registration[5] for the issuance of up to $300 million in medium-term notes. No such notes had been issued or were outstanding.

In February 2001, Deluxe paid off $100 million of its 8.55% long-term unsecured and unsubordinated notes, which it had issued in 1991.

---

[3]Deluxe Corporation Annual Report (2001), 25–26.

[4]Commercial paper was an unsecured, short-term obligation issued by a corporation, typically for financing accounts receivable and inventories. It was usually issued at a discount reflecting prevailing market interest rates, and its maturity ranged from 2 to 270 days.

[5]Shelf registration was a term used to describe the U.S. Securities and Exchange Commission's rule that gave a corporation the ability to comply with registration requirements up to two years before a public offering for a security. With a registration on the shelf, the company could quickly go to market with its offering when conditions became more favorable.

In January 2001, the company's board of directors approved a stock-repurchase program, which authorized the repurchase of up to 14 million shares of Deluxe common stock, or about 19% of total shares outstanding. By year-end, the company had spent about $350 million to repurchase 11.3 million shares. This program followed a share-repurchase program initiated in 1999, which called for the repurchase of 10 million shares, or about 12.5% of the firm's shares outstanding at the time. Deluxe funded these repurchases with cash from operations and from issuances of commercial paper. **Exhibit 1** summarizes the firm's share repurchase activity in recent years. Singh believed the board would continue to pursue an aggressive program of share repurchases.

In addition to possible buybacks and strategic acquisitions, Singh reviewed other possible demands on the firm's resources. He believed that cash dividends would be held constant for the foreseeable future. He also believed that capital expenditures would be about equal to depreciation for the next few years. Although sales might grow, working capital turns should decline, resulting in a reduction in net working capital in the first year, followed by increases later on. Both of those effects reflected the tight asset management under the new CEO. **Exhibit 4** gives a five-year forecast of Deluxe's income statement and balance sheet. This forecast was consistent with the lower end of analysts' projections for revenue growth and realization of the benefits of Deluxe's recent restructuring. The forecast assumed that the existing debt would be refinanced with similar debt, but did not assume major share repurchases. The forecast would need to be revised to reflect the impact of any recommended changes in financial policy.

Considerations in Assessing Financial Policy

In addition to assessing Deluxe's internal financing requirements, Singh recognized that his policy recommendations would play an important role in shaping the perceptions of the firm by bond-rating agencies and investors.

Bond Rating[6]

Deluxe's senior debt, which had matured in February 2001, had been rated A+ by Standard & Poor's and A1 by Moody's. (**Exhibit 5** presents the bond-rating definitions for this and other rating categories.) A+/A1 were investment-grade ratings, as were the next lower rating grades, BBB/Baa. Below that, however, were noninvestment-grade ratings (BB/Ba), which were often referred to as high yield or junk debt. Some large institutional investors (for example, pension funds and charitable trusts) were barred from investing in noninvestment-grade debt, and many individual

---

[6]A firm's bond rating, which was based on an analysis of the issuer's financial condition and profitability, reflected the probability of defaulting on the issue. The convention in finance was that the firm's bond rating referred to the rating on the firm's *senior* debt, with the understanding that any subordinated debt issued by the firm would ordinarily have a lower bond rating. For instance, Deluxe's senior debt had the split BBB/Baa3 rating, while its subordinated convertible bonds were rated BB/Ba. Standard & Poor's, Moody's Investors Service, and Fitch Investors Service were bond-rating services.

FIGURE 3 | Default Rates by Rating Category, 2001

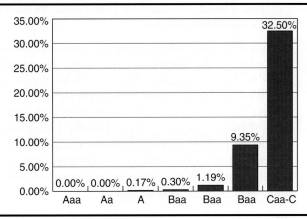

Source of data: Moody's Investors Service, February 2002.

investors shunned it as well. For that reason, the yields on noninvestment-grade debt over U.S. Treasury securities (i.e., spreads) were typically considerably higher than the spreads for investment-grade issues. For pertinent data on the rating categories, see **Figures 3** and **4.**

The ability to issue noninvestment-grade debt depended, to a much greater degree than did investment-grade debt, on the strength of the economy and on favorable credit market conditions. On that issue, Rajat Singh said:

> You don't pay much of a penalty in yield as you go from A to BBB. There's a range over which the risk you take for more leverage is de minimus. But you pay a big penalty as you

FIGURE 4 | Number of New Issues by Rating Category, 2005

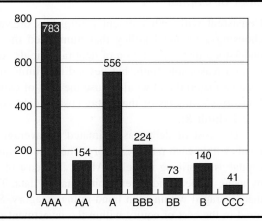

Source of data: Standard & Poor's *RatingsDirect.*

go from BBB to BB. The penalty is not only in the form of higher costs, but also in the form of possible damage to the Deluxe brand. We don't want the brand to be sullied by an association with junk debt.

For those reasons, Singh sought to preserve an investment-grade rating for Deluxe. But where in the investment-grade range should Deluxe be positioned? **Exhibit 6** gives the financial ratios associated with the various rating categories.

While the rating agencies looked closely at a number of indicators of credit quality, Deluxe's managers paid particular attention to the ratio of earnings before interest and taxes (EBIT) to interest expense. **Exhibit 7** illustrates Deluxe's EBIT-coverage ratios for the past 10 years. Singh's recommendations for the company would require the selection of an appropriate target bond rating. Thereafter, Singh would have to recommend to the board the minimum and maximum amounts of debt that Deluxe could carry to achieve the desired rating.

Flexibility

Singh was aware that choosing a target debt level based on an analysis of industry peers might not fully capture the flexibility that Deluxe would need to meet its own possible future adversities. Singh said:

> Flexibility is how much debt you can issue before you lose the investment-grade bond rating. I want flexibility, and yet I want to take advantage of the fact that, with more debt, you have lower cost of capital. I am very comfortable with Deluxe's strategy and internal financial forecasts for its business; if anything, I believe the forecasts probably underestimate, rather than overestimate, its cash flows. But let's suppose that a two-sigma adverse outcome would be an EBIT close to $200 million—I can't imagine in the worst of times an EBIT less than that.

Accordingly, Singh's final decision on the target bond rating would have to be one that maintained reasonable reserves against Deluxe's worst-case scenario.

Cost of Capital

Consistent with management's emphasis on value creation, Singh believed that choosing a financial policy that minimized the cost of capital was important. He understood that exploitation of debt tax shields could create value for shareholders— up to a reasonable limit, but beyond that limit, the costs of financial distress would become material and would cause the cost of capital to rise. Singh relied on Hudson Bancorp's estimates of the pretax cost of debt and cost of equity by rating category (see **Exhibit 8**).

The cost of debt was estimated by averaging the current yield-to-maturity of bonds within each rating category. The cost of equity (K_e) was estimated by using the capital asset pricing model (CAPM). The cost of equity was computed for each firm by using its beta and other capital market data. The individual estimates of K_e were then averaged within each bond-rating category. Singh reflected on the relatively flat trend in the cost of equity within the investment-grade range, and he understood that changes in leverage within the investment-grade range were not regarded as material to investors. Nonetheless, it remained for Singh to determine which rating category provided the lowest cost of capital.

Current Capital-Market Conditions

Any policy recommendations would need to acknowledge the feasibility of implementing those policies today as well as in the future. **Exhibit 9** presents information about current yields in the U.S. debt markets. The current situation in the debt markets was favorable as the U.S. economy continued its expansion. The equity markets seemed to be pausing after a phenomenal advance in prices. The outlook for interest rates was stable, although any sign of inflation might cause the Federal Reserve to lift interest rates. Major changes in taxes and regulations were in abeyance, at least until the outcome of the next round of presidential elections.

Conclusion

Rajat Singh leafed through the analyses and financial data he had gathered for his presentation to Deluxe Corporation's board of directors. Foremost in his mind were the words of the company's chief financial officer, Douglas Treff, who had said to a group of securities analysts barely a week earlier:

> Let me anticipate a question which many of you are pondering. What now? Our board of directors and the management team are committed to maximizing shareholder value. Our past actions have demonstrated that commitment. We have spun off a business, eFunds, at the end of 2000, to unleash the value of two different types of companies. Over the past 18 months, we have returned more than $600 million to shareholders through cash dividends and share repurchases. Therefore, be assured that we are evaluating options that will continue to create value for our fellow shareholders.[7]

Clearly, Singh's plan would have to afford Deluxe low costs and continued access to capital under a variety of operating scenarios in order for the firm to pursue whatever options it was considering. This would require him to test the possible effects of downside scenarios on the company's coverage and capitalization ratios under alternative debt policies. He reflected on the competing goals of value creation, flexibility, and bond rating. He aimed to recommend a financial policy that would balance those goals and provide guidance to the board of directors and the financial staff regarding the firm's target mix of capital. With so many competing factors to weigh, Singh believed that it was unlikely that his plan would be perfect. But then he remembered one of his mentor's favorite sayings: "If you wait until you have a 99% solution, you'll never act; go with an 80% solution."

---

[7]Fair Disclosure Financial Network, transcript of Earnings Release Conference Call, 18 July 2002.

EXHIBIT 1 | Deluxe Corporation's 10-Year Financial Summary (in millions of U.S. dollars except per-share values and numbers of shares)

	At Fiscal Years Ended December 31									
	1992	1993	1994	1995	1996	1997	1998	1999	2000	2001
Selected Income Statement Information										
Net sales	$1,534.4	$1,581.8	$1,747.9	$1,858.0	$1,895.7	$1,919.4	$1,931.8	$1,650.5	$1,262.7	$1,278.4
Operating expenses	$722.2	$739.5	$797.3	$819.4	$862.4	$806.7	$805.9	$688.9	$417.9	$421.1
Profit from operations	$812.2	$842.3	$950.6	$1,038.6	$1,033.3	$1,112.7	$1,125.9	$961.6	$844.8	$857.2
Interest expense	$15.4	$10.3	$11.3	$14.7	$12.0	$9.7	$9.7	$9.5	$10.8	$5.6
Net earnings	$202.8	$141.9	$140.9	$87.0	$65.5	$44.7	$143.1	$203.0	$161.9	$185.9
Common shares, end of year (000s)	83,797	82,549	82,375	82,364	82,056	81,326	80,481	72,020	72,555	64,102
Common shares repurchased (000s)	(2,197)	(1,341)	(1,191)	(1,414)	(1,715)	(1,833)	(9,573)	(48)	(11,332)	(3,898)
Common shares issued (000s)	949	1,167	1,181	1,106	985	988	1,112	583	2,890	1,255
Earnings per share[1]	$2.42	$2.09	$1.71	$1.15	$1.65	$2.15	$2.34	$2.64	$2.34	$2.70
Dividend per share	$1.34	$1.42	$1.46	$1.48	$1.48	$1.48	$1.48	$1.48	$1.48	$1.48
Selected Balance Sheet Information										
Working capital	$330.9	$386.9	$224.5	$130.4	$12.3	$108.1	$131.0	$167.8	$14.0	$116.6
Net property, plant, & equipment	$389.0	$401.6	$461.8	$494.2	$446.9	$415.0	$340.1	$294.8	$174.0	$149.6
Total assets	$1,199.6	$1,252.0	$1,256.3	$1,295.1	$1,176.4	$1,148.4	$1,171.5	$992.6	$649.5	$537.7
Long-term debt	$115.5	$110.8	$110.9	$111.0	$108.9	$110.0	$106.3	$115.5	$10.2	$10.1
Common stockholders' equity	$829.8	$801.2	$814.4	$780.4	$712.9	$610.2	$606.6	$417.3	$262.8	$78.6
Book value: LT debt/capital	12.2%	12.1%	12.0%	12.5%	13.3%	15.3%	14.9%	21.7%	3.7%	11.4%
Market value: LT debt/capital	2.9%	3.6%	4.9%	4.4%	3.9%	3.8%	3.5%	5.5%	0.6%	0.4%
Selected Valuation Information (year-end)										
Deluxe Corp. stock price	$46.75	$36.25	$26.38	$29.00	$32.75	$34.50	$36.56	$27.44	$25.27	$41.58
S&P 500 Composite Index	418.17	464.30	462.62	576.70	700.92	941.64	1,072.32	1,281.91	1,364.44	1,104.61
Deluxe Corp. average P/E[2]	17.60x	19.00x	17.40x	25.90x	20.60x	15.40x	14.30x	12.70x	10.20x	11.01x
S&P 500 Composite average P/E[2]	24.38x	24.11x	18.36x	16.92x	20.26x	23.88x	27.45x	31.43x	26.29x	29.50x
Deluxe Corp. market/book ratio	4.72x	3.73x	2.67x	3.06x	3.77x	4.60x	4.85x	4.74x	6.98x	33.91x
Deluxe Corp. Beta	1.00	1.00	1.00	0.95	0.90	0.95	0.85	0.90	0.90	0.85
Yield on 20-year T-bonds	7.67%	6.48%	8.02%	6.01%	6.73%	6.02%	5.39%	6.83%	5.59%	5.74%
Yield on 90-day T-bills	3.08%	3.01%	5.53%	4.96%	5.07%	5.22%	4.37%	5.17%	5.73%	1.71%
Total annual ret. on large co. stocks	7.67%	9.99%	1.31%	37.43%	23.07%	33.36%	28.58%	21.04%	−9.11%	−11.88%

[1]Primary earnings though 1997, then diluted.

[2]P/E ratios are computed on earnings before restructuring charges, litigation award, and other extraordinary items.

Sources of data: Standard & Poor's *Research Insight; Value Line Investment Survey;* Datastream Advance; Ibbotson Associates, *Stocks, Bonds Bills & Inflation Yearbook 2002.*

EXHIBIT 2 | Deluxe Corporation's Consolidated Statements of Income
(in millions of U.S. dollars)

	Years ended December 31	
	2001	**2000**
Revenue	$1,278.4	$1,262.7
Cost of goods sold	453.8	453.0
Selling, general, and admin. expense	514.4	518.2
Goodwill amortization expense	6.2	5.2
Asset impairment and disposition losses	2.1	7.3
Total costs	976.4	983.8
Profit/(loss) from operations	302.0	278.9
Interest income	2.4	4.8
Other income	(1.2)	1.2
Interest expense	(5.6)	(11.4)
Earnings/(loss) before taxes	297.6	273.4
Tax expense	111.6	104.0
Discontinued operations income/(loss)		(7.5)
Net earnings/(loss)	$ 185.9	$ 161.9

Source of data: Company regulatory filings.

EXHIBIT 3 | Deluxe Corporation's Consolidated Balance Sheets
(in millions of U.S. dollars)

	2001	2000
Assets		
Current assets		
Cash and cash equivalents	$ 9.6	$ 80.7
Marketable securities	—	18.5
Trade accounts receivable – net	37.7	46.0
Inventories	11.2	11.3
Supplies	11.1	11.8
Deferred income taxes	4.6	7.4
Prepaid expenses and other	9.9	12.0
Total current assets	84.0	187.8
Long-term investments	37.7	35.6
Property, plant, and equipment – net	151.1	174.0
Intangibles – net	115.0	134.5
Goodwill – net	82.2	88.4
Other noncurrent assets	67.9	36.2
Total assets	$537.8	$656.4
Liabilities and Stockholders' Equity		
Current liabilities		
Accounts payable	$ 52.8	$ 44.7
Accrued liabilities	162.9	148.5
Short-term debt	150.0	—
Long-term debt due within one year	1.4	100.7
Total current liabilities	367.1	293.9
Long-term debt	10.1	10.2
Deferred income taxes	44.9	51.1
Other long-term liabilities	37.0	38.3
Total liabilities	459.1	393.5
Common stockholders' equity		
Common shares	64.1	72.6
Additional paid-in capital	—	44.2
Retained earnings	14.6	146.2
Unearned compensation	0.1	0.1
Accum. other comprehensive income	—	(0.2)
Total common stockholders' equity	78.7	262.9
Total liabilities and stockholders' equity	$537.8	$656.4

Source of data: Company regulatory filings.

EXHIBIT 4 | Deluxe Corporation's Financial Forecast, 2002–06 (in millions of U.S. dollars)

	Actual	Projected				
	2001	2002	2003	2004	2005	2006
Annual increase in sales	1.2%	1.4%	1.6%	2.0%	2.2%	2.4%
Operating profit/sales	23.6%	26.6%	26.7%	26.7%	26.7%	26.7%
Tax rate	37.0%	38.0%				
Working capital/sales	9.1%	9.1%				
Dividend payout ratio		52.0%				
Income Statement						
Net sales	$1,278.4	$1,296.3	$1,317.0	$1,343.4	$1,372.9	$1,405.9
Operating profit	302.0	344.8	351.6	358.7	366.6	375.4
Interest expense, net	3.2	4.0	4.0	4.0	4.0	4.0
Pretax income	298.8	340.8	347.6	354.7	362.6	371.4
Tax expense	111.6	129.5	132.1	134.8	137.8	141.1
Net income	187.1	211.3	215.5	219.9	224.8	230.3
Dividends	94.9	94.9	94.9	94.9	94.9	94.9
Retentions to earnings	$ 92.2	$ 116.4	$ 120.7	$ 125.0	$ 129.9	$ 135.4
Balance Sheet						
Cash	$ 9.6	$ 124.3	$ 243.1	$ 365.8	$ 493.0	$ 625.4
Working capital (without debt)	116.6	118.2	120.1	122.5	125.2	128.2
Net fixed assets	151.1	151.1	151.1	151.1	151.1	151.1
Total assets	277.2	393.6	514.3	639.3	769.3	904.6
Debt (long- and short-term)	161.5	161.5	161.5	161.5	161.5	161.5
Other long-term liabilities	37.0	37.0	37.0	37.0	37.0	37.0
Equity	78.7	195.2	315.8	440.9	570.8	706.2
Total capital	$ 277.2	$ 393.6	$ 514.3	$ 639.3	$ 769.3	$ 904.6
Free Cash Flows						
EBIT		$ 344.8	$ 351.6	$ 358.7	$ 366.6	$ 375.4
Less taxes on EBIT		(131.0)	(133.6)	(136.3)	(139.3)	(142.6)
Plus depreciation		50.0	50.0	50.0	50.0	50.0
Less capital expenditures		(50.0)	(50.0)	(50.0)	(50.0)	(50.0)
Less additions to/plus reductions in working capital		(1.6)	(1.9)	(2.4)	(2.7)	(3.0)
Free cash flow		$ 212.2	$ 216.1	$ 220.0	$ 224.6	$ 229.7

Source: Case writer's analysis, consistent with forecast expectations of securities analysts.

EXHIBIT 5 | Standard & Poor's Bond-Rating Definitions

Long-Term Issue Credit Ratings: Issue credit ratings are based, in varying degrees, on the following considerations:

- Likelihood of payment? Capacity and willingness of the obligor to meet its financial commitment on an obligation in accordance with the terms of the obligation.
- Nature and provisions of the obligation.
- Protection afforded by and relative position of the obligation in the event of bankruptcy, reorganization, or other arrangements under the laws of bankruptcy and other laws affecting creditors' rights.

The issue-rating definitions are expressed in terms of default risk. As such, they pertain to senior obligations of an entity. Junior obligations are typically rated lower than senior obligations, to reflect the lower priority in bankruptcy, as noted above. (Such differentiation applies when an entity has both senior and subordinated obligations, secured and unsecured obligations, or operating company and holding company obligations.) Accordingly, in the case of junior debt, the rating may not conform exactly to the category definition.

AAA
An obligation rated AAA has the highest rating assigned by Standard & Poor's. The obligor's capacity to meet its financial commitment on the obligation is extremely strong.

AA
An obligation rated AA differs from the highest-rated obligations only to a small degree. The obligor's capacity to meet its financial commitment on the obligation is very strong.

A
An obligation rated A is somewhat more susceptible to the adverse effects of changes in circumstances and economic conditions than are obligations in the higher-rated categories. The obligor's capacity to meet its financial commitment on the obligation, however, is still strong.

BBB
An obligation rated BBB exhibits adequate protection parameters. However, adverse economic conditions or changing circumstances are more likely to lead to a weakened capacity of the obligor to meet its financial commitment on the obligation.

BB, B, CCC, CC, and C
Obligations rated BB, B, CCC, CC, and C are regarded as having significant speculative characteristics. BB indicates the least degree of speculation and C indicates the highest. While such obligations will likely have some quality and protective characteristics, those characteristics may be outweighed by large uncertainties or major exposures to adverse conditions.

Plus (+) or minus (−)
The ratings from AA to CCC may be modified by the addition of a plus (+) or a minus (−) sign to show the obligation's relative standing within the major rating categories.

Source: Standard & Poor's *Bond Guide,* 2001.

EXHIBIT 5 | Moody's Bond-Rating Definitions   (*continued*)

Aaa Bonds that are rated Aaa are judged to be of the best quality. They carry the smallest degree of investment risk and are generally referred to as gilt edge. Interest payments are protected by a large or by an exceptionally stable margin and principal is secure. While the various protective elements are likely to change, such changes as can be visualized are most unlikely to impair the fundamentally strong position of such issues.

Aa Bonds that are rated Aa are judged to be of high quality by all standards. Together with the Aaa group, they compose what are generally known as high-grade bonds. They are rated lower than the best bonds because margins of protection may not be as large as in Aaa securities or fluctuations of protective elements may be of greater amplitude or there may be other elements present that make the long-term risks appear somewhat larger than in Aaa securities.

A Bonds that are rated A possess many favorable investment attributes and are to be considered upper-medium-grade obligations. Factors giving security to principal and interest are considered adequate, but elements may be present that suggest a susceptibility to impairment sometime in the future.

Baa Bonds that are rated Baa are considered medium-grade obligations (i.e., they are neither highly protected nor poorly secured). Interest payment and principal security appear adequate for the present, but certain protective elements may be lacking or may be characteristically unreliable over any great length of time. Such bonds lack outstanding investment characteristics and, in fact, have speculative characteristics as well.

Ba Bonds that are rated Ba are judged to have speculative elements; their future cannot be considered as well assured as the higher-rated categories. Often, the protection of interest and principal payments may be very moderate and thereby not well safeguarded during both good and bad times over the future. Uncertainty of position characterizes bonds in this class.

B Bonds that are rated B generally lack the characteristics of the desirable investment. Assurance of interest and principal payments or of maintenance of other terms of the contract over any long period may be small.

Caa Bonds that are rated Caa are of poor standing. Such issues may be in default or there may be present elements of danger with respect to principal or interest.

Ca Bonds that are rated Ca represent obligations that are speculative in a high degree. Such issues are often in default or have other marked shortcomings.

C Bonds that are rated C are the lowest-rated class of bonds, and issues so rated can be regarded as having extremely poor prospects for ever attaining any real investment standing.

Source: *Mergent Annual Bond Record,* 2002.

EXHIBIT 6 | Key Industrial Financial Ratios by Rating Categories

Key Industrial Financial Ratios (Three-year medians 2000–02)	Investment Grade				Noninvestment Grade		
	AAA	AA	A	BBB	BB	B	
EBIT interest coverage (x)	23.4	13.3	6.3	3.9	2.2	1.0	
EBITDA interest coverage (x)	25.3	16.9	8.5	5.4	3.2	1.7	
Funds from operations/total debt (%)	214.2	65.7	42.2	30.6	19.7	10.4	
Free operating cash flow/total debt (%)	156.6	33.6	22.3	12.8	7.3	1.5	
Return on capital (%)	35.0	26.6	18.1	13.1	11.5	8.0	
Operating income/sales (%)	23.4	24.0	18.1	15.5	15.4	14.7	
Long-term debt/capital (%)	(1.1)	21.1	33.8	40.3	53.6	72.6	
Total debt/capital, incl. short-term debt (%)	5.0	35.9	42.6	47.0	57.7	75.1	

Standard & Poor's defined these ratios based on the book value of these items as follows:

EBIT interest coverage = EBIT/interest expense.

EBITDA interest coverage = (EBIT plus depreciation and amortization)/interest expense

Long-term debt/capital = long-term debt/(long-term debt + stockholders' equity)

Total debt/capital, incl. short-term debt = (short-term debt + long-term debt)/(short-term debt + long-term debt + stockholders' equity)

Source of data: Standard & Poor's *CreditStats*.

EXHIBIT 7 | Deluxe Corporation's Annual EBIT-Coverage Ratios

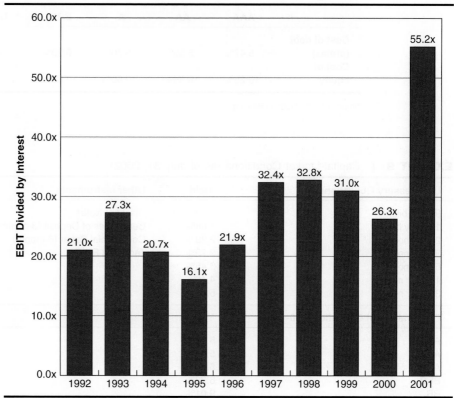

Source of data: Company regulatory filings; case writer's analysis.

EXHIBIT 8 | Capital Costs by Rating Category

	AAA	AA	A	BBB	BB	B
Cost of debt (pretax)	5.47%	5.50%	5.70%	6.30%	9.00%	12.00%
Cost of equity	10.25%	10.35%	10.50%	10.60%	12.00%	14.25%

Source of data: Hudson Bancorp.

EXHIBIT 9 | Capital-Market Conditions (as of July 31, 2002)

U.S. Treasury Obligations	Yield	Other Instruments	Yield
90-day bills	1.69%	Discount Notes	1.70%
180-day bills	1.68%	Certificates of Deposit (3-month)	1.72%
2-year notes	2.23%	Commercial Paper (6-month)	1.75%
3-year notes	2.79%	Term Fed Funds	1.78%
5-year notes	3.45%		
10-year notes	4.46%		
30-year notes	5.30%		

Corporate Debt Obligations (10-year)	Yield
AAA	5.51%
AA	5.52%
A	5.70%
BBB	6.33%
BB	9.01%
B	11.97%

Source of data: *Bloomberg LP, S&P's Research Insight, Value Line Investment Survey, Datastream Advance.*

Horizon Lines, Inc.

Even a small leak will sink a great ship[1]
　　—Benjamin Franklin

By April 1, 2011, the Horizon Lines 2010 annual report had been published with a statement from newly appointed CEO Stephen Fraser, explaining that the company expected to be in technical default on its debt. During the previous 50 years, Horizon Lines (Horizon) had revolutionized the global economy with the invention of containerized shipping and had become the largest U.S. domestic ocean carrier. By the beginning of 2007, however, Horizon was unprofitable, and its losses had increased each year since (**Exhibit 1**). As negative earnings mounted, so did Horizon's debt burden: Current liabilities had nearly quadrupled by the end of 2010 (**Exhibits 2 and 3**). The company had also suffered two major setbacks in the past six months: the loss of a key strategic alliance and $65 million paid out in criminal and civil fines.

Management's reaction had been to conserve cash by cutting the common dividend for 2010 by more than half and then eliminating it completely beginning in the first quarter of 2011. Investors responded accordingly; the company's stock price dropped from $5 per share at the start of 2011 to a recent price of $0.85. Bondholders also were concerned as the market price of the convertible notes had fallen to $0.80 on the dollar, raising the yield on the notes by over 20% (**Exhibit 4**).

Price Fixing in Puerto Rico

In October 2008, three Horizon executives and two executives from its competitor Sea Star Line pled guilty to crimes related to price fixing. A U.S. Department of Justice investigation revealed that for nearly six years, Horizon and Sea Star Line had colluded to fix prices, rig bids, and allocate customers. All five executives were sentenced to

---

[1]From Benjamin Franklin's "The Way to Wealth" essay written in 1758.

prison time, and Horizon began a long period of litigation that culminated in February 2011 when Horizon pleaded guilty to one felony count of violating the Sherman Antitrust Act. The court imposed a fine of $45 million to be paid out over the next five years.[2] On top of the criminal penalties, nearly 60 civil class-action lawsuits had also been filed against Horizon, which prompted the company to report a $20 million expense for legal settlements in 2009. In 2011, Horizon would begin payments on the criminal fine and expected to close out the civil claims with a payment of $11.8 million.

As a result of the legal difficulties, Horizon's board of directors announced that Chairman, President, and CEO Chuck Raymond would be leaving the company, and Stephen Fraser, a board member, would assume the roles of president and CEO.

The Jones Act

Consistent with most sectors in the transportation industry, shipping was greatly affected by government regulations. For almost a century, the U.S. domestic shipping market had been regulated by Section 27 of the Merchant Marine Act of 1920, more commonly known as the Jones Act.[3] The federal statute applied to maritime commerce traveling in U.S. waters between ports located on the U.S. mainland and in Alaska, Hawaii, and Puerto Rico. The law's purpose was to support the U.S. maritime industry by requiring that all goods transported by water between U.S. ports be carried on ships constructed and flagged in the United States.

In the last few decades, however, the economic conditions of the industry, in particular high labor rates in the United States, caused Jones Act vessels to have higher construction, maintenance, and operation costs than foreign vessels. This prompted critics to claim that the regulations were outdated and protectionist and that they hindered free trade and priced U.S. shipbuilders out of the international market. But the law continued to receive political support from every U.S. president since Woodrow Wilson, who had originally signed it into law. In reference to the current political climate, Horizon's 2010 annual report stated: "The ongoing war on terrorism has further solidified political support for the Jones Act, as a vital and dedicated U.S. merchant marine cornerstone for strong homeland defense, as well as a critical source of trained U.S. mariners for wartime support."[4]

Despite the extra costs associated with the Jones Act, it also created an attractive competitive landscape for existing container ship operators in the market. Although container shipping between ports in the contiguous United States was no longer competitive with inland trucking, Jones Act carriers had been able to maintain an operating advantage on trade routes between the U.S. mainland, Alaska, Hawaii, and Puerto Rico. As of 2008, only 27 vessels, 19 of which were built before 1985, were qualified by the Jones Act. The high capital investments and long delivery lead times associated with

---

[2]Horizon's payment schedule was $1 million due immediately, $1 million at the end of year one, $3 million at the end year two, $5 million at the end of year three, $15 million at the end of year four, and $20 million at the end of year five.

[3]Named after the bill's sponsor, U.S. Senator Wesley Jones.

[4]Horizon Lines annual report, 2010.

building a new containership created high barriers for new entrants. These barriers also caused the domestic market to be less fragmented and less vulnerable to overcapacity.

The Maersk Partnership

A major drawback of the Jones Act market was that very few goods were shipped back to the continental United States, leading to a severe imbalance in container utilization. This was particularly significant for Hawaii and Guam, because ships returning to the mainland had to travel a long distance with mostly empty containers. To alleviate this problem, Horizon entered into a strategic alliance with A.P. Moller-Maersk in the 1990s to share container space along the Hawaii and Guam lane. Under the terms of the agreement, Horizon used its vessels to ship a portion of its cargo in Maersk-owned containers on westbound routes. The cargo would be unloaded in Hawaii or Guam, and the empty containers would then be shipped to ports in China and Taiwan instead of directly back to the United States. After the vessels arrived in Asia, Maersk replaced the empty containers with loaded containers for Horizon to carry back to the West Coast of the United States.

This alliance was so beneficial that in 2006, Horizon entered into a long-term lease agreement with Ship Finance International Limited to charter five container vessels not qualified by the Jones Act to travel on its Asia-Pacific route. Horizon was obligated to charter each ship for 12 years from the date of delivery at an annual rate of $6.4 million per vessel. The economic conditions changed with the global recession of 2008, however, causing overcapacity in the international shipping market, which led to container freight rates falling significantly. Horizon's profitability also fell, due partly to top-line reductions but also to escalating fuel costs. Although Horizon was locked into its long-term lease until 2018–19, Maersk was able to unilaterally exit the strategic alliance in December 2010.

Shortly after termination of the partnership, Horizon attempted to cover its lease obligations by starting its own trans-Pacific shipping service. Unfortunately, by March 2011, freight rates continued to decline, and fuel costs continued to increase. Projections for the remainder of the year showed that eastbound freight rates would drop 35%, while the average price of fuel would increase 40%, which put the Pacific route into a significant operating-loss position.

Pushed by mounting operating losses, Horizon management decided to save money by shutting down its unprofitable routes in the Pacific and holding all five non-Jones Act vessels pier-side in a reduced operational state. Although Horizon would continue to incur leasing costs for those vessels for another eight or nine years, it eliminated most of the operating costs associated with the Pacific routes.

The Debt Structure

In 2007, when the future of the shipping business seemed bright and Horizon's stock was trading at an all-time high, the company completed a major round of refinancing to consolidate its debt into two sources. The first was a senior secured credit agreement that used all Horizon-owned assets as collateral. The senior credit facility included a $125 million term loan and a $250 million five-year revolving credit facility provided by a lending group of major banks. The second source was $330 million of unsecured, 4.25% convertible senior notes which, like the term loan, matured in 2012. The notes were primarily held by three large mutual fund companies: Legg Mason, Pioneer Investment Management, and Angelo Gordon & Co. **Exhibit 5** provides the details of Horizon's debt structure.

Both the senior credit facility and the 4.25% convertible notes carried covenants that specified a maximum leverage ratio and a minimum interest coverage ratio.[5] By the time 2010 results were released, the company's poor earnings performance plus its payments for the criminal fine and the civil settlements made it apparent that the company would be unlikely to satisfy these covenants during 2011. Tripping a debt covenant would put the company in technical default, giving debt holders the right to call the loan (i.e., demand immediate and full payment of the principal outstanding). Unless Horizon could negotiate a change to the covenants to remove the default, it would almost certainly have to seek the protection of the bankruptcy courts because it would be impossible to raise new debt or equity under such dire circumstances.

Although Horizon was not expected to miss an interest payment the following quarter, future interest and principal payments would be accelerating and would place an increasing strain on Horizon's ability to meet its cash obligations, regardless of whether the company satisfied the debt covenants. For example, the $125 million term loan required Horizon to make quarterly principal payments of $4.7 million through September 2011, at which point the principal payments escalated to $18.4 million until August 2012 when the loan matured. Interest payments on the senior credit facility were due semiannually (February and August) and averaged about 4.6%. The convertible notes carried a low coupon rate of 4.25%, but the $330 million principal would also be due in August 2012. **Exhibit 6** provides management's report of interest, principal, and other contractual obligations for 2011 and beyond. **Exhibit 7** shows current interest rates for government and corporate debt obligations.

Restructuring Options

On the operational side, in addition to shutting down the Pacific routes, Horizon had made attempts to reduce headcount, but this had had little impact, since much of the work force was protected by unions. The next step would be to divest underperforming business units or sell the entire business to a strategic buyer. Given the high barriers to entry for the domestic market and the general view that container traffic was relatively stable, finding a buyer was feasible, but finding a buyer that would pay a reasonable price would be difficult to execute in the near term. The net effect was that Horizon was expecting poor performance for 2011 as operating costs were rising, and shutting down the Pacific routes would add to those expenses for 2011. Longer term, the reduced operations were expected to decrease Horizon's revenues for 2012, but they would also allow the company to show positive EBIT starting in 2013 (**Exhibit 8**).

---

[5]The interest coverage ratio was defined as Adjusted EBITDA/Cash Interest, and the leverage ratio was computed as Senior Secured Debt/Adjusted EBITDA (annualized). Between the credit facility and the convertible notes, the tightest covenant requirements were a minimum interest coverage ratio of 2.75 × for each quarter of 2011 and a maximum leverage ratio of 3.25 × for each quarter of 2011.

Realistically, the only viable alternative to avoid a default in 2011 was for Horizon to restructure its capital structure. For a financial restructuring, there were three basic options available to Stephen Fraser and his management team.

Option 1: Issue New Equity

A straightforward way to inject capital into the business would be to issue new shares of common stock. Horizon could use the funds from the new stock offering to pay down its debt obligation and give the business additional capital to grow the Jones Act side of the business. This was relatively easy and required no negotiations with existing debt holders.

Option 2: File for Chapter 11

As a U.S. business, Horizon had the option of filing for protection under Chapter 11 of the U.S. Bankruptcy code.[6] Fraser could file immediately and rely on the bankruptcy judge to oversee the reorganization. Normally, the judge would request a plan of reorganization (POR) from management that specified how the company needed to be changed in order to emerge from Chapter 11 as an economically viable entity. The primary purpose of the POR was to present a blueprint of how to restructure the balance sheet to a manageable level of interest and principal payments. This meant that many of the debt claimants were asked to accept new securities that summed to less than the face value of their claim.

The amount of the *haircut* would depend upon the seniority of the claim. For example, a senior secured lender might receive full cash payment for its claim, whereas a junior unsecured lender might receive a combination of new debt and equity representing $0.40 on the dollar of the face value of the original debt. The judge would not allow senior claimants to take a larger haircut than any junior claimant, nor would the judge entertain a POR that was unlikely to receive the voting approval of all the impaired claimants. If the judge thought a POR was fair to all claimants and provided a viable capital structure for the company going forward, he or she could overrule a dissenting class of claimants in order to force a solution. In this regard, the judge played the role of mediator in a negotiation process that often involved many revisions to the POR before being accepted by all parties, or the judge exercised the right to *cram down* the plan in order to enact it.

A Chapter 11 bankruptcy was designed to give a failing company the best possible chance to restructure and continue operating as a viable enterprise. The courts served the purpose of intervening with bill collectors to protect the company from being forced to liquidate in order to make an interest or principal payment. The theory was that it was better to have an orderly reorganization within the court system that resulted in a viable company that could continue to pay its suppliers and employees than to allow the company to disintegrate in the chaos of a feeding frenzy of its creditors. Companies continued to operate normally while in Chapter 11, so most customers were not aware

---

[6]Matthias Hild, "A Managerial Primer on the U.S. Bankruptcy Code," UVA-QA-0633 (Charlottesville, VA: Darden Business Publishing, 2008) reviews Chapter 11 bankruptcy rules.

of the reorganization process. If the company needed additional capital to grow the business, it could simply increase the size of the new debt and equity offerings as part of the POR.

Option 3: Restructure the Debt Directly

This approach had the same objective as using Chapter 11. Negotiating a deal directly with the debt holders, however, had the advantage of being faster, and it avoided court costs. The typical Chapter 11 process took months or years to resolve and resulted in large legal fees for both company and claimants. To be successful, Horizon would need to exchange its existing debt for a combination of new notes and common shares. The swap would give the existing debt holders a reduced claim on the company, but it would be a claim that was much more likely to be serviced. At the same time, Horizon could ask creditors to accept a new set of covenants and a longer maturity to alleviate the short-term cash-flow crunch it currently faced. The net effect would be to lengthen the maturity of the outstanding debt plus reduce the overall amount of debt outstanding and therefore reduce the level of interest payments.

As part of the restructuring, Horizon also needed to receive new capital to pay off the senior credit facility and help grow the Jones Act business. The new capital could come from issuing shares to the public in addition to the shares distributed to the existing debt holders to satisfy their claims on the company. Horizon could also raise the capital by issuing new debt. Regardless of whether the new capital was debt or equity, it would be expensive and reflect the high risk associated with Horizon. For example, given the low stock price, it would require a large number of new shares to raise a meaningful amount of equity money. Also for such a risky situation, any new lender would require collateral for the debt plus an interest rate in the range of 10% to 15%.

Restructuring had several disadvantages. First, it would be unlikely that Horizon could successfully include any claimants other than the senior creditors. Like most companies with strong unions, Horizon offered a defined-benefit pension plan to its employees, and that plan was underfunded. A Chapter 11 proceeding could result in a reduction of the benefits paid to employees, which would reduce the company's own mandatory contributions to the plan. But such changes were very difficult to enact outside of the court system, so if Horizon opted to restructure its debt directly, it would need to focus solely on the claims of the senior credit facility and the convertible bonds. A second disadvantage was that a voluntary restructuring created a risk for the claimants. In particular, if Horizon were to declare bankruptcy shortly after the restructuring, the Chapter 11 proceedings would start from the newly restructured claims. Therefore, if debt holders had agreed to accept equity in lieu of all or part of their original debt claim, the courts would view the reduced debt claim as the relevant claim for the Chapter 11 proceedings. Once a claimant voluntarily agreed to a reduction of its original claim, that claim was gone forever.

Stephen Fraser was not in an enviable position. Regardless of the option he chose, the company's success was not guaranteed. Moreover, with the covenant default approaching, it was time to "right the ship," but a poor choice by Fraser at this point could take his company down and his career along with it.

EXHIBIT 1 | Consolidated Statement of Operations, December 31, 2008–10
(in thousands of U.S. dollars)

	2010	2009	2008
Operating Revenue	**1,162,505**	**1,124,215**	**1,270,978**
Operating expense			
Cost of services (excluding depreciation expense)	989,923	922,959	1,047,871
Depreciation and amortization	44,475	44,307	44,537
Amortization of vessel drydocking	15,046	13,694	17,162
Selling, general and administrative	83,232	97,257	103,328
Legal settlements	31,770	20,000	0
Miscellaneous expense and charges	3,909	3,710	12,018
Total operating expense	**1,168,355**	**1,101,927**	**1,224,916**
Operating (loss) income	(5,850)	22,288	46,062
Interest expense, net	(40,117)	(38,036)	(39,923)
Income tax and other (expense) benefit	(332)	(10,659)	4,214
Loss from discontinued operations	(11,670)	(4,865)	(12,946)
Net loss	**(57,969)**	**(31,272)**	**(2,593)**
Basic and diluted loss per share	(1.88)	(1.03)	(0.09)
Dividends declared per share	0.20	0.44	0.44

Data Source: Horizon Lines annual report, 2010.

EXHIBIT 2 | Consolidated Balance Sheet Statements, December 31, 2009–10
(in thousands of U.S. dollars)

	2010	2009
Assets		
Cash	2,751	6,419
Accounts receivable, net of allowance	111,887	115,069
Materials and supplies	29,413	30,254
Other current assets	21,638	30,059
Total current assets	165,689	181,801
Property and equipment, net	194,657	192,624
Goodwill and intangible assets, net	394,973	419,008
Other long-term assets	30,438	25,678
Total assets	785,757	819,111
Liabilities		
Accounts payable	43,413	42,372
Current portion of long-term debt*	508,793	18,750
Other accrued liabilities	115,895	115,697
Total current liabilities	668,101	176,819
Long-term debt, net of current portion*	7,530	496,105
Deferred rent, taxes & other liabilities	70,334	44,909
Total liabilities	745,965	717,833
Common stock**	345	341
Treasury stock, 3,800 shares at cost	(78,538)	(78,538)
Additional paid in capital	193,266	196,900
Accumulated deficit	(75,281)	(17,425)
Total stockholders' equity	39,792	101,278
Total liabilities & stockholders' equity	785,757	819,111

* Includes capital lease.

** Common stock, $0.01 par value, 100,000 shares authorized, 34,546 shares issued and 30,746 shares outstanding on December 26, 2010, and 34,091 shares issued and 30,291 shares outstanding on December 20, 2009.

Data Source: Horizon Lines annual report, 2010.

EXHIBIT 3 | Consolidated Cash Flow Statements, December 31, 2008–10
(in thousands of U.S. dollars)

	2010	2009	2008
Cash flows from operating activities			
Net (loss) income from continuing operations	(46,299)	(26,407)	10,353
Adjustments			
Depreciation	23,777	24,002	24,232
Amortization of intangibles	20,698	20,305	20,305
Amortization of vessel drydocking	15,046	13,694	17,162
Impairment charge	2,655	1,867	6,030
Restructuring charge	2,057	787	3,126
Amortization of deferred financing costs	3,412	2,947	2,693
Deferred income taxes	148	10,617	(4,153)
Gain on equipment disposals	(47)	(154)	(24)
Gain on sale of interest in joint venture	(724)	0	0
Loss on early modification/extinguishment of debt	0	50	0
Accretion on convertible notes	11,060	10,011	8,901
Stock-based compensation	2,122	3,096	3,651
Accounts receivable, net	1,301	13,710	7,931
Materials and supplies	807	(6,739)	7,636
Other current assets	(1,148)	1,247	23
Accounts payable	1,041	910	1,434
Accrued liabilities	5,581	(767)	(5,653)
Vessel rent	(3,898)	(4,874)	(4,883)
Vessel dry-docking payments	(19,159)	(14,735)	(13,913)
Accrued legal settlements	26,770	15,000	0
Other assets/liabilities	(768)	(3,486)	3,506
Net cash provided by operating activities	**44,432**	**61,081**	**88,357**
Cash flows from investing activities			
Purchases of equipment	(16,298)	(12,931)	(38,639)
Proceeds from the sale of interest in joint venture	1,100	0	0
Proceeds from sale of equipment	454	1,237	500
Net cash used in investing activities	**(14,744)**	**(11,694)**	**(38,139)**
Cash flows from financing activities			
Borrowing under revolving credit facility	108,800	64,000	78,000
Payments on revolving credit facility	(108,800)	(84,000)	(80,000)
Payments of long-term debt	(18,750)	(7,968)	(6,538)
Dividend to stockholders	(6,281)	(13,397)	(13,273)
Payment of financing costs	(75)	(3,492)	(139)
Common stock issued under employee stock purchase plan	111	104	38
Payments on capital lease obligation	(124)	0	(81)
Purchase of treasury stock	0	0	(29,330)
Proceeds from exercise of stock options	0	0	13
Net cash used in financing activities	**(25,119)**	**(44,753)**	**(51,310)**
Net change in cash from continuing operations	4,569	4,634	(1,092)
Net change in cash from discontinued operations	(8,237)	(3,702)	303
Net change in cash	**(3,668)**	**932**	**(789)**
Cash at beginning of year.	6,419	5,487	6,276
Cash at end of year.	2,751	6,419	5,487

EXHIBIT 4 | Horizon Lines (HRZ) Stock Price and Convertible Notes Price

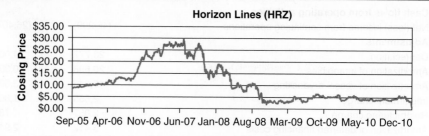

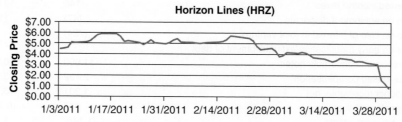

Recent Closing Prices and Yields for March 2011			
	Mar. 29	**Mar. 30**	**Mar. 31**
Common stock ($ per share)	1.62	1.27	0.85
4.25% convertible notes (per $100 face value)	91.1	90.0	80.0
4.25% convertible notes (yield to maturity)	10.8%	10.9%	20.4%

Data Sources: Yahoo! Finance, NYSE, and case writer estimates.

EXHIBIT 5 | Debt Structure* (in thousands of U.S. dollars)

	2010	2009
Term loan**	93,750	112,500
Revolving credit facility**	100,000	100,000
4.25% convertible senior notes***	313,414	302,355
Capital lease obligations	9,159	—
Total long-term debt	516,323	514,855

* Both the senior credit facility and the 4.25% convertible notes carried covenants that specified a maximum leverage ratio and a minimum interest coverage ratio. The interest coverage ratio was defined as Adjusted EBITDA/Cash Interest, and the leverage ratio was computed as Senior Secured Debt/Adjusted EBITDA (annualized). Between the credit facility and the convertible notes, the tightest covenant requirements were a minimum interest coverage ratio of 2.75 × for each quarter of 2011 and a maximum leverage ratio of 3.25 × for each quarter of 2011. For purposes of the covenants, EBITDA was adjusted to report legal settlements on a cash basis.

** The senior credit facility is provided by a lending group of major banks and is composed of the term loan and the revolving credit facility and is secured by substantially all of the assets of the company. Interest payments on the revolver are variable and are based on the three-month London Inter-Bank Offered Rate (LIBOR) plus 3.25%. Through the use of an interest rate swap, the term loan bears interest at a fixed rate of 4.52% per annum. The weighted average interest rate for the facility was 4.6% at the end of 2010. Remaining quarterly principal payments for the term loan are specified as $4.7 million through September 30, 2011, and $18.8 million until final maturity on August 8, 2012.

*** The notes are unsecured and mature on August 15, 2012. The aggregate principal amount of $330 million for the notes is recorded net of original issue discount. Each $1,000 of principal is convertible into 26.9339 shares of Horizon's common stock, which is the equivalent of $37.13 per share. The notes were primarily held by three large mutual fund companies: Legg Mason, Pioneer Investment Management, and Angelo Gordon & Co.

Data Sources: Horizon Lines 10-K filing, 2010, and case writer estimates.

EXHIBIT 6 | Contractual Obligations, 2011 and Beyond (in thousands of U.S. dollars)

	2011	2012	2013	2014	2015	2016	After 2016	Total Obligations
Principal and operating lease obligations								
Senior credit facility*	18,750	175,000						193,750
4.25% convertible senior notes*	—	330,000						330,000
Operating leases	100,373	105,681	105,681	67,770	67,770	67,770	143,035	658,080
Capital lease	1,629	1,307	1,307	756	756	756	2,647	9,158
Subtotal	120,752	611,988	106,988	68,526	68,526	68,526	145,682	1,190,988
Cash interest obligations**								
Senior credit facility	8,913	8,050						16,963
4.25% convertible senior notes	14,025	14,025						28,050
Capital lease	857	620	620	262	262	262	277	3,160
Subtotal	23,795	22,695	620	262	262	262	277	48,173
Legal settlements***	12,767	4,000	5,000	15,000	20,000			56,767
Other commitments	14,932	119	100					15,151
Total obligations	172,246	638,802	112,708	83,788	88,788	68,788	145,959	1,311,079

* Horizon has announced that it expects a covenant default on its debt. The company has until May 21, 2011, to obtain a waiver from the debt holders, which if not received could result in the holders' demanding acceleration of all principal and interest payments. In addition, due to cross-default provisions, such a default could lead to the acceleration of the maturity of all the company's scheduled principal and interest payments.

** Interest payments on the term loan portion of the senior credit facility are fixed via an interest rate swap at 4.52%. Interest payments on the revolver portion of the senior credit facility are variable and are computed as LIBOR plus 3.25%. The weighted average interest rate for the facility was 4.6% at the end of 2010. Interest on the 4.25% convertible senior notes is fixed and is paid semiannually on February 15 and August 15 of each year, until maturity on August 15, 2012.

*** Legal settlement for 2011 consists of a $1 million charge for the $45 million criminal fines and $11.767 million as final settlement of the civil lawsuits. The civil settlement was originally recorded as $20 million in 2009, of which $5 million was paid immediately, and the remainder was eventually settled as $11.767 million.

Data Sources: Horizon Lines 10-K filing, 2010, and case writer estimates.

EXHIBIT 7 | Interest Rates for March 31, 2011

U.S. Treasury Yields	
1-Year	0.19%
10-Year	3.17%
Corporate Yields	
6-Month LIBOR	0.41%
Prime	3.25%
AAA	4.14%
AA	4.35%
A	4.49%
BBB	4.99%
BB	6.52%
B	7.94%

Data Source: Yahoo! Finance.

EXHIBIT 8 | Operating Cash Flow Projections for 2011–15
(in thousands of U.S. dollars)

	2010	2011E	2012E	2013E	2014E	2015E
Operating Revenue*	1,162,505	1,220,630	915,473	942,937	971,225	1,000,362
Operating expense						
Cost of services (excluding depreciation expense)	989,923	1,074,155	778,152	782,638	786,692	800,289
Depreciation and amortization	59,521	59,521	59,521	59,521	59,521	59,521
Selling, general and administrative	83,232	87,394	65,545	67,512	69,537	71,623
Other charges	3,909	4,000	4,000	4,000	4,000	4,000
Total operating expense	1,136,585	1,225,069	907,218	913,670	919,750	935,433
EBIT (before legal settlements)	25,920	(4,439)	8,255	29,267	51,475	64,928
– Legal settlements (cash basis)	(5,000)	(12,767)	(4,000)	(5,000)	(15,000)	(20,000)
Adjusted EBIT	20,920	(17,206)	4,255	24,267	36,475	44,928
Adjusted EBITDA**	80,441	42,315	63,776	83,788	95,996	104,449
Assumptions:						
Cost of services/revenue	85%	88.0%	85.0%	83.0%	81.0%	80.0%
SG&A/revenue	7%	7.2%	7.2%	7.2%	7.2%	7.2%
Revenue growth		5.0%	−25.0%	3.0%	3.0%	3.0%
EBIT/revenue	1.8%	−1.4%	0.5%	2.6%	3.8%	4.5%

* Revenues for 2012 and beyond reflect the shutdown of unprofitable routes in the Pacific.

** Cash flow projections are computed using an "adjusted" EBITDA for which legal settlements are recorded on an expected cash basis. In contrast, GAAP requires EBIT to be computed based on settlement charges computed as the present value of the future payments and reported in the year of the settlement. Specifically, Horizon reported $31.77 million as legal settlements for 2010, which represented the present value of the $45 million to be received over the ensuing five years. Legal settlement for 2011 consists of a $1 million charge for the $45 million criminal fines and $11.767 million as final settlement of the civil lawsuits. Debt covenants use adjusted EBITDA for the leverage and interest coverage ratios.

Source: Case writer estimates.

Analysis of Financing Tactics: Leases, Options, and Foreign Currency

Carrefour S.A.

With total sales of (euros) EUR53.9 billion from more than 5,200 stores, Carrefour S.A. was Europe's largest retailer in the summer of 2002. Over the previous four years, Carrefour's growth, including several large acquisitions, had occurred almost entirely outside France. The company maintained retail operations in 26 countries across the globe.

In funding its ongoing expansion, Carrefour faced an immediate debt-financing requirement of EUR750 million. Historically, Carrefour management maintained a practice of funding capital needs in the same currency as the respective business operations. Its investment banks, Morgan Stanley and UBS-Warburg, however, had recently suggested that Carrefour consider borrowing in British pounds sterling through the eurobond market in order to take advantage of a temporary borrowing opportunity in that currency. As a basis of comparison, the investment bankers provided alternative rates across various currencies for a proposed 10-year Carrefour bond. The bankers estimated that the bond could be priced at par at a coupon rate of $5\frac{1}{4}$ in euros, $5\frac{3}{8}$ in British pounds, $3\frac{5}{8}$ in Swiss francs, or $5\frac{1}{2}$ in U.S. dollars.

Carrefour

In 1963 in the small French town of Sainte-Geneviéve-des-Bois, southeast of Paris, Carrefour transformed the world of retailing with the introduction of the "hypermarket" concept. This retail format combined a supermarket, drugstore, discount store, and gas station into one massive, one-stop-shopping megastore. The original Sainte-Geneviéve-des-Bois store boasted 2,500 square meters of retail space, 12 checkouts, and 400 parking spaces. Leveraging this concept, the company expanded rapidly in France and beyond, opening its first store outside France (Belgium) in 1969, and outside Europe (Brazil) in 1975. In addition to strong organic growth, Carrefour pursued selective acquisitions, including notable mergers with Euromarche and Montlaur in

1991 and Promodes in 1999. **Exhibit 1** provides a history of Carrefour's store portfolio from 1992 to 2001.

Carrefour was profitable in all major operating regions. In 2001, the company generated operating profits of EUR2.8 billion on total net sales of EUR69.5 billion. Of that profit, 5% originated in Asia, 2% originated in Latin America, and 26% originated in Europe outside France, with the remainder of profits coming from French operations. The regional-sales breakdown was 7% from Asia, 12% from Latin America, and 32% from Europe outside France. For Carrefour, 2001 marked an important milestone as the first year that total international sales exceeded total domestic French sales. Carrefour was the largest retailer in France, Belgium, Greece, and Spain. **Exhibit 2** details Carrefour's consolidated financial statements.

The company expected to maintain its expansion trajectory. Carrefour's CEO, Daniel Bernard, stated that in 2002 the company would increase sales by 5% on constant exchange rates and increase recurring net income by 10% to 15%. He asserted that the company would continue to gain market share in most of the countries where it operated, notably in Italy, Belgium, Brazil, and Argentina.

Carrefour's Financing Policy

With such broad international reach, Carrefour was highly disciplined with respect to its management of exchange rate risk. Within each country, Carrefour operated primarily within the local economy for sourcing its products. Any foreign-currency exposure on imported goods was generally hedged through forward contracts on the currency.

A *currency forward contract* was a financial agreement whose value was determined based on the difference between a predetermined forward rate and the prevailing spot rate at a particular point in the future. For example, suppose Carrefour purchased a U.S. dollar forward contract on EUR1 million in one year that was priced at (U.S. dollars) USD0.891 per euro. The gain on the contract in one year would be equal to 1,000,000 multiplied by the difference between the forward rate of USD0.891 and the prevailing dollar-to-euro exchange rate in one year (the spot rate). Suppose that the prevailing dollar-to-euro exchange rate was USD0.90 per euro. If the dollar appreciated to a dollar-to-euro exchange rate of USD0.85 in one year, Carrefour would gain USD41,429 on the forward contract [(USD0.891 − USD0.85) × 1,000,000]. Carrefour gained in this scenario because it owned a contract that gave it USD0.891 for every euro in the contract when the prevailing exchange rate only gave it USD0.85 per euro. If alternatively the dollar depreciated to a dollar-to-euro exchange rate of USD0.95, Carrefour would lose USD58,571 on the forward contract [(USD0.891 − USD0.95) × 1,000,000]. Carrefour lost in this scenario because it was locked into a contract that required it to receive only USD0.891 for every euro in the contract when the prevailing exchange rate gave them USD0.95 per euro. In summary, with this particular forward contract Carrefour gained if the dollar appreciated and lost if the dollar depreciated.

Banks offered forward rates based on the equivalent rate that could be synthetically locked in by borrowing and lending in the two currencies. For example, suppose that the prevailing dollar-to-euro exchange rate was USD0.90 per euro and the prevailing interbank one-year interest rate is 4% in dollars and 5% in euro. If the bank wanted a forward position of receiving dollars and paying euros, it could borrow in euros at 5%, convert the proceeds into dollars, and invest the dollars at 4%. In constructing this "synthetic forward contract," the bank would generate dollars from euros at a rate of (1.04)(USD0.90) ÷ (1.05) or USD0.891 per euro. Through borrowing in euros and investing in dollars the bank could simulate the same forward conversion of currency as that of a forward contract. Since the forward contract generated the same currency conversion as the synthetic forward contract, it was sensible that the fair forward rate for the USD/EUR exchange rate was determined by the same synthetic forward pricing formula:

$$f^T_{USD/EUR} = s_{USD/EUR} \frac{(1 + R_{USD,T})^T}{(1 + R_{EUR,T})^T}$$

where $f^T_{USD/EUR}$ is the forward rate for T-years, $s_{USD/EUR}$ is the prevailing spot exchange rate, and $R_{USD,T}$ and $R_{EUR,T}$ are the prevailing interbank interest rates for T-year maturity in dollars and euros, respectively. The pricing relationship applied to all currency combinations and maturities. Another way of arriving at the same forward contract pricing formula was to assume that in competitive markets the borrowing rate in one currency could not be meaningfully different than the rate achieved by borrowing in another currency and hedging the exchange rate risk with forward contracts. This condition was commonly called *covered interest rate parity*.[1]

In 2001, total Carrefour borrowings were EUR13.5 billion, of which EUR6.4 billion were in publicly traded bonds. Carrefour's debt was denominated in many currencies. **Exhibit 3** details the recent composition of Carrefour's borrowings by currency. Foreign-currency borrowing was generally hedged so that total debt requirements were currently 97% in euros.

Current Market Opportunities

As Carrefour management considered the bond-denomination decision, it also considered the current inflation, interest-rate, and exchange-rate environment.[2] Over the previous three years, long-term bond yields had declined in all four currencies. The Swiss franc's interest rate, however, had consistently been the lowest rate. The decision also hinged on future movements in exchange rates. Over the previous five years,

---

[1]Standard international finance theory prescribed that the forward rate represent an unbiased predictor of the future spot exchange rate. The empirical evidence overwhelming rejected this notion, finding that forward rates were poor and biased predictors of future exchange rates (see Ken Froot and Richard Thaler, "Anomalies: Foreign Exchange,"*Journal of Economic Perspectives* 4 [1990]: 179–92, for a readable summary of the empirical evidence). In fact, the research literature suggested that the current spot exchange rate was generally a better predictor of the future exchange rate than was the forward rate.

[2]Because the bonds would be offered in the eurobond market, they would be subject to similar issuance costs, liquidity, and specifications regardless of the currency denomination. Eurobonds uniformly followed an annual coupon convention.

the euro had depreciated against most major currencies. Should this trend continue, paying down foreign-currency debt with euro-denominated cash flow would become increasingly expensive. **Exhibits 4, 5,** and **6** provide information on trends in inflation, government-benchmark bond yields, and exchange rates in the various currencies. **Exhibits 7** and **8** provide information on prevailing current spot exchange rates and the yield curve.

EXHIBIT 1 | Total Number of Consolidated Stores

	1992	1993	1994	1995	1996	1997	1998	1999	2000	2001
France	485	546	828	840	761	805	1,256	1,703	1,726	1,295
Spain	40	43	46	50	53	56	58	1,858	1,939	1,952
Portugal	2	2	2	2	2	3	4	278	277	281
Italy	0	1	6	5	6	6	6	52	413	305
Turkey	0	1	1	1	1	2	2	14	46	99
Poland						1	3	13	23	60
Czech Republic								3	6	9
Slovakia									2	2
Belgium										129
Switzerland										8
Greece								146	323	338
Argentina	6	7	9	12	15	18	21	128	361	400
Brazil	28	29	33	38	44	49	59	152	189	222
Mexico			2	7	13	17	19	17	18	19
Chile							1	2	3	4
Colombia							1	2	3	5
United States	2									
Taiwan	5	7	8	10	13	17	21	23	24	26
Malaysia			1	1	2	3	5	6	6	6
China				2	3	7	14	20	24	24
Korea					3	3	6	12	20	22
Indonesia								1	5	7	8
Singapore						1	1	1	1	1
Hong Kong					1	2	4	4		
Thailand					2	6	7	9	11	15
Japan									1	3
Total	568	636	936	968	919	996	1,489	4,448	5,423	5,233

Source: Carrefour S.A., annual report, 2001.

EXHIBIT 2 | Financial Statements (in millions of euros)

	2001	2000
Sales, net of taxes	69,486	64,802
Cost of sales	53,875	49,920
Sales, general, and admin. exp.	11,729	11,236
Other income	645	763
Depreciation	1,702	1,685
EBIT	2,826	2,725
Interest expense	646	707
Income tax	586	650
Net income from recurring operations	1,594	1,369
Fixed assets	26,561	27,840
Inventories	5,909	5,716
Trade and supplier receivables	2,946	3,146
Other receivables	3,258	4,387
Cash and marketable securities	4,797	2,941
Total assets	43,470	44,031
Shareholders' equity	8,192	8,932
Provision for long-term liabilities	2,027	1,772
Borrowings	13,471	13,949
Trade payables and other debt	19,781	19,377
Total liabilities and shareholders' equity	43,470	44,031

EXHIBIT 3 | Breakdown of Borrowings by Currency
(in millions of euros)

		2001	2000
EUR	Euro	12,267	12,201
JPY	Japanese yen	342	90
USD	U.S. dollar	110	115
ARS	Argentine peso	238	903
CHF	Swiss franc	191	161
NOK	Norwegian kroner	61	61
TRY	Turkish lire	49	65
CNY	Chinese yuan	39	28
BRL	Brazilian real	35	143
MYR	Malaysian ringgit	29	70
COP	Colombian peso	26	7
TWD	Taiwanese dollar	25	71
KRW	South Korean won	15	30
	Others	15	3
	Total	13,471	13,949

Source: Company documents.

EXHIBIT 4 | Trends in Inflation Rates (GDP deflator)

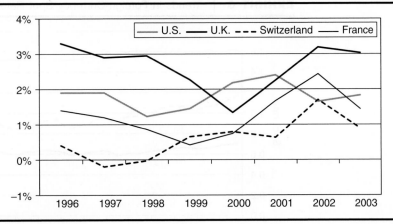

Data Source: Datastream.

EXHIBIT 5 | Trends in 10-Year Government-Benchmark Bond Yields

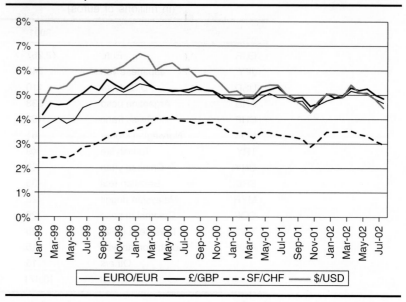

Data Source: Datastream.

EXHIBIT 6 | Trends in Foreign-Currency Spot Rates

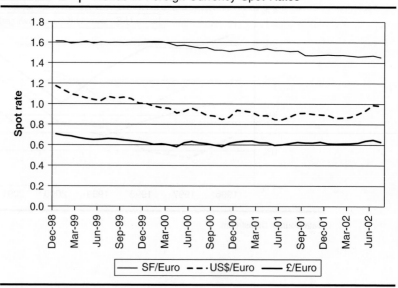

Data Source: Datastream.

EXHIBIT 7 | Cross-Exchange Rates (spot prices, 7/31/2002)

	EUR	GBP	CHF	USD
EUR	1.000	1.593	0.688	1.020
GBP	0.628	1.000	0.432	0.640
CHF	1.453	2.315	1.000	1.482
USD	0.980	1.562	0.675	1.000

Data Source: Datastream.

EXHIBIT 8 | Inter-bank Interest Rates by Currency Denomination[1] (percent)

Maturity	EUR	GBP	CHF	USD
1-year	3.514	4.258	1.125	2.099
2-year	3.816	4.622	1.713	2.767
3-year	4.110	4.910	2.172	3.432
4-year	4.342	5.088	2.498	3.922
5-year	4.530	5.190	2.743	4.308
6-year	4.688	5.249	2.948	4.619
7-year	4.819	5.292	3.120	4.873
8-year	4.928	5.331	3.267	5.081
9-year	5.017	5.358	3.394	5.264
10-year	5.087	5.374	3.499	5.413

[1]Rates equal to zero-curve fixed-to-floating swap rates.

Data Source: Datastream.

Baker Adhesives

In early June 2006, Doug Baker met with his sales manager Alissa Moreno to discuss the results of a recent foray into international markets. This was new territory for Baker Adhesives, a small company manufacturing specialty adhesives. Until a recent sale to Novo, a Brazilian toy manufacturer, all of Baker Adhesives' sales had been to companies not far from its Newark, New Jersey, manufacturing facility. As U.S. manufacturing continued to migrate overseas, however, Baker would be under intense pressure to find new markets, which would inevitably lead to international sales.

Doug Baker was looking forward to this meeting. The recent sale to Novo, while modest in size at 1,210 gallons, had been a significant financial boost to Baker Adhesives. The order had used up some raw-materials inventory that Baker had considered reselling at a significant loss a few months before the Novo order. Furthermore, the company had been running well under capacity and the order was easily accommodated within the production schedule. The purpose of the meeting was to finalize details on a new order from Novo that was to be 50% larger than the original order. Also, payment for the earlier Novo order had just been received and Baker was looking forward to paying down some of the balance on the firm's line of credit.

As Baker sat down with Moreno, he could tell immediately that he was in for bad news. It came quickly. Moreno pointed out that since the Novo order was denominated in Brazilian reais (BRL), the payment from Novo had to be converted into U.S. dollars (USD) at the current exchange rate.[1] Given exchange-rate changes since the time Baker Adhesives and Novo had agreed on a per-gallon price, the value of the payment was substantially lower than anticipated. More disappointing was the fact that Novo was unwilling to consider a change in the per-gallon price for the follow-on order. Translated into dollars, therefore, the new order would not be as profitable as the original order had initially appeared. In fact, given further anticipated changes in exchange rates the new order would not even be as profitable as the original order had turned out to be!

---

[1]The Brazilian currency is referred to as *real* in the singular (as in "the Brazilian real") and *reais* in the plural (as in "sales are denominated in reais").

Adhesives Market

The market for adhesives was dominated by a few large firms that provided the vast bulk of adhesives in the United States and in global markets. The adhesives giants had international manufacturing and sourcing capabilities. Margins on most adhesives were quite slim since competition was fierce. In response, successful firms had developed ever more efficient production systems which, to a great degree, relied on economies of scale.

The focus on scale economies had left a number of specialty markets open for small and technically savvy firms. The key to success in the specialty market was not the efficient manufacture of large quantities, but figuring out how to feasibly and economically produce relatively small batches with distinct properties. In this market, a good chemist and a flexible production system were key drivers of success. Baker Adhesives had both. The business was started by Doug Baker's father, a brilliant chemist who left a big company to focus on the more interesting, if less marketable, products that eventually became the staple of Baker Adhesives' product line. While Baker's father had retired some years ago, he had attracted a number of capable new employees, and the company was still an acknowledged leader in the specialty markets. The production facilities, though old, were readily adaptable and had been well maintained.

Until just a few years earlier, Baker Adhesives had done well financially. While growth in sales had never been a strong point, margins were generally high and sales levels steady. The company had never employed long-term debt and still did not do so. The firm had a line of credit from a local bank, which had always provided sufficient funds to cover short-term needs. Baker Adhesives presently owed about USD180,000 on the credit line. Baker had an excellent relationship with the bank, which had been with the company from the beginning.

Novo Orders

The original order from Novo was for an adhesive Novo was using in the production of a new line of toys for its Brazilian market. The toys needed to be waterproof and the adhesive, therefore, needed very specific properties. Through a mutual friend, Moreno had been introduced to Novo's purchasing agent. Working with Doug Baker, she had then negotiated the original order in February (the basis for the pricing of that original order is shown in **Exhibit 1**). Novo had agreed to pay shipping costs, so Baker Adhesives simply had to deliver the adhesive in 55-gallon drums to a nearby shipping facility.

The proposed new order was similar to the last one. As before, Novo agreed to make payment 30 days after receipt of the adhesives at the shipping facility. Baker anticipated a five-week manufacturing cycle once all the raw materials were in place. All materials would be secured within two weeks. Allowing for some flexibility, Moreno believed payment would be received about three months from order placement; that was about how long the original order took. For this reason, Moreno expected receipt of payment on the new order, assuming it was agreed upon immediately, somewhere around September 5, 2006.

Exchange Risks

With her newfound awareness of exchange-rate risks, Moreno had gathered additional information on exchange-rate markets before the meeting with Doug Baker. The history of the dollar-to-real exchange rate is shown in **Exhibit 2**. Furthermore, the data in that exhibit provided the most recent information on money markets and an estimate of the expected future (September 5, 2006) spot rates from a forecasting service.

Moreno had discussed her concerns about exchange-rate changes with the bank when she had arranged for conversion of the original Novo payment.[2] The bank, helpful as always, had described two ways in which Baker could mitigate the exchange risk from any new order: hedge in the forward market or hedge in the money markets.

Hedge in the Forward Market

Banks would often provide their clients with guaranteed exchange rates for the future exchange of currencies (forward rates). These contracts specified a date, an amount to be exchanged, and a rate. Any bank fee would be built into the rate. By securing a forward rate for the date of a foreign-currency-denominated cash flow, a firm could eliminate any risk due to currency fluctuations. In this case, the anticipated future inflow of reais from the sale to Novo could be converted at a rate that would be known today.

Hedge in the Money Markets

Rather than eliminate exchange risk through a contracted future exchange rate, a firm could make any currency exchanges at the known current spot rate. To do this, of course, the firm needed to convert future expected cash flows into current cash flows. This was done on the money market by borrowing "today" in a foreign currency against an expected future inflow or making a deposit "today" in a foreign account so as to be able to meet a future outflow. The amount to be borrowed or deposited would depend on the interest rates in the foreign currency because a firm would not wish to transfer more or less than what would be needed. In this case, Baker Adhesives would borrow in reais against the future inflow from Novo. The amount the company would borrow would be an amount such that the Novo receipt would exactly cover both principal and interest on the borrowing.

After some discussion and negotiation with the bank and bank affiliates, Moreno was able to secure the following agreements: Baker Adhesives' bank had agreed to offer a forward contract for September 5, 2006, at an exchange rate of 0.4227 USD/BRL. An affiliate of the bank, located in Brazil and familiar with Novo, was willing to provide Baker with a short-term real loan, secured by the Novo receivable,

---

[2]Though Baker Adhesives had a capable accountant, Doug Baker had decided to let Alissa Moreno handle the exchange-rate issues arising from the Novo order until they better understood the decisions and tradeoffs that needed to be made.

at 26%.[3] Moreno was initially shocked at this rate, which was more than three times the 8.52% rate on Baker's domestic line of credit; however, the bank described Brazil's historically high inflation and the recent attempts by the government to control inflation with high interest rates. The rate they had secured was typical of the market at the time.

The Meeting

It took Doug Baker some time to get over his disappointment. If international sales were the key to the future of Baker Adhesives, however, Baker realized he had already learned some important lessons. He vowed to put those lessons to good use as he and Moreno turned their attention to the new Novo order.

---

[3]Note that the loan from the bank affiliate was a 26% annual percentage rate for a three-month loan (the bank would charge exactly 6.5% on a three-month loan, to be paid when the principal was repaid). The effective rate over three months was, therefore, 6.5%. The 8.52% rate for Baker's line of credit was an annual percentage rate based on monthly compounding. The effective monthly rate was, therefore, $8.52\% \div 12 = 0.71\%$, which implies a $(1.0071)^3 - 1 = 2.1452\%$ effective rate over three months.

EXHIBIT 1 | Novo Price Calculation on Initial Order
(figures in U.S. dollars unless otherwise specified)

Labor	6,000
Materials	32,500
Manufacturing overhead	4,000
Administrative overhead	2,000
Total costs	44,500
Profit margin (12%)	6,068
Cost plus profit margin in dollars	50,568
Conversion (USD/BRL)	0.4636
Cost plus markup (BRL)	109,077
Amount (gallons)	1,210
Quoted price per gallon (BRL)	90.15

Notes:

The exchange rate used in the calculation was obtained from the *Wall Street Journal*.

Overhead was applied based on labor hours.

The raw materials expense was based on the original cost (book value) of the materials.

The rounded price of BRL90.15 per gallon was used in negotiations with Novo. Thus, for the final order, Novo was billed a total of BRL90.15 × 1,210 = BRL109,081.50.

Source: Created by case writer.

EXHIBIT 2 | Exchange Rate and Money-Market Information

Exchange Rates for the Real as of June 5, 2006 (USD/BRL)

Bid on real	0.4368
Ask for real	0.4371
Consensus forecast bid for September 5, 2006	0.4234
Consensus forecast ask for September 5, 2006	0.4239

Standard Deviation of Monthly Exchange-Rate Changes

2005	3.36%
Year to date 2006	6.53%

Interbank Rates (annual effective rates)

Brazil	19.47%
United States	5.08%

Data Source: *Wall Street Journal.*

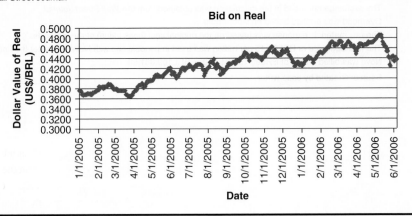

Source: Created by case writer.

J&L Railroad

It was Saturday, April 25, 2009, and Jeannine Matthews, chief financial officer at J&L Railroad (J&L), was in the middle of preparing her presentation for the upcoming board of directors meeting on Tuesday. Matthews was responsible for developing alternative strategies to hedge the company's exposure to locomotive diesel-fuel prices for the next 12 months. In addition to enumerating the pros and cons of alternative hedging strategies, the board had asked for her recommendation for which strategy to follow.

Fuel prices had always played a significant role in J&L's profits, but management had not considered the risk important enough to merit action. As the board reviewed the details of the company's performance for 2008 in February, they discovered that, despite an increase of $154 million in rail revenues, operating margin had shrunk by $114 million, largely due to an increase in fuel costs (**Exhibits 1** and **2**). Having operating profit fall by 11% in 2008 after it had risen 9% in 2007 was considered unacceptable by the board, and it did not want a repeat in 2009.

Recently in a conversation with Matthews, the chairman of the board had expressed his personal view of the problem:

> Our business is running a railroad, not predicting the strength of an oil cartel or whether one Middle East nation will invade another. We might have been lucky in the past, but we cannot continue to subject our shareholders to unnecessary risk. After all, if our shareholders want to speculate on diesel fuel prices, they can do that on their own; but I believe fuel-price risk should *not* be present in our stock price. On the other hand, if the recession continues and prices drop further, we could increase our profit margins by not hedging.

Diesel-fuel prices had peaked in early July 2008 but then had trended downward as a result of the worldwide recession and softening demand. By January 2009, diesel-fuel prices had fallen to their lowest level since early 2005. At February's meeting, the board had decided to wait and see how the energy markets would continue to react to the recession and softening demand. By March, however, oil and diesel-fuel prices had begun to rebound, so the board charged Matthews with the task of proposing a hedging policy at the meeting on April 28.

This disguised case was revised and updated by Rick Green based on an earlier version adapted from a Supervised Business Study written by Jeannine Lehman under the direction of Professor Kenneth Eades. Funding was provided by the L. White Matthews Fund for finance case writing. Copyright © 1994 by the University of Virginia Darden School Foundation, Charlottesville, VA. All rights reserved. *To order copies, send an e-mail to sales@dardenbusinesspublishing.com. No part of this publication may be reproduced, stored in a retrieval system, used in a spreadsheet, or transmitted in any form or by any means—electronic, mechanical, photocopying, recording, or otherwise—without the permission of the Darden School Foundation.* Rev. 8/09.

It was industry practice for railroads to enter into long-term contracts with their freight customers, which had both good and bad effects. On the positive side, railroads could better predict available resources by locking in revenues in advance. On the negative side, fixed-price contracts limited railroads' profit margins and exposed them to potentially large profit swings if any of their costs changed. In this regard, diesel fuel was a particularly troublesome cost for railroads, because it represented a large cost item that also was difficult to predict due to the volatility of fuel prices.

An ideal solution to the fuel-price risk would be for railroads to enter into long-term fixed-price contracts with their fuel suppliers. A fixed-price contract with suppliers when combined with the fixed-price contracts with freight customers would serve to steady future profits. Moreover, by contracting with fuel suppliers to deliver all of J&L's fuel needs at a fixed price, management could be assured of meeting its fuel budget numbers at year's end. At times, fuel suppliers had agreed to such contracts, but over the years, J&L had not been satisfied with the results. The problem was that when fuel prices had risen substantially, many suppliers walked away from their commitments leaving J&L with a list of three unattractive options:

1. *Force compliance*: J&L could take the supplier to court to enforce the contract; however, many suppliers were thinly capitalized, which meant that the legal action against them could put them into bankruptcy. As a result, J&L might get little or nothing from the supplier and yet would be saddled with significant legal fees.

2. *Negotiate a new price*: This usually meant that J&L would agree to pay at or near the current market price, which was equivalent to ignoring the original contract; plus it set a bad precedent for future contracts.

3. *Walk away and buy the fuel on the open market from another supplier*: This choice avoided "rewarding" the supplier for defaulting on its contract but was functionally equivalent to never having the contract in the first place.

Based on this history, J&L's board decided to "assume the fuel suppliers are not the answer to our fuel price problem." The board then asked Matthews to explore other alternatives to manage the fuel risk and preserve J&L's relationships with the fuel suppliers.

Mathews had determined that, if J&L were to hedge, it could choose between two basic strategies. The first was to do the hedging in-house by trading futures and options contracts on a public exchange. This presented a number of tradeoffs, including the challenge of learning how to trade correctly. The second was to use a bank's risk management products and services. This would cost more but would be easier to implement. For either alternative, she would need to address a number of important details, including how much fuel to hedge and how much risk should be eliminated with the hedge.

Railroad Industry

Railroads hauled record amounts of freight in 2006 and 2007, and began to encounter capacity constraints. In 2008, the industry hauled nearly two billion tons of freight, although rail traffic declined due to weakness in the economy. The transportation of coal was by far the number one commodity group carried. Other significant commodity groups were chemicals, farm products, food, metallic ores, nonmetallic minerals, and lumber, pulp, and paper products.

Freight and unit trains had expanded the industry since deregulation in the 1980s. Rail carriers served as long-distance haulers of *intermodal* freight, carrying the freight containers for steamship lines, or trailers for the trucking industry. *Unit* train loads were used to move large amounts of a single commodity (typically 50 or more cars) between two points using more efficient locomotives. A unit train would be used, for example, to move coal between a coal mine and an electric generating plant.

Several factors determined a railroad's profitability: government regulation, oligopolistic competition within the industry, and long-term contracts with shippers and suppliers. The railroad industry had a long history of price regulation; the government had feared the monopolistic pricing that had driven the industry to the brink of ruin in the 1970s. Finally recognizing the intense competition among most rail traffic, Congress passed the Staggers Rail Act of 1980, allowing railroads to manage their own assets, to price services based on market demand, and earn adequate revenues to support their operations. America's freight railroads paid almost all of the costs of tracks, bridges, and tunnels themselves. In comparison, trucks and barges used highways and waterways provided and maintained by the government.

After the Staggers Act was passed, railroad fuel efficiency rose 94%. By 2009, a freight train could move a ton of freight 436 miles on a single gallon of locomotive diesel fuel, approximately four times as far as it could by truck. The industry had spent considerable money on the innovative technology that improved the power and efficiency of locomotives and produced lighter train cars. Now, a long freight train could carry the same load as 280 trucks while at the same time producing only one-third the greenhouse-gas emissions.[1]

Market share was frequently won or lost solely on the basis of the price charged by competing railroads. Although rarely more than two or three railroads competed for a particular client's business, price competition was often fierce enough to prohibit railroads from increasing freight prices because of fuel-price increases. But, as fuel prices during 2008 climbed higher and faster than they had ever done before, there was some discussion in the railroad industry regarding the imposition of fuel surcharges when contracts came up for renewal. So far, however, none of the major carriers had followed up the talk with action.

J&L Railroad

J&L Railroad was founded in 1928 when the Jackson and Lawrence rail lines combined to form one of the largest railroads in the country. Considered a Class I railroad, J&L operated approximately 2,500 miles of line throughout the West and the Midwest. Although publicly owned, J&L was one of the few Class I railroads still managed by the original founding families. In fact, two of the family members still occupied seats on its board of directors. During the periods 1983–89, 1996–99, and 2004–08, J&L had invested significant amounts of capital into replacing equipment and refurbishing roadways. These capital expenditures had been funded either through internally

---

[1] Association of American Railroads, http://www.freightrailworks.org.

generated funds or through long-term debt. The investment in more efficient locomotives was now paying off, despite the burden of the principal and interest payments.

J&L had one of the most extensive intermodal networks, accounting for approximately 20% of revenues during the last few years, as compared to the Class I industry average of 10%. Transportation of coal, however, had accounted for only 25% to 30% of freight revenues. With the projected increase in demand for coal from emerging economies in Asia, management had committed to increase revenues from coal to 35% within three years. That commitment was now subject to revision due to slowing global economic activity and the recent fall in energy prices.

Exchange-Traded Contracts

J&L's exposure to fuel prices during the next 12 months would be substantial. Matthews estimated that the company would need approximately 17.5 million gallons of diesel fuel per month or 210 million gallons for the coming year. This exposure could be offset with the use of heating oil futures and option contracts that were traded on the New York Mercantile Exchange (NYMEX) (**Exhibits 3** and **4**). NYMEX did not trade contracts on diesel fuel, so it was not possible to hedge diesel fuel directly. Heating oil and diesel fuel, however, were both distillates of crude oil with very similar chemical profiles and highly correlated market prices (**Exhibit 5**). Thus, heating-oil futures were considered an excellent hedging instrument for diesel fuel.

Futures allowed market participants to contract to buy or sell a commodity at a future date at a predetermined price. If market participants did not want to buy a commodity today based on its *spot price*, the current market price, they could use the futures market to contract to buy it at a future date at the futures price. A futures price reflected the market's forecast of what the spot price was expected to be at the contract's maturity date. Many factors influenced the spot price and futures prices, both of which changed constantly depending on the market news. With current market conditions, the futures market was expecting price to trend up from the spot of $1.36 to an average of $1.52 over the next 12 months.

A trader who wanted to buy a commodity would take a "long" position in the contract, whereas a seller would take a "short" position. Because J&L's profits fell when fuel prices increased, the company could offset its exposure by taking long positions in heating-oil futures. For example, instead of waiting two months to buy fuel on the open market at the going price, J&L could enter into the July futures contract on April 25 to buy heating oil at $1.4138/gallon (**Exhibit 3**). Therefore, when the contract matured in two months,[2] J&L could buy heating oil at exactly $1.4138/gallon regardless of the price of heating oil at the time. This could work for or against J&L depending on whether prices rose or fell during the two months. For example, if at maturity of the contract, heating oil was selling at $1.4638, J&L would have benefited by $.05/gallon by owning the futures. If heating oil was selling for $1.3638 at maturity, J&L would have lost $.05/gallon on the futures. In either case, however, J&L

---

[2] NYMEX futures expired on the last trading day of the previous month; therefore, the July futures matured on June 30, 2009.

would pay exactly $1.4138 per gallon and would face no uncertainty about the net price paid after entering into the July futures contract.

Fuel producers or distributors who wanted to fix their selling price would take a short position in the fuel futures. Alternatively, the seller might be a speculator who believed that the spot price of fuel at maturity would end up being lower than the current futures price. In either case, futures was a zero-sum game because one party's gain exactly equals the other party's loss. As long as the futures price was an unbiased estimate of the future spot price, the *expected* payoff at maturity was zero for both the long and short side of the contract. Thus, although the buyer and seller were required to pay a modest fee to the exchange to enter a futures contract, no money was exchanged between buyers and sellers at the outset. If the futures price increased over time, the buyer would collect, and if the futures price decreased, the seller would collect. When the contract matured, it was rare for the buyer to request physical delivery of the commodity, rather the vast majority of contracted futures were cash settled.

NYMEX futures created a few problems for J&L management. First, because J&L would have to use heating-oil contracts to hedge its diesel-fuel exposure, there would be a small amount of risk created by the imperfect match of the prices of the two commodities. This "basis," however, was minimal owing to the high correlation historically between the two price series. Of greater concern was that NYMEX contracts were standardized with respect to size and maturity dates. Each heating-oil futures contract was for the delivery of 42,000 gallons and matured on the last business day of the preceding month. Thus, J&L faced a maturity mismatch because the hedge would only work if the number of gallons being hedged was purchased specifically on the day the futures contract matured. In addition, J&L faced a size mismatch because the number of gallons needed in any month was unlikely to equal an exact multiple of 42,000 gallons.

Some institutional features of NYMEX futures contracts had to be considered as well. NYMEX futures were "marked to market" daily, which meant that every investor's position was settled daily, regardless of whether the position was closed or kept open. Daily marking-to-market limited the credit risk of the transaction to a single day's movement of prices. To further reduce the credit risk, the exchange required margin payments as collateral. When a contract was initially opened, both parties were required to post an initial margin equal to approximately 5% or less of the contract value. At the end of each trading day, moneys were added or subtracted from the margin account as the futures trader's position increased or decreased in value. If the value of the position declined below a specified maintenance level, the trader would be required to replenish the margin to its initial margin level. Thus, the combination of daily marking-to-market and the use of margins effectively eliminated any credit risk for exchange-traded futures contracts. Still, the daily settlement process created a cash-flow risk because J&L might have to make cash payments well in advance of the maturity of a contract.

In addition to futures contracts, it was possible to buy NYMEX options on the futures. A call option gave the buyer the right, but not the obligation, to go long on the underlying commodity futures at a given price (the strike price) on or before the expiration date. A *put* option gave the buyer the right to go short on the futures at the strike price. The typical futures option expired a few days prior to the expiration of the underlying futures contract to give the counterparties time to offset their positions on the futures exchange. Options were offered at a variety of strike prices and maturities (**Exhibit 4**). Unlike the underlying futures contract, puts and calls commanded a market price called the *premium*. A call premium increased as the spread of the futures price over the strike price increased, whereas a put premium increased as the spread of the strike price over the futures price increased. The premiums of both puts and calls were higher for options with more time to maturity. Thus, unlike the futures, option buyers had to pay the premium to buy the contract in addition to both buyer and seller paying a fee for the transaction.

The Risk-Management Group at Kansas City National Bank

Walt Bernard, vice president of the risk management group of Kansas City National Bank, (KCNB) had recently given a presentation to J&L senior management in which he described the wide range of risk-management products and techniques available to protect J&L's profit margin. Each technique used a particular financial product to hedge by various degrees J&L's exposure to diesel-fuel price changes. The products offered by KCNB were completely financial in design (i.e., no actual delivery of the commodity took place at maturity). To hedge diesel fuel, KCNB offered No. 2 heating-oil contracts, the same commodity traded on the NYMEX. Also similar to trading on the NYMEX, working with KCNB meant that J&L could continue to do business as usual with its suppliers and perform its hedging activities independently.

The primary risk-management products offered by KCNB were commodity swaps, caps, floors, and collars (see **Exhibit 6** for cap and floor quotes). KCNB's instruments were designed to hedge the *average* price of heating oil during the contract period. By contrast, NYMEX futures and options were contracts designed against the spot price in effect on the last day of the contract. In a commodity swap, the bank agreed to pay on the settlement date if the average price of heating oil was above the agreed-upon swap price for the year. Conversely, J&L would have to pay the bank if the average price was below the contracted swap price. Thus, a swap was essentially a custom-fit futures contract, with KCNB rather than NYMEX carrying the credit risk. Because the swap was priced on the average heating-oil price, settlement occurred at the end of the swap (12 months in J&L's case) rather than daily as with NYMEX futures. In addition, KCNB would not require J&L to post a margin but would charge a nominal up-front fee as compensation for accepting J&L's credit risk. KCNB was currently quoting the 12-month swap price for heating oil as $1.522/gallon.

KCNB also offered commodity options, referred to as caps, floors, and collars. A *cap* was essentially a call option; a *floor* was a put option; and a *collar* was the combination of a cap and a floor. For a cap, KCNB agreed to pay the excess of the realized average fuel price over the cap's "strike price." If the average fuel price never reached the strike price, KCNB would pay nothing. As for any option, J&L would need to pay KCNB a premium for the cap. The cap premium varied according to how far the strike price was above the expected price. If the strike was close to the expected price implied by the futures contracts, J&L would have to pay a relatively high premium. If J&L was willing to accept some risk by contracting for a strike price that was significantly higher than the expected average price, the premium would be smaller. In any case, the cap would allow J&L to take advantage of price decreases and yet still be protected from price increases above the cap's strike price.

A commodity collar was used to limit the movement of prices within the range of the cap and floor strike prices. By choosing a collar, J&L would be selling a floor while simultaneously buying a cap. KCNB agreed to pay the excess, if any, of the average heating-oil price over the cap strike price. Conversely, J&L would have to pay if the average price fell below the floor strike price. Collars could be designed to have a minimal up-front cost by setting the cap and floor strike prices so that the revenue derived from selling the floor exactly offset the premium for buying the cap. If J&L management wanted to guard against prices rising above a certain price (the cap's strike price) but were willing to give up the benefit of prices falling below a certain level (the floor's strike price), a collar could be the logical choice.

Matthews's Choice

Jeannine Matthews had decided to recommend that J&L hedge its fuel costs for the next 12 months, at least to some extent. Her analysis revealed that despite using more efficient equipment, the cost of fuel as a percentage of revenues had increased every year since 2001 (**Exhibit 7**). The immediate questions to be answered were: How much fuel should be hedged, and how should the hedge be structured?

Bernard had presented Matthews with a myriad of possibilities, each of which provided some degree of profit protection. A commodity swap, for example, could be used to completely fix the price of fuel for the next year. If the price of diesel fuel ended up falling below the swap price, however, the hedge would be more of an embarrassment than a benefit to Matthews. Defending a newly initiated hedging policy would be difficult if J&L's profits lagged those of other railroads because of a failure to capture lower fuel costs.

Then there was the issue of how much fuel to hedge. If the economy experienced a slowdown, J&L would experience a drop in rail loads, which would result in using less than the 210 million gallons currently expected. If the hedge was constructed based on more fuel than needed, it was conceivable that J&L could end up paying to settle its position with the bank for fuel that it could not use. At the same time, it was also possible that the economy would pick up, and J&L would end up having to buy a significant amount of fuel on the open market without the benefit of a hedge.

Instead of a swap, Matthews could use a cap to eliminate the risk of high fuel prices. This would seem to alleviate the problem of over- or under-hedging because the cap would only be exercised if it was profitable (i.e., if prices rose beyond the cap's strike price). At that point, J&L would prefer to have been over-hedged because the company would get a higher payoff from the cap. The biggest concern about the cap strategy was that the price of heating oil might not rise high enough to trigger the cap, in which case the premium paid for the cap would have only served to reduce profits with no offsetting benefits. Another alternative was to enter into a collar, which could be structured to have a zero cost; however, a collar carried a hidden cost because it gave up the savings if fuel prices happened to fall below the floor's strike price.

Matthews knew that it was important for her to keep in mind that all of KCNB's product could be mimicked using NYMEX futures and options. In fact, maybe there was a creative way to combine NYMEX securities to give J&L a better hedge than provided by KCNB's products. Regardless of what she recommended, Matthews realized that she needed to devise a hedging strategy that would give J&L the maximum benefit at the lowest cost and would not prove to be an embarrassment for her or J&L.

EXHIBIT 1 | Consolidated Income Statement, 2006–08 (in millions of dollars) December 31

	2008	2007	2006
Revenues by market group:			
Coal	$1,080	$ 871	$ 857
Merchandise	1,907	1,954	1,878
Intermodal	714	722	725
Total operating revenues	3,701	3,547	3,461
Expenses:			
Compensation and benefits	987	939	970
Purchased service and rent	588	571	581
Fuel	603	430	403
Depreciation	296	285	271
Materials and other	313	294	295
Total operating expenses	2,787	2,519	2,520
Operating income:	914	1,028	941
Other income	40	34	55
Interest expense, net	(163)	(162)	(175)
Income (loss) before income taxes:	791	900	820
Income tax provision	(297)	(310)	(276)
Net income	$ 494	$ 589	$ 545

Source: Main Street Trading data.

EXHIBIT 2 | Consolidated Balance Sheets, 2007–08 (in millions of dollars)
December 31

Assets	2008	2007
Current assets:		
Cash	$ 227	$ 76
Receivable net	320	347
Materials and suppliers, at average cost	71	65
Deferred income taxes, current	55	70
Other current assets	62	58
Total current assets	735	616
Properties:		
Investment	654	726
Property, road and structures, net	8,184	7,940
Other assets	101	336
Total assets	$9,674	$9,618
Liabilities and shareholders' equity		
Current liabilities:		
Accounts payable	$ 419	$ 419
Current portion of long-term debt	96	75
Income taxes payable	81	87
Other accrued expenses	178	136
Total current liabilities	774	717
Long-term debt	2,275	2,207
Deferred income taxes	2,344	2,366
Other liabilities and reserves	747	750
Total liabilities	6,140	6,040
Shareholders' equity:		
Common stock	135	140
Additional paid-in capital	618	539
Accumulated other comprehensive income (loss)	(347)	(147)
Retained income	3,128	3,046
Total shareholders' equity	3,534	3,578
Total liabilities and shareholders' equity	$9,674	$9,618

Source: Main Street Trading data.

EXHIBIT 3 | NYMEX Heating Oil Exchange Futures (in dollars per gallon) April 24, 2009

Month	Last
May '09	$1.368
Jun '09	$1.386
Jul '09	$1.414
Aug '09	$1.443
Sep '09	$1.472
Oct '09	$1.502
Nov '09	$1.533
Dec '09	$1.563
Jan '10	$1.593
Feb '10	$1.614
Mar '10	$1.626
Apr '10	$1.629
May '10	$1.638

Spot = $1.360

Each heating-oil futures contract was for the delivery of 42,000 gallons and matured on the last business day of the preceding month (e.g., the June 2009 contract expires May 29, 2009).

Source: New York Mercantile Exchange data.

EXHIBIT 4 | NYMEX Heating Oil Call Option Premiums (in dollars per gallon) April 24, 2009

Strike Price	Aug. '09 Calls	Oct. '09 Calls	Dec. '09 Calls	Feb. '10 Calls	May '10 Calls
1.36	0.196	0.265	0.326	0.376	0.394
1.40	0.175	0.244	0.303	0.353	0.371
1.45	0.151	0.219	0.277	0.326	0.344
1.50	0.131	0.196	0.253	0.301	0.319
1.55	0.113	0.176	0.230	0.277	0.295
1.60	0.098	0.158	0.210	0.255	0.272
1.65	0.084	0.142	0.192	0.235	0.252
1.70	0.072	0.127	0.175	0.216	0.233
Expiry date	7/28/2009	9/25/2009	11/24/2009	1/26/2010	4/27/2010
Days to expiry	95	154	215	278	369
Futures price	$1.443	$1.502	$1.563	$1.614	$1.638
Treasury yield	0.11%	0.17%	0.31%	0.38%	0.49%

Source: Main Street Trading data.

EXHIBIT 5 | Diesel Fuel versus Heating Oil Prices (in dollars per gallon)
January 2007 to March 2009

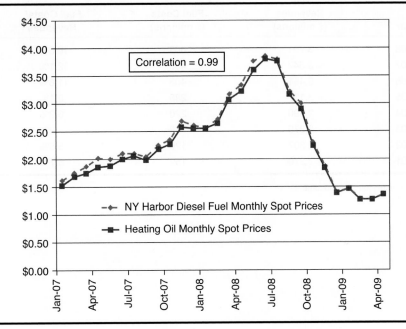

Source: Graph created by case writer using data from Energy Information Association.

EXHIBIT 6 | KCNB Cap and Floor Prices (in dollars per gallon)
April 24, 2009

Strike Price	1-Year Cap	1-Year Floor
1.40	0.201	0.079
1.45	0.172	0.101
1.50	0.147	0.125
1.55	0.125	0.152
1.60	0.105	0.182
1.65	0.088	0.215
1.70	0.073	0.250

Note: Cap and floors prices are based on the average daily closing price of heating fuel for
one year.

Data Source: Company documents.

EXHIBIT 7 | Fuel Costs 2001–08

Year	Rail Revenues ($ millions)	Fuel Costs ($ millions)	Fuel Costs/ Revenues	Gallons (millions)
2008	3,701	603	16.3%	205.1
2007	3,547	430	12.1%	205.6
2006	3,461	403	11.6%	216.6
2005	3,137	285	9.1%	170.0
2004	2,690	220	8.2%	191.2
2003	2,379	189	7.9%	216.1
2002	2,307	126	5.5%	179.4
2001	2,270	152	6.7%	206.4

Data Source: Company documents.

Primus Automation Division, 2002

In early 2002, Tom Baumann, an analyst in the Marketing and Sales Group of the Factory Automation Division of Primus Corporation, had to recommend to the division sales manager, Jim Feldman, the terms under which Primus would lease one of its advanced systems to Avantjet Corporation, a manufacturer of corporate-jet aircraft. Specifically, Baumann was weighing a choice among four alternative sets of lease terms.

The problem of analyzing and setting lease terms was relatively new to Baumann and had arisen only a month earlier, when Avantjet informed Baumann and Feldman that its pending purchase of the factory-automation system had been put on indefinite hold. Avantjet's CEO had just ordered a moratorium on any capital expenditures that might negatively affect Avantjet's income statement and balance sheet. Baumann was not completely surprised by Avantjet's decision. Just recently, the *Wall Street Journal* had singled out Avantjet's declining stock price and worsening balance sheet as an example of manufacturers' deteriorating condition during the economic recession.

Only three months earlier, Baumann and Feldman had won an apparent competition for Avantjet's business over Primus's leading competitors, Faulhaber Gmbh of Germany and Honshu Heavy Industries of Japan. Baumann feared that Avantjet's temporizing would give those two competitors an opportunity to renew their selling efforts to Avantjet.

Feldman challenged Baumann to find a way to make the sale: "Help me salvage this deal or we won't make our sales budget for the year. Also, given the steep competition, we might lose the customer altogether on future sales." Baumann explored a range of creative financing terms, such as leasing, that might remove Avantjet's reluctance to proceed. He concluded that structuring the transaction as a lease might save the deal. Now, choosing the annual lease payment remained the only detail to be settled before returning to Avantjet with a proposal.

This case was prepared by Robert Hengelbrok, under the supervision of Robert F. Bruner and with the assistance of Sean D. Carr. It was written as a basis for class discussion rather than to illustrate effective or ineffective handling of an administrative situation. Copyright © 2005 by the University of Virginia Darden School Foundation, Charlottesville, VA. All rights reserved. *To order copies, send an e-mail to* sales@dardenbusinesspublishing.com. *No part of this publication may be reproduced, stored in a retrieval system, used in a spreadsheet, or transmitted in any form or by any means—electronic, mechanical, photocopying, recording, or otherwise—without the permission of the Darden School Foundation.*

Primus Automation Division

Primus Automation, a division of a large, worldwide manufacturing and services firm, was an innovative producer of world-class factory-automation products and services, with operations in the United States, Europe, and Asia. Primus's products included programmable controllers, numerical controls, industrial computers, manufacturing software, factory-automation systems, and data communication networks.

The business environment had changed dramatically over the past year. Slower economic growth, coupled with increased competition for market share, had been forecast for the next few years. Still, a recent resurgence in the U.S. manufacturing base—due to the weakened dollar driving up U.S. exports—was spurring factory automation. Cross-continental industry alliances and an accelerated rate of new product introductions had heightened industry rivalries.

Primus Automation's objectives were to maintain leadership in market share, increase sales by 15% a year, and achieve its targets for net income and working capital turnover. Those objectives were to be realized by providing the most responsive customer service, attaining a strong share position in the high volume-growing segments, and offering leading-technology products based on industry standards.

Meeting the objectives required stimulating the demand by creating new incentives for purchasing automation equipment. Many of the unsophisticated users of automation equipment in the United States needed to be educated in analyzing capital expenditures, tax incentives, and alternative methods for acquiring the needed equipment. Division executives had discussed various asset-financing approaches as a means of assisting with the placement of their systems.

Asset-Financing Approaches

Baumann discussed with Primus's division executives the variety of ways a firm might acquire the use of a Primus Automated Factory System. First, the customer could purchase a system with cash or with borrowed funds, either unsecured or collateralized by the equipment. Second, the firm could acquire the equipment through a conditional sale in which the title would pass to the firm upon the receipt of the final payment. Finally, the customer could lease the equipment in one of two ways: (1) via a cancelable *operating lease,* which would carry a term that was less than the economic life of the property; or (2) via a noncancelable financial *capital lease* that would span the entire economic life of the property.

Capital versus Operating Leases

Baumann reviewed his notes on the rules defining the two types of leases. To be classified as a capital lease under the guidelines of Financial Accounting Standards Board (FASB) Statement No. 13,[1] the lease had to meet one or more of the following four criteria:

---

[1] *Statement of Financial Accounting Standards No. 13: Accounting for Leases,* Financial Accounting Standards Board (November 1976), 7–9.

a. Ownership of the asset transferred by the end of the lease term.

b. The lease contained a bargain-purchase option, whereby the lessee had to pay the fair market value for the property at the end of the lease.

c. The lease term was equal to 75% or more of the economic life of the property.

d. The present value of the lease payments over the lease term was equal to or greater than 90% of the fair market value of the leased property at the beginning of the lease.

If the lease qualified as a capital lease, then the lessee would be required to depreciate the equipment by showing it as an asset and a liability on its balance sheet. The lessee could not deduct the lease payment from its income taxes. At the end of the lease, the lessee retained ownership and bore the risk of early changes in the asset's value.

If the lease met none of the foregoing criteria, it would be classified as an operating lease. As an operating lease, the lease payments would be treated as an ordinary expense, deductible from taxable income. The leased property would not appear on the lessee's balance sheet and, after the lease term, would revert to the lessor.

Primus Automation had never before offered leasing and was unfamiliar with the actual workings of leasing arrangements. Fortunately, the Equipment Finance Division of Primus's parent company had extensive leasing expertise and assisted Baumann in his research. As he dug out some of the information that the division had sent him, Baumann realized that this was the first application of his efforts and he wanted to make sure he understood all the nuances involved with leasing.

Avantjet

Baumann had heard that Avantjet's vice president of operations was determined to get an automation system to cut costs and accelerate his company's production line. A large backlog of orders for both new jets and the retrofitted older models had put new demands on production. Without such a system, it would be very difficult to meet promised deliveries. In addition, Baumann knew that Avantjet's capital-budgeting process included all major expenditures—new construction and capital leases—but excluded operating leases.

The risk of obsolescence and the ability to upgrade equipment weighed heavily in Avantjet's decision. Overall, the most important factor was cash flow, because Avantjet wanted to avoid any additional unplanned expenditures in 2002. Avantjet was very capital intensive and was only marginally profitable because it was so highly leveraged. (**Exhibits 1** and **2** show Avantjet's income statement and balance sheet.)

With that in mind, Baumann wondered how he was going to find a way to resolve all the issues. He knew that many companies had turned to leasing to address some of those concerns. Although many of the large firms in the airframe industry were not as cash strapped as the small- and medium-sized shops, it was worthwhile to find out what classes of customers would benefit financially from leasing. Baumann surmised that tax rates and cost-of-capital disparities between the lessor and lessee might be critical drivers in any lease arrangement.

Primus's Competitors

Several months earlier, when Avantjet was reviewing system proposals from Primus, Honshu, and Faulhaber, Baumann and Feldman learned from Avantjet that all three systems were roughly equivalent but differed in pricing. **Table 1** summarizes the pricing options then available:

TABLE 1 | Summary of the available pricing options (in USD)

System Manufacturer	Purchase Price of System If Avantjet Were to Buy	Quoted Annual Lease Expense and Guaranteed Residual Value[2] for 5-Year Operating Lease
Faulhaber Gmbh	$759,000	$170,000; 15% residual value
Honshu Heavy Industries	$737,000	$163,000; 24% residual value
Primus Automation Division	$715,000	Not previously quoted

Baumann had learned from industry newsletters that foreign manufacturers sometimes exploited their allegedly lower costs of capital as a competitive weapon in designing financing terms for their customers. Baumann wondered whether this was apparent in the lease terms proposed by Faulhaber and Honshu, and planned to estimate the effective lease costs under their respective proposals.

Primus's Lease Proposal

The particular deal that Feldman had called Baumann about was a proposal for a $715,000 factory-automation system. This equipment would enable Avantjet to operate a group of workstations from a central control site while gaining valuable feedback and planning capabilities. Realizing that he had to find out more about Avantjet's motives for delaying the project, Baumann quizzed Feldman about Avantjet's performance and requirements. Feldman told Baumann that Avantjet's last CEO had been replaced by a senior executive from outside the firm who was more concerned about the bottom line and the balance sheet than he was about making capital expenditures that had long paybacks.

With that in mind, Baumann began to assess this particular deal. The price of the total package was $715,000. Baumann assumed that Avantjet's primary alternative to leasing was to borrow the purchase price of the equipment on a five-year, interest-bearing term loan payable in equal annual amounts due at the end of each year. The Equipment Finance Division also quoted Baumann four alternatives for a five-year operating lease with equal annual payments (due at the beginning of each year) that varied depending on Avantjet's actual tax rate and cost of debt. At the end of the lease

---

[2]Residual value was the estimated fair value of a leased asset at the end of the lease term. Because future values were difficult to predict, residual values were often highly subjective. Equipment leases typically stipulated a guaranteed residual value.

term, renewal was subject to negotiation between the two parties. Factory-automation equipment was classified as technological equipment with a five-year life. Five-year MACRS[3] depreciation rates, based on the full value of the property, were as follows in **Table 2:**

TABLE 2 | 5-year MACRS

Income Tax Depreciation Rate Schedule	
Year	Percentage
1	20.00
2	32.00
3	19.20
4	11.52
5	11.52

In order to structure it as an operating lease, the Equipment Finance Division required an 11.2729% residual guarantee from Baumann's division. Baumann did not know how sensitive to the residual assumption the results would be. Because his division was trying to move into leasing to bolster sales, he figured that it might be willing to assume some of the risk of the equipment's value declining substantially in five years. Primus Automation might also have to assist the Equipment Finance Division in remarketing the equipment to another user, if a new lease were not signed when the original lease expired. (**Exhibit 3** lists the various pricing and leasing terms.)

To analyze leasing scenarios, Baumann created a leasing model (**Exhibits 4** and **5**) for computing the net present value (NPV) and the internal rate of return (IRR) of cash flows to get a better understanding of which alternative would be the least costly to Avantjet. The scenario with the lowest present value would be the cheapest financing alternative. The IRR represented the effective cost of the lease financing. If that rate were below the after-tax cost of debt, leasing would be the more attractive method of financing.

Although Baumann guessed that Avantjet had about the same borrowing cost as Primus (about 9.5%), he suspected that Avantjet was in a lower tax bracket. Baumann decided to run some sensitivity analyses with a zero marginal tax rate. With such a low tax rate, Avantjet could not fully exploit the tax savings on interest and depreciation.

Small- and medium-sized firms probably paid higher interest rates than Primus and could save money if Primus financed the equipment and passed on some of the financing savings to them. Leasing terms might be adjusted to exchange tax benefits for lower lease rates. Baumann's analysis used the after-tax cost of debt as the discount rate, but Baumann thought he might want to use a higher discount rate, perhaps the

---

[3]MACRS stood for modified accelerated cost recovery system. It was a method of accelerated depreciation allowed under the U.S. Tax Code. Under MACRS, depreciation deductions were determined without regard to the asset's residual value.

weighted-average cost of capital, based on the greater risk involved with leasing high-technology equipment.

A thorough sensitivity analysis based on various discount and tax rates might help to determine under what circumstances a customer might want to lease. Sample calculations for four lease rates that Primus might offer different customers are presented in **Exhibit 6.** With a variety of options and scenarios to propose to Avantjet, depending on actual tax and hurdle rates, Baumann believed that Primus had a good chance of resurrecting the deal and meeting its sales goals for 2002. Moreover, this experience would assist Primus in offering lease proposals to its future customers.

EXHIBIT 1 | Avantjet's Statement of Income ($000)

	2001	2000	1999
Sales	$576,327	$575,477	$432,522
Other income	9,985	6,976	9,677
Gross income	586,312	582,453	442,199
Cost of goods sold	425,076	423,443	325,016
Selling, general, & admin.	43,624	36,215	35,632
Research & development	13,773	12,873	9,064
Interest	84,062	87,259	27,002
Total expenses	566,535	559,790	396,714
Income before taxes	19,777	22,662	45,485
Taxes	9,690	11,105	22,288
Net income	$ 10,087	$ 11,557	$ 23,197

Source: Company records.

EXHIBIT 2 | Avantjet's Balance Sheet ($000)

	2001	2000
Assets		
Current assets:		
Cash and temporary investments	$ 19,918	$ 27,263
Accounts receivable	37,791	37,307
Inventories	310,180	323,101
Prepaid expenses	13,928	13,362
Total current assets	381,817	401,033
Property, plant, and equipment:		
Land	2,245	2,245
Buildings	30,654	30,229
Machinery and equipment	26,932	21,244
Furniture and fixtures	1,683	1,520
Construction in progress	1,668	885
	63,182	56,123
Less accumulated depreciation	12,634	8,267
Net property, plant, and equipment	50,548	47,856
Other assets	640,369	648,339
Total assets	$1,072,734	$1,097,228
Liabilities and stockholders' equity		
Current liabilities:		
Long-term debt	$ 592	$ 563
Accounts payable	42,355	38,760
Notes payable	4,750	5,764
Accrued compensation, interest, and other liabilities	39,627	43,855
Deposits and progress payments	146,964	160,946
Total current liabilities	234,288	249,888
Long-term notes payable to banks	646,633	671,225
Deferred income taxes	42,661	41,498
	689,294	712,723
Common stockholders' equity:		
Common stock	3,385	3,027
Capital in excess of par value	74,081	69,770
Retained earnings	72,017	62,156
Less common stock in treasury	(331)	(336)
Total stockholders' equity	149,152	134,617
Total liabilities and stockholders' equity	$1,072,734	$1,097,228

Source: Company records.

EXHIBIT 3 | Terms under Hypothetical Leasing and Buy-and-Borrow Strategies

Terms Under Hypothetical Buy-and-Borrow and Leasing Strategies	
Loan ("Buy-and-Borrow") 5-year term loan Payment in arrears	
Equipment cost	$715,000
Cash down payment	$0
Loan amount	$715,000
Lease 5-year net lease	Annual payments (in advance)
Leasing option #1	$155,040
Leasing option #2	$160,003
Leasing option #3	$162,350
Leasing option #4	$164,760
Both Methods	
Guaranteed residual value: (required by Primus Equipment Finance Division)	11.2729%
Investment tax credit	0%
Depreciation	5-year MACRS

EXHIBIT 4 | Sample Calculation of the Present Value of Cash Outflows: Scenario A, Lease Payment 2 ($160,003)[1]

| Tax rate: | 34.00% | Equipment cost: $715,000 |
| Pretax interest rate | 9.50% | Lease payment: $160,003 |

Year	Interest Payment after Tax[2]	Principal Payment[2]	Five-Year MACRS[3] Depr. Rate	Depr. before Tax	Depr. Tax Savings	Residual Cash Flow after Tax[4]	Loan Cash Outflow[5]	Lease Cash Outflow[6]
0							$ 0	$105,602
1	$ 44,831	$118,287	20.00%	$143,000	($48,620)		$114,498	$105,602
2	$ 37,414	$129,524	32.00%	$228,800	($77,792)		$ 89,146	$105,602
3	$ 29,293	$141,829	19.20%	$137,280	($46,675)		$124,447	$105,602
4	$ 20,400	$155,303	11.52%	$ 82,368	($28,005)		$147,698	$105,602
5	$ 10,663	$170,057	11.52%	$ 82,368	($28,005)	($67,199)	$ 85,515	$ 0
Sum	$142,600	$715,000	94.24%	$673,816	($229,097)	($67,199)	$561,303	$528,010
NPV							**$469,273**	**$469,273**

[1]This table illustrates the calculation of net present value (NPV) for the two methods of equipment financing: the loan financing alternative (also called buy-and-borrow) and the lease financing. Because these cash flows are net outflows or expenses, the alternative with the lower net present value will be more attractive to the customer.

[2]See "Loan Amortization Table."

[3]Modified Accelerated Cost Recovery System (MACRS).

[4]The residual cash flow equals the sale proceeds less the tax expense on the gain or loss from the sale. The tax expense equals the tax rate times the differences between sale proceeds and net book value of the asset (see separate calculation below).

[5]Loan cash flows are the sum of after-tax interest payments, principal payments, depreciation tax shield (shown as a negative value because it reduces expenses), and value captured from the sale of the residual asset (also negative). Loan-financing cash flows occur *in arrears*.

[6]Lease cash flows equal the assumed lease payment less the tax shield. Lease payments are made *in advance*.

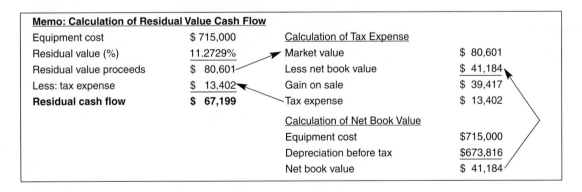

Memo: Calculation of Residual Value Cash Flow			
Equipment cost	$ 715,000	Calculation of Tax Expense	
Residual value (%)	11.2729%	Market value	$ 80,601
Residual value proceeds	$ 80,601	Less net book value	$ 41,184
Less: tax expense	$ 13,402	Gain on sale	$ 39,417
Residual cash flow	**$ 67,199**	Tax expense	$ 13,402
		Calculation of Net Book Value	
		Equipment cost	$715,000
		Depreciation before tax	$673,816
		Net book value	$ 41,184

EXHIBIT 5 | Sample Calculation of the Internal Rate of Return: Scenario A, Lease Payment 2 ($160,003)[1]

Year	Lease Payment after Tax[2]	Forgone Tax Savings Associated with Depreciation[2]	Forgone Residual Value after Tax[2]	Initial Purchase Price Saved	Lease Payment Less Incremental Cash Flow
0	($105,602)			$715,000	$609,398
1	($105,602)	($48,620)			($154,222)
2	($105,602)	($77,792)			($183,394)
3	($105,602)	($46,675)			($152,277)
4	($105,602)	($28,005)			($133,607)
5	$0	($28,005)	($67,199)		($95,204)
Sum	($528,010)	($229,097)	($67,199)	$715,000	($109,307)
IRR					**6.27%**

[1]This table illustrates the calculation of the internal rate of return (IRR) associated with lease financing. The IRR is the effective after-tax cost of the lease financing and is useful for comparison with the cost of alternative forms of financing. Because this is a calculation based on *costs* to the customer, a lower IRR will be more attractive to the customer.

[2]See "Sample Calculation of the Present Value of Cash Outflows."

EXHIBIT 6 | Summary Table of the NPV and IRR for the Four Tax and Cost-of-Capital Scenarios

Scenario	A	B	C	D
Effective tax rate	34.0%	34.0%	0.0%	0.0%
Pretax cost of debt	9.5%	13.0%	9.5%	13.0%
After-tax cost of debt	6.27%	8.58%	9.50%	13.00%
NPV of loan ("borrow-and-buy")	$469,273	$484,546	$663,800	$671,253
IRR of loan ("borrow-and-buy")	6.27%	8.58%	9.50%	13.00%
Leasing option #1	$155,040	$155,040	$155,040	$155,040
NPV of leasing option #1	$454,717			
IRR of lease	5.32%			
Lease advantage over borrowing	$ 14,556			
Leasing option #2	$160,003	$160,003	$160,003	$160,003
NPV of leasing option #2	$469,273			
IRR of lease	6.27%			
Lease advantage over borrowing	$0			
Leasing option #3	$162,350	$162,350	$162,350	$162,350
NPV of leasing option #3	$476,156			
IRR of lease	6.72%			
Lease advantage over borrowing	($6,883)			
Leasing option #4	$164,760	$164,760	$164,760	$164,760
NPV of leasing option #4	$483,225			
IRR of lease	7.19%			
Lease advantage over borrowing	($13,952)			
Faulhaber Gmbh				
NPV of loan				
NPV of lease				
IRR of lease				
Lease advantage over borrowing				
Honshu Heavy Industries				
NPV of loan				
NPV of lease				
IRR of lease				
Lease advantage over borrowing				

Note: Calculations for shaded cells are presented in Exhibits 4 and 5.

Mogen, Inc.

On January 10, 2006, the managing director of Merrill Lynch's Equity-Linked Capital Markets Group, Dar Maanavi, was reviewing the final drafts of a proposal for a convertible debt offering by MoGen, Inc. As a leading biotechnology company in the United States, MoGen had become an important client for Merrill Lynch over the years. In fact, if this deal were to be approved by MoGen at $5 billion, it would represent Merrill Lynch's third financing for MoGen in four years with proceeds raised totaling $10 billion. Moreover, this "convert" would be the largest such single offering in history. The proceeds were earmarked to fund a variety of capital expenditures, research and development (R&D) expenses, working capital needs, as well as a share repurchase program.

The Merrill Lynch team had been working with MoGen's senior management to find the right tradeoff between the conversion feature and the coupon rate for the bond. Maanavi knew from experience that there was no "free lunch," when structuring the pricing of a convertible. Issuing companies wanted the conversion price to be as high as possible and the coupon rate to be as low as possible; whereas investors wanted the opposite: a low conversion price and a high coupon rate. Thus, the challenge was to structure the convert to make it attractive to the issuing company in terms of its cost of capital, while at the same time selling for full price in the market. Maanavi was confident that the right balance in the terms of the convert could be found, and he was also confident that the convert would serve MoGen's financing needs better than a straight bond or equity issuance. But, he needed to make a decision about the final terms of the issue in the next few hours, as the meeting with MoGen was scheduled for early the next morning.

Company History

Founded in 1985 as MoGen (Molecular Genetics) the company was among the first in the biotechnology industry to deliver on the commercial promises of emerging sciences, such as recombinant DNA and molecular biology. After years of research, MoGen emerged with two of the first biologically derived human therapeutic drugs, RENGEN and MENGEN, both of which helped to offset the damaging effects from chemotherapy for cancer patients undergoing treatment. Those two MoGen products were among the first "blockbuster" drugs to emerge from the nascent biotechnology industry.

By 2006, MoGen was one of the leading biotech companies in an industry that included firms such as Genentech, Amgen, Gilead Sciences, Celgene, and Genzyme. The keys to success for all biotech companies were finding new drugs through research and then getting the drugs approved by the U.S. Food and Drug Administration (FDA). MoGen's strategy for drug development was to determine the best mode for attacking a patient's issue and then focusing on creating solutions via that mode. Under that approach, MoGen had been able to produce drugs with the highest likelihood of both successfully treating the patient as well as making the company a competitive leader in drug quality. In January 2006, MoGen's extensive R&D expenditures had resulted in a portfolio of five core products that focused on supportive cancer care. The success of that portfolio had been strong enough to offset other R&D write-offs so that MoGen was able to report $3.7 billion in profits in 2005 on $12.4 billion in sales. Sales had grown at an annual rate of 29% over the previous five years, and earnings per share had improved to $2.93 for 2005, compared with $1.81 and $1.69 for 2004 and 2003, respectively (**Exhibits 1** and **2**).

The FDA served as the regulating authority to safeguard the public from dangerous drugs and required extensive testing before it would allow a drug to enter the U.S. marketplace. The multiple hurdles and long lead-times required by the FDA created a constant tension with the biotech firms who wanted quick approval to maximize the return on their large investments in R&D. Moreover, there was always the risk that a drug would not be approved or that after it was approved, it would be pulled from the market due to unexpected adverse reactions by patients. Over the years, the industry had made progress in shortening the approval time and improving the predictability of the approval process. At the same time, industry R&D expenditures had increased 12.6% over 2003 in the continuing race to find the next breakthrough product.

Like all biotech companies, MoGen faced uncertainty regarding new product creation as well as challenges involved with sustaining a pipeline of future products. Now a competitive threat of follow-on biologics or "biosimilars" began emerging. As drugs neared the end of their patent protection, competitors would produce similar drugs as substitutes. Competitors could not produce the drug exactly, because they did not have access to the original manufacturer's molecular clone or purification process. Thus, biosimilars required their own approval to ensure they performed as safely as the original drugs. For MoGen, this threat was particularly significant in Europe, where several patents were approaching expiration.

Funding Needs

MoGen needed to ensure a consistent supply of cash to fund R&D and to maintain financial flexibility in the face of uncertain challenges and opportunities. MoGen had cited several key areas that would require approximately $10 billion in funding for 2006:

1. *Expanding manufacturing and formulation, and fill and finish capacity*: Recently, the company had not been able to scale up production to match increases in demand for certain core products. The reason for the problem was that MoGen outsourced most of its formulation and fill and finish manufacturing processes, and these off-shore companies had not been able to expand their operations quickly enough. Therefore, MoGen wanted to remove such supply risks by increasing both its internal manufacturing capacity in its two existing facilities in Puerto Rico as well as new construction in Ireland. These projects represented a majority of MoGen's total capital expenditures that were projected to exceed $1 billion in 2006.

2. *Expanding investment in R&D and late-stage trials*: Late-stage trials were particularly expensive, but were also critical as they represented the last big hurdle before a drug could be approved by the FDA. With 11 late-stage "mega-site" trials expected to commence in 2006, management knew that successful outcomes were critical for MoGen's ability to maintain momentum behind its new drug development pipeline. The trials would likely cost $500 million. MoGen had also decided to diversify its product line by significantly increasing R&D to approximately $3 billion for 2006, which was an increase of 30% over 2005.

3. *Acquisition and licensing*: MoGen had completed several acquisition and licensing deals that had helped it achieve the strong growth in revenues and earnings per share (EPS). The company expected to continue this strategy and had projected to complete a purchase of Genix, Inc., in 2006 for approximately $2 billion in cash. This acquisition was designed to help MoGen capitalize on Genix's expertise in the discovery, development, and manufacture of human therapeutic antibodies.

4. *The stock repurchase program*: Due to the highly uncertain nature of its operations, MoGen had never issued dividends to shareholders but instead had chosen to pursue a stock repurchase program. Senior management felt that this demonstrated a strong belief in the company's future and was an effective way to return cash to shareholders without being held to the expectation of having a regular dividend payout. Due to strong operational and financial performance over the past several years, MoGen had executed several billion dollars worth of stock repurchases, and it was management's intent to continue repurchases over the next few years. In 2005, MoGen purchased a total of 63.2 million shares for an aggregate $4.4 billion.[1] As of December 31, 2005, MoGen had $6.5 billion remaining in the authorized share repurchase plan, of which management expected to spend $3.5 billion in 2006.

---

[1]Through various share repurchase programs authorized by the board of directors, MoGen had repurchased $4.4 billion, $4.1 billion, and $1.8 billion of MoGen common stock in 2005, 2004, and 2003, respectively.

With internally generated sources of funds expected to be $5 billion (net income plus depreciation), MoGen would fall well below the $10 billion expected uses of funds for 2006. Thus, management estimated that an offering size of about $5 billion would cover MoGen's needs for the coming year.

Convertible Debt

A convertible bond was considered a hybrid security, because it had attributes of both debt and equity. From an investor's point of view, a convert provided the safety of a bond plus the upside potential of equity. The safety came from receiving a fixed income stream in the form of the bond's coupon payments plus the return of principal. The upside potential came from the ability to convert the bond into shares of common stock. Thus, if the stock price should rise above the conversion price, the investor could convert and receive more than the principal amount. Because of the potential to realize capital appreciation via the conversion feature, a convert's coupon rate was always set lower than what the issuing company would pay for straight debt. Thus, when investors bought a convertible bond, they received less income than from a comparable straight bond, but they gained the chance of receiving more than the face value if the bond's conversion value exceeded the face value.

To illustrate, consider a convertible bond issued by BIO, Inc., with a face value of $1,000 and a maturity of five years. Assume that the convert carries a coupon rate of 4% and a conversion price of $50 per share and that BIO's stock was selling for $37.50 per share at the time of issuance. The coupon payment gives an investor $40 per year in interest (4% × $1,000), and the conversion feature gives investors the opportunity to exchange the bond for 20 shares (underlying shares) of BIO's common stock ($1,000 ÷ $50). Because BIO's stock was selling at $37.50 at issuance, the stock price would need to appreciate by 33% (conversion premium) to reach the conversion price of $50. For example, if BIO's stock price were to appreciate to $60 per share, investors could convert each bond into 20 shares to realize the bond's conversion value of $1,200. On the other hand, if BIO's stock price failed to reach $50 within the five-year life of the bond, the investors would not convert, but rather would choose to receive the bond's $1,000 face value in cash.

Because the conversion feature represented a right, rather than an obligation, investors would postpone conversion as long as possible even if the bond was well "in the money." Suppose, for example, that after three years BIO's stock had risen to $60. Investors would then be holding a bond with a conversion value of $1,200; which is to say, if converted they would receive the 20 underlying shares worth $60 each. With two years left until maturity, however, investors would find that they could realize a higher value by selling the bond on the open market, rather than converting it. For example, the bond might be selling for $1,250; $50 higher than the conversion value. Such a premium over conversion value is typical, because the market recognizes that convertibles have unlimited upside potential, but protected downside. Unlike owning BIO stock directly, the price of the convertible bond cannot fall lower than its bond value—the value of the coupon payments and principal payment—but its conversion value could rise as high as the stock price will take it. Thus, as long as more upside potential is possible, the premium price will exist, and investors will have the incentive to sell their bonds, rather than convert them prior to maturity.[2]

Academics modeled the value of a convertible as the sum of the straight bond value plus the value of the conversion feature. This was equivalent to valuing a convert as a bond plus a call option or a warrant. Although MoGen did not have any warrants outstanding, there was an active market in MoGen options (**Exhibit 3**). Over the past five years, MoGen's stock price had experienced modest appreciation with considerable variation (**Exhibit 4**).

MoGen's Financial Strategy

As of December 31, 2005, the company had approximately $4 billion of long-term debt on the books (**Exhibit 5**). About $2 billion of the debt was in the form of straight debt with the remaining $1.8 billion as seven-year convertible notes. The combination of industry and company-specific risks had led MoGen to keep its long-term debt at or below 20% of total capitalization. There was a common belief that because of the industry risks, credit-rating agencies tended to penalize biotech firms by placing a "ceiling" on their credit ratings. MoGen's relatively low leverage, however, allowed it to command a Standard and Poor's (S&P) rating of A+, which was the highest rating within the industry. Based on discussions with S&P, MoGen management was confident that the company would be able to maintain its rating for the $5 billion new straight debt or convertible issuance. For the current market conditions, Merrill Lynch had estimated a cost to MoGen of 5.75%, if it issued straight five-year bonds. (See **Exhibit 6** for capital market data.)

MoGen's seven-year convertible notes had been issued in 2003 and carried a conversion price of $90.000 per share. Because the stock price was currently at $77.98 per share, the bondholders had not yet had the opportunity to exercise the conversion option.[3] Thus, the convertibles had proven to be a low-cost funding source for MoGen, as it was paying a coupon of only 1.125%. If the stock price continued to remain below the conversion price, the issue would not be converted and MoGen would simply retire the bonds in 2010 (or earlier, if called) at an all-in annual cost of 1.125%.[4]

---

[2]If BIO paid a dividend on its stock and if the dividend cash flow exceeded the coupon payment, investors might convert prior to maturity in order to capture the higher cash flow afforded by owning the stock.

[3]Like most convertibles, MoGen's seven-year notes were callable. This meant that MoGen had the right to buy back the bonds at a given call price at a 10% or 15% premium over face value. The call provision was often used as a means to force the bondholders to convert their bonds into stock. For example, assume a bond was callable at "110" (10% over face value) and the underlying stock price had appreciated so that the bond price had risen to a 20% premium over face value. If the company called the bond at 110, investors would choose to convert, to keep the 20% premium rather than accept the 10% call premium from the company.

[4]Interest expense for convertibles was tax deductible just like interest on straight bonds. Thus, the 1.125% coupon rate would represent an after-tax cost of about 0.78%, for a 40% tax rate. Convertible bondholders had no voting rights prior to converting the bonds into equity.

On the other hand, if the stock price appreciated substantially by 2010, then the bond-holders would convert and MoGen would need to issue 11.1 shares per bond out-standing or approximately 20 million new shares. Issuing the shares would not necessarily be a bad outcome, because it would amount to issuing shares at $90 rather than at $61, the stock price at the time of issuance.[5]

Since its initial public offering (IPO), MoGen had avoided issuing new equity, except for the small amounts of new shares issued each year as part of management's incentive compensation plan. The addition of these shares had been more than offset, however, by MoGen's share repurchase program, so that shares outstanding had fallen from 1,280 million in 2004, to 1,224 million in 2005. Repurchasing shares served two purposes for MoGen: (1) It had a favorable impact upon EPS by reducing the shares outstanding; and (2) It served as a method for distributing cash to shareholders. Although MoGen could pay dividends, management preferred the flexibility of repur-chasing shares. If MoGen were to institute a dividend, there was always the risk that the dividend might need to be decreased or eliminated during hard times which, when announced, would likely result in a significant drop of the stock price.

Merrill Lynch Equity-Linked Origination Team

The U.S. Equity-Linked Origination Team was part of Merrill Lynch's Equity Capital Markets Division that resided in the Investment Banking Division. The team was the product group that focused on convertible, corporate derivative, and special equity transaction origination for Merrill Lynch's U.S. corporate clients. As product experts, members worked with the industry bankers to educate clients on the benefits of uti-lizing equity-linked instruments. They also worked closely with derivatives and convertible traders, the equity and equity-linked sales teams, and institutional investors including hedge funds, to determine the market demand for various strategies and securities. Members had a high level of expertise in tax, accounting, and legal issues. The technical aspects of equity-linked securities were rigorous, requiring significant financial modeling skills, including the use of option pricing models, such as Black-Scholes and other proprietary versions of the model used to price convertible bonds. Within the equities division and investment banking, the team was considered one of the most technically capable and had proven to be among the most profitable busi-nesses at Merrill Lynch.

Pricing Decision

Dar Maanavi was excited by the prospect that Merrill Lynch would be the lead book runner of the largest convertible offering in history. At $5 billion, MoGen's issue would represent more than 12% of the total proceeds for convertible debt in the United States during 2005. Although the convert market was quite liquid and the Merrill Lynch team was confident that the issue would be well received, the unprecedented

---

[5]The impact of conversion was reported in fully *diluted* earnings per share that was computed using the po-tential shares outstanding, including shares issued in the event of a conversion.

size heightened the need to make it as marketable as possible. Maanavi knew that MoGen wanted a maturity of five years, but was less certain as to what he should propose regarding the conversion premium and coupon rate. These two terms needed to be satisfactory to MoGen's senior management team while at the same time being attractive to potential investors in the marketplace. **Exhibit 7** shows the terms of the offering that had already been determined.

Most convertibles carried conversion premiums in the range of 10% to 40%. The coupon rates for a convertible depended upon many factors, including the conversion premium, maturity, credit rating, and the market's perception of the volatility of the issuing company's stock. Issuing companies wanted low coupon rates and high conversion premiums, whereas investors wanted the opposite: high coupons and low conversion premiums. Companies liked a high conversion premium, because it effectively set the price at which its shares would be issued in the future. For example, if MoGen's bond was issued with a conversion price of $109, it would represent a 40% conversion premium over its current stock price of $77.98. Thus, if the issue were eventually converted, the number of MoGen shares issued would be 40% less than what MoGen would have issued at the current stock price. Of course, a high conversion premium also carried with it a lower probability that the stock would ever reach the conversion price. To compensate investors for this reduced upside potential, MoGen would need to offer a higher coupon rate. Thus, the challenge for Maanavi was to find the right combination of conversion premium and coupon rate that would be acceptable to MoGen management as well as desirable to investors.

There were two types of investor groups for convertibles: fundamental investors and hedge funds. Fundamental investors liked convertibles, because they viewed them as a safer form of equity investment. Hedge fund investors viewed convertibles as an opportunity to engage in an arbitrage trading strategy that typically involved holding long positions of the convertible and short positions of the common stock. Companies preferred to have fundamental investors, because they took a longer-term view of their investment than hedge funds. If the conversion premium was set above 40%, fundamental investors tended to lose interest because the convertible became a more speculative investment with less upside potential. Thus, if the conversion premium were set at 40% or higher, it could be necessary to offer an abnormally high coupon rate for a convertible. In either case, Maanavi thought a high conversion premium was not appropriate for such a large offering. It could work for a smaller, more volatile stock, but not for MoGen and not for a $5 billion offering.

Early in his conversations with MoGen, Maanavi had discussed the accounting treatment required for convertibles. Recently, most convertibles were being structured to use the "treasury stock method," which was desirable because it reduced the impact upon the reported fully diluted EPS. To qualify for the treasury stock method the convertible needed to be structured as a net settled security. This meant that investors would always receive cash for the principal amount of $1,000 per bond, but could receive either cash or shares for the excess over $1,000 upon conversion. The alternative method of accounting was the if-converted method, which would require MoGen to compute fully diluted EPS, as if investors received shares for the full amount of the bond when they converted; which is to say the new shares equaled the principal amount divided by the conversion price per share. The treasury stock method, however, would allow MoGen to report far fewer fully diluted shares for EPS purposes because it only included shares representing the *excess* of the bond's conversion value over the principal amount. Because much of the issue's proceeds would be used to fund the stock repurchase program, MoGen's management felt that using the treasury stock method would be a better representation to the market of MoGen's likely EPS, and therefore agreed to structure the issue accordingly (see "conversion rights" in **Exhibit 7**).

In light of MoGen management's objectives, Maanavi decided to propose a conversion premium of 25%, which was equivalent to conversion price of $97.000.[6] MoGen management would appreciate that the conversion premium would appeal to a broad segment of the market, which was important for a $5 billion offering. On the other hand, Maanavi knew that management would be disappointed that the conversion premium was not higher. Management felt that the stock was selling at a depressed price and represented an excellent buy. In fact, part of the rationale for having the stock repurchase program was to take advantage of the stock price being low. Maanavi suspected that management would express concern that a 25% premium would be sending a bad signal to the market: a low conversion premium could be interpreted as management's lack of confidence in the upside potential of the stock. For a five-year issue, the stock would only need to rise by 5% per year to reach the conversion price by maturity. If management truly believed the stock had strong appreciation potential, then the conversion premium should be set much higher.

If Maanavi could convince MoGen to accept the 25% conversion premium, then choosing the coupon rate was the last piece of the pricing puzzle to solve. Because he was proposing a mid-range conversion premium, investors would be satisfied with a modest coupon. Based on MoGen's bond rating, the company would be able to issue straight five-year bonds with a 5.75% yield. Therefore, Maanavi knew that the convertible should carry a coupon rate noticeably lower than 5.75%. The challenge was to estimate the coupon rate that would result in the debt being issued at exactly the face value of $1,000 per bond.

---

[6] Although the conversion premium would be determined in advance of the issuance, the conversion price would be determined based on the stock price on the issuance day. For example, a 25% conversion premium would lead to a conversion price of $100, if MoGen's stock price were to rise to $80 on the date of issuance.

EXHIBIT 1 | Consolidated Income Statements
(in millions of dollars, except per share)

	2005	2004	2003
Total Revenues	**$12,430**	**$10,550**	**$8,356**
Operating expenses:			
Cost of sales	2,082	1,731	1,341
Research and development	2,314	2,028	1,655
Write-off of acquired research and development	0	554	0
Selling, general, and administrative	2,790	2,556	1,957
Amortization of acquired intangible assets	347	333	336
Other items, net	49	0	(24)
Total operating expenses	7,582	7,202	5,265
Operating Income	**4,848**	**3,348**	**3,091**
Interest expense, net	20	47	82
Income before income taxes	4,868	3,395	3,173
Provision for income taxes	1,194	1,032	914
Net income	**$3,674**	**$2,363**	**$2,259**
Earnings per share:			
Basic	$2.97	$1.86	$1.75
Diluted	$2.93	$1.81	$1.69
Shares used in calculation of earnings per share (millions):			
Basic	1,236	1,271	1,288
Diluted	1,258	1,320	1,346

EXHIBIT 2 | Consolidated Balance Sheets
(in millions of dollars)

	2005	2004	2003
Current Assets			
Cash and short-term investments	5,255	5,808	5,123
Receivables	1,769	1,461	1,008
Inventories	1,258	888	713
Other current assets	953	1,013	558
Total current assets	9,235	9,170	7,402
Long-Term Assets			
Net property, plant, and equipment	5,038	4,712	3,799
Intangible assets and goodwill	14,237	14,558	14,108
Other assets	787	781	804
Total Assets	29,297	29,221	26,113
Current Liabilities			
Current portion of long-term debt	–	1,173	–
Accounts payable	596	507	327
Other accrued liabilities	2,999	2,477	2,129
Total current liabilities	3,595	4,157	2,456
Long-Term Liabilities			
Long-term debt	3,957	3,937	3,080
Deferred taxes and other	1,294	1,422	1,188
Total liabilities	8,846	9,516	6,724
Shareholders' Equity			
Common capital ($0.0001 par value)	0.122	0.126	0.128
Capital surplus	23,561	22,078	19,995
Retained earnings	(3,110)	(2,373)	(606)
Total Shareholders' Equity	20,451	19,705	19,389
Total Liabilities and Shareholders' Equity	29,297	29,221	26,113
Common shares outstanding (millions)	1,224	1,260	1,284

EXHIBIT 3 | MoGen Option Data: January 10, 2006
(MoGen closing stock price = $77.98)

	Exercise Date	Days to Maturity	Exercise Price	Closing Price	Open Interest	Volume
Call	4/22/2006	102	$75	$6.60	3,677	52
Call	4/22/2006	102	$80	$3.85	6,444	98
Call	1/20/2007	375	$75	$10.70	6,974	143
Call	1/20/2007	375	$80	$7.75	9,790	3
Put	4/22/2006	102	$75	$2.70	9,529	10
Put	4/22/2006	102	$80	$5.00	8,512	5
Put	1/20/2007	375	$75	$4.65	5,175	10
Put	1/20/2007	375	$80	$6.90	4,380	0

EXHIBIT 4 | MoGen Stock Price for 2001 to 2005

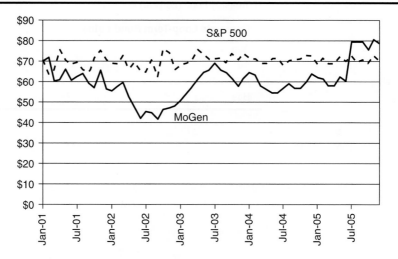

Performance Summary for 2001 to 2005

	MoGen	S&P 500
Five-year appreciation	12.2%	−8.6%
Annual appreciation (average)	2.4%	−1.7%
Annualized volatility	27.0%	14.9%

EXHIBIT 5 | Long-Term Debt as of December 31, 2005 (in millions of dollars)

1.125% convertible notes due in 2010	$1,759
4.85% notes due 2014	1,000
4.00% notes due 2009	998
6.5% debt securities due 2007	100
8.1% notes due 2097	100
Total borrowings	$3,957

EXHIBIT 6 | Capital Market Data for January 2006

U.S. Government Yields

Treasury bill (1-year)	4.45%
Treasury note (5-year)	4.46%
Treasury bond (20-year)	4.65%

Corporate Long-Term Bond Yields

Aaa	5.29%
Aa	5.45%
A	5.79%
Baa	6.24%

EXHIBIT 7 | Selected Terms of Convertible Senior Notes

Notes offered	$5,000,000,000 principal amount of Convertible Senior Notes due February 1, 2011.
Interest & payment dates	The annual interest rate of _____ would be payable semiannually in arrears in cash on January 1 and July 1 of each year, beginning July 1, 2006.
Conversion rights	Holders will be able to convert their notes prior to the close of business on the business day before the stated maturity date based on the applicable conversion rate.
	The conversion rate will be ____ shares of common stock per $1,000 principal amount. This is equivalent to a conversion price of ____ per share of common stock.
	Upon conversion, a holder will receive an amount in cash equal to the lesser of (i) the principal amount of the note, and (ii) the conversion value. If the conversion value exceeds the principal amount of the note on the conversion date, MoGen will deliver cash or common stock or a combination of cash and common stock for the conversion value in excess of $1,000.
Ranking	The notes will rank equal in right of payment to all of MoGen's existing and future unsecured indebtedness and senior in right to payment to all of MoGen's existing and future subordinated indebtedness.
Use of proceeds	We estimate that the net proceeds from this offering will be approximately $4.9 billion after deducting estimated discounts, commissions, and expenses. We intend to use the net proceeds for our share repurchase program as well as for working capital and general corporate purposes.

## PART 8

Valuing the Enterprise: Acquisitions and Buyouts

Methods of Valution for Mergers and Acquisitions

This note addresses the methods used to value companies in a merger and acquisitions (M&A) setting. It provides a detailed description of the discounted-cash-flow (DCF) approach and reviews other methods of valuation, such as market multiples of peer firms, book value, liquidation value, replacement cost, market value, and comparable transaction multiples.

Discounted-Cash-Flow Method

Overview

The DCF approach in an M&A setting attempts to determine the *enterprise value* or value of the company, by computing the present value of cash flows over the life of the company.[1] Because a corporation is assumed to have infinite life, the analysis is broken into two parts: a forecast period and a terminal value. In the *forecast period*, explicit forecasts of free cash flow that incorporate the economic costs and benefits of the transaction must be developed. Ideally, the forecast period should comprise the interval over which the firm is in a transitional state, as when enjoying a temporary competitive advantage (i.e., the circumstances where expected returns exceed required returns). In most circumstances, a forecast period of five or ten years is used.

The *terminal value* of the company, derived from free cash flows occurring after the forecast period, is estimated in the last year of the forecast period and capitalizes

---

[1]This note focuses on valuing the company as a whole (i.e., the enterprise). An estimate of equity value can be derived under this approach by subtracting interest-bearing debt from enterprise value. An alternative method not pursued here values the equity using residual cash flows, which are computed as net of interest payments and debt repayments plus debt issuances. Residual cash flows must be discounted at the cost of equity.

This note was prepared by Susan Chaplinsky, Professor of Business Administration, and Michael J. Schill, Associate Professor of Business Administration, with the assistance of Paul Doherty (MBA '99). Portions of this note draw on an earlier note, "Note on Valuation Analysis for Mergers and Acquisitions" (UVA-F-0557).

the present value of all future cash flows beyond the forecast period. To estimate the terminal value, cash flows are projected under a steady-state assumption that the firm enjoys no opportunities for abnormal growth or that expected returns equal required returns following the forecast period. Once a schedule of free cash flows is developed for the enterprise, the weighted average cost of capital (WACC) is used to discount them to determine the present value. The sum of the present values of the forecast period and the terminal value cash flows provides an estimate of company or enterprise value.

Review of DCF basics

Let us briefly review the construction of free cash flows, terminal value, and the WACC. It is important to realize that these fundamental concepts work equally well when valuing an investment project as they do in an M&A setting.

Free cash flows: The free cash flows in an M&A analysis should be the expected incremental operating cash flows attributable to the acquisition, before consideration of financing charges (i.e., prefinancing cash flows). Free cash flow equals the sum of net operating profits after taxes (NOPAT), plus depreciation and noncash charges, less capital investment and less investment in working capital. NOPAT captures the earnings after taxes that are available to all providers of capital. That is, NOPAT has no deductions for financing costs. Moreover, because the tax deductibility of interest payments is accounted for in the WACC, such financing tax effects are also excluded from the free cash flow, which is expressed in **Equation 1**:

$$FCF = NOPAT + Depreciation - CAPEX - \Delta NWC \qquad (1)$$

where:

- *NOPAT* is equal to *EBIT* $(1-t)$ where t is the appropriate marginal (not average) cash tax rate, which should be inclusive of federal, state, local, and foreign jurisdictional taxes.
- *Depreciation* is noncash operating charges including depreciation, depletion, and amortization recognized for tax purposes.
- *CAPEX* is capital expenditures for fixed assets.
- ΔNWC is the increase in net working capital defined as current assets less the non-interest-bearing current liabilities.[2]

The cash-flow forecast should be grounded in a thorough industry and company forecast. Care should be taken to ensure that the forecast reflects consistency with firm strategy as well as with macroeconomic and industry trends and competitive pressure.

---

[2]The net working capital should include the expected cash, receivables, inventory, and payables levels required for the operation of the business. If the firm currently has excess cash (more than is needed to sustain operations), for example, the cash forecast should be reduced to the level of cash required for operations. Excess cash should be valued separately by adding it to the enterprise value.

The forecast period is normally the years during which the analyst estimates free cash flows that are consistent with creating value. A convenient way to think about value creation is whenever the return on net assets (RONA)[3] exceeds the WACC.[4] RONA can be divided into an income statement component and a balance sheet component:

$$RONA = NOPAT/Net\ Assets$$

$$= NOPAT/Sales \times Sales/Net\ Assets$$

In this context, value is created whenever earnings power increases (NOPAT/Sales) or when asset efficiency is improved (Sales/Net Assets). In other words, analysts are assuming value creation whenever they allow the profit margin to improve on the income statement and whenever they allow sales to improve relative to the level of assets on the balance sheet.

Terminal value: A terminal value in the final year of the forecast period is added to reflect the present value of all cash flows occurring thereafter. Because it capitalizes all future cash flows beyond the final year, the terminal value can be a large component of the value of a company, and therefore deserves careful attention. This can be of particular importance when cash flows over the forecast period are close to zero (or even negative) as the result of aggressive investment for growth.

A standard estimator of the terminal value (TV) in the final year of the cash-flow forecast is the constant growth valuation formula (**Equation 2**).

$$Terminal\ Value = FCF^{Steady\ State} \div (WACC - g) \qquad (2)$$

where:

- $FCF^{Steady\ State}$ is the steady-state expected free cash flow for the
- *WACC* is the weighted average cost of capital
- *g* is the expected steady-state growth rate of $FCF^{Steady\ State}$ in perpetuity

The free cash-flow value used in the constant growth valuation formula should reflect the steady-state cash flow for the year after the forecast period. The assumption of the formula is that in steady state, this cash flow will grow in perpetuity at the steady-state growth rate. A convenient approach is to assume that RONA remains constant in perpetuity; that is, both profit margin and asset turnover remain constant in perpetuity. Under this assumption, the analyst grows all financial statement line items (i.e., revenue, costs, assets) at the expected steady-state growth rate. In perpetuity, this assumption makes logical sense in that if a firm is truly in steady state, the financial statements should be growing, by definition, at the same rate.

---

[3]In this context, we define net assets as total assets less non-interest-bearing current liabilities or equivalently as net working capital plus net fixed assets. A similar relationship can be expressed using return on capital (ROC). Because the uses of capital (working capital and fixed assets) equal the sources of capital (debt and equity), it follows that RONA (return on net assets) equals roc and therefore, ROC = NOPAT/(Debt + Equity).

[4]WACC is discussed later in this note as the appropriate discount rate used for the free cash flows.

Discount rate: The discount rate should reflect the weighted average of investors' opportunity cost (WACC) on comparable investments. The WACC matches the business risk, expected inflation, and currency of the cash flows to be discounted. In order to avoid penalizing the investment opportunity, the WACC also must incorporate the appropriate target weights of financing going forward. Recall that the appropriate rate is a blend of the required rates of return on debt and equity, weighted by the proportion of the firm's market value they make up (**Equation 3**).

$$WACC = W_d\, k_d\, (1-\,t)\, +\, W_e\, k_e \qquad (3)$$

where:

- k_d is the required yield on new debt: It is yield to maturity.
- k_e is the cost of equity capital.
- W_d, W_e are target percentages of debt and equity (using market values of debt and equity).[5]
- t is the marginal tax rate.

The costs of debt and equity should be going-forward market rates of return. For debt securities, this is often the yield to maturity that would be demanded on new instruments of the same credit rating and maturity. The cost of equity can be obtained from the Capital Asset Pricing Model (CAPM) (**Equation 4**).

$$k_e = R_f + \beta\ (R_m - R_f) \qquad (4)$$

where:

- R_f is the expected return on risk-free securities over a time horizon consistent with the investment horizon. Most firm valuations are best served by using a long maturity government bond yield.

- $R_m - R_f$ is the expected market risk premium. This value is commonly estimated as the average historical difference between the returns on common stocks and long-term government bonds. For example, Ibbotson Associates estimated the geometric mean return between 1926 and 2007 for large capitalization U.S. equities between 1926 and 2007 was 10.4%. The geometric mean return on long-term government bonds was 5.5%. The difference between the two implies a historical market-risk premium of about 5.0%. In practice one observes estimates of the market risk premium that commonly range from 5% to 8%.

- β or beta is a measure of the systematic risk of a firm's common stock. The beta of common stock includes compensation for business and financial risk.

---

[5]Debt for purposes of the WACC should include all permanent, interest-bearing debt. If the market value of debt is not available, the book value of debt is often assumed as a reasonable proxy. The shorter the maturity of the debt and the closer the correspondence between the coupon rate and required return on the debt, the more accurate the approximation.

The M&A Setting

No doubt, many of these concepts look familiar. Now we must consider how they are altered by the evaluation of a company in an M&A setting. First, we should recognize that there are two parties (sometimes more) in the transaction: an acquirer (buyer or bidder) and a target firm (seller or acquired). Suppose a bidder is considering the potential purchase of a target firm and we must assess whether the target would be a good investment. Some important questions arise in applying our fundamental concepts:

1. *What are the potential sources of value from the combination? Does the acquirer have particular skills or capabilities that can be used to enhance the value of the target firm? Does the target have critical technology or other strengths that can bring value to the acquirer?*

   Potential sources of gain or cost savings achieved through the combination are called synergies. Baseline cash-flow projections for the target firm may or may not include synergies or cost savings gained from merging the operations of the target into those of the acquirer. If the base-case cash flows do not include any of the economic benefits an acquirer might bring to a target, they are referred to as *stand-alone* cash flows. Examining the value of a target on a stand-alone basis can be valuable for several reasons. First, it can provide a view of what the target firm is capable of achieving on its own. This may help establish a floor with respect to value for negotiating purposes. Second, construction of a stand-alone DCF valuation can be compared with the target's current market value. This can be useful in assessing whether the target is under- or overvalued in the marketplace. Given the general efficiency of markets, however, it is unlikely that a target will be significantly over- or undervalued relative to the market. Hence, a stand-alone DCF valuation allows analysts to calibrate model assumptions to those of investors. By testing key assumptions relative to this important benchmark, analysts can gain confidence that the model provides a reasonable guide to investors' perception of the situation.

2. *What is the proper discount rate to use?*

   The discount rate used to value the cash flows of the target should compensate the investor/acquiring firm for the risk of the cash flows. Commonly, the cost of capital of the target firm provides a suitable discount rate for the stand-alone and merger cash flows. The cost of capital of the target firm is generally more appropriate as a discount rate than the cost of capital of the acquiring firm because the target cost of capital generally better captures the risk premium associated with bearing the risk of the target cash flows than does the cost of capital of the acquiring firm. If the target and acquirer are in the same industry, they likely have similar business risk. Because in principle the business risk is similar for the target and the acquirer, either one's WACC may be justifiably used. The use of the target's cost of capital also assumes that the target firm is financed with the optimal proportions of debt and equity and that these proportions will continue after the merger.

Additional information on the appropriate discount rate can be obtained by computing the WACCs of firms in the target's industry. These estimates can be summarized by taking the average or median WACC. By using the betas and financial structures of firms engaged in this line of business, a reliable estimate of the business risk and optimal financing can be established going forward.

Sometimes an acquirer may intend to increase or decrease the debt level of the target significantly after the merger—perhaps because it believes the target's current financing mix is not optimal. The WACC still must reflect the business risk of the target. A proxy for this can be obtained from the unlevered beta of the target firm's equity or an average unlevered beta for firms with similar business risk. The target's premerger unlevered beta must then be relevered to reflect the acquirer's intended postmerger capital structure.

To unlever a firm beta, one uses the prevailing tax rate (T) and the predeal debt-to-equity ratio (D/E) of the firm associated with the beta estimate (β_L) to solve **Equation 5**:

$$\beta_u = \beta_L / [1 + (1 - T)\, D/E] \tag{5}$$

Next, one uses the unlevered beta estimate (β_u) or average unlevered beta estimate (if using multiple firms to estimate the unlevered beta) to relever the beta to the new intended debt-to-equity ratio (D/E^*) (**Equation 6**):

$$\beta'_L = \beta_u [1 + (1 - T)\, D/E^*] \tag{6}$$

The result is a relevered beta estimate (β'_L) that captures the business risk and the financial risk of the target cash flows.

The circumstances of each transaction will dictate which of these approaches is most reasonable. Of course, if the target's business risk somehow changes because of the merger, some adjustments must be made to all of these approaches on a judgment basis. The key concept is to find the discount rate that best reflects the business and financial risks of the target's cash flows.

3. *After determining the enterprise value, how is the value of the equity computed?*

    This is a straightforward calculation that relies upon the definition of enterprise value as the value of cash flows available to *all* providers of capital. Because debt and equity are the sources of capital, it follows that enterprise value (V) equals the sum of debt (D) and equity (E) values (**Equation 7**):

$$V = D + E \tag{7}$$

Therefore, the value of equity is simply enterprise value less the value of existing debt (**Equation 8**):

$$E = V - D \tag{8}$$

where debt is the market value of all interest-bearing debt outstanding at the time of the acquisition. For publicly traded targets, the value of the share price can be computed by simply dividing the equity value by the numbers of shares of stock outstanding.

4. *How does one incorporate the value of synergies in a DCF analysis?*

Operating synergies are reflected in enterprise value by altering the stand-alone cash flows to incorporate the benefits and costs of the combination. Free cash flows that include the value an acquirer and target can achieve through combination and are referred to as combined or *merger* cash flows.

If the acquirer plans to run the acquired company as a stand-alone entity, as in the case of Berkshire Hathaway purchasing a company unrelated to its existing holdings (e.g., Dairy Queen), there may be little difference between the stand-alone and merger cash flows. In many strategic acquisitions, however, such as the Pfizer/Wyeth and InBev/Fujian Sedrin Brewery mergers, there can be sizeable differences.

How the value of these synergies is split among the parties through the determination of the final bid price or premium paid is a major issue for negotiation.[6] If the bidder pays a premium equal to the value of the synergies, all the benefits will accrue to target shareholders, and the merger will be a zero net-present-value investment for the shareholders of the acquirer.

Example of the DCF Method

Suppose Company A has learned that Company B (a firm in a different industry but in a business that is strategically attractive to Company A) has retained an investment bank to auction the company and all of its assets. In considering how much to bid for Company B, Company A starts with the cash-flow forecast of the stand-alone business drawn up by Company B's investment bankers shown in **Table 1**. The discount rate used to value the cash flows is Company B's WACC of 10.9%. The inputs to WACC, with a market risk premium of 6%, are shown in **Table 2**.

On a stand-alone basis, the analysis in **Table 1** suggests that Company B's enterprise value is $9.4 million.

Now suppose Company A believes that it can make Company B's operations more efficient and improve its marketing and distribution capabilities. In **Table 3**, we incorporate these effects into the cash-flow model, thereby estimating a higher range of values that Company A can bid and still realize a positive net present value (NPV) for its shareholders. In the merger cash-flow model of the two firms in **Table 3**, Company B has added two percentage points of revenue growth, subtracted two percentage points from the COGS[7]/Sales ratio, and subtracted one percentage point from SG&A/Sales ratio relative to the stand-alone model. We assume that all of the merger synergies will be realized immediately and therefore should fall well within the five-year forecast period. The inputs to target and acquirer WACCs are summarized in **Table 3**.

Because Company A and Company B are in different industries, it is not appropriate to use Company A's WACC of 10.6% in discounting the expected cash flows. Despite the fact that after the merger, Company B will become part of Company A,

---

[6] The premium paid is usually measured as: (Per-Share Bid Price—Market Price for Target Shares Before Merger) ÷ Market Price for Target Shares Before Merger.

[7] Cost of Goods Sold.

TABLE 1 | Valuation of Company B as a stand-alone unit. (assume that Company A will allow Company B to run as a stand-alone unit with no synergies)

Revenue growth	6.0%	Steady state growth	5.9%
COGS	55%	WACC	10.9%
SG&A	20%	Tax rate	39%
Net working capital (NWC)	22%		

	Year 0	Year 1	Year 2	Year 3	Year 4	Year 5	Year 6 Steady State
Revenues ($ thousands)	9,750	10,000	10,600	1,236	11,910	12,625	13,370
COGS		5,500	5,830	6,180	6,551	6,944	
Gross profit		4,500	4,770	5,056	5,360	5,681	
SG&A		2,000	2,120	2,247	2,382	2,525	
Depreciation		1,000	1,000	1,000	1,000	1,000	
EBIT		1,500	1,650	1,809	1,978	2,156	
Less taxes		(585)	(644)	(706)	(771)	(841)	
NOPAT		915	1,007	1,103	1,207	1,315	1,393
Add: depreciation		1,000	1,000	1,000	1,000	1,000 ⎫	664
Less: capital expenditures		(1,250)	(1,250)	(1,250)	(1,250)	(1,250) ⎬	
Less: Increase in NWC		(55)	(132)	(140)	(148)	(157)	(164)
= Free cash flow		610	625	713	809	908	565
Terminal value						11,305	
Free Cash Flows + Terminal Value		610	625	713	809	12,213	
Enterprise Value PV$_{10.9\%}$ (FCF) =	9,396						
NWC (22% Sales)	2,145	2,200	2,332	2,472	2,620	2,777	2,941
NPPE (+ CAPEX − Depr. each year)	10,000	10,250	10,500	10,750	11,000	11,250	11,914
Operating margin [NOPAT/Sales]		9.2%	9.5%	9.8%	10.1%	10.4%	10.4%
PPE turnover [Sales/NPPE]		0.98	1.01	1.05	1.08	1.12	1.12
RONA [NOPAT/(NWC+NPPE)]		7.3%	7.8%	8.3%	8.9%	9.4%	9.4%

Year 6 Steady-State Calculations:
Sales = Year 5 Sales × (1+ Steady-State Growth) = 12,625 × 1.059 = 13,370
NOPAT = Year 5 NOPAT × (1+ Steady-State Growth) = 1,315 × 1.059 = 1,393
NWC = Year 5 NWC × (1 + Steady-State Growth) = 2,777 × 1.059 = 2,941
NPPE = Year 5 NPPE × (1+ Steady-State Growth) = 11,250 × 1.059 = 11,914
Increase in NPPE = Capital Expenditures less Depreciation = 11,250 − 11,914 = −664
Year 5 Terminal Value = Steady-State FCF ÷ (WACC − Steady-State Growth) = 565 (0.109 − 0.059) = 11,305

we do not use Company A's WACC because it does not reflect the risk associated with the merger cash flows. In this case, one is better advised to focus on "where the money is going, rather than where the money comes from" in determining the risk associated with the transaction. In other words, the analyst should focus on the target's risk and financing (not the buyer's risk and financing) in determining the appropriate

TABLE 2 | Inputs to WACC.

	Bidder A-Co.	Target B-Co.
Bond rating	A	BBB
Yield to maturity of bonds—k_d	7.2%	7.42%
Tax rate	39.0%	39.0%
After-tax cost of debt—$k_d(1 - t)$	4.39%	4.53%
Beta	1.05	1.20
Cost of equity—k_e	12.18%	13.08%
Debt as % of capital—W_d	20.0%	25.0%
Equity as % of capital—W_e	80.0%	75.0%
10-year treasury bond yield	5.88%	5.88%
Market risk premium	6.0%	6.0%
WACC	10.6%	10.9%

discount rate. The discount rate should reflect the expected risk of the cash flows being priced and not necessarily the source of the capital.

Notice that the value with synergies, $15.1 million, exceeds the value as a stand-alone entity by $5.7 million. In devising its bidding strategy, Company A would not want to offer the full $15.1 million and concede all the value of the synergies to Company B. At this price, the NPV of the acquisition to Company A is zero. The existence of synergies, however, allows Company A leeway to increase its bid above $9.4 million and enhance its chances of winning the auction.

Considerations for Terminal Value Estimation

In the valuation of both the stand-alone and merger cash flows, the terminal value contributes the bulk of the total cash-flow value (if the terminal value is eliminated, the enterprise value drops by about 75%). This relationship between terminal value and enterprise value is typical of firm valuation because of the ongoing nature of the life of a business. Because of the importance of the terminal value in firm valuation, the assumptions that define the terminal value deserve particular attention.

In the stand-alone Company B valuation in **Table 1**, we estimated the terminal value using the constant-growth valuation model. This formula assumes that the business has reached some level of steady-state growth such that the free cash flows can be modeled to infinity with the simple assumption of a constant growth rate. Because of this assumption, it is important that the firm's forecast period be extended until such a steady state is truly expected.[8] The terminal-value growth rate used in the valuation is 5.9%. In this

---

[8]The steady state may only be accurate in terms of expectations. The model recognizes that the expected terminal value has risk. Businesses may never actually achieve steady state due to technology innovations, business cycles, and changing corporate strategy. The understanding that the firm may not actually achieve a steady state does not preclude the analyst from anticipating a steady-state point as the best guess of the state of the business at some point in the future.

TABLE 3 | Valuation of Company B with synergies.
(assume that Company B merges with Company A and realizes operational synergies)

Revenue growth	8.0%	Steady-state growth	5.9%
COGS	53%	WACC	10.9%
SG&A	19%	Tax rate	39%
Net working capital (NWC)	22%		

	Year 0	Year 1	Year 2	Year 3	Year 4	Year 5	Year 6 Steady State
Revenues ($ thousands)	9,750	10,000	10,800	11,664	12,597	13,605	14,408
COGS		5,300	5,724	6,182	6,676	7,211	
Gross profit		4,700	5,076	5,482	5,921	6,394	
SG&A		1,900	2,052	2,216	2,393	2,585	
Depreciation		1,000	1,000	1,000	1,000	1,000	
EBIT		1,800	2,024	2,266	2,527	2,809	
Less Taxes		(702)	(789)	(884)	(986)	(1,096)	
NOPAT		1,098	1,235	1,382	1,542	1,714	1,815
Add: Depreciation		1,000	1,000	1,000	1,000	1,000 ⎫	
Less: Capital expenditures		(1,250)	(1,250)	(1,250)	(1,250)	(1,250) ⎬	(664)
Less: Increase in NWC		(55)	(176)	(190)	(205)	(222) ⎭	(177)
= Free cash flow		793	809	942	1,086	1,242	974
Terminal value						19,490	
Free cash flows + terminal value		793	809	942	1,086	20,732	
Enterprise Value PV$_{10.9\%}$ (FCF) =	15,140						
NWC (22% sales)	2,145	2,200	2,376	2,566	2,771	2,993	3,170
NPPE (+ CAPEX − Depr. each year)	10,000	10,250	10,500	10,750	11,000	11,250	11,914
Operating margin [NOPAT/sales]		11.0%	11.4%	11.9%	12.2%	12.6%	12.6%
PPE turnover [sales/NPPE]		0.98	1.03	1.09	1.15	1.21	1.21
RONA [NOPAT/(NWC+NPPE)]		8.8%	9.6%	10.4%	11.2%	12.0%	12.0%

Year 6 Steady-State Calculations:
Sales = Year 5 Sales × (1 + Steady-State Growth) = 13,605 × 1.059 = 14,408
NOPAT = Year 5 NOPAT × (1 + Steady-State Growth) = 1,714 × 1.059 = 1,815
NWC = Year 5 NWC × (1 + Steady-State Growth) = 2,993 × 1.059 = 3,170
NPPE = Year 5 NPPE × (1 + Steady-State Growth) = 11,250 × 1.059 = 11,914
Increase in NPPE = Capital Expenditures less Depreciation = 11,250 − 11,914 = −664
Year 5 Terminal Value = Steady-State FCF ÷ (WACC − Steady-State Growth) = 974 (0.109 − 0.059) = 19,490

model the analyst assumes that the steady-state growth rate can be approximated by the long-term risk-free rate (i.e., the long-term Treasury bond yield). Using the risk-free rate to proxy for the steady-state growth rate is equivalent to assuming that the expected long-term cash flows of the business grow with the overall economy (i.e., nominal expected growth rate of GDP). Nominal economic growth contains a real growth component plus an inflation rate component, which are also reflected in long-term government bond yields.

For example, the Treasury bond yield can be decomposed into a real rate of return (typically between 2% and 3%) and expected long-term inflation. Because the Treasury yield for our example is 5.9%, the implied inflation is between 3.9% and 2.9%. Over the long term, companies should experience the same real growth and inflationary growth as the economy on average, which justifies using the risk-free rate as a reasonable proxy for the expected long-term growth of the economy.

Another important assumption is estimating steady-state free cash flow that properly incorporates the investment required to sustain the steady-state growth expectation. The steady-state free-cash-flow estimate used in the merger valuation in **Table 3** is \$974,000. To obtain the steady-state cash flow, we start by estimating sales in **Equation 9**:[9]

$$Sales^{Steady\ State} = Sales^{Year\ 5} \times (1 + g) = 13,605 \times 1.059 = 14,408 \qquad (9)$$

Steady state demands that all the financial statement items grow with sales at the same steady-state rate of 5.9%. This assumption is reasonable because in steady state, the enterprise should be growing at a constant rate. If the financial statements did not grow at the same rate, the implied financial ratios (e.g., operating margins or RONA) would eventually widely deviate from reasonable industry norms.

The steady-state cash flow can be constructed by simply growing all relevant line items at the steady-state growth rate as summarized in **Tables 1** and **3.** To estimate free cash flow we need to estimate the steady-state values for NOPAT, net working capital, and net property, plant and equipment. By simply multiplying the Year 5 value for each line item by the steady-state growth factor of 1.059, we obtain the steady-state Year 6 values.[10] Therefore, to estimate the steady-state change in NWC we use the difference in the values for the last two years (**Equation 10**):

$$\Delta NWC^{Steady\ State} = NWC^{Year\ 5} - NWC^{Steady\ State} = 2,993 - 3,170 = -177 \quad (10)$$

This leaves depreciation and capital expenditure as the last two components of cash flow. These can be more easily handled together by looking at the relation between sales and net property, plant, and equipment where NPPE is the accumulation of capital expenditures less depreciation. **Table 3** shows that in the steady-state year NPPE has increased to 11,914. The difference of NPPE gives us the net of capital expenditures and depreciation for the steady state (**Equation 11**):

$$\Delta NPPE^{Steady\ State} = NPPE^{1995} - NPPE^{Steady\ State} = 11,250 - 11,914 = -664 \quad (11)$$

Summing the components gives us the steady-state free cash flow (**Equation 12**):

$$
\begin{aligned}
FCF^{Steady\ State} &= NOPAT^{Steady\ State} + \Delta NPPE^{Steady\ State} + \Delta NWC^{Steady\ State} \quad (12)\\
&= \quad 1,815 \qquad\qquad -664 \qquad\qquad\quad -176\\
&= 974^{11}
\end{aligned}
$$

---

[9] Note that **Tables 1** and **3** summarize the steady-state calculations.

[10] Alternatively, we can compute NOPAT using Year 5's NOPAT/Sales ratio of 12.6% or net working capital using the same 22% of sales relation used throughout the analysis. As long as the ratios are constant and linked to the steady-state sales value, the figures will capture the same-steady state assumptions.

[11] Note that we can demonstrate that the cash-flow estimation process is consistent with the steady-state growth if we were to do these same calculations, using the same growth rate for one more year, the resulting FCF would be 5.9% higher (i.e., $974 \times 1.059 = 1,031$).

Therefore, by maintaining steady-state growth across the firm, we have estimated the numerator of the terminal value formula that gives us the value of all future cash flows beyond Year 5 (**Equation 13**):

$$Terminal\ Value^{Year\ 5} = FCF^{Steady\ State} \div (WACC - g)$$
$$= 974 \div (0.109 - 0.059) = 19,490 \qquad (13)$$

The expression used to estimate steady-state free cash flow can be used for alternative assumptions regarding expected growth. For example, one might also assume that the firm does not continue to build new capacity but that merger cash flows grow only with expected inflation (e.g., 3.9%). With this scenario, the calculations are similar but the growth rate is replaced with the expected inflation. Even if capacity is not expanded, investment must keep up with growth in profits to maintain a constant expected rate of operating returns.

Finally, it is important to acknowledge that the terminal value estimate embeds assumptions about the long-term profitability of the target firm. In the example in **Table 3**, the implied steady-state RONA can be calculated by dividing the steady-state NOPAT by the steady-state net assets (NWC + NPPE). In this case, the return on net assets is equal to 12.0% [1,815 ÷ (3,170 + 11,914)]. Because in steady state the profits and the assets will grow at the same rate, this ratio is estimated to remain in perpetuity. The discount rate of 10.9% maintains a benchmark for the steady-state RONA. Because of the threat of competitive pressure, it is difficult to justify in most cases a firm valuation where the steady-state RONA is substantially higher than the WACC. Alternatively, if the steady-state RONA is lower than the WACC, one should question the justification for maintaining the business in steady state if the assets are not earning the cost of capital.

Market Multiples as Alternative Estimators of Terminal Value

Given the importance attached to terminal value, analysts are wise to use several approaches when estimating it. A common approach is to estimate terminal value using market multiples derived from information based on publicly traded companies similar to the target company (in our example, Company B). The logic behind a market multiple is to see how the market is currently valuing an entity based on certain benchmarks related to value rather than attempting to determine an entity's inherent value. The benchmark used as the basis of valuation should be something that is commonly valued by the market and highly correlated with market value. For example, in the real estate market, dwellings are frequently priced based on the prevailing price per square foot of comparable properties. The assumption made is that the size of the house is correlated with its market value. If comparable houses are selling at $100 per square foot, the market value for a 2,000-square-foot house is estimated to be worth $200,000. For firm valuation, current or expected profits are frequently used as the basis for relative market multiple approaches.

Suppose, as shown in **Table 4**, that there are three publicly traded businesses that are in the same industry as Company B: Company C, Company D, and Company E. The respective financial and market data that apply to these companies are shown in

TABLE 4 | Comparable companies to target company.

	Company C	Company D	Company E
Industry	Industry Z	Industry Z	Industry Z
Stage of growth	Mature	Mature	High Growth
EBIT ($ in thousands)	$ 3,150	$ 2,400	$ 750
Net earnings	1,500	1,500	150
Equity value	14,000	11,400	3,000
Debt value	2,800	3,000	3,500
Enterprise value	$16,800	$14,400	$6,500
Enterprise value/EBIT	5.3	6.0	8.7
Equity value/net earnings	9.3	7.6	20.0

Table 4. The enterprise value for each comparable firm is estimated as the current share price multiplied by the number of shares outstanding (equity value) plus the book value of debt. Taking a ratio of the enterprise value divided by the operating profit (EBIT), we obtain an EBIT multiple. In the case of Company C, the EBIT multiple is 5.3 times, meaning that for every $1 in current operating profit generated by Company C, investors are willing to pay $5.3 of firm value. If Company C is similar today to the expected steady state of Company B in Year 5, the 5.3-times-EBIT multiple could be used to estimate the expected value of Company B at the end of Year 5, the terminal value.[12]

To reduce the effect of outliers on the EBIT multiple estimate, we can use the information provided from a sample of comparable multiples. In sampling additional comparables, we are best served by selecting multiples from only those firms that are comparable to the business of interest on the basis of business risk, economic outlook, profitability, and growth expectations. We note that Company E's EBIT multiple of 8.7 times is substantially higher than the others in **Table 4**. Why should investors be willing to pay so much more for a dollar of Company E's operating profit than for a dollar of Company C's operating profit? We know that Company E is in a higher growth stage than Company C and Company D. If Company E profits are expected to grow at a higher rate, the valuation or capitalization of these profits will occur at a higher level or multiple. Investors anticipate higher future profits for Company E and consequently bid up the value of the respective capital.[13]

Because of Company E's abnormally strong expected growth, we decide that Company E is not a good proxy for the way we expect Company B to be in Year 5.

---

[12] We assume in this example that current multiples are the best proxies for future multiples. If there is some reason to believe that the current multiple is a poor or biased estimate of the future, the market multiples must be adjusted accordingly. For example, if the current profits are extraordinarily small or large, a multiple based on such a distorted value will produce an artificial estimate of the expected future value. A more appropriate multiple will use a nondistorted or "normalized" profit measure.

[13]See **Appendix** for an example of the relationship between market multiples and the constant-cash-flow growth model.

We choose, consequently, to not use the 8.7 times EBIT multiple in estimating our terminal value estimate. We conclude instead that investors are more likely to value Company B's operating profits at approximately 5.7 times (the average of 5.3 and 6.0 times). The logic is that if investors are willing to pay 5.7 times EBIT today for operating profit of firms similar to what we expect Company B to be in Year 5, this valuation multiple will be appropriate in the future. To estimate Company B's terminal value based on our average EBIT multiple, we multiply the Year 5 stand-alone EBIT of $2.156 million by the average comparable multiple of 5.7 times. This process provides a multiple-based estimate of Company B's terminal value of $12.2 million. This estimate is somewhat above the constant-growth-based terminal value estimate of $11.3 million.

While the importance of terminal value motivates the use of several estimation methods, sometimes these methods yield widely varying values. The variation in estimated values should prompt questions on the appropriateness of the underlying assumptions of each approach. For example, the differences in terminal value estimates could be due to:

1. a forecast period that is too short to have resulted in steady-state performance;

2. the use of comparable multiples that fail to match the expected risk, expected growth, or macroeconomic conditions of the target company in the terminal year; or

3. an assumed constant growth rate that is lower or higher than that expected by the market.

The potential discrepancies motivate further investigation of the assumptions and information contained in the various approaches so that the analyst can "triangulate" to the most appropriate terminal-value estimate.

In identifying an appropriate valuation multiple, one must be careful to choose a multiple that is consistent with the underlying earnings stream of the entity one is valuing. For example, one commonly used multiple based on net earnings is called the price-earnings or P/E multiple. This multiple compares the value of the equity to the value of net income. In a valuation model based on free cash flow, it is typically inappropriate to use multiples based on net income because these value only the equity portion of the firm and assume a certain capital structure.[14] Other commonly used multiples that are appropriate for free-cash-flow valuation include EBITDA (earnings before interest, tax, depreciation, and amortization), free cash flow, and total capital multiples.

Although the market-multiple valuation approach provides a convenient, market-based approach for valuing businesses, there are a number of cautions worth noting:

1. Multiples can be deceptively simple. Multiples should provide an alternative way to triangulate toward an appropriate long-term growth rate and not a way to avoid thinking about the long-term economics of a business.

2. Market multiples are subject to distortions due to market misvaluation and accounting policy. Accounting numbers further down in the income statement

---

[14] Only in the relatively rare case of a company not using debt would the P/E ratio be an appropriate multiple.

(such as net earnings) are typically subject to greater distortion than items high on the income statement. Because market valuations tend to be affected by business cycles less than annual profit figures, multiples can exhibit some business-cycle effects. Moreover, business profits are negative, the multiples constructed from negative earnings are not meaningful.

3. Identifying closely comparable firms is challenging. Firms within the same industry may differ greatly in business risk, cost and revenue structure, and growth prospects.

4. Multiples can be computed with different timing conventions. Consider a firm with a December 31 fiscal year (FY) end that is being valued in January 2005. A trailing EBIT multiple for the firm would reflect the January 2005 firm value divided by the 2004 FY EBIT. In contrast, a current-year EBIT multiple (leading or forward EBIT multiple) is computed as the January 2005 firm value divided by the 2005 EBIT (expected end-of-year 2006 EBIT).[15] Because leading multiples are based on expected values, they tend to be less volatile than trailing multiples. Moreover, leading and trailing multiples will be systematically different for growing businesses.

Transaction Multiples for Comparable Deals

In an M&A setting, analysts look to comparable transactions as an additional benchmark against which to assess the target firm. The chief difference between transaction multiples and peer multiples is that the former reflects a "control premium," typically 30% to 50%, that is not present in the ordinary trading multiples. If one is examining the price paid for the target equity, transactions multiples might include the Per-Share Offer Price Target Book Value of Equity Per Share, or Per-Share Offer Price Target Earnings Per Share. If one is examining the total consideration paid in recent deals, one can use Enterprise Value EBIT. The more similarly situated the target and the more recent the deal, the better the comparison will be. Ideally, there must be several similar deals in the last year or two from which to calculate median and average transaction multiples. If there are, one can glean valuable information about how the market has valued assets of this type.

Analysts also look at premiums for comparable transactions by comparing the offer price to the target's price before the merger announcement at selected dates, such as 1 day or 30 days, before the announcement. A negotiator might point to premiums in previous deals for similarly situated sellers and demand that shareholders receive "what the market is paying." One must look closely, however, at the details of each transaction before agreeing with this premise. How much the target share price moves upon the announcement of a takeover depends on what the market had anticipated before the announcement. If the share price of the target had been driven up in the days or weeks before the announcement on rumors that a deal was forthcoming, the

---

[15] Profit figures used in multiples can also be computed by cumulating profits from the expected or most recent quarters.

control premium may appear low. To adjust for the "anticipation," one must examine the premium at some point before the market learns of (or begins to anticipate the announcement of) the deal. It could also be that the buyer and seller in previous deals are not in similar situations compared with the current deal. For example, some of the acquirers may have been financial buyers (leveraged buyout [LBO] or private equity firms) while others in the sample were strategic buyers (companies expanding in the same industry as the target.) Depending on the synergies involved, the premiums need not be the same for strategic and financial buyers.

Other Valuation Methods

Although we have focused on the DCF method, other methods provide useful complementary information in assessing the value of a target. Here, we briefly review some of the most popularly used techniques.

Book Value

Book-value valuation may be appropriate for firms with commodity-type assets valued at market, stable operations, and no intangible assets. Caveats are the following:

- This method depends on accounting practices that vary across firms.
- It ignores intangible assets like brand names, patents, technical know-how, and managerial competence.
- It ignores price appreciation due, for instance, to inflation.
- It invites disputes about types of liabilities. For instance, are deferred taxes equity or debt?
- Book value method is *backward-looking*. It ignores the positive or negative operating prospects of the firm and is often a poor proxy for market value.

Liquidation value

Liquidation value considers the sale of assets at a point in time. This may be appropriate for firms in financial distress, or more generally, for firms whose operating prospects are highly uncertain. Liquidation value generally provides a conservative lower bound to the business valuation. Liquidation value will depend on the recovery value of the assets (e.g., collections from receivables) and the extent of viable alternative uses for the assets. Caveats are the following:

- It is difficult to get a consensus valuation. Liquidation values tend to be highly appraiser-specific.
- It relies on key judgment: How finely one might break up the company: Group? Division? Product line? Region? Plant? Machines?
- Physical condition, not age, will affect values. There can be no substitute for an on-site assessment of a company's real assets.
- It may ignore valuable intangible assets.

Replacement-cost value

In the 1970s and early 1980s, during the era of high inflation in the United States, the U.S. Securities and Exchange Commission required public corporations to estimate replacement values in their 10-K reports. This is no longer the case, making this method less useful for U.S. firms, but still is useful for international firms where the requirement continues. Caveats are the following:

- Comparisons of replacement costs and stock market values ignore the possible reasons for the disparity: overcapacity, high interest rates, oil shocks, inflation, and so on.

- Replacement-cost estimates are not highly reliable, often drawn by simplistic rules of thumb. Estimators themselves (operating managers) frequently dismiss the estimates.

Market value of traded securities

Most often, this method is used to value the equity of the firm (E) as Stock Price Outstanding Shares. It can also be used to value the enterprise (V) by adding the market value of debt (D) as the Price Per Bond Number of Bonds Outstanding.[16] This method is helpful if the stock is actively traded, followed by professional securities analysts, and if the market efficiently impounds all public information about the company and its industry. It is worth noting the following:

- Rarely do merger negotiations settle at a price below the market price of the target. On average, mergers and tender offers command a 30% to 50% premium over the price one day before the merger announcement. Premiums have been as high as 100% in some instances. Often the price increase is attributed to a "control premium." The premium will depend on the rarity of the assets sought after and also on the extent to which there are close substitutes for the technology, expertise, or capability in question, the distribution of financial resources between the bidder and target, the egos of the CEOs involved (the hubris hypothesis), or the possibility that the ex ante target price was unduly inflated by market rumors.

- This method is less helpful for less well-known companies with thinly or intermittently traded stock. It is not available for privately held companies.

- The method ignores private information known only to insiders or acquirers who may see a special economic opportunity in the target company. Remember, the market can efficiently impound only *public* information.

---

[16] Since the market price of a bond is frequently close to its book value, the book value of debt is often used as a reasonable proxy for its market value. Conversely, it is rare that book value per share of equity is close enough to its market price to serve as a good estimate.

Summary Comments

The DCF method of valuation is superior for company valuation in an M&A setting because it:

- Is not tied to historical accounting values. It is forward-looking.
- Focuses on cash flow, not profits. It reflects noncash charges and investment inflows and outflows.
- Separates the investment and financing effects into discrete variables.
- Recognizes the time value of money.
- Allows private information or special insights to be incorporated explicitly.
- Allows expected operating strategy to be incorporated explicitly.
- Embodies the operating costs and benefits of intangible assets.

Virtually every number used in valuation is *measured with error*, either because of flawed methods to describe the past or because of uncertainty about the future. Therefore:

- No valuation is "right" in any absolute sense.
- It is appropriate to use several scenarios about the future and even several valuation methods to limit the target's value.

> *Adapt to diversity:* It may be easier and more accurate to value the divisions or product lines of a target, rather than to value the company as a whole. Recognize that different valuation methods may be appropriate for different components.
>
> *Avoid analysis paralysis:* Limit the value quickly. Then if the target still looks attractive, try some sensitivity analysis.

Beyond the initial buy/no buy decision, the purpose of most valuation analysis is to support negotiators. Knowing value boundaries and conducting sensitivity analysis enhances one's flexibility to respond to new ideas that may appear at the negotiating table.

APPENDIX

Description of Relationship between Multiples of Operating Profit and Constant Growth Model

One can show that cash-flow multiples such as EBIT and EBITDA are economically related to the constant growth model. For example, the constant growth model can be expressed as follows:

$$V = \frac{FCF}{WACC - g}$$

Rearranging this expression gives a free-cash-flow multiple expressed in a constant growth model:

$$\frac{V}{FCF} = \frac{1}{WACC - g}$$

This expression suggests that cash-flow multiples are increasing in the growth rate and decreasing in the WACC. In the following table, one can vary the WACC and growth rate to produce the implied multiple.

		WACC	
	8%	10%	12%
0%	12.5	10.0	8.3
2%	16.7	12.5	10.0
4%	25.0	16.7	12.5
6%	50.0	25.0	16.7

(Growth, left axis label)

American Greetings

This year American Greetings is demonstrating to naysayers that the greeting card space is not dead. The company has accelerated top line through a combination of organic growth and acquisitions, and year to date revenues are trending well ahead of our forecast. However, the growth has come at a cost that is also far greater than we had anticipated . . . In Q3 marketing spending increased by a surprising $10 million . . . The company also accelerated investment spending in the digital space to support the growth of recently launched cardstore.com. In addition, [American Greetings] has incurred . . . incremental expenses this year to roll out new doors in the dollar store channel . . .

—Jeff Stein, Managing Director, Northcoast Research

It was New Years Day 2012 and the weather was unseasonably warm in Cleveland, Ohio, headquarters for American Greetings Corporation. But while temperatures were up, the same could not be said of American Greetings stock price. Over the past several months, American Greetings' share price had been cut in half to a year-end closing price of $12.51 (see **Exhibit 1**).

American Greetings management historically had turned to share buybacks at times of low equity valuation. With current valuation levels, management was considering going into the market with a $75 million repurchase program. The decision hinged on how the future of the enterprise was expected to play out. If the share price reasonably reflected the bleak prospects of American Greetings, management should preserve cash for future needs. If, on the other hand, American Greetings stock was simply temporarily out of favor, the buyback plan presented a prudent defensive strategy.

American Greetings

With $1.7 billion in revenue, American Greetings was the second largest greeting card publisher in the United States. To meet the changing times, American Greetings sold greeting cards through traditional retail channels as well as electronically through a number of company websites. In addition to gift cards, American Greetings marketed giftwraps, candles, party goods, candles, and other giftware. To strengthen its business,

This case was prepared by Michael J. Schill, Robert F. Vandell Research Associate Professor of Business Administration. Copyright © 2011 by the University of Virginia Darden School Foundation, Charlottesville, VA. All rights reserved. *To order copies, send an e-mail to* sales@dardenbusinesspublishing.com. *No part of this publication may be reproduced, stored in a retrieval system, used in a spreadsheet, or transmitted in any form or by any means—electronic, mechanical, photocopying, recording, or otherwise—without the permission of the Darden School Foundation.*

the company owned and maintained the following major brands: American Greetings, Carlton Cards, Gibson, Recycled Paper Greetings, Papyrus, and DesignWare. American Greetings owned the rights to a variety of popular characters, including Strawberry Shortcake, the Care Bears, Holly Hobbie, the Get Along Gang, and the Nickelodeon characters. The company was able to generate additional revenue by licensing the rights to these characters. Overall, management positioned American Greetings as a leader in social expression products that assisted "consumers in enhancing their relationships to create happiness, laughter, and love."

The company had a long affiliation with the founding Sapirstein family. Shortly after immigrating to the United States in 1905, Jacob Sapirstein, a Polish entrepreneur, launched a business with the help of his young family distributing German manufactured postcards in Cleveland. The business leadership was passed on to Jacob's oldest son Irving Stone and then to Irving's son-in-law, Morry Weiss. In 2003, Morry's sons Zev and Jeffrey Weiss were appointed as chief executive officer and president, respectively. Morry Weiss continued to serve as chairman of the board of directors.

Despite the strong family affiliation, American Greetings was widely held in the public equity markets with over 11,000 shareholders including large positions by such institutional investors as the British investment fund MAM Investments (10.6% of American Greetings shares) and US funds Dimensional Fund Advisors (10.5%), BlackRock (7.9%), and LSV Asset Management (6.7%). Dividend payments to investors had been on an upward trend in recent years, rising from 12 cents per share in 2004 to 56 cents in 2010.

Exhibits 2 and **3** provide American Greetings' detailed financial statements. Since American Greetings' fiscal year ended in February, the figures for 2011, for example, included estimated results through February 2012.

Greeting Cards

Two players, Hallmark and American Greetings, dominated the U.S. greetings card industry. Hallmark was the larger of the two and privately held by the Hall family. Total worldwide revenue for Hallmark was $4 billion. From its headquarters in Kansas City, Missouri, Hallmark had aggressively expanded its business internationally with operations in over 100 countries. Hallmark maintained licensing agreements with independent "Hallmark Gold Crown" retail stores that marketed Hallmark products. Hallmark owned ancillary businesses such as the crayon maker, Crayola, and the cable network channel, Hallmark Channel. Other card companies, such as Detroit-based Avanti Press, had found successful niches in the $6 billion U.S. greeting card market.

The industry analyst firm Mintel maintained that the overall greeting card market had contracted by 9% since 2005 and that the contraction would continue (see **Exhibit 4**). Mintel's best case forecast called for a 4% market decline over the next four years while its worst-case scenario called for a 16% decline. The market contraction was thought to be driven by the substitution of other forms of social expression products for greeting cards due to the ease of such alternative forms as smart phones, electronic social networking, and digital imaging which impacted the traditional Christmas card market. The rapid expansion of social media networks such as

Facebook provided even stronger challenges to electronic cards. An industry survey found that the substitution to social media networking was particularly acute among younger demographics (see **Exhibit 5**). Analysts expected the trend to continue as the ease of digital communication substituted for traditional forms of social expression.

The industry had responded to the substantive technological shift with important market innovations. The two dominant greeting card companies, Hallmark and American Greetings, had created an extensive collection of electronic cards that made it easy for customers to send cards electronically. Card manufacturers maintained websites that allowed consumers to purchase paper greeting cards on the Internet via computer or smart phone and have the physical cards delivered directly to the recipient. Kiosks had been placed in retail stores that allowed customers to create custom cards. Distribution had expanded to build a substantive presence in the expanding "dollar stores" retail channel where greeting cards were reported to be a top-selling item.

Despite the challenges, large numbers of people continued to buy greeting cards. In a recent survey, fifty-two percent of U.S. respondents had purchased a greeting card in the past three months. This figure was down from 59% who had responded affirmatively in 2006.[1]

Valuation

With an end of year close of $12.51 per share, American Greetings' PE ratio was at 6 times, its enterprise value to EBITDA ratio was at 3.5 times, and market-to-book ratio was below one. All of these valuation ratios were at the bottom of American Greetings' comparable group (see **Exhibit 6**). American Greetings' management believed its valuation suggested an opportunity, but low levels also signaled a concern from the industry on the prospects of the company. For example, equity analysts at Standard and Poor's maintained a "Hold" recommendation on the stock, claiming:

We see [American Greetings' 2012] sales increasing 2.5% to $1.73 billion. . . . We see demand benefitting from increased promotional spending in a more stable economic environment as the company pursues growth within the discount distribution channel . . . acquisitions . . . [and] international sales . . . We expect margins to narrow . . . reflecting a shift in customer mix toward the discount channel, increasing marketing costs to spur demand, distribution expansion costs, and expenses related to plans to move AM's headquarters building. While we believe channel migration will result in a permanent negative margin shift, we do not believe transition costs related to expanded distribution efforts will be a factor in the long term.[2]

Value Line analyst, Orly Seidman, held a more optimistic view with expectations of steady margins and steady long-term growth:

The company has been improving the product pipeline. Management should continue to follow consumer and societal trends to better brand its offerings. It has shifted its focus from its core segment to pursue noncard merchandise. Product innovation, stronger retail partnerships, and

---

[1] Mintel, "Greeting Cards and E-Cards—US," Survey, February 2011.

[2] American Greetings Corp., Standard and Poor's, Stock Report, December 27, 2011.

sell-diversified portfolio ought to drive customer interest in its goods. Technological enhancements will likely remain key to its long-term approach. Over the past few quarters, [American Greetings] rolled out several complementary interactive products (i.e., mobile apps) and should continue to bolster its digital position.[3]

It was clear that there was substantial disagreement regarding the future growth trajectory and operating margins for the company. Over the past several years, revenue growth had been near to below zero. This year, however, revenue growth was anticipated to be over 7% (see **Exhibit 7**). Similarly, operating margins that had been abnormally low two to five years ago had improved to 9% recently.

A bullish view held that American Greetings would be able to maintain operating margins at 9% and achieve long-term ongoing revenue growth of 3%. A bearish view held that American Greetings' prospective revenue growth would be near zero into the future and that margins would continue to erode to a long-term rate of 6%. The expectation was that recent investments would generate some future working capital efficiency for American Greetings, but there was little evidence that fixed asset turnover would improve.

Management understood that returns and growth were challenging to achieve in early 2012. Yields on U.S. Treasury Bills and Bonds were at historic lows of 0.1% and 2.8%, respectively (see **Exhibit 8**). In such an environment, investors would richly reward returns of even small magnitudes.

---

[3] Orly Seidman, American Greetings, Value Line Investment Survey, November 11, 2011.

EXHIBIT 1 | American Greetings Share Price

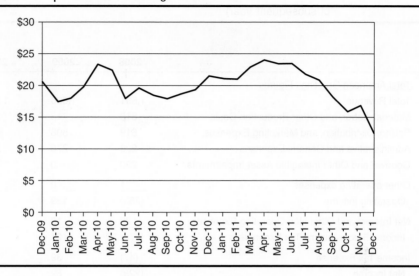

EXHIBIT 2 | American Greetings Income Statement (USD millions; Fiscal year ends February of subsequent year)

	2008	2009	2010	2011 (Est) (Ends Feb 2012)
Total American Greetings Figures				
Total Revenue	1,691	1,636	1,593	1,677
Material, Labor, and Other Production Costs	810	713	682	743
Selling, Distribution, and Marketing Expenses	619	508	478	526
Administrative and General Expenses	226	276	261	258
Goodwill and Other Intangible Asset Impairments	290	0	0	0
Other operating expenses	1	0	3	(6)
Operating Income	(253)	139	175	157
Net Interest and Other Non Operating Expenses	22	18	19	28
Income Before Income Tax Expense	(275)	121	156	129
Income Tax Expense	(47)	39	69	47
Net Income	(228)	82	87	82
Earnings Per Share (Basic)	(4.89)	2.07	2.18	2.22
Dividends per Share	0.60	0.36	0.56	0.60
Average Number of Shares Outstanding (Millions)	46.5	39.5	40.0	38.50
By Business Unit				
Operating Segment Net Sales				
North American Social Expression Products	1,095	1,235	1,191	1,215
International Social Expression Products	271	254	262	344
Retail Operations	179	12		
AG Interactive	83	80	78	68
Operating Segment Earnings				
North American Social Expression Products	70	236	218	148
International Social Expression Products	(78)	17	20	20
Retail Operations	(19)	(35)		
AG Interactive	(162)	11	14	14
Total Revenue by Product Category				
Everyday Greeting Cards	704	764	753	823
Seasonal Greeting Cards	357	369	377	408
Gift Packaging	240	221	223	239
Other Revenue	44	38	32	32
All Other Products	345	244	207	176

Source: Company accounts; Management and case writer estimates

EXHIBIT 3 | American Greetings Balance Sheet (USD millions; Fiscal year end February 28 of subsequent year)

	2009 (Feb 2010)	2010 (Feb 2011)	2011 (Est) (Feb 2012)
Cash and Cash Equivalents	138	216	172
Trade Accounts Receivable	136	120	130
Inventories	164	180	190
Prepaid Expenses	148	128	131
Other Current Assets	94	57	54
Total Current Assets	679	701	677
Net Property, Plant and Equipment and Other Assets	850	832	859
Total Assets	1,529	1,533	1,536
Debt Due within One Year	1	—	—
Accounts Payable	95	87	87
Other Current Liabilities	272	255	255
Current Liabilities	369	343	343
Long-term Debt and Other Liabilities	525	441	441
Shareholders' Equity	636	749	752
Total Liabilities and Shareholders' Equity	1,530	1,532	1,536

Source: Company accounts; Management and case writer estimates

EXHIBIT 4 | Total U.S. Greeting Cards Sales (Actual and forecast estimation)

	Sales at current prices		Index
	$million	% annual change	2005 = 100
2005	6,537		100
2006	6,420	−1.8	98
2007	6,285	−2.1	96
2008	6,266	−0.3	96
2009	6,149	−1.9	94
2010	5,935	−3.5	91
2011 (Est.)	5,838	−1.6	89
2012 (Est.)	5,711	−2.2	87
2013 (Est.)	5,596	−2.0	86
2014 (Est.)	5,478	−2.1	84
2015 (Est.)	5,359	−2.2	82

EXHIBIT 5 | Feelings about e-Cards Usage Change Among 2000 Respondents, by Age (October 2010)

	All	By Age Category					
		18–24	25–34	35–44	45–54	55–64	65+
Question 1.In the last year I have sent more e-cards than I used to	22%	17%	26%	20%	22%	21%	24%
Question 2. In the last year I have sent fewer e-cards than I used to because I send greetings over social networking sites such as Facebook	20%	26%	27%	21%	19%	15%	13%

Source: Mintel

EXHIBIT 6 | Comparable Firms (End of 2011, Millions Except Share Price)

	Share Price	Shares Outstanding	Total Cash	Total Debt	Revenue	EDITDA
American Greetings	12.51	38.32	86	235	1,660	204
Blyth	56.80	8.22	182	101	984	48
Central Garden & Pet	8.16	48.04	28	461	1,650	109
Consolidated Graphics	48.28	10.24	7	197	1,050	122
CSS Industries	19.92	9.73	10	0	453	30
Deluxe	22.76	50.93	31	742	1,420	359
Fossil	79.36	61.79	288	15	2,570	525
Lancaster Colony	69.34	27.26	162	0	1,090	156
McCormick & Company	50.42	133.05	73	1,250	3,700	650
McGraw-Hill	44.97	278.00	973	1,200	6,250	1,670
Meredith	32.65	44.79	26	250	1,350	240
RR Donnelley & Sons	14.43	178.50	450	345	10,610	1,290
Scholastic	29.97	31.05	114	215	1,950	189
Scotts Miracle-Gro	46.69	60.83	128	1,060	2,820	391
Tupperware Brands	55.97	56.13	138	621	2,580	431

	ROA	ROE	Beta	S&P Bond Rating	Moody's Bond Rating
American Greetings	7%	11%	1.63	BB+	Ba2
Blyth	4%	9%	1.60		
Central Garden & Pet	5%	5%	1.55		B3
Consolidated Graphics	5%	10%	1.45		
CSS Industries	4%	2%	1.36		
Deluxe	13%	55%	1.85	B	B1
Fossil	19%	28%	1.62		
Lancaster Colony	14%	19%	0.42		
McCormick & Company	9%	24%	0.24	A−	A2
McGraw-Hill	14%	44%	0.99		
Meredith	7%	15%	1.75		
RR Donnelley & Sons	5%	-7%	2.02		
Scholastic	6%	8%	1.04	BB−	
Scotts Miracle-Gro	10%	20%	0.96		
Tupperware Brands	12%	34%	1.52		Baa3

Source: Yahoo! Finance

EXHIBIT 7 | American Greetings Operating Performance (For fiscal year end February 28 of subsequent year)

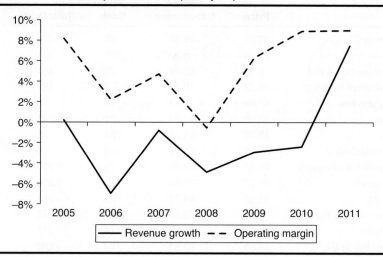

EXHIBIT 8 | Capital Market Data

	Yield
30-day Treasury Bill	0.1%
10 year Treasury Bond	2.8%
10-year Corporate Bonds of Industrial Companies	
AAA	2.8%
AA	2.9%
A+	3.2%
A	3.3%
A−	3.5%
BBB+	3.8%
BBB	4.1%
BBB−	4.6%
BB+	5.8%
BB	6.5%
BB−	6.5%
B+	6.8%
B	8.4%
B−	9.0%
	5-year forecast
U.S. Real GDP annual growth rate	3.3%
U.S. GDP annual deflator rate	1.8%
Consumer Price Index annual rate	2.2%

Arcadian Microarray Technologies, Inc.

In August 2005, negotiations neared conclusion for a private equity investment by Sierra Capital Partners in Arcadian Microarray Technologies, Inc. The owners of Arcadian, who were also its senior managers, proposed to sell a 60% equity interest to Sierra Capital for $40 million. The proceeds of the equity sale would be used to finance the firm's growth. Sierra Capital's due diligence study of Arcadian had revealed a highly promising high-risk investment opportunity. It remained for Rodney Chu, a managing director with Sierra Capital, to negotiate the specific price and terms of investment. Chu aimed to base his negotiating strategy on an assessment of Arcadian's economic value and to structure the interests of Sierra Capital and the managers of Arcadian to create the best incentives for value creation.

Chu's analysis so far had focused on financial forecasting of equity cash flows. The final steps would be to estimate a terminal value for the company (also called "continuing value") and to discount the cash flows and terminal value to the present. He also sought an assessment of forecast assumptions. In that regard, he requested help from Paige Simon, a new associate with Sierra Capital.

Sierra Capital Partners

Sierra Capital, located in Albuquerque, New Mexico, had been organized in 1974 as a hedge fund, though over the years it had a successful record of private equity investments and had gradually shifted its activities to this area. The firm had $2 billion under management, and its portfolio consisted of 64 investments, about evenly split between venture capital investments and participations in leveraged buyouts. Sierra Capital focused almost entirely on the life sciences sector. Like other investors, however, the firm had been burned by several flameouts following the boom in biotechnology stocks in 2000, when many rising young firms' blockbuster discoveries failed to materialize. Sierra Capital's mantra now when evaluating investments was, "NRDO: no research, development only."

Arcadian Microarray Technologies, Inc.

Following the completion of the Human Genome Project[1] in 2003, which sought to map the entire human DNA sequence[2], several companies had developed technologies for researchers to exploit that mountain of data. Specifically, those new products helped scientists find the links between the variations in a person's genetic code and their predisposition to disease. It was hoped that ultimately this would usher in an era when disease diagnosis, treatment, and prevention could be tailored to an individual's unique genetic identity.

Arcadian Microarray Technologies, Inc.,[3] headquartered in Arcadia, California, was founded in 2003 by seven research scientists, two of whom had been major contributors to the Human Genome Project itself. The team had developed a unique DNA scanning device in the form of a waferlike glass chip that could allow scientists to analyze thousands of human genes or gene fragments at one time, rather than individually. The gene chips, also called DNA microarrays, made it possible to identify specific sequence variations in an individual's genes, some of which could be associated with disease. Arcadian's business consisted of two segments:

- *DNA microarrays.* Arcadian's DNA microarrays were created using semiconductor-manufacturing technology. The chips were only a few centimeters in size, and had short, single-stranded DNA segments spread across their surface. Arcadian's chips were unique because they could hold up to one billion DNA types—more than any other microarray currently available. That was ground-breaking technology that would afford low-cost and virtually error-free detection of a wide range of medical conditions. Development of the chip technologies was finished, and the products were moving rapidly through the Food and Drug Administration (FDA) approval process; because of their noninvasive and diagnostic nature, they might be available for sale within 12 months.

- *Human therapeutics.* The search for vaccines and antibiotics with which to fight incurable diseases was potentially the most economically attractive segment, and Arcadian leveraged its leading-edge DNA-testing platform to conduct proprietary research in this area. Management's long-term strategy was to use external funding (through joint venture arrangements with well-capitalized pharmaceutical firms)

---

[1]The Human Genome Project (HGP), completed in April 2003, was an international research program to map and understand all human genes. The HGP revealed that there are probably between 30,000 and 40,000 human genes, and the research provided detailed information about their structure, organization, and function.

[2]Sequencing is a means of determining the exact order of the chemical units within a segment of DNA.

[3]Genomics is the study of an organism's genome and its use of genes. A genome is an organism's complete set of deoxyribonucleic acid (DNA), a chemical compound that contains the genetic instructions needed to develop and direct the activities of every organism. Each of the estimated 30,000 genes in the human genome carries information for making all the proteins required by an organism, a process called *gene expression*.

to the fullest extent possible to carry the firm until its first major proprietary breakthrough. But despite external funding, Arcadian still faced significant capital requirements stemming from investment in infrastructure, staffing, and its own proprietary research program.

Arcadian's management believed that applications for its DNA microarray technology would pay off dramatically and quickly: by the year 2013 they believed the firm's revenues (namely, sales of proprietary products, underwritten research, and royalties) would top $1 billion. Rodney Chu was less optimistic, believing that the FDA approval process would slow down the commercialization of Arcadian's new products. The cash flow forecasts of management and of Chu are given in **Exhibits 1** and **2.** Chu assumed the firm would not finance itself with debt; thus, the forecasted free cash flows were identical with equity cash flows.

In assessing Arcadian, Chu looked toward two publicly held companies in the general field of molecular diagnostics.

- *Affymetrix, Inc.,* based in Santa Clara, California, was the pioneer in the development of DNA microarrays and was at that time the world's leading provider of gene expression technology. Its patented GeneChip® product was widely used for molecular biology research and had been cited in more than 3,000 peer-reviewed publications. On December 27, 2004, Affymetrix's GeneChip was the first microarray approved by the FDA for in-vitro use, which represented a major step toward the use of DNA microarrays in a clinical setting. The firm's beta was 1.30; its price/expected earnings ratio was 50.09; its price/book ratio was 8.56; price/sales was 7.49; and price/free cash flow was 97.50. The firm had $120 million in debt outstanding. The firm's sales had grown from $290 million in 2002, to $301 million in 2003, to $346 million in 2004, and to an expected $380 million in 2005. The company paid no dividend.

- *Illumina, Inc.* of San Diego, California, developed a microarray design that attached hundreds of thousands of biological sensors to submicroscopic glass beads that could seek out and latch onto specific sequences of DNA. The company's proprietary BeadArray technology used fiber optics to achieve this miniaturization of arrays that enabled a new scale of experimentation. With negative historical and expected earnings, the firm's price/earnings ratio was meaningless; however, the firm traded at 8.46 times book value, and 8.82 times sales. Illumina's revenues were $10 million in 2002, $28 million in 2003, and $51 million in 2004, and were expected to be about $73 million in 2005.

Having been burned by the biotech bust, securities analysts were now cautious about the fledgling gene diagnostics industry. "The human genome period ushered in a new wealth of information about our genes and at the time there was a lot of hoopla about the ability to cure disease," said one analyst. "In reality, human biology and genetics are complicated."[4] DNA-based medical testing, made possible by gene

---

[4]Aaron Geist, analyst with Robert W. Baird & Co., quoted in "Success Is All in the Genes," *Investor's Business Daily,* 18 July 2005, A12.

expression diagnostic technology, was at the edge of the legal envelope, and the field was quickly being flooded with entrepreneurial research scientists. The FDA approval process was at best uncertain in this area, and established firms experienced internal clashes over direction.

The Idea of Terminal Value

To assist him in the final stages of preparing for the negotiations, Rodney Chu called in Paige Simon, who had just joined the firm after completing an undergraduate degree. To lay the groundwork for the assignment, Chu began by describing the concept of terminal value:

> CHU: Terminal value is the lump-sum of cash flow at the *end* of a stream of cash flows—that's why we call it "terminal." The lump sum represents either (a) the proceeds to us from exiting the investment, or (b) the present value (at that future date) of all cash flows beyond the forecast horizon.

> SIMON: Because they are way off in the future, terminal values really can't be worth worrying about, can they? I don't believe most investors even think about them.

> CHU: Terminal values are worth worrying about for two reasons. First, they are present in the valuation of just about every asset. For instance, in valuing a U.S. Treasury bond, the terminal value is the return of your principal at the maturity of the bond.

> SIMON: Some investors might hold to maturity, but the traders who really set the prices in the bond markets almost never hold to maturity.

> CHU: For traders, terminal value equals the proceeds from selling the bonds when you exit from each position. You can say the same thing about stocks, currencies, and all sorts of hard assets. Now, the second main reason we worry about terminal value is that in the valuation of stocks and whole companies, terminal value is *usually a very big value driver.*

> SIMON: I don't believe it. Terminal value is a distant future value. The only thing traders care about is dividends.

> CHU: I'll bet you that if you took a random sample of stocks—I'll let you throw darts at the financial pages to choose them—and looked at the percentage of today's share price *not* explained by the present value of dividends for the next five years, you would find

> | Simon's first task: Present and explain the data in **Exhibit 3.** |

> that the unexplained part would dominate today's value. I believe that the unexplained part is largely due to terminal value.[5]

> SIMON: I'll throw the darts, but I still don't believe it—I'll show you what I find.

---

[5]The unexplained part could also be due to option values that are not readily captured in a discounted cash flow valuation.

Varieties of Terminal Values

CHU: We can't really foresee terminal value, we can only *estimate* it. For that reason, I like to draw on a wide range of estimators as a way of trying to home in on a best guess of terminal value. The estimators include (a) accounting book value, (b) liquidation value, (c) multiples of income, and (d) constant growth perpetuity value. Each of those has advantages and disadvantages, as my chart here shows (**Exhibit 4**). I like the constant growth model best and the book value least, but they all give information, so I look at them all.

SIMON: Do they all agree?

CHU: They rarely agree. Remember that they are imperfect estimates. It's like picking the point of central tendency out of a scatter diagram or triangulating the height of a tree, using many different points of observation from the ground. It takes a lot of careful judgment because some of the varieties of terminal value are inherently more trustworthy than others. From one situation to the next the different estimators have varying degrees of appropriateness. In fact, even though I usually disregard book value, there are a few situations in which it might be a fair estimate of terminal value.

SIMON: Like what?

CHU: Give it some thought; you can probably figure it out. Give me some examples of where the various estimators would be appropriate or inappropriate. But remember that no single estimator will give us a "true" value. Wherever possible, we want to use a variety of approaches.

> Simon's second task: Consider the approaches described in **Exhibit 4.**

Taxes

SIMON: What about taxes in terminal values? Shouldn't I impose a tax on the gain inherent in any terminal value?

CHU: Sure, if you are a taxpaying investor and if it is actually your intent to exit the investment at the forecast horizon. But lots of big investors in the capital markets (such as pension funds and university endowments) do not pay taxes. And other investors really do not have much tax exposure because of careful tax planning. Finally, in mergers and acquisitions analysis and most kinds of capital budgeting analysis, the most reasonable assumption is to *buy and hold,* in perpetuity. Overall, the usual assumption is *not* to tax terminal values. But we all need to ask the basic question at the start of our analysis, is the investor likely to pay taxes?

Liquidation vs. Going Concern Values

SIMON: Now I'm starting to get confused. I thought "terminal" meant the end— and now you're talking about value in perpetuity. If terminal value is really the ending value, shouldn't we be talking about a *liquidation value*? Liquidation values are easy to estimate: we simply take the face value of net working capital, add the proceeds of selling any fixed assets, and subtract the long-term debt of the company.

CHU: *Easy* isn't the point. We have to do what's economically sensible. For instance, you wouldn't want to assume that you would liquidate Microsoft in three years just because that's as far into the future as you can forecast. Microsoft's key assets are software, people, and ideas. The value of those will never get captured in a liquidator's auction. The real value of Microsoft is in a stream of future cash flows. When we come to a case such as Microsoft, we see the subtlety of "terminal value"—in the case of *most* companies, it means "continuing value" derived from the going concern of the business. Indeed, many assets live well beyond the forecast horizon. Terminal value is just a summary (or present value) of the cash flows beyond the horizon.

SIMON: So when would you use liquidation value?

CHU: I've seen it a lot in corporate capital budgeting, cases like machines, plants, natural resources projects, etc. The assets in those cases have definite lives. But companies and *businesses* are potentially very long-lived and should be valued on a going concern basis. But I still look at liquidation value because I might find some interesting situations where liquidation value is higher than going concern value. Examples would be companies subject to oppressive regulation or taxation and firms experiencing weird market conditions—in the late 1970s and early 1980s, most oil companies had a market value *less* than the value of their oil reserves. You don't see those situations very often, but still it's worth a look.

Market Multiples and Constant Growth Valuation

SIMON: Aren't multiples the best terminal value estimators? They are certainly the easiest approach.

CHU: I use them, but they've got disadvantages, as my chart (**Exhibit 4**) shows. They're easy to use, but too abstract for my analytical work. I want to get really close to the assumptions about value, and for that reason, I use this version of the constant growth valuation model to value a firm's assets:

$$TV_{Firm} = \frac{FCF \times (1 + g_{FCF}^{\infty})}{WACC - g_{FCF}^{\infty}}$$

"FCF" is free cash flow. "WACC" is weighted average cost of capital. And "g^{∞}" is the constant growth rate of free cash flows to infinity. This model was derived from an infinitely long DCF valuation formula.

$$PV_{Firm} = \frac{FCF_0 \times (1 + g_{FCF}^{\infty})}{(1 + WACC)} + \frac{FCF_0 \times (1 + g_{FCF}^{\infty})^2}{(1 + WACC)^2}$$

$$+ \frac{FCF_0 \times (1 + g_{FCF}^{\infty})^3}{(1 + WACC)^3} + \dots + \frac{FCF_0 \times (1 + g_{FCF}^{\infty})^{\infty}}{(1 + WACC)^{\infty}}$$

If the growth rate is constant over time, this infinitely long model can be condensed into the easy-to-use constant growth model.

When I'm valuing equity instead of assets, I use the constant-growth valuation formula, but with equity-oriented inputs:

$$TV_{Equity} = \frac{Residual\ cash\ flow \times (1 + g_{RCF}^{\infty})}{Cost\ of\ equity - g_{RCF}^{\infty}}$$

Residual Cash Flow (RCF) is the cash flow which equity-holders can look forward to receiving—a common name for RCF is dividends. A key point here is that the growth rate used in this model should be the growth rate appropriate for the type of cash flow being valued; and the capital cost should be appropriate for that cash flow as well.

You may have seen the simplest version of the constant growth model—the one that assumes zero growth—which reduces to dividing the annual cash flow by a discount rate.

SIMON: Sure, I have used a model like that to price perpetual preferred stocks. In the numerator, I inserted the annual dividend; in the denominator I inserted whatever we thought the going required rate of return will be for that stream.

CHU: If you insert some positive growth rate into the model, the resulting value gets bigger. In a growing economy, the assumption of growing free cash flows is quite reasonable. Sellers of companies always want to persuade you of their great growth prospects. If you buy the optimistic growth assumptions, you'll have to pay a higher price for the company. But the assumption of growth can get unreasonable if pushed too far. Many of the abuses of this model have to do with the little infinity symbol, ∞: the model assumes *constant growth at the rate, g, to infinity.*

"Peter Pan" Growth: WACC < g

SIMON: Right! If you assume a growth rate greater than WACC, you'll get a *negative* terminal value.

CHU: That's one instance in which you cannot use the constant growth model. But think about it: WACC less than g *can't* happen; a company cannot grow to infinity at a rate greater than its cost of capital. To illustrate why, let's rearrange the constant growth formula to solve for WACC:

$$WACC = \frac{FCF_{Next\ period}}{Value\ of\ firm_{Current\ period}} + g_{FCF}^{\infty}$$

If WACC is less than *g*, then the ratio of FCF divided by the value of the firm would have to be *negative.* Since the value of the healthy firm to the investors cannot be less than zero,[6] the source of negativity must be FCF—that means the firm is absorbing rather than throwing off cash. Recall that in the familiar constant growth terminal value formula, FCF is the flow that compounds to infinity at the rate g. Thus, if FCF is negative, then the entire stream of FCFs must be negative—the company is like Peter Pan: *it never grows up;* it never matures to the point where it throws off positive cash flow. That is a crazy implication because investors would not buy securities in a firm that never paid a cash return. In short, you cannot use the constant growth model where WACC is less than g, nor would you want to because of the unbelievable implications of that assumption.

Using Historical Growth Rates; Setting Forecast Horizons

CHU: A more common form of abuse of this model is to assume a very high growth rate, simply by extrapolating the past rate of growth of the company.

SIMON: Why isn't the past growth rate a good one?

CHU: Companies typically go through life cycles. A period of explosive growth is usually followed by a period of maturity and/or decline. Take a look at the three deals in this chart (**Exhibit 5**): a startup of an animation movie studio in Burbank, California; a bottling plant in Mexico City, and a high-speed private toll road in Los Angeles.

- **Movie studio.** The studio has a television production unit with small but steadily growing revenues and a full feature-length film production unit with big but uncertain cash flows. The studio does not reach stability until the 27th year. The stability is largely due to the firm's film library, which should be sizable by then. After year 27, exploiting the library through videos and re-releases will act as a shock absorber, dampening swings in cash flow due to the production side of the business. Also, at about that time, we can assume that the studio reaches production capacity.

- **Bottling plant.** The bottler must establish a plant and an American soda brand in Mexico, which accounts for the initial negative cash flows and slow growth. Then, as the brand takes hold, the cash flows increase steeply. Finally, in year 12, the plant reaches capacity. After that, cash flows grow mainly at the rate of inflation.

- **Toll road.** The road will take 18 months to build, and will operate at capacity almost immediately. The toll rates are government-regulated, but the company will be allowed to raise prices at the rate of inflation. The cash flows reach stability in year 3.

A key point of judgment in valuation analysis is to *set the forecast horizon at that point in the future where stability or stable growth begins.* You can't use past rates

---

[6]This is a sensible assumption for healthy firms, under the axiom of the limited liability of investors: investors cannot be held liable for claims against the firm, beyond the amount of their investment in the firm. However, in the cases of punitive government regulations or an active torts system, investors may be compelled to "invest" further in a losing business. Examples would include liabilities for cleanup of toxic waste, remediation of defective breast implants, and assumption of medical costs of nicotine addiction. In those instances, the value of the firm to investors could be negative.

of growth of cash flows in each of these three projects because the explosive growth of the past will not be repeated. Frankly, over long periods of time, it is difficult to sustain cash flow growth much in excess of the economy. If you did, you would wind up owning everything!

SIMON: So at what year in the future would you set the horizon and estimate a terminal value for those three projects? And what growth rate would you use in your constant growth formula for them? Uh-oh. I know: "Figure it out for yourself."

> Simon's third task:
> Assess the forecast
> horizons for the
> three projects.
> See **Exhibit 5.**

Growth Rate Assumption

CHU: There are two classic approaches for estimating the growth rate to use in the constant-growth formula. The first is to use the self-sustainable growth rate formula,

$$g^\infty = ROE \times (1 - DPO)$$

That equation assumes that the firm can only grow as fast as it adds to its equity capital base (through the return on equity, or "ROE," less any dividends paid out, indicated through the dividend payout ratio, or "DPO"). I'm not a big fan of that approach because most naive analysts simply extrapolate *past* ROE and DPO without really thinking about the future. Also it relies on accounting ROE and can give some pretty crazy results.[7]

The second approach assumes that nominal growth of a business is the sum of *real growth* and *inflation*. In more proper mathematical notation the formula is

$$g^\infty_{Nominal} = [(1 + g^\infty_{Units}) \times (1 + g^\infty_{Inflation})] - 1$$

That formula uses the Fisher Formula, which holds that the nominal rate of growth is the product of the rate of inflation and the "real" rate of growth[8]. We commonly think of real growth as a percentage increase in units shipped. But in rare instances, real growth could come from price increases due, for instance, to a monopolist's power over the market. For simplicity, I just use a short version of the model (less precise, though the difference in precision is not material):

$$g^\infty_{Nominal} = g^\infty_{Units} + g^\infty_{Inflation}$$

Now, this formula focuses you on two really interesting issues: the real growth rate in the business, and the ability of the business to pass along the effects of inflation. The consensus inflation outlook in the United States today calls for about a 2% inflation rate indefinitely. We probably have not got the political consensus in the United States to drive inflation to zero, and the Federal Reserve has shown strong resistance to letting inflation rise much higher. Well, if inflation

---

[7] For a full discussion of the self-sustainable growth rate model, see "A Critical Look at the Self-Sustainable Growth Rate Concept" (UVA-F-0951).

[8] Economist Irving Fisher derived this model of economic growth.

is given, then the analyst can really focus her thinking on the more interesting issue of the real growth rate of the business.

The real growth rate is bound to vary by industry. Growth in unit demand of consumer staple products (such as adhesive bandages) is probably determined by the growth rate of the population—less than 1% in the United States. Growth in demand for luxury goods is probably driven by growth of real disposable income— maybe 3% today. Growth in demand for industrial commodities like steel is probably about equal to the real rate of growth of GNP—about 3% on average through time. In any event, all of those are small numbers.

When you add those real growth rates to the expected inflation rate today, you get a small number—that is intuitively appealing since over the very long run, the increasing maturity of a company will tend to drive its growth rate downward.

Terminal Value for Arcadian Microarray Technologies

CHU: We're negotiating to structure an equity investment in Arcadian. We and management disagree on the size of the cash flows to be realized over the next 10 years (see **Exhibits 1** and **2**). I'm willing to invest cash on the basis of *my* expectations, but I'm also willing to agree to give Arcadian's management a contingent payment if they achieve *their* forecast. To begin the structuring process, I needed valuations of Arcadian under their and our forecasts. We have the cash flow forecasts, and we both agree that the weighted average cost of capital (WACC) should be 20%—that's low for a typical venture capital investment, but given that Arcadian's research and development (R&D) partners are bearing so much of the technical risk in this venture, I think it's justified. All I needed to finish the valuation was a sensible terminal value assumption—I've already run a sensitivity analysis using growth rates to infinity ranging from 2% to 7% (see **Exhibit 6**). The rate at which the firm grows will place different demands on the need for physical capital and net working capital— the higher the growth rate, the greater the capital require-ments. So, in computing the terminal value using the constant growth model, I adjusted the free cash flow for these different capital requirements. Here are the scenarios I ran (in millions of U.S. dollars):

| Simon's fourth task: Interpret **Exhibit 6.** |

Nominal Growth Rate to Infinity	Capital Expenditures in Terminal Year, Net of Depreciation	Net Working Capital Investment in Terminal Year
2%	$0 million	$0 million
3%	−$ 5	−$3
4%	−$12	−$5
5%	−$15	−$7
6%	−$20	−$8
7%	−$28	−$9

Arcadian's management believes that they can grow at 7% to infinity, assuming a strong patent position on breakthrough therapeutics. I believe that a lower growth rate is justified, though I would like to have your recommendation on what that rate should be. Should we be looking at the population growth rate in the United States (about 1% per year), or the real growth rate in the economy (about 3% per year), or the historical real growth rate in pharmaceutical industry revenues (5% per year)? Are there other growth rates we should be considering?

> Simon's fifth task: What drives g^∞?

We ought to test the reasonableness of the DCF valuations against estimates afforded by other approaches. Estimates of book and liquidation values of the company are not very helpful in this case, but multiples estimates would help. Price/earnings (P/E) multiples for Arcadian are expected to be 15 to 20 times at the forecast horizon—that is considerably below the P/Es for comparable companies today, but around the P/Es

> Simon's sixth task: Estimate terminal values using multiples and prepare present-value estimates using them.

for established pharmaceutical companies. Price/book ratios for comparable companies today are around 8.5 times; Arcadian's book value of equity is $3.5 million. Please draw on any other multiples you might know about. We do not foresee Arcadian paying a dividend for a long time.

SIMON: That makes me skeptical about the whole concept. Terminal value for a high-tech company will be an awfully mushy estimate. How do you estimate growth? How sensitive is terminal value to variations in assumed growth rates? And with several terminal value estimates, how do you pick a "best guess" figure necessary to complete the DCF analysis? And once you've done all that, how far apart are the two valuations?

CHU: You need to help me find intelligent answers to those questions. Please let me have your recommendations about terminal values, their assumptions, and ultimately, about what you believe is a sensible value range today for Arcadian, from our standpoint and management's. By "value range," I mean high and low estimates of value for the equity of Arcadian that represent the bounds within which we will start negotiating (the low value), and above which we will abandon the negotiations.

> Simon's seventh task: Triangulate value ranges and recommend a deal structure.

Conclusion

Later, Rodney Chu reflected on the investment opportunity in Arcadian. It looked as if management's asking price was highly optimistic; $40 million would barely cover the cash deficit Sierra had projected for 2005. That implied that further rounds of financing would be needed for 2006 and beyond. But buying

> Chu's task: Assess early exit values and their impact on the decision.

into Arcadian now was like buying an option on future opportunities to invest—the price of that option was high, but the potential payoff could be immense if the examples of Affymetrix and Illumina were accurate reflections of the potential value creation in this field. Indeed, it was reasonable to assume that Arcadian could go public in an initial public offering (IPO) shortly after a major breakthrough pharmaceutical was announced. An IPO would accelerate the exit from this investment. If an IPO occurred, Sierra Capital would not sell its shares in Arcadian, but instead would distribute the Arcadian shares tax-free to clients for whom Sierra Capital was managing investments. Chu wondered how large the exit value might be, and what impact an early exit would have on the investment decision.

EXHIBIT 1 | Arcadian Microarray Technologies Cash Flow Forecast, by Arcadian Management (values in millions of U.S. dollars)

	Actual 2004	2005	2006	2007	2008	2009	2010	2011	2012	2013	2014
INCOME STATEMENT											
Sales											
Clinical microarrays	$0	$1	$15	$56	$107	$181	$249	$274	$282	$285	$289
Research microarrays	2	12	28	45	75	110	135	165	190	210	225
Royalties and other revenue	0	0	2	13	52	106	146	166	174	186	189
Human therapeutics	0	0	0	0	8	57	171	250	330	352	362
Total sales	**2**	**13**	**45**	**114**	**242**	**454**	**701**	**855**	**976**	**1,033**	**1,065**
Cost of sales	7	10	21	41	84	159	246	322	335	350	361
Gross profits	**(5)**	**3**	**24**	**73**	**158**	**295**	**455**	**533**	**641**	**683**	**704**
Contract revenue	16	21	23	15	12	4	3	3	3	3	3
Operating expenses											
Research & development	14	20	24	18	21	21	32	43	51	52	50
Selling, general, & admin.	12	15	24	45	93	176	259	323	369	372	349
Total expenses	**26**	**35**	**48**	**63**	**114**	**197**	**291**	**366**	**420**	**424**	**399**
Other income	3	2	2	0	(3)	(10)	(25)	(38)	(43)	(37)	(20)
Income before taxes	**(12)**	**(9)**	**1**	**25**	**53**	**92**	**142**	**132**	**181**	**225**	**288**
Taxes	0	0	5	9	19	32	57	76	89	90	85
Net income	**($12)**	**($9)**	**($4)**	**$16**	**$35**	**$60**	**$85**	**$56**	**$92**	**$135**	**$203**
FREE CASH FLOW											
Net income	($12)	($9)	($4)	$16	$35	$60	$85	$56	$92	$135	$203
Noncash items	0	1	2	2	6	10	18	19	15	8	(1)
Working capital	(4)	(8)	(12)	(22)	(63)	(101)	(118)	(100)	(61)	1	39
Capital expenditures	(15)	(6)	(5)	(23)	(53)	(93)	(111)	(98)	(66)	(10)	(10)
Free cash flow	**($31)**	**($22)**	**($19)**	**($27)**	**($76)**	**($124)**	**($126)**	**($123)**	**($20)**	**$134**	**$231**

Source: Case writer's analysis.

EXHIBIT 2 | Arcadian Microarray Technologies Cash Flow Forecast, by Sierra Capital Analysts (values in millions of U.S. dollars)

	Actual 2004	2005	2006	2007	2008	2009	2010	2011	2012	2013	2014	2015
INCOME STATEMENT												
Sales												
Clinical microarrays	$0	$0	$2	$11	$22	$36	$56	$71	$85	$95	$106	$114
Research microarrays	2	4	11	22	40	59	89	135	145	160	185	199
Royalties and other revenue	0	1	4	7	12	15	25	50	60	75	91	105
Human therapeutics	0	0	0	0	0	0	0	14	56	80	110	140
Total sales	**2**	**5**	**17**	**40**	**74**	**110**	**170**	**270**	**346**	**410**	**492**	**558**
Cost of sales	7	17	20	25	39	54	72	96	124	142	154	160
Gross profits	**(5)**	**(12)**	**(3)**	**15**	**35**	**56**	**98**	**174**	**222**	**268**	**338**	**398**
Contract revenue	16	22	22	15	12	4	4	4	4	4	4	4
Operating expenses												
Research & development	14	23	25	27	29	33	37	44	52	53	54	58
Selling, general, & admin.	12	21	25	32	44	64	87	104	127	138	136	136
Total expenses	**26**	**44**	**50**	**59**	**73**	**96**	**124**	**147**	**179**	**191**	**191**	**194**
Other income	3	0	0	1	(1)	(2)	(2)	(3)	(2)	0	0	3
Income before taxes	**(12)**	**(34)**	**(31)**	**(29)**	**(27)**	**(38)**	**(24)**	**28**	**45**	**80**	**152**	**210**
Taxes	0	0	(0)	1	4	(13)	4	11	15	27	39	48
Net income	**($12)**	**($34)**	**($31)**	**($30)**	**($31)**	**($25)**	**($28)**	**$17**	**$30**	**$53**	**$112**	**$162**
FREE CASH FLOW												
Net income	($12)	($34)	($31)	($30)	($31)	($25)	($28)	$17	$30	$53	$112	$162
Noncash items	2	3	3	3	4	6	8	10	14	18	20	23
Working capital	(6)	(6)	(6)	(7)	(14)	(17)	(19)	(20)	(28)	(16)	(6)	(6)
Capital expenditures	(15)	(9)	(9)	(9)	(10)	(11)	(15)	(18)	(24)	(27)	(28)	(30)
Free cash flow	**($31)**	**($46)**	**($43)**	**($43)**	**($51)**	**($47)**	**($54)**	**($11)**	**($8)**	**$28**	**$98**	**$149**

Source: Case writer's analysis.

EXHIBIT 3 | Paige Simon's Dart-Selected Sample of Firms with Analysis of Five-Year Dividends as a Percentage of Stock Price

	Recent Price	Annual Dividend	Projected Five-Year Dividend Growth (%)	Beta	Equity Cost	Present Value of Five Years' Dividends	Percent of Market Price Not Attributable to Dividends
BNSF	$53	$0.64	13.0%	0.95	11.2%	3.36	94%
Caterpillar	49	0.80	10.0	1.20	12.6	3.74	92
Cooper Industries	67	1.40	0.0	1.20	12.6	4.98	93
Cummins, Inc.	82	1.20	1.0	1.35	13.4	4.30	95
Deluxe Corporation	33	1.48	1.5	0.80	10.4	5.79	82
RR Donnelley	34	1.04	3.5	0.95	11.2	4.21	88
Dun & Bradstreet	64	0.00	0.0	0.80	10.4	0.00	100
Eaton Corp.	63	1.08	13.5	1.10	12.0	5.62	91
Emerson Electric Co.	70	1.60	7.5	1.10	12.0	7.08	90
Equifax	33	0.11	3.5	1.10	12.0	0.44	99
FedEx Corporation	81	0.29	13.0	1.10	12.0	0.00	100
Fluor Corporation	63	0.64	4.0	1.20	12.6	2.54	96
Honeywell Int'l. Inc.	34	0.75	3.0	1.35	13.4	2.84	92
Illinois Tool Works, Inc.	82	1.00	8.5	1.05	11.7	4.58	94
Kelly Services	29	0.40	11.0	0.95	11.2	1.99	93
ServiceMaster	14	0.43	2.5	0.80	10.4	1.73	87
Sherwin-Williams Co.	46	0.68	11.0	1.00	11.5	3.36	93
Smurfit-Stone Cont. Co.	10	0.00	0.0	1.30	13.1	0.00	100
Tenneco	17	0.00	0.0	1.75	15.5	0.00	100
Weyerhauser Co.	68	1.60	7.5	1.15	12.3	7.03	90
						Average	93%

Note: To illustrate the estimate of 94% for Burlington Northern, the annual dividend of $0.64 was projected to grow at 13.0% per year to $0.72 in 2006, $0.82 in 2007, $0.92 in 2008, $1.04 in 2009, and $1.18 in 2010. The present value of those dividends discounted at 11.2% was $3.36. That equaled about 6% of Burlington Northern's stock price, $53.00. The complement, 94%, is the portion of market price not attributable to dividends.

Source of data: *Value Line Investment Survey* for prices, dividends, growth rates, and betas. Other items calculated by case writer.

EXHIBIT 4 | Key Terminal Value Estimators

Approach	Advantages	Disadvantages
Book Value	—Simple —"Authoritative"	—Ignores some assets and liabilities —Historical costs: backward-looking —Subject to accounting manipulation
Liquidation Value	—Conservative	—Ignores "going concern" value —(Dis)orderly sale?
Replacement Value	—"Current"	—Replace *what?* —Subjective estimates
Multiples, Earnings Capitalization —**Price/Earnings** —**Value/EBIT** —**Price/Book**	—Simple —Widely used	—"Earnings" subject to accounting manipulation —"Snapshot" estimate: may ignore cyclical, secular changes —Depends on comparable firms: ultimately just a measure of relative, not absolute value
Discounted Cash Flow	—Theoretically based —Rigorous —Affords many analytical insights —Cash focus —Multiperiod —Reflects time value of money	—Time-consuming —Risks "analysis paralysis" —Easy to abuse, misuse —Tough to explain to novices

EXHIBIT 5 | Cash Flows of Three Deals with Differing Rates of Development (values in millions of U.S. dollars)

Year	Movie Studio	Bottling Plant	Toll Road
1	($20)	($20)	($20)
2	(40)	(60)	90
3	(60)	(100)	169
4	(20)	5	172
5	0	10	176
6	20	20	179
7	30	40	183
8	50	65	187
9	75	115	190
10	100	150	194
11	90	180	198
12	80	190	202
13	60	200	206
14	55	204	210
15	70	208	214
16	85	212	219
17	95	216	223
18	105	221	227
19	130	225	232
20	150	230	237
21	140	234	241
22	160	239	246
23	190	244	251
24	225	249	256
25	240	254	261
26	230	259	266
27	255	264	272
28	260	269	277
29	265	275	283
30	270	280	288
31+	Steady growth to infinity.		

Projected Cash Flows by Investment

Toll road

Bottling plant

Movie studio

Millions of Dollars / Year

Source : Case writer's analysis.

EXHIBIT 6 | Sensitivity Analysis of Arcadian Terminal Value and Present Value By Variations in Terminal Value Scenarios (values in millions of U.S. dollars)

Arcadian's View

	2%	3%	4%	5%	6%	7%
Annual growth rate to infinity	**2%**	**3%**	**4%**	**5%**	**6%**	**7%**
Weighted average cost of capital	20%	20%	20%	20%	20%	20%
Annual capex (net of depr'n.) 2015	$0	($5)	($12)	($15)	($20)	($28)
Annual addition to NWC 2015	—	(3)	(5)	(7)	(8)	(9)
Adjusted free cash flow 2015	202	194	185	180	174	165
Terminal value 2014	1,142	1,173	1,200	1,257	1,314	1,355
PV of terminal value 2014	185	189	194	203	212	219
PV free cash flows 2005–2014	($151)	($151)	($151)	($151)	($151)	($151)
Total Present Value	**$33**	**$38**	**$43**	**$52**	**$61**	**$68**

Sierra Capital's View

	2%	3%	4%	5%	6%	7%
Annual growth rate to infinity	**2%**	**3%**	**4%**	**5%**	**6%**	**7%**
Weighted average cost of capital	20%	20%	20%	20%	20%	20%
Annual capex (net of depr'n.) 2016	$0	($5)	($12)	($15)	($20)	($28)
Annual addition to NWC 2016	—	(3)	(5)	(7)	(8)	(9)
Adjusted free cash flow 2016	185	177	168	163	157	148
Terminal value 2015	1,049	1,073	1,093	1,142	1,189	1,219
PV of terminal value 2015	141	144	147	154	160	164
PV free cash flows 2005–2015	($118)	($118)	($118)	($118)	($118)	($118)
Total Present Value	**$23**	**$26**	**$29**	**$35**	**$42**	**$46**

Source: Case writer's analysis.

Jetblue Airways IPO Valuation

My neighbor called me the other day and she said, "You have an interesting little boy." Turns out, the other day she asked my son Daniel what he wanted for Christmas. And he said, "I want some stock." "Stock?" she said. "Don't you want video games or anything?" "Nope," he said. "I just want stock. JetBlue stock."

—David Neeleman

CEO and Founder, JetBlue Airways

It was April 11, 2002, barely two years since the first freshly painted JetBlue plane had been rolled out at the company's home base at New York City's John F. Kennedy Airport (JFK). JetBlue's first years had been good ones. Despite the challenges facing the U.S. airline industry following the terrorist attacks of September 2001, the company remained profitable and was growing aggressively. To support JetBlue's growth trajectory and offset portfolio losses by its venture-capital investors, management was ready to raise additional capital through a public equity offering. **Exhibits 1** through **4** provide selections from JetBlue's initial public offering (IPO) prospectus, required by the SEC to inform investors about the details of the equity offering.

After nearly two weeks of road-show meetings with the investment community, the JetBlue management team had just finished its final investor presentation and was heading for Chicago's Midway Airport. With representatives of co-lead manager Morgan Stanley and the JetBlue board patched in on a conference call, it was time for the group to come to an agreement on the offering price of the new shares. The initial price range for JetBlue shares, communicated to potential investors, was $22 to $24. Facing sizable excess demand for the 5.5 million shares planned for the IPO, management had recently filed an increase in the offering's price range ($25 to $26). But even at that price range, most of the group thought the stock faced "blow-out" demand.

After months of preparation, it was time to set the price. The underwriters were anxious to distribute the shares that evening, and NASDAQ was prepared for JBLU (the company's ticker symbol) to begin trading on the exchange in the morning.

JetBlue Airways

In July 1999, David Neeleman, 39, announced his plan to launch a new airline that would bring "humanity back to air travel." Despite the fact that the U.S. airline industry had witnessed 87 new-airline failures over the previous 20 years, Neeleman was convinced that his commitment to innovation in people, policies, and technology could keep his planes full and moving.[1] His vision was shared by an impressive new management team and a growing group of investors. David Barger, a former vice president of Continental Airlines, had agreed to become JetBlue's president and COO. John Owen had left his position as executive vice president and former treasurer of Southwest Airlines to become JetBlue's CFO. Neeleman had received strong support for his business plan from the venture-capital community. He had quickly raised $130 million in funding from such high-profile firms as Weston Presidio Capital, Chase Capital Partners, and Quantum Industrial Partners (George Soros's private-equity firm).

In seven months, JetBlue had secured a small fleet of Airbus A320 aircraft and initiated service from JFK to Fort Lauderdale, Florida, and Buffalo, New York. By late summer of 2000, routes had been added to two other Florida cities (Orlando and Tampa), two other northeastern cities (Rochester, New York, and Burlington, Vermont), and two California cities (Oakland and Ontario). The company continued to grow rapidly through early 2002, and was operating 24 aircraft flying 108 flights per day to 17 destinations.

JetBlue's early success was often attributed to Neeleman's extensive experience with airline start-ups. As a University of Utah student in his early 20s, Neeleman began managing low-fare flights between Salt Lake City and Hawaii. His company, Morris Air, became a pioneer in ticketless travel, and was later acquired by low-fare leader Southwest Airlines. Neeleman stayed only briefly at Southwest, leaving to assist in the launching of Canadian low-fare carrier WestJet while waiting out the term of his "noncompete" agreement with Southwest. Simultaneously, Neeleman also developed the e-ticketing system Open Skies, which was acquired by Hewlett-Packard in 1999.

Neeleman acknowledged that JetBlue's strategy was built on the goal of fixing everything that "sucked" about airline travel. He offered passengers a unique flying experience by providing new aircraft, simple and low fares, leather seats, free LiveTV at every seat, preassigned seating, reliable performance, and high-quality customer service. JetBlue focused on point-to-point service to large metropolitan areas with high average fares or highly traveled markets that were underserved. JetBlue's operating strategy had produced the lowest cost per available-seat-mile of any major U.S. airline in 2001—6.98 cents versus an industry average of 10.08 cents.

With its strong capital base, JetBlue had acquired a fleet of new Airbus A320 aircraft. JetBlue's fleet not only was more reliable and fuel-efficient than other airline

---

[1]Jeff Sweat, "Generation Dot-Com Gets Its Wings," *Information Week* (January 1, 2001).

fleets, but also afforded greater economies of scale because the airline had only one model of aircraft. JetBlue's management believed in leveraging advanced technology. For instance, all its pilots used laptop computers in the cockpit to calculate the weight and balance of the aircraft and to access their manuals in electronic format during the flight. JetBlue was the first U.S. airline to equip cockpits with bulletproof Kevlar doors and security cameras in response to the September 11 hijackings.

JetBlue had made significant progress in establishing a strong brand by seeking to be identified as a safe, reliable, low-fare airline that was highly focused on customer service and by providing an enjoyable flying experience. JetBlue was well positioned in New York, the nation's largest travel market, with approximately 21 million potential customers in the metropolitan area. Much of JetBlue's customer-service strategy relied on building strong employee morale through generous compensation and passionately communicating the company's vision to employees.

The Low-Fare Airlines

In 2002, the low-fare business model was gaining momentum in the U.S. airline industry. Southwest Airlines, the pioneer in low-fare air travel, was the dominant player among low-fare airlines. Southwest had successfully followed a strategy of high-frequency, short-haul, point-to-point, low-cost service. Southwest flew more than 64 million passengers a year to 58 cities, making it the fourth-largest carrier in America and in the world. Financially, Southwest had also been extremely successful—in April 2002, Southwest's market capitalization was larger than all other U.S. airlines combined (**Exhibits 5** and **6** provide financial data on Southwest Airlines).

Following the success of Southwest, a number of new low-fare airlines emerged. These airlines adopted much of Southwest's low-cost model, including flying to secondary airports adjacent to major metropolitan areas and focusing on only a few types of aircraft to minimize maintenance complexity. In addition to JetBlue, current low-fare U.S. airlines included AirTran, America West, ATA, and Frontier. Alaska Air, an established regional airline, was adopting a low-fare strategy. Many of the low-fare airlines had been resilient in the aftermath of the September 11 attacks. (**Exhibit 7** shows current market-multiple calculations for U.S. airlines.) Low-fare airlines had also appeared in markets outside the United States, with Ryanair and easyJet in Europe and WestJet in Canada. (**Exhibit 8** provides historical growth rates of revenue and equipment for low-fare airlines.)

The most recent IPOs among low-fare airlines were of non-U.S. carriers. Ryanair, WestJet, and easyJet had gone public with trailing EBIT multiples of 8.5×, 11.6×, and 13.4×, respectively, and first-day returns of 62%, 25%, and 11%, respectively.[2]

---

[2]The "first-day return" was the realized return based on the difference between the IPO share price and the market share price at the close of the first day of exchange-based trading. The term "trailing EBIT (earnings before interest and taxes) multiple" was defined as (Book debt + IPO price × Post-IPO shares outstanding)/(Most recent year's EBIT). The term "leading EBIT multiple" referred to an EBIT multiple based on a future year's forecast EBIT.

The IPO Process

The process of "going public" (selling publicly traded equity for the first time) was an arduous undertaking that usually required about three months. **Exhibit 9** provides a timeline for the typical IPO.[3] A comment on the IPO process by JetBlue CFO John Owen can be found at http://it.darden.virginia.edu/JetBlue/streaming_links.htm.

Private firms needed to fulfill a number of prerequisites before initiating the equity-issuance process. Firms had to generate a credible business plan; gather a qualified management team; create an outside board of directors; prepare audited financial statements, performance measures, and projections; and develop relationships with investment bankers, lawyers, and accountants. Frequently, firms held "bake-off" meetings to discuss the equity-issuance process with various investment banks before selecting a lead underwriter. Important characteristics of an underwriter included the proposed compensation package, track record, analyst research support, distribution capabilities, and aftermarket market-making support.

After the firm satisfied the prerequisites, the equity-issuance process began with an organizational or "all-hands" meeting, which was attended by all the key participants, including management, underwriters, accountants, and legal counsel for both the underwriters and the issuing firm. The meeting was designed for planning the process and reaching agreement on the specific terms. Throughout the process, additional meetings could be called to discuss problems and review progress. Following the initiation of the equity-issuance process, the Securities and Exchange Commission (SEC) prohibited the company from publishing information outside the prospectus. The company could continue established, normal advertising activities, but any increased publicity designed to raise awareness of the company's name, products, or geographical presence in order to create a favorable attitude toward the company's securities could be considered illegal. This requirement was known as the "quiet period."

The underwriter's counsel generally prepared a "letter of intent," which provided most of the terms of the underwriting agreement but was not legally binding. The underwriting agreement described the securities to be sold, set forth the rights and obligations of the various parties, and established the underwriter's compensation. Because the underwriting agreement was not signed until the offering price was determined (just before distribution began), both the firm and the underwriter were free to pull out of the agreement anytime before the offering date. If the firm did withdraw the offer, the letter of intent generally required the firm to reimburse the underwriter for direct expenses.

The SEC required that firms selling equity in public markets solicit its approval. The filing process called for preparation of the prospectus (Part I of the registration statement), answers to specific questions, copies of the underwriting contract, company charter and bylaws, and a specimen of the security (all included in Part II

---

[3]This section draws from Michael C. Bernstein and Lester Wolosoff, *Raising Capital: The Grant Thornton LLP Guide for Entrepreneurs;* Frederick Lipman, *Going Public;* Coopers and Lybrand, *A Guide to Going Public;* and Craig G. Dunbar, "The Effect of Information Asymmetries on the Choice of Underwriter Compensation Contracts in IPOs" (PhD diss., University of Rochester, n.d.).

of the registration statement), all of which required the full attention of all parties on the offering firm's team. One of the important features of the registration process was the performance of "due-diligence" procedures. Due diligence referred to the process of providing reasonable grounds that there was nothing in the registration statement that was significantly untrue or misleading, and was motivated by the liability of all parties to the registration statement for any material misstatements or omissions. Due-diligence procedures involved such things as reviewing company documents, contracts, and tax returns; visiting company offices and facilities; soliciting "comfort letters" from company auditors; and interviewing company and industry personnel.

During this period, the lead underwriter began to form the underwriting "syndicate," which comprised a number of investment banks that agreed to buy portions of the offering at the offer price less the underwriting discount. In addition to the syndicate members, dealers were enlisted to sell a certain number of shares on a "best-efforts" basis. The dealers received a fixed reallowance, or concession, for each share sold. The selling agreement provided the contract among members of the syndicate. The agreement granted power of attorney to the lead underwriter, and stipulated the management fee that each syndicate member was required to pay the lead underwriter, the share allocations, and the dealer reallowances or concessions. Because the exact terms of the agreement were not specified until approximately 48 hours before selling began, the agreement did not become binding until just before the offering. The original contract specified a range of expected compensation levels. The selling agreement was structured so that the contract became binding when it was orally approved via telephone by the syndicate members after the effective date.

The SEC review process started when the registration statement was filed and the statement was assigned to a branch chief of the Division of Corporate Finance. As part of the SEC review, the statement was given to accountants, attorneys, analysts, and industry specialists. The SEC review process was laid out in the Securities Act of 1933, which aspired to "provide full and fair disclosure of the character of securities sold in interstate commerce."[4] Under the Securities Act, the registration statement became effective 20 days after the filing date. If, however, the SEC found anything in the registration statement that was regarded as materially untrue, incomplete, or misleading, the branch chief sent the registrant a "letter of comment" detailing the deficiencies. Following a letter of comment, the issuing firm was required to correct and return the amended statement to the SEC. Unless an acceleration was granted by the SEC, the amended statement restarted the 20-day waiting period.

While the SEC was reviewing the registration statement, the underwriter was engaged in "book-building" activities, which involved surveying potential investors to construct a schedule of investor demand for the new issue. To generate investor interest, the preliminary offering prospectus, or "red herring" (so called because the prospectus was required to have "Preliminary Prospectus" on the cover in red ink), was printed and offered to potential investors. Underwriters generally organized a one- or two-week "road-show" tour during this period. The road shows allowed managers

---

[4]Preamble, Securities Act of 1933.

to discuss their investment plans, display their management potential, and answer questions from financial analysts, brokers, and institutional investors in locations across the country or abroad. Finally, companies could place "tombstone ads" in various financial periodicals announcing the offering and listing the members of the underwriting syndicate.

By the time the registration statement was ready to become effective, the underwriter and the offering firm's management negotiated the final offering price and the underwriting discount. The negotiated price depended on perceived investor demand and current market conditions (e.g., price multiples of comparable companies, previous offering experience of industry peers). Once the underwriter and the management agreed on the offering price and discount, the underwriting agreement was signed, and the final registration amendment was filed with the SEC. The company and the underwriter generally asked the SEC to accelerate the final pricing amendment, which was usually granted immediately over the telephone. The offering was now ready for public sale. The final pricing and acceleration of the registration statement typically happened within a few hours.

During the morning of the effective day, the lead underwriter confirmed the selling agreement with the members of the syndicate. Following confirmation of the selling agreement, selling began. Members of the syndicate sold shares of the offering through oral solicitations to potential investors. Because investors were required to receive a final copy of the prospectus with the confirmation of sale and the law allowed investors to back out of purchase orders upon receipt of the final prospectus, the offering sale was not realized until underwriters actually received payment. Underwriters would generally cancel orders if payment was not received within five days of the confirmation.

SEC Rule 10b-7 permitted underwriters to engage in price-stabilization activities for a limited period during security distribution. Under this rule, underwriters often posted stabilizing bids at or below the offer price, which provided some price stability during the initial trading of an IPO.

The offering settlement, or closing, occurred seven to ten days after the effective date, as specified in the underwriting agreement. At this meeting, the firm delivered the security certificates to the underwriters and dealers, and the lead underwriter delivered the prescribed proceeds to the firm. In addition, the firm traditionally delivered an updated comfort letter from its independent accountants. Following the offering, the underwriter generally continued to provide valuable investment-banking services by distributing research literature and acting as a market maker for the company.

The IPO Decision

There was some debate among the JetBlue management team regarding the appropriate pricing policy for the IPO shares. Morgan Stanley reported that the deal was highly oversubscribed by investors (i.e., demand exceeded supply). Analysts and reporters were overwhelmingly enthusiastic about the offering. (**Exhibit 10** contains a selection of recent comments by analysts and reporters.) Given such strong demand, some members of the group worried that the current pricing range still left too much money on the table. Moreover, they believed that raising the price would send a strong signal of confidence to the market.

The contrasting view held that increasing the price might compromise the success of the deal. In management's view, a successful offering entailed not only raising the short-term capital needs, but also maintaining access to future capital and providing positive returns to the crew members (employees) and others involved in directed IPO share purchases. Because maintaining access to capital markets was considered vital to JetBlue's aggressive growth plans, discounting the company's IPO price seemed like a reasonable concession to ensure a successful deal and generate a certain level of investor buzz. Being conservative on the offer price seemed particularly prudent considering the risks of taking an infant New York airline public just six months after 9/11. (**Exhibit 11** provides forecasts of expected aggregate industry growth and profitability; **Exhibit 12** shows the share-price performance of airlines over the past eight months.)

By April 2002, the U.S. economy had been stalled for nearly two years. The Federal Reserve had attempted to stimulate economic activity by reducing interest rates to their lowest level in a generation. Current long-term U.S. Treasuries traded at a yield of 5%, short-term rates were at 2%, and the market risk premium was estimated to be 5%.

Based on the JetBlue management team's forecast of aircraft acquisitions, **Exhibit 13** provides a financial forecast for the company.[5]

---

[5]In pricing IPO shares, it was appropriate to divide the total equity value of the firm by the premoney shares outstanding. In the case of JetBlue, the number of premoney shares outstanding was 35.1 million. This number included the automatic conversion of all convertible redeemable preferred shares into common shares.

EXHIBIT 1 | Selections from JetBlue Prospectus

The Offering	
Common stock offered	5,500,000 shares
Use of proceeds	We intend to use the net proceeds, together with existing cash, for working capital and capital expenditures, including capital expenditures related to the purchase of aircraft.
Dividends	We have not declared or paid any dividends on our common stock. We currently intend to retain our future earnings, if any, to finance the further expansion and continued growth of our business.
Proposed NASDAQ National Market symbol	JBLU

Results of Operations

	Three Months Ended				
Operating Statistics:	Dec 31, 2000	Mar 31, 2001	Jun 30, 2001 (unaudited)	Sep 30, 2001	Dec 31, 2001
Revenue passengers	523,246	644,419	753,937	791,551	926,910
Revenue passenger miles (in thousands)	469,293	600,343	766,350	863,855	1,051,287
Available seat miles (in thousands)	623,297	745,852	960,744	1,131,013	1,370,658
Load factor	75.3%	80.5%	79.8%	76.4%	76.7%
Breakeven load factor	79.4%	73.2%	70.6%	74.6%	76.2%
Aircraft utilization (hours per day)	11.8	13.1	13.1	12.8	11.8
Average fare	$ 90.65	$ 96.15	$ 101.01	$ 101.66	$ 99.37
Yield per passenger mile (cents)	10.11	10.32	9.94	9.29	8.76
Passenger revenue per available seat mile (cents)	7.61	8.31	7.93	7.10	6.72
Operating revenue per available seat mile (cents)	7.85	8.56	8.16	7.30	6.97
Operating expense per available seat mile (cents)	8.03	7.55	7.01	6.93	6.68
Departures	4,620	5,283	6,332	6,936	7,783
Average stage length (miles)	833	871	937	1,007	1,087
Average number of operating aircraft during period	9.2	10.5	13.2	15.9	19.4
Full-time equivalent employees at period end	1,028	1,350	1,587	1,876	2,116
Average fuel cost per gallon (cents)	103.38	86.03	83.24	79.53	60.94
Fuel gallons consumed (in thousands)	8,348	9,917	12,649	14,958	17,571
Percent of sales through jetblue.com during period	32.6%	37.6%	39.4%	45.1%	51.3%

EXHIBIT 2 | Balance Sheets of JetBlue Airways (in thousands of dollars)

	December 31	
	2001	2000
ASSETS		
Cash and cash equivalents	$117,522	$34,403
Receivables, less allowance	20,791	21,633
Inventories, less allowance	2,210	1,133
Prepaid expenses and other	3,742	2,744
Total current assets	144,265	59,913
Flight equipment	364,681	163,060
Predelivery deposits for flight equipment	125,010	91,620
	489,691	254,680
Less accumulated depreciation	9,523	2,334
	480,168	252,346
Other property and equipment	29,023	18,290
Less accumulated depreciation	4,313	1,632
	24,710	16,658
Total property and equipment	504,878	269,004
Other Assets	24,630	15,211
Total Assets	$673,773	$344,128

	December 31	
	2001	2000
LIABILITIES		
Accounts payable	$24,549	$12,867
Air traffic liability	51,566	27,365
Accrued salaries, wages and benefits	18,265	5,599
Other accrued liabilities	15,980	5,255
Short-term borrowings	28,781	15,138
Current maturities of long-term debt	54,985	24,800
Total current liabilities	194,126	91,024
Long Term Debt	290,665	137,110
Deferred Credits & Other Liabilities	10,708	6,595
Convertible Redeemable Preferred Stock	210,441	163,552
COMMON STOCKHOLDERS' EQUITY	44	44
Additional paid-in capital	3,889	487
Accumulated deficit	(33,117)	(54,684)
Unearned compensation	(2,983)	—
Total common stockholders' equity (deficit)	(32,167)	(54,153)
Total Liabilities & Common Stockholders' Equity	$673,773	$344,128

EXHIBIT 3 | Statements of Operations of JetBlue Airways
(in thousands of dollars, except per-share amounts)

	Year Ended December 31		
	2001	**2000**	**1999**
Operating Revenues			
Passenger	$310,498	$101,665	$ —
Other	9,916	2,953	—
Total Operating Revenues	320,414	104,618	—
Operating Expenses			
Salaries, Wages and Benefits	84,762	32,912	6,000
Aircraft Fuel	41,666	17,634	4
Aircraft Rent	32,927	13,027	324
Sales and Marketing	28,305	16,978	887
Landing Fees and Other Rents	27,342	11,112	447
Depreciation and Amortization	10,417	3,995	111
Maintenance Materials and Repairs	4,705	1,052	38
Other Operating Expenses	63,483	29,096	6,405
Total Operating Expenses	293,607	125,806	14,216
Operating Income (Loss)	26,807	(21,188)	(14,216)
Other Income (Expense)			
Airline Stabilization Act Compensation	18,706	—	—
Interest Expense	(14,132)	(7,395)	(705)
Capitalized Interest	8,043	4,487	705
Interest Income and Other	2,491	2,527	685
Total Other Income (Expense)	15,108	(381)	685
Income (Loss) Before Income Taxes	41,915	(21,569)	(13,531)
Income Tax Expense (Benefit)	3,378	(239)	233
Net Income (Loss)	38,537	(21,330)	(13,764)
Preferred Stock Dividends	(16,970)	(14,092)	(4,656)
Net Income (Loss) Applicable to Common Stockholders	$21,567	($35,422)	($18,420)
Earnings (Loss) Per Common Share:			
Basic	$9.88	($27)	($37)
Diluted	$1.14	($27)	($37)
Pro forma basic (unaudited)	$1.30		

EXHIBIT 4 | Statements of Cash Flows of JetBlue Airways
(in thousands of dollars)

	Year Ended December 31		
	2001	2000	1999
Cash Flows From Operating Activities			
Net income (loss)	$38,537	($21,330)	($13,764)
Adjustments to reconcile net income (loss) to net cash provided by (used in) operating activities:			
Depreciation	9,972	3,889	111
Amortization	445	106	—
Deferred income taxes	3,373	—	—
Other, net	5,960	3,892	619
Changes in certain operating assets and liabilities:			
Decrease (increase) in receivables	430	(21,622)	—
Increase in inventories, prepaid expenses and other	(2,120)	(3,354)	(340)
Increase in air traffic liability	23,788	26,173	—
Increase in accounts payable and other accrued liabilities	30,894	15,070	6,818
Net cash provided by (used in) operating activities	111,279	2,824	(6,556)
Cash Flows From Investing Activities			
Capital expenditures	(233,775)	(205,759)	(12,463)
Predelivery deposits for flight equipment, net	(54,128)	(27,881)	(50,713)
Increase in security deposits	(1,952)	(7,939)	(5,302)
Purchases of short-term investments	—	(20,923)	—
Proceeds from maturities of short-term investments	—	21,392	—
Other, net	—	(20)	1,026
Net cash used in investing activities	(289,855)	(241,130)	(67,452)
Cash Flows From Financing Activities			
Proceeds from issuance of convertible redeemable preferred stock	29,731	51,322	80,671
Proceeds from issuance of common stock	25	130	69
Proceeds from issuance of long-term debt	185,000	137,750	—
Proceeds from short-term borrowings	28,781	15,138	—
Proceeds from aircraft sale and leaseback transactions	72,000	70,000	—
Repayment of long-term debt	(35,254)	(18,577)	—
Repayment of short-term borrowings	(15,138)	—	—
Other, net	(3,450)	(1,300)	—
Net cash provided by financing activities	261,695	254,463	80,740
Increase In Cash And Cash Equivalents	83,119	16,157	6,732
Cash and cash equivalents at beginning of year	34,403	18,246	11,514
Cash and cash equivalents at end of year	$117,522	$34,403	$18,246

EXHIBIT 5 | Selections from Value Line Tear Sheet for Southwest Airlines

Recent stock price	$20.69			
P/E ratio	49.3			
Dividend yield	0.1%			
Beta	1.10			
Financial statement forecast	2001	2002E	2003E	2005E/2007E
Total debt (in millions)	$1,842			
Revenue (in millions)	$5,555	$6,000	$7,100	$10,300
Operating margin	17.1%	18.0%	24.5%	27.0%
Tax rate	31.0%	38.5%	38.5%	38.5%
Common shares outstanding (in millions)	776.8	785.0	795.0	815.0

EXHIBIT 6 | Southwest Airlines: Current Debt Outstanding

Issue	Moody's Rating	Amount Outstanding	Maturity Date	Yield to Maturity
Short-term bank debt	NA	$475 million	NA	NA
Floating rate secured notes	NA	$200 million	2004	NA
Private notes 5.10–6.10	NA	$614 million	2006	NA
Floating rate French Bank debt	NA	$52 million	2012	NA
8.75 Note	Baa1	$100 million	Oct-2003	5.65%
8.00 Note	Baa1	$100 million	Feb-2005	5.91%
7.875 Debenture	Baa1	$100 million	Sep-2007	7.41%
7.375 Debenture	Baa1	$100 million	Feb-2027	8.68%
Capital leases	NA	$109 million	NA	NA

Data Source: Mergent's Bond Record; Southwest Annual Report.

EXHIBIT 7 | Recent Valuation Multiples

	Actual for 2001						Estimates for 2002	
	Price/ Share	Book Equity/ Share	Book Debt/ Share	EBITDA*/ Share	EBIT/ Share	Earnings/ Share	EBIT/ Share	Earnings/ Share
	(1)	(2)	(3)	(4)	(5)	(6)	(7)	(8)
AirTran	6.6	0.5	4.0	1.2	0.8	0.3	0.8	0.3
Alaska Air	29.1	32.1	33.8	3.3	(1.7)	(1.5)	2.7	(0.8)
America West	3.5	12.5	10.2	(4.3)	(6.2)	(4.4)	(4.5)	(4.1)
AMR	22.3	35.1	69.3	(7.0)	(16.2)	(11.5)	12.4	(3.9)
ATA	15.0	10.8	32.9	8.5	(2.0)	(2.6)	(6.4)	(7.2)
Continental	26.2	20.9	82.0	9.8	1.4	(1.6)	11.1	(1.2)
Delta	29.3	32.7	70.3	(1.4)	(11.8)	(9.9)	8.4	(3.1)
Frontier	17.0	5.4	0.0	3.2	3.0	2.0	0.6	0.4
Midwest	14.6	8.3	2.7	(0.1)	(1.6)	(1.1)	1.6	0.8
Northwest	15.7	(5.1)	66.9	1.6	(4.4)	(5.0)	7.2	(2.5)
Ryanair	32.1	5.5	3.3	1.3	0.9	0.7	1.2	0.9
Southwest	18.5	5.3	1.8	1.5	1.1	0.7	1.4	0.7
United	13.5	59.6	186.2	(37.0)	(56.1)	(39.6)	N/A	(15.4)
WestJet	15.9	2.8	1.0	2.1	1.3	0.8	1.6	0.6

	Trailing					Leading	
	Market to book multiple	Total capital multiple	EBITDA multiple	EBIT multiple	PE Multiple	EBIT multiple	PE multiple
	[1/2]	[(1+3)/(2+3)]	[(1+3)/4]	[(1+3)/5]	[1/6]	[(1+3)/7]	[1/8]
AirTran	13.5	2.4	8.6	13.0	25.3	13.9	20.0
Alaska Air	0.9	1.0	19.2	(37.1)	(19.3)	23.3	(38.8)
America West	0.3	0.6	(3.2)	(2.2)	(0.8)	(3.0)	(0.8)
AMR	0.6	0.9	(13.1)	(5.7)	(1.9)	7.4	(5.7)
ATA	1.4	1.1	5.6	(23.8)	(5.7)	(7.5)	(2.1)
Continental	1.3	1.1	11.0	77.0	(16.7)	9.8	(22.4)
Delta	0.9	1.0	(71.6)	(8.4)	(3.0)	11.8	(9.4)
Frontier	3.2	3.2	5.3	5.7	8.4	26.6	45.9
Midwest	1.8	1.6	(298.3)	(11.0)	(13.5)	11.2	17.4
Northwest	(3.1)	1.3	51.6	(18.8)	(3.1)	11.5	(6.3)
Ryanair	5.8	4.0	26.4	38.5	44.0	30.3	34.1
Southwest	3.5	2.9	13.4	18.6	27.6	14.3	28.4
United	0.2	0.8	(5.4)	(3.6)	(0.3)	N/A	(0.9)
WestJet	5.6	4.4	8.1	12.7	19.6	10.6	26.9

Data Source: Actual numbers for 2001 are from company annual reports. Estimates for 2002 are from Value Line when available, otherwise consensus analyst estimates are used. All stock prices are quoted as of December 31, 2001. Ryanair figures are based on the respective American Deposit Receipt prices. Westjet figures are in Canadian dollars. One US dollar = 1.5870 Canadian dollars as of March 31, 2002. The calculation procedure for the valuation multiples is defined in the lower panel based on the numbered variables defined in the upper panel.

EXHIBIT 8 | Historical Annual Growth Rates for Low-Fare Airlines

Year	$ Revenue Growth					$ Gross Equipment Growth				
	AirTran	ATA	Frontier	Ryanair	Southwest	AirTran	ATA	Frontier	Ryanair	Southwest
1972					−20%					177%
1973					5%					55%
1974					28%					61%
1975					32%					54%
1976					51%					35%
1977					101%					59%
1978					42%					66%
1979					46%					68%
1980					32%					57%
1981					35%					27%
1982					45%					23%
1983					18%					35%
1990					10%					17%
1991					14%					11%
1992					20%		11%			28%
1993		1%			21%	2204%	24%			36%
1994	456%	21%	49%		18%	175%	23%	186%		13%
1995	186%	18%	125%	20%	13%	−40%	5%	66%	25%	11%
1996	−4%	2%	39%	N/A	10%	−4%	4%	26%	15%	19%
1997	49%	20%	56%	N/A	16%	108%	17%	50%	29%	12%
1998	18%	21%	105%	39%	19%	15%	22%	50%	11%	9%
1999	−20%	39%	79%	68%	19%	24%	15%	43%	21%	14%
2000	35%	23%	237%	N/A	16%	7%	−1%	−6%	N/A	19%
2001	−22%	−58%		N/A	12%					−2%

EXHIBIT 9 | Lifecycle of a Typical U.S. IPO Transaction

Event time (in days)	Event
<0	Underwriter selection meeting.
0	Organizational "all-hands" meeting. "Quiet period" begins.
15–44	Due diligence. Underwriter interviews management, suppliers, and customers; reviews financial statements; drafts preliminary registration statement. Senior management of underwriter gives OK on issue.
45	Registration (announcement) date. Firm files registration statement with SEC; registration statement is immediately available to the public.
45–75	SEC review period. SEC auditor reviews for compliance with SEC regulations. Underwriter assembles syndicate and prepares road show.
50	Distribute preliminary prospectus (red herring).
60–75	Road show. Underwriters and issuing firm's management present offering to interested institutional investors and build book of purchase orders.
75–99	Letters of comment received from SEC; amendments filed with SEC.
99	Effective date. Underwriter and firm price offering. SEC gives final approval of registration statement.
100	Public offering date. Stock issued and begins trading.
108	Settlement date. Underwriter distributes proceeds to issuing firm.
After market	Underwriter may support new equity by acting as market maker and distributing research literature on issuing firm.

EXHIBIT 10 | Selected Quotations of Analysts and Reporters

"The bottom line is really very simple. Neeleman saw a gaping hole and flew a plane through it. Get on this baby, because this is as close to a sure thing as it gets." —Lisa DiCarlo, *Forbes*

"People are going to have a high appetite for JetBlue stock." —Ray Neidl, ABN Amro

"JetBlue took to the skies in 2000 and surprised the airline sector when it reported its first profit only a year later. Passengers are drawn to the low fares, leather seats and free live TV on board. And Wall Street admires JetBlue for its experienced management team and winning formula, one made popular by the success of Southwest Airlines." —Suzanne Pratt, *Nightly Business Report*

"JetBlue is off to a good start. But to say it deserves the valuation of Southwest, which has not had a year without profits for 27 years, might be a stretch." —Jim Corridore, Standard & Poor's

"JetBlue has a management team with real expertise, and they're executing very well." —Marc Baum, IPO Group

"It's a very young company that's still going to need to make a lot of investment over the next 5 to 10 years, There's not going to be a lot of free cash flow." —Jonathan Schrader, Morningstar

"What's important here is that the business model is solid and they aren't deviating from it." —Helane Becker, Buckingham Research

"Everyone I've talked to that's flown with them has been delighted." —Jim Broadfoot, Ivy Emerg. Growth Fund

"This is an industry where the failure rate is very high for new entrants." —Patrick Murphy, former Assistant Secretary, Department of Transportation

"It's a fantastic airline. It's also something that you need to personally experience . . . There's live TV, all-leather seats that are comfortable, and the crew has an attitude that is one of service. It's ingrained and installed in them and as a result, they treat passengers differently. I think they have cornered the market on perhaps the way flying ought to be." —Clark Snyder, LiveTV

Sources: *BusinessWeek, BBC News, Nightly Business Report, New York Metro.*

EXHIBIT 11 | Historical Financial Performance and Analysts' Financial Forecasts
for Air-Transport Industry

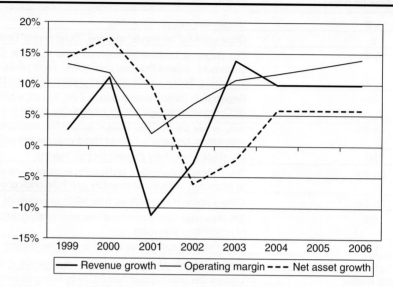

Source: Adapted from Value Line Investment Survey, March 2002.

EXHIBIT 12 | Recent Share-Price Performance for Airlines

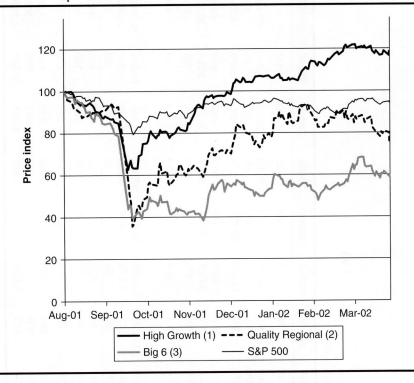

Notes:

1. High-growth airlines include Southwest Airlines, Ryanair, easyJet, and WestJet.
2. Quality regional airlines include Atlantic Coast and Skywest.
3. Big 6 airlines include American, Continental, Delta, Northwest, United, and US Airways.

EXHIBIT 13 | JetBlue Financial Forecast (dollars in millions)

	2001	2002E	2003E	2004E	2005E	2006E	2007E	2008E	2009E	2010E
Number of aircraft	21	34	48	62	74	86	98	108	113	117
$ Revenue/plane	$15.3	$17.6	$18.4	$19.2	$20.1	$21.0	$21.9	$22.8	$23.8	$24.9
Expected inflation rate		16%	4%	4%	4%	4%	4%	4%	4%	4%
Operating margin	8.4%	13.3%	15.2%	15.2%	15.2%	15.2%	15.2%	15.2%	15.2%	15.2%
$ Depreciation per aircraft	$0.5	$0.5	$0.5	$0.6	$0.6	$0.6	$0.7	$0.7	$0.7	$0.8
$ Net capex per incremental aircraft	$21.3	$22.3	$23.5	$24.6	$25.9	$27.1	$28.5	$29.9	$31.4	$33.0
Expected inflation rate		5%	5%	5%	5%	5%	5%	5%	5%	5%
NWC turnover (revenue/NWC)	9.4	9.4	9.4	9.4	9.4	9.4	9.4	9.4	9.4	9.4
Financial forecast										
Revenue	$320	$600	$884	$1,192	$1,485	$1,802	$2,114	$2,466	$2,694	$2,912
Cash expenses	283	502	723	975	1,215	1,474	1,753	2,016	2,202	2,380
Depreciation	10	18	26	36	45	54	65	75	83	90
EBIT	27	80	134	181	226	274	326	375	410	443
Taxes (Tax rate = 34%)	9	27	46	62	77	93	111	127	139	151
NOPAT	18	53	89	120	149	181	215	247	270	292
Capital expenditure	234	290	328	345	310	326	342	299	157	132
Net working capital	34	63	94	126	157	191	227	261	285	308
Fixed assets	530	802	1,104	1,413	1,679	1,950	2,227	2,451	2,526	2,568

Data Source: JetBlue management forecast and case writer analysis.

Rosetta Stone: Pricing the 2009 IPO

We are changing the way the world learns languages.
  —Tom Adams

It was mid-April 2009. Tom Adams, president and CEO of Rosetta Stone, Inc. (Rosetta Stone), the language learning software company, reached for his iPhone to contact Phil Clough of private equity fund ABS Capital. Adams and Clough had been discussing plans to take Rosetta Stone public for some time. The wait was finally over.

In the wake of the 2008 financial crisis, the market for initial public offerings (IPOs) evaporated. By early spring the market was showing its first encouraging signs. Just a week prior, Chinese online videogame developer Changyou.com had listed on the NASDAQ at a price to EBITDA of 6.5 times followed by a one-day jump of 25%, and the online college Bridgeport Education was currently circulating its plans to go public at a range of 10 to 12 times EBITDA.

Having received preliminary approval of its registration filings with the U.S. Securities and Exchange Commission (SEC), Rosetta Stone was authorized to sell 6.25 million shares, a 30% stake in the company. **Exhibits 1** and **2** provide financial statements from Rosetta Stone's IPO prospectus, required by the SEC to inform investors about the details of the equity offering. Half of the shares were to be new shares and the other half were shares to be sold by existing shareholders. Rosetta Stone management had circulated an estimated price range of $15 to $17 per share, representing a price to EBITDA of about 8 times. Demand for the shares was strong, and some analysts believed that Rosetta Stone was leaving money on the table. Yet with world financial and product markets still in turmoil, there was a strong case to be made for prudence.

This case was written by Associate Professor Michael J. Schill with the assistance of Suprajj Papireddy (MBA '10), Tom Adams (Rosetta Stone), and Phil Clough (MBA '90 and ABS Capital). It was written as a basis for class discussion rather than to illustrate effective or ineffective handling of an administrative situation. Copyright © 2009 by the University of Virginia Darden School Foundation, Charlottesville, VA. All rights reserved. *To order copies, send an e-mail to* sales@dardenbusinesspublishing.com. *No part of this publication may be reproduced, stored in a retrieval system, used in a spreadsheet, or transmitted in any form or by any means—electronic, mechanical, photocopying, recording, or otherwise—without the permission of the Darden School Foundation.*

Economic Conditions

The previous year had been a dramatic one for the world economy. Prices on global credit and equity markets had been in free fall. The U.S. equity market was down over 50% from its peak in October 2007 (see **Exhibit 3** for details of the recent price history of U.S. equity market returns in total and for select industries). The collapse of world financial markets had preceded deterioration in economic activity worldwide, including dramatic shifts in real estate values, unemployment levels, and discretionary consumer spending. The severity of economic conditions had prompted massive intervention by world governments with dramatic policy changes, particularly by the U.S. federal government. The economic and political conditions were frequently compared with those of the Great Depression of the 1930s. With the crisis in full swing, investors had flocked to U.S. Treasuries for security, pushing down yields on these instruments to historic lows (see **Exhibit 4**). Heightened investor risk aversion had expanded the risk premium for all securities. The general market risk premium was currently estimated at 6.5% or 8.5%, respectively, depending on whether long-term or short-term government yields were used in estimating the risk-free rate.

In February and March of 2009, there had been some evidence of improvement in financial and economic conditions. Wholesale inventories were in decline. New-home sales were beginning to rise. The equity market had experienced a rally of over 20% in recent weeks. Yet many money managers and analysts worried that such economic green shoots were only a temporary rally in a longer-running bear market. There was strong concern that the magnitude of government spending would spur inflation in the U.S. dollar. GDP growth was still negative, corporate bankruptcy rates and unemployment were at historic highs, and many believed the economic void was just too big for a quick recovery to be feasible. A *Wall Street Journal* survey of U.S. economists suggested that the economy was expected to generate positive growth in the last half of 2009.[1] In contrast, a survey of U.S. corporate executives stated that less than a third of respondents expected to see an economic upturn in 2009.[2] The debate regarding the economic future of the world economy raged on.

Rosetta Stone

In the 1980s, Allen Stoltzfus, an economics professor, real estate agent, and history buff, was frustrated with his slow progress in mastering the Russian language. He was enrolled in a conventional classroom Russian course but found it much less effective than the process he had used to learn German while living in Germany years before. Seeking to produce a more natural language learning method, Stoltzfus envisioned using computer technology to simulate the way people learn their native language—with pictures and sounds in context. Rather than learning the language by translating one language to another, his approach would be to use

[1]Phil Izzo, "Obama, Geithner Get Low Grades From Economists," *Wall Street Journal,* March 11, 2009.

[2]"Economic Conditions Snapshot, March 2009: McKinsey Global Survey Results," *McKinsey Quarterly,* March 2009.

electronic technology to encourage people to think in the target language from the beginning. He sought the aid of his brother-in-law, John Fairfield, who had received graduate training in computer science. Together they explored the concept of how a computer could be made to facilitate language learning. Stoltzfus and Fairfield founded Fairfield Language Technologies in Harrisonburg, Virginia, in 1992. The emergence of CD-ROM technology in the 1990s made the project feasible. The company released its first retail language training software product in 1999 under the name Rosetta Stone.[3]

The Rosetta Stone series of CD-ROMs provided users with an effective way of learning new languages. The software utilized a combination of images, text, and sound to teach various vocabulary terms and grammatical functions intuitively by matching images with the spoken word. Following the way children learn their first language, the company called this method of teaching languages the *Dynamic Immersion* method: "dynamic" because digital technology and the teaching method powerfully engaged the learner in an interactive learning process, and "immersion" because learners anywhere, from any language background, started at the very beginning and studied exclusively in the target language. A recent research study provided scientific evidence that the language test scores of students that completed 55 hours of Rosetta Stone training performed comparably to those who had completed an entire semester of a good quality college language course.[4] Rosetta Stone users were broadly satisfied with the experience and regularly recommended the software to others.

After focusing initially on school and government sales, the company began aggressively pursuing the retail market in 2001. Following the death of Stoltzfus in 2002, the company hired an outsider, 31-year-old Tom Adams, as chief executive. Adams brought an international dimension to the small-town, rural company: A native of Sweden who had grown up in England and France, he was fluent in Swedish, English, and French. He had studied history at Bristol University in the United Kingdom and had earned an MBA from INSEAD in France. Prior to arriving in Harrisonburg, Adams had been a commodity merchant in Europe and China.

Adams got right to work by entering new markets and scaling up the current business; from 2004 to 2005, the revenues of the company nearly doubled, from $25 million to $48 million. Acknowledging the need for capital and professional support as the company expanded, Adams solicited a capital infusion from the private equity market. In 2006, two firms, ABS Capital Partners and Norwest Equity Partners, made major equity investments in the company. As part of the recapitalization, the name of the company was changed from Fairfield Language Technologies to Rosetta Stone, Inc., to match the signature product. Over the ensuing two years, revenue continued to expand aggressively, rising to $81 million in 2006, $137 million in 2007, and

---

[3]The name *Rosetta Stone* referred to a black basalt tablet discovered in 1799 by a French engineer in Napoleon's army near the Egyptian town of Rosetta. The tablet contained an inscription of a single text in three languages—two Egyptian scripts (hieroglyphic and demotic) and ancient Greek—thus enabling 19th century scholars to decipher Egyptian scripts conclusively for the first time.

[4]Roumen Vesselinov, "Measuring the effectiveness of Rosetta Stone," working paper, City University of New York, January 2009.

$210 million in 2008. Since Adams's arrival, the compound annual growth rates of Rosetta Stone's revenue and operating profit were at 70% and 98%, respectively, and the company employed over 1,200 people. By early 2009, Rosetta Stone was the most recognized language learning software brand in the world. Millions of language learners in more than 150 countries were using the Rosetta Stone software. The company offered self-study language learning solutions in 31 languages to its customers. (**Exhibit 5** lists the language training software currently offered by the company.) In 2008, approximately 80% of Rosetta Stone revenue was accounted for by retail consumers, 20% by institutions. Institutional customers included educational institutions, government and military institutions, commercial institutions, and not-for-profit institutions.

In a few short years, Rosetta Stone had successfully developed a strong brand; its kiosks with bright yellow boxes had become an institution in U.S. airports, and its print advertising in travel publications included a popular print ad of a young farm boy holding a Rosetta Stone box, the copy reading, "He was a hardworking farm boy. She was an Italian supermodel. He knew he would have just one chance to impress her." The unaided awareness of the Rosetta Stone brand was over seven times that of any other language learning company in the United States. Leveraging a strong brand, steady customer base, and diverse retail network, Rosetta Stone had maintained positive profitability in 2008 despite the severe economic downturn and, in both average orders of bundled products and services and in units sold, even had experienced increases.

The company expanded its product line by increasing the number of languages and levels offered and broadened the language learning experience by introducing Rosetta Studio and Rosetta World. Rosetta Studio allowed each Rosetta Stone learner to schedule time to chat with other learners and with a native-speaking coach to facilitate language practice, motivation, and confidence. Rosetta World connected a virtual community of language learners to practice their skills through a collection of games and other dynamic conversation opportunities. Adams envisioned a substantial growth trajectory for the company with a multitude of ways to leverage its novel learning technology and expand its geographic reach. With a fixed development cost, Adams expected the strategy to continue to increase company operating margins and expand revenue, but he recognized that, as the company continued to show strong profit and growth, the incentive for competition to attempt to gain market share would intensify. **Exhibit 6** provides three video excerpts of an interview with Adams in which he describes the future of Rosetta Stone.

Industry Overview

The worldwide language learning industry was valued at more than $83 billion, of which more than $32 billion was for self-study learning, according to a Nielsen survey. The U.S. market, from which Rosetta Stone generated 95% of its revenue, was estimated to be more than $5 billion for total language learning and $2 billion for self-study learning. The total language learning market was expected to expand as proficiency in multiple languages was becoming increasingly important due to trends in globalization and immigration. The self-study market, particularly through electronic delivery, was expected to dominate the industry expansion given that self-study was increasingly accepted by language learning and travel enthusiasts.

The language learning industry had historically been dominated by specialized language schools that taught languages through conventional classroom methods. The largest player in the market was privately held Berlitz International. Berlitz taught languages in its classrooms using the Berlitz Method of Language Instruction, which advocated immersion in the target language, among other things, and according to company literature, offered programs and services through more than 470 centers in over 70 countries. Auralog, a French company, was another important competitor in the industry. Both Berlitz and Auralog offered electronic software packages that provided quality language training software.

Just as Rosetta Stone had developed the Rosetta World product, businesses such as LiveMocha, Babalah, and Palabea had also adopted a social media approach, connecting language learners through the Internet, but these sites tended to be secondary enrichment sources for language learners.

Major software companies with deep pockets represented the most important potential threat. Although the novelty of Rosetta Stone's approach shielded it from many of the existing players in the industry, the entry of a company such as Apple or Microsoft into the language learning market had the potential to thwart Rosetta Stone's aspiration of dominating global language learning.

The IPO Process[5]

The process of *going public*—selling publicly traded equity for the first time—was an arduous undertaking that, at a minimum, required about three months. (**Table 1** provides a timetable for the typical IPO. **Exhibit 6** links to video of Adams describing the specific ways Rosetta Stone management prepared the company to go public.)

Before initiating the equity-issuance process, private firms needed to fulfill a number of prerequisites: generate a credible business plan; gather a qualified management team; create an outside board of directors; prepare audited financial statements, performance measures, and projections; and develop relationships with investment bankers, lawyers, and accountants. Frequently, firms held "bake-off" meetings to discuss the equity-issuance process with various investment banks before selecting a lead underwriter. Important characteristics of an underwriter included the proposed compensation package, track record, analyst research support, distribution capabilities, and aftermarket market-making support.

After the firm satisfied the prerequisites, the equity-issuance process began with a meeting of all the key participants (management, underwriters, accountants, and

[5]This section draws from Michael C. Bernstein and Lester Wolosoff, *Raising Capital: The Grant Thornton Guide for Entrepreneurs* (Chicago: Irwin Professional Publishing, 1995); Frederick Lipman, *Going Public* (Roseville, CA: Prima, 1994); Coopers and Lybrand, *A Guide to Going Public* 2nd edition (New York: Coopers & Lybrand, 1997); and Craig G. Dunbar, "The Effect of Information Asymmetries on the Choice of Underwriter Compensation Contracts in IPOs" (PhD diss., University of Rochester, n.d.).

TABLE 1 | Timetable for typical U.S. IPO (in days).

Prior to Day 1: **Organizational "all-hands" meeting**	1 2 3 4 5 6 7 8 9 10 11 12 13 14	**1–14: Quiet period**	
15–44: Due diligence Underwriter interviews management, suppliers, and customers; reviews financial statements; drafts preliminary registration statement. Senior management of underwriter gives OK on issue.	15 16 17 18 19 20 21 22 23 24 25 26 27 28 29 30 31 32 33 34 35 36 37 38 39 40 41 42		
45: Registration (announcement) **50: Prospectus (*red herring*)**	43 44 **45** 46 47 48 49 **50** 51 52 53 54 55 56 57 58 59 60 61 62 63 64 65 66 67 68 69 70	**45–75: SEC review period** SEC auditor reviews for compliance with SEC regulations. Underwriter assembles syndicate and initiates road show.	
76–89: Letters of comment received from SEC; amendments filed with SEC. **90: Effective date; shares offered**	71 72 73 74 75 76 77 78 79 80 81 82 83 84 85 86 87 88 89 **90** **91** 92 93 94 95 96 97 **98**	**76–89: Road show** Preliminary price range set. Under- writers, issuing firm's management present deal to institutional investors, build book of purchase orders. **91: Trading begins** **98: Settlement**	

Source: Created by case writer based on industry standards.

legal counsel for both the underwriters and the issuing firm) to plan the process and reach agreement on specific terms. Throughout the process, additional meetings could be called to discuss problems and review progress.

Following the initiation of the equity-issuance process, the SEC prohibited the company from publishing information outside the prospectus. The company could continue established, normal advertising activities, but any increased publicity designed to raise awareness of the company's name, products, or geographical presence in order to create a favorable attitude toward the company's securities could be considered illegal. This requirement was known as the *quiet period*.

The underwriter's counsel generally prepared a letter of intent that provided most of the terms of the underwriting agreement but was not legally binding. The underwriting agreement described the securities to be sold, set forth the rights and obligations of the various parties, and established the underwriter's compensation. Because the underwriting agreement was not signed until the offering price was determined (just before distribution began), both the firm and the underwriter were free to pull out of the agreement any time before the offering date. If the firm did withdraw the offer, the letter of intent generally required the firm to reimburse the underwriter for direct expenses.

The SEC required that firms selling equity in a public market solicit the market's approval. The filing process called for preparation of the prospectus (Part I of the registration statement), answers to specific questions, copies of the underwriting contract, company charter and bylaws, and a specimen of the security (all included in Part II of the registration statement), all of which required the full attention of all parties on the offering firm's team.

One of the important features of the registration process was the performance of due-diligence procedures. *Due diligence* referred to the process of providing reasonable grounds that there was nothing in the registration statement that was significantly untrue or misleading and was motivated by the liability of all parties to the registration statement for any material misstatements or omissions. Due-diligence procedures involved such things as reviewing company documents, contracts, and tax returns; visiting company offices and facilities; soliciting "comfort letters" from company auditors; and interviewing company and industry personnel.

During this period, the lead underwriter began to form the underwriting *syndicate*, which comprised a number of investment banks that agreed to buy portions of the offering at the offer price less the underwriting discount. In addition to the syndicate members, dealers were enlisted to sell a certain number of shares on a "best-efforts" basis. The dealers received a *fixed reallowance*, or concession, for each share sold. The selling agreement provided the contract to members of the syndicate, granted power of attorney to the lead underwriter, and stipulated (a) the management fee that each syndicate member was required to pay the lead underwriter, (b) the share allocations, and (c) the dealer reallowances or concessions. Because the exact terms of the agreement were not specified until approximately 48 hours before selling began, the agreement would not become binding until just before the offering. The original contract specified a range of expected compensation levels; the selling agreement was structured so that the contract became binding when it was orally approved via telephone by the syndicate members after the effective date.

The SEC review process started when the registration statement was filed and the statement was assigned to a branch chief of the Division of Corporate Finance. As part of the SEC review, the statement was given to accountants, attorneys, analysts, and industry specialists. The SEC review process was laid out in the Securities Act of 1933, which according to its preamble aspired to "provide full and fair disclosure of the character of securities sold in interstate commerce." Under the Securities Act, the registration statement became effective 20 days after the filing date. If, however, the SEC found anything in the registration statement that was regarded as materially untrue, incomplete, or misleading, the branch chief sent the registrant a *letter of comment* detailing the deficiencies. Following a letter of comment, the issuing firm was required to correct and return the amended statement to the SEC. Unless an acceleration was granted by the SEC, the amended statement restarted the 20-day waiting period.

While the SEC was reviewing the registration statement, the underwriter was engaged in "book-building" activities, which involved surveying potential investors to construct a schedule of investor demand for the new issue. To generate investor interest, the preliminary offering prospectus or "red herring" (so called because the prospectus was required to have the words *preliminary prospectus* on the cover in red ink) was printed and offered to potential investors. During this period, underwriters generally organized a one- to two-week "road show" tour, which enabled managers to discuss their investment plans, display their management potential, and answer questions from financial analysts, brokers, and institutional investors in locations across the country or abroad. Finally, companies could place "tombstone ads" in various financial periodicals announcing the offering and listing the members of the underwriting syndicate.

By the time the registration statement was ready to become effective, the underwriter and the offering firm's management negotiated the final offering price and the underwriting discount. The negotiated price depended on perceived investor demand and current market conditions (e.g., price multiples of comparable companies, previous offering experience of industry peers). Once the underwriter and the management agreed on the offering price and discount, the underwriting agreement was signed, and the final registration amendment was filed with the SEC. The company and the underwriter generally asked the SEC to accelerate the final pricing amendment, which was usually granted immediately by phone. The offering was now ready for public sale. The final pricing and acceleration of the registration statement typically happened within a few hours.

During the morning of the effective day, the lead underwriter confirmed the selling agreement with the members of the syndicate. Following confirmation of the selling agreement, selling began. Members of the syndicate sold shares of the offering through oral solicitations to potential investors. Because investors were required to receive a final copy of the prospectus with the confirmation of sale, and the law allowed investors to back out of purchase orders upon receipt of the final prospectus, the offering sale was not realized until underwriters actually received payment. Underwriters would generally cancel orders if payment was not received within five days of the confirmation.

SEC Rule 10b-7 permitted underwriters to engage in price stabilization activities for a limited period during security distribution. Under this rule, underwriters often posted stabilizing bids at or below the offer price, which provided some price stability during the initial trading of an IPO.

The *offering settlement*, or closing, occurred seven to ten days after the effective date, as specified in the underwriting agreement. At this meeting, the firm delivered the security certificates to the underwriters and dealers, and the lead underwriter delivered the prescribed proceeds to the firm. In addition, the firm traditionally delivered an updated comfort letter from its independent accountants. Following the offering, the underwriter generally continued to provide valuable investment-banking services by distributing research literature and acting as a market maker for the company.

Pricing the Rosetta Stone IPO

Adams had a preference for a strong balance sheet and cash position for the company. As a private company, corporate investment was limited by the amount of capital the company could borrow from private sources. With constrained resources, Adams was concerned that Rosetta Stone was an attractive takeover target for a company with the needed resources. Led by Phil Clough at ABS Capital, the private equity investors were anxious to recognize the gains achieved through the Rosetta Stone investment.

In March, the board had discussed the matter and yielded the IPO decision to Adams. Despite the uncertainty of taking a relatively young company public in the most volatile markets in decades, Adams was inclined to move forward with the deal. The fourth quarter financials continued to show impressive performance, with a 53% expansion in revenue despite the global economic contraction. (**Exhibit 7** details the historical financial performance of the company along with historical internally generated values of Rosetta Stone shares.) Advisors at Morgan Stanley had shared their view that Rosetta Stone was one of only a handful of companies that currently had a shot at a successful IPO. Senior management had been preparing the systems and organization of the company for public company status for years. Adams saw the IPO event as significant opportunity to establish business credibility and build the Rosetta Stone brand in a global marketplace. His decision was to launch.

Over the following week or two, senior management and bankers visited prospective investors on the east and west coasts of the United States and in Europe. The investor response was highly enthusiastic, with investors commonly asking to "max out" their allocation in the deal. By the end of the road show, Morgan Stanley reported that the book was more than 25 times oversubscribed, meaning that the underwriters maintained orders for 25 shares for every Rosetta Stone share being offered in the deal.

Adams was delighted that many investors appeared to share his vision of Rosetta Stone's unique capacity to play a substantial role in the global language learning market. Such a trajectory implied revenue growth rates of 20% to 35% for some time. Other analysts were more skeptical, predicting revenue growth of around 15% for the next five years and then tapering down to a long-term growth rate of 3% to 4%. Adams believed that the operating leverage in the organization allowed margins to continue to improve for some time; others believed that competitive pressure would soon drive margins down. (**Exhibit 8** provides one view of how the financials were expected to play out in the years to come.) In the debt market, Rosetta Stone faced a prevailing borrowing rate of about 7.5%. The marginal corporate tax rate for the company was 38%. **Exhibit 9** details the current ownership structure of the company and details the new shares to be sold in the offering, which would grow the total number of shares outstanding from 17.2 million to 20.3 million.[6]

Comparable multiples played an important role in the valuation of IPO firms. **Exhibit 10** provides financial data on a broad set of industry comparable firms. Adams liked K12 Inc. as a comparable match, but acknowledged that no other firm perfectly matched Rosetta Stone's business strategy, skill set, risk profile, or growth potential. Still, there was some debate regarding whether Rosetta Stone would be positioned as a technology company or an educational company. See **Exhibit 6** for a link to video excerpts of Adams and Clough discussing this topic.

---

[6]To avoid the dilution of the value of securities of pre-IPO investors, it was appropriate in pricing IPO shares to divide the total premoney equity value of the firm by the premoney shares outstanding. In the case of Rosetta Stone, the number of premoney shares outstanding was 17.19 million. Since the pre-IPO investors held claim on the ongoing business, a valuation based on the ongoing business represented a premoney valuation. Valuations based on postmoney shares required adding the value of the new IPO shares to the ongoing business valuation prior to dividing by the postmoney shares.

EXHIBIT 1 | Rosetta Stone Income Statement (in thousands of dollars)[1]

	2004	2005	2006	2007	2008
Revenue	$25,373	$48,402	$91,570	$137,321	$209,380
Cost of revenue	3,968	8,242	12,744	20,687	28,676
Gross profit	21,405	40,160	78,826	116,634	180,704
Operating expenses:					
Sales and marketing	11,303	22,432	46,549	65,437	93,384
Research and development	1,833	2,819	8,158	12,893	18,387
Acquired in-process research and development	0	0	12,597	0	0
General and administrative	6,484	8,157	16,732	29,786	39,577
Lease abandonment	0	0	0	0	1,831
Transaction-related expenses	0	0	10,315	0	0
Total operating expenses	19,620	33,408	94,351	108,116	153,179
Income from operations	1,785	6,752	−15,525	8,518	27,525
Other income and expense:					
Interest income	84	38	613	673	454
Interest expense	0	0	−1,560	−1,331	−891
Other income	120	134	63	154	239
Interest and other income (expense), net	204	172	−884	−504	−198
Income before income taxes	1,989	6,924	−16,409	8,014	27,327
Income tax expense (benefit)	66	143	−1,240	5,435	13,435
Net income	1,923	6,781	−15,169	2,579	13,892
Preferred stock accretion	0	0	−159	−80	0
Net income attributable to common stockholders	$1,923	$6,781	−$15,328	$2,499	$13,892

Data Source: Rosetta Stone preliminary prospectus (Form S-1/A, filed March 17, 2009), U.S. SEC.

[1]Depreciation and amortization expense was reported as $6.5, $7.8, and $7.1 million, respectively, for 2006, 2007, and 2008.

EXHIBIT 2 | Rosetta Stone Balance Sheet (in thousands of dollars)

	As of December 31	
Assets	**2007**	**2008**
Cash and cash equivalents	$22,084	$30,660
Accounts receivable	11,852	26,497
Inventory, net	3,861	4,912
Prepaid expenses and other current assets	3,872	6,598
Deferred income taxes	848	2,282
Total current assets	42,517	70,949
Property and equipment, net	13,445	15,727
Goodwill	34,199	34,199
Intangible assets, net	13,661	10,645
Deferred income taxes	6,085	6,828
Other assets	469	470
Total assets	110,376	138,818
Liabilities and stockholders' equity		
Accounts payable	4,636	3,207
Accrued compensation	4,940	8,570
Other current liabilities	11,421	21,353
Deferred revenue	12,045	14,382
Current maturities of long-term debt	3,400	4,250
Total current liabilities	36,442	51,762
Long-term debt	9,909	5,660
Deferred revenue	894	1,362
Other long-term liabilities	6	963
Total liabilities	47,251	59,747
Commitments and contingencies	5,000	0
Common stock outstanding	51,038	56,038
Additional paid-in capital	8,613	10,814
Accumulated income (loss)	−1,470	12,422
Accumulated other comprehensive loss	−56	−203
Total stockholders' equity	58,125	79,071
Total liabilities and stockholders' equity	$110,376	$138,818

Data Source: Rosetta Stone prospectus.

EXHIBIT 3 | Value of $1 invested in January 1998

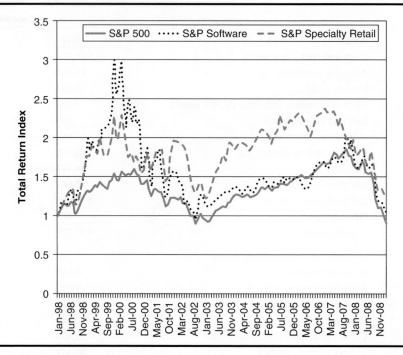

Source: Created by case writer with data from Morningstar.

EXHIBIT 4 | U.S. Yield Curve Data (in percent)

Date	Yields				
	3-month	1-year	5-year	10-year	30-year
1/30/2009	0.24	0.51	1.85	2.87	3.58
2/27/2009	0.26	0.72	1.99	3.02	3.71
3/31/2009	0.21	0.57	1.67	2.71	3.56
4/1/2009	0.22	0.58	1.65	2.68	3.51
4/2/2009	0.22	0.59	1.74	2.77	3.57
4/3/2009	0.21	0.60	1.87	2.91	3.70
4/6/2009	0.20	0.60	1.90	2.95	3.73
4/7/2009	0.20	0.60	1.87	2.93	3.72
4/8/2009	0.18	0.59	1.83	2.86	3.66
4/9/2009	0.18	0.60	1.90	2.96	3.76

Data Source: U.S. Department of the Treasury.

EXHIBIT 5 | Language Coverage of Rosetta Stone Products (2008)

	Instructional software			Audio companion		
	Level 1	Level 2	Level 3	Version 1	Version 2	Version 3
Arabic	●	●	●	●		●
Chinese (Mandarin)	●	●	●	●	●	
Danish	●	●	●	●		●
Dutch	●	●	●	●		●
English (UK)	●	●	●	●		●
English (U.S.)	●	●	●	●		●
Farsi (Persian)	●	●	●	●		●
French	●	●	●	●		●
German	●	●	●	●		●
Greek	●	●	●	●		●
Hebrew	●	●	●	●		●
Hindi	●	●	●	●		●
Indonesian	●				●	
Irish	●	●	●	●		●
Italian	●	●	●	●		●
Japanese	●	●	●	●		●
Korean	●	●	●	●		●
Latin	●				●	
Pashto	●				●	
Polish	●	●	●	●		●
Portuguese (Brazil)	●	●	●	●		●
Russian	●	●	●	●		●
Spanish (Latin America)	●	●	●	●		●
Spanish (Spain)	●	●	●	●		●
Swahili	●				●	
Swedish	●	●	●	●		●
Tagalog	●	●			●	
Thai	●	●			●	
Turkish	●				●	
Vietnamese	●				●	
Welsh	●				●	

Data Source: Rosetta Stone prospectus.

EXHIBIT 6 | Video Exhibit Links

Video Exhibit 1. What is the future for Rosetta Stone?
Interview with Tom Adams, CEO, Rosetta Stone, Inc.

(http://www.youtube.com/watch?v=FjxZ6VhWPBw)

Video Exhibit 2. What does it take to go public?
Interview with Tom Adams, CEO, Rosetta Stone, Inc.

(http://www.youtube.com/watch?v=QVl9NNgmT7U)

Video Exhibit 3. What kind of business is Rosetta Stone?
Interview with Tom Adams, CEO, Rosetta Stone, Inc. and
Phil Clough, Managing General Partner, ABS Capital Partners

(http://www.youtube.com/watch?v=Lnilib9UJx0)

EXHIBIT 7 | Rosetta Stone Historical Financial Performance, 2006 to 2008 (in thousands of dollars except percent and share value)

	2006	2007	2008
Revenue	91,570	137,321	209,380
Revenue growth	89%	50%	52%
EBITDA	1,290	16,318	34,625
EBITDA margin	1.4%	11.9%	16.5%
Total debt		13,309	9,910
Total equity		58,125	79,071
Total capital		71,434	88,981
Capital turnover		1.92	2.24
Return on capital		11.9%	30.9%
Estimated share value[1]	$6.08	$11.19	$17.49

[1]Estimated by Rosetta Stone board of directors based on multiple of EBITDA for industry comparables.

EXHIBIT 8 | Financial Forecast for Rosetta Stone (in millions of dollars)

	2008A	2009E	2010E	2011E	2012E	2013E	2014E	2015E	2016E	2017E	2018E
Revenue growth	52.5%	35.0%	35.0%	30.0%	25.0%	23.0%	21.0%	18.0%	13.0%	10.0%	5.0%
Gross margin	86.3%	86.0%	86.0%	85.0%	84.0%	83.0%	82.0%	81.0%	80.0%	79.0%	78.0%
SGA exp / revenue	63.5%	63.5%	63.5%	63.0%	63.0%	62.5%	62.5%	62.5%	62.5%	62.5%	62.5%
R&D exp / revenue	8.8%	9.0%	9.0%	8.5%	8.5%	8.5%	8.5%	8.0%	8.0%	8.0%	8.0%
Capital expenditures	7.0	5.0	8.0	9.0	9.5	10.0	11.0	11.0	9.0	8.0	5.0
NPPE turnover	13.5	15.0	15.2	15.4	15.6	15.8	16.0	16.2	16.4	16.8	17.3
NWC turnover	8.9	9.0	9.0	9.0	8.5	8.5	8.0	8.0	8.0	8.0	8.0
Revenue	209.4	282.7	381.6	496.1	620.1	762.7	922.9	1,089.0	1,230.6	1,353.6	1,421.3
Gross profit	180.7	243.1	328.2	421.7	520.9	633.1	756.8	882.1	984.5	1,069.4	1,108.6
SGA expense	133.0	179.5	242.3	312.5	390.7	476.7	576.8	680.6	769.1	846.0	888.3
R&D expense	18.4	25.4	34.3	42.2	52.7	64.8	78.4	87.1	98.4	108.3	113.7
EBIT	29.4	38.2	51.5	67.0	77.5	91.5	101.5	114.3	116.9	115.1	106.6
Net working capital	23.4	31.4	42.4	55.1	73.0	89.7	115.4	136.1	153.8	169.2	177.7
Net PPE	15.7	18.8	25.1	32.2	39.7	48.3	57.7	67.2	75.0	80.6	82.2

Source: Case writer analysis.

EXHIBIT 9 | Principal and Selling Stockholders
(in thousands except percent)

Name of beneficial owner	Shares owned prior to offering		Shares offered in IPO
Entities affiliated with ABS Capital Partners	7,556.1	44.0%	1,889.6
Norwest Equity Partners VIII	4,940.0	28.7%	1,235.4
Tom Adams (President, CEO)	743.7	4.3%	
Eric Eichmann (COO)	146.3	0.9%	
Brian Helman (CFO)	91.0	0.5%	
Greogory Long (CPO)	106.2	0.6%	
Michael Wu (General Counsel)	45.5	0.3%	
Patrick Gross (Director)	20.7	0.1%	
John Coleman (Director)	16.2	0.1%	
Laurence Franklin (Director)	16.2	0.1%	
Other owners	3,507.6	20.4%	
New IPO shares			3,125.0
Total shares	17,189.5		6,250.0

Source: Rosetta Stone prospectus.

EXHIBIT 10 | Financial Data for Industry Comparables[1]

	Recent Price	Number of shares (in millions)	Debt (in millions)	Beta	Revenue growth	Income growth	Price/EPS 2008	Price/EPS 2009	EV/EBITDA 2008	EV/EBITDA 2009
For-profit education										
Apollo Group, Inc.	63.81	160.15	0.0	0.60	15%	491%	19.2	14.5	9.7	7.2
American Public Education Inc.	37.56	18.06	0.0	NA	55%	54%	42.4	29.3	20.5	13.8
Corinthian Colleges, Inc.	16.88	86.45	31.9	0.75	16%	78%	28.7	18.1	11.6	7.8
Career Education Corp.	21.05	90.09	1.7	0.70	-2%	9%	19.5	20.0	6.8	6.8
Capella Education	50.34	16.69	0.0	0.55	20%	32%	31.5	23.4	13.4	10.3
Strayer Education	168.01	13.88	0.0	0.55	25%	24%	33.2	25.8	17.8	14.1
DeVry Inc.	42.47	71.64	20.0	0.55	17%	33%	23.2	17.5	12.5	9.6
ITT Educational Services Inc.	101.6	38.56	150.0	0.60	17%	45%	19.0	13.6	10.1	7.4
K12 Inc.	15.29	28.86	13.7	NA	61%	44%	18.3	35.4	13.4	8.7
Grand Canyon Education, Inc.	14.72	45.47	32.1	NA	62%	126%	NA	24.3	30.2	11.5
New Oriental Ed. & Tech. Group, Inc.	50.33	149.19	0.0	1.20	43%	-3%	32.9	24.5	23.8	17.2

Data Source: SEC filings, Value Line Investment Survey, and other analyst reports.

[1]The reported multiples are based on the same valuation numerator but with 2008 actual profits or 2009 expected profits, respectively.

EXHIBIT 10 | Financial Data for Industry Comparables (*Continued*)

	Recent Price	Number of shares (in millions)	Debt (in millions)	Beta	Revenue growth	Income growth	Price/EPS 2008	Price/EPS 2009	EV/EBITDA 2008	EV/EBITDA 2009
Internet										
Activision Blizzard, Inc.	$10.03	1,359	$0.0	NA	124%	340%	18.5	17.2	6.9	6.9
Amazon.com, Inc.	74.71	429	74.0	1.10	29%	24%	53.8	47.9	27.1	23.6
Dice Holdings Inc.	3.2	62.21	60.2	NA	9%	2%	12.3	25.7	4.5	6.9
drugstore.com, Inc.	1.3	97.36	2.1	1.65	8%	63%	NA	NA	NA	91.1
eBay	14.32	1,287.81	0.0	1.15	11%	−22%	12.8	17.1	7.0	8.1
Google	379.5	315.25	0.0	0.90	31%	9%	23.6	20.7	13.2	11.3
GSI Commerce	14.93	47.93	195.9	1.15	29%	−2%	NA	NA	12.2	10.6
TechTarget Inc.	2.38	41.75	0.0	1.45	20%	−117%	NA	NA	8.8	11.3
WebMD Health Corp.	25.58	57.58	0.0	0.85	15%	114%	45.8	46.0	18.1	16.4
Electronic Arts Inc.	19.16	322	0.0	0.90	15%	55%	NA	24.1	NA	11.5
Yahoo! Inc.	14.02	1,393.35	0.0	1.00	3%	−78%	32.6	37.3	10.2	10.3
Software										
Adobe Systems	23.64	524.27	350.0	1.20	13%	−41%	14.9	22.9	8.6	12.6
ArcSight Inc.	14.15	31.5	0.0	NA	34%	509%	NA	52.8	39.2	21.8
Intuit	25.35	320.53	998.1	0.90	15%	9%	19.5	16.2	9.2	7.9
Microsoft	18.83	8891	0.0	0.80	18%	−32%	10.2	12.0	5.9	6.8
Omniture	13.54	75.05	13.2	1.30	107%	37%	NA	NA	16.4	9.6
Salesforce.com	37.36	122.43	0.0	1.20	44%	93%	NA	57.7	35.0	20.7
Symantec	16.47	819.92	1,766.0	0.90	5%	−234%	9.4	9.5	4.7	4.9
McAfee Inc.	34.49	153.72	0.0	1.00	22%	77%	26.1	24.1	12.3	10.1
Vmware Inc.	29.6	389.86	450.0	NA	42%	62%	27.1	33.9	21.0	23.8

Data Source: SEC filings, Value Line Investment Survey, and other analyst reports.

EXHIBIT 10 | Financial Data for Industry Comparables (*Continued*)

For-Profit Education	
Apollo Group, Inc.	Education programs for working adults at the high school, undergraduate, and graduate levels, online and on-campus through subsidiaries.
American Public Education Inc.	Online postsecondary education degree programs and certificate programs including national security, military studies, intelligence, homeland security, criminal justice, technology, business administration and liberal arts; primarily serves military and public service communities.
Corinthian Colleges, Inc.	Private, for-profit postsecondary education degree programs in healthcare, electronics, and business.
Career Education Corporation	North American private, for-profit postsecondary education in information technologies, visual communication and design technologies, business studies, and culinary arts.
Capella Education Company	Online postsecondary education services company; doctoral, master's and bachelor's programs through their subsidiary.
Strayer Education, Inc.	Holding company of Strayer University, which offers undergraduate and graduate degree programs in business administration, accounting, information technology, education, and public administration to working adults.
DeVry, Inc.	North American higher education programs, offering associate, bachelor's and master's degree programs in technology; healthcare technology; business, and management; also offers online secondary education to school districts and medical education.
ITT Educational Services, Inc.	Technology-based postsecondary degree programs in the United States.
K12 Inc.	Technology-based education company; proprietary curriculum, software and educational services created for online delivery to students in kindergarten through 12th grade.
Grand Canyon Education, Inc.	Online undergraduate and graduate degree programs in education, business, and healthcare.
New Oriental Education & Technology Group, Inc.	Foreign language training and test preparation courses in the United States and the People's Republic of China; development and distribution of primary and secondary educational content and technology.

Data Source: Adapted from company sources.

EXHIBIT 10 | Financial Data for Industry Comparables (*Continued*)

Internet	
Activision Blizzard, Inc.	Interactive entertainment software and peripheral products.
Amazon.com, Inc.	Diversified online retailer with emphasis on books.
Dice Holdings Inc.	Career services and recruiting.
drugstore.com, Inc.	Online drugstore.
eBay Inc.	Online trading community.
Google Inc.	Web-based search engine and global technology company.
GSI Commerce, Inc.	E-commerce business developer/operator.
TechTarget	Industry-specific portal operator.
WebMD Health Corp.	Health information services for consumers, physicians, healthcare professionals, employers, and health plans.
Electronic Arts Inc.	Interactive entertainment software and peripheral products.
Yahoo! Inc.	Internet media company providing Web navigation, aggregated information content, communication services, and commerce.

Software	
Adobe Systems Incorporated	Computer software products and technologies.
ArcSight, Inc.	Security and compliance management solutions.
Intuit Inc.	Business and financial management software solutions.
Microsoft Corporation	Operating system software, server application software, business and consumer applications software, software development tools, and Internet/intranet software; also video game consoles and digital music entertainment devices.
Omniture, Inc.	Online business optimization software.
Salesforce.com, Inc.	Application services that permit sharing of on-demand customer information .
Symantec Corporation	Security, storage, and systems management solutions.
McAfee Inc.	Computer security solutions.
VMware Inc.	Virtual infrastructure solutions.

Data Source: Adapted from company sources.

The Timken Company

In 2002, The Timken Company was considering acquiring the Torrington Company from Ingersoll-Rand. The acquisition would make a clear statement to the market about Timken's commitment to remain a worldwide leader in the bearing industry by combining more than 100 years of bearing manufacturing and development experience. Because the two companies shared many of the same customers but had few products in common, customers would surely appreciate that Timken's sales representatives could meet more of their needs. Timken's potential annual cost savings from consolidating manufacturing facilities and processes were estimated to be more than $80 million. If the price paid for Torrington were too high, Ingersoll-Rand, rather than Timken, would capture the value of the synergies. In addition, given the large size of the acquisition, Timken was concerned about the impact on its balance sheet. If Ingersoll-Rand demanded a cash deal and if Timken raised the money with new debt, the increased leverage would almost certainly prompt credit agencies to downgrade Timken's investment-grade rating.

The Bearing Industry

Bearings of various sizes and specifications found their way into everything from space shuttles to household appliances, automobiles, dentist drills, roller skates, and computer disk drives. In 2001, U.S. establishments involved in ball- and roller-bearing manufacturing employed more than 33,000 workers.

The bearing industry was facing a variety of complex problems. Policies favoring the steel industry did not always consider the best interests of the bearing industry, which, as manufacturers of secondary steel products, was in the middle of the production chain. Because bearings were essential components of military and civilian machinery and equipment, the federal government had historically been a major customer. Nonetheless, foreign competitors had taken business away from U.S. companies by selling bearings of equal quality at lower prices. The intensity of the competition at times resulted in charges by U.S. firms of illegal dumping practices by foreign competitors. Found guilty of such practices, those companies often turned around and either opened or bought plants in the United States to supply their American customers.

Shipments of ball and roller bearings grew steadily during the 1990s, peaking in 1998 at more than $5.8 billion. Although 1999 and 2000 remained relatively strong, the value of shipments dropped dramatically in 2001, sinking to $5.3 billion, the lowest since 1995. Reasons included the economic recession, decreased automotive demand, and the terrorist attacks on September 11, 2001. There had been moderate growth in the sector in 2002, led by automotive production, which had risen 5% due to sales incentives, including 0% financing. Overall, the bearings-industry demand was expected to soften as automotive demand had begun to decrease in late 2002 and was generally expected to remain flat for 2003. Thus, the bearings industry appeared to be in a cyclical trough from which many analysts predicted a more widespread recovery in 2003 of about 2% to 3% growth.

Bearings worldwide were doing significantly better. Orders had increased globally and were forecast to grow 6.5% a year through 2005, to $42 billion. With supply levels remaining high worldwide, prices overall were stable and not expected to rise in 2003. Conversely, prices for imports were expected to increase in 2003. As bearings from China came into the United States, selling at below-market prices, the federal government had levied antidumping duties of up to 59.3%. Antidumping payments to Timken amounted to $50 million in 2002 ($30 million in 2001).

The major industry players included Timken, SKF, and NSK, Ltd. Sweden-based Aktiebolegat SKF controlled 20% of the world market in bearings, which was more than twice the market share held by its closest competitors. In 2002, its sales were $4.8 billion, up 18.2% from 2001, and the company employed 39,000 workers. NSK, Ltd., based in Tokyo, produced bearings for the automotive, information technology, and electronics industries. In 2002, NSK's sales reached $3.62 billion and employment topped 22,000, spread across 50 subsidiaries worldwide. In 2002, Timken reported a net income of $38.7 million on sales of $2.55 billion (**Exhibit 1**) and assets of $2.75 billion (**Exhibit 2**). Two-thirds of Timken's sales came from bearings, and about 20% of its sales were from outside the United States. Timken had operations in 25 countries and employed nearly 18,000 workers.

The Timken Company

In 1898, veteran St. Louis carriage-maker Henry Timken patented a design for tapered roller bearings (bearings enclosed between a pair of concentric rings) to facilitate the motion of carriage axles. The following year, Timken and his sons, William and Henry (H. H.), founded The Timken Roller Bearing Axle Company, which was the beginning of what was to become a global manufacturer of highly engineered bearings, alloy and specialty steel, and related components. In 1902, the company moved to Canton, Ohio, to be near the growing steelworks in Pittsburgh, Pennsylvania, and the new automobile factories in Buffalo, New York, Cleveland, Ohio, and Detroit, Michigan. In 1908, with the debut of the Ford Model T, the Timkens' business soared. In 1917, the company began making its own steel for bearings.

Timken stock was sold to the public for the first time in 1922. World War II created increased demand for Timken's products, and the company opened several new plants. H. H. Timken's son, W. Robert Timken, became president in 1960 and chair in 1968. The company continued to grow during the 1960s, when it opened plants in Brazil and France. In 1970, the company adopted its current name, the Timken Company. W. R. Timken Jr., grandson of the founder, became chair in 1975.

In 1982, with increasing competition from Europe and Japan, the company suffered its first loss since the Depression. During the years that followed, Timken engaged in joint ventures, acquisitions, and investments in the United States as well as various locations around the world, including the United Kingdom, Europe, India, China, Africa, and Australia. In 1999, Timken cut production capacity to 80%, and began to consolidate operations and restructure into global business units. The company closed plants in Australia, restructured operations in South Africa (cutting about 1,700 jobs), and outsourced its European distribution to a company in France. In early 2001, the company announced that it would lay off more than 7% of its work force.

Timken business units

In 2002, the company operated three segments: the Automotive Group, the Industrial Group, and the Steel Group. The Automotive and Industrial Groups designed, manufactured, and distributed a range of bearings and related products and services. Automotive Group customers included original-equipment manufacturers (OEMs) of passenger cars and trucks, ranging from light- and medium-duty to heavy-duty trucks and their suppliers. Industrial Group customers included both OEMs and distributors for agricultural, construction, mining, energy, mill, machine-tooling, aerospace, and rail applications. The Steel Group designed, manufactured, and distributed different alloys in both solid and tubular sections, as well as custom-made steel products, for both automotive and industrial applications, including bearings.

Automotive and Industrial Groups: The tapered roller bearing was Timken's principal product in the antifriction industry segment. It consisted of four components: the cone, the cup, the cage, and the tapered rollers. The roller bearing contained many individual and highly toleranced components. When properly applied to a qualified axle journal, it became a system whose function was to carry the weight of the railcar and its cargo reliably, with minimal rolling resistance. The bearing stack comprised both load-carrying and non-load-carrying components. Certain components of the bearing were designed to carry the load. Those components safely carried the weight of the railcar and its cargo with a minimum of rolling resistance. The non-load-carrying components positioned the bearing laterally on the axle and provided the force necessary to achieve proper bearing clamp. Although they did not directly carry the weight of the railcar and its cargo, those components were critical to overall bearing performance. Sometimes called auxiliary components, they completed the bearing stack. Timken manufactured or purchased those components and then sold them in a variety of configurations and sizes.

The company's aerospace and superprecision facilities produced high-performance ball bearings and cylindrical bearings for ultra high-speed and ultra high-accuracy applications in the aerospace, medical and dental, computer disk drive, and other industries. Those bearings utilized ball- and straight-rolling elements and were in the superprecision end of the bearing industry. A majority of Timken's aerospace and superprecision products were custom-designed bearings and spindle assemblies. They often involved specialized materials and coatings for use in applications that subjected the bearings to extreme speed and temperature.

The company competed with domestic manufacturers as well as foreign manufacturers of antifriction bearings, including SKF, INA-Holding Schaeffler KG, NTN Corporation, Koyo Seiko Company, Ltd., and NSK, Ltd. Timken's principal competitors in aerospace products included Ellwood Specialty, Slater/Atlas, and Patriot.

Steel Group: Steel products included steels of low and intermediate alloy, vacuum-processed alloys, tool steel, and some carbon grades. Those products were available in a range of solid and tubular sections with a variety of lengths and finishes. They were used in an array of applications, including bearings, automotive transmissions, engine crankshafts, oil drilling, aerospace, and other similarly demanding applications. Approximately 13% of Timken's steel production was devoted to its bearing operations.

Timken also produced custom-made steel products, including alloy and steel components for automotive and industrial customers. That business provided the company with the opportunity to further expand its market for tubing and to capture higher value-added steel sales. It also enabled Timken's traditional tubing customers in the automotive and bearing industries to take advantage of higher-performing components that cost less than alternative products. Custom-made products were a growing portion of the company's steel business.

Timken's worldwide competitors in seamless mechanical tubing included Copperweld, Plymouth Tube, V & M Tube, Sanyo Special Steel, Ovako Steel, and Tenaris. Competitors in steel-bar products included such North American producers as Republic, Mac Steel, North Star Steel, and a variety of offshore steel producers that imported into North America. Competitors in the precision-steel market included Metaldyne, Linamar, and such overseas companies as Showa Seiko, SKF, and FormFlo. High-speed steel competitors in North America and Europe included Erasteel, Bohler, and Crucible. Tool-and-die steel competitors included Crucible, Carpenter Technologies, and Thyssen.

Ingersoll-Rand

Ingersoll-Rand was an $8.9 billion global diversified manufacturer of industrial and commercial equipment and components. It traced its history to 1871, when Simon Ingersoll patented a steam-powered rock drill, a watershed event that led to the formation of the Ingersoll Rock Drill Company. In 1872, Albert Rand started Rand & Waring Drill and Compressor Company, and changed the name to Rand Drill Company in 1879. Later that year, the first Rand air compressor was introduced. In 1885, the Sergeant Drill Company was formed when Henry Sergeant left the Ingersoll Rock Drill Company. In 1888, the Ingersoll Rock Drill Company merged with the Sergeant Drill Company to form the Ingersoll-Sergeant Drill Company. In 1905,

Ingersoll-Sergeant merged with Rand Drill to form Ingersoll-Rand, headquartered in New York City.

In the 1960s, the company completed nine acquisitions, including The Torrington Company in 1968. In 1985, the Fafnir Bearing Division of Textron was purchased and merged with Torrington. Those acquisitions made Ingersoll-Rand (IR) the largest U.S. bearing manufacturer. Over the ensuing 20 years, IR continued in acquisition mode until, in 2002, the company consisted of four segments: Climate Control, Industrial Solutions, Infrastructure, and Security and Safety.

Climate Control Segment

This segment accounted for 25% of consolidated sales and 17% of income among all segments (segment income). Climate Control produced transport temperature units and heating-ventilation and air-conditioning systems for trucks, buses, and passenger railcars.

Infrastructure Segment

This segment accounted for 27% of consolidated sales and 28% of segment income. Infrastructure produced equipment for the construction, renovation, and repair of public works and private projects, as well as golf carts and utility vehicles.

Security and Safety Segment

This segment accounted for 15% of consolidated sales and 43% of segment income. Security and Safety produced a broad array of commercial and residential security and safety products, including steel doors, electronic-access control systems, and personnel-attendance systems.

Industrial Solutions Segment

This segment accounted for 33% of consolidated sales and 22% of segment income. A group of diverse businesses, Industrial Solutions was divided into three major subsegments: Air Solutions, Engineered Solutions, and Dresdner-Rand. Air Solutions made such products as motion-control components, gas and other compressors, and fluid products. In 2002, Air Solutions reported revenues of $1.3 billion. Engineered Solutions, with sales of $1.2 billion, comprised IR's worldwide operations relating to precision bearings and motion-control components. Dresdner-Rand, with sales of $1.024 billion, produced energy-conversion technology for the oil, gas, and chemical industries.

In early 2002, IR decided to divest the Engineered Solutions segment (Torrington). Strategically, that decision appeared to be consistent with the company's desire to allocate capital to higher potential growth and higher return service businesses, where IR could leverage its cross-selling strategy. IR could not justify allocating substantial capital resources to maintain a leading competitive position in a consolidating, relatively slow-growth industry. Moreover, from an end-market standpoint, the divestiture would reduce IR's exposure to the North American automotive markets.

In 2002, IR reported a loss of $173.5 million on sales of $8.9 billion (**Exhibit 3**) and assets of $10.8 billion (**Exhibit 4**).

The Torrington Company

Founded in 1866 as Excelsior Needle Company, a maker of sewing-machine needles, The Torrington Company was an old-line industrial firm. In 1866, the sewing-machine industry was in its infancy, and Excelsior used a new technology to make the first uniform needles for sewing machines. By the turn of the century, the company expanded into making needles for a wide variety of fabric-sewing, shoemaking, and knitting machines. It later moved into other products, including spokes, marine engines, spark plugs, carburetors, and carpet sweepers, together with a new line of ball bearings for the fledgling automobile industry. During World War II, Torrington developed needle bearings for many military products, including the B-29 Super Fortress bomber, which contained more than 2,000 of the small bearings. Over the decades, Torrington expanded into Europe and Asia before it was acquired by Ingersoll-Rand in 1969.

Torrington operated its business in two segments that were familiar to Timken: automotive and industrial. Sales were approximately equal across the two segments. The OEM business focused on higher-margin niche products.

Torrington's 2002 sales were split as follows: 73% in North America, 17% in Europe, and 10% elsewhere. The company employed 10,500 workers at 27 plants worldwide, and served many diverse end-use markets, including automotive, consumer, general industrial, construction, agricultural, and natural resources. The company's products included spherical roller bearings, radial cylindrical roller bearings, planetary gear shafts, engine bearings, assembled camshafts, radial ball bearings, precision ball screws, radial tapered ball bearings, steering-column shafts, sensor bearings, thrust roller bearings, and needle rollers.

In 2002, revenues and operating income for IR's Torrington Division were $1.204 billion and $85.2 million, respectively, and were expected to reach $1.65 billion and $116.7 million by 2007 (**Exhibit 5**).

Timken's Operating and Financial Strategies

In 2002, Timken was involved in a companywide restructuring, which included consolidating operations into global business units to reduce costs and to set the stage for international growth. In addition, Timken was planning to add new products to its portfolio to become more than a supplier of bearings. Within the industry, this strategy was called "bundling." The strategy arose in response to the reality that foreign competitors were making simple products at substantially lower costs than U.S. companies could produce them. To differentiate their products and command higher margins, Timken and other companies had begun to enhance their basic product with additional components in order to more precisely meet customers' needs with a higher-value-added product.

Bundling was not designed solely to fight imports. Bearing manufacturers were increasingly assembling customized products that took one standard part and surrounded it with casings, pins, lubrication, and electronic sensors. In many cases, manufacturers offered installation and maintenance services, as well as ongoing engineering, all in the name of offering products and services the imports were not offering.

In the 1990s, bundling began in earnest in the auto industry, where parts suppliers saw it as a way to increase profits and to make themselves indispensable to increasingly demanding and cost-conscious auto manufacturers. According to a survey of auto-parts suppliers by the University of Michigan and Oracle Corporation, companies that sold integrated systems posted better results than did those making only commodity products. The bundling process could also benefit buyers by reducing the number of suppliers and relieving them of routine labor- and cost-intensive tasks such as finishing and assembly.

Like other auto suppliers, Timken began bundling prelubricated, preassembled bearing packages for car makers in the early 1990s. Industrial business customers, which accounted for about 38% of Timken's sales, had begun putting the same pressure on their suppliers: Cut prices or lose business to lower-priced foreign producers. Customers not only wanted higher-value-added products, but they also wanted their suppliers to handle an increasing number of tasks.

Over the past 10 years, Timken had experienced significant variation in its financial performance. Earnings per share (EPS) had peaked at $2.73 in 1997, but had hit a low in 2001, with a loss of $0.69 per share. Dividends had steadily increased until 1998, when they remained flat until the loss in 2001 led to the dividends' being cut to $0.52 in 2002. With 2002 EPS at $0.63, Timken's dividend payout had risen to a very demanding 83%. At the same time, Timken's leverage, as measured by total debt to capital, had steadily risen from a low of 20.5% in 1995 to a high of 43.1% in 2002. The trend of increasing leverage had prompted the rating agencies to place Timken's BBB rating on review. Timken considered it a priority to carry an investment-grade debt rating in order to maintain access to the public debt markets at reasonable interest rates.

Torrington as a Potential Acquisition

Timken originally approached Ingersoll-Rand to purchase only the industrial side of Torrington's business. Such a purchase would have represented substantial growth of that market for Timken while reducing Timken's exposure to the auto industry, which continued to be a concern to management. Early in 2002, as the initial negotiations progressed and Timken's management team got a closer look at Torrington, it concluded that Torrington's automotive business was stronger than originally thought, prompting the company to begin pursuing the purchase of Torrington in its entirety. Although such an acquisition would be considerably larger than initially intended, it was consistent with management's desire to increase market share within the global bearing industry.

If Timken succeeded in acquiring Torrington, the combined companies would become the third-largest producer of bearings in the world, and it would have many complementary products. Timken, the inventor of the tapered roller bearing, and Torrington, the pioneer and leading global producer of needle roller bearings, had only a 5% overlap in their product offerings. Conversely, the two companies' customer lists overlapped by approximately 80%. Thus, it was expected that the combined companies would be able to create more value for customers with a more complete product line and, eventually, more effective new-product development. Torrington had sophisticated needle-bearing solutions for automotive power-train applications, which complemented Timken's existing portfolio of tapered roller bearings and precision-steel components for wheel ends and drivelines. Industrial customers required a broad range of industrial solutions and services involving tapered and needle roller bearings as well as cylindrical, spherical, and ball bearings.

Timken's cylindrical bearings, which reduced friction in giant dump trucks and industrial mills, provided an example of how Timken could benefit from acquiring Torrington and its product lines. Timken's cylindrical bearings could be married with flap-like parts from Torrington that lubricated moving pieces. Previously, Timken's customers had been combining the friction and lubrication functions themselves. By assuming that task, Timken hoped to distinguish itself from its foreign competitors and add enough value to increase margins.

On a broader level, Timken executives planned to use the company's international distribution network to deliver Torrington products under the well-known Timken brand name and increase its range of products for aftermarket customers. With that acquisition, Timken would increase its penetration of the global bearing market from 7% to 11%. The company would offer a broader range of complementary products, and its customer base would become larger and more diverse, with more end-use applications and significant cross-selling opportunities. In addition, being number three in the industry would help give Timken more clout in negotiations with customers and suppliers.

Of particular interest to Timken's executives were the expected annual cost savings of $80 million by the end of 2007. According to Ward J. Timken, "There will be certain redundancies in sales forces. You can identify where some of the areas will be." In addition to reducing the combined sales forces, Timken expected to realize significant purchasing synergies by giving much larger volume to a reduced list of suppliers in exchange for price reductions. Before the $80 million in cost savings could be realized, however, certain other costs associated with integrating the two companies were likely to be incurred. One industry analyst estimated that those integration costs would total $130 million over the first couple of years following the merger.

Regardless of the price paid for Torrington, Timken would face significant challenges regarding the financing of the deal. Both Moody's and Standard & Poor's had placed Timken's ratings of Baa1/BBB on review. In view of Torrington's size, Timken knew it would be very difficult to raise the needed cash without significantly raising the level of debt on the books. For example, if IR agreed to sell Torrington for $800 million (analysts' estimated minimum value for the company) and Timken raised the entire amount with a debt offering, Timken's leverage ratios would suffer enough to virtually guarantee that Timken would lose its investment-grade rating.[1] This was particularly troubling, not only because Timken would be forced to borrow the money

---

[1] **Exhibit 6** reports the median financial ratios for industrial firms by S&P industrial debt-rating categories. Investment-grade ratings included AAA, AA, A, and BBB.

at "high-yield" rates, but also because the availability of future funds could become limited for companies carrying non-investment-grade ratings.

In light of the size of the transaction, Timken management concluded that the ideal capital structure needed to be a combination of debt and equity financing. Timken could do this by issuing shares to the public to raise cash and/or by issuing shares directly to IR as consideration for Torrington. **Exhibit 7** compares the stock performances of IR and Timken with the S&P Industrials Index for 1998–2002. Timken's prior equity issuance occurred in 1987, when it raised $63.4 million for 7.2 million shares.[2] Over the past five years, Timken had relied solely on debt to raise $140 million for refunding existing debt and for investment purposes. With the company's stock currently trading around $19 a share, it would require almost double the shares issued in 1987 to raise the same amount of money today.

Information on bearing-industry companies is reported in **Exhibit 8**. **Exhibit 9** depicts government- and corporate-bond yields as of December 2002.

---

[2] The actual number of shares issued (1.8 million) has been adjusted for 2-for-1 stock splits in 1988 and 1997.

EXHIBIT 1 | Timken Corporate Income Statements, 2001–02 ($ in millions, except percentages)

	2001	2002	2001	2002
Total operating revenue	2,447.2	2,550.1	100.0%	100.0%
Cost of goods sold	(2,046.5)	(2,080.5)		
Gross profit	400.7	469.6	16.4%	18.4%
Sales, general, and administrative	(363.7)	(358.9)		
Impairment and restructuring expenses	(54.7)	(32.1)		
Operating profit	(17.7)	78.6	−0.7%	3.1%
Interest expense (net of interest income)	(31.3)	(29.9)		
Receipt of Continued Dumping and Subsidy				
Offset Act payment	29.5	50.2		
Other nonoperating expenses	(7.5)	(13.4)		
Income before tax	(27.0)	85.5		
Income taxes	(14.8)	(34.1)		
Net income before cumulative effect of accounting change	(41.7)	51.4	−1.7%	2.0%
Cumulative effect of accounting change	0.0	(12.7)		
Net income	(41.7)	38.73		
EBIT (before nonrecurring)	37.0	110.7		
Depreciation	152.5	146.5		
Capital expenditures	102.3	90.7		

EXHIBIT 2 | Timken Balance Sheet ($ in millions)

	2001	2002
Assets		
Cash	33.4	82.1
Receivables	307.8	361.3
Inventory	429.2	488.9
Other current assets	58.0	36.0
Total current assets	**828.4**	**968.3**
Net property, plant, and equipment	1,305.3	1,226.2
Other assets	399.4	553.9
Total assets	**$2,533.1**	**$2,748.4**
Liabilities		
Accounts payable	258.0	296.5
Current portion of long-term debt	42.4	111.1
Notes payable	2.0	0.0
Other current liabilities	338.8	226.5
Total current liabilities	**641.2**	**634.1**
Long-term debt	368.2	350.1
Deferred tax liability	742.0	1,155.1
Total liabilities	**$1,751.3**	**$2,139.3**
Shareholders' equity	781.7	609.1
Total liabilities and owners' equity	**$2,533.1**	**$2,748.4**

EXHIBIT 3 | Ingersoll-Rand and Torrington Comparative Income Statements, 2001–02
($ in millions, except percentages)

	Ingersoll-Rand			
	2001	**2002**	**2001**	**2002**
Net sales	$8,604.2	$8,951.3	100.0%	100.0%
Cost of goods sold	6,736.5	6,826.5		
Gross profit	1,867.7	2,124.8	21.7%	23.7%
Selling and administrative expenses	1,370.5	1,439.8		
Restructuring charges	73.7	41.9		
Operating income	423.5	643.1	4.9%	7.2%
Net interest expense	(268.8)	(241.0)		
Minority interests	(20.7)	(14.4)		
Earnings before income taxes	134.0	387.7		
(Benefit)/provision for income taxes	(48.1)	20.3		
Earnings from continuing operations	182.1	367.4		
Discontinued operations (net of tax)	64.1	93.6		
Cumulative effect of accounting changes	0.0	(634.5)		
Net earnings	$ 246.2	($173.5)	2.9%	−1.9%

	Torrington			
	2001	**2002**	**2001**	**2002**
Sales	$1,004.3	$ 1,204	100.0%	100.0%
Operating Income	$ 78.0	$ 85.2	7.8%	7.1%

EXHIBIT 4 | Ingersoll-Rand Balance Sheet ($ in millions)

	2001	2002
Assets		
Cash	$ 114.0	$ 342.2
Receivables	1,359.8	1,405.3
Inventory	1,143.9	1,983.8
Deferred tax asset	321.2	0.0
Other current assets	760.2	381.1
Total current assets	**3,699.1**	**4,112.4**
Net property, plant, and equipment	1,289.5	1,279.9
Goodwill	4,807.5	4,005.5
Intangible assets	848.1	890.9
Other assets	489.6	520.9
Total assets	**$11,133.8**	**$10,809.6**
Liabilities		
Accounts payable	$ 701.6	$ 2,347.4
Accrued expenses	1,470.7	1,155.5
Short-term debt	561.9	0.0
Other current liabilities	249.3	295.2
Total current assets	**2,983.5**	**3,798.1**
Long-term debt	2,900.7	2,092.1
Minority interests	107.6	115.1
Other noncurrent liabilities	1,225.4	1,326.1
Total liabilities	**7,217.2**	**7,331.4**
Shareholders' equity	**3,916.6**	**3,478.2**
Total liabilities and owners' equity	**$11,133.8**	**$10,809.6**

EXHIBIT 5 | Torrington Financial Summary and Projections, 1999–2007 ($ in millions)

	1999	2000	2001	2002	2003E	2004E	2005E	2006E	2007E
Net sales	$1,239.5	$1,161.0	$1,004.3	$1,204	$1,282.0	$1,365.3	$1,454.1	$1,548.6	$1,649.2
Operating income	$ 145.7	$ 172.6	$ 78.0	$ 85.2	$ 90.7	$ 96.6	$ 102.9	$ 109.5	$ 116.7
Sales Growth		−6.3%	−13.5%	19.9%	6.5%	6.5%	6.5%	6.5%	6.5%
Operating Margin	11.8%	14.9%	7.8%	7.1%	7.1%	7.1%	7.1%	7.1%	7.1%
Capital Expenditures	$ 84.0	$ 85.0	$ 45.0	$ 41.0	$ 175.0	$ 130.0	$ 140.0	$ 150.0	$ 160.0
Depreciation Expense	$ 75.0	$ 77.0	$ 79.0	$ 80.0	$ 84.2	$ 90.0	$ 96.0	$ 102.0	$ 108.5

Data Source: Case writer estimates based on stock analysts' reports.

EXHIBIT 6 | Select Financial Ratios by S&P Credit-Rating Categories (median value for industrial companies, 2000–02)

	AAA	AA	A	BBB	BB	B	CCC
EBIT interest coverage (×)	23.4	13.3	6.3	3.9	2.2	1.0	0.1
EBITDA interest coverage (×)	25.3	16.9	8.5	5.4	3.2	1.7	0.7
EBITDA/sales (%)	23.4	24.0	18.1	15.5	15.4	14.7	8.8
Total debt/capital (%)	5.0	35.9	42.6	47.0	57.7	75.1	91.7

Ratio Definitions:

EBIT interest coverage = EBIT/interest expense

EBITDA interest coverage = EBITDA/interest expense

EBITDA/sales = EBITDA/sales

Total debt/capital = (Long-term debt plus current maturities and other short-term borrowings)/(Long-term debt plus current maturities and other short-term borrowings + Shareholders' equity)

EXHIBIT 7 | Timken, Ingersoll-Rand, and S&P 500 Stock Performance Indexed to Timken's January 1998 Price (1998–2002)

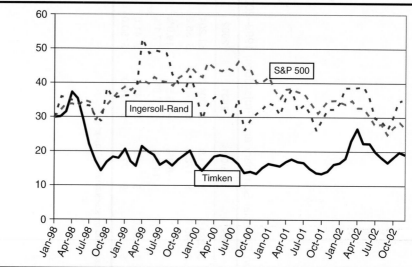

EXHIBIT 8 | Financial Data on Companies in Bearing Industry

Bearing Companies	Beta	Debt*	Sales*	EBITDA*	Net Income*	EBITDA Interest Coverage	Number of Shares*	Price per Share	EBITDA/ Sales	Enterprise Value/ EBITDA	Debt Rating
Kaydon Corp.	1.25	$ 72.4	$ 279.4	$ 60.1	$ 25.4	3.6	30.3	$20.0	21.5%	11.3	
NN, Inc.	0.85	$ 53.1	$ 180.2	$ 26.2	$ 4.7	6.5	15.4	$ 9.3	14.5%	7.5	
Timken	1.10	$461.2	$2,550.1	$257.2	$ 51.5	8.6	63.4	$16.8	10.1%	5.9	BBB
Commercial Metals	0.63	$255.6	$2,441.5	$138.2	$ 40.5	5.2	28.0	$17.9	5.7%	5.5	BBB
Metals Usa, Inc.	0.38	$128.7	$ 943.7	$ 4.0	$ 48.8	0.2	20.2	—	0.4%	—	
Mueller Industries	1.08	$ 18.2	$ 955.3	$123.9	$ 71.2	84.9	34.3	$25.9	13.0%	7.3	BBB
Precision Castparts Corp.	1.10	$612.4	$2,117.2	$389.6	$159.4	6.2	52.8	$21.7	18.4%	4.5	
Quanex Corp.	0.75	$ 75.6	$ 994.4	$127.0	$ 55.5	5.2	16.4	$34.7	12.8%	5.1	
Worthington Ind.	0.49	$290.9	$2,219.9	$188.0	$ 75.2	2.4	85.9	$18.7	8.5%	10.1	BBB

*Millions

EXHIBIT 9 | Capital Market Information (December 2002)

Government	Yield
Short term	1.86%
Intermediate	3.55%
Long-term	4.97%

Industrials	Yield
AAA	5.22%
AA	5.38%
A	5.84%
BBB	7.23%
BB	9.69%
B	10.84%

Sun Microsystems

Oracle will be the only company that can engineer an integrated system-application to disk—where all the pieces fit together so the customers do not have to do it themselves . . . Our customers benefit as their systems integration costs go down while system performance, reliability and security go up.

— Larry Ellison, CEO, Oracle Corporation[1]

It was the first time in the last two weeks that Margaret Madison, a member of Oracle's corporate development team, had not stayed in the office until two in the morning. At the close of business earlier that day, Friday, April 17, 2009, Oracle had put in an offer of $7.38 billion, or $9.50 per share, to acquire Sun Microsystems. Only nine months into her position, Madison, a recent MBA graduate, had found herself to be a member of Oracle's valuation team, assessing a potential merger with Sun. The journey, however, was not over yet. Sun had a number of potential suitors, IBM standing prominently among them, and Madison and her colleagues expected IBM to counter Oracle's offer.

Oracle, a California-based business software company, was one of the world's largest and most reputable sellers of database management systems and other related software. With $23.6 billion in annual revenue, the company was a leviathan, led forward with lightning speed by the only CEO Oracle had ever had, Larry Ellison. Sun was nothing to scoff at either. Once the darling of Silicon Valley, it had fallen on tough times but was still competitive. Sun had started as a hardware and servers producer, but over the years, it had established a solid position in the software industry with its Java programming language, Solaris operating system, and MySQL database management software. Combining these two companies had the potential to create the Wal-Mart of the enterprise software industry. Ellison "had a vision for creating an end-to-end vendor [that] clients go to for all their technology" needs.[2]

---

[1] "Oracle Buys Sun," Oracle Corporation press release, April 20, 2009.

[2] Jerry Hirsch and Alex Pham, "With IBM Out, Oracle Jumps in to Buy Sun for $7.4 Billion," *Los Angeles Times*, April 21, 2009.

Oracle's bid of $9.50 per share was more than a 40% premium over Sun's $6.69 closing price that day. But only a few weeks prior, IBM—Oracle's chief rival in the $15 billion database software business—had offered $9.40 per share for Sun. The talks had stalled due to antitrust concerns, employment contracts, and the final price, which opened a window of opportunity for Oracle to step in and ensure that Sun did not fall into a competitor's hands.

Oracle had been on a successful shopping spree over the past several years. The ability to acquire 10% margin companies and turn them into 40% margin companies had distinguished Ellison and his team as ruthless cost-cutters who planned ahead well before making purchases. As a member of the corporate development team, Madison knew that better than anyone else. She had spent the last few weeks carefully poring over every part of Sun's financials, business lines, R&D figures, and personnel expenditures. Today was a break from the 20-hour work days, the sight of empty Chinese food cartons, documents strewn across the table, and weary-eyed bankers. Today had been a better day, but only delivered brief respite to the team. All the questions they had worked on so diligently still remained. Had they considered everything? Was the final offer appropriate? If competitors upped their bids, how much more could Oracle offer?

Competitive Landscape

The technology industry had historically comprised three sectors: hardware, software and services, and storage and peripherals. In 2008, revenue generated by these three segments was $411 billion,[3] $2,239 billion,[4] and $160 billion,[5] respectively. In total, the value of the industry was roughly $2.8 trillion, or about one-fifth of U.S. GDP.

The computer hardware market consisted of personal computers (PCs) (roughly half of sales), servers, mainframes, and workstations (**Exhibit 1**). Although customer loyalty was relatively low, brand awareness was high, which somewhat restricted new entry into the market. Business customers were typically tied to specific hardware manufacturers through long-term contracts, which led to significant switching costs. Individuals were less fettered and had minimal switching costs, but only represented a small percentage of the market. Computer hardware was a necessity for individuals and businesses alike, making demand strong and consistent.[6] With weak rivalry among players, the market had enjoyed a healthy 4.8% growth over the previous few years and was expected to grow at the same pace until 2013.

The software and services segment was the largest part of the IT industry. The industry was peppered with thousands of competitors large and small, young and mature, fun and serious. It offered a wide array of products ranging from heavyweight

---

[3] Datamonitor, "Global Computer Hardware: Industry Profile," December 2008.

[4] Datamonitor, "Global Software & Services: Industry Profile," March 2009.

[5] Datamonitor, "Global Computer Storage & Peripherals: Industry Profile," March 2009.

[6] Major producers of computer hardware included Dell, Hewlett-Packard (HP), Sun, IBM, and Apple. Some (e.g., Dell and HP) were fairly diversified and offered a swath of hardware products. Others (e.g., Sun and IBM) marketed their products almost exclusively to business customers. Apple was unique because it dealt mainly with retail customers.

software, such as Microsoft Windows, to small applications; services also ran the gamut, ranging from large-scale consulting products to small projects, such as website development and design for local businesses. Some competitors had a large Internet presence (e.g., Google or YouTube), whereas other niche players operated small tools, such as online surveys (**Exhibit 2**). Only the heavyweights enjoyed some customer loyalty. Major software and services providers—Microsoft, IBM, HP, and Oracle—had stable and rather predictable revenues and notable market share (**Exhibit 3**). This software and services segment outpaced the hardware and storage and peripherals segments, growing at 12.2% annually between 2004 and 2008, and it was expected to maintain a healthy annual growth rate of 10.4% until 2013.[7]

The smallest segment—computer storage and peripherals—included data storage components, computer processors, and other peripherals (e.g., printers). The market was dominated by storage devices, such as hard drives. Combined, HP, Toshiba, and IBM commanded about half of the market. Historic sales growth rates of storage and peripherals mirrored that of the computer hardware segment.

In the 1990s, the IT industry resembled a tiered cake, with one or two heavyweights controlling each tier. These tiers were essentially technology swim lanes with little competition from other firms. For example, Cisco controlled the networking hardware market; Sun and HP were known for manufacturing servers. The business software segment belonged to SAP, while Oracle led in databases. IBM, a longtime hardware company, had moved into consulting and services. Everyone knew that HP laptops ran Windows operating systems but used Toshiba hard drives. Commercial clients bought Sun servers and ran Oracle database management software. There was relatively little overlap between these rival giants.[8]

At the dawn of the new millennium, the industry started to change. Lines between segments were becoming blurred; former allies encroached on each other's turf, and customers were forced to deal with fewer suppliers. The success of Apple's concept of a one-stop shop for consumers to acquire hardware, software, and even peripherals with a tightly controlled distribution channel forced large technology companies to reconsider their strategic approaches to business development. "The maturing tech industry has set giant companies on a collision course, as once-disparate technologies take on new capabilities in a 'convergence' of computers, software and networking."[9] Companies such as Apple and Dell moved away from PC manufacturing to other consumer devices, such as mobile phones, printers, and cameras. By the end of 2008, Apple, a long-standing competitor in the PC segment, derived only one-third of its total revenue from computers and laptops.[10] But simple deviation from historical products was a drop in the bucket. Battles were breaking out all across the industry. In 2009, Cisco, a manufacturer of networking hardware, announced it would start building its own servers, thus stepping into the territory of its longtime ally HP, which dominated the

---

[7] "Global Software & Services: Industry Profile," March 2009.

[8] "Mr. Ellison Helps Himself," *Economist*, April 23, 2009.

[9] Ben Worthen and Justin Scheck, "As Growth Slows, Ex-Allies Square Off in a Tech Turf War," *Wall Street Journal,* March 16, 2009, A1

[10] Apple, Inc., annual report, 2008.

server market. HP itself took aggressive steps to compete with IBM in the technological outsourcing segment by acquiring Electronic Data Systems in 2008. Microsoft attempted to take over Yahoo, thereby eyeing Google's domain. Dell was rumored to be in the final stages of developing a "data-center management software that [would] compete with existing offerings by HP, IBM and others."[11] Oracle was on a long-term shopping spree expanding from database management software to an array of products. (See **Exhibit 4** for company descriptions and **Exhibit 5** for sales growth.)

"In the past, when big tech companies crossed over into others' businesses, they often dismissed it as 'co-opetition,' meaning they planned to compete in some areas and cooperate in others."[12] With healthy growth of the technology industry and consumer hunger for new gadgets, there was plenty of revenue to go around. But the financial crisis, beginning in 2007, changed the landscape. The looming recession shrunk sales all across the industry and forced technology companies to explore every opportunity for extra revenue.

Oracle

In 1977, Larry Ellison, Bob Miner, and Ed Oates, three twentysomething software engineers, left Ampex Inc. to start a new venture, Software Development Laboratories.[13] Ellison became the head of the fledgling firm. Within a year, the team had designed the first relational database management system (RDBMS) under the code name "Oracle." Early adopters of the technology included government, military, and intelligence entities (including the U.S. Central Intelligence Agency) and innovative businesses, such as Bell Telephone Laboratories. The original product and all the following versions of Oracle capitalized heavily on the revolution of electronic record keeping that hit U.S. corporations in the 1970s. By 2009, all large U.S. corporations without exception were using database management products in every aspect of their business: back office, front office, client relationships, Internet, and so on. Every set of records that companies kept required a database server and an application that would search through data quickly and efficiently providing managers with information on demand. Both the software for keeping the data in an easily accessible format and the tools to speedily search through that data were Oracle's bread and butter. Every heartbeat of a corporation, every step it took involved a database management system: payroll, sales, supply chain decisions, and travel reimbursements, to name a few.

Oracle's relationships with clients did not stop at merely developing and distributing the RDBMS software. The company provided continued support to its clients through constant improvements in its software, customized customer support and training, and on-site installation and tune-up of the applications to a particular client's needs. Oracle targeted high-end customers because it had a lot to offer them. Apart from being the best among competitors in data access speed, Oracle also provided

---

[11]Worthen and Scheck.

[12] Worthen and Scheck.

[13] Justin Rohrlich, "Rags to Riches CEOs: Larry Ellison," *Minyanville.com,* November 18, 2009, http://www.minyanville.com/businessmarkets/articles/oracle-ibm-ellison-ampex-sdl-billionaire/11/18/2009/id/25369 (accessed November 2, 2010).

best-in-class data security protection. Its early versions could be installed and used on any type of computer, running any operating system. This was a revolutionary move that catapulted Oracle's sales early on.

Oracle went public in 1986 on the NASDAQ. Although its journey had not been smooth at all times, Ellison had always managed to turn the company around. He had a vision to create a company that would dominate the "desktop of business users" market. As early as the 1980s, Oracle had aimed to create customized applications for business users built upon the core product: Oracle RMDBS. Over time, the company had gained significant presence in developing applications for supply chain management, manufacturing, financials, project systems, market management, and human resources, which were highly popular among Oracle's customers.[14]

By 2000, Oracle sales had topped $10 billion. Despite a dip in sales during the dot-com bubble, Oracle had remained highly profitable. For a brief period, Ellison was the wealthiest man in the world. Oracle's success continued into the new millennium. Between 2000 and 2005, the top line grew annually at 2.9%, operating profit increased at 5.5%, and the margin improved by nearly 400 basis points. These healthy profits led to a significant accumulation of cash, which in turn allowed Oracle, under Ellison's leadership, to become a serial acquirer.

Since 2005, Oracle had spent more than $30 billion on over 50 bolt-on acquisitions (see **Exhibit 6** for select transactions), only a few of which were intended to refine and innovate Oracle's core database product line. Other acquisitions had allowed Oracle to aggressively move into new areas that would complement its current offerings and allow it to compete in the middleware, applications, and industry-specific software arenas. The most transformational move was in the applications space, where Oracle had snapped up PeopleSoft, Siebel, and Hyperion, all of which provided enterprise management solutions.[15] Oracle's 2008 acquisition of BEA Systems, a middleware company that utilized service-oriented architecture infrastructure to better link databases and software applications, was notable because it provided Oracle with additional flexibility to link all the products in its portfolio.[16] By early 2009, Oracle had become the biggest supplier of commercial software.

Sun Microsystems

Sun Microsystems, Inc., established in 1982 by three Stanford graduate students, built desktop computers and workstations. Sun entered the market at a time when pairing proprietary hardware, operating systems, and software was the norm. Sun broke new ground with its UNIX-based Solaris, which made its computers compatible with many other software and hardware products available on the market.[17] Sun's success, similar to Oracle, was attributed to rapid computerization of the companies' records where

---

[14] Michael Abbey, *Oracle 9i: A Beginner's Guide,* (Berkeley, CA: McGraw-Hill, 2002).

[15] Oracle Corporation, "Oracle Corporate Timeline," http://www.oracle.com/timeline/index.html (accessed November 2, 2010).

[16]"Oracle to Acquire BEA Systems," Oracle Corporation press release, January 16, 2008.

[17] "Sun Microsystems, Inc., Company History," http://www.fundinguniverse.com/company-histories/ Sun-Microsystems-Inc-Company-History.html (accessed November 2, 2010).

new workstations rapidly replaced the behemoth "minicomputers." From 1985 to 1989, Sun grew at average annual rate of 145%, reaching the status of fastest-growing company in America. The next step in Sun's stardom was due to its development, in 1989, of a new chipset based on scalable performance architecture (SPARC). Sun's SPARCs enhanced existing products by allowing it to create the smallest and fastest workstations on the market at the time. Combining the high-quality hardware with excellent on- and off-site customer service was a recipe for success.

Alongside the best-in-its-class workstations, Sun had been the proud owner of the Solaris operating system, which successfully competed with Microsoft Windows in the corporate world and was treasured by many in the industry. In 1995, the company had also developed the Java programming language, which customers universally loved and had become an industry standard for developing software for web applications. Virtually all PCs and eventually mobile phones required Java, which Sun licensed for a small fee. In 1997, Oracle converted to Sun's Java programming language, thus allowing its applications to be easily used by web developers. Oracle had also adopted the Linux operating system.

Sun went public in 1986 with a solid product offering dominated by its hardware sales. It had thrived until the turn of the century, when competition and market trends had turned against the company. After an altercation with Microsoft in the late 1990s, Sun was forced to make Java and Solaris available to users gratis. The burst of the dot-com bubble had hit Sun hard by almost annihilating its high-end hardware sales to the financial sector. The economic downturn following the dot-com bust had forced financial conglomerates to cut costs and move to lower-end hardware offered by Sun's competitors.[18] Companies had also started to shy away from the SPARC proprietary chip line favoring more widely used chips from Intel and Advanced Micro Devices. Sun's product mix had begun to move from predominantly hardware to a mix of hardware, software, and services, but waning hardware sales were not offset by gains in other offerings.[19]

Sun tried to leverage its acclaimed software systems to boost hardware sales by making Java (and later Solaris) an open-source platform in 2007. Open-source software allowed developers to adjust the platform to their specifications and thus provided a greater ability to adapt systems to a variety of tasks. The rationale for changing was to compete with Symbian and Microsoft in the mobile phone market and to increase the number of users. Sun had also expected this move would lead to greater adoption of the Solaris platform in the corporate world and drive hardware sales in uncaptured markets.[20] In reality, these moves failed to garner the sales Sun had anticipated. Sun was losing consumers on the high end to IBM and on the low end to Dell and HP,

---

[18] Matthew Karnitschnig, "IBM in Talks to Buy Sun in Bid to Add to Web Heft," *Wall Street Journal,* March 18, 2009.

[19] Sun Microsystems, Inc., Form 10-K, September 27, 1999. In 1999, Sun generated $9.6 billion in revenue from its hardware segment, while software and services added $1.6 billion. Ten years later, in 2009, Sun's business mix had changed dramatically; the Systems and Services segments were expected to generate $6.7 and $4.7 billion in revenue, respectively.

[20] Connie Guglielmo, "Sun Makes Java Free, Expands Mobile-Phone Software," *Bloomberg Online,* Bloomberg, May 8, 2007.

and nothing seemed to be able to change the trend.[21] In January 2008, Sun decided to move in yet another direction by announcing it would acquire MySQL AB for $1 billion. The company's core product was open-source database management software, touted as the world's most popular. MySQL was widely used by companies, such as Facebook, that ran websites on thousands of servers. By adding MySQL, Sun had hoped to find new outlets for its existing product lines and also to distribute MySQL through current channels.[22]

All the efforts to revive the once-glorious company were undermined by the financial crisis in 2007. In 2008, facing a banking industry on the brink of collapse and finding themselves unable to borrow to finance their immediate needs, companies reined in capital expenditures; naturally, computer and software updates were put on the back burner. In November 2008, well into the swing of the crisis, Sun announced plans to reduce its work force by approximately 15%.[23] Sales in 2009 were expected to drop by 17.5% from $13.9 billion to about $11.4 billion. Sun was expected to record a charge of $1.5 billion for goodwill impairment. The company that once had a reputation for turning laboratory successes into profits was headed into a tailspin. At that point, company management started to look for a potential suitor.

Oracle Eyes Sun

Ellison was one of those suitors who believed in the future of Sun as a part of Oracle. In his opinion, many smaller companies were doomed due to slowing revenue growth and the desire by clients to work with fewer suppliers. Armed with a respected management team and a war chest of more than $8 billion in cash,[24] Oracle aggressively pursued acquisition. Oracle had followed Sun for some time, hoping to capitalize on Sun's misfortunes by getting specific assets or the entire company at a deflated price (**Exhibit 7**). On March 12, 2009, Oracle contacted Sun about acquiring some assets. Within a week, while Sun was mulling Oracle's offer, a rumor surfaced that IBM was considering taking over Sun. On April 6, 2009, news broke that IBM and Sun had been in serious merger talks for more than a month. But the negotiations did not end in a deal, and Oracle did not wait long to step in. After all, the combination of Oracle's databases and Sun's servers had driven both companies' sales for much of 1990s. Both companies formed a united front against Microsoft, exploiting Solaris and Java as foundations for business software.

Ellison's stated vision was to transform Oracle into the Apple for the business customer by delivering high-quality, seamlessly integrated consumer products where software and hardware components were developed in conjunction, thus minimizing the customer setup process.

Strategically, the merger would combine Oracle's dominant position in the software space with Sun's expertise in hardware and networking (**Exhibit 8**). The move

[21] Morningstar, "Sun Microsystems, Inc.," *Morningstar,* October 31, 2008.

[22] "Sun to Acquire MySQL." Sun Microsystems, Inc., press release, January 16, 2008.

[23] "What's Next after IBM-Sun Merger Talks Fizzle?," *EE Times Asia,* April 8, 2009.

[24] Oracle Corporation, Form 10-Q, February 28, 2009.

also added the prized Java, MySQL, and Solaris platforms to Oracle's portfolio. The cannibalization of software products, though possible, was expected to be minimal. Although core Oracle products and MySQL were both database management systems, they appealed to different customers and were not in competition: Oracle could sell its software to the high-end clients while effectively serving smaller clients well. The corporate development team was sure that Oracle could capitalize on Sun's customer base and service contracts. The move made perfect sense strategically; the only matter to be determined was the price. That's where Madison and her valuation team stepped in.

Fortunately, Madison had already collected plenty of information needed to put a price on Sun; she had gathered it when Oracle had first showed interest. She had market data for comparable companies (**Exhibit 9**), the appropriate yields (**Exhibit 10**), balance sheets for both Sun and Oracle (**Exhibits 11** and **12**, respectively), and historic financials for Oracle (**Exhibit 13**). With Oracle entering into a confidentiality agreement with Sun, she had also received access to proprietary information. Madison and her team had spent a great deal of time looking at Sun's historical record and carefully developed projections for its future performance as a standalone company (**Exhibit 14**), which she knew would be the cornerstone of crafting a firm valuation.

The next step was to determine how much extra value Oracle could generate by making Sun's operations more efficient, cutting outdated and inefficient products and departments, streamlining remaining product lines, and introducing new synergistic systems. Knowing that a significant percentage of anticipated merger synergies were never realized historically, Madison and her team were fairly conservative with their estimates.

Cost cutting was the easy part. Having restructured and implemented lean operations in a line of past acquisitions, Madison and her colleagues were pros at trimming the fat. They knew Oracle could reduce Sun's staff by 20% to 25%, slash SG&A expenses by 22% to 32%, and allocate a significant amount for other restructuring costs. Estimating sales forecasts, potential new product lines, and software licensing was a completely different story, which necessitated bringing the marketing, sales, and R&D people on board.

First of all, Oracle team members expected Sun to initially lose some customers as a result of the merger. They knew that uncertainty of product offerings would push some customers to delay purchases and some to switch to competitors. After all, nobody wanted to buy an expensive piece of computer equipment only to find later that it would not be supported by the new owners of the company. Another issue was the lower-end customers that Oracle had never dealt with before. The marketing team expected these customers to hesitate to buy from Oracle for fear of being pushed into buying more expensive products. Marketing specialists knew that rivals would use similar arguments in aggressively pursuing Sun's clients. The only thing Oracle could do on this front was to minimize the extent of customer attrition. Oracle's marketing department was already working on a plan to reassure low- and high-end customers alike of continued service.

The second order of business was Sun's precious software. Although the open-source software could be downloaded free of charge, customers could elect to pay for product support and updates. The software had been particularly attractive during the recession. Market surveys, which Oracle had quietly conducted, suggested that customers might be open to paying a small fee for software downloads. The quality of Sun's software was so well known and appreciated by the market that the Oracle team was certain to increase its revenue stream from software licensing. The bigger source of revenue, however, was in the potential new products at the intersection of Sun and Oracle technologies. After all, most of Oracle's systems were built using Java and ran on the Solaris operating system.

The R&D team brainstormed on combining Oracle's products and Sun's hardware and software. Oracle had a long-standing plan to build Exadata machines that could handle both online transactions and data warehousing. Initially, the company had planned to use HP's hardware, but the opportunities Sun offered were too good to miss. Oracle engineers were positive that combining Oracle software with Flash-Wire technology, which Sun possessed, and then putting it on Sun hardware, could create a transaction-processing database machine. This machine would be twice as fast as its predecessor and, with high probability, much faster than machines produced by its closest rival, IBM.

When Madison put a bottom line to the dollar value of all the potential synergies the merger could generate, the numbers were rather impressive. But the merger would also be costly. The team's calculations suggested that integration charges would be close to $1.1 billion in aggregate, with most (about $750 million) incurred in 2010. It also anticipated an initial loss in operating income of about $45 million, due to loss of customers and/or delayed purchases. Cost cutting, licensing income, new products, and the addition of the "integrated application-to-disk" service had the potential to boost operating profit by as much as $900 million per year. Preferring to remain conservative, Madison assumed that such synergies would kick in gradually over a three-year time horizon starting in 2011.

The Decision

As Madison drove from San Francisco to her Redwood City, California, office the following morning, she wondered if her teammates had accounted for everything. She knew they were conservative in most of the financial projections, but they remained merely estimates. If rivals such as IBM placed a competitive bid for Sun over the weekend, Madison's team and manager would go over the estimates yet again, evaluating every aspect of the due diligence Oracle conducted in its effort to acquire Sun.

EXHIBIT 1 | Global Computer Hardware Sales

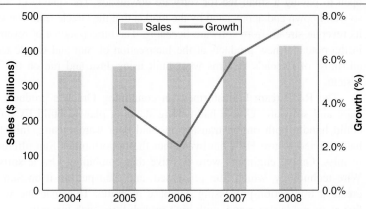

Global Computer Hardware Sales: 2004–08

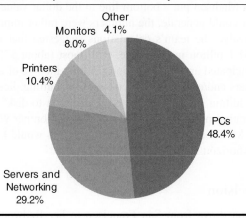

Global Computer Hardware Sales by Product: 2008

Data Source: Datamonitor, "Global Computer Hardware: Industry Profile," December 2008.

EXHIBIT 2 | Global Software & Services Sales

Global Software & Services Sales: 2004–08

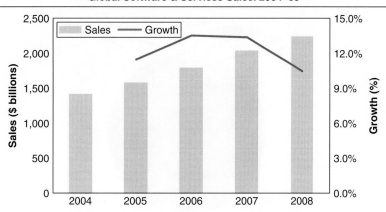

Global Software & Services Sales by Product: 2008

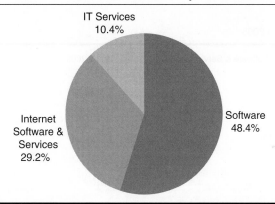

Data Source: Datamonitor, "Global Software & Services: Industry Profile," March 2009.

EXHIBIT 3 | Global Software & Services Sales by Share, 2008

Global Software & Services Sales by Share: 2008

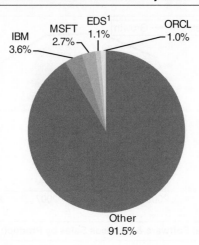

[1]EDS was acquired by HP in 2008

Data Source: Datamonitor, "Global Software & Services: Industry Profile," March 2009.

EXHIBIT 4 | IT Industry Companies

	Description	Key Products	Notable Acquisitions
Primarily Hardware			
Advanced Micro Devices	Develops and manufactures semiconductors and microprocessors	×86 microprocessors, microprocessors for computers and servers	×ATI Technologies (2006)
Apple	Designs, manufactures and markets personal computers, related software and mobile communication and entertainment devices	Macintosh computers, iPhones, iPods, music related products	
Dell	Offers a wide range of computers and related products	Desktop and laptop computers, software and peripherals, servers	*EqualLogic (2008)
EMC	Provides enterprise storage systems, software, networks and services	Information storage, VMware	
Hewlett-Packard	Provides imaging and printing systems, computing systems, and information technology for business and home	Consulting services, enterprise storage and servers, personal computers, digital cameras, printers and ink	*Compaq (2002) *EDS (2008)
Intel	Designs and manufactures computing and communications components and platforms	Microprocessors, chipsets, motherboards, platforms	
International Business Machines	Offers computer solutions through the use of advanced information technology	Consulting services, middleware, servers, laptops	
NetApp	Provides storage and data management solutions	Filers	
Sun Microsystems	Provides products, services and support for building and maintaining network computing environments	Enterprise systems and services, storage and software platforms Java, Solaris and MySQL	*MySQL (2008)
Primarily Software			
Adobe Systems	Develops, markets and supports computer software products and technology	Creative solutions, Acrobat	
Microsoft	Develops, manufactures, licenses, sells and supports software products	Windows, business and server software, gaming and handheld devices	
Novell	Provides Network and Internet directory software and services	Enterprise networking software	
Oracle	Supplies software for enterprise information management	Relational databases, middleware software, applications, related services	*People Soft (2005) *Siebel Systems (2006) *Hyperion Solutions (2007) *BEA Systems (2008)
Red Hat	Develops and provides open source software and services	Linux	

Sources: Industry reports and Bloomberg.

EXHIBIT 5 | Relative Sales Growth, 2000–08

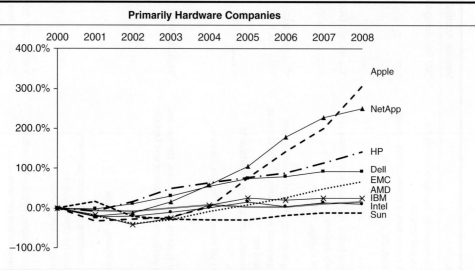

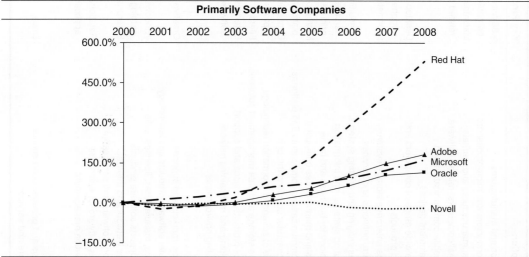

Data Source: Compustat.

EXHIBIT 6 | Selected Acquisitions Completed by Oracle, 2005–08

Target	Completion Date	Deal Size ($MM)	Product Catgory	Core Products
PeopleSoft	January 2005	10,300.0	Applications	Human resource management systems and customer relationship management software
Retek Inc.	April 2005	630.0	Industry Solutions	Management software for the retail industry
G-Log	September 2005	N/A	Industry Solutions	Logistics and transportation management software
Siebel Systems Inc.	January 2006	5,946.5	Applications	Customer relationship management, business intelligence and data integration software
360Commerce	January 2006	N/A	Industry Solutions	Open-store and multil-channel solutions software
Portal Software Inc.	April 2006	233.7	Industry Solutions	Billing and revenue management solutions for communications and media industry
Mantas Inc.	October 2006	122.6	Industry Solutions	Fraud and compliance software for financial institutions
Stellent Inc.	November 2006	398.7	Middleware	Content management software solutions
MetaSolv Inc.	October 2006	217.7	Industry Solutions	Customer relationship software for the communications industry
Hyperion Solutions Corp.	March 2007	3,292.1	Applications	Performance management software
Agile Software Corp.	May 2007	480.1	Applications	Product life cycle software for the industrial products, electronics and high-tech, and life science industries
BEA Systems Inc.	January 2008	8,056.0	Middleware	Enterprise infrastructure software
Skywire Software LLC	June 2008	N/A	Industry Solutions	Web-based insurance, financial and enterprise management software
Primavera Software Inc.	October 2008	N/A	Applications	Project, program and portfolio management software

Source: SDC Platinum.

685

EXHIBIT 7 | Relative Stock Performance, January 3, 2006, to April 16, 2009

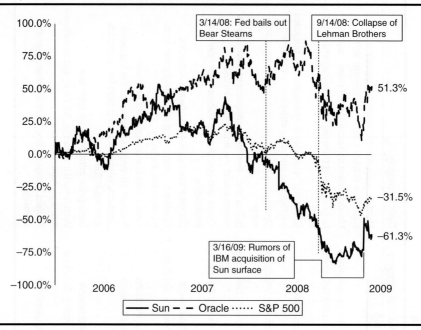

Data Sources: Yahoo! Finance and Wharton Research Database Service.

EXHIBIT 8 | Comparing Oracle and Sun Microsystems (in billions of U.S. dollars)

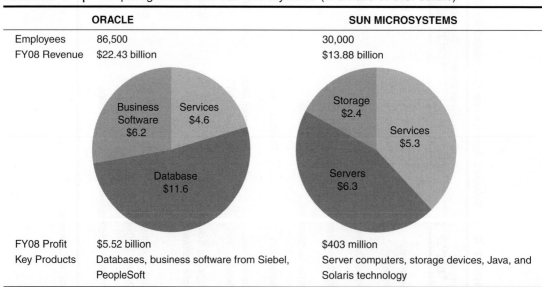

	ORACLE	SUN MICROSYSTEMS
Employees	86,500	30,000
FY08 Revenue	$22.43 billion	$13.88 billion

ORACLE pie: Business Software $6.2, Services $4.6, Database $11.6

SUN MICROSYSTEMS pie: Storage $2.4, Services $5.3, Servers $6.3

	ORACLE	SUN MICROSYSTEMS
FY08 Profit	$5.52 billion	$403 million
Key Products	Databases, business software from Siebel, PeopleSoft	Server computers, storage devices, Java, and Solaris technology

Data Source: Don Clark and Ben Worthen, "Oracle Snatches Sun, Foiling IBM," *Wall Street Journal,* April 21, 2009.

EXHIBIT 9 | IT Companies' Financial Data (market data as of April 17, 2009)

	Ticker	Stock Price ($)	Shares Out (MM)	Market Cap ($MM)	BV Debt ($MM)	Levered Beta	Bond Rating	Cash & Investments ($MM)	LTM Sales ($MM)	LTM EBIT ($MM)	LTM EBITDA ($MM)	LTM Earnings ($MM)
Primarily Hardware												
Advanced Micro Devices	AMD	3.56	609	2,168	4,988	2.19	B	933	5,808	(1,955)	(732)	(3,098)
Apple	AAPL	123.42	889	109,713	—	1.11	—	24,490	37,096	7,984	8,739	5,728
Dell	DELL	11.06	1,944	21,505	2,011	1.12	A2	9,546	61,101	3,190	3,959	2,478
EMC	EMC	12.81	2,041	26,142	3,404	1.39	—	6,446	14,876	1,569	2,626	1,346
Hewlett-Packard	HPQ	36.30	2,416	87,708	20,458	1.25	A2	10,140	118,697	10,354	14,175	8,050
Intel	INTC	15.60	2,562	39,967	1,988	1.20	A1	8,840	37,586	8,954	13,570	5,292
International Business Machines	IBM	101.27	1,343	136,052	33,925	0.93	A1	12,907	103,630	16,715	22,165	12,334
NetApp	NTAP	17.59	330	5,808	1,265	1.80	—	2,604	3,464	116	286	101
Sun Microsystems	JAVA	6.69	739	4,941	1,257	1.73	Ba1	3,061	13,438	(2,231)	(1,757)	n/a
Primarily Software												
Adobe Systems	ADBE	24.70	524	12,944	350	1.32	—	2,018	3,476	961	1,231	809
Microsoft	MSFT	19.20	8,896	170,795	2,000	0.99	Aaa	31,447	61,981	22,128	24,485	17,232
Novell	NOVL	3.94	343	1,353	122	1.50	B1	1,067	940	10	55	(15)
Oracle	ORCL	19.06	5,046	96,180	11,238	1.27	A2	12,624	23,630	8,406	10,291	5,739
Red Hat	RHT	18.32	190	3,482	—	1.20	BB	663	628	80	119	85

Data Sources: Yahoo! Finance, Moody's, Bloomberg, and company filings. Market data as of April 17, 2009.

EXHIBIT 10 | Relevant Security Yields, April 2009

Corporate Bond Yields

AAA	5.50%
AA	5.77%
A+	6.27%
A	6.35%
A−	6.50%
BBB+	7.54%
BBB	7.62%
BBB−	8.64%
BB+	11.42%
BB	11.49%
BB−	11.70%
B+	13.28%
B	14.70%
B−	15.46%

U.S. Treasury Yields

180-Day	0.34%
1-Year	0.54%
3-Year	1.22%
5-Year	1.71%
10-Year	2.82%
30-Year	3.66%

Data Sources: Mergent Bond Record, U.S. Treasury, and Ibbotson Associates.

EXHIBIT 11 | Sun Microsystems Historical and Projected Balance Sheet
(in millions of U.S. dollars)

	Fiscal Year-End June 30		
	2007	2008	2009E
Assets			
Current Assets			
Cash[(1)]	3,620	2,272	1,876
Marketable Debt Securities	2,322	1,038	1,185
Net Receivables	2,964	3,019	2,258
Inventory	524	680	566
Deferred Prepaid Taxes [(2)]	200	216	188
Other Current Assets	1,058	1,218	995
Total Current Assets	10,688	8,443	7,068
Property, Plant, & Equipment, Net	1,504	1,611	1,616
Goodwill	2,514	3,215	1,743
Intangible Assets	633	565	269
Other Noncurrent Assets	499	506	536
Total Assets	**15,838**	**14,340**	**11,232**
Liabilities & Equity			
Current Liabilities			
Accounts Payable Including Accrued Payroll	2,222	2,121	1,600
Short/Current Long-Term Debt	1	—	554
Deferred Taxes[(2)]	2,047	2,236	2,341
Other Current Liabilities Including Warranty Reserve	1,182	1,311	1,126
Total Current Liabilities	5,451	5,668	5,621
Long-Term Debt	1,264	1,265	695
Deferred Long-Term Charges[(2)]	659	683	635
Other Noncurrent Liabilities[(3)]	1,285	1,136	976
Total Liabilities	8,659	8,752	7,927
Stockholders' Equity			
Common Stock	6,987	7,391	7,582
Treasury Stock	(311)	(2,726)	(2,569)
Retained Earnings	189	430	(2,055)
Other Stockholders' Equity	314	493	347
Total Stockholders' Equity	7,179	5,588	3,305
Total Liabilities & Equity	**15,838**	**14,340**	**11,232**

Data Sources: Company filings and case writer estimates.

[(1)](Sun Microsystems') long-term strategy is to maintain a minimum amount of cash and cash equivalents in subsidiaries for operational purposes and to invest the remaining amount of our cash in interest-bearing and highly liquid cash equivalents and marketable debt securities.

[(2)]Deferred taxes and related accounts are not expected to vary with sales or continue to accumulate as a company growth.

[(3)]Includes deferred settlement income from Microsoft as of June 30, 2009, 2008, 2007, and 2006, long-term tax liabilities as of June 30, 2009, 2008, 2007, and 2006, and long-term restructuring liabilities.

EXHIBIT 12 | Oracle Historical and Projected Balance Sheet
(in millions of U.S. dollars)

	Fiscal Year-End May 31		
	2007	2008	2009E
Assets			
Current Assets			
Cash & Cash Equivalents	7,020	11,043	12,624
Net Receivables	4,589	5,799	4,430
Inventory	—	—	—
Other Current Assets	1,274	1,261	1,527
Total Current Assets	12,883	18,103	18,581
Property, Plant, & Equipment, Net	1,603	1,688	1,922
Goodwill	13,479	17,991	18,842
Intangible Assets	5,964	8,395	7,269
Other Noncurrent Assets	643	1,091	802
Total Assets	**34,572**	**47,268**	**47,416**
Liabilities & Equity			
Current Liabilities			
Accounts Payable	315	383	271
Short/Current Long-Term Debt	1,358	1,001	1,001
Other Current Liabilities	7,714	8,645	7,877
Total Current Liabilities	9,387	10,029	9,149
Long-Term Debt	6,235	10,235	9,237
Deferred Long-Term Charges	1,121	1,218	480
Other Noncurrent Liabilities	910	2,761	3,460
Total Liabilities	17,653	24,243	22,326
Stockholders' Equity			
Common Stock	10,293	12,446	12,980
Treasury Stock	—	—	—
Retained Earnings	6,223	9,961	11,894
Other Stockholders' Equity	403	618	216
Total Stockholders' Equity	16,919	23,025	25,090
Total Liabilities & Equity	**34,572**	**47,268**	**47,416**

Data Sources: Company filings and case writer estimates.

EXHIBIT 13 | Oracle Historical and Projected Income Statement (in millions of U.S. dollars)

	Fiscal Year-End May 31		
	2007	2008	2009E
Software Revenues	14,211	17,843	18,877
Services Revenues	3,785	4,587	4,375
Net Revenue	17,996	22,430	23,252
Selling, General, & Administrative	8,790	10,468	10,217
Research & Development	2,195	2,741	2,767
Amortization of Intangible Assets	878	1,212	1,713
Other Operating Expense	159	165	234
Total Operating Expense	12,022	14,586	14,931
Operating Income	5,974	7,844	8,321
Income Tax on Operations	1,709	2,316	2,380
Net Operating Profit After Tax	4,265	5,528	5,941
Effective Corporate Tax Rate	28.6%	29.5%	28.6%

Data Sources: Company filings and case writer estimates.

EXHIBIT 14 | Sun Microsystems Historical and Projected Income Statement (in millions of U.S. dollars)

	2007	2008	2009E	Fiscal Year-End June 30 2010E	2011E	2012E	2013E	2014E
Net Revenue	13,873	13,880	11,449	12,665	13,047	13,526	13,885	14,243
Cost of Sales	7,608	7,425	6,718	7,685	7,583	7,735	7,889	8,075
Gross Margin	6,265	6,455	4,731	4,980	5,464	5,791	5,996	6,168
Selling, General, & Administrative	3,851	3,955	3,461					
Research & Development	2,008	1,834	1,648					
Impairment of Goodwill	—	—	1,460					
Other Operating Expense	97	294	398					
Total Operating Expense	5,956	6,083	6,967	4,839	4,992	5,121	5,249	5,372
Operating Income	309	372	(2,236)	141	472	670	747	796
Depreciation & Amortization	517	476	474	536	456	470	487	500
as % of Prior Year PP&E	34.4%	29.5%	29.3%	30.0%	30.0%	30.0%	30.0%	30.0%
Net PP&E	1,611	1,616	1,788	1,520	1,566	1,623	1,666	1,709
as % of Sales	11.6%	11.6%	15.6%	12.0%	12.0%	12.0%	12.0%	12.0%

Data Sources: Company filings and case writer estimates.

Hershey Foods Corporation: Bitter Times in a Sweet Place

Hershey's chocolate. Like baseball and apple pie, it was an American icon. So when Hershey's largest shareholder proposed selling the company in early 2002, the residents of Hershey, Pennsylvania, the state attorney general, legislators, and current and former Hershey employees reacted with alarm. For them, the idea of selling the "Great American Chocolate Bar" was an insult to a beloved American institution and a threat to the principles on which Milton Hershey had built his company.

Unlike most large corporations, Hershey Foods' majority shareholder was not a corporate raider, institutional investor, or multinational, but rather the Hershey Trust Company, which owned 77% of its voting stock. The trust had been endowed by a gift, in 1918, by Milton Hershey himself, with the objective of supporting the Milton Hershey School, an institution for orphans in Hershey, Pennsylvania. Nevertheless, in March 2002, the Hershey Trust's board of trustees decided that the school would be better served if its holdings were less concentrated in Hershey stock. Therefore, the Hershey Trust announced its decision to sell its entire stake in Hershey Foods, which effectively put the corporation up for sale.

Six months after making its decision to explore a potential sale, the board of the Hershey Trust Company was examining two serious offers: a joint bid from Cadbury Schweppes PLC and Nestlé S.A. and an independent bid from the Wm. Wrigley Jr. Company. The primary question for the board's 17 members was whether the bidders had accurately valued Hershey and, if so, whether the economic value created through the deal was consistent with the board's obligation to safeguard Hershey's legacy of community involvement.

This case was prepared by Sean Carr (MBA '03) and Gustavo Rodriguez (MBA '03), under the supervision of Professors Kenneth M. Eades, Chris Muscarella (Penn State University), and Samuel C. Weaver (Lehigh University). It was written as a basis for class discussion rather than to illustrate effective or ineffective handling of an administrative situation. Copyright © 2004 by the University of Virginia Darden School Foundation, Charlottesville, VA. All rights reserved. *To order copies, send an e-mail to sales@dardenbusinesspublishing.com. No part of this publication may be reproduced, stored in a retrieval system, used in a spreadsheet, or transmitted in any form or by any means—electronic, mechanical, photocopying, recording, or otherwise—without the permission of the Darden School Foundation.* Rev. 02/11.

The Confectionary Industry

In 2001, the U.S. confectionary industry was worth $24 billion. Chocolate products accounted for 55% of that market; gum, 12%; and nonchocolate candy, 32%. The consumption of all confectionery had stagnated in the United States during the past four years, and the consumption of chocolate, in particular, had declined during the previous year. Despite the disappointing trend in the U.S. market, several factors had helped a few key industry players grow during this period:

- Developing innovative products with high consumer appeal and price per pound
- Identifying and acquiring target companies to execute expansion strategies
- Developing operations and/or distribution systems in new countries

With a market share of 30%, Hershey led the U.S. market for candy and gum in 2001, followed by M&M Mars, Inc. (Masterfoods Corp.) at 17.1%, Wm. Wrigley Jr. Co. at 6.6%, and Nestlé at 6.5%. The other players sharing the remaining 40% of the market included Cadbury Schweppes, World's Finest Chocolate, Inc., and Tootsie Roll Industries, Inc.

With its aggressive introduction of new products, Wrigley posted a 12.3% growth in revenues over the previous year. Wrigley, the largest producer of chewing gum in the world, had recently introduced Wrigley Eclipse Flash Strips, which accounted for some of the company's impressive performance and moved it from fourth to third place in U.S. rankings. Nestlé showed 6.5% sales growth, and Mars and Hershey each showed 1.4% growth.

Milton Snavely Hershey: Entrepreneur

Milton Snavely Hershey was born to a German-Mennonite family in south-central Pennsylvania, on September 13, 1857, shortly before the outbreak of the American Civil War. In his youth, Hershey was a poor student, and after transferring among seven different schools, he dropped out before reaching the fourth grade. As a young adult, Hershey developed an interest in becoming a confectioner, and in 1886, he opened the Lancaster Caramel Company in Lancaster, Pennsylvania, which specialized in caramels made with fresh milk.

Because he believed there would be great demand for affordable, mass-produced chocolate, Hershey sold his caramel business for $1 million in 1900, but retained the firm's chocolate-making machines. Attracted by central Pennsylvania's ample supplies of water, dairy farms, and hard-working immigrants, Hershey used the proceeds from the sale to purchase 1,200 acres of farmland and to break ground for the Hershey factory on March 2, 1903. Upon its completion, in December 1904, Hershey had built the largest chocolate factory in the world, and the Hershey Chocolate Company was born.

Hershey, Pennsylvania: From Factory to Company to Town

Hershey enjoyed making money, but he "wanted it used for a purpose of enduring good." (A sign on his office wall read "Business Is a Matter of Human Service.") Influenced by utopian "manufacturing communities" of the time, Milton Hershey decided to surround his business enterprise with a model town. In the pastures surrounding his new factory, Hershey mapped out a village, with tree-lined streets whose names evoked the exotic lands of the cocoa bean, including Trinidad, Caracas, and Ceylon (Sri Lanka). Milton Hershey created the Hershey Improvement Company, a division of Hershey Chocolate, which built a complete infrastructure, including roads, sewers, utilities, houses, and public buildings. In 1906, the village of Derry Church, Pennsylvania, was renamed Hershey.

The development of Hershey, Pennsylvania, followed the ebb and flow of the company's fortunes. Following financial difficulties in 1920, Milton Hershey reorganized and refinanced his company, creating three new entities:

- Hershey Chocolate Corporation, which acquired all the chocolate properties;
- Hershey Corporation, which acquired the company's 65,000 acres of sugar-cane fields and eight sugar-processing plants in Cuba;
- Hershey Estates, which continued the work of the Hershey Improvement Company.

Through Hershey Estates, the Hershey Chocolate Company played an ever-larger role in the lives of Hershey's citizens. By 1927, Hershey Estates had a hand in more than 30 nonchocolate interests, including the telephone company, a department store, the hospital, and the cemetery. See **Exhibit 1** for a list of Hershey Estates' enterprises.

Milton Hershey's dedication to his employees and the residents of the town was steadfast. During the Great Depression, despite a 50% drop in sales, Hershey refused to lay off any local employees. Instead, between 1929 and 1939, he launched a series of massive building projects that resulted in the construction of most of Hershey's major buildings, including the Hershey Community Center, the lavish Hotel Hershey, the high school, the Hershey Sports Arena, Hershey Stadium, and the Hershey Chocolate Corporation headquarters, at 19 East Chocolate Avenue.

Hershey Estates served the town well but operated at a financial loss. During Milton Hershey's lifetime, profit for the Estates division was never a primary consideration. In fact, after 1927, Milton Hershey relied on profits from the company's Cuban sugar operations to provide the capital for his many construction projects. Following Hershey's death, in 1945, pressure grew to reduce Hershey Chocolate's involvement in the town. In the 1960s, owing to increased regulation, competition for financing, and a poor business climate, Hershey Estates divested its electric, water, sewer, and telephone utilities. The lumberyard and creamery were also sold, the ballroom torn down, the pool filled in, and the community center turned over to Hershey Foods for office space.

In 1970, after years of benign neglect, Hershey Estates began to focus on Hersheypark, an amusement park, as a revenue generator, and approved a five-year plan to revitalize it. Later, Hershey Estates was renamed Hershey Entertainment and Resorts Company (HERCO), and committed itself to managing Hershey's entertainment properties. See **Exhibit 2** for a description of HERCO's businesses.

Milton Hershey's Commitment: The Milton Hershey School

In 1909, at the suggestion of his wife, Kitty, the unschooled Milton Hershey created a residence and school for homeless boys. In 1918, three years after his wife's death, the childless Milton Hershey bequeathed his entire personal fortune to the Milton Hershey School, including thousands of acres of land and all his stock in the Hershey Chocolate Company. The Hersheys designated the newly created Hershey Trust Company as the sole trustee for the school. According to the deed of trust, the trustee was responsible for managing the trust's considerable endowment and for reporting to the school's managers. Ever since the bequest, the Hershey Trust Company had had a controlling interest in every major Hershey entity. Moreover, the school's managers and the trust's board comprised the same 17 individuals. Hershey Foods' board, however, was, for the most part, an independent entity with only one of its nine members also serving on the trust's board. See **Exhibit 3** for an organizational chart.

By 2002, the Milton Hershey School (MHS) admitted both boys and girls without regard to race and provided instruction from kindergarten through the 12th grade. MHS enrolled 1,300 students, who lived on the school's 1,400-acre campus. Annual spending per student was $96,000, which included housing, food, clothing, and medical care. MHS's endowment, administered by the Hershey Trust Company, had grown from its initial bequest of $60 million to approximately $5.4 billion, making it one of the largest educational endowments in the United States. See **Exhibit 4** for a comparison of private educational endowments.

Hershey Foods Corporation

Milton Hershey learned that the secret of mass production for his chocolate lay in the manufacture of huge quantities of one item, standardized in design, and with a continuity of streamlined output that held down costs. The plain milk-chocolate bar and the milk-chocolate bar with almonds were the bread and butter of the Hershey Chocolate Company. With this recipe, Hershey had generated sales of $5 million by 1911, more than eight times the company's first-year revenues. By 1921, Hershey's sales had soared to $20 million.

In 1937, the quartermaster of the United States Army asked the Hershey Chocolate Corporation to develop a military-ration bar that could meet the needs of soldiers in the field. The requirements for the bar were that it should weigh about four ounces, be able to withstand high temperatures, and taste "just a little better than a boiled potato." The result was the Field Ration D. By the end of World War II, Hershey was producing 24 million units of Field Ration D per week.

And so, while other confectioners were forced to limit or even cease production during the war, the Hershey Chocolate Corporation was winning millions of loyal consumers, as well as a place in American history. Between 1940 and 1945, more than three billion units of Field Ration D bars were made and distributed to soldiers around the world.

Shortly after the end of World War II, Milton S. Hershey died at age 88, on October 13, 1945. Hershey's passing, however, did not diminish the strength of his business. By 1951, sales had grown to $154 million, and by 1962, sales had reached $183 million. In 1963, the Hershey Chocolate Corporation undertook its first major acquisition when it purchased the H. B. Reese Candy Company, Inc., makers of Reese's Peanut Butter Cups. This move began a string of acquisitions by Hershey that would continue for the next 25 years.

During the 1960s, Hershey diversified by acquiring several major pasta manufacturers, including San Giorgio Macaroni, Inc., and Delmonico Foods, Inc. By the 1980s, the company had become the largest pasta manufacturer in the United States. This diversification away from chocolate products led to a change in the company's name to Hershey Foods Corporation in 1984. By 1999, however, the company had changed its strategy again and sold its U.S. pasta business, the Hershey Pasta Group, to New World Pasta, LLC, for $450 million plus equity.

By 2002, Hershey remained the number-one candy maker in the United States, with sales comprising roughly 80% chocolate and 20% nonchocolate foods. Its largest customer was Wal-Mart, which represented 17% of the company's total sales. Other major Hershey customers included Kmart, Target, Albertsons, and CVS. Sales outside the United States accounted for 10% of total revenues. According to *Money* magazine, Hershey Foods' stock ranked as the 28th-best performer of the last 30 years, with annualized returns of 17.4%.

The Hershey Trust Company Considers a Sale

Over the years, both the composition and the size of Hershey Trust's board of directors had changed (see **Exhibits 5** and **6**). In particular, the trust's board had expanded from 10 members, in 1990, to 17 members, in 2002, and the composition of the board had shifted toward education professionals, Hershey School alumni, and various public-sector leaders. The board's mandate, however, remained that of serving the interests of the Milton Hershey School, the primary beneficiary of the trust's endowment. The endowment had grown from Milton Hershey's original gift of $60 million of Hershey stock to its current level of $5.4 billion. Beginning in the 1990s, Hershey Foods had reduced the concentration in Hershey shares through a share-repurchase program. In all, Hershey Foods repurchased $1.2 billion of its own shares so that, by 2002, only 58.6% of the endowment comprised Hershey Foods' shares. The trust's large holding amounted to 31% of Hershey Foods' common shares and 77% of the stockholders' votes.[1]

---

[1] In 1984, Hershey Foods introduced "super voting stock" (10 votes per share) for the trust, which consolidated its majority ownership of Hershey Foods Corporation. To compensate for the superior voting rights, the class B common stock received a 10% lower dividend than the regular common stock. If the trust's stake in Hershey Foods ever dropped below 15%, its special voting stock reverted to common. With the exception of Hershey and a select group of other firms, the New York Stock Exchange did not allow companies to maintain dual classes of common stock.

During the past 16 years, Hershey's stock had shown variable performance, but had significantly outperformed Standard & Poor's 500-stock index by an average of 6.8% per year (see **Exhibit 7**).[2] Despite the overall strong investment performance of the trust and its gradual diversification away from Hershey shares, by early 2002 there was an increasing concern among board members that the trust was compromising its fiduciary responsibility by concentrating a disproportionate amount of the endowment fund in the shares of Hershey Foods Corporation. Therefore, during a meeting in March 2002, the trust's board voted 15–2 to "explore a potential sale" of its holdings in Hershey Foods.

The board believed that a sale of the trust's entire stake in Hershey Foods would garner a higher premium than if its shares were sold piecemeal; therefore, the decision to sell was tantamount to putting Hershey Foods Corporation on the block. According to Robert C. Vowler, president and CEO of the Hershey Trust Company, the trust planned to invest the profits from the sale in a variety of U.S. equities and fixed-income and international securities to provide more "straight lines of return and not the volatility of one stock."

Following the March board meeting, a delegation from the trust told the chairman and CEO of Hershey Foods Corporation, Richard H. Lenny, to begin the process of finding suitable bidders for the company. But Lenny opposed the idea of a sale and asked for time to make a counterproposal. In May, Lenny presented a stock-buyback offer to the head of the trust's investment committee, J. Robert Hillier, who also sat on the board of Hershey Foods. The plan called for Hershey Foods to purchase half of the trust's shares at a 10% premium. Hershey Foods would also help the trust sell the remainder of its shares over the next three to five years. The trust's board, however, rejected the plan on the ground that the 10% premium was insufficient.

On July 25, 2002, a day that would become known by those opposed to the sale as Black Thursday, the trust made public its decision to sell its portion of the outstanding shares of Hershey Foods Corporation. Following news of the announcement, Hershey's stock price soared from $63 to $79 per share. In the ensuing weeks, rumors swirled about potential bidders. Among the names to emerge were the Wm. Wrigley Jr. Company, Nestlé S.A., Cadbury Schweppes PLC, Kraft Foods, the Coca-Cola Company, and PepsiCo.

Swift Reaction

The prospect of a sale of Hershey Foods, an American icon and the paternalistic benefactor of a town, produced a groundswell of opposition by employees, local businesses, and politicians who feared Hershey would become part of someone else's global empire. Many residents of Hershey, Pennsylvania, whose population of 22,400 included 6,200 Hershey employees, were concerned that the legacy of Hershey's involvement in the community would be compromised and many jobs might be lost. Community leaders organized rallies and developed a Web site, www.friendsofhershey.org, gathering 6,500 signatures of people opposed to the sale.

---

[2]According to *Money* magazine, Hershey Foods ranked as the 28th-best-performing stock of the past 30 years.

The controversy over the proposed sale of Hershey Foods became increasingly public as protests by company employees and retirees and Milton Hershey School alumni came to the attention of Pennsylvania's attorney general, whose office oversaw trusts and charities in the state. On August 12, the attorney general filed a petition asking that any sale of Hershey Foods be subject to approval by the Dauphin County Orphan's Court, which had jurisdiction over charitable trusts. On August 24, the attorney general sought an injunction to stop the sale altogether.[3]

The issues underlying the controversy emerged during the ensuing court proceedings:

Jack Stover, lawyer for the Hershey Trust Company: "[The injunction] causes irreparable harm to us. . . . It ties the hands of the Trustees with regard to its single largest asset . . . Who in the courtroom has not read in the paper what happens in today's economy when you invest too heavily in a single stock?"

Judge James Gardner Collins: "What makes the attorney general's office better financial managers than the board of the Hershey Trust, and literally the worldwide experts they have hired as well?"

Jerry Pappert, deputy attorney general: "Because we're managing different clients. We're managing the interests of the public, and we have an opportunity and a duty under law to make sure that the ultimate beneficiary of the trust, the public, is not harmed."

During the injunction hearings, several former Hershey Foods executives testified against the sale, including Richard Zimmerman, former CEO of Hershey Foods, and Bruce McKinney, former CEO of HERCO. Representative James Sensenbrenner (R-Wis.), chairman of the House Judiciary Committee, asked the Federal Trade Commission to scrutinize carefully any antitrust implications of the potential sale of Hershey Foods.

The Bids: Wrigley and Nestlé—Cadbury Schweppes

By September 14, 2002, the final date by which bids could be submitted, the Hershey Trust Company board was considering two serious offers: a $12.5 billion bid from the Wm. Wrigley Jr. Company and a $10.5 billion joint-bid from Nestlé S.A. and Cadbury Schweppes PLC.

The Wm. Wrigley Jr. Company

The world's largest maker of chewing gum had been based in Chicago since 1892, when William Wrigley, while working as a salesman for his family's soap factory, began offering customers chewing gum. In 1898, he merged his company with one of his suppliers to form the Wm. Wrigley Jr. Company, and by 1910, the firm's spearmint gum was the leading U.S. brand.

As late as 1961, the company still offered its original five-cent price and product line. But by 1971, as it faced competitive and economic pressures, the company

---

[3]The attorney general, Mike Fisher, was a Republican candidate for governor of Pennsylvania at the time.

increased its price to seven cents and launched several new products, including the following:

- Big Red (1975)
- Orbit, a sugar-free gum (1977)
- Hubba Bubba (1978)
- Extra (1980)

Wrigley continued to expand its business by launching operations in Eastern Europe and China (1993). In 1999, Bill Wrigley, a member of the fourth generation of Wrigleys to lead the company, became president and CEO. After 2000, the company focused on testing innovative gums with such attributes as cough suppression and teeth whitening.

In 2002, the Wrigley family owned about 35% of the company and controlled 60% of its voting shares. With 2001 revenues of $2.4 billion, Wrigley commanded a 50% share of the global gum market, and sold its products in more than 150 countries. Nearly all its revenues were derived from gum. Wrigley's Web site described its business strategy as follows:

> Wrigley is committed to achieving generational growth and prosperity for our stakeholders. To achieve this mission, we are executing against a long-term strategic business plan based on six key objectives. Those objectives include:

- Boosting our core chewing gum business
- Expanding business geographically and into new channels
- Diversifying our product line in "close to home" areas
- Focusing on innovation in our products, marketing, and business processes
- Delivering the highest quality at lowest costs
- Growing and developing our Wrigley people around the world

The Wm. Wrigley Jr. Company offered $12.5 billion ($7.5 billion in stock and $5.0 billion in cash) for 100% of the outstanding shares of Hershey Foods Corporation. The Hershey Trust Company would exchange its Hershey shares for cash and shares in the new company, to be renamed Wrigley-Hershey. This offer, the equivalent of $89 per share, represented a 42% premium over Hershey's preannouncement stock price. The deal included commitments to the Hershey community, including assurances of job retention at Hershey Foods' plants in Derry Township.

Some analysts speculated that Wrigley management was assuming it could put Hershey products into its product mix and sell them internationally. Although it was unlikely that Wrigley could achieve significant cost savings, management hoped to generate higher sales volumes. Wrigley had been successful in selling chewing gum internationally and was hoping to do the same with Hershey's chocolates.

Nestlé S.A.

Nestlé S.A. was founded in 1843, when Henri Nestlé purchased a factory in Vevey, Switzerland, that made products ranging from nut oils to rum. In 1904, the company began selling chocolates, and one year later merged with the Anglo-Swiss Company, retaining the Nestlé name. During World War I, the company developed a water-soluble "coffee cube," and the idea became one of the company's most popular products, Nescafé. Nestlé continued to introduce popular products during the next four decades, including Nestlé's Crunch bar (1938), Quik drink mix (1948), and Taster's Choice instant coffee (1966).

In the 1970s, the company expanded its product line by acquiring a 49% stake in Gesparal, a holding company that controlled the French cosmetics firm L'Oréal. In the 1980s, Nestlé continued its expansion by acquiring the U.K. chocolate company Rowntree, maker of Kit Kat (licensed to Hershey Foods Corporation). In the 1990s, Nestlé completed several more acquisitions, including Butterfinger, Baby Ruth candies, Source Perrier water, and Alpo pet food. Simultaneously, Peter Braceck-Letmathe, named CEO in 1997, divested Nestlé's noncore businesses such as Contadina tomato products and Libby's canned-meat products.

After acquiring Ralston Purina, in 2001, Nestlé consolidated its position as the world's number-one food company. Nestlé had become a leader in coffee (Nescafé), bottled water (Perrier), and pet food (Ralston Purina) and an important player in the cosmetics industry. Through its stake in Alcon, Inc., Nestlé also participated in ophthalmic pharmaceuticals, contact-lens solutions, and equipment for ocular surgery.

Nestlé's strategy, according to its Web site, was as follows:

> Nestlé's strategic priorities are focused on delivering shareholder value through the achievement of sustainable, capital-efficient, and profitable long-term growth. The combination of our four-pillar strategy and efficiency programmes will deliver market-share growth and margin improvement.
>
> Our four-pillar strategy is based on:
>
> - Operational performance
> - Product innovation and renovation
> - Product availability
> - Consumer communication

Through this strategy, Nestlé had been able to establish itself as both an international and a local company. With nearly 470 factories in 84 countries, many of Nestlé's brands were unique to particular countries. Nestlé had been successful at satisfying local tastes with local products. In the future, the company planned to expand into specialty nutritional foods and ice cream.

Cadbury Schweppes PLC

In 2002, Cadbury Schweppes was a major global player in both the beverage and confectionary industries. With bottling and partnership operations in 10 countries and licensing agreements in 21 more, Cadbury Schweppes was the third-largest soft-drink company by sales volume in the world. Its confectionary products were manufactured in 25 countries and sold in almost 200, making it the fourth-largest confectioner in the industry.

Both Schweppes Ltd. and Cadbury Group Ltd. had sought new markets since their founding in the nineteenth century. The two companies merged in 1969, giving birth to one of the biggest players in the candy and soft-drink sectors. The new company, Cadbury Schweppes PLC, began a continuous program of worldwide expansion. By 2001, the company derived 45% of its revenues from the Americas, 38% from Europe, and 12% from Asia. Cadbury Schweppes employed more than 41,000 people worldwide.

According to its Web site, Cadbury Schweppes' governing objective was the growth of shareowner value through "focusing on the beverages and confectionary businesses, developing robust and sustainable positions in regional markets, and growing organically and by acquisition."

Since the mid-1980s, acquisitions and divestments had played a key role in Cadbury Schweppes' expansion plans. Key transactions included the acquisition of Dr. Pepper/Seven-Up, Hawaiian Punch, Snapple Beverage Group, and Kraft Foods' candy business in France.

The Nestlé–Cadbury Schweppes offer for Hershey Foods was $10.5 billion in cash. At $75 a share, this offer represented a significantly lower premium than that offered by Wrigley. Moreover, the bid was complicated by the fact that Nestlé received royalties from Hershey for U.S. sales of its Kit Kat and Rolo brands. The licensing arrangement had been negotiated between Rowntree and Hershey prior to Nestlé's acquisition of Rowntree. Because the licensing agreement was structured to continue in perpetuity, Hershey valued the licensing of the two brands at approximately $1 billion. An important aspect of the agreement, however, was that a change of ownership of Hershey would transfer all rights to the two brands back to Nestlé. Therefore, according to the agreement, regardless of who won the bidding battle for Hershey, Nestlé stood to gain the value of the licensing agreement.

The deal included a provision making Hershey, Pennsylvania, the headquarters of Cadbury Schweppes' operations in the United States and calling it the "chocolate capital of the world." With new production facilities and distribution capabilities in the United States, however, they expected to reduce costs by consolidating operations and reducing workforces. See **Exhibit 8** for a summary of the bidders' financials.

The Hershey Trust Company Board Decides

In essence, the board faced both an economic and a governance decision. On the economic side, the board needed to determine the value of Hershey as a stand-alone entity compared with the bids being offered. See **Exhibit 9** for Hershey's historical financials, **Exhibit 10** for Hershey management's financial forecasts,[4] and **Exhibit 11** for industry comparables. On the governance side, the board needed to decide whether selling Hershey compromised the board's original mandate from Milton Hershey.

---

[4]Forecasts were made by Hershey management for the company as a stand-alone entity prior to the announcement by Hershey Trust and the bids by Wrigley and Nestlé–Cadbury Schweppes.

EXHIBIT 1 | Businesses Operated by Hershey Estates (1927)

Hershey Baking Company	Hershey Greenhouse and Nursery
Hershey Cemetery	Hershey Hospital
Hershey Cold Storage	Hershey Laundry
Hershey Community Building	Hershey Museum
Hershey Community Inn	Hershey Park
Hershey Community Theatre	Hershey Park Golf Club
Hershey Country Club	Hershey Rose Garden
Hershey Dairy	Hershey Sewerage Company
Hershey Department Store	Hershey Telephone Company
Hershey Electric Company	Hershey Transit Company
Hershey Experimental Candy Kitchen	Hershey Water Company
Hershey Feed and Grain	Hershey Zoo
Hershey Farms	Hotel Hershey
Hershey Farming Implements	Coal
Hershey Filling Station	Real Estate
Hershey Garage	

Source: Hershey Community Archives.

EXHIBIT 2 | Businesses Operated by Hershey Entertainment and Resorts (2002)

HERSHEYPARK is a popular theme park boasting 60 rides and several entertainment venues. Milton Hershey himself built the park as a leisure opportunity for Hershey workers and their families.

ZOOAMERICA North American Wildlife Park has on exhibit more than 200 animals indigenous to North America.

HERSHEYPARK Arena was once host to the American Hockey League **HERSHEY BEARS**. In 2002 the team left the 3,000-seat arena to play at GIANT Center.

HERSHEYPARK Stadium attracts 30,000 audience members to its Summer Concert Series and other events.

THE STAR PAVILION at HERSHEYPARK Stadium is an outdoor amphitheater designed for musical perform-ances; its capacity is 7,200.

HERSHEY BEARS, the oldest American Hockey League franchise, is a frequent Calder Cup winner.

THE HOTEL HERSHEY, a AAA Four Diamond hotel, is known for its rich history. Since its construction in 1933, by it has grown to include 234 guest rooms and almost 25,000 square feet of event space.

HERSHEY Lodge and Convention Center is an even larger hotel and conference facility, with 667 guest rooms and 100,000 square feet of event space.

HERSHEY'S CHOCOLATE TOWN CAFÉ's chocolate theme reflects its Hershey's Chocolate World location. It is managed by HERSHEY® Resorts and owned by Hershey Foods Corporation.

BELLA LUNA is Hershey's authentic Italian Deli.

HERSHEY Highmeadow Campground offers visitors a chance to enjoy 55 acres of Pennsylvania countryside, on either open campsites or in the comfort of a log cabin.

HERSHEY Nursery has handled the landscaping needs of area homes and businesses since 1905.

Source: Hershey Entertainment and Resorts Company.

EXHIBIT 3 | Hershey Entities Organizational Chart (2002)

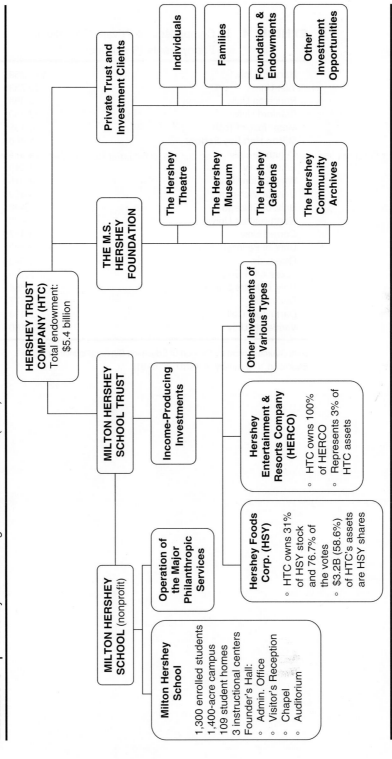

Source: Hershey Trust Company.

EXHIBIT 4 | Comparison of Private Educational Endowments ($ millions)

Harvard Univ.	$18,259
Yale Univ.	10,739
Princeton Univ.	8,359
Stanford Univ.	8,250
Mass. Inst. of Tech.	6,135
Milton Hershey School	**5,400**
Columbia Univ.	4,324
Emory Univ.	4,249
Washington Univ.	4,018
Univ. of Michigan	3,689
Univ. of Chicago	3,492
Northwestern Univ.	3,470
Cornell Univ.	3,437
Univ. of Pennsylvania	3,382
Rice Univ.	3,243
Texas A&M Univ.	3,193
Univ. of Notre Dame	2,884
Duke Univ.	2,577
Dartmouth Coll.	2,414
Vanderbilt Univ.	$2,160

Data Source: Voluntary Support of Education Survey (Council for Aid to Education, a subsidiary of RAND, 2000–01).

EXHIBIT 5 | Boards of Directors for Hershey Trust and Hershey Foods Corporation (1990)

1990 Hershey Trust Board of Directors[1]		1990 Hershey Foods Board of Directors	
Kenneth V. Hatt	Chairman of the Board of Hershey Trust Co. & Milton Hershey School Board of Managers	Richard. A. Zimmerman	Chairman and CEO Hershey Foods Corporation
Richard. A. Zimmerman	Chairman and CEO of Hershey Foods Corporation	Kenneth V. Hatt	Chairman of the Board Hershey Trust Company
Kenneth L Wolfe	President and Chief Operating Officer Hershey Foods Corporation	Kenneth L. Wolfe	President and Chief Operating Officer Hershey Foods Corporation
William R. Fisher	President of the Milton Hershey School and board of directors of The Hershey Bank	Howard O. Beaver, Jr.	Retired Chairman of the Board Carpenter Technology Corporation Reading, PA
Rod J Pera	Managing partner in the Harrisburg law firm of McNees, Wallace & Nurick, counsel to all Hershey entities.	John F. Burlingame	Retired Vice Chairman of the Board and Executive Officer GE Company Stamford, Connecticut
John F. Rineman	Executive vice president of the Pennsylvania Medical Society	Thomas C. Graham	President USS a division of USX Corporation Pittsburgh, PA
J. Bruce McKinney	President, CEO and chairman of the board of Hershey Entertainment & Resort Co. (HERCO)	John. C. Jamison	Dean of the Graduate School of Business Administration College of William and Mary, Williamsburg, VA
William H Alexander	Chairman of H. B. Alexander Constr-uction Company. Director of family business programs at Snider Entre-preneurial Center, Wharton School, University of Pennsylvania.	Dr. Sybil C. Mobley	Dean of the School of Business and Industry Florida Agricultural and Mechanical University Tallahassee, Florida
Ronald D. Glosser	President of Hershey Trust Co	Francine I. Neff	Vice President and Director NETS Inc. privately held investment management company Albuquerque, NM
C. McCollister Evarts	Dean, Penn State Milton S. Hershey Medical College	John. M. Pietruski	Retired Chairman of the Board and CEO Sterling Drug Inc. New York, NY
Juliet C Rowland	President and CEO, Ohio United Way	H. Robert Sharbaugh	Retired Chairman and CEO Sun Company, Radnor, PA
		Joseph P. Viviano	President Hershey Chocolate USA

[1]All Hershey Trust board members also serve on the board of directors of the Milton Hershey School.

EXHIBIT 6 | Boards of Directors for Hershey Trust and Hershey Foods Corporation (2001)

2001 Hershey Trust Board of Directors[2]		2001 Hershey Foods Board of Directors	
Robert C. Vowler	President and CEO, Hershey Trust Company	Richard H. Lenny	Chairman, President and CEO, Hershey Foods Corporation
J. Robert Hillier, FAIA	Chairman and Founder of Hillier Group (architects)	J. Robert Hillier, FAIA	Chairman and Founder, The Hillier Group (architects)
A. John Gabig, Esq.	Chairman of MHS Board of Managers	Jon A. Bosia	Chairman and CEO, Lincoln National Corporation
William L. Lepley	President and CEO of Milton Hershey School	Robert H. Campbell	Chairman and CEO (ret.), Sunoco Inc.
William H. Alexander	Chairman of H. B. Alexander Construction Company. Director of family business programs at Snider Entrepreneurial Center, Wharton School, University of Pennsylvania.	Gary P. Coughlan	Sr. VP Finance and CFO (ret.), Abbott Laboratories Inc.
		Bonnie Hill	President and CEO, The Times Mirror Foundation
Lucy D. Hackney, Esq.	Former Policy adviser, General Services Admin	John C. Jamison	Chairman, Mallardee Associates
Wendy D. Puriefoy	Public Education Network	Mackey J. McDonald	Chairman, President and CEO, VF Corporation
W. Don Cornwell	Granite Broadcasting Co.	John M. Pietruski	Chairman, Texas Biotechnology Corporation
A. Morris Williams, Jr.	President, Williams & Company		
Michael W. Matier	Institutional Research & Planning, Cornell U.		
Rev. John S. McDowell, Jr.	St. James the Less Episcopal Church		
Anthony J. Colistra	Superintendent, Cumberland Valley School Dist.		
Robert F. Cavanaugh	Managing director, DLJ Real Estate Partners		
Joan S. Lipsitz, Ph.D.	Independent education consultant		
Hilary C. Pennington	Co-founder, Jobs for the Future		
Juliet C. Rowland	President and CEO, Ohio United Way		

[2]All Hershey Trust board members also serve on the board of directors of the Milton Hershey School.

EXHIBIT 7 | Hershey Stock-Price Performance (1986–2001)

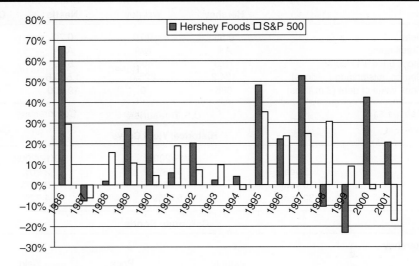

	Average Stock Returns*	
	1997–2001 (5 years)	1986–2001 (16 years)
Hershey	16.4%	18.8%
	(32.7%)	*(24.9%)*
S&P 500	9.0%	12.0%
	(19.5%)	*(14.7%)*

*Standard deviation of returns in parentheses.

EXHIBIT 8 | Bidding Companies' Financial Data

	Hershey	Wrigley	Nestle	Cadbury Schweppes
Beta	0.55	0.70	0.70	0.60
Credit rating	A+	N/A	AAA	BBB
Stock price 9/17/2002	73.8	49.5	51.9	28.5
Shares outstanding (millions)	134.2	225.0	1,550.6	502.5
Book value of debt ($ millions)	885	0	19,500	3,543

U.S. Treasuries

Historical Yield Curve

	8/19/2002	9/17/2002
5 year	3.38%	2.90%
10 year	4.28%	3.82%
30 year	5.05%	4.73%

Corporate Bonds[1]

Hershey

Maturity	Price	Yield
8/15/2012	117.7	4.69
2/15/2021	137.1	5.56
2/15/2027	119.4	5.73

Wrigley

No debt

Nestlé

Maturity	Price	Yield
6/15/2025	125.4	5.84

Cadbury Schweppes[1]

Maturity	Price	Yield
12/15/2005	100.6	4.31

[1]Cadbury Schweppes bonds in British pounds sterling. All other bonds denominated in U.S. dollars.

EXHIBIT 9 | Historical Financial Statements of Hershey Foods Corporation (in millions of dollars)

Income Statement	1996	1997	1998	1999	2000	2001
Sales	$3,989.3	$4,302.2	$4,435.6	$3,970.9	$4,221.0	$4,137.2
Cost of sales	2,302.1	2,488.9	2,625.1	2,354.7	2,471.2	2,668.5
Gross profit	1,687.2	1,813.3	1,810.6	1,616.2	1,749.8	1,468.7
Selling, marketing, and administrative	1,124.1	1,183.1	1,167.8	1,057.8	1,127.2	1,056.1
Operating income	563.1	630.2	642.8	558.4	622.7	412.6
Gain (loss) on sale of business	(35.4)	—	—	243.8	—	—
Earnings before interest and tax	527.8	630.2	642.8	802.1	622.7	412.6
Interest expense	48.0	76.3	85.7	74.3	76.0	69.1
Pretax income	479.7	554.0	557.1	727.9	546.6	343.5
Income taxes	206.6	217.7	216.1	267.6	212.1	136.4
Net income	$ 273.2	$ 336.3	$ 341.0	$ 460.3	$ 334.5	$ 207.1

Balance Sheet	1996	1997	1998	1999	2000	2001
Cash and cash equivalents	$ 61.4	$ 54.2	$ 39.0	$ 118.1	$ 32.0	$ 134.1
Accounts receivable trade	294.6	360.8	451.3	352.8	379.7	361.7
Inventories	475.0	505.5	493.2	602.2	605.2	512.1
Other current assets	155.2	114.2	150.4	207.0	278.5	159.5
Total current assets	986.2	1,034.8	1,134.0	1,280.0	1,295.3	1,167.5
Property, plant, and equipment, net	1,601.9	1,648.2	1,648.1	1,510.5	1,585.4	1,534.9
Goodwill	566.0	551.8	530.5	450.2	474.4	388.7
Other tangible assets	30.7	56.3	91.6	106.0	92.6	156.3
Total assets	$3,184.8	$3,291.2	$3,404.1	$3,346.7	$3,447.8	$3,247.4
Accounts payable	$ 134.2	$ 146.9	$ 156.9	$ 136.6	$ 149.2	$ 133.0
Accrued liabilities	368.1	391.2	311.9	364.7	359.5	465.5
Short-term debt	315.0	257.5	346.0	211.6	258.1	7.9
Total current liabilities	817.3	795.7	814.8	712.8	766.9	606.4
Long-term debt	655.3	1,029.1	879.1	878.2	877.7	877.0
Other long-term liabilities	327.2	346.5	346.8	330.9	327.7	361.0
Deferred income taxes	224.0	267.1	321.1	326.0	300.5	255.8
Total liabilities	2,023.8	2,438.4	2,361.8	2,248.0	2,272.7	2,100.2
Stockholders' equity	1,161.0	852.8	1,042.3	1,098.6	1,175.0	1,147.2
Total liabilities and equity	$3,184.8	$3,291.2	$3,404.1	$3,346.7	$3,447.8	$3,247.4

EXHIBIT 10 | Forecast Financial Statements of Hershey Foods Corporation as Stand-Alone Entity (in millions of dollars)

Income Statement	2002	2003	2004	2005	2006	2007	2008	2009	2010	2011
Sales	$4,343.9	$4,561.0	$4,789.1	$5,028.5	$5,280.0	$5,544.0	$5,821.2	$6,112.2	$6,417.8	$6,738.7
Cost of sales	2,541.2	2,622.6	2,705.8	2,841.1	2,983.2	3,132.3	3,289.0	3,453.4	3,626.1	3,807.4
Selling, general & administrative	1,164.2	1,222.4	1,283.5	1,347.7	1,415.0	1,485.8	1,560.1	1,638.1	1,720.0	1,806.0
Operating income (EBIT)	638.5	716.1	799.8	839.8	881.8	925.8	972.1	1,020.7	1,071.8	1,125.4
Taxes	252.2	282.9	315.9	331.7	348.3	365.7	384.0	403.2	423.4	444.5
Net operating profit after tax (NOPAT)	386.3	433.2	483.9	508.1	533.5	560.1	588.1	617.5	648.4	680.8
Sales growth	5.0%	5.0%	5.0%	5.0%	5.0%	5.0%	5.0%	5.0%	5.0%	5.0%
EBIT/sales	14.7%	15.7%	16.7%	16.7%	16.7%	16.7%	16.7%	16.7%	16.7%	16.7%
Balance Sheet										
Total current assets	1,194.6	1,254.3	1,317.0	1,382.9	1,452.0	1,524.6	1,600.8	1,680.9	1,764.9	1,853.2
Goodwill	388.7	388.7	388.7	388.7	388.7	388.7	388.7	388.7	388.7	388.7
Net property, plant, equipment, and other	1,737.5	1,824.4	1,915.6	2,011.4	2,112.0	2,217.6	2,328.5	2,444.9	2,567.1	2,695.5
Non-interest-bearing current liabilities	543.0	570.1	598.6	628.6	660.0	693.0	727.6	764.0	802.2	842.3
Curr. assets/sales	27.5%	27.5%	27.5%	27.5%	27.5%	27.5%	27.5%	27.5%	27.5%	27.5%
NIBCL/sales	12.5%	12.5%	12.5%	12.5%	12.5%	12.5%	12.5%	12.5%	12.5%	12.5%
NPPE, other/sales	40.0%	40.0%	40.0%	40.0%	40.0%	40.0%	40.0%	40.0%	40.0%	40.0%

Source: Case writer estimates.

712

EXHIBIT 11 | Industry Comparables

Company Name	Exchange	Book Value of debt ($millions)	Common Shares Outstanding (millions)	Stock Price (9/17/02)	Market Cap ($millions)	Debt/ Equity	EBIT ($millions)	Enterprise Value/EBIT Multiple
Cadbury Schweppes PLC -ADS	NYSE	3,543	503	28.5	14,296	0.25	1,501	11.9
Hershey Foods Corp	NYSE	885	134	73.8	9,905	0.09	413	26.1
Jm Smucker Co	NYSE	150	50	37.6	1,862	0.08	59	33.9
Nestlé S A -Spon ADR	OTC	19,500	1,551	51.9	80,399	0.24	3,007	33.2
Sanfilippo John B & Son	NSDQ	52	9	6.7	61	0.85	18	6.1
Sherwood Brands Inc	AMEX	1	4	4.5	17	0.07	1	17.2
Tootsie Roll Industries Inc	NYSE	8	52	31.0	1,610	0.00	101	16.1
Wrigley (Wm) Jr Co	NYSE	0	225	49.5	11,135	0.00	583	19.1

Flinder Valves and Controls Inc.

In early May 2008, W. B. "Bill" Flinder, president of Flinder Valves and Controls Inc. (FVC), and Tom Eliot, chairman and chief executive officer of RSE International Corporation (RSE), were planning to negotiate a possible acquisition of FVC by RSE. Serious discussions for combining the two companies had started in March of that year, following casual conversations that dated back to late 2007. Those initial talks focused on the broad motives for each side to do a deal, and on the management issues, including compensation, in the new firm. What still remained was to negotiate a final term sheet on which the definitive agreement would be drafted and signed.

In the background, the past 12 months had been associated with mounting difficulty for the U.S. economy. The industries within which RSE and FVC operated were not immune from these effects. A recent analyst report summarized the market view for industrial manufacturing.

> Tighter borrowing standards and a severely weakened housing sector are weighing on the domestic economy, prompting consumers to cut back on spending and industrial manufacturers to reduce production. A similar situation now seems to be taking hold in western Europe.[1]

Both corporate leaders were concerned about the opportunities and risks of doing a deal in this increasingly challenging environment.

Flinder Valves and Controls Inc.

Flinder Valves and Controls, located in Southern California, manufactured specialty valves and heat exchangers. FVC maintained many standard items, but nearly 40% of its volume and 50% of its profits were derived from special applications for the defense and aerospace industries. Such products required extensive engineering experience of a kind only a few firms were capable of providing. FVC had a reputation for engineering excellence in the most complex phases of the business and, as a result, often did prime contract work on highly technical devices for the government.

---

[1] *Value Line Investment Survey,* April 25, 2008.

FVC was an outgrowth of a small company organized in 1980 for engineering and developmental work on an experimental heat-exchanger product. In 1987, as soon as the product was brought to the commercial stage, Flinder Valves and Controls Inc. was organized to acquire the properties, both owned and leased, of the engineering corporation. The president of the predecessor company, Bill Flinder, continued as the president of FVC. Eventually, the company acquired the patents it had licensed.

The raw materials used by the company were obtainable in ample supply from a number of competitive suppliers. Marketing arrangements presented no problems. Sales to machinery manufacturers were made directly by a staff of skilled sales engineers. The Auden Company, a large firm in a related field, was an important foreign distribution channel under a nonexclusive distributor arrangement. About 15% of FVC's sales came from Auden. Foreign sales through Auden and directly through FVC's own staff accounted for 30% of sales. Half the foreign sales originated in emerging economies, mainly Brazil, Korea, and Mexico. The other half originated in the United Kingdom, Italy, and Germany.

Although competitive erosion in the mid-2000s had temporarily interrupted FVC's sales growth, better economic conditions in the markets of developed countries, together with FVC's recent introduction of new products for the aerospace and defense industries, offered the company excellent prospects for improved performance. Sales in the first quarter of 2008 grew 23% over the corresponding period in 2007, at a time when many of FVC's competitors experienced limited growth prospects. **Exhibits 1** and **2** show the most recent financial statements for FVC.

FVC's plants, all of modern construction, were organized for efficient handling of small production orders. The main plant was served by switch tracks in a 15-car dock area of a leading railroad and also by a truck area for the company's own fleet of trucks. From 2005 to 2007, net additions to property totaled $7.6 million.

Bill Flinder, an outstanding researcher in his own right, had always stressed the research and development involved in improved products, with patent protection, although the company's leadership was believed to be based on its head start in the field and its practical experience.

FVC's success had brought numerous overtures from companies looking for diversification, plant capacity, management efficiency, financial resources, or an offset to cyclical business. For instance, when Flinder Valves was taken public in 1996, Auden Company, which later became a holder of 20% of FVC common stock, advanced a merger proposal. Rumors of possible antitrust action by the U.S. Department of Justice had circulated after the news of the proposed merger became public, and Auden withdrew from the discussions. FVC received various proposals from 1998 on, but none reached the stage of working out an agreement until the advances of RSE International Corporation.

FVC had come to RSE's attention with the FVC's disclosure of a U.S. government contract. FVC was to develop an advanced hydraulic-controls system, code-named "widening gyre," for use in numerous military applications. The technology was still in research and development, but was expected to have broad commercial value if the results were found to be economically successful.

RSE International Corporation

Tom Eliot had founded RSE International in 1970, grown it, taken it public, and firmly rooted it as a Russell 1000 company. In response to what he perceived to be the firm's growth challenges for the next decade, Eliot had persuaded RSE's board that the company should follow a policy of focused diversification, which would be achieved by an aggressive growth-by-acquisition program designed to create opportunities and entries into more dynamic markets than the ones RSE then served.

In 2008, RSE manufactured a broad range of products including advanced industrial components as well as chains, cables, nuts and bolts, castings and forgings, and other similar products. RSE then sold them (mostly indirectly) to various industrial users. One division produced parts for aerospace propulsion and control systems with a broad line of intermediate products. A second division produced a wide range of nautical navigation assemblies and allied products. The third division manufactured a line of components for missile and fire-control systems. These products were all well regarded by RSE's customers, and each was a significant factor in its respective market. **Exhibit 3** shows the RSE balance sheets for 2007; **Exhibit 4** presents the income statements from 2003 to 2007.

The company's raw material supply (sheets, plates, and coils) of various metals came from various producers. RSE International's plants were ample, modern, well-equipped with substantially newer machinery, and adequately served by railroad sidings. The firm was considered a low-cost producer that possessed unusual production knowledge. It was also known as a tough competitor.

Eliot and his management team had initiated several changes to help increase RSE's profit margins. Chief among them, in late 2006, had been the implementation of Project CORE, a business wide initiative to improve and unify the corporate wide information systems. This project had already identified numerous opportunities for improving profits and sales. As a result, RSE's latest sales and earnings forecasts projected a steady increase over the next five years. The current plan (excluding merger growth) called for sales to hit $3 billion within five years (**Exhibit 5**). Despite Eliot's confidence and optimism for the future of the company, he believed that the stock market still undervalued his firm's shares.

The Situation

During the early part of 2008, a series of group meetings had taken place between Tom Eliot and Bill Flinder and their respective advisers. It seemed clear to both parties that both FVC and RSE could profit from the merger. By early May, a broad outline of the merger seemed to be developing. Flinder Valves was to become a subsidiary of RSE International—the deal would be structured in such a way as to preserve FVC's identity. The two sides had explored some of the governance and compensation issues in the merger. Flinder would be retained along with his top management team and all other employees. No layoffs were contemplated. This reflected RSE's intention to invest in and grow the FVC operation. FVC's solid management team was one of the factors that had attracted RSE in the first place, and Eliot wanted to keep the same management in place after the merger. Flinder would receive a generous option-based incentive bonus that could result in a salary increase of between $50,000 and $200,000 per year. Because Flinder was 62 years old and nearing retirement, the compensation package was meant to retain him in the coming years as he trained a new chief executive.

The price of the deal was less clear. FVC's shares traded on the NASDAQ, whereas RSE's traded on the American Stock Exchange. The market capitalizations for FVC and RSE were approximately $100 million and $1.4 billion, respectively. Both companies had experienced recent rapid rises in share price due to strong performance despite the weak economic environment. **Exhibit 6** shows recent share prices for Flinder Valves and RSE.[2]

The financial advisors had collected a variety of relevant capital-market data. **Exhibit 7** provides valuation information on exchange-listed comparables for Flinder Valves and RSE. **Exhibit 8** presents information on recent related acquisitions. **Exhibit 9** presents historical money-market and stock-return data through May 2008. RSE's debt was currently rated Baa.

Flinder had shared FVC's current corporate-financial-statement forecast with Eliot but had emphasized that it did not include any benefits of the merger or the benefits of promising new technologies, such as the widening gyre (**Exhibit 10**). The reluctance to include the widening gyre project stemmed from the substantial uncertainty remaining regarding its potential economic benefits.

The companies had yet to settle on the form of consideration, either cash or RSE stock, that would best serve the parties to the deal. Eliot expected that RSE had the financial capacity to borrow the entire amount through its existing credit facilities. Roughly 70% of the Flinder Valves stock was held by its board of directors and their families, including the 20% owned by the Auden Company and 40% owned by Bill Flinder. The Auden Company did not object to the merger, but it had given notice that it would sell any RSE shares received in the deal. The Auden Company was about to undertake a new expansion of its own, and its executives were not disposed to keeping tag ends of minority interests in a company such as RSE. They saw no reason, however, for not maintaining their satisfactory business relationships with the Flinder Valves enterprise if it became a division of RSE International.

---

[2]RSE International's stock had a beta of 1.25; the beta for FVC was 1.00, based on the most recent year's trading prices. Both companies faced a marginal tax rate of approximately 40%.

EXHIBIT 1 | Consolidated Balance Sheet as of December 31, 2007 for Flinder Valves and Controls (dollars in thousands)

Assets		
Cash	$ 1,884	
U.S. Treasury tax notes and other Treasury obligations	9,328	
Due from U.S. government	868	
Accounts receivable net	2,316	
Inventories, at lower of cost or market	6,888	
Other current assets	116	
Total current assets		$21,400
Investments		1,768
Land	92	
Buildings	6,240	
Equipment	18,904	
Less: allowance for depreciation	7,056	
Total plant, property, and equipment—gross	$18,180	
Construction in process	88	
Total plant, property, and equipment—net*		18,268
Patents		156
Cash value of life insurance		376
Deferred assets		156
Total assets		42,124
Liabilities and Stockholders' Equity		
Accounts payable	2,016	
Wages and salaries accrued	504	
Employees' pension cost accrued	208	
Tax accrued	72	
Dividends payable	560	
Provision for federal income tax	1,200	
Total current liabilities		4,560
Deferred federal income tax		800
Common stock at par (shares authorized and outstanding 2,440,000 shares)	1,220	
Capital surplus	7,180	
Earned surplus	28,364	
Total equity		36,764
Total liabilities and stockholders' equity		42,124

*Equivalent land in the area had a market value of $320,000, and the building had an estimated market worth of $16,800,000. Equipment had a replacement cost of approximately $24,000,000 but a market value of about $16,000,000 in an orderly liquidation.

EXHIBIT 2 | Summary of Consolidated Earnings and Dividends for Flinder Valves and Control
(dollars in thousands)

	2003	2004	2005	2006	2007	(Unaudited) Three months ended 3/30	
						2007	2008
Sales	$36,312	$34,984	$35,252	$45,116	$49,364	$11,728	$14,162
Cost of goods sold	25,924	24,200	24,300	31,580	37,044	8,730	10,190
Gross profit	10,388	10,784	10,952	13,536	12,320	2,998	3,972
administrative	2,020	2,100	2,252	2,628	2,936	668	896
Other income—net	92	572	108	72	228	14	198
Income before taxes	8,460	9,256	8,808	10,980	9,612	2,344	3,274
Taxes	3,276	3,981	3,620	4,721	4,037	1,009	1,391
Net income	5,184	5,275	5,188	6,259	5,575	1,335	1,883
Cash dividends	1,680	2,008	2,016	2,304	2,304	576	753
Depreciation	784	924	1,088	1,280	1,508	364	394
Capital expenditures	1,486	1,826	2,011	2,213	2,433	580	640
Working capital needs	1,899	3,492	−1,200	4,289	4,757	1,130	1,365
Ratio analysis							
Sales	100.0	100.0	100.0	100.0	100.0	100.0	100.0
Cost of goods sold	71.4	69.2	68.9	70.0	75.0	74.4	72.0
Gross profit	28.6	30.8	31.1	30.0	25.0	25.6	28.0
administrative	5.6	6.0	6.4	5.8	5.9	5.7	6.3
Other income—net	0.3	1.6	0.3	0.2	0.5	0.1	1.4
Income before federal taxes	23.3	26.5	25.0	24.3	19.5	20.0	23.1
Net income	14.3	15.1	14.7	13.9	11.3	11.4	13.3

EXHIBIT 3 | Consolidated Balance Sheet for RSE International as of December 31, 2007 (dollar figures in thousands)

Assets

Cash		$ 46,480
U.S. government securities, at cost		117,260
Trade accounts receivable		241,760
Inventories, at lower of cost or market		179,601
Prepaid taxes and insurance		2,120
Total current assets		587,221
Investment in wholly-owned Canadian subsidiary		158,080
Investment in supplier corporation		104,000
Cash value of life insurance		3,920
Miscellaneous assets		2,160
Property, plant, and equipment, at cost:		
Buildings, machinery, equipment	671,402	
Less: allowances for depreciation and amortization	260,001	
Property, plant, and equipment—net	411,402	
Land	22,082	
Property, plant, equipment, and land—net		433,484
Patents, at cost, less amortization		1,120
Total assets		$1,289,985

Liabilities and Stockholders' Equity

Notes payable to bank		$ 5,795
Accounts payable and accrued expenses		90,512
Payrolls and other compensation		38,399
Taxes other than taxes on income		3,052
Provision for federal taxes on income refund, estimated		32,662
Current maturities of long-term debt		30,900
Total current liabilities		201,320
Note payable to bank[1]		119,100
Deferred federal income taxes		29,668
2% cumulative convertible preferred stock, $20 par,		27,783
1,389,160 shares outstanding[2]		
Common stock, $2 par; 96,000,000 shares authorized;		125,389
62,694,361 shares issued		
Capital surplus[3]		21,904
Retained earnings		764,821
Total equity		939,897
Total liabilities and stockholders' equity		$1,289,985

[1]$150,000,000 note, payable semiannually beginning June 30, 2008; $30,900,000 due within one year, shown in current liabilities. One covenant required the company not to pay cash dividends, except on preferred stock, or to make other distribution on its shares or acquire any stock, after December 31, 1999, in excess of net earnings after that date.

[2]Issued in January 2007; convertible at rate of 1.24 common share to one preferred share; redeemable beginning in 2012; sinking fund beginning in 2016.

[3]Resulting principally from the excess of par value of 827,800 shares of preferred stock over the pay value of common share issues in conversion in 2007.

EXHIBIT 4 | Summary of Consolidated Earnings and Dividends for RSE International (dollars in thousands)

	2003	2004	2005	2006	2007
Net sales	$1,623,963	$1,477,402	$1,498,645	$1,980,801	$2,187,208
Cost of products sold	1,271,563	1,180,444	1,140,469	1,642,084	1,793,511
Gross profit	352,400	296,958	358,176	338,717	393,697
Selling, general, and administrative	58,463	69,438	74,932	87,155	120,296
Earnings before federal income taxes	293,937	227,520	283,244	251,562	273,401
Tax expense	126,393	95,558	116,130	101,882	109,360
Net earnings	167,544	131,962	167,114	149,679	164,041
Depreciation	19,160	20,000	21,480	24,200	26,800
Cash dividends declared	85,754	77,052	53,116	77,340	92,238

EXHIBIT 5 | Forecast Financial Statements for RSE International for the Years Ended December 31, 2007–12 (dollars in thousands except per-share figures)

	Actual	Projected				
	2007	2008	2009	2010	2011	2012
Sales	$2,187,208	$2,329,373	$2,480,785	$2,642,037	$2,813,769	$2,996,658
Cost of goods sold	1,793,510	1,920,085	2,064,243	2,216,470	2,367,290	2,537,259
Gross profit	393,698	409,288	416,542	425,567	446,479	459,399
Selling, general, and admin.	120,296	129,786	139,481	151,027	161,315	169,826
Income before tax	273,402	279,502	277,061	274,540	285,164	289,573
Tax expense	109,361	111,801	110,824	109,816	114,066	115,829
Net income	164,041	167,701	166,237	164,724	171,098	173,744
Cash dividends	92,238	102,082	108,714	115,779	125,185	133,313
Depreciation	26,800	27,950	29,770	31,700	33,170	35,960
Net PPE	389,321	426,522	459,404	498,497	541,109	587,580
Net working capital	422,597	447,956	486,428	528,407	574,238	624,303
Earnings per share[1]	$2.62	$2.60	$2.58	$2.56	$2.66	$2.70
Divs. per share common stock[1]	$1.42	$1.58	$1.69	$1.80	$1.94	$2.07
Div. per share preferred stock[2]	$0.40					

[1]62,694,361 common shares in 2007. Thereafter, 64,416,919 shares reflecting conversion of the preferred stock.

[2]1,389,160 preferred shares in 2007. Conversion into 1,722,558 shares of common stock assumed in 2008.

EXHIBIT 6 | Market Prices of Flinder Valves and RSE International Corporation

	Flinder Valves and Controls			RSE International Corporation				
	Common Stock			Common Stock			Preferred Stock	
	High	Low	Close	High	Low	Close	High	Low
2003	$16.25	$8.75	$15.00	$12.31	$10.05	$11.88		
2004	24.75	14.00	22.63	14.36	11.77	13.16		
2005	25.00	20.00	22.25	12.81	9.27	11.13		
2006 Quarter Ended:								
March 31	24.38	20.75	21.50	14.13	12.83	13.95		
June 30	22.75	20.38	21.00	13.69	12.04	11.78		
September 30	22.75	20.38	21.50	12.83	10.48	11.26		
December 31	24.36	20.13	21.00	12.39	11.26	11.87		
2007 Quarter Ended:								
March 31	23.50	20.00	21.75	11.60	10.20	10.67	13.61	12.21
June 30	23.63	19.88	22.00	11.60	10.90	10.90	13.15	12.04
September 30	22.75	20.00	22.50	13.61	11.13	13.61	14.22	12.37
December 31	30.00	22.25	28.50	17.01	13.30	16.78	17.32	13.77
2008 Quarter Ended:								
March 31	32.13	26.00	31.50	20.73	15.08	20.69	17.32	13.98
May 1, 2008	$39.75	$38.90	$39.75	$22.58	$18.30	$21.98	$17.63	$15.35

EXHIBIT 7 | Market Information on Firms in the Industrial Machinery Sector

	Price/ Earnings Ratio	Beta	Dividend Yield	Expected Growth Rate to 2010	Debt/ Capital
Cascade Corp. Manufactures loading engagement devices	10.5	0.95	1.7%	5.1%	29%
Curtiss-Wright Corporation Manufactures highly engineered, advanced technologies that perform critical functions	17.2	1.0	0.7	12.3	36%
Flowserve Corp. Makes, designs, and markets fluid handling equipment (pumps, valves, and mechanical seals)	20.8	1.3	1.0	27.0	30%
Gardner Denver Manufacturers stationary air compressors, vacuum products, and blowers	10.9	1.3	Nil	NMF	19%
Idex Corp. Manufactures a wide range of pumps and machinery products	16.1	1.05	1.5	10.8	22%
Roper Inds. Manufacturers energy systems and controls, imaging equipment, and radio frequency products	19.7	1.2	0.5	10.8	29%
Tecumseh Products Manufactures compressors, condensers, and pumps	38.2	1.05	Nil	NMF	8%
Watts Industries Manufactures and sells an extensive line of valves for the plumbing and heating and water quality markets	15	1.3	1.5	8.4	32%

NMF = not meaningful figure.

Source: *Value Line Investment Survey,* April 25, 2008.

EXHIBIT 8 | Information on Selected Recent Mergers

Effective Date	Acquirer	Business	Target	Business
5/25/2006	Armor Holdings Inc	Law enforcement equip	Stewart & Stevenson	Turbine-driven products
6/26/2006	Bouygues SA	Construction	Alstom SA	Power generation equip
9/20/2006	Boeing Co	Aircraft	Aviall Inc	Vehicle parts
11/10/2006	Daikin Industries Ltd	Air conditioning sys	OYL Industries Bhd	Airconditioners
12/8/2006	Oshkosh Truck Corp	Heavy duty trucks	JLG Industries Inc	Excavators/telehandlers
4/11/2007	Rank Group Ltd	Investment holding co	SIG Holding AG	Packaging/plastics machinery
6/22/2007	Meggitt PLC	Aerospace/defense system	K&F Industries Holdings	Aircraft braking systems
7/31/2007	BAE Systems Inc	Electronic systems	Armor Holdings Inc	Law enforcement equip
12/3/2007	Carlyle Group LLC	Private equity firm	Sequa Corp	Aircraft engine component
12/20/2007	ITT Corp	Pumps/valves	EDO Corp	Electn system products
2/6/2008	London Acquisition BV	Investment holding co	Stork NV	Components
6/5/2008	Ingersoll-Rand Co Ltd	Industrial machinery/equip	Trane Inc	Air conditioners

Acquirer	Target	Transaction Size ($mm)	Target Net Sales Last 12 Months ($mm)	Equity Value/ Target Net Income	Enterprise Value/ Target Net Sales	Enterprise Value/ Target Operating Income	Enterprise Value/ Target Cash Flow	Premium 4 Weeks Prior to Announce- ment Date (%)
Armor Holdings Inc	Stewart & Stevenson	1,123	726	65.3	1.12	33.1	23.7	40.6
Bouygues SA	Alstom SA	2,467	17,679	nmf	1.48	77.9	22.5	–1.2
Boeing Co	Aviall Inc	2,057	1,371	28.9	1.53	18.7	14.9	27.2
Daikin Industries Ltd	OYL Industries Bhd	1,152	1,581	27.6	1.41	21.5	16.8	19.4
Oshkosh Truck Corp	JLG Industries Inc	3,252	2,289	20.5	1.30	11.9	10.7	52.3
Rank Group Ltd	SIG Holding AG	2,314	1,418	38.6	1.56	64.8	14.2	19.3
Meggitt PLC	K&F Industries Holdings	1,802	424	20.3	4.26	13.1	10.8	13.5
BAE Systems Inc	Armor Holdings Inc	4,328	2,805	30.5	1.71	17.1	14.3	29.3
Carlyle Group LLC	Sequa Corp	2,007	2,181	34.4	1.25	20.6	12.5	63.3
ITT Corp	EDO Corp	1,678	945	86.8	1.99	34.0	23.9	40.5
London Acquisition BV	Stork NV	2,347	2,153	17.1	0.02	na	na	35.2
Ingersoll-Rand Co Ltd	Trane Inc	9,751	8,328	21.2	1.39	14.9	11.6	na

na = not available.

Data Source: Thomson Financial's *SDC Platinum.*

EXHIBIT 9 | Capital Market Interest Rates and Stock Price Indexes
(averages per year except April 2008, which offers closing values for
April 25, 2008)

	2006	2007	April 2008
U.S. Treasury Yields			
3-month bills	4.70%	4.40%	1.28%
30-year bonds	5.00%	4.91%	4.52%
Corporate Bond Yields by			
Aaa	5.59%	5.56%	5.58%
Aa	5.80%	5.90%	5.96%
A	6.06%	6.09%	6.32%
Baa	6.48%	6.48%	6.98%
Stock Market			
S&P 500 Index	1,418	1,468	1,398
Price/earnings ratio	17.7×	18.3×	17.4×
Industrial Machinery Stocks			
Price/earnings ratio	13.9×	14.0×	
Dividend yield	1.4%	1.4%	
Historical return premium of equity over government debt (1926–2007)			
Geometric average	5.5%		
Arithmetic average	7.2%		

Data Source: *Value Line Investment Survey,* 25 April 2008; *Federal Reserve Bulletin;* Compustat.

EXHIBIT 10 | Forecast of Financial Statements for Flinders Control and Valve for Years Ended
December 31, 2008–12 (dollars in thousands)

	Actual	Projected				
	2007	2008	2009	2010	2011	2012
Sales	$49,364	$59,600	$66,000	$73,200	$81,200	$90,000
Cost of goods sold	37,044	43,816	48,750	54,104	59,958	66,200
Gross profit	12,320	15,784	17,250	19,096	21,242	23,800
administrative	2,936	3,612	4,124	4,564	5,052	5,692
Other income, net	228	240	264	288	320	352
Income before taxes	9,612	12,412	13,390	14,820	16,510	18,460
Taxes	4,037	4,965	5,356	5,928	6,604	7,384
Net income	$ 5,575	$ 7,447	$ 8,034	$ 8,892	$ 9,906	$11,076
Depreciation	$ 1,508	$ 1,660	$ 1,828	$ 2,012	$ 2,212	$ 2,432
Net PPE	$18,268	$22,056	$24,424	$27,088	$30,049	$33,306
Net Working capital	$16,840	$20,331	$22,515	$24,971	$27,700	$30,702

Source: FVC Analysis.

Palamon Capital Partners/ TeamSystem S.p.A.

We want to make money by investing in change.
—Louis Elson, Managing Partner, Palamon

In February 2000, Louis Elson looked over the London skyline and reflected on the international private equity industry and the investment processes that would be necessary for success in this increasingly competitive field. Elson, a managing partner of the U.K.-based private equity firm Palamon Capital Partners, was specifically considering an investment in TeamSystem S.p.A., an Italian software company. Palamon was interested in TeamSystem for the growth opportunity that it represented in a fast-changing market. Palamon had an opportunity to purchase a 51% stake in TeamSystem for (euro) EUR25.9 million. In preparing a recommendation to his colleagues at Palamon, Elson planned to assess TeamSystem's strategy, value the firm, identify important risks, evaluate proposed terms of the investment, and consider alternative exit strategies.

International Private Equity Industry

The international private equity industry was segmented into three sectors. Venture capital funds made high-risk early-stage investments in startup companies. Generalist private equity funds provided expansionary funding or transitional funding that allowed small companies to grow and eventually go public. And leveraged buyout funds financed the acquisitions (often by management) of pre-existing companies that had the capacity to take on debt and make radical improvements in operations.

This case was prepared by Chad Rynbrandt from interviews, under the direction of Robert F. Bruner, with the assistance of Sean D. Carr. Some details have been simplified for expositional clarity. The cooperation of Palamon Capital Partners is gratefully acknowledged, as is the financial support of the Batten Institute. Copyright © 2001 by the University of Virginia Darden School Foundation, Charlottesville, VA. All rights reserved. *To order copies, send an e-mail to* sales@dardenbusinesspublishing.com. *No part of this publication may be reproduced, stored in a retrieval system, used in a spreadsheet, or transmitted in any form or by any means—electronic, mechanical, photocopying, recording, or otherwise—without the permission of the Darden School Foundation.* Rev. 12/05.

Private equity funds raised capital primarily from individual investors, pension funds, and endowments that were interested in more attractive risk/return investment propositions than the public capital markets offered. Funds existed all over the world, but, not surprisingly, North America had the largest number of funds and largest dollar value of capital invested as of 1999. Europe and Asia had the next largest private equity industries. **Exhibit 1** presents the number and dollar values of private equity funds by global geographic region.

Most private equity markets saw rapid growth in the 1990s. In Europe, the amount of new capital raised grew from EUR4.4 billion in 1994 to EUR25.4 billion in 1999. Correspondingly, the amount of capital invested by the funds more than quadrupled from EUR5.5 billion to EUR25.1 billion over the same period. **Exhibit 2** summarizes the amount of new capital raised and the amount invested through the 1990s. Some key players in the mid-market sector in Europe included Duke Street Capital (EUR650 million fund based in the United Kingdom), Mercapital (EUR600 million fund based in Spain), and Nordic Capital (EUR760 million fund based in Sweden). Large investment banks such as Dresdner, Deutsche Bank, and Banca de Roma also had notable private equity presences.

Louis Elson and Palamon Capital Partners

Louis Elson began working in private equity in 1990, when he joined E.M. Warburg, Pincus & Co. Soon after joining the firm, he began focusing on European transactions and, in 1992, decided to relocate permanently to Europe. Elson became a partner of Warburg, Pincus in 1995 and was an integral part of a team that built a US$1.3 billion portfolio of equity investments for the firm. The portfolio contained more than 40 investments in seven different European countries. In late 1998, Elson and another of his partners, Michael Hoffman, saw a unique window of opportunity in the European private equity industry. They believed that the European economic landscape was changing in a way that benefited smaller, middle-market companies. Therefore, Elson and Hoffman recruited two additional partners and began laying the foundation for what would eventually become Palamon Capital Partners.

By August 1999, Elson and Hoffman had raised a fund of EUR440 million. They accomplished that despite macroeconomic obstacles like the Russian debt default by marketing their unique pan-European private equity experience. With the fund closed, Elson and Hoffman grew the Palamon team to nine professionals. They hired people with experience in private equity, investment banking, corporate finance, and management consulting. Consistent with Elson and Hoffman's original vision, the Palamon team used their breadth of experience to build a portfolio of investments that would provide investors with a unique risk profile and substantial long-term returns. Essentially, Palamon was a generalist private equity fund that served the segment of investor that was interested in less risk than venture capital, but more risk than the leveraged buyout funds. Accordingly, Palamon targeted a 35% return on a single portfolio investment, and 20% to 25% blended net return on a portfolio, with an investment horizon of approximately six years. Louis Elson said:

> Our investors include large American public sector pension funds, corporate pension funds, major financial institutions, and large endowment funds. They look for us to beat the return on the S&P Index by 500 basis points per year on average. We have the best chance of getting funded again if we can beat this target, adjusting of course for risk. We look to pick up good businesses at attractive prices, and then add value through active involvement with them.

Like other generalist funds, Palamon's investment strategy was to make "bridge" investments in companies that wanted to move from small, private ownership to the public capital markets. Unlike many private equity funds, however, Palamon did not restrict itself to one specific European country, nor did it limit its scope to one industry. Instead, Palamon focused more broadly on small to mid-sized European companies in which it could acquire a controlling stake for between EUR10 million and EUR50 million.

For companies that fit Palamon's profile, the transition from private to public ownership required both funding and management ability. Palamon, therefore, complemented its financial investments with advisory services to increase the probability that the portfolio companies would successfully make it to the public markets. Elson was optimistic about Palamon's investment strategy. As Elson sat in his office, Palamon was finalizing its first investment, a Spanish Internet content company, Lanetro, S.A., and had three other investments (including TeamSystem) in the pipeline.

Investment Process

Palamon's investment process began with the development of an investment thesis that would typically involve a market undergoing significant change, which might be driven by deregulation, trade liberalization, new technology, demographic shifts, and so on. Within the chosen market, Palamon looked for attractive investment opportunities, using investment banks, industry resources, and personal contacts. The search process was time-consuming, with only 1% of the opportunities making it through to the next phase, due diligence, which involved thorough research into the history, performance, and competitive advantages of the investment candidate. Typically, only one company made it through that final screen to provide Palamon with a viable investment alternative.

Palamon brought its deal-making experience to bear in shaping the specific terms of investment. Carefully tailored agreements could increase the likelihood of a successful outcome, both by creating the right incentives for operating managers to achieve targets, and by timing the delivery of cash returns to investors in ways consistent with the operating strategy of the target. Deal negotiations covered many issues including price, executive leadership, and board composition. Once a deal had been completed, Palamon then offered value-added support to management.

To close the process, Palamon searched for the best exit alternative, one that would help them fully realize a return on the fund's investment. Classic exit alternatives included sale of the firm through an initial public offering in a stock market, and sale of the firm to a strategic buyer. **Exhibit 3** provides more detail about Palamon's process and the firm's investment screening criteria.

TeamSystem, S.p.A.

Palamon's theme-based search generated the opportunity to invest in TeamSystem, S.p.A. In early 1999, even before Palamon's fund had been closed, Elson had concluded that the payroll servicing industry in Italy could provide a good investment opportunity because of the industry's extreme fragmentation and constantly changing regulations. History had shown that governments in Italy adjusted their policies as often as four times a year. For Palamon, the space represented a ripe opportunity to invest in a company that would capitalize on the need of small companies to respond to this legislative volatility. With the help of a boutique investment bank and industry contacts, Palamon approached two leading players in the market. Neither company was suitable to Palamon, but both identified their most respected competitor as TeamSystem. Palamon approached TeamSystem directly and found a good fit. Due diligence was done and, by the end of the year, a specific investment proposal had taken shape. It was the one Elson now considered.

TeamSystem was founded in 1979 in Pesaro, Italy. Since its founding, the company had grown to become one of Italy's leading providers of accounting, tax, and payroll management software for small-to-medium-size enterprises (SMEs). Led by cofounder and CEO Giovanni Ranocchi, TeamSystem had built up a customer base of 28,000 firms, representing a 14% share of the Italian market.

TeamSystem offered its customers a compelling value proposition. The company's software integrated a business's financial information and automated tedious and complex administrative functions. The software also enabled SMEs and their financial advisors to stay on top of the frequently changing regulatory environment. To that end, TeamSystem continually invested in development to keep its software current. Customers were given access to product upgrades in exchange for a yearly maintenance fee that the company collected (in addition to the initial purchase price of the software). TeamSystem had excelled in customer service and developed loyal customers. Nearly 95% of its customers renewed their maintenance contracts every year.

In 1999, TeamSystem generated sales of (lira) ITL60.5 billion (EUR31.3 million) and EBIT (earnings before interest and taxes) of ITL18.5 billion (EUR9.5 million). Those results continued a strong pattern of growth for TeamSystem. Since 1996, sales had grown at an annualized rate of 15% and operating margins improved. As a result, EBIT had grown at an annualized rate of 31.6% over the same period. **Exhibit 4** provides additional detail on TeamSystem's historical sales and profitability from 1996 through 1999. **Exhibit 5** contains balance sheet information for the same period.

As Elson looked through the numbers, he noted the current lack of debt on TeamSystem's balance sheet. In his opinion, that represented an opportunity to bring TeamSystem to a more effective capital structure that might lower the company's cost of capital. Elson also noted the "pro forma" label on both financial statements. TeamSystem, given its private ownership and multicompany structure, did not have audited consolidated financial information for the previous five years.

Industry Profile

The Italian accounting, tax, and payroll management software industry in which TeamSystem operated was highly fragmented. More than 30 software providers vied for the business of 200,000 SMEs with the largest having a 15% share of the market (TeamSystem ranked number two with its 14% share.) All of the significant players in the industry were family-owned companies that did not have access to international capital markets. **Exhibit 6** shows 1998 revenues for the nine largest players.

Analysts predicted that two things would characterize the future of the industry—consolidation and growth. Consolidation would occur because few of the smaller companies would be able to keep up with the research and development demands of a changing industry. Analysts pointed to three acquisitions in 1998–99 as the start of that trend. As for growth, experts predicted 9% annual growth over the period 1999–2002. That growth would come primarily from increased PC penetration among SMEs, greater end-user sophistication, and continued computerization of administrative functions.

The Transaction

After reviewing TeamSystem's past performance and the state of the industry, Elson returned his attention to the specifics of the TeamSystem investment. The most recent proposal had offered EUR25.9 million for 51% of the common (or ordinary) shares in a multipart structure that also included a recapitalization to put debt on the balance sheet:

- Palamon would invest ITL50.235 billion (EUR25.9 million) in the ordinary shares (i.e., common equity) of TeamSystem S.p.A. Those shares would be purchased from existing shareholders of TeamSystem. Giovanni Rannochi would maintain a 20% shareholding, while noncore employees would be diluted from holdings ranging from 3% to 8% to just 1% each after completion.

- More than half of TeamSystem's ITL28.5 billion of cash was to be distributed to existing shareholders via two dividend payments before Palamon's investment: an ITL8.5 billion dividend to existing TeamSystem shareholders in April 2000, and a ITL6.5 billion dividend to be paid at time of closing. A cash balance of ITL 13.5 billion would remain.

- With Palamon's assistance, TeamSystem would borrow ITL46 billion from Deutsche Bank, in a seven-year loan, offering a three-year principal repayment holiday and an initial cost of 1.0% over base rates (Italian government bonds). Shareholders would receive the proceeds of the debt at time of closing in another special dividend.

- Excess real estate would be sold by TeamSystem, thus removing the distraction of unrelated property investments. A group of existing shareholders had made an offer to purchase ITL2.1 billion of real estate at book value if the transaction closed.

The sources and uses of funds in the transaction are summarized in **Exhibit 7.** An income statement and balance sheet for TeamSystem, pro forma the transaction, are given in **Exhibits 8** and **9.** Palamon, as a majority shareholder, would have full effective control of TeamSystem, although the existing shareholders would have a number of minority protection rights. For example, Palamon would be unable to dismiss Ranocchi for a two-year period. But Palamon would have the ability to deliver 100% of the shares of the company to a trade buyer should that be the appropriate exit. Furthermore, more than 40% of the cash to be paid to the departing shareholders would be held in escrow for a period of at least two years, under Palamon's control.

Valuation

To properly evaluate the deal, Elson had to develop a view about the value of Team-System. He faced some challenges in that task, however. First, TeamSystem had no strategic plan or future forecast of profitability. Elson only had four years of historical information. If Elson were to do a proper valuation, he would need to estimate the future cash flows that TeamSystem would generate given market trends and the value that Palamon could add. His best guess was that TeamSystem could grow revenues at 15% per year for the next few years, a pace above the expected market growth rate of 9%, followed by a 6% growth rate in perpetuity.[1] He also thought that Palamon's professionals could help Ranocchi improve operating margins slightly. Lastly, Elson believed that a 14% discount rate would appropriately capture the risk of the cash flows. That rate reflected three software companies' trading on the Milan stock exchange, whose betas averaged 1.44 and unlevered betas averaged 1.00.

The second challenge Elson faced was the lack of comparable valuations in the Italian market. Because most competitors were family-owned, there was very little market transparency. The nearest matches he could find were other European and U.S. enterprise resource planning (ERP)[2] companies and accounting software companies. The financial profiles of those comparable firms are contained in **Exhibits 10** and **11**. See also exchange rates and capital market conditions in **Exhibits 12** and **13**. Looking through the data, Elson noticed the high growth expectations (greater than 20%) for the software firms and correspondingly high valuation multiples.

Risks

Elson was concerned about more than just the valuation, however. He wanted to carefully evaluate the risks associated with the deal, specifically:

- *TeamSystem's management team might not be able to make the change to a more professionally run company.* The investment in TeamSystem was a bet on a small private company that Elson hoped would become a dominant, larger player. The CEO, Ranocchi, had successfully navigated the last five years of growth, but had, by his own admission, created a management group that relied on him for almost every decision. From conversations and interviews, Elson concluded that Ranocchi

---

[1]This was roughly the sum of an expected long-term inflation rate in the euro of 3%, and long-term real economic growth in Europe of 3%.

[2]Enterprise resource planning (ERP) systems were commercial software packages that promise the seamless integration of all the information flowing through a company: financial, accounting, supply chain, customer, and human resources information.

could take the company forward, but he had concerns about the ability of the supporting cast to deliver in a period of continued growth.

- *TeamSystem was facing an inspection by the Italian tax authorities.* The inspection posed a financial risk, and therefore could serve as a significant distraction for management. Further, because it was "open-ended," the inspection might delay the company's ability to go public. Elson had quantified the risk, however, through sensitivity and scenario analysis, and believed that the expected monetary impact of the inspection was low.

- *The company might not be able to keep up with technological change.* While the company had begun to adapt to technological changes such as new programming languages, it still had some products on older platforms that would require significant reprogramming. In addition, the Internet posed an immediate threat if TeamSystem's competitors adapted to it more quickly than TeamSystem did.

Finally, Elson wanted to make sure that he could capture the value that TeamSystem might be able to create in the next few years. Exit options were, therefore, also an important consideration.

Conclusion

Elson looked at all the information that covered his desk and pondered the recommendation he should make to his partners. How much was a 51% stake really worth? What might explain the valuation results? What nonprice considerations should he make part of the deal? How might Palamon feasibly capture the value from the investment? Were the risks serious enough to compromise the value of the investment?

EXHIBIT 1 | Size of Regional Private Equity Markets, 1999

Region	Number of Funds	Total Value of Funds (in U.S.D millions)
North America	8,376	892,598
Europe	2,556	160,749
Asia	1,360	60,582
Middle East	130	6,469
Australia/Oceania	155	5,741
Central/South America	42	5,044
Africa	13	1,711

Source of data: Thomson Securities Data/Venture Xpert.

EXHIBIT 2 | Historical Data on European Private Equity Market

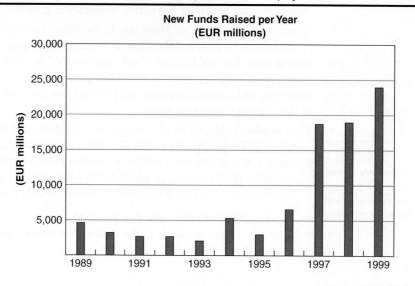

New Funds Raised per Year
(EUR millions)

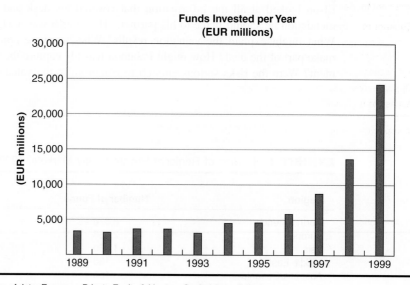

Funds Invested per Year
(EUR millions)

Source of data: European Private Equity & Venture Capital Association.

EXHIBIT 3 | Screening Criteria and Investment Process

Investment Process

Palamon utilizes an investment process that has been proven over the past decade through economic cycles and across geographic regions. The process is underpinned by a core set of investment principles, which can be summarized by stage of the investment process.

- Determination of Investment Focus—Identify sectors undergoing significant changes, develop industry knowledge, and take a contrarian stance when appropriate.
- Pro-Active Deal Sourcing—Proactively pursue investment opportunities within identified sectors.
- Rigorous Due Diligence—Execute comprehensive yet focused company due diligence; concentrate on "deal breakers" early on.
- Sophisticated Deal Structuring—Base structuring on a sound knowledge of local practices without relying necessarily on ineffective customs; align objectives with the entrepreneur; avoid excess leverage.
- Value-Added Support—Provide strategic direction to portfolio companies; make international network of advisors and expertise available to management teams; commit to longer time horizons sufficient to ensure scope for company growth.
- Proven Realization Strategies—Prepare for liquidity events; utilize in-house expertise to access public market capital or organize trade sales, creating exit options for all shareholders.

Investment Screening Criteria

The partners of Palamon are especially rigorous in their investment selection criteria, identifying those characteristics that will foster high growth combined with manageable risk. The following key elements are sought in each investment made:

- Superior management with unique capabilities and experience
- Leadership in core markets which are either expanding robustly or are experiencing dislocation due to technological, regulatory, or competitive changes
- High potential for operating leverage
- Opportunity to access alternative markets
- Access to undervalued assets

Source: http://www.palamon.com/ (accessed 19 December 2005).

EXHIBIT 4 | TeamSystem S.p.A. Pro Forma Historical Income Statement
(values in ITL millions)

	1996	1997	1998	1999
Total sales	39,665	42,922	50,694	60,499
Cost of materials	(9,979)	(11,430)	(12,258)	(15,179)
Cost of service	(9,380)	(8,692)	(10,889)	(12,389)
Rents and leasing	(328)	(394)	(1,493)	(1,553)
Total operating cost	(19,687)	(20,516)	(24,640)	(29,121)
Salaries	(4,875)	(5,382)	(6,282)	(7,151)
Social contributions	(1,855)	(2,047)	(1,917)	(2,011)
Other personnel costs	(456)	(481)	(572)	(753)
Total personnel costs	(7,186)	(7,910)	(8,771)	(9,915)
Other operating costs	(2,793)	(3,052)	(3,133)	(1,339)
EBITDA	9,999	11,444	14,150	20,124
Depreciation & amortization	(1,052)	(1,427)	(1,355)	(1,636)
EBIT	8,947	10,017	12,795	18,488
Interest expense	(185)	(144)	(154)	(210)
Non-op income	1,800	1,305	1,132	1,283
Pretax profit	10,563	11,178	13,773	19,562
Taxes	(5,870)	(6,699)	(6,437)	(9,525)
Earnings before minorities	4,693	4,479	7,336	10,036
Elimination of intercompany invest	(30)	(13)	(139)	(287)
Net income	4,663	4,466	7,197	9,749

Source: Palamon memorandum.

EXHIBIT 5 | TeamSystem S.p.A. Pro Forma Historical Balance Sheet
(values in ITL millions)

	1996	1997	1998	1999
ASSETS				
Cash	13,092	19,134	21,144	28,513
Marketable securities				
Receivables	13,257	14,957	16,328	19,443
Inventory	1,333	1,087	1,195	1,235
Total current assets	27,682	35,178	38,667	49,191
Intangible assets	14	22	18	21
Land, PP&E	4,962	2,080	2,489	3,681
Other tangible assets	729	668	1,140	2,055
Deferred costs	327	1,947	1,738	1,865
Securities and other	1,434	1,173	1,229	1,226
Total assets	35,148	41,068	45,281	58,039
LIABILITIES				
Accounts payable	7,661	8,932	8,969	9,669
Tax and other payables	6,796	9,827	8,660	9,956
Deferred income and accruals	1,200	1,127	1,257	4,156
Long-term liabilities	2,688	2,094	2,235	3,055
Total liabilities	18,345	21,980	21,121	26,836
SHAREHOLDERS' EQUITY AND MINORITY INTEREST				
Capital	4,580	4,580	4,580	4,580
Reserves	6,636	9,442	11,662	15,884
Operating income	4,584	4,405	7,132	9,660
(Less special dividend)				
Total shareholders' equity	15,800	18,427	23,374	30,124
Minority interest	1,003	661	786	1,079
Total shareholders' equity and minority interest	16,803	19,088	24,160	31,203
Total shareholders' equity and liabilities	35,148	41,068	45,281	58,039

Source: Palamon memorandum.

EXHIBIT 6 | Revenues for Top Companies in Italian Payroll Software Industry, 1998

Company	Revenues (ITL billions)
TeamSystem	50.7
Inaz Paghe	47.0
Osra	38.0
Sistemi	37.0
Zuchetti	36.0
Esa Software	35.0
Omega Data	34.4
Axioma	26.0
Dylog Italia	25.0

Source: Palamon memorandum.

EXHIBIT 7 | Sources/Uses of Cash in Proposed Leveraged Restructuring (values in ITL millions)

Sources:	
Debt	46,000
Excess cash	15,000
	61,000
Uses:	
Special dividend—April 2000	8,500
Special dividend—closing	52,500
	61,000

Note: This table refers strictly to the leveraged recapitalization of TeamSystem. Ignored in this table are (1) the ITL50.235 billion purchase of shares by Palamon from investors in TeamSystem and (2) a purchase of TeamSystem real estate for ITL2.1 billion by investors. Palamon would not receive any of the special dividends.

EXHIBIT 8 | TeamSystem S.p.A. Pro Forma Income Statement
(values in ITL millions)

	1996	1997	1998	1999	2000	2001	2002	2003	2004	2005	2006	2007	growth
					15%	15%	15%	6%	6%	6%	6%	6%	
Total sales	39,665	42,922	50,694	60,499	69,573	80,009	92,011	97,532	103,383	109,586	116,162	123,131	
Cost of materials	(9,979)	(11,430)	(12,258)	(15,179)									
Cost of service	(9,380)	(8,692)	(10,889)	(12,389)									
Rents and leasing	(328)	(394)	(1,493)	(1,553)									
Total operating cost	(19,687)	(20,516)	(24,640)	(29,121)	(31,308)	(36,004)	(41,405)	(43,889)	(46,523)	(49,314)	(52,273)	(55,409)	45.00% of sales
Salaries	(4,875)	(5,382)	(6,282)	(7,151)									
Social contributions	(1,855)	(2,047)	(1,917)	(2,011)									
Other personnel costs	(456)	(481)	(572)	(753)									
Total personnel costs	(7,186)	(7,910)	(8,771)	(9,915)	(10,784)	(12,401)	(14,262)	(15,117)	(16,024)	(16,986)	(18,005)	(19,085)	15.50% of sales
Other operating costs	(2,793)	(3,052)	(3,133)	(1,339)	(2,783)	(3,200)	(3,680)	(3,901)	(4,135)	(4,383)	(4,646)	(4,925)	4.00% of sales
EBITDA	9,999	11,444	14,150	20,124	24,699	28,403	32,664	34,624	36,701	38,903	41,237	43,712	
Depreciation & amortization	(1,052)	(1,427)	(1,355)	(1,636)	(835)	(900)	(975)	(1,010)	(1,046)	(1,085)	(1,126)	(1,170)	25.00% of PP&E and Intang
EBIT	8,947	10,017	12,795	18,488	23,863	27,503	31,689	33,614	35,655	37,818	40,111	42,542	
Interest expense	(185)	(144)	(154)	(210)	(3,160)	(3,160)	(3,160)	(2,765)	(1,975)	(1,185)	(395)	—	6.87% interest
Non-op income	1,800	1,305	1,132	1,283	561	1,157	1,855	2,091	2,408	2,813	3,310	4,507	5.00% return on mkt secur
Pretax profit	10,563	11,178	13,773	19,562	21,265	25,500	30,383	32,939	36,088	39,446	43,026	47,049	
Taxes	(5,870)	(6,699)	(6,437)	(9,525)	(10,207)	(12,240)	(14,584)	(15,811)	(17,322)	(18,934)	(20,652)	(22,584)	48.00% of pre-tax profit
Earnings before minorities	4,693	4,479	7,336	10,036									
Elimination of intercompany invest	(30)	(13)	(139)	(287)									
Net income	4,663	4,466	7,197	9,749	11,058	13,260	15,799	17,129	18,766	20,512	22,373	24,465	

Source: Case writer's analysis.

EXHIBIT 9 | TeamSystem S.p.A. Pro Forma Balance Sheet (values in ITL millions)

	1996	1997	1998	1999	2000	2001	2002	2003	2004	2005	2006	2007	
ASSETS													
Cash	13,092	19,134	21,144	28,513	13,500	15,202	17,482	18,531	19,643	20,821	22,071	23,395	19.0% of sales
Marketable securities					11,224	23,143	37,096	41,816	48,165	56,253	66,196	90,144	PLUG
Receivables	13,257	14,957	16,328	19,443	20,872	24,003	27,603	29,259	31,015	32,876	34,848	36,939	30.0% of sales
Inventory	1,333	1,087	1,195	1,235	1,391	1,600	1,840	1,951	2,068	2,192	2,323	2,463	2.0% of sales
Total current assets	27,682	35,178	38,667	49,191	46,988	63,948	84,021	91,557	100,891	112,142	125,438	152,941	
Intangible assets	14	22	18	21	20	20	20	20	20	20	20	20	
Land, PP&E	4,962	2,080	2,489	3,681	1,581	1,581	1,581	1,581	1,581	1,581	1,581	1,581	
Other tangible assets	729	668	1,140	2,055	1,739	2,000	2,300	2,438	2,585	2,740	2,904	3,078	2.5% of sales
Deferred costs	327	1,947	1,738	1,865	2,087	2,400	2,760	2,926	3,102	3,288	3,485	3,694	3.0% of sales
Securities and other	1,434	1,173	1,229	1,226	1,391	1,600	1,840	1,951	2,068	2,192	2,323	2,463	2.0% of sales
Total assets	35,148	41,068	45,281	58,039	53,807	71,549	92,523	100,473	110,245	121,962	135,751	163,776	
LIABILITIES													
Accounts payable	7,661	8,932	8,969	9,669	11,132	12,802	14,722	15,605	16,541	17,534	18,586	19,701	16.0% of sales
Tax and other payables	6,796	9,827	8,660	9,956	11,132	12,802	14,722	15,605	16,541	17,534	18,586	19,701	16.0% of sales
Deferred income and accruals	1,200	1,127	1,257	4,156	3,479	4,000	4,601	4,877	5,169	5,479	5,808	6,157	5.0% of sales
Long term liabilities	2,688	2,094	2,235	3,055	46,000	46,000	46,000	34,500	23,000	11,500	—	—	
Total liabilities	18,345	21,980	21,121	26,836	71,742	75,604	80,044	70,587	61,252	52,047	42,980	45,559	
SHAREHOLDERS' EQUITY AND MINORITY INTEREST													
Capital	4,580	4,580	4,580	4,580	4,580	4,580	4,580	4,580	4,580	4,580	4,580	4,580	
Reserves	6,636	9,442	11,662	15,884	24,544	(24,398)	(11,138)	4,661	21,789	40,555	61,067	83,440	
Operating income	4,584	4,405	7,132	9,660	11,058	13,260	15,799	17,129	18,766	20,512	22,373	24,465	
(Less special dividend)					(61,000)								
Total shareholders' equity	15,800	18,427	23,374	30,124	(19,818)	(6,558)	9,241	26,369	45,135	65,647	88,020	112,486	3.5% of equity
Minority interest	1,003	661	786	1,079	1,883	2,504	3,238	3,517	3,859	4,269	4,751	5,732	
Total shareholders' equity and minority interest	16,803	19,088	24,160	31,203	(17,935)	(4,054)	12,479	29,886	48,994	69,915	92,771	118,218	
Total shareholders' equity and liabilities	35,148	41,068	45,281	58,039	53,807	71,549	92,523	100,473	110,245	121,962	135,751	163,776	

DEBT REPAYMENT

	2000	2001	2002	2003	2004	2005	2006
Starting balance	46,000						
Principal due	0%	0%	0%	25%	25%	25%	25%
Payment	—	—	—	(11,500)	(11,500)	(11,500)	(11,500)

Source: Case writer's analysis.

EXHIBIT 10 | Valuation Measures for Publicly Traded Enterprise Resource Planning (ERP) Software Companies

	Adjusted Market Value[a] as a Multiple of:			Equity Market Value as a Multiple of:			Long-Term Projected EPS Growth[b]	CY 1999 P/E to LTGR	Growth Rates 1 Year		Long-Term Margins	
	Long-Term Revenues	Long-Term Op. Inc.	EPS	Cal. 1999 EPS Est.[b]	Cal. 2000 EPS Est.[b]	Cal. 2001 EPS Est.[b]			Rev.	EBIT	EBIT	Net
Tier 1—Large ERP Players												
Baan	4.0 ×	NM	NM	NM	NM	NM	26%	NM	8.2%	NM	−38.0%	−40.2%
JD Edwards	1.6 ×	26.2 ×	37.9 ×	NM ×	95.0 ×	74.9 ×	27%	NM	44.2%	77.0%	6.2%	5.0%
Oracle	6.8 ×	32.0 ×	47.8 ×	42.1 ×	34.4 ×	27.8 ×	24%	143%	23.6%	32.7%	21.2%	14.6%
Peoplesoft	2.3 ×	23.6 ×	NM	NM	54.8 ×	44.3 ×	24%	231%	61.1%	41.7%	9.9%	2.1%
SAP	8.3 ×	42.1 ×	75.2 ×	61.9 ×	45.8 ×	36.6 ×	25%	182%	41.9%	17.4%	19.7%	11.1%
Low	1.6 ×	23.6 ×	37.9 ×	42.1 ×	34.4 ×	27.8 ×	24%	143%	8.2%	17.4%	−38.0%	−40.2%
Mean	4.6 ×	31.0 ×	53.6 ×	52.0 ×	57.5 ×	45.9 ×	25%	185%	35.8%	42.2%	3.8%	−1.5%
High	8.3 ×	42.1 ×	75.2 ×	61.9 ×	95.0 ×	74.9 ×	27%	231%	61.1%	77.0%	21.2%	14.6%
Tier 2—Middle Market Accounting Software Companies												
Great Plains Software Inc.	4.8 ×	8.1 ×	56.1 ×	48.2 ×	37.8 ×	28.0 ×	35%	108%	57.5%	590.5%	58.9%	9.5%
Intuit Inc.	5.8 ×	42.8 ×	43.6 ×	62.4 ×	52.4 ×	43.2 ×	21%	247%	12.8%	40.1%	13.6%	16.3%
Epicor Software	1.5 ×	NM	NA	54.2 ×	18.1 ×	14.2 ×	28%	66%	NA	NA	−10.0%	10.2%
Sage Group PLC	16.0 ×	58.5 ×	84.3 ×	71.1 ×	58.2 ×	43.0 ×	35%	165%	25.9%	26.6%	27.4%	17.7%
Symix	0.7 ×	8.2 ×	12.6 ×	13.5 ×	12.1 ×	9.4 ×	28%	43%	48.4%	68.0%	8.4%	5.1%
Low	0.7 ×	8.1 ×	12.6 ×	13.5 ×	12.1 ×	9.4 ×	21%	43%	12.8%	26.6%	−10.0%	−10.2%
Mean	5.8 ×	29.4 ×	49.2 ×	49.9 ×	35.7 ×	27.6 ×	29%	126%	36.2%	181.3%	19.7%	7.7%
High	16.0 ×	58.5 ×	84.3 ×	71.1 ×	58.2 ×	43.2 ×	35%	247%	57.5%	590.5%	58.9%	17.7%
Tier 3—Others												
Agresso	0.8 ×	40.2 ×	42.0 ×	15.6 ×	7.7 ×	3.5 ×	121%	6%	266.4%	3209.1%	2.1%	1.8%
Intentia	1.6 ×	−69.2 ×	NM	62.1 ×	29.5 ×	NA	NA	NA	51.7%	115.6%	−2.4%	−5.5%
Navision	17.6 ×	79.6 ×	126.9 ×	41.6 ×	32.0 ×	NA	NA	NA	91.5%	137.9%	22.1%	14.0%
Brain International	3.1 ×	NM	NM	72.7 ×	31.8 ×	NA	NA	NA	23.1%	−66.0%	−0.2%	1.1%
Low	0.8 ×	−69.2 ×	42.0 ×	15.6 ×	7.7 ×	3.5 ×	121%	6%	23.1%	−66.0%	−2.4%	−5.5%
Mean	5.8 ×	16.9 ×	84.5 ×	48.0 ×	25.3 ×	3.5 ×	121%	6%	108.2%	849.2%	5.4%	2.9%
High	17.6 ×	79.6 ×	126.9 ×	72.7 ×	32.0 ×	3.5 ×	121%	6%	266.4%	3209.1%	22.1%	14.0%

[a]Based on adjusted market capitalization, which is defined as equity market value + long-term debt − cash & equivalents.

[b]Based on I/B/E/S estimates.

Source of: Thomson Financial's *Datastream Advance*.

EXHIBIT 11 | Financial Data for Selected Enterprise Resource Planning (ERP) Software Companies (values in USD thousands, except per-share data)

	Equity Market Value	Long-Term Debt	Cash & Equiv.	Adjusted Market Value[a]	Revenues	Op. Inc.	EPS	Cal. 2000 EPS Est.[b]	Cal. 2001 EPS Est.[b]	Book Value	Total Assets
Tier 1—Large ERP Players											
Baan	2,637,618	200,546	121,697	2,716,467	674,664	(256,446)	$ (1.35)	$ 0.08	$ 0.10	112,821	696,510
JD Edwards	1,829,385	—	211,782	1,617,603	1,001,263	61,842	$ 0.45	$ 0.18	$ 0.23	583,996	950,473
Oracle	62,282,746	301,140	2,562,764	60,021,122	8,827,252	1,872,881	$ 0.87	$ 1.21	$ 1.50	3,695,267	7,259,654
Peoplesoft	3,611,452	—	498,155	3,113,297	1,333,095	131,978	$ 0.05	$ 0.26	$ 0.32	664,292	1,440,605
SAP	41,907,460	718,858	693,411	41,932,907	5,052,321	995,535	$ 5.33	$ 8.76	$ 10.96	2,096,138	4,083,069
Tier 2—Middle Market Accounting Software Companies											
Great Plains Software	767,893	—	123,683	644,210	134,907	79,489	$ 0.86	$ 1.28	$ 1.72	133,193	180,252
Intuit Inc.	6,476,010	36,043	1,761,200	4,750,853	814,889	111,009	$ 2.15	$ 1.79	$ 2.17	1,673,405	2,469,865
Epicor Software	154,977	—	47,304	107,673	73,688	(7,333)	NA	$ 0.21	$ 0.27	122,196	199,735
Sage Group	5,997,648	136,046	78,171	6,055,523	377,477	103,595	$ 0.58	$ 0.83	$ 1.13	11,187	650,375
Symix	84,421	4,109	3,261	85,269	123,010	10,374	$ 0.91	$ 0.95	$ 1.22	36,749	73,346
Tier 3—Others											
Agresso	88,554	1,398	18,680	71,272	85,973	1,771	$ 0.04	$ 0.24	$ 0.53	40,804	89,789
Intentia	557,217	36,833	12,655	581,395	352,988	(8,400)	$ (0.72)	$ 0.74	NA	104,085	275,714
Navision	655,707	—	6,285	649,422	36,875	8,155	$ 0.20	$ 0.80	NA	9,540	25,127
Brain International	256,499	19,991	39,283	237,207	76,686	(164)	$ 0.13	$ 1.26	NA	65,365	107,844

[a]Based on adjusted market capitalization, which is defined as equity market value + long-term debt − cash & equivalents.
[b]Based on I/B/E/S estimates.
Source of data: Datastream.

EXHIBIT 12 | Recent ITL/EUR Exchange Rates

On January 1, 1999, the European Community fixed the ITL/EUR conversion rate at LIT 1,936.27. The exchange rates that follow were estimated through euro vs. dollar exchange rates,[1] and are proxies for open market rates of exchange.

Date	ITL/EUR
September 1999	1696.3
October 1999	1740.1
November 1999	1901.8
December 1999	1912.6
January 2000	2055.0

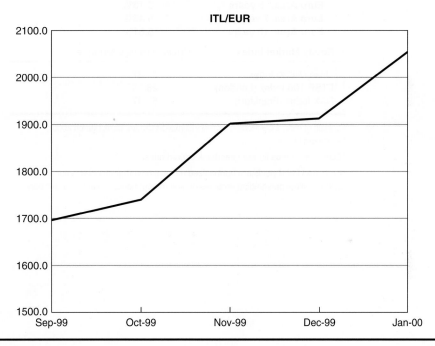

ITL/EUR

Source: Bloomberg LP.

[1]For instance, in September 1999, the EUR/USD exchange rate was 1.0684, and the ITL/USD exchange rate was 1812.32. Dividing the ITL/USD rate by the EUR/USD rate yields an implied ITL/EUR rate of 1696.3.

EXHIBIT 13 | Capital-Market Conditions, February 2000

Instrument	Yield
EURIBOR[1]	
90-day	3.41%
6-month	3.78%
1-year	4.11%
Government Bonds	
(euro-denominated)	
Italy, April 2004	6.00%
Italy, July 2007	5.87%
Italy, March 2011	9.25%
Euro Area,[2] 5 years	5.16%
Euro Area, 7 years	5.45%
Euro Area, 10 years	5.61%

Equity Market Index	Price/Earnings Multiple
Milan MIB30 Index	37.87
FTSE 100 Index (London)	28.75
DAX Index (Frankfurt)	57.47

Sources of data: *ECB Monthly Bulletin,* European Central Bank (March 2000); Bloomberg LP.

[1]EURIBOR stands for euro interbank offered rates.

[2]Euro area bond yields are harmonized national government bond yields weighted by the nominal outstanding amounts of government bonds in each maturity band.

Purinex, Inc.

To lead the world in discovering, developing & commercializing novel therapeutic compounds acting on the purine receptors in order to save and improve patients' lives.

Company mission statement

In June 2004, Purinex, Inc., a pharmaceutical company with several clinically and commercially promising drugs in development, had reached a turning point. Sometime in the next four to twelve months, the company stood an excellent chance of securing a partnership with a major pharmaceutical company. That partnership, if secured, would enable Purinex to develop one of its leading compounds into a drug for the treatment of one of the world's deadliest and most widespread diseases. The company had no sales or earnings, however, and there was only enough cash on hand to last 11 months.

Gilad Harpaz, Purinex's chief financial officer, believed that if a partnership deal came through, the company would be in an excellent position to carry out its mission. Moreover, securing a deal was practically a prerequisite for any eventual initial public offering,[1] which was an attractive exit strategy for many of the company's investors. But, as things stood, it was unclear whether the firm could stay afloat until such a partnership could be consummated.

Harpaz believed that the company could either attempt to secure financing now or wait until it struck a partnership deal. "But if we wait," Harpaz thought, "the terms of a deal would get a lot worse." Harpaz, a former officer in the Israeli special forces who had earned a graduate degree in business, considered how to structure this decision. What were the probabilities that a collaboration with a pharmaceutical company would actually happen? How would the company stay above water until that occurred? Besides insolvency, what were the other risks to the company under these circumstances?

---

[1]An initial public offering (IPO) was the first sale of stock to the public by a private company. IPOs were often issued by smaller, younger companies seeking capital to expand, but could also be done by large privately owned companies looking to become publicly traded.

Purinex, Inc.

Purinex was a drug-discovery and -development company based in Syracuse, New York, that sought to commercialize therapeutic compounds based on its purine drug-development platform. Purine was a naturally occurring molecule that played an important role in numerous biochemical processes. Purinex had developed a process for creating small molecules that acted as selective agonists (activators) or antagonists (blockers) for specific purine receptors in the cell membrane.[2] These molecules could initiate physiological responses or block the activation of receptors by endogenously produced signaling molecules. Purinex's goal was to develop products that evoked a receptor-specific pharmacodynamic effect without producing undesirable outcomes that could result from interactions with other receptors.

The company had 14 employees and maintained a chemistry laboratory a few miles from its main office. Purinex's intellectual-property portfolio consisted of more than 35 patents pending or issued in the purine field. The company planned to take its new receptor-selective drugs into clinical trials to address a broad range of potential indications. In June 2004, the most promising indications for its compounds were for the treatment of diabetes and sepsis.

Diabetes

Diabetes was a long-term condition that affected the body's ability to process glucose and hampered its use of other nutrients, such as protein and fat. Glucose, a common product of digestion, circulated in the blood to the body's cells, where it served as one of the chief sources of energy. Diabetes disrupted the body's mechanisms for moving glucose out of the bloodstream and using it in cells. As a result, levels of blood glucose (blood sugar) stayed excessively high, leading to serious health complications over time.

High levels of blood glucose affected the eyes, kidneys, and the nervous system. In addition, diabetes increased the risk of atherosclerosis, which narrowed arteries, especially those carrying blood to the heart, brain, and legs. Diabetes affected more than 100-million people worldwide, and was among the most common causes of death and disability in North America and Europe. Purinex had a patent on the use of any purine antagonist for the treatment of diabetes and its related conditions within the United States. The company had also developed a series of proprietary antagonist molecules that showed great promise in preclinical studies of diabetes. Potential annual sales for this drug were believed to be $4 billion.

Sepsis

Sepsis was a serious medical condition caused by a severe infection leading to a systemic inflammatory response. The more critical subsets of sepsis included severe sepsis (sepsis with acute organ dysfunction) and septic shock (sepsis with refractory arterial

---

[2]An *agonist* promoted certain kinds of cellular activity by binding to a cell's receptor. An *antagonist* prevented certain types of cellular reactions by blocking other substances from binding to a cell's receptor.

hypotension). Septicemia was sepsis of the bloodstream (blood poisoning) and was caused by bacteremia, which was the presence of bacteria in the bloodstream. The systemic inflammatory response syndrome led to widespread activation of inflammation and coagulation pathways. This could progress to dysfunction of the circulatory system and, even under optimal treatment, into multiple-organ dysfunction syndrome and, eventually, death.

Sepsis was more common and more dangerous in the elderly, immunocompromised, and critically ill patients. It occurred in 2% of all hospitalizations, and accounted for as much as 25% of intensive care unit (ICU) bed utilization. It was a major cause of death in ICUs worldwide, with mortality rates that ranged from 20% for sepsis to 40% for severe sepsis to more than 60% for septic shock. In the United States, sepsis was the leading cause of death in noncoronary ICU patients, and the tenth leading cause of death overall. One problem in the management of septic patients was the delay in administering the right treatment after the sepsis had been diagnosed.

One of Purinex's agonists for the treatment of sepsis had been shown (in animals) to have limited side effects and to be fast acting and effective at treating sepsis, even if treatment were significantly delayed after onset of the disease. Further, it had been proved safe in humans in a phase I clinical trial. Harpaz estimated that annual sales for this product could be around $500 million.

Development of Pharmaceutical Drugs

In 2005, the pharmaceutical industry remained one of the world's most dynamic economic sectors, with more than $530 billion in global sales. Although pharmaceuticals continued to grow faster than most other segments of the economy, some analysts predicted a softening in its growth over the next five years. As part of an effort to remain competitive, many large pharmaceutical firms had moved aggressively to partner with smaller firms in the biotechnology sector[3] in order to identify the next generation of drug candidates. In recent years, the U.S. biotechnology industry had mushroomed, as sector revenues grew from $8 billion, in 1992, to nearly $40 billion, at the end of 2003.

Collectively, the biotechnology industry devoted a higher percentage of its sales to research and development (R&D) than did any other major U.S. industry. According to Standard & Poor's, R&D spending by biotechnology firms was close to 40% of the industry's revenues. This high percentage was largely because many biotechnology companies did not generate revenues. R&D spending by public biotechnology companies was $17 billion in 2003 and $12.5 billion in 2002. Among the reasons for the high R&D costs was that the drug development and approval process was lengthy and risky. According to a June 2001 study by the Boston Consulting Group (BCG), the total cost to develop a new human-therapeutic compound was $880 million; a 2003 report by Tufts University placed that cost at $897 million (in 2000 dollars).

---

[3]In its broadest sense, *biotechnology* referred to the use of biological processes to solve problems or to make useful products, agribusiness, biology-based environmental remediation, biodefense, and drug research and development by small pharmaceutical firms.

The BCG report estimated that drug-development failures accounted for 75% of the total R&D cost.

While the total development time for a drug was highly variable, it took 10 to 15 years, on average, to move a drug from preclinical development to marketing approval. The process for discovering, developing, and gaining approval for new therapeutics consisted of several distinct steps: early discovery, preclinical development, clinical trials, and regulatory filing and review. **Exhibit 1** illustrates schematically the phases of development for a new compound.

According to a number of studies, the preclinical phase accounted for about 40% of the time and resources required to bring a new compound to market. The preclinical stage included target identification, target validation, assay development,[4] primary and secondary screening, lead optimization, and preclinical studies. The significant challenges of the preclinical phase were exemplified by a rule of thumb adopted by Pfizer, Inc. On average, it took about 7 million primary screen candidates to produce one new chemical entity.

In the United States, the drug-approval process was overseen by the Food and Drug Administration (FDA), which required extensive testing to ensure drug safety and efficacy. The drug manufacturer had to undertake three sequential sets of clinical tests before applying for regulatory approval. The FDA estimated that, out of every 20 drugs that entered clinical testing, on average, 13 or 14 would successfully complete phase I. Of those, about 9 would complete phase II; only 2 would likely survive phase III. On average, only 5% to 10% of drugs entering clinical trials were ultimately approved for marketing, often after several attempts.

Access to Capital

Given the magnitude of R&D requirements, early-stage biotechnology firms needed sufficient access to capital. Typically, biotechnology entities were funded through seed money from individual angel investors[5] or venture-capital[6] (VC) firms. According to Burrill & Company, a private merchant bank specializing in life sciences, funding from such sources for North American biotechnology firms was $2.6 billion in 2002 and more than $2.8 billion in 2003. A recent report by Standard & Poor's indicated that funding for most biotechnology firms would remain attractive, but "...we see deal terms remaining clearly less attractive than the valuation premiums that were commanded in 2000, when the market was in a euphoric state."

---

[4]An assay was a test that measured a biological response or assessed physical attributes, or, as here, referred to a screening process for new drug candidates.

[5]Angel investors were individuals who provided financing to small start-ups or entrepreneurs. Angel investors were often friends or relatives of the firm's principals, but they could also be sophisticated and experienced investors. Angel investors were rarely involved in the firm's management, but they could add value through their contacts and expertise.

[6]Venture capital was a broad term that referred to the financing provided by professional/institutional investors to start-up firms and small businesses with perceived growth potential. Venture capital was often a very important source of funding for new firms that might not have access to capital markets and that usually entailed high risk for investors, but that had the potential for above-average returns.

If a firm had a promising investigational drug candidate, it could also seek an alliance with a larger pharmaceutical or biotechnology company. The larger company could provide up-front fees, R&D funding, milestone payments,[7] royalties,[8] and, possibly, copromotion rights. In addition, the company could supply production facilities or sales organizations, often in return for marketing rights under licensing arrangements. **Exhibit 2** describes the terms of recent partnership deals between biotechnology and pharmaceutical firms. **Exhibit 3** provides the median and mean values of a broad sample of those deals at each stage of the drug development process.

The number of collaborative agreements between "Big Pharma" (large-capitalization pharmaceutical firms) and biotechnology entities had increased steadily in recent years. According to Burrill & Company, such partnering arrangements had reached $8.9 billion in 2003, up from $7.5 billion in 2002. These partnering deals were expected to surpass $10 billion in 2004. **Exhibit 4** depicts the relative proportion of funding sources for North American biotechnology firms in 2003.

Investment and Financing Decisions

In June 2004, Purinex had a broad range of technologies under development, two of which had applications appropriate for partnership deals with a larger pharmaceutical company: a preclinical stage antagonist program for the treatment of diabetes and an agonist program for the treatment of sepsis that had completed a phase I clinical trial.

Over the past several months, Purinex had initiated discussions with several, large, well-capitalized pharmaceutical companies regarding a possible collaboration for both compounds. Two companies had come forward with preliminary term sheets: one sought a deal for the treatment of sepsis, and the other wanted a deal for diabetes. Each proposed deal would entitle Purinex to receive a combination of up-front fees, milestone payments, and royalties, as described in **Table 1**:

TABLE 1 | Combinations of monies to be received for each deal.

	Sepsis	Diabetes
Up-front	$5 million	$8 million
Milestones (total, undiscounted[9])	$108 million	$80 million
Royalty	10.0%	12.0%

---

[7]Milestone payments were a series of payments made upon the successful completion of certain triggering events in the drug development process.

[8]A royalty was a payment to an owner for the use of property, especially patents, copyrighted works, or franchises. Royalties were usually calculated as a percentage of the revenues obtained through the use of the property.

[9]Harpaz's initial practice was to assess partnership deal terms on an undiscounted basis; but where time allowed and forecast assumptions were available, he would do further analysis.

Harpaz believed there was about a 75% chance that Purinex would secure a partnership with a pharmaceutical company for either sepsis or diabetes sometime during the next four to twelve months. If that partnership occurred, he estimated a 60% probability that it would be a deal for sepsis. If a partnership did not occur during the next four to twelve months, Harpaz believed there was a very strong chance—perhaps a 95% probability—that a different partnership with a third company for the diabetes application would occur about a year later. This later deal would likely have half the value of the one he was currently considering.

Harpaz thought it unlikely that Purinex would form partnership deals for both sepsis and diabetes. The company's management believed it was important for Purinex to retain at least one of those programs in order to maintain the firm's viability as a strategic acquisition target or as a possible IPO candidate ("so as not to sell off all of the crown jewels," he thought). Therefore, he believed the two deals were mutually exclusive.

Harpaz remained very concerned that Purinex had only $700,000 in cash on hand. The firm's burn rate[10] was about $60,000 a month (Purinex had no sales or earnings other than income from federal research grants, which offset about $100,000 of the company's $160,000 in monthly expenses). Because the sepsis and diabetes partnerships were so uncertain in the short term, Harpaz was considering three options for his firm. Each option came with its own risks:

- **Venture-capital round:** Purinex could seek to raise a one-time round of financing from a VC firm. VC firms had expressed serious interest in biotechnology investments lately, and Purinex showed great promise. Harpaz believed it would take about three months to secure $10 million from a VC firm, and that VC firms would likely give the company a premoney valuation[11] of $15 million. The VC financing would come with a significant number of restrictions, including preferences for board appointments, antidilution rights, liquidity, participation, and positive and negative covenants.

- **Wait six months:** Purinex could simply wait in the expectation that either the sepsis deal or the diabetes deal would come through. Purinex's current owners would then retain complete control of the company, which Harpaz believed could be valued at $25 million. While Purinex had about twelve months of cash available, the company could only wait about six months before securing additional financing. If either the sepsis or the diabetes deal failed to happen during the next six months, Purinex would be forced into a down-round[12] scenario with potential investors.

---

[10]The burn rate was the rate at which a new company depleted its capital to finance operations before it began to generate a positive cash flow. The burn rate was usually quoted in terms of cash spent per month.

[11]Premoney valuation was the value of a company before external financing alternatives were added to its balance sheet.

[12]A down round was a round of financing in which investors purchased stock from a company at a lower valuation than the one placed on the company by earlier investors. Down rounds caused the dilution of economic value for existing investors, which often meant that the company founders' stock or options were worth much less or possibly nothing at all. For start-up firms in a down round, VC firms would typically impose more onerous covenants, dictate a lower premoney valuation, and even remove current management.

Under those dire circumstances, Harpaz believed that the premoney valuation for Purinex would drop to $8 million or possibly as low as $5 million.

- **Angel round:** A third option for the company would be to undertake another one-time round of financing from a number of angel investors. Harpaz did not think Purinex could raise as much from angel investors as it could from VC firms—probably only $2 million. But with angel investors, Harpaz could probably ensure a higher firm valuation—about $17.5 million—and a diverse group of angels would not demand many preferences. It would take about six months to complete an angel round of financing.

In the back of his mind, Harpaz knew that if the firm were well capitalized, it would have a better chance of securing a collaboration with a major pharmaceutical firm and getting a better deal;[13] there was a "credibility value" in being adequately funded. How could the firm survive until that happened? What was the best way to finance the firm, yet also maximize the value of the firm today? Certainly, there was value in having the founders and current principals maintain control of the company, but what was that worth? "There are certain risks we're willing to take, and certain ones we're not," Harpaz thought to himself. "We are in the technology risk business, not the finance risk business." How could he evaluate all those risk-and-return scenarios?

---

[13]Harpaz believed that a round of VC funding could possibly increase the value of a pharma deal by 10%.

EXHIBIT 1 | The Drug-Development Process

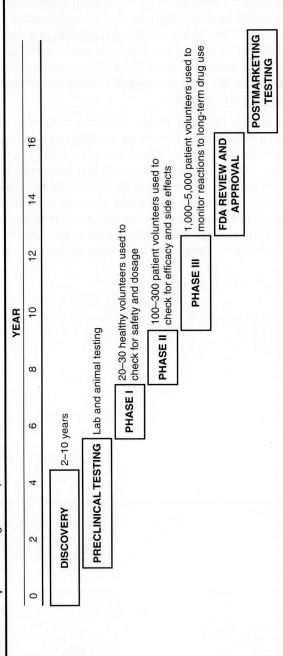

Source of data: Ernst & Young, LLP, *Biotechnology Industry Report: Convergence 2000* (cited in the *Guide to Biotechnology*, The Biotechnology Industry Organization [BIO]).

EXHIBIT 2 | Recent Biotechnology/Pharmaceutical Partnering Deals

Companies	Date	Details of the Deals
Curagen/TopoTarget	Jun–04	Histone deacetylase inhibitor: $5 million (m) in equity, $5m in license fees, plus $41m in milestones and royalties; deal includes rights to follow-up compounds at $1m license fee and $30m in milestones per product
Serono/4SC	May–04	Licenses worldwide rights to small-molecule dihydroorotate dehydrogenase inhibitors for autoimmune disorders—up-front, R&D funding and milestones, plus undisclosed royalties
Arqule/Roche	Apr–04	E2F pathway: $15m up-front, $276m in milestones, plus undisclosed royalties
Lundbeck/Merck	Feb–04	Gaboxadol, sleep deprivation: $70m up-front plus $200m in milestones plus royalties plus copromotion rights to undisclosed Merck product
Biostratum/NovoNordisk	Jan–04	Cancer project focused on Anti-laminin 5 antibodies: $80m milestones per antibody plus royalties and undisclosed royalties
Array Biopharma/AZ	Dec–03	Oncology: $10m up-front, $85m milestones, R&D funding plus milestones
Neurogean/Merck	Dec–03	Neurology/pain: $42m up-front, $118m in milestones, plus R&D funding plus milestones
MorphoSys/Pfizer	Dec–03	Five-year license, $50m in potential milestones plus royalties
Actelion/Merck	Dec–03	Renin inhibitor: $10m up-front, $262m in milestones
Neurosearch/GSK	Dec–03	Central nervous system area: $82m in guaranteed payments plus $200m in "bioworld payments"

Source of data: Credit Suisse First Boston.

EXHIBIT 3 | Mean and Median Terms of Partnership-Deal Licensing
(in millions of dollars)

	Preclinical Stage	Phase I	Phase II	Phase III
Total Value				
Mean	$82.7	$268.0	$212.3	$227.0
Median	$57.0	$200.4	$179.5	$247.5
Up-front				
Mean	$30.2	$32.6	$44.6	$42.7
Median	$19.0	$11.7	$25.0	$32.0
Milestones				
Mean	$72.9	$213.0	$196.6	$241.7
Median	$62.0	$184.6	$120.0	$200.0

Source of data: Credit Suisse First Boston, citing *Biocentury* (2003–February 2004).

EXHIBIT 4 | Financings in the North American Biotechnology Industry, 2003

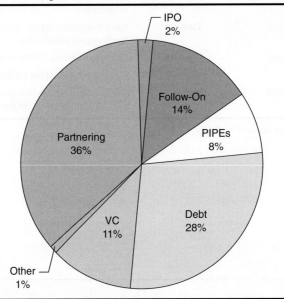

Source of data: Burrill & Company.

Note: PIPEs were private investments in public entities.

Medfield Pharmaceuticals

Susan Johnson, founder and CEO of Medfield Pharmaceuticals, had planned to spend the first few weeks of 2011 sorting out conflicting recommendations for extending the patent life of the company's flagship product, Fleximat, which was scheduled to go off patent in two years. With only three other products in Medfield's lineup of medications, one of which had only just received U.S. Food and Drug Administration (FDA) approval, strategic management of the company's product pipeline was of paramount importance. But a recent $750 million offer to purchase the company had entirely shifted her focus.

The offer was not a complete surprise. The pharmaceutical industry landscape had changed considerably since Johnson, formerly a research scientist, had founded Medfield 20 years earlier.[1] Development costs were rising, patents were running out, and new breakthroughs seemed ever more difficult to obtain. The industry was now focused on mergers and acquisitions, restructuring, and other strategies for cost-cutting and survival. Smaller firms like Medfield were being gobbled up by the major players all the time. Companies with approved products or products in the later stages of development, such as Medfield, were especially likely targets.

While she no longer owned a controlling interest in the firm and could not force a particular decision, Johnson recognized that as CEO, founder, and largest single investor, she would be expected to offer an opinion and that her opinion would be extremely influential. It was also clear that determining the value of the company, and therefore whether the offer was reasonable, would necessitate a careful review of the company's existing and potential future products, and no one understood these as well as Johnson.

Of course, for Johnson, this was more than simply a financial decision. She believed strongly, as did other employees, particularly among the research staff, that Medfield was engaged in work that was important, and she took great pride in the firm's accomplishments. Medfield's corporate culture was explicitly oriented toward the end goal of improving patients' health, as evidenced by its slogan: "We Bring Wellness." This was

---

[1] Except where otherwise noted, general statistics and information about the pharmaceutical industry come from Plunkett Research, http://www.plunkettresearch.com.

an important value that Johnson had consciously and specifically built into the firm's culture. Both Johnson's parents were doctors and ran a small family-oriented practice that they had taken over from Johnson's maternal grandfather in the town where Johnson was raised. The idea of bettering lives through medicine was one Johnson had grown up with.

Current Product Lines

The company had experienced excellent growth over the years and in 2009 had 290 employees, total sales of $329 million (primarily in the United States), and a net income of $58 million. See **Exhibits 1** and **2** for financial information. The company manufactured and sold three primary drugs; all but one had substantial patent life remaining. Two were for pain management and the third was for auto-immune diseases. A fourth drug, also for pain management, had been approved and was ready for distribution. Due to its strong marketing and sales force, Medfield enjoyed an excellent reputation with both physicians and hospitals.

The company's leading seller—responsible for 64% of its revenues—was Fleximat. Fleximat was a monoclonal antibody used to treat pain and swelling in patients with ulcerative colitis, rheumatoid arthritis, and Crohn's disease, an ongoing disorder that caused painful inflammation of the digestive tract. Fleximat had proved to be much more effective than competing sulfa-based drugs (such as sulfasalazine) in treating those patients—particularly juveniles—who had an inadequate response to conventional therapies for Crohn's disease. Fleximat, however, was due to go off patent in two years.

The other three products were as follows:

- *Lodamadal* was an extended-release tablet for once-daily treatment of moderate to severe pain in patients requiring continuous, around-the-clock opioid therapy for an extended period of time. It was in the class of medications called opiate agonists, which worked by changing the way the body sensed pain. This drug accounted for 12% of Medfield's revenues.

- *Orsamorph* was a morphine sulfate sustained-release tablet designed to treat more intense pain. This was a popular drug in hospitals and accounted for 24% of revenues; it had eight years of patent life left.

- *Reximet* treated acute migraines. Reximet, which would begin selling in 2012, was a single tablet containing sumatriptan succinate, a 5-HT 1B/1D agonist, and naproxen sodium, a non-steroidal anti-inflammatory drug. Reximet had proved effective in treating arthritis and joint pain.

The Pharmaceutical Industry

Globally, the pharmaceutical industry was a powerhouse, generating billions in revenues. The U.S. pharmaceutical manufacturing industry, at the core of the global business, had historically enjoyed high profits. Yearly, from 1995 through 2002, it was the most profitable industry in the United States, and drug manufacturers had experienced three times more profitability than the median of all *Fortune* 500 companies in 2004.[2]

---

[2]Haiden A. Huskamp, "Prices, Profits, and Innovation: Examining Criticisms of New Psychotropic Drugs' Value," *Health Affairs* 25, no. 3 (2006).

Drug companies made money by bringing "blockbuster" drugs to market, relying on the period during which they were protected by patent to make significant revenues and focusing on mass-market drugs that treated a wide variety of ailments. Traditional pharmaceutical companies, several of which had existed since the 19th century, discovered and created new drugs using organic chemistry and natural compounds, but biotechnology companies—which used gene-splicing to produce their drugs had been on the rise since the mid-1970s. These companies often created "orphan drugs" that focused on rare diseases affecting a small percentage of the population.[3]

In 2009, the pharmaceutical industry had approximately 1,500 companies with combined annual revenues of $200 billion. At the top of the drug-company pile were Abbott, Bristol-Myers Squibb, Eli Lilly and Company, Johnson & Johnson, Pfizer, and Merck. More than 80% of pharmaceutical revenue was brought in by the 50 largest companies.

But the pharmaceutical industry had found itself at a crossroads as the first decade of the 21st century wound down. With the economic downturn, impending health-care-reform legislation, and many drugs losing their patents, drug companies had to determine how best to boost their bottom line. Most alarming to many of the major pharmaceutical companies was the imminent expiration of patents; estimates were that from 2009 to 2016, losses from these expirations would benefit generics to the tune of $140 billion.[4] As a result, the large pharmaceuticals were turning to various options to stay viable, including restructuring, cutting internal R&D, adding biologics,[5] building generic units, entering emerging markets, and looking at M&A. Many large companies were bulking up their products by buying or licensing drugs from other companies or acquiring smaller outfits.

New drug approvals had also taken a dive. In 2009, there were only 25 new drugs[6] that received approval from the Center for Drug Evaluation and Research at the FDA. In contrast, during the mid-1990s, more than twice that number had been approved. The cost of bringing a drug to market was high: The latest figure (2005) was $1.3 billion, as compared with $802 million in 2001, $300 million in 1991, and $100 million in 1979. In general, only 2 in 10 approved medicines recouped R&D costs.

The pharmaceutical industry—particularly in the 1990s and in the first decade of the 21st century—had come under criticism both from the public and the government, not only for the high price of branded drugs, but also for some of its tactics and strategies. Various manufacturers were accused of, among other things, withholding data from the FDA; manipulating certain data to achieve specific results (as Merck was accused of doing with Vioxx); hiring physician opinion leaders at great cost to promote its products; lavishing gifts, meals, and other luxuries on physicians in an

---

[3]An example of an orphan drug was Rituxan, which had been developed by Genentech and Biogen to treat people suffering from non-Hodgkin's lymphoma—a relatively small market.

[4]Ian Mawhinney, "2020: A New Drug Delivery Landscape," *Drug Discovery and Development* 12, no. 10 (December 2009): 32.

[5]Biologics were created using biological processes, such as T-cell activation or stimulation of blood components, rather than chemical synthesis.

[6]This number refers to traditional pharmaceuticals, which were discovered via organic chemistry; there were nine approvals of biologics in 2009.

attempt to get them to prescribe a particular drug; and promoting drugs for off-label use. Drug companies had become the whipping posts for practically everyone, from presidents to consumer activists to the general public.

The Generic Equation

U.S. patent policy gave drug manufacturers a 20-year protection from the date of the original patent (usually filed early in the research process), plus 14 years from the date of FDA approval. Once the patent expired, the medication was fair game and other companies could make generic forms of it. In the United States, the modern system of generics came into being in 1984, after passage of the Drug Price Competition and Patent Term Restoration Act (or the Hatch-Waxman Act), which significantly changed the pharmaceutical patent landscape. The legislation's purpose was to ensure that generics were more widely available and to ensure adequate incentives for investing in the development of new drugs. The act expedited the process of generics reaching the market by letting manufacturers file an abbreviated new drug application with the FDA. The act also granted concessions to the brand manufacturers, allowing them to increase the patent time.

Generics were, on average, 50% to 75% cheaper than the branded drug, and in many cases, the price difference was much bigger. This disparity benefited consumers tremendously but had the opposite effect on name-brand pharmaceutical firms. Sales of blockbuster drugs could plunge 80% or more the first year after a generic competitor entered the market. In 2009, the generics' share of the market was 74%, compared with 49% in 2000. In 2008, generics manufacturers Teva Pharmaceuticals and Mylan Laboratories topped the list of producers of dispensed prescriptions in the United States at 494.2 million and 307.7 million, respectively, beating out Pfizer and Merck.[7] Of that top ten, six were generics manufacturers.

Generics received a big boost in 2006, when Wal-Mart pharmacies, primarily to fight mail-order pharmacies, began offering deeply discounted generic brands for a flat $4 per month. Other large chains with pharmacies (e.g., Kroger, Target, and Walgreens) jumped on the $4 generic bandwagon. The popularity of these programs led to still-deeper discounts and even some free medication over the following years. Wal-Mart offered 90-day supplies of some generic drugs for $10, and grocery chain Publix offered free generic antibiotics for up to 14 days. Competition was fierce among manufacturers of generic drugs, resulting in heavy discounting.

Given this change in the competitive landscape, toward the end of the first decade of the 21st century, many major pharmaceutical companies were branching out by producing generics, not only of their own brands but also those of other companies. This represented an attempt to introduce a subtle form of differentiation into the mostly cost-leader-focused generics market; brand-name companies that produced generics could charge slightly more for the promise of quality, as opposed to no-name generic producers, whose selling point was rock-bottom prices. Among others, Pfizer (with its

---

[7]Business Monitor International, "Competitive Landscape," *United States Pharmaceuticals & Healthcare Report Q1 2010,* 62.

generics division Greenstone), Schering-Plough (which created a generic subsidiary, Warrick Pharmaceuticals), Novartis, Sanofi-Aventis, and GlaxoSmithKline were manufacturing copycat drugs from other companies; the latter two targeted non-U.S. markets. Obviously, independent generic manufacturers were not pleased with this practice.

Fleximat Strategies

As Johnson considered the state of the industry and Medfield's specific situation, her attention increasingly focused on Fleximat—the firm's core product but biggest source of uncertainty. Aside from simply letting Fleximat's patent lapse and losing sales to the inevitable generic substitutes, Johnson knew the company had several possible alternative actions. Of these, Johnson believed four approaches stood out:

1. Launch a renewed marketing effort. This would include becoming more aggressive in Medfield's current tactics. Johnson was well aware of how successful AstraZeneca's commercials for Nexium had been, which featured apparently suicidal people standing on cliffs, desperate for heartburn relief, and diners at fancy restaurants mishearing a waiter describe the gastric distress that would follow after they ate their meals.

2. Engage in evergreening tactics. This essentially would allow the firm to maintain the benefits of patents through aggressive litigation. For example, a manufacturer could "stockpile" patent protections by taking out many separate patents (each good for 20 years), legitimate or not, on various components or attributes of one of its products. Components covered could include the color of the medication, a particular chemical reaction when the drug is taken and metabolized, or dose amounts. The firm would then defend these with legal actions that would impede the development and sale of generics.

3. Manufacture the generic form of Fleximat in-house. Medfield could also partner with a large generic manufacturer. This would be the easiest approach and would lead to the widest use of Fleximat by patients, but it would generate little in the way of financial benefits to the firm.

4. Reformulate Fleximat. This was the practice of "reinventing" a drug to "improve" it and thus stave off the generics. It meant reconfiguring the medication so it was different enough for FDA approval and a new patent, although this often could be done without substantially changing the medication itself. Methods to extend the patent life of the compound could include slightly changing the formulation, dosage, or labeling. See **Exhibit 3** for examples of drug reformulation.

Of these four alternatives, reformulation struck Johnson as likely the most beneficial to Medfield; however, there were notable risks. The most famous reformulation controversy had been the case of AstraZeneca's Nexium (a.k.a. "the purple pill"). AstraZeneca (AZ) released the patented heartburn drug Prilosec in 1981. It was one of the company's biggest blockbuster drugs. As patent expiration loomed, AZ got FDA approval in February 2001 for the reformulation of Prilosec into a newly patented drug called Nexium, also a heartburn prescription and very similar to Prilosec. AZ then ceased promoting Prilosec and began aggressively pushing Nexium. Two years later, the FDA approved an over-the-counter (OTC) version of Prilosec, which had exclusivity in the OTC market until 2006.

As a result of this reformulation, Walgreen Company sued AstraZeneca for antitrust violations, claiming the pharmaceutical company had deliberately switched "the market from its heartburn prescription drug Prilosec just as that patent was about to expire to its newly approved drug Nexium, which had a fresh patent."[8] Walgreen's lawsuit alleged that AZ manipulated the market, taking the emphasis off Prilosec, which had generic competition, and placing it on Nexium, which had a patent until 2014 and no generic competition, and that in doing so, the company eliminated choices for patients. Furthermore, Walgreen argued that there was little difference between Prilosec and Nexium and that AZ's switching of them was exclusionary and violated the Sherman Antitrust Act. Walgreen also claimed that AZ was guilty of further exclusionary action when it introduced the OTC version of Prilosec and received a three-year exclusivity grant from the FDA. In addition, Walgreen contended that AstraZeneca engaged in prohibited exclusionary conduct when it introduced Prilosec OTC and obtained an FDA grant of exclusivity for three years.

Ultimately, all five complaints in the lawsuit were dismissed for "failure to state a claim," and the federal district court judge asserted, among other things, that instead of having taken away drug choices, as Walgreen claimed, AZ had created additional choices (Prilosec OTC and Nexium). The court also made the point that antitrust laws do not evaluate the quality of a particular drug—whether superior or inferior; new products could only affect the market share if customers preferred them. Finally, the court did not find that AZ had interfered with Walgreen's freedom to compete; in other words, the court found that AZ was not guilty of illegal antitrust activity. While there was only one study that demonstrated superiority of Nexium, it had been sponsored by AstraZeneca.[9]

Nevertheless, while not considered racketeering in the courts, the process of reformulation came under increasing public scrutiny. According to author Malcolm Gladwell, Nexium had become a "symbol of everything that is wrong with the pharmaceutical industry":

> The big drug companies justify the high prices they charge—and the extraordinary profits they enjoy—by arguing that the search for innovative, life-saving medicines is risky and expensive. But Nexium is little more than a repackaged version of an old medicine. And the hundred and twenty dollars a month that AstraZeneca charges isn't to recoup the costs of risky research and development; the costs were for a series of clinical trials that told us nothing we needed to know, and a half-billion-dollar marketing campaign selling the solution to a problem we'd already solved.[10]

---

[8]"Prilosec/Nexium Antitrust Claims Dismissed: No Antitrust Violation for Introducing New Drugs to the Market," *Judicial View,* https://www.judicialview.com/Court-Cases/Antitrust/Prilosec-Nexium-Antitrust-Claims-Dismissed/No-Antitrust-Violation-for-Introducing-New-Drugs-to-the-Market/5/2666 (accessed September 1, 2011).

[9]Esomeprazole (Nexium) provided improved acid control versus omeprazole (Prilosec) in patients with symptoms of gastroesophageal reflux disease.

[10]Malcolm Gladwell, "High Prices: How to Think About Prescription Drugs," *New Yorker,* October 25, 2004, 86.

Furthermore, in a front-page article that first revealed AZ's initiative to reformulate its expiring medication, the *Wall Street Journal* concluded that "the Prilosec pattern, repeated across the pharmaceutical industry, goes a long way to explain why the nation's prescription drug bill is rising an estimated 17% a year even as general inflation is quiescent.[11]

The Value of Medfield

As Johnson sat down to contemplate the acquisition offer, she began to look at the company's portfolio of drugs in a new light. Rather than therapies for ailments, they were sources of cash flow. Fortunately, whereas the R&D process was notoriously unpredictable, once a product was approved, the future was relatively clear. This future could be summarized as follows:

- For 20 years, the product would be patent-protected, and from the initial sales level, sales would grow at about 2% a year. When the patent expired, sales would decline 50% in each of the following three years and then would have effectively negligible sales in the fourth year.

- The direct cost of sales would be 23%.

- Direct marketing costs were 27% of revenue and Medfield typically spent 19% of revenue on future R&D.

- The company estimated other general and administrative expenses would be about 4% of sales. A large portion of this expense category was tied directly or indirectly to sales and little of the cost was reasonably classified as fixed.

- Capital expenditures were typically close to depreciation levels so that net changes in plant and equipment associated with a given product could be ignored. Similarly, net working capital tended to be very small and could be ignored.

- The marginal tax rate for the firm was 32% and Johnson estimated that 8.5% was a reasonable discount rate (cost of capital) for this industry.

Johnson had recently requested a forecast of the firm's financials based on approved products. This forecast (**Exhibit 4**) included a forecast for Reximet starting with initial sales of $80 million. This forecast was generated largely as a tool for examining the prospects associated with products already in existence and to allow her to gauge the possible impact of Fleximat going off patent. Clearly, the forecast did not include the operating effects of adding new products to the lineup. While generated for an alternate purpose, the forecast was built from the assumptions listed above, and Johnson wondered if this forecast could also form a reasonable basis for valuing the company.

As Johnson contemplated her analysis, she immediately recognized that she needed to reach some decision regarding extending the patent life of Fleximat. The simplest and most obvious approach was to reformulate the drug. Her research team

---

[11]Gardiner Harris, "Prilosec's Maker Switches Users To Nexium, Thwarting Generics," *Wall Street Journal,* June 6, 2002, 1.

was reasonably certain that if it focused its efforts on changing the shape of the pill and applying an easier-to-swallow coating, a reformulation push in 2011 and 2012 at a cost of $35 million a year would likely generate a suitable reformulation. This reformulation would very likely leave the pharmacology of the medication unchanged. Of course, getting users to opt for the reformulation would require a strong marketing campaign above what was typical. She estimated the firm would have to spend $25 million annually for five years starting in 2011 (the first year getting the market ready for the reformulation) to ensure the success of the reformulation. A reformulation would not, of course, prevent some erosion in sales. Johnson estimated that when the patent expired in 2013, the drug would still see a 50% decline in sales, but after that, sales would grow at 2% a year for eight years. After that eight-year period, she reasonably expected that sales would dissipate in a manner similar to drugs going off patent (three years of 50% declines before dissipating entirely).

Big Decisions

Johnson had started the company with a simple mission: to find and develop medicines that would make lives better. Fleximat, she knew, had brought untold relief to children suffering from Crohn's disease, and this was particularly important to her because her nephew had Crohn's disease and Johnson had witnessed the incurable, chronic disease firsthand. For this reason, she wondered how the potential sale of the company might transform Medfield. The focus on making lives better, she hoped, would remain unchanged since the effectiveness of Medfield's drugs was the core source of its demand. She also expected the research staff and structures would be only slightly altered given that the team she had put together was quite effective; whereas a typical firm might have to spend $50 million for five years to develop a new product such as Reximet, her team could probably do it for $35 million a year.[12]

It was clear to Johnson that this offer was a great opportunity for her to exit the business on a high note. Given that Medfield was about to roll out Reximet and that it had two other products with substantial patent lives remaining, the company was a good catch for a potential buyer. Johnson also realized that the state of early-stage product development at Medfield was quite weak at the time. None of its new products was in late-stage trials. The fact was that the offer would leave her extremely wealthy and it would afford her a graceful exit from her venture. Of course, in deference to the many other owners, she had to put aside her own cares and evaluate the offer in the spirit of a financial transaction. This was a big decision—likely the largest of her life.

---

[12]Research costs at Medfield were lower, and development times were shorter than they were for the typical large pharmaceutical company given that Medfield targeted small markets; Medfield was not seeking the next blockbuster drug.

EXHIBIT 1 | Medfield Pharmaceuticals Annual Income Statement[1]
(in thousands of dollars)

	2007	2008	2009	2010
Revenue	223,721	261,253	300,556	329,203
Cost of Goods Sold	55,788	65,724	75,241	76,472
Gross Profit	167,933	195,529	225,315	252,731
SG&A Expenses	71,586	82,446	97,542	105,166
Research and Development	42,175	54,078	57,535	62,457
	113,761	136,524	155,077	167,623
Earnings Before Interest and Taxes	54,172	59,005	70,238	85,108
Interest	984	1,385	1,403	1,457
	53,188	57,620	68,835	83,651
Income Taxes	16,457	18,982	22,495	25,875
Net Income	36,731	38,638	46,340	57,776

Note: The company has negligible depreciation and amortization.

[1]All exhibits were created by the case writer.

EXHIBIT 2 | Medfield Pharmaceuticals Balance Sheet
(in thousands of dollars)

	2007	2008	2009	2010
Cash	21,465	28,227	29,542	32,251
Receivables	28,815	39,568	39,117	41,927
Inventory	24,704	24,316	27,859	30,559
	74,984	92,111	96,518	104,737
Property and Equipment	102,977	118,553	127,498	129,171
Other Assets	45,937	49,312	61,569	67,718
	223,898	259,976	285,585	301,626
Accounts Payable	25,187	26,460	27,070	30,142
Accrued Expenses	39,236	52,634	55,256	59,850
Current LTD	2,882	3,373	3,801	4,501
	67,305	82,467	86,127	94,493
LTD	17,069	23,609	25,278	26,850
Equity	139,524	153,900	174,180	180,283
	223,898	259,976	285,585	301,626

EXHIBIT 3 | Drug Reformulation Methods

AstraZeneca	To create Nexium, AstraZeneca cut Prilosec in half and changed its color (modest change, basically repackaging) and thus maintained a patented brand.
GlaxoSmithKline	As GlaxoSmithKline lost its patent on Paxil, an antidepressant, the company developed a new version (Paxil CR) that patients took just once a day, rather than twice. (Even though a Paxil generic weakened sales of Paxil CR, the company stuck with the extended-release version because it was a better fit for people with depression, who tended not to take their medication.)
Eli Lilly and Company	As Eli Lilly's patent expired on the antidepressant Prozac, the company introduced Prozac Weekly (again, easier and more efficient for patients with depression). Nonetheless, the $182 million sales of Prozac Weekly paled in comparison to the $2 billion sales that the daily Prozac, when patented, had brought in.
Schering-Plough	Schering-Plough launched Clarinex, a tweaked version of Claritin, its blockbuster antihistamine, the same year that Claritin lost patent protection. Schering-Plough also beat the generic companies at their own game by launching Claritin as an OTC drug within days of losing its patent. (Nonetheless, though Claritin was making $3 billion in sales when it lost patent exclusivity, the combined OTC Claritin and Clarinex sales were $1 billion—only a third of peak [and patented] prescription Claritin sales.)
Pfizer	Pfizer created an under-the-tongue version of Xanax (formerly just a pill), which provided faster delivery into the system, thus changing the method of delivery.
Elan	Drugmaker Elan used Nanocrystal technology for a 600% improvement in the bioavailability of compounds that dissolved poorly in water. Patients would still take the medication orally, but it allowed for a lower required dosage, smaller and more convenient dosage forms, and faster rates of absorption. For example, Elan reformulated Bristol-Myers Squibb's liquid Megace so it was not so thick and so that HIV/AIDS patients could drink less of it and more easily. Novartis created a patch delivery system with the Alzheimer's drug Exelon.

EXHIBIT 4 | Financial Forecast Based on Existing Products (in millions of dollars, unless otherwise noted)

| | | | Direct Marketing General and Admin. | | | | Taxes Discount Rate | | 32.0% | |
| | Costs of Sales 23.0% Research 19.0% | | | | 27.0% 4.0% | | | | 8.5% | |
	2010	2011	2012	2013	2014	2015	2016	2017	2018	2019
Fleximat										
Sales	210.56	214.77	219.07	109.53	54.77	27.38				
Cost of Sales	47.46	49.40	50.39	25.19	12.60	6.30				
Lodamadal										
Sales	39.67	40.47	41.28	42.10	42.94	43.80	21.90	10.95	5.48	
Cost of Sales	10.55	9.31	9.49	9.68	9.88	10.07	5.04	2.52	1.26	
Orsamorph										
Sales	78.97	80.55	82.16	83.80	85.48	87.19	88.93	90.71	92.52	94.37
Cost of Sales	18.46	18.53	18.90	19.27	19.66	20.05	20.45	20.86	21.28	21.71
Reximet										
Sales			80.00	81.60	83.23	84.90	86.59	88.33	90.09	91.89
Cost of Sales			18.40	18.77	19.14	19.53	19.92	20.32	20.72	21.14
Total Sales	329.20	335.79	422.50	317.04	266.42	243.27	197.43	189.99	188.09	186.27
Cost of Sales	76.47	77.23	97.18	72.92	61.28	55.95	45.41	43.70	43.26	42.84
Research	62.46	63.80	80.28	60.24	50.62	46.22	37.51	36.10	35.74	35.39
Direct Marketing	91.22	90.66	114.08	85.60	71.93	65.68	53.31	51.30	50.78	50.29
General and Administrative	13.94	13.43	16.90	12.68	10.66	9.73	7.90	7.60	7.52	7.45
Taxes	27.15	29.01	36.50	27.39	23.02	21.02	17.06	16.41	16.25	16.09
NOPAT	57.96	61.65	77.57	58.21	48.91	44.66	36.25	34.88	34.53	34.20